French Women
and the
Age of Enlightenment

French Women
and the
Age of Enlightenment

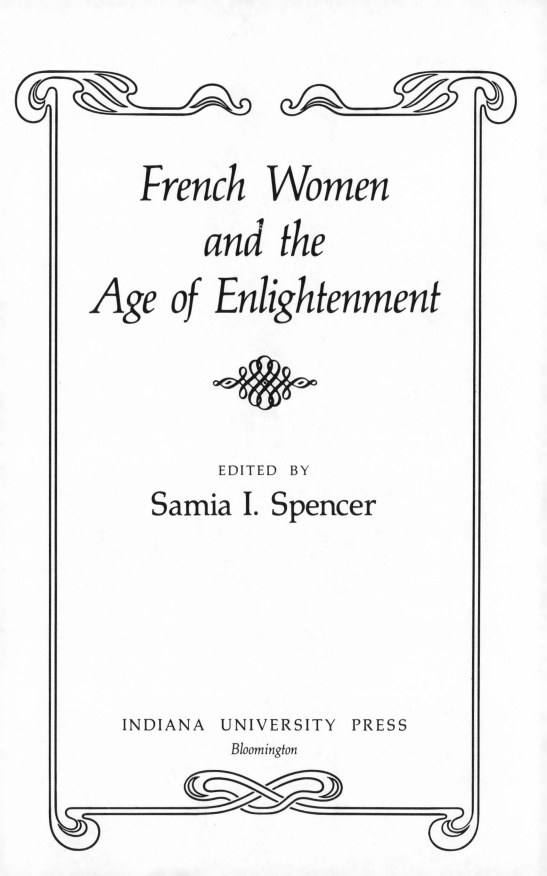

EDITED BY

Samia I. Spencer

INDIANA UNIVERSITY PRESS

Bloomington

Publication of this anthology has been supported by institutional grants from:
Auburn University
Boston College
North Carolina State University
Russell Sage College
Southern Connecticut State University
The University of Alabama in Birmingham

Manufactured in the United States of America

Library of Congress Cataloging in Publication Data
Main entry under title:

French women and the Age of Enlightenment.
Includes bibliographical references.
1. Women—France—History—18th century—Addresses, essays, lectures.
2. Women—France—Social conditions—Addresses, essays, lectures. I. Spencer,
Samia I., 1943-
HQ1149.F8F73   1984   305.4'0944   83-48403
ISBN 0-253-32481-5
ISBN 0-253-20725-8 (pbk.)
2 3 4 5 6 96 95 94 93 92

Contents

Part III: Women and Culture

Part IV: Creative Women and Women Artists

Part V: <u>The Philosophes</u>: Feminism and/or Antifeminism?

Part VI: Portrayal of Women in French Literature

Part VII: Portrayal of French Women in Other European Literatures

FOREWORD

The eighteenth century—particularly in France—was one of the richest periods in the history of the western world. That our culture and institutions are so deeply rooted in its legacy may be a reason for the increasing number of scholarly studies devoted to this century.

One area, however, has not received the full attention it deserves: the contributions of eighteenth-century French women to the history and thought of their time. Documents of the century indicate, and subsequent studies confirm, that—with the possible exception of the present century—French women have never been so influential and prolific as they were in the Age of Enlightenment. Recently, a new generation of historians and literary scholars—women in particular—has greatly enhanced our understanding and appreciation of eighteenth-century French women. Most of these studies, however, are limited to a particular aspect of women's activities. The purpose of this anthology is to include in a single volume a comprehensive view of French women's political, social, cultural, literary, artistic, and scientific accomplishments. It is our hope that this initial effort will stimulate additional research culminating in an accurate, fair, and balanced history of eighteenth-century France, one in which the contributions of all her citizens—female and male—will be recognized.

The present volume would not have been possible without the dedication, support, suggestions, and faith of its contributors. For nearly five years, we shared our ideas and goals, our energy and lives. During the creation of the book, two children, Sarah Thomas Boss and Matthew James Prather, were born, and two friends were taken from us. In June 1980, Hélène Monod-Cassidy succumbed after a long illness, before her contribution to *French Women and the Age of Enlightenment* could be realized. A year and a half later, one of the strongest supporters of this project, Leonora Cohen Rosenfield, died before seeing the book come to life.

Particular thanks are extended to the many friends and colleagues who took a personal interest in the project and made invaluable recommendations. Mary M. Millman, whose mastery of the English language and stylistics is unsurpassed, spent many hours on the careful reading and editing of several chapters of the book. Glenn Anderson of the Ralph Brown Draughon Library checked hundreds of references, dates, titles, and other bibliographical details. In all the years that I have known him, he has never been unable to answer any of my questions, no matter how complicated. Bettye Campbell, Lula Jones, Kathy Kickliter, and Carolyn McCormick showed competence, care, understanding and infinite patience throughout the lengthy process of typing and correcting the manuscript.

Special appreciation goes to Dr. Chester C. Carroll, the Auburn University Research Grant-in-Aid Committee, and the Humanities Fund of the School of Arts and Sciences for their financial assistance in the research, the preparation, and the publication of this volume. I am particularly indebted to Dr. Paul F. Parks, Vice President for Research at Auburn University, not only for making this book possible but also for his broad vision, his commitment to excellence, and his generous and unequivocal support of research in language and literature.

I would like to recognize the important role of the University of Illinois library in making possible the research for my own chapter on "Women and Education." I was granted an extended loan of the rare and irreplaceable eighteenth-century works that were essential to my study. Throughout the years that the books were lent to me, I enjoyed the full cooperation and confidence of the library's professional and considerate personnel.

Last but not least, I would like to express my affectionate gratitude to my husband, Bill, without whose total and uncompromising support this book could not have been brought to life.

SAMIA I. SPENCER

PREFACE
Perilous Visibilities

In 1793, five women were publicly beheaded in Paris for alleged crimes against the state. They were not, to be sure, the only victims of the Revolutionary Tribunal established that year to defend the beleaguered young Republic against real or imaginary "traitors" (its free use of that democratic instrument of punishment—the guillotine— is legendary), but these five women form a symbolic configuration because of the diverse positions they occupied in society. Marie-Antoinette sat at the pinnacle of power and prestige. Mme du Barry was, by contrast, a woman of the *petit peuple*; yet her career as courtesan raised her to the rank of pseudoqueen when she became the mistress of Louis XV and the center of a brilliant and elegant court. A well-read, idealistic woman from the artisan stratum of society, Mme Roland, had, with her husband, been at the center of political power and intrigue. Charlotte Corday achieved fame and death in a single day when she assassinated the sanguinary and fanatic Marat. A semi-aristocratic, convent-bred provincial girl, she was, like Mme Roland, a child of the Enlightenment and an early admirer of revolutionary ideals. Most unexpected of all was Olympe de Gouges, the only one of these women who could be considered a feminist. A political agitator and illiterate who emerged from the ranks of the unruly Paris "populace," she claimed for all French women equal rights with men as citizens of the new France.

It was also in 1793 that the government abolished the Society of Republican Women organized a few months earlier. The Age of Enlightenment, in its encounter with political realities, was bearing strange fruits, unforeseen by its then departed fathers. Among the first casualties, in addition to the ancien régime, were the high expectations of a number of women for whom, in its early stages, the Revolution had seemed a propitious moment for initiating changes in their legal, social, political, and intellectual status. How necessary these changes were will be documented by *French Women and the Age of Enlightenment*.

One would be tempted to take the five feminine figures cited before
as emblematic of the differing postures of women in an era of
violence—women in the limelight, willingly or unwillingly—and of the
fate they underwent. Although this is a temptation, it is not my
purpose and would, in fact, contravene the spirit of the book. *French
Women and the Age of Enlightenment* is a collection of essays that are strictly
informative and nonspeculative in nature. What the events of 1793
underscore, as I see it, is the appropriateness of the overall title. The
essays dramatize the connection between the liberal ideas of the
philosophes—diverse as they were—and the emergence of a pervasive
feminine presence and consciousness that the "New Regime" found
intolerable. Some 150 years were to pass before women would be
allowed access to positions of power and authority—to say nothing of
the granting of their rights. Perilous, indeed, was the visibility of
women in the Age of Enlightenment; the events of 1793 clearly
signaled that women were expected to keep out of the public arena—
and a grievous and serious setback that proved to be.

The chapters in this collection are the work of twenty-eight women
scholars, eighteenth-century specialists who were prompted by their
sense of the paucity of research in their field of specialization. The
eighteenth century as such, and most particularly eighteenth-century
France, has always received much distinguished scholarly attention in
the U. S., both from historians and literary scholars. But as Samia I.
Spencer, the admirable editor of this volume points out, the "contributions of eighteenth-century French women" have been inadequately
treated. The nostalgic view of the eighteenth century as a century of
feminine supremacy—a view formulated by the Goncourt brothers
toward the end of the nineteenth century—became quite pervasive.
Much work was done on the salons and the women who hosted the
"great men" of the day. But enormous gaps remained in our
knowledge of the women themselves, the restraints they suffered,
and the "feminine condition" as such.

The new emphasis on social history and women's studies points to
other realities behind the stereotypes. The purpose of this book, as
Professor Spencer describes it, is to collect and disseminate the more
recent knowledge that has accrued. The contributors had a difficult
task, indeed, but an essential one—not so much to refute past work as
to produce a more accurate and stimulating view of the climate of
France at a particularly difficult and paradoxical moment in her
history. Whatever the difficulties, and I shall come to them later, they
have been met in a straightforward fashion. The contributors do not
cover the same material, nor do they adhere to the same method of
presentation. They do have one thing in common: like the *philosophes*,

they write lucidly, "for everybody in everybody's language"—in keeping with their overriding purpose of providing accurate and unbiased information.

It would be impossible to survey the essays presented. I shall comment briefly on the structure of the book, which begins with a survey of the infrastructure of the eighteenth century—the socio-political institutions and mores—and then moves on to the cultural area. The difficulties are obvious. There is first the vastness and complexity of the topic. Secondly, there is the problem of defining the period to be dealt with. Some contributors view the eighteenth century as revolving around the Revolution; others seem to take the Revolution as a terminal date. Certain figures seem to have been incompletely presented—Mme Roland, for instance, as a political figure and, curiously, Mme de Staël, both of whom were so deeply marked by the Enlightenment. There is some overlap in the essays, which is unavoidable when a variety of scholars treat a number of related items. All in all, the divergencies among viewpoints are slight, and the respect for a tradition of scholarship based on the study of primary sources is everywhere apparent. Although no contribution is controversial or aggressive in tone, the overall effect is to "deconstruct" the rather complacent, stereotyped image of the century ensconced in many a French school manual. One comes a little closer to an understanding of how so much brilliance capsized into so much savagery as the old order gave way to the new.

The book is divided into seven parts, each comprising separate chapters that approach a specific topic from different angles. The first two parts deal with "Women and Political Life" and "Women in Society." They are rich in information on "Women and the Law," "Women and Politics," "Women, Democracy, and Revolution in Paris," "Women and the Family," "Women and Education," "Women and Work," and, last but not least important, "Women Versus Clergy, Women Pro Clergy." The latter two essays bring new materials culled from the exploration of archives, and, between them, explode or substantiate stereotypes while underscoring the common constraints under which all women existed.

Part III holds its own surprises as it explores the pervasive and little-studied presence of women in the arts, as performers mainly but also as practitioners, a topic that leads to some humorous treatment of the symbolic representation of "Woman as Muse." The problem of "Women in Science," about which there is a paucity of information, is dealt with by concentration on a single figure, that of Mme du Châtelet. One remembers, of course, the activities of Mme de Warens as depicted by Rousseau.

The discussions of the women writers in Part IV—novelists, memorialists, *épistolières*—again point to a surprising paucity of information. The contributors suggest that research in this area be directed at producing profiles and bibliographies. The high esteem and widespread success enjoyed in their time by the few professional women painters raises the question of their later disappearance from the annals of painting. The portrayal of their work offered in this section reveals a far more lively activity than one might have expected.

The last three parts depict women from diverse perspectives: through the *Encyclopedia;* as rather vaguely theorized by the greater *philosophes*—Montesquieu, Voltaire, Diderot and Rousseau; and as glimpsed in eighteenth-century literature. In a sweeping finale, we are given images of the French eighteenth-century woman as portrayed in the literatures of England, Germany, Russia, and Spain. These sections do not pretend to be exhaustive, but they stimulate the reader and offer inspiration for further research. As a conclusion, we are given a carefully weighed, not overly optimistic estimate of the "legacy" passed on to the nineteenth century—concepts of woman's nature, role, potential, and place.

This collection of essays opens up many avenues of speculation. One wonders, for instance, about the marked differences in style between the great figures of the seventeenth century: the hard-riding, hard-plotting *grandes dames* of *la Fronde*, the independent and fastidious *précieuses,* and the dignified self-sufficiency of the two great aristocratic writers, Mme de Lafayette and Mme de Sévigné, who outclassed all but the two or three great writers among their contemporaries.

Another avenue of thought opens as we compare the "feminism-antifeminism" rhetoric of the eighteenth century to our own. This rhetoric is quite obviously no longer ours, postulated as it was upon a heritage of basic assumptions concerning "human nature," personality, the presence of an autonomous feminine "subject" and others. In transition between the Christian version of "woman" and the relativism and pragmatism of a segment of eighteenth-century thought, feminism—by female or male thinkers—is defined in simple, age-old terms: are women as potentially capable of reasoning as men? Should their education reflect their differing "roles"? Feminism is defined in terms of a recognition of woman as equal in status to man, man himself being the model of mankind. It is this ultimately male model that some French women reject today along with the term feminism itself. These contemporary women are like their predecessors in regard to the *philosophes;* they are the disciples of a new constellation of thinkers: Lacan, Derrida, Deleure, Foucault. From our vantage point today, we are tempted to attribute the "failure" of eighteenth-century feminism to the naïveté of the views concerning the male-female relationship of all but the most sophisticated of its male thinkers—Choderlos de Laclos and the marquis de Sade. In this realm, the eighteenth century was less innovative than might appear.

French Women and the Age of Enlightenment is a solid contribution, as much to our knowledge of what we still have to learn about women in history as to our sense of cultural history itself. It is furthermore an example of collaborative scholarship that deserves to be widely emulated. For my part, I see it as a sure sign that women in the U. S. are now fully visible, integrated, and confident members of the century-old "community of scholars."

GERMAINE BRÉE

French Women
and the
Age of Enlightenment

ᴚ Elizabeth Fox-Genovese

Introduction

> Since women find the paths to fame and power closed to members of their sex, they achieve these goals via other routes, using their charms as compensation.
> —Mme de Lambert (*Oeuvres*, pp. 69-70)

D URING the eighteenth century, foreign observers identified the women of France as a distinct and probably dangerous species. The essays by Katharine M. Rogers, Charlotte C. Prather, Carolyn Hope Wilberger, and Eva M. Kahiluoto Rudat, which conclude this volume, demonstrate that, national and cultural differences notwithstanding, English, German, Russian, and Spanish visitors concurred that French women differed—unfavorably—from those at home. According to David Hume, the French nation "gravely exalts those, whom nature has subjected to them, and whose inferiority and infirmities are absolutely incurable." Melchior Grimm, that dauntless chronicler of the Parisian literary scene, was similarly disturbed by the libertine social mores, social influence, and political power of French women, whose unwarranted behavior threatened proper family and civic structure. In their different ways, Russian and Spanish commentators recognized the power and attraction of French culture, but they also recognized the wide freedom of French women as disruptive of traditional values.

These views instructively point to the special quality of women's status in eighteenth-century France. All foreigners, apparently, saw the French case as one of excess, as a deviation from the norm. No matter, for the moment, that the norms of, say, England and Russia differed considerably from each other. The recognized divergence of French women from all norms presents a paradox, for, by common agreement, French women were seen to enjoy power and freedom that correspond imperfectly to the modern view of the constraints that hedged in their lives.

Edmond and Jules de Goncourt, who, in 1862, wrote the first comprehensive interpretation—and the first modern cultural and social portrait—of *La Femme au dix-huitième siècle,* called attention to the paradox, even if they did not explore it fully. "When during the eighteenth century," they begin, "the woman is born, she is not received into life by the joy of a family. . . . she is a benediction that they accept as a deception."[1] There follows as grim a picture as one cõuld want of the neglect and disadvantages that attended the girl's education, premature marriage, and unhappy domestic circumstances. Yet, toward the end of the study, they apparently reverse ground. In a chapter entitled "The Domination and the Intelligence of the Woman," they baldly assert that in the eighteenth century the woman

> is the principle that governs, the reason that directs, the voice that commands. She is the universal and fatal cause, the origin of events, the source of things. . . . Nothing escapes her, and she holds everything, the King and France, the will of the sovereign and the authority of opinion.[2]

Not merely does she rule the kingdom, appoint to ministries, reverse diplomatic alliances, award seats in the Academy, patronize arts and letters, she rules in the home as well: madame's, not monsieur's, dinner is served.

The Goncourt brothers do not fully explain this paradox of power and enslavement, of being and nothingness, but historians of women cannot afford to gloss over it so lightly. Nor can we afford to submit to the even greater temptation and dismiss it as illusion, for the flattering portrait that the Goncourts drew of eighteenth-century French women is as one with that of Hume and Grimm, except for interpretation. Where Hume and Grimm and their contemporaries saw disorder rampant, the Goncourts saw the triumph of grace and culture—what Norbert Elias has called "the civilizing process."[3] Detractors and celebrators alike were looking at the same women, describing the same patterns of behavior, and evaluating the same culture. Modern historians no longer look at eighteenth-century France through the same filters nor do they ask the same questions.

The Goncourts considered the woman of the eighteenth century as the embodiment of the ineffable grace and elegance that was eighteenth-century France—the world capital of civilization. Many of their predecessors and successors—the scholars and men of letters who edited innumerable volumes of women's letters and memoirs and wrote of the salons and of the lives of eighteenth-century French women—explicitly identified their work as an attempt to recapture the sweetness of life in that final flowering of aristocratic society before the Revolutionary holocaust destroyed everything worth living for. In their effort to recapture and to celebrate the grace and charm of life under the ancien régime, they were even prepared to reclassify what many would have considered deviant female behavior as yet another manifestation of the superior values encoded in aristocratic culture. Thus, the modern reader, who might expect the defense of pre-Revolutionary society to be accompanied by a paean to female submissiveness, may be surprised by Charles Henry's impassioned assessment of Julie de Lespinasse's irregular life: "Mademoiselle de Lespinasse's salon evaporated with her; but the hostess lived in the memory of contemporaries as one of the superior incarnations of passion, as the symbol of a time that has fled very fast and very far." The discovery and publication of her letters, which Henry is editing, ensure her a place in posterity and "she will live as long as passion; she will live beside Sapho, beside St. Theresa, beside Héloïse, beside those rare beings who wrote strongly for having lived strongly."[4] Henry accepts the identification of extraordinary women with aristocratic society and culture and finds ways of praising them despite their deviations from norms of female docility.

Other nineteenth- and early twentieth-century historians of traditional French society, apparently more impressed with the dangers of celebrating female independence whatever the mitigating social context, refused to accept the Julie de Lespinasses and their kind as representative of true aristocratic values. Thus, Edmond Pilon and Georges Lenôtre, following Charles de Ribbe, insisted that the froth of Parisian society ill represented—in fact, deviated from—the true character of the ancien régime, which they believed rested upon deep and stable family values. For them, the Revolution constituted not the assault of mediocre individualism and uniformity on style and distinction but the assault of the instrumentalism and disorder of the market on organic social and personal relations.[5]

Whatever their differences, these two interpretations concur in repudiating the Revolution and in celebrating aristocratic, in contrast to bourgeois, society and culture. They both restrict their serious attention to that small part of pre-revolutionary French society that might be called *le pays civilisé*. Recent historians have increasingly directed their attention to the vast numbers of French people who could not claim membership in that elite group. Social history concentrates on rural populations, on the urban poor, on criminals, even on the mercantile bourgeoisie, and similar groups whose participation in the dazzling culture of the France of the Enlightenment seems to have been marginal at best. Even students of the Enlightenment proper are turning their attention to the sociology of culture, to less prominent authors, to the dissemination of literary artifacts, and to related questions far removed from the classical literary studies of high culture.[6] In addition, feminist scholars have insisted that all of these scholarly trends must be re-viewed from the perspective of women since none of them takes any necessary account of women's experience and perceptions.

Feminist scholars in particular and scholars who study women in general have yet to reach agreement about the proper framework for the study of women. With the rapid development of the field of

women's history, the study of "women worthies" has fallen into
disrepute.[7] There is a general assumption that women's experience
can best be captured through the study of groups of women, perhaps
especially women of the popular classes, although it is also recognized
that much can be learned about more privileged women, provided they
are studied with the proper methods. In recent years, historians of
women have drawn heavily upon the methods of social and cultural
anthropology and, in some measure, demography to recreate women's
universes and cultures as well as their place in society at large. If such
studies are still in their infancy, they are already yielding splendid
results.[8] But, however rich they may be individually, these studies
collectively do not exhaust the complex problems of women in the age
of the French Enlightenment. As literary scholars properly insist, we
must also explore the vicissitudes of women's relation to high culture
and trace the uneven trajectory of women's own voices. Social history,
like historical anthropology, helps to establish the conditions or
structures of women's lives but cannot alone reveal the meanings
women ascribed to their lives.

Modern feminism has forged a series of questions about women's
lives, especially about the nature and sources of the powers and
freedoms women enjoy, which are totally foreign to the concerns of
the Goncourts and their colleagues. Ironically, those questions relate
rather more closely—if inversely—to the concerns of Hume and
Grimm, who worried especially about women's sexual freedom and
intellectual authority. Grimm, for example, insisted that literary
activity should be a male prerogative. In his opinion, Prather reminds
us, any woman who aspired to write should veil her thoughts in
"delicacy" and "modesty." Female authorship—with all the authority
the term implies—was more or less explicitly assimilated to female
sexuality, and both were discouraged.

Grimm and Hume, not unlike Jean-Jacques Rousseau and Restif de
La Bretonne, were appalled by what they viewed as the lawlessness
and unruliness of at least some eighteenth-century French women.
They saw a pervasive failure of delicacy and modesty; they shuddered
at female sexual license; they reproved women's intrusion into
intellectual and political life. Modern feminist scholars, in contrast, are
more impressed with the persisting legal and social barriers—not to
mention misogynic attitudes—that hampered women's independent
action and even women's cultural production. Because modern
feminist scholars find the social, political, and cultural domination of
women by men so decisive, we have difficulty accepting the Goncourts'
judgment that women themselves dominated eighteenth-century
French society. Today, it seems obvious that eighteenth-century
French women exercised power and enjoyed prestige on the sufferance

of men—that the sphere of independent female action was circumscribed indeed and, according to some, even shrinking. Few would
dispute the influence of the galaxy of notable eighteenth-century
women who have mesmerized historians and critics since their own
day: Mme du Maine, Mme de Tencin, Mme de Pompadour, Mme
d'Epinay, Mme Geoffrin, Mme du Deffand, Mlle de Lespinasse, Mme
du Châtelet, and so many more. But today we question the extent of
that influence, the terms on which it was exercised, women's own
perceptions of their roles, and the implications that the roles of some
had for the fate of women as a group.

So far, there has been very little meeting ground between the old
history of women worthies and the new social history of women. Even
the old, conservative tradition of family history has not fed directly
into the new social history. For French scholars, attitudes toward the
Revolution as the great rupture in national development remain
subject to conflict, although the overt celebrants of the society of the
ancien régime are less vociferous, or at least less outspoken, than was
common at the beginning of this century. Overall, the competing
claims of social history and the history of ideas, the competing
judgments of the French Revolution, and the precarious status of the
history of women in the French academy have combined to delay the
appearance of a history of women in eighteenth-century France. We
have nothing for the eighteenth century that can be compared with
Carolyn Lougee's fine book, *Le Paradis des Femmes*, on women in the
salons in the seventeenth century.[9] We have no modern history of
Mme de Pompadour or the role of women in the French court. We
have no history of women's participation in Parisian and provincial
academies, their submission of essays for prize competitions, their
participation in the societies of agriculture, or their attendance at
public courses, such as those offered by the Musée of Bordeaux.[10]
Evelyne Sullerot's *Histoire de la presse féminine en France des origines à 1848*
offers an indispensable introduction to an important topic but cannot
substitute for separate studies by the editors, contributors, and
readers of various periodicals.[11] Pierre Fauchery and Paul Hoffmann
provide massive overviews of the depiction of women in the novel and
the thought of the Enlightenment respectively, but neither devotes
serious attention to the contributions of women themselves.[12] Léon
Abensour's monumental study, *La Femme et le féminisme avant la révolution*,
remains, more than forty years after its initial publication, the most
comprehensive and learned history of women in eighteenth-century
French society and culture.[13] No modern synthesis has replaced it,
although recent historical and literary studies move beyond Abensour
if only in using sources and asking questions that he did not. Ironically,
the extraordinary visibility of a constellation of eighteenth-century

French women appears to have deterred scholars from assessing the experience of French women as a group, whatever the differences that separated them. Modern feminists have understandably reacted against the tradition that, with approbation or disgust, took the women of the Parisian elite as a proxy for woman. Yet, ultimately, no general history of women in eighteenth-century French culture and society will be possible until we can understand those women in their own society and in relation to women of other times and places—until, in short, we can restore them to the possible experience of women in the eighteenth century. This volume represents a first installment in that project.

Eighteenth-century France does not fit neatly into such vague categories as traditional or modern. The legal and political structures of the ancien régime had evolved from the feudalism of medieval France without any radical breaks.[14] Although the rise of absolutism, the commercialization of office, and the successive waves of legal reform and institutional innovation had superseded many feudal institutions, as a rule, new institutions had been superimposed on the old without eradicating them. Some withered from lack of use, and others were subject to conversion; but the basic structure of estates, like the basic property relations, persisted.[15] This complex history has provoked innumerable interpretations of French development that are not of immediate concern here. Certain general patterns emerge; but specific changes affected different groups of women differently, and the differences command attention first. To the extent that eighteenth-century France bore a strong corporatist imprint, women lived their lives as women of specific corps or social groups.[16] Estate membership constituted the overriding distinction, but within estates, there were important regional and social differences. Adrienne Rogers underscores the importance of regional difference in women's standing at law. Within the third estate alone, women might be bourgeoises of a specific city (and which city could make a difference), might be members of a guild, might be members of a rural *communauté d'habitants*. These different identifications, and many more, shaped women's social position and, presumably, their self-perceptions as women. They also erected perceptual barriers to a single, uniform notion of women that would invite women's identification with each other as members of a gender. We have only to recall Arthur Young's searing picture of the grim lives and premature aging of peasant women to recognize that the circumstances of their lives hardly invited them to identify with the fashionable denizens of Paris society, if, indeed, they had heard of them.[17]

The Church and the State constituted the principal institutions that sought to cut across local and social particularisms, and even they did so unevenly. Michel de Certeau's pioneering study of the standardization of language at the time of the French Revolution offers a healthy caution to those who are tempted to seek some precocious, uniform national culture under the ancien régime.[18] From the early seventeenth century on, the State had pursued a policy of self-aggrandizement that extended from purification and standardization of official language to what Saint-Simon, and, after him, de Tocqueville, would see as a leveling of its subjects.[19] Saint-Simon was primarily worried about the devaluing of the status of the old nobility of the sword and the rise of nobles of the robe and mere bourgeois to positions of power and influence. De Tocqueville, for his part, noted the growing institutional uniformity of the eighteenth century, which, he believed, foreshadowed the work of the Revolution. The ultimate significance of these judgments remains questionable. However much the nobility was being dissolved into a new elite, noble status persisted; and, as late as the second half of the eighteenth century, the nobility staged a defense of the prerogatives of blood not merely in the ideology of *race* propounded by Boulainvilliers but also in such practical matters as exemption from specific forms of taxation and monopoly of key forms of military service.[20] And however great the progress of centralization, the diversity of localities and social groups remained important, as did a staggering variety of special privileges.

The growth of absolutism promoted a tendency toward a sharp delineation of women's status, at least at the upper levels of society. The most notable feature was surely the explicit patriarchalism of royal law. As Adrienne Rogers suggests, royal law distinctly fostered primogeniture (normally male) in particular and men's dominance of property and the family unit in general. This tendency should be understood as a policy of male domination in contrast to the persisting models of community of goods between spouses and equal inheritance among heirs that much customary law permitted.[21]

The growing centralization and bureaucratization of royal government also circumscribed women's political roles. The piecemeal exclusion of women from politics had begun at least in the High Middle Ages. The "invention" of the Salic law in the fourteenth century retroactively established their unfitness to govern the realm, or, perhaps more portentously, to inherit rights of sovereignty. As delegates of families and as members of the royal court, women had continued to participate actively in the political life of the realm. During the religious wars of the second half of the sixteenth century and the Fronde of the mid-seventeenth century, women had actively championed political factions. The roster of queens and princesses of the blood is impressive. From the beginnings of the personal reign of Louis XIV on, however, their roles were severely circumscribed. Mme de Maintenon stands alone, and the domestic cast of her role, like the domestic values she prescribed in her educational program at St. Cyr, augur a new attitude toward women's relation to political life. Her most notable eighteenth-century successor, Mme de Pompadour, would display a more flamboyant style but would also exercise her considerable influence purely on the basis of her personal relation with the king.

There would be no return from Louis XIV's policy of professionalization of government. The *conseil du roi*, the ministries, the bureaux, the intendancies would all be staffed by men and, increasingly, to the disgust of the Saint-Simons, by men who were specialists or professionals, albeit of inherited or acquired noble status. It should also be noted that women, barred from the law, never belonged to the judiciary, which played such important political and administrative roles and served as the nursery of intendants. Even the lower institutions of government, which might be taken to reflect custom as much as royal policy, excluded women. We have no record of female *jurats, échevins,* or *capitouls;* none of female *syndics de village.* Women were being progressively excluded from any roles of governance that they might have played in guilds. Some noble women retained rights to be elected to the Estates General or to send delegates, but even this residual right rarely found expression and could be expected to succumb to the weight of the royal policy of the uniform masculinization of government. After the long hiatus in representation under absolutism—the Estates General last met in 1614—no woman figured among the elected deputies in 1789.[22]

French absolutism confirms the general rule that systematic state building tends to disfranchise women and the special rule that pre-bourgeois European state building tended to be self-consciously patriarchal.[23] It also, with respect to political life, strengthens the case of those who argue for a deterioration in women's status with the emergence of modern institutions and the growth of capitalism, although that long history cannot simply be subsumed under an undifferentiated model of patriarchalism.[24] Susan P. Conner's essay demonstrates that noblewomen did not passively accept their growing exclusion from politics. She also charts a significant progression in female political goals and style. Mme du Maine emerges as the last of that tradition of noblewomen, perhaps best exemplified by the Grande Mademoiselle for the Fronde, who sought to organize and advance the claims of a political faction that aspired to control the crown itself. Yet Mme de Tencin, Mme du Maine's contemporary, cannot be understood as a successor to the tradition—her political dabblings were purely personal. Mme de Pompadour, the great political woman of the century, did pursue policies, in contrast to whims, but could work only through her personal influence with the king. Her impact should not be minimized, but, as Conner argues, it cannot be credited to the account of the political influence of women as women. Pompadour provoked much of the rising chorus of protest against women's unseemly and disruptive political influence, but she stood alone in her time and had no successor. Marie-Antoinette never demonstrated political skill on the scale of her political commitments; and in her principal political role as symbol of the female presence in the realm, she failed miserably.[25]

Harriet B. Applewhite's and Darline Gay Levy's essay underscores the changing structure of women's political participation in the eighteenth century. The deep current of female politics that they find surfacing during the Revolution had popular rather than aristocratic roots. Recent work in the history of popular protest under the ancien régime has established the importance and ubiquity of women's participation in and even leadership of protest movements, especially bread riots, and their vigorous defense of the notions of moral economy and *taxation populaire*.[26] In essential respects, women's participation in popular politics was analogous to the political activity of aristocratic women. Common (often poor) women, like noble (even more often, rich) women, entered the political arena as representatives of families, corporations, communities, as, in short, representatives of particularist groups. Yet common women may also have claimed political roles on the basis of their gender. They did not necessarily have any more advanced ideas than their privileged sisters about the political rights of women as individuals, in the sense of the nascent ideology of the rights of man; but they did belong to a tradition in which the ideology of gender, of male and female spheres, carried great weight. As women, they were responsible for important aspects of collective life; as women, they would act collectively to defend the families' food supply or their own marketing rights. No more than aristocratic women do common women fit neatly into the model of modern feminism. If common women defended the interests of women as women, their understanding of those rights was more indebted to traditional corporatism than to modern individualist thought. In the eighteenth century, aristocratic women were far more likely than their common sisters to have a notion of their own aspirations as individuals, but their concept of individualism probably had more to do with the seventeenth-century concept of *gloire*, of individual excellence or heroism, than with the universal claims of bourgeois individualism.[27] And they assuredly assimilated that concept of individualism to their assumptions about the prerogatives of birth, or caste. They aspired to individual power within traditional institutions, to personal interests within their corps, but hardly to defend the individual rights of all women as women. Nothing in their experience would have led them to identify with the *tricoteuses* of the Faubourg St. Antoine or the *citoyennes républicaines révolutionnaires*.[28]

The Revolution constituted a watershed in the history of women's political and legal status as in so much else. Applewhite and Levy cogently argue that during the Revolution the women of Paris contributed decisively to forging a new concept of legitimacy. They show that Parisian women's pursuit of their special responsibilities for the well-being of the Parisian populace merged with and expanded the growing ideas of democracy and sovereignty of the people. To the fight for popular sovereignty, the women of Paris brought the idea of women's active charge of women's sphere—its public extensions as well as its domestic ones. The march on Versailles in October of 1789 also reveals their commitment to an enlightened patriarchalism, which they did not see as contradictory to popular democracy. The queen, as the baker's wife, stood as their symbol of the female dimension of legitimate royalty. The events of the Revolution also offered Parisian women a rapidly expanding language of democratic politics. Their engagement in the practical creation of popular sovereignty not merely reflected their long-standing roles as women but also modified their conception of those roles and of the nature of female citizenship.[29] Ultimately, the Mountain did them in. The Jacobins' idea of political democracy did not include female citizenship. In fact, it rested squarely on the ideal of female domesticity. The Terror pronounced a harsh judgment on disorderly women, whatever their political persuasion; the guillotine indiscriminately claimed the lives of Marie-Antoinette, Mme Roland, and Olympe de Gouges.

The Revolution brought the triumph of a universal ideal of womanhood and considerable uniformity to the external conditions of women's lives. Severe class differences persisted, but women of all classes were subject to the male dominance propounded by the Napoleonic Code and were excluded from the official politics of the nation. Claire G. Moses's concluding essay traces the complex implications of this legacy for nineteenth-century feminism. The Revolution also contributed to the consolidation and dissemination of a single ideal of womanhood that had been slowly germinating under the ancien régime. New attitudes toward women manifest throughout the eighteenth century, like important changes in women's experience, help to account for the contradictory assessments of women's status. The various strands that would constitute the post-Revolutionary ideology of womanhood can all be identified under the ancien régime, as many of the essays demonstrate; but the unified, dominant image did not take shape until the system of estates, local privilege, and corporations had been abolished.[30]

Historians of women constantly debate whether social, political, economic, and intellectual change—especially the great revolutions—benefit, hinder, or are irrelevant to women. The French Revolution, itself the result of eighteenth-century change in all areas, promoted distinct changes in women's lives; but, as my essay on women and work attempts to show, the changes are hard to label as improvement or deterioration, much less to assess uniformly for all groups. The principal lessons to be drawn from an investigation of women's work have implications for women's experience in general. They are: that separate spheres, far from having been invented by the Revolutionary bourgeoisie or capitalism, had been the norm throughout French history and marked rural life as sharply as urban; that women customarily contributed at least their fair share to all household economies; that women's work had only exceptionally netted women the power, prestige, or remuneration that men's work netted men; that the tightening grip of the monarchy on economic life in general and the guilds in particular tended to reinforce male dominance, even when, by abolishing guilds or establishing *métiers libres*, it promoted a free market in labor power; that the erosion of traditional communities —rural or urban—exposed women to risk more than it opened paths of advancement and independence to them; that before, during, and after the Revolution women's work remained primarily a facet of household economies and rarely permitted a woman a comfortable, independent living; that professionalization in all areas tended to disadvantage women by officially excluding them and reducing their family contributions to unpaid domestic labor; that working-class women's wage labor did not significantly modify gender relations within or without the family. In short, the study of women's work suggests that the changes of the eighteenth century pointed toward a reorganization of the relation between women's work and society, primarily because of men's growing dependence upon salaries and wages, but did not necessarily advantage or disadvantage women in a consistent manner. Cultural and ideological changes yielded similarly mixed results.

Those who like to celebrate the power and status enjoyed by women in "traditional" French society must take account of Ian Maclean's judgment that the dominant culture's view of women was profoundly negative and did not improve during the Renaissance or, indeed, the seventeenth century.[31] Officially, woman remained an imperfect man, a weak vessel, a victim of her body in general and her uterus in particular, the equivalent of an idiot or a child. The eighteenth century itself did little to change that verdict, although it softened its consequences and, eventually, came to idealize the very women it demeaned. But eighteenth-century thought also included a distinct feminist current, which reached its high point in Condorcet's writings and the political claims of women such as Olympe de Gouges and Etta Palm d'Aelders.[32] A rising tide of opinion in favor of a positive, if

subordinate, domestic role for women blocked that current. The
project for women corresponded to the predilections of Rousseau and
Grimm.

Ruth Graham's essay on women and the clergy explores the
complexity of women's relation to religion during the period. In
theology and ideology, the Church, like the State, promoted a
universal model of womanhood; but in practice, also like the State, it
sustained very different relations with different groups of women.
Graham explores the special relation of women to Jansenism, not
merely the Jansenism of the nuns of Port-Royal, who cultivated a
special form of individual piety and austerity, but also the Jansenism of
the women of Paris, who embraced it as an expression and legitimation
of their own forms of piety and enthusiasm for which the orthodox
Church hierarchy had scant patience. The full story of women and
religion in the eighteenth century remains to be told, but we can
already discern a steady growth in female teaching and charitable
orders and the beginnings of the special responsibility of women for
ministering to the sick, the needy, and the young. Michel Vovelle has
found, at least for Provence, that the eighteenth century witnessed a
steady decline in the visible signs of men's religious devotions but not
women's.[33] Graham shows that by the middle of the Revolutionary
period there was evidence of that special identification of women with
religion that would characterize the nineteenth century. This is not
the place to total the balance sheet of assets and liabilities that women
gained from this association, but its existence is worth noting both as
an important change and as a harbinger of such nineteenth-century
offshoots as Auguste Comte's deification of Clotilde de Vaux. Women
gained some prestige in the eyes of the Church and expanding
opportunities to act in defense of religious values; but their improved
position, like their improved position in the home, came at a time when
men were more and more associated with a secular public sphere that
provided new opportunities for individual authority and advancement
but largely excluded women.

The growing interest in women's education, on the part of both men
and women, expressed the conflicting and changing attitudes toward
women. Mme de Maintenon and Fénelon had inaugurated the tradition of domestic and maternal education for women in the late
seventeenth century. Eighteenth-century writers, especially after
mid-century, developed their core ideas in conjunction with the
general concerns of enlightened social thought. Eighteenth-century
pedagogy for women sought to reconcile the sensationalist psychology
of Locke and others with a commitment to woman's different (inferior
and then special) nature and, following Rousseau, her maternal
destiny and obligation.[34] Samia I. Spencer's essay calls attention to the

genuine explosion of interest in the education of women among all social groups. The values that eighteenth-century educators sought to instill in women seem to have been remarkably similar across class lines. The differences in goals for women of different classes consisted especially in the amount of education, rather than the function of education. For although women, as Spencer argues, "acquired an unspoken right to knowledge and education" and no longer risked ridicule as *savantes* for any learning they might acquire, they were also subject to stringent spoken, as well as unspoken, constraints on the uses to which they should put that education.

In education, as in so much else, the mid-century appears to have been a turning point.[35] At about the time that the nation, in Voltaire's phrase, "set itself to reasoning about grain," it also set itself to propounding programs for improved education. In the earlier part of the century, improved education for at least individual noble- and elite women seems to have been accepted, although never institutionalized and never available to all. One has only to think of the spelling errors of Mme de Graffigny. Education for such women can probably be linked to the growth of enlightened thought in polite society; but even the most learned and enlightened women, as Linda Gardiner shows in the case of Emilie du Châtelet, suffered under special burdens that hampered their full and equal participation in the world of science and scholarship. It is the familiar story of women's picking up what advanced education they could—especially Latin and mathematics, normally not considered necessary for girls—from the tutors of their brothers or friends of the family.[36] Female learning constituted the exception and was closely associated with inappropriate female power; if learned women were no longer ridiculed in aristocratic society, they were often isolated and mistrusted. The eighteenth century witnessed the final flowering of the community of aristocratic amateurs in which women might find at least a precarious foothold.[37] Scientific learning was coming to require more professional training, and, following the Revolution, that training would become the monopoly of the university system that excluded women. Before the Revolution, the tendency was already apparent.

Female learning could be inculcated and contained within the private world of aristocratic polite society, but its implications of authoritative female individualism threatened the values and self-esteem of the emerging group of professional men of letters. Women themselves were well aware that their knowledge and scholarly accomplishments would not necessarily yield them approbation. We are back to Grimm and Rousseau, not to mention Diderot; but as these thinkers and many others began to point out, female education did not have to result in female learning, much less in female authority. The growing consensus about the appropriate purpose and content of women's education must be understood in the context of the changing model of womanhood that was taking shape at the end of the ancien régime.

We must juxtapose the mounting critique of the self-cultivation and self-assertion of privileged women with the indisputable progress in female literacy in general and women's education in particular. François Furet and Jacques Ozouf, like Daniel Roche and others, have demonstrated that a real, if unevenly distributed, progress in female literacy characterized the eighteenth century. Paris and northern France led the rest of the country both in literacy and in the rate of its increase throughout the eighteenth century. But as a certain level of literacy was attained, the rate of its increase slowed in those regions that had previously lagged in absolute figures. During the eighteenth century, within the more advanced regions, the literacy of women lagged behind that of men, but the rate of increase for women surpassed that of men. Even within the advanced regions, the class differentials in literacy were considerable, and the literacy of women always fell short of that of men. Measurement of literacy depends upon the kinds of sources used; marriage contracts and inventories after death bias findings in favor of the propertied—even among the lower classes—and, hence, in favor of literacy. Parisian criminal records reveal an appallingly low level of literacy among the women whose experience they document.[38]

The considerable increases in literacy testify to the success of the schooling activities of the Church. During the century, the number of teaching orders proliferated, and women's teaching orders explicitly undertook the schooling of girls. As Spencer shows, the efforts for girls did not equal those for boys, and the rule of strict gender segregation in early education was clearly not always observed, primarily for lack of resources and facilities. Nonetheless, Roche asserts that in Paris schooling reached close to one hundred percent of the population.[39] Even where the education of girls was successfully implemented, it focused on the inculcation of religious and domestic values. The education of girls can thus appropriately be interpreted as a self-conscious exercise in social control, understood not merely as an imposition of accommodation and docility but also as the cultivation of specific female roles. The mounting agreement that women's social mission lay in motherhood and domesticity also helps to account for the spiraling attacks on convent education for privileged women. Boarding at convent schools was held to remove girls from the beneficial influence of their mothers and to expose them to the corrupting influences of convent life. It artificially separated them from the world so that, upon their release, they could be expected to engage in flagrantly inappropriate behavior, in particular, sexual adventures. Diderot's famous picture is only the most dramatic manifestation of a general current of opinion.[40] By the end of the century, the general reflection on female pedagogy—to which women themselves, notably Mme de Genlis and Mme Campan, made important contributions—had yielded substantial agreement on the domestic education of girls and the role of women as domestic educators. The post-Revolutionary writings of Mme Necker de Saussure, Mme de Remusat, and others thus reflected the thought and experience of the closing years of the ancien régime.[41]

The insistence upon domestic education for girls, ideally provided by their mothers, grew apace with a congeries of new ideals of family life. Cissie Fairchilds argues that Lawrence Stone's model of the appearance of the conjugal family and affective domesticity in England can be applied to France, at least in the second half of the century. She may overstate a good case, for room remains for difference of opinion, at least with respect to the generalization of the model in pre-Revolutionary France. But there can be no doubt that, at least following 1760, various strata of French society were drawn to the models of domesticity offered by English novels as well as by Jean-Jacques Rousseau. Nor can there be any doubt that Fairchilds' model triumphed and was rapidly disseminated among the upper classes immediately following the Revolution.[42] For the pre-Revolutionary period, however, there is some evidence that older, more patriarchal attitudes and behavior persisted among some segments of the nobility. This counterpoint includes such phenomena as fathers' continuing recourse to *lettres de cachet* to discipline recalcitrant sons, notably but far from exclusively, Victor Riqueti's imprisonment of his headstrong son Honoré; the persistence of early, and arranged, marriages for noble daughters; and the continued recourse to both wet nurses for infants and convent education for girls. Helen Maria Williams justified the early phases of the Revolution on the specific grounds that the monarchy reflected and guaranteed the illegitimate powers of fathers, which were most dramatically expressed in the fathers' interference with their children's legitimate desire to marry for love.[43]

Fairchilds does point to an important current: some members of the nobility converted to the ideals of domesticity. Significantly, the numbers of noble infants sent out to nurse and those who died with wet nurses declined. The infatuation with the idea of motherhood, especially the idea of mothers' nursing their own children, progressed rapidly. The difficulty lies with our uncertain ability to document accurately the incidence of conjugal domesticity in contrast to conjugal arrangements, cynicism, and callousness. Nor can we categorically affirm that the nobility alone paved the way for the generalization of the practice of domesticity. Only after the Revolution can we point with confidence to the institutionalization of the complex of ideas including domesticity, mothers' nursing, maternal education, and marriage for affection, if not love. All of the ideas were present before the Revolution, but, without a clear social foundation, they were probably implemented piecemeal by different social groups and different individuals within groups.[44]

The ideals of domestic and maternal womanhood nonetheless provide the focal point for the refiguration of the concept of woman and the roles of women in the closing decades of the ancien régime. With the erosion of traditional forms of social stratification and identification, it appeared to many that women were breaking free of their social moorings. Conjugal domesticity and motherhood were gradually seen to offer the perfect molds within which to reconfine female sexuality and female authority. They also had the advantages of offering women a new and flattering image of themselves, control of their own sphere—however marginalized—and a model with which women of different social and economic backgrounds could identify. Although precise chronological lines cannot be drawn, it would appear that in the early part of the century female individualism was associated with the growing freedom and education of aristocratic women, but not with a feminist discourse. In the second part of the century, the preoccupation with male individualism promoted some exploration of the claims of feminism, understood as universal female individualism, but concentrated even more on developing the ideal of woman as a willing domestic mirror.[45]

The thought of the Enlightenment wrestled with the theoretical problems of woman's nature and appropriate social and political roles. Some consideration of women constitutes an integral part of most of the leading Enlightenment texts on social theory. Yet, as heirs to the time-honored notions of female inferiority, Enlightenment thinkers normally continued to view women as weak, troublesome, shrewish, false, vindictive, ill-suited for friendship, coquettish, vain, superficial, deceitful, and, in general, lesser humans. As Sara Ellen Malueg demonstrates, the numerous articles on women in the *Encyclopédie* are riddled with such views, although some of the authors, notably the chevalier de Jaucourt, did argue for women's strong qualities and adult capacities. If the *Encyclopédie* offers no coherent feminist agenda, its plates graphically depict women's active participation in various forms of productive and social life. This contradiction between text or interpretation and visual representation offers a splendid image of the contradictions between women's diverse social roles and the dominant discourse on women. To the extent that the women whose productive activities were depicted belonged to the third estate, men of letters— even when they themselves were of bourgeois origin—may have had difficulty seeing that productive activity as female and may have resisted associating the diversity of women's activities with a discourse on women's nature. Even if the eighteenth century could see women's social contributions, it apparently had trouble naming them, especially within the context of a concept of woman.

Pauline Kra's article on Montesquieu and Blandine L. McLaughlin's article on Diderot explore the specific attitudes toward women of two of the century's leading theorists. Both articles draw upon and extend an important body of recent scholarship on women in the thought of the Enlightenment. Both demonstrate that it would be impossible to label either Montesquieu or Diderot a feminist in the modern sense, or even in the classical equal rights sense of a Condorcet. Both Montesquieu and Diderot take the problem of woman seriously, both betray considerable sympathy for women, and both end with the assumption that women are destined to find happiness in an enlightened domesticity. Montesquieu forcefully insists that the status of women constitutes an important measure of the freedom and level of civilization of any society. Yet, ultimately, his attitudes toward women, like his liberalism, remain tied to the older noble tradition; and although he assumes that women will, even under the monarchy where they are the freest, pursue their lives within the family and under the direction of husbands and fathers, he appears unthreatened by female sexuality, initiative, and intelligence.[46] Diderot, in contrast, bears the distinct marks of nascent bourgeois misogyny. His recognition of the liabilities under which women suffer never leads him to deny their inferiority, much less to seek their equality in dignity and authority with men. Upon close reading, his views approximate those of Rousseau and Grimm. He joins those who are engaged in modernizing traditional notions of separate spheres to conform to the needs of bourgeois men exposed to all the anxieties and pressures of self-promotion in a competitive market. In this spirit, he writes to his daughter Angélique, foreshadowing post-Revolutionary ideas of domesticity, and echoing peasant custom: "External affairs are his, those of the interior are yours." And, as McLaughlin also quotes him, for men like himself, a woman must be "the mother of his children . . . the unique individual under the sky who feels his caresses and whose soul responds fully to his."

Modern feminist scholarship properly draws attention to the deep misogynistic currents that inform the thought of men like Diderot and Rousseau. Yet, however deeply those views were indebted to traditional misogyny, they also represent a genuine transformation of traditional thinking about women. The early part of the century had bequeathed to men a double anxiety that they tended to confound. On the one hand, they were worried about what Ruth P. Thomas identifies as female eroticisms and female sexualities breaking out of

their prisons—the harem of Montesquieu's *Lettres Persanes;* on the other
hand, they were worried about what Nancy K. Miller has identified as
the "male anxiety about the self in an unheroic world."[47] The thought
of many of the *philosophes* merges in this respect with the domestic
message of the novel to forge a new model of female confinement. But
the search for this new model led to a new idealization of women's
roles within their newly assigned spheres. The representation of
women as muses or as suicides or as edifying examples, discussed here
by Roseann Runte, Ruth Thomas, and Vera G. Lee, all confirm this
mixed denigration and idealization of women that characterized the
second half of the century in particular.

The steady, if uneven, appearance of the new image of women
gradually triumphed over older views. In this perspective, it is possible
to see the marquis de Sade's views of women as the dramatization of
the conflict between that unbridled female sexuality that so worried
the eighteenth century and the agents of its containment. It is almost
as if Sade used female sexuality as a metaphor for female individualism,
although one cannot but wonder whether he did not have in mind the
heroic individualism of the older aristocratic tradition. Alice M.
Laborde insists that Sade's concept of pleasure must be reconsidered in
relation to his concept of property and that we recognize his deep
hostility to treating women as property. The nature and extent of his
feminism remains a subject of heated debate, but we do not have to
cast Sade as a champion of women, much less as a feminist, to
recognize that he perceived the possibilities for the oppression of
women inherent in the idealization of their virtue by anxious males.
Nonetheless, his personal war with the enforcers of female virtue
strongly suggests that Sade was more concerned with his own
struggle with those agents of conformity than with the independence
or dignity of women.

Rousseau, as Gita May suggests, forces us to clarify our understanding of women's relations to the new values that were emerging from
the transformation of the dominant male culture. In recent years,
Rousseau has not merely been accorded a key place in eighteenth-
century thought but has also come in for sharp attack from feminist
critics. The two trends are not unrelated. From the vantage point of
the late twentieth century, Rousseau appears as the decisive prophet
of male individualism in a competitive, capitalist society. That compelling, subjective perspective shaped his treatment of women, in which
modern feminists recognize the prototype for their own subjection
and exclusion from authoritative individualism. "Made for man's
delight," Sophie offends contemporary women's—especially feminists'—
ambitions and self-respect.[48] Yet, May insists, we must confront the
deep admiration that so many accomplished women of the late

eighteenth and early nineteenth centuries accorded Rousseau. The possible reasons for this admiration are many, and not all invalidate contemporary feminists' hostility to him. If women like Mme Roland and Mme de Staël were drawn to Julie as a romantic heroine, their attraction could have resulted from an unconscious temptation to surrender and even to destroy themselves—at the hands of men. Women's relation to romantic love—like men's—has ever been conflicting and composed, at least in part, of a desire to merge to the point of self-obliteration. But there are other possibilities. The picture of Julie's reign, through the giving and withholding of approbation and affection, at Clarens must have been seductive to many. Today we may read of her domestic rule through the disabused eyes of those just escaping from the suburban wasteland in which women's dominion of the home ultimately resulted. But for eighteenth-century women, that dominion was new and must have looked preferable to subjection in the home. And if we legitimately doubt that either death for love or pastoral domesticity exhausted the ambitions of Mme Roland or Mme de Staël, we would do well to remember that they could have read the *Confessions* as a model of self-investigation and self-creation that women—extraordinary women—as well as men could emulate. History and society, not natural law, barred women from full and equal participation in individualism.

The changes in women's position in eighteenth-century society and the changes in the concept of woman in eighteenth-century culture do not amount to clear progress or deterioration. In society and culture, women's domestic and maternal destiny persisted, albeit somewhat refashioned. The only indisputable marks of progress for women— aside from a growing freedom from death in childbirth and, for poor women, from death from starvation—appear to have been literacy and education. Eighteenth-century French women themselves provide the most forceful testimony to the limitations of women's literacy and education as an unambiguous source of female empowerment, but, whatever their perceptions of those limitations, women in growing numbers exercised their powers of self-expression. Nor were those powers limited to the written word.

The chapters by Barbara G. Mittman on women in the theatre arts, Ursula M. Rempel on women in music, and Danielle Rice on women in the visual arts offer an important and revealing perspective on the relation of women to culture. In these arenas, as elsewhere, it is difficult not to be impressed by the subtle changes in women's position. If the ancien régime did little to encourage the achievements of women as individuals, its corporate structure did offer them certain kinds of possibilities even as it imposed constraints.

Raymond Williams and others have suggested that the modern idea of the artist, like the modern idea of genius, took shape toward the middle of the eighteenth century in conjunction with the general ideology of individualism. Previously, artists had produced and performed within the context of guilds, workshops, and an elaborate system of patronage.[49] The emergence of the concept of the artist as creator should be associated with the development of the market, in particular an urban market, for literature and *objets d'art*. From the chapters on music, visual arts, and the theatre, it would appear that these general changes had a special impact on women. Especially in music and the visual arts, women appear to have acquired training and pursued success in the context of family traditions and workshops. If they enjoyed less independent authority than did their male peers, they nonetheless benefited from a supportive structure that permitted them to exercise their craft. And even though official policy discouraged their official recognition—it was ruled in 1706 that no more women would be admitted to the Académie des Beaux-Arts—some women continued to be admitted to the Académie throughout the eighteenth century.

The theatre presents an especially fascinating case. Throughout the century, women had a special association with both public and private theatres. In the private sphere, women, notably Mme de Pompadour, presided over every aspect of theatrical production. This arena offered them the opportunity to produce, direct, and act. But as this tradition with its prohibitive costs was nearing its end, the public tradition of the actress as exemplary dangerous woman was coming into its own. Throughout the ancien régime, public actresses experienced the negative effects of corporate identity; they literally lost civil rights. But they were also beginning to emerge from that corporate background into the full light of public glorification. The actress as public woman captures the full complexity of the female condition. Exalted, recognized as gifted, showered with acclaim, actresses were also the quintessential women at risk. The very exercise of their talent, especially its public display, cut them off from all the normal protections. Freed of constraint, they became fair game for exploitation. In mobilizing their womanhood as actresses, they tore the veils from both their sexuality and their intelligence. Their authority was revealed as the occasion for their vulnerability.

The nineteenth-century mythology of the actress, dancer, and courtesan belongs to another book. It is, nonetheless, worth evoking briefly if only to call attention to the contradictory models of female accomplishment and self-expression. These occupations permitted women a certain freedom denied to their domestic sisters. The female sexuality that nineteenth-century culture would do so much to disguise and contain was, for these women, the essence of their success. They displayed what other women were supposed to hide. Yet their very success depended upon their exhibition of themselves as women. Their cultural authority was contradicted by their dependence upon pleasing as women. Their lives revolved around the paradox of goddess and whore. The veils of femininity under which they affirmed their individual initiative constituted an open contradiction of any authoritative individualism.

Authoritative individualism lay at the core of the struggles of literary women. Everything encouraged—indeed, coerced—them to speak through the models of womanhood proffered by the dominant culture. Even the Goncourts, in their catalogue of female domination and intelligence, do not suggest that women contributed to or shaped the culture of the century except by indirection. As *salonnières*, as patronesses, as arbiters of taste, women functioned as mediators and as facilitators of male authority and genius. To a remarkable degree, the women writers of the century did observe at least the outward proprieties of "modesty" and "delicacy" that Grimm prescribed. Yet women did write and did find covert ways of conveying their own standards and judgments. The eighteenth century witnessed the delineation—if not the origins—of what would become a distinctive female literary tradition. As letter writers, memorialists, and novelists, eighteenth-century women groped for their own voices and contributed to what was beginning to define itself as a female perspective on the world.

Judith Curtis, in her chapter on the letter writers, eschews literary judgment for its own sake in favor of presenting the letters as testimonials to the daily concerns of these individual women as women. The common themes she identifies include depression and ill health and a concern with the nature and availability of happiness *(bonheur)*. Women's letters precisely straddle the borders of women's domestic lives; Janus-like, they mediate women's spontaneous self-expression and women's crafted self-representation. Daniel Roche reminds us that during the eighteenth century, letter writing became common among various strata of the Parisian population. The new services of the *messageries* and the *postes* permitted easy exchange of notes. Surely women's growing literacy encouraged their participation in the exchange of messages. For most women, letters emanated from and translated the concerns of their domestic lives. The unpublished correspondence of Mme Chazot Duplessy of Bordeaux to her newly married daughter, Mme de Cursol, tells of daily events and offers advice on everything from sexual relations to the proper disciplining of servants.[50] Serge Chassagne has recently published the correspondence of Mme de Maraise, a bourgeoise married to one of the owners of the Jouy manufacture, who, he claims, "mediated" between the world of Parisian enlightenment and Jouy. A consummate businesswoman, Mme de Maraise was not on that account distracted from her domestic and maternal responsibilities. Her letters mix business and family affairs with domestic chat and local gossip in a manner that faithfully captures the multiple concerns of the households of the commercial and manufacturing bourgeoisie—and especially captures the role of women in that world. In the midst of the business reports and the chat, she occasionally sets forth her views on the nature and value of friendship or the responsibilities of motherhood in phrases that echo the new sensibility of the closing decades of the ancien régime.[51]

Perhaps because Mme de Maraise is so indispensable to her world, so busy, and so satisfied with her lot, her letters are less concerned with the problem of *bonheur* than those of the women Curtis discusses. For the period during which she was writing, the great female problems of love, loneliness, and age did not press her to consider the vicissitudes of female *bonheur*. But for her, as for other women, letter writing had become an important part of her life. Her human networks were reinforced by written exchanges, and participation in those networks was, more or less explicitly, pushing her to represent herself in words.

The memorialists, discussed in Susan R. Kinsey's chapter, take verbal self-representation one step beyond the mixed spontaneity and artifice of the letter writers. The memorialists commit themselves to a unified work, not just vignettes of a life. The late eighteenth century witnessed the appearance of the autobiography as the self-conscious creation of a self. Rousseau's *Confessions* is, in this sense, taken to mark the emergence of a new genre. The memorial, which already had a venerable history, can also be viewed as a construction of a self, but it is a self in relation to, or as an observer of, events of general significance. It is as if in the autobiography the self becomes the history as well as the observer, and women dared not plunge directly into that self-revelation. The memorial offered them the opportunity to exercise authority through the ordering and interpreting of events. Even more than the place they ascribed to themselves, the fact of recording established—however indirectly—their authorship. In the memorial, the implied "I" of the recording subject is more important than the frequently demure or self-effacing "I" of the reported self as participant. The memorial offered women the chance to comment on public events and to interpret the motivations and the actions of the makers of history. As Kinsey states, a woman's *gloire* depended, by the time of the Revolution, on her anonymity. We are back, by another route, to the paradox of power and submission. As it became more plausible to see women as a group, to press gender identification across class barriers, it became less acceptable for women to seek *gloire* as individuals, for to do so would be, implicitly, to claim the possibility of *gloire* for their gender.

The Revolution dramatically restricted women's access to public events after its own explosive momentum had been spent. Mme Roland simultaneously signals the end of an aristocratic tradition—to which, without the Revolution, she could never have adhered—and inaugurates a tradition of bourgeois domesticity. The Revolution opened the stage of politics to the men of her class and, for a brief moment, to some women. Even so, Mme Roland's influence on those events was through men; her acquaintance with the actors was in her own domestic space. But through her *Mémoires*, she, like the other memorialists who preceded her, claimed history for female scrutiny and judgment.

Like letters and memorials, women's novels took their place on the circumference of female consciousness, at the fringe of that hole of silence, the unwritten female autobiography. Joan Hinde Stewart, in her chapter on the novelists, explores the variety of female fictions that appeared during the eighteenth century and, as they increased in number, established the core of a female literary tradition that would henceforth be, in Stewart's paraphrase of Virginia Woolf, continuous. In France, as in England, the eighteenth century witnessed women's appropriation of the novel. No matter that men would continue to use the genre and that some of its greatest manifestations would be written by men, prose fiction became a female preserve. But women's appropriation of the novel corresponded with mounting attacks on female authorship. Women novelists resorted to innumerable strata-gems to propound and simultaneously to disguise their views. Their use of letters and of history as modes of displacement or of concealment of direct self-assertion underscores the links between the different forms of women's writing. But by the end of the century, women novelists had increasingly opted in favor of contemporary, domestic settings. Their reworking of conventions, their subtle subversions, their simultaneous assertion and denial of authoritative female subjectivity, all came to mark their works, however diverse, as facets of an emerging tradition. Women's novels resolutely testify to the growing importance of women's status as women, rather than as members of particularist groups. Women's fictions, taken as a group, can be read for an alternate—and sometimes dissenting—interpretation of the triumph of bourgeois values.

Women's novels are increasingly scanned for evidence of women's distinct values and judgments—and should be. But the decoding of women's voices should be undertaken with caution. Women did develop a distinct culture within a culture, but because the dominant culture so resolutely denied their authority—their purposeful exercise of authorship—they resorted to fictions and cast themselves as scribes. The novels can tell us much, but they can never entirely replace that missing autobiography. Adélaïde-Gillette Billet Dufresnoy, in her autobiographical novel, *La Femme auteur ou les inconvénients de la célébrité* (1812), insisted that authorship cost a woman all respectability and social acceptance.[51] Authorship lost her family, friends, and love. The very act of writing, she suggested, constitutes a violation of modesty and delicacy in the eyes of the world. Authoritative individualism violates womanhood and deprives women of all rights to protection without yielding them the advantages of independent dignity. As Mme de Genlis, who had enjoyed a remarkable career prior to the Revolution, wrote in her *Discours sur la suppression des couvents* in 1790, "A woman needs support; she can only be esteemed for quiet and domestic virtues, and a spotless reputation." For Genlis, as for Billet Dufresnoy, the victory of male individualism had imposed the universality of female domesticity.[52]

Through the novel, women educated each other in the conditions and psychological snares of their domestic lives. This education scrupulously reflected the changing mores of the eighteenth century, even as it reflected women's conception of their own worth and strength. Kinsey quotes Mme Roland's report in her *Mémoires* of her own answer to the Académie de Besançon's topic, "How the education of women can contribute to making men better." Roland, with the gains of the Revolution in mind, insists upon the importance of improving both sexes by good laws. "So," she concludes, "I clearly said how it appeared to me that women should be, but I added that they could only be made so in another order of things."

The Revolution did inaugurate a new order of things, although many of the changes that it would consolidate had been advocated by one or another group throughout the eighteenth century. The order it inaugurated for women emphasized domesticity, motherhood, and self-effacement. The juxtaposition of the Goncourts' picture of the domination and intelligence of the woman of the eighteenth century with the retiring bourgeois *mère de famille* suggests loss of power and status. But, as this book makes clear, the Goncourts' picture requires revision. Even the most brilliant and dazzling eighteenth-century women suffered the constraints of the explicit patriarchalism of the ancien régime. They did profit from the opportunities afforded by a hierarchical social system and exaggerated by that system's disintegration. Their post-Revolutionary sisters experienced the full authoritarianism of a social system determined to establish its own legitimacy and to correct the excesses of its predecessor. But the new forms of confinement, accompanied as they were by a more flattering image of women, by greater unity of experience among women, and by the emergence of a genuine female literary tradition, offered new possibilities.

NOTES

1. Edmond et Jules de Goncourt, *La Femme au dix-huitième siècle*, 2 vols. (Paris: Flammarion & Fasquelle, n.d.), vol. 1. p. 11.
2. Ibid., vol. 2, p. 97.
3. Norbert Elias, *The Civilizing Process: The History of Manners*, translated by Edmund Jephcott (New York: Urizen Books, 1978), esp. Part Two, "Sociogenesis of the Concept of *Civilization* in France."
4. Charles Henry, "Étude sur Mademoiselle de Lespinasse," in Julie de Lespinasse, *Lettres inédites à Condorcet, à d'Alembert, à Guibert, au comte de Crillon*, edited by Charles Henry (1887; Geneva: Slatkine, 1971), pp. 34-35. The spelling of Sapho and Theresa are his own. See also Julie de Lespinasse, *Lettres*, edited by Eugène Asse (1886; Geneva: Slatkine, 1971).
5. Edmond Pilon, *La Vie de famille au XVIIIe siècle*, édition revue, augmentée et précédée d'une introduction, par G. Lenôtre (Paris: Henri Jonquières, 1928); Charles de Ribbe, *La Famille et la société en France* (Paris: Albanel, 1873).
6. Among many, see Robert Darnton, *The Business of Enlightenment: A Publishing History of the ENCYCLOPÉDIE 1775-1800* (Cambridge, Mass.: Harvard University Press, 1979); François Furet et al., *Livre et société*, 2 vols. (Paris: Mouton, 1965 and 1970); Daniel Roche, *Le Peuple de Paris* (Paris: Aubier, 1981); Olwen H. Hufton, *The Poor of Eighteenth-Century France 1750-1789* (Oxford: Oxford University Press, 1974); Yves Castan, *Honnêteté et relations sociales en Languedoc (1715-1780)* (Paris: Plon, 1974); J. P. Gutton, *Domestiques et serviteurs dans la France de l'ancien régime* (Paris: Aubier, 1981).
7. Natalie Zemon Davis, "'Women's History' in Transition: The European Case," *Feminist Studies* 3, no. 3/4 (Spring-Summer 1976):83-103.
8. Natalie Zemon Davis, *Society and Culture in Early Modern France* (Stanford: Stanford University Press, 1975). Davis's essays on women in this volume are exemplary, but see also Suzanne Wemple, *Women in Frankish Society: Marriage and the Cloister 500 to 900* (Philadelphia: University of Pennsylvania Press, 1981).
9. Carolyn Lougee, *Le Paradis des Femmes: Women, Salons, and Social Stratification in Seventeenth-Century France* (Princeton: Princeton University Press, 1977). For a brief, graceful overview, see Vera Lee, *The Reign of Women in Eighteenth-Century France* (Cambridge, Mass.: Schenkman, 1975), and for a recent interpretive essay, which does not substitute for the much-needed general study, see Pierre Darmon, *Mythologie de la femme dans l'ancienne France, XVIe-XVIIe siècles* (Paris: Le Seuil, 1983).
10. Mme Gacon-Dufour belonged to the Société d'Agriculture de Paris in the 1780s and reported to it on her experiments with doves. Mme Roland reports in her *Mémoires* of submitting an essay for the prize competition sponsored by the Académie de Besançon. See Susan Kinsey's chapter in this volume. On women's interest in the courses offered by the Musée de Bordeaux in the late 1780s, see "Plumatif des délibérations commencé le 13 juin 1787," MS. 829, vol. xiv, Bibliothèque de la ville de Bordeaux. The entry for August 1, 1787 reads: "The abbot Sebathier asked if it would be permitted to the young ladies who had followed his courses of mathematics and

astronomy to compete for prizes like the young men. It was determined that they would compete but that they would first take a special exam." For Mme Gacon-Dufour, see Elizabeth Fox-Genovese and Eugene D. Genovese, *Fruits of Merchant Capital: Slavery and Bourgeois Property in the Rise and Expansion of Capitalism* (New York: Oxford University Press, 1983), chapter 11.

11. Evelyne Sullerot, *Histoire de la presse féminine en France des origines à 1848* (Paris: Armand Colin, 1966).

12. Pierre Fauchery, *La Destinée féminine dans le roman européen du dix-huitième siècle: 1713-1807. Essai de gynécomythie romanesque* (Paris: Armand Colin, 1972); Paul Hoffmann, *La Femme dans la pensée des lumières* (Paris: Éditions Orphrys, 1977).

13. Léon Abensour, *La Femme et le féminisme avant la révolution* (1923; Geneva: Slatkine, 1977).

14. C. B. A. Beherns, *The Ancien Régime* (London: Thames and Hudson, 1967), pp. 9-24, limits the applicability of the term to the period 1748-1789; Pierre Goubert, *The Ancien Régime: French Society, 1600-1750,* translated by Steve Cox (New York: Harper and Row, 1974) offers a more expanded view.

15. For a general overview, see Roland Mousnier, *The Institutions of France under the Absolute Monarchy 1598-1789,* translated by Brian Pearce (Chicago: University of Chicago Press, 1979).

16. E. Lousse, *La Société d'ancien régime: Organisation et représentation corporatives* (Louvain: Editions Universitas, 1952).

17. Arthur Young, *Travels in France during the Years 1787, 1788, 1789,* edited by Jeffrey Kaplow (Garden City, N.Y.: Doubleday, 1969), pp. 22-25.

18. Michel de Certeau, Dominique Julia, Jacques Revel, *Une Politique de la langue. La Révolution française et les patois: L'Enquête de Grégoire* (Paris: Gallimard, 1975).

19. Louis de Rouvroy, Duke of Saint-Simon, *Memoirs of Louis XIV and His Court and the Regency,* 3 vols. (New York: F. T. Collier, 1910); Alexis de Tocqueville, *L'Ancien Régime et la révolution,* Introduction de Georges Lefebvre, 2 vols. (Paris: Gallimard, 1952). On the dictionary prepared by the Académie Française following 1634, see Jacques Boulenger, *The Seventeenth Century in France* (New York: Capricorn Books, 1963). On the crown's promotion of courtesy and manners, see Orest Ranum, "Courtesy, Absolutism, and the Rise of the French State," *Journal of Modern History* 52, no. 3 (September 1980):426-451.

20. David Bien, "La réaction aristocratique avant 1789: l'exemple de l'armée," *Annales: économies, sociétés, civilisations* 29 (1974):23-48 and 505-534.

21. For a recent general summary, see James F. Traer, *Marriage and the Family in Eighteenth-Century France* (Ithaca: Cornell University Press, 1980). See also Paul Ourliac and J. de Malafosse, *Le Droit familial,* vol. 3 of *Histoire du droit privé* (Paris: Presses universitaires de France, 1968).

22. Abensour, *La Femme et le féminisme,* pp. 325-352. A full history of women's political rights and their exercise of those rights under the ancien régime has still to be written. Women participated in many particularist and corporate bodies in early modern France, and there is evidence that noblewomen who held fiefs exercised the powers of justice and representation that belonged to them, although rarely in person. All of these rights belonged to a corporate status or, in the case of noblewomen, to the land—not to individuals; and all of women's political participation declined sharply under absolutism.

23. Martin King Whyte, *The Status of Women in Preindustrial Societies* (Princeton: Princeton University Press, 1978); Gordon Schochet, *Patriarchalism in Political Thought: The Authoritarian Family and Political Speculation and Attitudes Especially in Seventeenth-Century England* (Oxford: Basil Blackwell, 1975).

24. Elizabeth Fox-Genovese, "Property and Patriarchy in Classical Bourgeois Political Theory," *Radical History Review* 4, nos. 2-3 (Spring-Summer 1977): 36-59; idem, "Placing Women's History in History," *New Left Review* 133 (May-June 1982):5-29.

25. G. P. Gooch, "Maria Theresa and Marie-Antoinette," in his *Maria Theresa and Other Studies* (London: Longmans, Green, & Co., 1951). Gooch draws heavily on the correspondence between mother and daughter to provide an illuminating view of Marie-Antoinette.

26. Among many, see Olwen Hufton, "Women in Revolution, 1789-1796," *Past and Present* 53 (1971):90-108; George Rudé, *The Crowd in the French Revolution* (Oxford: Oxford University Press, 1959). See also the references in the chapter by Harriet B. Applewhite and Darline Gay Levy and my own chapter in this volume.

27. Ian Maclean, *Woman Triumphant: Feminism in French Literature 1610-1652* (Oxford: Oxford University Press, 1977).

28. On the *citoyennes républicaines*, see Marie Cerati, *Le Club des citoyennes républicaines révolutionnaires* (Paris: Éditions sociales, 1966). In fact, the threatening political behavior of lower class women may have helped to convert their aristocratic—and even bourgeois—sisters to the virtues of domesticity.

29. Cerati, *Le Club;* Darline Gay Levy and Harriet B. Applewhite, "Women of the Popular Classes in Revolutionary Paris," in *Women, War and Revolution,* edited by Carol R. Berkin and Clara M. Lovett (New York: Holmes and Meier, 1980), pp. 9-36; Mary Durham Johnson, "Old Wine in New Bottles: The Institutional Changes for Women of the People During the French Revolution," in ibid., pp. 107-144; *Women in Revolutionary Paris 1789-1795* edited and translated by Darline Gay Levy, Harriet B. Applewhite, and Mary Durham Johnson (Urbana: University of Illinois Press, 1979); Paule-Marie Duhet, *Les Femmes et la révolution* (Paris: Julliard, 1971); Olivier Blanc, *Olympe de Gouges* (Paris: Syros, 1981); Elizabeth Racz, "The Women's Rights Movement in the French Revolution," *Science and Society* 16 (1951-52); Ruth Graham, "Loaves and Liberty: Women in the French Revolution," in *Becoming Visible. Women in European History,* edited by Renate Bridenthal and Claudia Koonz (Boston: Houghton Mifflin, 1977); Jane Abray, "Feminism in the French Revolution," *American Historical Review* 80, no. 1 (February 1975):43-62. For brief, recent summaries, see Jean Rabaut, *Histoire des féminismes français* (Paris: Stock, 1978), pp. 53-75; and Maïté Albistur and Daniel Armogathe, *Histoire du féminisme français,* 2 vols. (Paris: Éditions des femmes, 1977), vol. 1, pp. 306-346.

30. Fox-Genovese and Genovese, chapter 11; Barbara Corrado Pope, "Revolution and Retreat: Upper-Class French Women after 1789," in Berkin and Lovett, pp. 215-236; Margaret H. Darrow, "French Noblewomen and the New Domesticity, 1750-1850," *Feminist Studies* 5, no. 1 (1979):41-65. Cf. Linda K. Kerber, *Women of the Republic: Intellect and Ideology in Revolutionary America* (Chapel Hill: University of North Carolina Press, 1980).

31. Ian Maclean, *The Renaissance Notion of Woman: A Study in the Fortunes of Scholasticism and Medical Science in European Intellectual Life* (Cambridge: Cambridge University Press, 1980).

32. David Williams, "The Politics of Feminism in the French Enlightenment," in *The Varied Pattern: Studies in the 18th Century,* edited by Peter Hughes and David Williams (Toronto: A. M. Hakkert, Ltd., 1971), pp. 333; Abensour, *La Femme et le féminisme;* idem; *Histoire générale du féminisme des origines à nos jours* (1921; Geneva: Slatkine, 1979), pp. 178-204; Edwin R. Hedman, "Early French Feminism: From the Eighteenth Century to 1848" (Ph.D. diss., New York University, 1954), esp. pp. 46-65; Georges Ascoli, "Essai sur l'histoire des idées féministes

en France du XVIe siècle à la Révolution," *Revue de Synthèse Historique* 13 (July-December 1906):25-57, 99-106, and 167-184.

33. Michel Vovelle, *Piété baroque et déchristianisation en Provence au XVIIIe siècle* (Paris: Plon, 1973).

34. Madeleine Danielou, *Madame de Maintenon éducatrice* (Paris: Bloud & Gay, 1946); *Fénelon on Education* edited by H. C. Barnard (Cambridge: Cambridge University Press, 1966); Paul Rousselot, *Histoire de l'éducation des femmes en France,* 2 vols. (n.d.; repr. New York: Burt Franklin, 1971), vol. 2, pp. 1-91; Lougee, *Le Paradis des Femmes.*

35. Harvey Chisick, *The Limits of Reform in the Enlightenment: Attitudes toward the Education of the Lower Classes in Eighteenth-Century France* (Princeton: Princeton University Press, 1981), sees a decisive increase in interest in popular education about 1769 but makes no mention of women in his otherwise thoughtful study. See also comte de Luppe, *Les Jeunes Filles à la fin du XVIII siècle* (Paris: Edouard Champion, 1925); Georges Snyders, *La Pédagogie en France aux XVIIe et XVIIIe siècles* (Paris: Presses universitaires de France, 1965); Roger Chartier, Dominique Julia, and Marie-Madeleine Compère, *L'Éducation en France du XVIe au XVIIIe siècle* (Paris: CDU & SEDES, 1976); Rousselot, *Histoire de l'éducation des femmes en France;* J. Morange and J.-F. Chassaing, *Le Mouvement de réforme de l'enseignement en France 1760-1798* (Paris: Presses Universitaires de France, 1974).

36. Cf. *Female Scholars: A Tradition of Learned Women before 1800,* edited by J. R. Brink (Montreal: Eden Press, 1980).

37. Evelyn Gordon Bodek, "Salonnières and Bluestockings: Educated Obsolescence and Germinating Feminism," *Feminist Studies* 3, nos. 3/4 (Spring/Summer 1976):185-199; Myra Reynolds, *The Learned Lady in England, 1650-1760* (Boston: Houghton Mifflin, 1920).

38. François Furet and Jacques Ozouf, *Lire et écrire: L'Alphabétisation des Français de Calvin à Jules Ferry,* 2 vols. (Paris: Éditions de Minuit, 1977) vol. 1, pp. 9-115, passim; Roche, pp. 204-241, passim.

39. Roche reports that 4/5 of female petty criminals could not sign their names and that only 7 percent of the women arrested on the roads of the Ile de France by the guards of the *Maréchaussée* could do so.

40. Denis Diderot, *La Religieuse,* in *Oeuvres romanesques,* edited by Henri Benac (Paris: Garnier, 1962).

41. Claire de Rémusat, *Essai sur l'éducation des femmes* (Paris: L'Advocat, 1824); Albertine Necker de Saussure, *L'Éducation progressive* (Paris: Pauline Frères, 1844).

42. See Fairchilds' chapter in this volume, and Lawrence Stone, *The Family, Sex, and Marriage in England, 1500-1800* (New York: Harper and Row, 1977). See also Pope, "Revolution and Retreat"; Fox-Genovese and Genovese, *Fruits of Merchant Capital;* Darrow, "French Noblewomen."

43. Helen Maria Williams, *Letters from France . . .* (Dublin: G. Chambers, 1794).

44. The ideals of marriage for love and domesticity can also be found among the emerging class of professional intellectuals and minor administrators. See *The Memoirs of P. S. Du Pont de Nemours,* edited and translated by Elizabeth Fox-Genovese (Wilmington, Del.: Scholarly Resources, 1984).

45. See, for example, David Williams, "The Fate of French Feminism: Boudier de Villemert's *Ami des femmes,*" *Eighteenth-Century Studies* 14, no. 1 (Fall 1980):37-55.

46. Opinions on Montesquieu differ considerably, but it seems difficult to assimilate him fully to the modern tradition of feminism. See Sheila Mason,

"The Riddle of Roxanne," in *Woman and Society in Eighteenth-Century France*, edited by Eva Jacobs et al. (London: Athlone Press, 1979), pp. 28-41; R. F. O'Reilly, "Montesquieu anti-feminist," *Studies on Voltaire and the Eighteenth Century*, vol. 102 (1973), pp. 143-156; Jeannette Geffiaud Rosso, *Montesquieu et la fémininité* (Pisa: Libreria Goliardica Editrice, 1977). On Diderot, see Robert Niklaus, "Diderot and Women," in Jacobs et al., pp. 69-82; Eva Jacobs, "Diderot and the Education of Girls," in ibid.; Arthur Wilson, "'Treated Like Imbecile Children' (Diderot): The Enlightenment and the Status of Women," in *Woman in the 18th Century and Other Essays*, edited by Paul Fritz and Richard Morton (Toronto: Samuel Stevens Hakkert & Co., 1976), pp. 89-104.

47. Nancy K. Miller, *The Heroine's Text: Readings in the French and English Novel 1722-1782* (New York: Columbia University Press, 1980), p. 151.

48. Victor G. Wexler, "'Made for Man's Delight': Rousseau an Antifeminist," *American Historical Review* II (1976):266-291. See also Tony Tanner, "Julie and 'La maison paternelle': Another Look at Rousseau's La Nouvelle Héloïse," *Daedalus* 105 (1976):23-45.

49. Raymond Williams, *Culture and Society 1780-1950* (London: Chatto and Windus, 1958).

50. Mme Chazot Duplessy, *Correspondance, MS. 1201*, Bibliothèque de la ville de Bordeaux.

51. *Une Femme d'affaires au XVIIIe siècle*, edited by Serge Chassagne (Paris: Privat, 1981); Roche, pp. 213-214.

52. Adélaïde-Gillette Billet Dufresnoy, *La Femme auteur ou les inconvénients de la célébrité* (Paris: Béchet, 1812); and Mme de Genlis, *Discours sur la suppression des couvents* (Paris: Onfrois, 1790), p. 26.

 I

Women and Political Life

🦋 Adrienne Rogers

Women and the Law

Historically, French eighteenth-century law is divided into three main periods: Old Law, Intermediate Law, and the law as promulgated under the Civil Code of 1804. Old Law prevailed until the Revolution; Intermediate Law was promulgated as a result of the Revolution of 1789; and the Civil Code of 1804, known as the Napoleonic Code, remained in effect without further modifications until late in the nineteenth century.[1]

Old Law refers to more than one set of laws governing all of France. The country was divided into two regions separated by a line from La Rochelle on the west coast to the Swiss frontier: to the north of this line was the region of customary law, and to the south of it was the region of written law.[2] Generally, written law was an outgrowth of Roman law, whereas the region of customary law reflected Germanic influence.[3] In view of the large geographic area involved, it is clear that customs imposed a great variety of law in "the" region of customary law.

Customary law is defined as being of oral origin and nature. It is based on customs that are old (of at least forty years' duration), reasonable, and acceptable, as evidenced by the fact that people have been willing to practice them for a long time.[4] A custom may be written down and made into law, but this does not make it any less a custom.[5]

Written law was an outgrowth, beginning in the eleventh century, of local southern customs combined with aspects of Roman law. The law of this geographical area was more unified than the laws of the regions governed by custom. Both written and customary law had in common their jurisdiction: both governed relationships between individuals not governed by canon law. For example, though marriage was considered a sacrament, those aspects of marriage that dealt with property matters, such as dowry and other financial aspects of the marital partnership, contractual obligations, wills, and inheritances, were under the jurisdiction of civil law. In addition, penal law was in large part incorporated into civil law.[6]

Whether written or customary, Old Law was that of an absolute Catholic monarchy, which therefore recognized the jurisdiction of canon law for church-related matters, such as the sacrament of marriage. It upheld the feudal social structure, awarding privileges to some at the expense of others. It upheld certain property notions, such as primogeniture, which was intended to maintain unity of properties rather than disperse land holdings.[7] It supported corporations and guilds.

Intermediate Law had two phases: the Revolutionary phase, from the time of the Constituent Assembly to the time of the Convention, and the period from the Directory through the Consulate. The Revolution affected civil law in three ways. Politically, the overthrow of an absolute Catholic monarchy meant, in law, the overthrow of those institutions that previously upheld that monarchy. Freedom of conscience took away the influence of canon law on civil law; abolition of feudal privilege was intended to eliminate not only class distinctions but also the possibility of keeping large landholdings in a few hands. Abolishing corporations was intended to encourage freedom of commerce.[8]

The Civil Code of 1804 included many concepts drawn from Old Law, both written and customary; but the spirit of the Civil Code drew inspiration from Intermediate Law in separating Church and State, in stressing individualism and the rights of man, and in consolidating men's political and economic rights. Changes in laws governing inheritance created a class of small landholders, breaking down bases for feudalism. Instituting divorce and freedom from paternal supervision at age twenty-one increased individual liberty.[9] In terms of the history of the law, the inauguration of the Civil Code marks the end of the eighteenth century.

Prior to the Revolution, women's civil rights varied according to socioeconomic class and marital status, as well as geography. The never-married woman had the right to handle her personal financial affairs herself, including taking legal action, buying, selling, and transferring her assets.[10] In terms of what she might inherit, however, her rights changed depending on historical period (Old Regime, Revolutionary, or post-Revolutionary period), geography, and socioeconomic class.

The laws governing inheritance were varied. The south of France, under the influence of Roman law, and customary law of Paris saw all children as equally eligible to inherit, regardless of sex. There is a paradox in that this was true for common people; the exception was for nobles, for whom primogeniture, inheritance by the eldest son exclusively, was the rule. However, in the absence of any son, an eldest daughter could inherit in accordance with the *droit d'aînesse*. This right, which originated in feudalism, was abrogated under Intermediate Law. Elsewhere in France, customs and law regarding rights of single daughters to inherit varied widely, sometimes depending on whether they were dowered, on the existence of brothers, or the single daughter remaining single and continuing to live in her father's house.[11]

When a woman married, she ceased to be an individual and became a member of a partnership that was considered, as a sacrament, to be a permanent, indissoluble bond, sanctified by the Church. If, in this partnership of the couple called *communauté* two individuals were molded together as one, it would nonetheless be erroneous to suppose that the two individuals were equal. A more accurate description would be the assimilation of one by the other. Theologically, it was determined that the union need have only one head, and that head, naturally, had to be the husband. This assumption was unquestionable and, for the most part, unquestioned. Human law upheld and applied divine law; the husband was seen as head of the marriage partnership and, therefore, was entitled to be obeyed.

What benefits might the wife expect from the partnership? Eighteenth-century legal experts saw the wife's subjection to her husband as tempered by the husband's profound affection for his companion, by the respect of a man for the mother of his children. This was the spirit of the law, but the letter of the law was another matter.[12] The married woman was, in fact, an inferior, a virtual slave, whose person and assets were given over to the absolute control of another party.[13]

The legal relationship of marriage partners varied, depending upon where the marriage took place. *Communauté, régime dotal,* or *régime normand* were bases for marriage contracts. The idea of *communauté* had undergone an evolution. In the thirteenth century, for example, the "communality" or partnership was real. The husband was master of the couple's legal assets, but only those; participation of both spouses was necessary for any transactions involving real property, such as sales, leases, disposal of fiefs, and mortgages. In all these instances, the wife's signature always appeared next to the husband's. Furthermore, in connection with running her household, the wife's expenses were part of the partnership's funds, and her debts as well as her husband's were liable to suit by creditors. From the sixteenth century on, under the influence of Roman law, the notion of marriage partnership took on an entirely different character. Certain reforms were introduced; and whether favorable or unfavorable to women, they made clear that, thereafter, the legal personhood of the married woman had less value than the husband's. The definition of marriage partnership changed from one in which there was an association of equals to one in which the husband had total power over the wife's assets; the wife had nothing unless specifically protected by a marriage contract.[14] The general overriding principle was that a married woman could do nothing without her husband's consent, and this would be the case up to and including the Napoleonic Code as well as in legislation deriving from it.[15]

In the south of France, under influence of Roman law, the *régime dotal*, or dowry system, prevailed. A woman's dowry comprised real and liquid assets. Any additional non-dowry funds belonging to the woman, called *paraphernaux*, were her own to do with as she wished without her husband's permission.[16]

The dowry was part of the couple's assets, but it was not to be used up; it was like a principal sum that might generate income. The income could be used by the husband, but the principal needed to be maintained intact or restored by the husband if he used any of it, to invest, for example. Protected from squandering by either husband or wife, it became part of the family patrimony and, upon death of the husband, was to revert to the wife or her heirs if she predeceased the husband. More discussion of what occurred after the husband's death will be taken up in the section on widowhood.

Under the Old Regime, and therefore under Old Law, marriage contracts found much favor in all classes but especially in the nobility and in the bourgeoisie. The purpose of the marriage contract was to establish how the marriage would be regulated financially: in a community property partnership; not in a partnership but with assets each brought to the marriage clearly designated, as well as stipulations as to their transfer to heirs with the death of their owners; in a dowry system, in which the definition of those assets constituting the dowry was spelled out clearly and what was to become of it when the husband or wife died was designated; or in the so-called Norman system, which prevailed in Normandy and which absolutely outlawed the notion of partnership in the sense of a wife participating as a partner.[17]

The preference for various matrimonial regulations was divided according to region, with the region of written law using the dowry system, the region of customary law following the example of Paris (where marriage was considered a partnership with assets and acquisitions held in common), and Normandy forbidding partnership.

The marriage contract stipulated exactly what the couple's financial arrangements were to be. Persons making the stipulations might be the couple's parents as well as outsiders, such as uncles, grandparents, or others who wished to make some provision for gifts to the husband or wife. The partners themselves might make gifts to each other. The basic principle underlying drafting of marriage contracts was that the notary drawing up the documents was free to include any provisions the clients might wish, so long as these were not contrary to law or accepted notions of propriety.[18] The following is an example of such an unthinkable clause: "Thus, the wife cannot be named head of household."[19] And yet, there were situations in which women were allowed to be so considered, although they were very few and always among the very well-off.[20]

Though, generally speaking, the husband had control over the goods of the wife, she might, under certain conditions, regain control of them. She might do so, for example, if she got a legal separation. In order to do that, she needed to prove that her husband was willfully dissipating her fortune and endangering the value of her dowry. Mere mismanagement of the fortune was not adequate cause. Error was permissible for the husband but obviously not for the wife since she was "protected" against making any mistakes by having the matter taken out of her hands altogether. Allowing the woman recovery of her fortune because her husband was mismanaging it was tantamount to acknowledging her capacity to judge what he was doing; to do that would have been to undermine the basic underlying principles of feminine incompetence and male superiority.[21]

Even with a legal separation, a woman could have absolute control only over those goods specified in the separation agreement. Should she wish to sell or mortgage property, or even collect on an inheritance, she needed her husband's permission. However, an interesting exception was made for a woman who had brought no dowry to the marriage but who had earned money in the exercise of some profession; she had the right, in the separation agreement, to have her earnings protected from liability for the husband's debts.

In addition to economic separation (*séparation des biens*), there was also physical separation (*séparation de corps*). This was not easy to obtain either. A husband's infidelity was not sufficient cause to obtain a separation.[22] Neither prolonged absence nor disappearance of the husband could release the woman from marriage. She had to follow wherever he went to live within the country, but not if he was leaving the country permanently and renouncing citizenship or if he had committed a crime and was fleeing to escape punishment.[23]

The grounds for separation were limited to "bad treatment" and "defamation." Bad treatment was interpreted only as being life-endangering or inimical to health to the point of threatening the possibility of recovery. Defamation was defined as a husband publicly defaming his wife's reputation. He might do this by obtaining a *lettre de cachet* and having his wife unjustifiably imprisoned for adultery, for example.[24]

Although a husband's adultery was not grounds for separation, a wife's adultery carried severe penalties. In the sixteenth century, adulterous women were whipped, subjected to public humiliation, and

locked up in a convent for two years. In the eighteenth century, the
adulterous woman was not subjected to public whipping and humiliation; but a vengeful husband could have her locked up for two years,
and if, after that time, he did not see fit to take her back, she could be
kept locked up in the convent for the rest of her life. All a husband
needed do to have the wife imprisoned for the first two years was to
obtain a *lettre de cachet;* to lock her away forever and take possession of
her fortune required a family council. As a legally dead person, her
fortune would be divided, with two-thirds going to her children or her
relatives and one-third to the monastery. Thus, the decision to
condemn her to life imprisonment was in the hands of the very people
who would benefit financially from her imprisonment.

Another alternative a husband might use if he caught his wife
flagrante delicto was to kill her:

> the right of a husband to kill a spouse caught in the act of being
> unfaithful is no longer spelled out in the law. But there is, in the
> eighteenth century, a jurisprudence which favors the deceived husband
> . . . "The husband," writes one legal expert, "does not have the right to
> kill his wife, but, if he does so, he quite readily obtains a pardon."[25]

As mothers, married women did not have authority over children
with respect to their upbringing, their education, or their marriage. A
father could oppose a child's marriage and give no justification for
doing so. If a widowed mother objected, she had to justify her decision,
and it could be overruled by other relatives.[26] Mothers or grandmothers
might be appointed guardians, but with many restrictions. A mother
might, for example, lose guardianship if other relatives objected to a
marriage the mother approved. In two instances, despite the influence
of Roman law, a woman might be a guardian: she might be named
guardian of her brothers and sisters, or if her husband were
"extravagant, violently insane, or under interdict," she might be
named his guardian.[27]

Though single women appeared to be in a more favorable legal
position than married ones, they were disadvantaged because of
unequal possibilities of sharing in the family fortune. Widows would
seem to have been the women most favored. They had whatever
advantages there may have been to having been married and the
presumably greater advantages of being free of the authority of a
husband. At the same time, a widow regained possession and control
of her dowry as well as her share of the marriage partnership's assets.

Theoretically, the widow was entitled to do entirely as she chose
with what she inherited, but in Normandy, for example, her decisions
were subject to the approval of some masculine relative of the
deceased husband. As for disposing of her own fortune, if she lived in
the region of written law, she could make a will; but in the region of

customary law, the practice varied. In many provinces, a woman's will had to be validated by her husband while he was alive. If the husband was away, incapacitated, a minor, or refused his permission, she could get the will validated by a magistrate. In the province of Hainaut, a woman could not make a will even if her husband authorized it; to "protect" the wife from possible undue influence by the husband, she had no right to make a will at all.

> It is therefore quite obvious that customs which award the husband maximum control over the wife's assets and which, on the other hand, naturally take all possible precautions to protect the wife's assets both during her life and after her death against incursions by her husband, are steeped in a violently antifeminist spirit.
>
> Among these customs, certain ones which remain in full force up until the French Revolution, reveal the full extent of the contempt in which the weaker sex was held, on the one hand by Roman law and on the other by Germanic custom which became feudal [custom or law].[28]

Upon the death of her husband, a new widow was not freed of personal contraints any more than of economic constraints. Her personal life was subject to close scrutiny. A widowed provincial noblewoman, for example, was subjected to "her relatives, father, mother, brothers, and sisters, who oversee her conduct and punish her with as much severity as a husband 'should she fail to live up to [the requirements of] honor'."[29]

In contrast to a widower, "the widowed woman is not ... mistress of her person, of her fortune, and of her actions. The fortune a woman inherits from her husband is not hers to give or to transfer to whomever she sees fit."[30]

The Edict of 1560 on Second Marriages sought to prevent widows from making disproportionate gifts of assets acquired from the first husband to a second. The idea was to prevent the widow from depriving her children of their inheritance on behalf of a second husband. This edict was modified in May 1586, when it was decided that the Edict on Second Marriages was applicable to husbands as well as to wives. The origin of the edict actually was a case concerning a remarried widower. In this instance, the law was equally applied to both sexes.[31]

Generally, however, the effects of being widowed were different for women and men. Abensour points out that the Edict on Second Marriages was concerned not only with keeping the original family fortune intact but also with keeping the widow in the state of widowhood that seemed most proper from a theological point of view. In this instance, canon law was not without influence on civil law.[32]

A widow who remarried was penalized, too, in losing the Right of Habitation if she had had it. The reasoning was that the family of the first husband would look askance at the prospect of husband number two living with the widow in the home provided by husband number one and that it was the obligation of the second husband, as it had been of the first, to provide her with a home appropriate to her station.[33]

When it came to remarrying, a widower could marry whomever he chose, regardless of social status. A widow, however, could not marry someone of a lower station without risking loss of her share in the first marriage partnership.

With respect to proper observance of a period of mourning, the widower might risk raised eyebrows if he did not appear to be mourning appropriately, but a widow risked a great deal more; she might be taken to court and deprived of the money she had inherited. Thus, the law, if not customs, in every way restricted the widow's freedom. Concern with morality—but a different morality for each sex—and the assumption that the woman is a weaker being than a man, justified these restrictions.[34]

Many women, unable to support themselves adequately in their work, or unable to support themselves at all, were forced to seek financial contributions of some sort from men. Discounting marriage as the first example of subjection to a man in exchange for "protection," there existed a hierarchy of prostitution. Opera stars and actresses were its aristocracy.[35] Its middle class consisted of the dancers and singers of lesser status as well as women who worked in the fashion or lingerie trades and some lower middle-class girls. Finally, the *filles du monde*, such as those who plied their trade in the Palais-Royal or in outlying suburban areas, were the lowest rung of the prostitution ladder.[36]

There were also houses of prostitution whose madams were liable to severe penalties, such as being whipped, pilloried, marched through the city with a sign on their chests announcing their profession; but these penalties were seldom applied, and madams apparently flourished.[37]

Lower-level prostitutes were less fortunate. It is estimated that there were at least twenty thousand prostitutes in Paris alone. Despite the fact that women resorted to prostitution much more out of necessity that any love of debauchery or "pleasure" seeking, legislators

> inspired by Christian dogma and Roman law continue to see in prostitution only vice, crime, shameful illness . . . [they] seek only to punish women's misconduct and to forestall its regrettable effects. They therefore set out in detail repressive legislation whose general tenets have been upheld long past the Revolution and up to our own time.[38]

A prostitute had absolutely no individual rights or liberty. She was constantly in danger of being rounded up either for medical examination or to be sent to prison at La Salpêtrière or Bicêtre. Conditions were so terrible in these prisons—starvation diet of bread and broth, hard labor, overcrowded conditions—that some women committed suicide rather than be subjected to them.[39] However, in Paris, "easy-going customs, a certain tolerance, and the cult of pleasure, tempered the rigidity of Christian anathema."[40]

Prostitutes in the provinces were subjected to even more stringent laws because local municipalities added their own laws to royal edicts. There was usually a forced-labor prison to which prostitutes were condemned after periodic roundups. Other penalties they might incur were: bread and water for three months, expulsion, beggars' prisons, whipping, and exhibition to public view in an iron cage. Almost everywhere they were listed on a register of known prostitutes and kept under surveillance thereafter.[41]

> Thus, female prostitution, despite some of its triumphant aspects, demonstrates beautifully the flagrant inferiority of the condition of women. Pushed into hell by the lack of adequate work opportunities which might allow them to earn their living, and the absurdly low salaries to be found in the available work, women, from the very moment of their "fall" became outlaws subjected with no safeguards to the whim of a brutal and capricious police force and condemned ever after to degradation. As many an author has noted, "a poorly constructed society takes out its own failings on them."[42]

What is not mentioned specifically here is that prostitution was judged to be a crime of which only women were guilty, as though it were possible to commit that crime without participation of a male partner. Nowhere is any thought given to the notion that if the woman was guilty of a crime in being a prostitute the man who used her was no less so.

The situation for unwed mothers was different. Influenced by the government's vested interest in the birthrate, the law acknowledged that an unwed mother became "that way" with assistance from a male partner and, therefore, decreed that she was entitled to demand reparation.[43] Up until 1730, the seducer could be condemned to death unless the woman agreed to marry him. In 1730, a royal ordinance abrogated the law permitting marriage between seducer and seducee as an alternative to the death penalty, thereby making the death penalty mandatory. In practice, however, it was seldom applied.

In provincial courts, thousands of women filed complaints against seducers—masters who took advantage of servants, priests who seduced parishioners, soldiers, tax collectors, schoolmasters—but, though the law gave women the right to complain, it was a rare instance when the courts hearing these cases inflicted any penalties on the guilty men. For the most part, the penalty was a fine to cover the woman's lying-in costs. Many young women did not accuse their seducers because they were too embarrassed to acknowledge their vulnerability publicly.[44]

When it came to unwed mothers, the government was keen on seeing to it that prospective children were born alive and in good health. An edict of Henry II, dated 1556 and still in effect in the eighteenth century, required unmarried pregnant women to declare their pregnancy to appropriate royal officers. The magistrate taking the declaration could not require the girl to identify the putative father. In the event that she failed to comply with the law by declaring her pregnancy and the child died unbaptized, she was subject to the death penalty. The death penalty was not always enforced, however; it was sometimes commuted to exile or branding.

In accordance with some old customs, an unmarried pregnant woman might find herself subjected to close surveillance. She might, at any time and with no forewarning, be subjected to an examination by a midwife accompanied by witnesses seeking to ascertain that the pregnancy was proceeding normally and well and without interference or negligence on her part. The Parlement of Dijon, in 1705 and again in 1715, and the Parlement of Paris, in 1761, sought to abolish this practice, which had led to such abuses as subjecting young women merely suspected of being pregnant to visits, whether there were any basis for the suspicion or not. After the practice was abolished by law in 1761, it still went on, since there is record of it happening as late as 1776.[45]

Despite all precautions, the number of babies killed remained very high, especially in rural areas. Foundling homes were established on the eve of the Revolution to discourage infanticides; and in Paris, once the foundling home was in existence, the rate of infanticide did drop to almost nothing.[46] However, the number of children abandoned to the home increased dramatically, and the mortality rate among them was high.[47]

Like prostitution in the cities, other criminal activities in rural areas resulted from poverty. Women were as guilty as men of smuggling, breaking and entering, highway robbery, and counterfeiting; and they were subject to the same penalties. In some impoverished provinces, such as lower Brittany, female robber bands of all ages roamed the countryside. Neither severe penalties nor charitable institutions had any restraining effect.[48]

Some crimes had a political basis, rooted in the abuses of the Old Regime. Tax collectors trying to collect the *dîme* in Provence were beaten with iron pipes by women as well as men and left for dead. A rent collector in Périgord was attacked by women who pulled his hair, threw ashes in his eyes, and destroyed his papers. "Exasperation against feudal tyranny, against the abusive weight of taxes, is felt as much by women as by men. Incidents such as these demonstrate it clearly."[49] Between 1718 and 1788, 252 women were imprisoned for political crimes of various sorts, including espionage and political conspiracy.[50]

Under the Old Regime, women had all the negative obligations of citizenship, such as paying taxes, including the labor tax, and being subjected to the same penalties as any other felon if they committed crimes. They were also subject to penalties men were not subject to in civil matters, such as adultery, and in "criminal" matters, such as prostitution. As for positive rights as citizens, a woman's status reflected that of her husband or father, so that noblewomen sometimes exercised a function related to their feudal position regardless of sex. By the eighteenth century, certain rights that women had exercised by custom in the Middle Ages had fallen into disuse. For example, in the Middle Ages, noblewomen had acted as peers and had even arbitrated vassals' disputes and participated in parlements, but by the eighteenth century, they could not hold any judicial offices. Access to all professions and the rights to litigate, to bear witness in court, to have guardianship of minors, to have one's signature considered legally binding and valid, to witness a will, to make a will—these rights were enjoyed by Frenchwomen of the eighteenth century either to a limited extent or not at all.[51]

As early as the end of 1788, when the king called together the Estates General, a few women petitioned in hope that they might "have a share in the benefits of liberty."[52] In December 1789, women were excluded from "the right to vote."[53] In the Constitution of 1791, the Constituent Assembly denied women citizenship, grouping them with other "passive" citizens, such as "children, minors, and convicted felons."[54] Again, women were expected to assume responsibilities of citizenship without privileges of citizenship and were subject to all penalties for disobeying the law.[55] A number of political clubs, both mixed-sex and exclusively female, were active throughout France. Although these clubs did not necessarily specify women's suffrage as a goal, they were concerned with improving women's status with respect to marriage laws, education and employment opportunities, and equality before the law.[56] When the activism of women's groups became too aggressive, the Convention outlawed the groups on November 4, 1793; on May 24, 1795, it further decreed that women were to be denied right of assembly and were required to stay home.[57] It is scarcely surprising then that there were women who felt that it had not been worthwhile to have a revolution.[58]

If the Revolution had not provided women with all rights of citizenship they had expected or hoped for, it did, nonetheless, bring about some changes. With the abolition of feudal rights, women in general were no longer excluded from possibilities of inheriting, per decree of April 8, 1791, handed down April 15. The law of January 7, 1794 (17 nivose an II) altered restrictions on gifts between spouses whether in first or second marriages. On June 13, 1793, the Convention awarded women the right to share equally in communal property: "The division of community property will be effected per head of household, of whatever age or sex, present or absent." Each department was to have a book listing widows and mothers with children who required assistance; however, more substantial economic assistance was lacking.[59]

With secularization of the law, marriage became a civil contract subject to termination. Perhaps because of the civil contract concept, the clientele of notaries for preparation of marriage contracts became more extensive and comprised more lower-class and less well-off people. Contracts that specified assets of the wife as distinct from the husband's also allowed her to dispose of her property, but, generally, marriage contracts written under Revolutionary law contained the same underlying principles and the same standard clauses as those written under Old Law.[60]

Because marriage was considered a civil contract and no longer a sacrament, the influence of canon law was removed and divorce became possible. By law of September 20, 1792, divorce became obtainable by mutual agreement, on grounds of incompatibility, or on other specific grounds.[61] The relative ease in obtaining a divorce turned out to be more favorable to men than to women, since women were more often in the position of abandoned spouse. "Women had observed how frequent was the risk of finding oneself abandoned, over forty . . . without the resource of a profession which might allow them to live independently."[62]

Custody of children in the event of divorce by mutual consent or on grounds of incompatibility was usually awarded to the mother, except that boys over age seven were awarded to the father and parents could make other arrangements that suited them. In the event of divorce other than by mutual consent or on grounds of incompatibility, a family council decided all matters concerning children including custody. Both parents were liable for child support in accordance with their ability to pay, regardless of who had custody.[63]

Another outcome of Revolutionary law was the suppression of religious orders in February 1790. For those women who suddenly found themselves cast out into the world—unmarried and probably unmarriageable, with no skills or opportunities for employment, and unprepared in any way for secular life—the enforced dissolution of convents was clearly not to their benefit. Even if they, or other unemployed women, participated in national workshops, their salaries were lower than men's.[64]

Unwed mothers who, unassisted, supported their children for ten years were entitled to financial assistance from the government at the end of that time. As for assistance from the putative father, it might take the form of lying-in costs for the mother and cost of feeding the child, assuming that the father was identified. The unwed mother was allowed to seek to identify him. (In the instance cited earlier of unwed mothers having to declare their pregnancy but not the identity of the father of the child, the intended protection from identification seems to have been for the benefit of the putative father rather than the unwed mother.)

As for bastards, Revolutionary law, like that of the Old Regime, saw them as having no family. At first, the Convention considered children out of wedlock as equally entitled to inherit as legitimate offspring, provided they were not the result of an incestuous or an adulterous coupling. By 1796, the law restricted the rights of bastards to inherit and forbade seeking out the identity of the father.[65] "The benefits derived by women from the Revolution were not commensurate with the efforts put forth by them for the new society . . . And their situation was to get worse with the Thermidorian Reaction, as well as the perverted, muscular, boot-clad form the Revolution assumed under the Consulate and the Empire."[66]

The Napoleonic Code reflected, insofar as women were concerned, Napoleon's misogyny. From early youth to the end of his life on St. Helena, he did not deviate in his view of women's purpose on earth: childbearing, or of their role in marriage: dependence and submission. Article 213 of the Napoleonic Code sums up these attitudes: "The husband owes his wife protection; the wife owes her husband obedience." The married woman had become a legal minor—forbidden to take legal action, buy, sell, inherit, have identity papers, work, or have a bank account. There were a few actions she might legally undertake without her husband's permission: act as parent to children from a preceding marriage and accept gifts intended for them; acknowledge, herself alone, children she had had out of wedlock prior to the marriage; and make or revoke a will or a gift in her husband's favor—for she had the right to make a will. Under the Napoleonic Code, the least favored women were clearly married women; the more favored were the never-married, widows, and divorcees, who had essentially the same civil rights as men.

During the first year of the Consulate, there were 698 divorces to 3,215 marriages. Under the Napoleonic Code, the law of September 20, 1792, was altered. Divorce was still possible but could be obtained only after a long and difficult procedure. Divorce by mutual consent was still possible, but it took a long time and entailed many obligations.

As for political rights, Napoleon's view was clearcut: only disorder could result if women did anything other than remain submissive and dependent. The Napoleonic Code was supposed to be an outgrowth of the Revolution; its laws were supposed to create equal opportunities for all Frenchmen. And they did—for all French men. As for women, their existence was acknowledged before the law only when it came to collecting taxes from them, sending them to prison, or sending them to the guillotine.

For the next century and a half, the fate of the French woman was sealed. Under the Old Regime, her status was, because of custom, not everywhere rigidly defined. In the state governed by Napoleon and his legal code, her destiny was controlled and restricted by law. Once again, she was an eternal minor; once again, she was legally a nothing.[67]

NOTES

1. Jean Carbonnier, *Les Personnes*, vol. 1 of *Droit civil* (Paris: Presses universitaires de France, 1974), pp. 60, 67.

2. Arlette Lebigre, *Histoire des institutions et des faits sociaux jusqu'en 1789* (Paris: Le cours de droit, 1974), p. 208.

3. Carbonnier, p. 60.

4. Lebigre, p. 191.

5. Carbonnier, p. 20.

6. Lebigre, p. 208.

7. Carbonnier, p. 61.

8. Ibid., p. 62.

9. Ibid., p. 66.

10. Léon Abensour, *La Femme et le féminisme avant la révolution* (Paris: Ernest Leroux, 1923), p. 25.

11. Ibid., pp. 26-28.

12. Ibid., p. 7.

13. Ibid., p. 8.

14. Ibid., p. 15.

15. Ibid., p. 17. An exception accepted under both written and customary law was the woman merchant, who had all legal rights necessary for carrying on business. Her financial obligations were binding on the marriage partnership.

16. Ibid. In the region of written law as well as in Normandy, Auvergne, and la Marche, women were allowed control of nondowry funds.

17. Jacques Lelièvre, *La Pratique des contrats de mariage chez les notaires au Châtelet de Paris de 1769 à 1804* (Paris: Cujas, 1959), p. 14.

18. Ibid., p. 13.

19. Ibid., p. 14.

20. Ibid., pp. 265-269.

21. Abensour, *La Femme et le féminisme*, p. 20.

22. Ibid., p. 10.

23. Ibid., p. 11. There was even unresolved debate concerning the question of venereal disease, and it finally was left in the hands of the presiding magistrate to decide whether a wife had grounds for demanding a separation if

her husband had contracted venereal disease prior to or outside of the marriage.

24. Ibid., p. 11.

25. Ibid., p. 9. Stringent space restrictions prevent the integration here of a discussion of the disparities between law and custom. In fact, husbands did not always take advantage of the law to prosecute unfaithful wives; custom often dictated that spouses, especially among the aristocracy in and around Paris, agree to go their separate ways once suitably legitimate heirs had been produced.

26. Ibid., p. 24.

27. Ibid., p. 31.

28. Ibid., p. 21.

29. Ibid., p. 136.

30. Ibid., p. 23.

31. Lebigre, p. 171.

32. Abensour, La Femme et le féminisme, p. 23.

33. Lelièvre, p. 125.

34. Abensour, La Femme et le féminisme, p. 24.

35. Ibid., p. 229.

36. Ibid., pp. 232-233.

37. Ibid., pp. 233-234.

38. Ibid., pp. 233-234.

39. Ibid., p. 235.

40. Ibid., p. 236.

41. Ibid., p. 236. A Dutchwoman, Mme de Combé, sought to rehabilitate prostitutes by placing them in convent-like homes, but these, under the supervision of nuns, were not very different from prisons.

42. Ibid., p. 237.

43. Ibid., p. 256. In some instances, a married man who seduced a girl might find his own marriage annulled and himself adjudged to be the husband of the accuser or required to provide her with a dowry.

44. Ibid., p. 257.

45. Ibid., pp. 25-26.

46. Ibid., p. 259.

47. Elisabeth Badinter, L'Amour en plus (Paris: Flammarion, 1980), p. 132. Badinter also has a lengthy discussion of "legitimate" infanticide, i.e., infants sent to wet nurses. The infant survival rate was very low.

48. Abensour, La Femme et le féminisme, pp. 245-246. The involvement of women in smuggling and in the manufacture of contraband salt was so great that the government, by royal ordinances of 1680 and 1688, had to take repressive measures against female salt smugglers. It declared them susceptible to the same penalties and the same fines as male salt smugglers.

49. Ibid., pp. 248-249.

50. Ibid., p. 255.

51. Ibid., pp. 29-30.

52. Léon Abensour, Histoire générale du féminisme des origines à nos jours (Paris: Librairie Delagrave, 1921), p. 179.

53. Paule-Marie Duhet, Les Femmes et la révolution 1789-1794 (Paris: Julliard, 1971) p. 223.

54. Ibid., pp. 165-166.

55. Ibid., p. 166.

56. Abensour, Histoire, pp. 198-201.

57. Ibid., p. 203.

58. Duhet, p. 164.

59. Ibid., p. 172. See Lelièvre, p. 179, for more detailed discussion of changes enacted by the law of January 7, 1794.

60. Lelièvre, p. 388.

61. Jean Rabaut, *Histoire des féminismes français* (Paris: Stock, 1978), p. 73.

62. Ibid., p. 79.

63. Lelièvre, p. 189.

64. Rabaut, p. 74.

65. Ibid., pp. 73-74.

66. Ibid., p. 75.

67. Alain Decaux, *Histoire des Françaises* (Paris: Librairie académique Perrin, 1972), vol. 2, pp. 616-620.

Susan P. Conner

Women and Politics

"Politics are like a labyrinth," wrote William Gladstone. They lure participants into a maze. They entangle the curious, they ensnarl the unwary, they obsess the ambitious. While Gladstone was writing about nineteenth-century politics, the politics of eighteenth-century France were no different. Strategies, tactics, and struggles for influence were conducted in the serpentine passages and corridors to power.

The eighteenth century, which is generally dated from the death of Louis XIV in 1715, was a period of sporadic international war, political intrigue, religious controversy, and diplomatic revolution. In France, controversies from previous centuries appeared again. The Jansenist and Jesuit quarrel reemerged, and political sparring between the legitimate and legitimized heirs of Louis XIV became entangled with the insurrections of Parlement. Other problems affecting politics included the fiscally disastrous schemes of John Law, continuing provincial discontentment with taxes, and an unstable international scene.

According to contemporaries, eighteenth-century politics had also fallen under the influence of women. Looking back over the century, portrait painter Mme Vigée-Lebrun wrote, "The women reigned then, the Revolution dethroned them."[1] The influence that women exerted, however, did not originate in the law. As Montesquieu observed, women had accumulated power through conspiracy. Such a base of power might be viewed as ephemeral, but to the *philosophe*, women had become "an estate within the state." That was a fact worthy of note to Montesquieu, and his fictional characters in *Lettres persanes* told his readers about it. "Anyone at the court, in Paris, or in the provinces," said Rica, "who judges the ministers, magistrates, and prelates without knowing the women who govern them is like a man who can easily tell that a machine works, but who has no knowledge of the inner springs."[2] Although *Lettres persanes* had been written in 1721 to point out the peccadillos and serious failings of the court, society, and government of Louis XIV, no one could fail to see the parallels with the Regency and reign of Louis XV.

Later historians have continued to echo many of the generalizations that eighteenth-century courtiers and writers made. Like Edmond and Jules de Goncourt, they seemed to be saying of the eighteenth-century woman: "[She] is the principle who governs, the reason which directs, and voice who commands."[3] Voilà the reign of women. Or was it?

Indeed, the role of women in eighteenth-century French politics cannot be treated so simply. A great deal of the problem lies in what the term "politics" means, because it has remained undefined and elusive in most of the literature of the period. It begs for a definition that neither excludes those participants outside the power structure nor reads twentieth-century expectations into the analysis. For our purposes then, politics and political involvement will be defined as activities that take place either within formal government institutions or through informal channels to power. Those informal paths may include any type of pressure on the governing group, either collectively or by individuals inside or outside the formal structure. The activity must be conscious, organized, and leading toward some legal change or governmental response.[4] The question of women and politics in eighteenth-century France becomes a question of whether "political personalities" existed among the women of the century and whether those women influenced affairs of state.

Over the years, writers on eighteenth-century France have talked about "political" women in various ways, particularly as *salonnières,* as working-class women who acted collectively prior to the Revolution, and as individual women of the elite who independently attempted to influence French politics. In reality, the *salonnières* should not be discussed in studies of political women. Their inclusion has actually been a case of mistaking visibility with political power. Scarcely on the periphery of politics, the *salonnières* were prominent not in politics but in social circles as inheritors of the tradition of the *précieuses* of the previous century. Like their predecessors, they continued to discuss controversial topics and to surround themselves with men of learning. Some continued to revolt against contemporary marriage customs; some studied literature that promoted equality between the sexes, although not particularly as feminists; and some wrote pamphlets and books that frequently contained political overtones.[5] In the last half of the century, for example, women's writings defended their sex with renewed vigor and force. Mme de Puisieux (*La Femme n'est pas inférieure à l'homme,* 1750-51), Mme Gacon-Dufour (*Mémoire pour le sexe féminin,* 1787), and Mme de Coicy (*Les Femmes comme il convient de les voir,* 1785) challenged the assumptions about the intellectual and physical attributes of women and about their economic position in society.[6] But the *salonnières* and writers did not step beyond their salons and discussions. They took no political action, and, therefore, they cannot be considered political women. Their study should be undertaken elsewhere.

Collective behavior of another type, however, was occurring at the same time in France. Evidence abounds documenting outbreaks of *taxation populaire*, bread riots, and localized challenges to conscription and taxation that were taking place throughout the century. But was this a form of collective political action in which women participated? On this question, scholars disagree radically. To Jeffrey Kaplow, the crowds of pre-Revolutionary Paris were "pre-political."[7] Women, many of whom participated frequently, were drawn into demonstrations because of their economic misfortunes. As wives and mothers who could not feed their families, they demanded that the government intervene to assist them. There was no desire for political change; there was no conscious challenge to the system. The women were instead governed by fears of famine and insecurity that drove them to riot. To Kaplow, no collective action to change the political system occurred until the Revolution took place.[8] Other scholars, however, disagree. Darline Levy and Harriet Applewhite suggest that eighteenth-century demonstrations were politically motivated and were directed with "a certain modicum of political skill."[9] Working-class women had discovered that they had the power to threaten the governing authority. Violence, although outside the formal system, could conceivably effect change. According to Levy and Applewhite, the women participants, therefore, could not be "pre-political" beings.

The answer to this question of political action probably lies somewhere in between the two positions. While an undeveloped political consciousness existed, the political organization to carry out change did not. Throughout the century, years of dearth and famine were also years of bread riots, in particular during the years 1725, 1739-1740, 1752, 1768, and the *guerre des farines* of 1775; however, the demonstrations made no lasting change, and the institution of the government was not challenged. On that count, George Rudé pointed out, "The main lesson of 1775 was, in short, that . . . no isolated movement of wage-earners, artisans and village poor could hope to yield revolutionary results."[10] Yet riots had continued throughout the century, led by people who had no legal rights to participate in the governing process or to challenge it. By the time of the Revolution, a metamorphosis had taken place, and the result was politically explosive. The scarcity of bread was consciously understood to be bound to the institution of the government. From 1789 on, demonstrations were no longer localized, and political as well as economic goals were evident. Popular violence became a "political tool" of the laboring men and women.[11] The *sans-jupons* and the club women of the Revolution became the inheritors of this political transformation.

Although the *salonnières* of eighteenth-century France remained outside the realm of political action and the wage-earning poor women of Paris can at best be described as marginally political, a handful of women did influence the affairs of state and wield political power. These few political personalities were extremely visible in French affairs. They were the women whom Montesquieu and his compatriots believed were dominating politics. "Since Francis I," wrote Melchior Grimm, echoing Montesquieu's observations, "women have played an important role in the court. In the only country in Europe where custom, not law excludes women from succession to the throne, it is unique that they nevertheless can reign as regents and rule, in fact, as wives and mistresses."[12] Grimm was correct that for several centuries tradition within the elite and royal society had given a few highly placed women an avenue to power. In the sixteenth century, Margaret of Angoulême and Catherine de Medici established a tradition of political involvement followed by Marie de Medici, her favorite Leonora Galigaï, Anne of Austria, and Mme de Maintenon in the seventeenth century. From religious disputes to domestic and foreign affairs to women's questions, their influence was present.

During the eighteenth century, the influence of women continued to be an individual effort. These few *femmes de la haute société*, however, were notorious rather than noteworthy for their work, and rather than being models for later feminists, their methods generally have been regarded with scorn. All were born into the nobility, frequented it, or were granted titles. All of them were also influence peddlers, inveterate seductresses, or coquettes, who seemed to represent the abuses of the ancien régime and who had no interest in pursuing social or political changes that would have supported equality between the sexes. All of these women consciously laid plans to increase their power over politics and the men who made decisions concerning affairs of state. Because of the legal exclusion of women from the government, their influence came through informal channels to power. In the pre-Revolutionary eighteenth century, women and politics were synonymous with intrigue.

A catalog of eighteenth-century political women is short: Mme du Maine, a venomously ambitious *intrigante* who sought the downfall of the regent; Mme de Tencin, a former canoness and the mistress of Guillaume Dubois, the first minister; and Mme de Pompadour, the ambitious *maîtresse en titre* of Louis XV who strove to be first minister. Only a few others might be considered, but their influence was never so great: Mme de La Tournelle, better known as the duchesse de Châteauroux; Mme du Barry; and Marie-Antoinette. Their reputations for perfidy, in fact, exceeded their deeds.

Chronologically, the first of the *intrigantes* was Anne Louise Bénédicte de Bourbon-Condé, duchesse du Maine (1676-1753). She was a princess of the blood and the wife of the duc du Maine, who was one of the legitimized sons *(légitimés)* of Louis XIV. The tiny, spirited duchess was obsessed with promoting her husband in circles of government because his elevation would increase her own power and prestige. But on the death of the Grand Monarch, Maine's position was suddenly and severely challenged by Philippe, duc d'Orléans, who assumed power. Cleverly, the regent removed the duc du Maine from the Conseil de Régence. He accepted his demotion, but the duchess was neither so unassuming or acquiescent as her husband.[13]

What the duchesse du Maine feared was further erosion of her husband's position and, therefore, of her own. She enjoyed the fame brought to her by the *grandes nuits de Sceaux,* and she began to recruit others who were discontented with the regent and his government. Shortly, what began as a personal vendetta against the duc d'Orléans became linked to the spread of inflammatory literature, to a power struggle between the dukes and nonducal nobility of France, and to conspiracy.

The clash began on February 22, 1717, when the dukes, encouraged by the princes of the blood, presented their petition to revoke all privileges granted to the *légitimés.* Mme du Maine then took action. Feverishly involved, she began to collect evidence to support her husband's claim. As she worked late into the night with memoirs, documents, and huge tomes of legal documents spread around her, she envisioned herself as the chief advocate for all wronged noblemen, the engineer of a new *fronde.*[14] Neither the nobles nor Mme du Maine expected the regent to call for a confrontation, but the duc d'Orléans could not expect to hold power if he allowed the dissident nobles to question his authority. The duchesse du Maine, however, chose to ignore the actions of the regent and Parlement, and she continued to lead the agitation that kept Paris in a furor. When Parlement convened in a less than conciliatory mood, the duc du Maine was stripped of his right of succession. Crying like a crazed fury, Mme du Maine retired to her estate, where she engaged in planning a conspiracy to depose the regent and to humiliate the pretentious princes of the blood and dukes.[15]

In her haste to find redress, the duchesse du Maine committed a number of capital errors. First, she did not realize that the regent never allowed women to concern themselves with governmental affairs. The comment that he had made to the comtesse de Sabran was already legendary: "Look at yourself, see if so pretty a face should talk business."[16] Second, she never understood that fomenting the controversy between the nonducal nobles and the princes of the blood would place her husband in a no-man's land between them. Third, the duchess indulged herself in conspiracy as if there would be no cost and as if she could withdraw from it at whim. The court at Sceaux became a *foyer de conspirateurs*, allegedly spawning propaganda and obscene parodies of the court at Versailles.[17]

From the time of her return to Sceaux, Mme du Maine's confused negotiations with Spanish agents began. Using white ink, secret contacts, a circuitous route including a Jesuit priest, a Belgian adventurer, and Cardinal Julio Alberoni, the duchess hoped to use Spanish influence to restore the will of Louis XIV. As the conspiracy developed during the summer of 1718, it included all of the following elements: to raise the people of Paris and the provinces in revolt against the duc d'Orléans; to arrest and kidnap the regent and imprison him in a Spanish fortress; to convoke the Estates General and reestablish their alleged historic rights; to turn the regency nominally over to the king of Spain, Philip V, a grandson of Louis XIV, who would serve with a Council of State. His lieutenant to administer the Kingdom of France was to be the duc du Maine. In separate maneuvers, the young and adventurous duc de Richelieu planned to turn the garrisons in Bayonne over to the Spanish, and Breton leaders promised support to the duchess if troops would aid them in their own uprising.[18]

In spite of her care to maintain secrecy, the duchess could not hide the nocturnal meetings with fellow conspirators. Initially, the cabal had seemed to be no more than a "conspiracy of grammarians."[19] Those who were knowledgeable had joked about the plots, but the regent finally decided to take action against such insubordination. On August 26, 1718, by *lit de justice*, the duc du Maine was stripped of his remaining special privileges.[20] Unaware of her responsibility in their misfortune, Mme du Maine redoubled her efforts to enlist the aid of the Spanish. The nocturnal meetings continued; the coterie of conspirators increased, including Spanish ambassador Antoine-Guidice, prince de Cellamare, who was committed to a program to unseat the regent and to destroy the Quadruple Alliance that had been sealed in August. Before the conspirators could complete their work, however, abbé Dubois acted to collect the incriminating evidence and to ferret out the conspirators. In total, several hundred people were implicated, among them the duc and duchesse du Maine and members of their household staff.[21]

On December 29, 1718, Mme du Maine was arrested and sent to the château of Dijon where she was formally imprisoned. Under pressure from the regent, she dictated a lengthy confession concerning her activities. Making herself appear almost as an innocent bystander, she said that she had been "seduced by the talk of many evil-intentioned persons" into entering the conspiracy.[22] Regardless of the extent of her guilt, the duc d'Orléans and abbé Dubois had achieved several victories. The vocal, acerbic, and annoying duchess was silent; and the rumblings of the nonducal nobility had been quieted for the moment. Dubois publicized the lilliputian kingdom of the duchess as a gargantuan empire of treasonous pro-Spanish dissidents. It was a pretext badly needed for a declaration of war. The peace party was discredited, and on January 10, 1719, France declared war on Spain.

Eleven months later, Mme du Maine was freed, and she returned to Sceaux, where she reopened her salon. Perhaps it was less brilliant and exciting, as one contemporary observed, but conspiracy and personal vendettas had proved to be a failure.[23] The duchesse du Maine relinquished her proverbial cloak and dagger to take up literature again instead of espionage.

Contemporary to the duchesse du Maine was the equally colorful Claudine Alexandrine Guérin de Tencin (1681-1749).[24] Like other women who attempted to make a mark on French politics, Mme de Tencin was ambitious and clever. In 1712 on moving to Paris, she became feverishly active in salon society, and shortly later, it was said that she held the first place in society—not because of her literary enterprise but because of her sexual conquests. Most of her liaisons had one thing in common: they were men of influence who might possibly help to advance her brother's career. The problem, as she saw it, was that her brother, the cardinal Pierre Guérin de Tencin, was not ambitious. In the words of a contemporary, "she had passed to her brother all the ambition she would have had, had her sex permitted it."[25]

In a well-known, but brief escapade, Mme de Tencin began her excursion into politics by seducing the regent. It quickly became clear, however, that the regent "did not like prostitutes who spoke of business between the sheets."[26] Soon after her episode with the duc d'Orléans, she became the mistress of abbé Dubois. At first secret, the affair became public after Dubois became an archbishop and cardinal. There is little question that the relationship influenced him, because he appointed the scarcely known cardinal de Tencin as religious advisor and confessor for John Law, the new, non-Catholic Contrôleur Général of France. Once Law was converted, the Tencin fortunes increased. Interestingly, the brokerage firm that Mme de Tencin had opened two months earlier began to prosper with assets totalling 3,356,892 *livres*.[27] Cardinal de Tencin was next charged with handling delicate matters in Rome, and his sister expected that an episcopate would soon be his. But the untimely death of Dubois in 1723 was a horrible blow to her plotting.

In the controversy between Jansenists and Jesuits, Mme de Tencin hoped to find a new avenue for her brother's advancement by allowing him to court both the king and the pope. Although the church council called for that purpose was held officially at Embrun, people said that it met "officiously" in Mme de Tencin's salon in Paris. On the other side of the controversy, fifty members of Parlement issued their own "consultation" proclaiming the invalidity of the council. Throughout Paris, songs, limericks, and obscene writings against Mme de Tencin circulated. Although she had stopped her immoral and dissolute behavior after her imprisonment in the Bastille, her detractors gathered ammunition against her.[28] She was possessed by the devil, they said, a "monster enriched by impudence and larceny."[29] Tempers became so inflamed that cardinal de Fleury demanded her exile from Paris until peace between the factions could be restored.

Several months later, Fleury allowed Mme de Tencin to return to Paris. When the seemingly contrite woman asked him to define a "rule of conduct" for her, Fleury reminded her: "Your sex confines you naturally within certain limits, which I should not have to recall to your memory."[30] She immersed herself in literary pursuits and turned her attention for nearly a decade to collecting *ses bêtes*, the menagerie of famous writers who frequented her salon.

In 1742, when cardinal de Tencin seemed destined to become the successor to Fleury, Mme de Tencin reentered politics by trying to ingratiate herself with the king's new mistress, Mme de La Tournelle. In the midst of her efforts, Fleury died, and Mme de Tencin became a liability to her brother as the infamies about her reappeared. The king chose no first minister for the remainder of his reign, but he turned over to the comte de Maurepas the portfolio that cardinal de Tencin had hoped to receive.[31]

For the remainder of her life, Mme de Tencin was committed to finding a niche in the court where she might influence politics in favor of her brother. Scores of letters passed between Mme de Tencin and the king's courtiers recommending a league of mutual benefit between the king's mistress and cardinal de Tencin. By 1743, however, the *religieuse défroquée* was considered an innocuous old woman; yet, as often as people sneered at her petty intrigues, they made sure that she would never again exert any influence. Mme de La Tournelle, no doubt, had once feared the power of Mme de Tencin and had written: "In spite of her cleverness, she cannot hide her obsession with power. She intrigues and forms cabals everywhere. . . . She has ambitions to put her brother in the ministry of foreign affairs, and God knows, she would be involved in everything if he were placed there."[32] Like Mme du Maine, Mme de Tencin's egocentric meddling in politics had failed, and she was remembered distastefully as an *intrigante*.

From the 1740s until the time of the Revolution, the few politically active women were found in the monarch's intimate circle. A *roi fainéant* of sorts, Louis' passions included hunting and women, not politics. For that reason, courtiers such as the duc de Richelieu hoped to influence policy decisions. Although the king had enunciated a firm stand against allowing women to play pseudoministerial roles, his sexual appetite was well known. Richelieu hoped to use his passion for mistresses to affect affairs of state.

Initially, Louis XV toyed with his mistresses—one Mailly-Nesle sister followed by another. The women appeared to be only whims until his eyes fell upon the youngest of the sisters, Marie-Anne de Mailly-Nesle (1717-1744), who became Mme de La Tournelle and later duchesse de Châteauroux. Unlike her sisters, she was exceedingly ambitious, impressionable, and under the tutelage of her cousin, the duc de Richelieu. It was only a matter of time until she replaced her sister in the king's bed and in his confidence.

Although the duchesse de Châteauroux did not affect politics through her own ingenuity, she set the stage for her successor. Her proximity to Louis XV made her exceedingly valuable, and Richelieu used that relationship to bring success to his martial policy. Frederick the Great also saw her as a tool to ensure that Franco-Prussian relations would remain firm. He wrote to her, or perhaps to her vanity, with simple persuasion: "Prussia can never know the debt it owes you."[33] Although her role in politics had been brief, erratic, and under the sway of Richelieu, Louis XV had allowed women to influence him. The time had come for another woman to emerge, the most politically influential woman of the reign of Louis XV. She was Jeanne Poisson, the future marquise de Pompadour.

According to her own stories, Jeanne Poisson (1721-1764) was reared from her youth to become a *morceau de roi*. Her education was impeccable, and her future was carefully planned. After several carefully arranged meetings with the king in the Forest of Sénart, she was introduced officially into court society in April of 1745. Initially, the youthful mistress shaped few political decisions. But Pompadour instructed herself in affairs of state, and she began to influence the choice of ministers and, thereby, the direction of French politics. In the end, her dislike of Frederick II, whose libelous verses annoyed her, and her displeasure with the Jesuits formed the basis of her own policy. It was not an easy path, and she once told her confidante, "My life is perpetual warfare."[34] As she was confronted by each of her implaccable enemies—the duc de Richelieu, the comte de Maurepas, and the d'Argenson brothers—it appeared that it might be a battle lost.

After the Peace of Aix-la-Chapelle in 1748, Pompadour became a part of the political scene. Epigrams, pamphlets, and the infamies of the *poissonades* circulated throughout Paris and within the court. It is doubtful that she played any role, even the most minor, in determining the provisions of the unpopular treaty, but to her name were attached the foulest accusations. She believed that one of her greatest enemies was the comte de Maurepas, who had a powerful influence over the king. In a brief power play, however, it was Pompadour who brought about his downfall.[35]

By 1750, it appeared that Pompadour monitored everything that was directed to the king. The more she instructed herself in politics, the more it seemed that she "intended to govern France as first minister." Her library of over 3,500 volumes gave evidence of the seriousness with which she took her task. While she worked to maintain her power, Pompadour also promoted some of the men around whom French history would be made—cardinal de Bernis, who became ambassador to Venice, and the comte de Stainville, who became ambassador to Rome. Like the Paris brothers, these men were devoted to Pompadour, supporting her against rivals and against detractors.[36]

The most damaging flaw in Pompadour's character was that she was too easily flattered. Her vanity, especially her belief that she was a "woman of state," began to overshadow her reasoning. There is certainly no doubt that by 1755 she saw herself as Mme de Maintenon's successor—the spiritual and political advisor to the king and a woman who, she believed, had transcended the role of mistress. More and more, she assumed a watchful eye over the monarch. She required that all ministers make their appointments through her; she turned them away, regardless of the cause, if the king appeared "jaundiced." She kept herself abreast of the news through Robert Janelle, *intendant des postes*, who reported on virtually everything that passed through the mail. Everything, it seemed, had to fall under her guardianship from her patronage of rococo ornamentation to her excursions into royal entrepreneurship and her occasional supervisory role at the Parc aux Cerfs. Likewise, she saw no paradox in promoting Voltaire and Quesnay while becoming a devoted communicant and correspondent with the pope.

After Pompadour was granted the position of *dame du palais de la reine* in 1756, she proceeded more fully with her other plans, which had been under way for some months. Her incursion into the political domain had not gone unnoticed by certain foreign diplomats, who knew the value of courting the king's favorite. Prince von Kaunitz, who had already established a positive relationship with the king's mistress during his earlier sojourns in Paris, decided to capitalize on "the reign of Madame de Pompadour," who seemed to be pro-Austrian. Other later circumstances, including the Convention of Westminster between Prussia and England, also favored the Austrians in their negotiations. A European war was brewing, the colonial controversy took on more serious overtones, and the authority of the king had been compromised in his dealings with Parlement. Pompadour, like Châteauroux before her, knew that successes on the battlefield would do much to restore the favor of the king. So, in the chambers of a vain woman at a very important moment in French fortune, the Austrian chancellor found a receptive audience for the *renversement des alliances* (diplomatic revolution).

It would be incorrect to blame Pompadour for the entire pro-Austrian policy and the calamitous war that resulted, but there is no doubt that she encouraged and supported the policy. Austrian Ambassador Georg Adam von Starhemberg prevailed upon her closeness to the king, and Maria Theresa prevailed upon her vanity. The ploy succeeded; and, in the words of a contemporary, "a letter from Maria Theresa turned Madame de Pompadour's head [toward] this monstrous alliance."[37] In September of 1755, the secret political dealings were formalized in a meeting on the grounds of Pompadour's summer residence at Bellevue. Pompadour, Bernis, and Starhemberg agreed on the basic provisions of what became the Treaty of Versailles that was signed on May 1, 1756. Starhemberg laid the credit at Pompadour's doorstep: "We owe everything to her, and it is to her that we must look for everything in the future. She likes recognition and deserves it."[38]

French politics were again torn by the unrest of the Parlement de Paris. Supplies for the Seven Years War, which had just opened, were scarce, and money was scarcer, according to Bernis. Pompadour studied the campaigns daily and allegedly marked troop movements with her beauty spots. But she was also waging a personal war against Lieutenant-General of Police Marc René d'Argenson ("a reciprocal hatred," a contemporary called it). On January 5, 1757, in the midst of the *malaise profond*, an attempt was made on the king's life. Damiens' attack with a pen knife was not fatal, but the king believed it to be so serious that he called for his confessor. Secluded, but out of danger, it appeared that the king was ready to divest himself of the marquise. He was in the hands of his doctors, counsellors, and churchmen, who, without doubt, were opposed to Pompadour. But again Pompadour remained, and Minister of Marine Machault and the comte d'Argenson were forced to leave Versailles. D'Argenson was the last of her implaccable enemies who had had enough power to endanger her position.[39]

Louis knew d'Argenson to be the rogue that he was, but in the midst of the war, France could spare neither Machault nor d'Argenson. Their replacements were nonentities—the marquis de Paulmy and Peirenc de Moras, who were unprepared for the weight of their task. In forcing the confrontation, Pompadour had created a ministerial crisis, but she was unaware of the crisis because she was preoccupied with her personal command of the situation. "With the confidence of a child," wrote Bernis astutely, "Madame de Pompadour believed that all would go well with her help." She named ambassadors; she promoted her favorite generals. Janelle and Chief of Police Berryer provided her with information on domestic affairs.[40]

The war dragged on, the French command was not unified, and jealousies obstructed the effectiveness of the command. At Rossbach and Crefeld, France suffered humiliation. It should have been clear to Pompadour that one of two changes needed to be made: either a unified generals' command had to be created or France needed to sue for the most favorable terms. Bernis supported the latter plan, but Pompadour resisted because she clung to the child-like faith that the French armies would be exonerated by a brilliant victory.[41] It was inevitable that she and Bernis would come into conflict over the course of the war. Bernis recommended turning policy decisions over to a committee. Being a realist, he also reserved a role for Pompadour: she could still control many appointments and make presentations to the king. To the marquise, however, "the scheme amounted to taking the reins of government out of her hands."[42]

As Bernis lost credibility with Pompadour and the king, he still hoped to retain his position on the king's council while turning over his portfolio to the duc de Choiseul, but Pompadour would not have it. On October 9, 1757, Bernis resigned from the department of foreign affairs. On the tenth, Bernis received his cardinal's hat, the one appointment that he had long coveted. He knew that Pompadour had been influential, and he wrote to her: "I owe it to you. I owe you nearly everything."[43] But too slowly did Bernis let loose of his interest in government. His policies clashed with the interests of the king, who hoped to bring victory out of the defeats of the French Army. In November, Bernis received his *lettre d'ordre* from the king, sending him to his abbey at Soissons.

No other ministerial changes occurred during the remaining years of Pompadour's life, and contemporaries remarked that the king had chosen to play a more active role in affairs of state. Yet the warning was always present: "You can secretly count on the king, but, in spite of all his attachment for you, his politics could force him perhaps to sacrifice you to his mistress and his ministers."[44] When Pompadour died in 1764, ministers wondered whether another mistress would try to slip on the shoes of the woman who had been "first minister."

Jeanne Bécu, who became the duchesse du Barry, was presented in court in 1769. Although she toyed with ministers, members of the court never saw her as Pompadour's successor. Never did she pattern herself after Pompadour or Mme de Maintenon. Louis XV also turned less to his mistress for advice and more to his ministers Choiseul and later René-Nicolas de Maupeou.

In 1775, a year after Louis XVI and Marie-Antoinette were crowned, the *Gazette de Hollande* reported that the age of mistresses had ended. But there was yet one woman, Marie-Antoinette, who attempted to play a role in affairs of state. As a queen, her position was more legitimate than her predecessors, but her meddling in politics to insure plush sinecures for her personal favorites and her making and unmaking of ministers were played more in the role of a traditional mistress. As the political climate changed, her meddling was tolerated even less than the political interference of those women who had preceded her. The disgraces of ministers like Turgot were laid at her doorstep. All expenditures were blamed on her, even though she did not attempt to dictate policy or to play the role of first minister. In many ways, however, she was like Pompadour; but the time for Pompadours had passed, and Marie-Antoinette was neither as serious nor as skilled as the marquise.

Among the many comments on women and politics in eighteenth-century France, Sainte-Beuve's remark is probably the most favorable. In describing Pompadour, he said simply, "She did no worse than any other favorite would have done in a period when France had no great statesmen."[45] These women, who lacked education in foreign and domestic affairs, played politics with the conviction that personal satisfaction was paramount. Only Pompadour sincerely wanted to sit at the bargaining table, but even she had no desire to serve as a model for those women who might follow her. Neither she nor the others wanted to expand opportunities for women or to create a more egalitarian system. They were, without doubt, products of the ancien régime. Not surprisingly then, their brand of "woman power" was condemned by the Revolution. Except for Mme du Maine, their influence could not be separated from their sex. According to feminists, the women in whom political power had rested had simply prostituted themselves for power.

NOTES

1. Elizabeth Vigée-Lebrun, *Memoirs of Madame Vigée Lebrun* (New York: Doubleday, Page and Company, 1903), p. 49.

2. Charles Louis de Secondat, baron de La Brède et de Montesquieu, *Lettres persanes* (Paris: Garnier, 1960), p. 236.

3. Edmond and Jules de Goncourt, *La Femme au dix-huitième siècle*, 2 vols. (Paris: Flammarion, 1929), vol. 2, p. 97.

4. Mary Stanley and Victoria Schuck, "In Search of Political Women," *Social Science Quarterly* 55, no. 3 (December, 1974):637; Jeane Kirkpatrick, *Political Woman* (New York: Basic Books, 1974), p. 217.

5. See Vera Lee, *The Reign of Women in 18th Century France* (Cambridge, Mass.: Schenkman Publishing Co., 1975) and Carolyn Lougee, *Le Paradis des Femmes: Women, Salons and Social Stratification in 17th Century France* (Princeton: Princeton University Press, 1976).

6. Léon Abensour, *La Femme et le féminisme avant la révolution* (Geneva: Slatkine-Megariotis Reprints, 1977), pp. 358-359.

7. Jeffrey Kaplow, *The Names of Kings: The Parisian Laboring Poor in the Eighteenth Century* (New York: Basic Books, Inc., 1972), p. 153.

8. Ibid., p. 159.

9. Darline Gay Levy and Harriet B. Applewhite, "Women of the Popular Classes in Revolutionary Paris, 1789-1795," in *Women, War and Revolution*, edited by Carol R. Berkin and Clara M. Lovett (New York: Holmes and Meier Publishers, 1980), p. 11.

10. George Rude, *Paris and London in the Eighteenth Century: Studies in Popular Protest* (New York: The Viking Press, 1970), p. 67.

11. Louise Tilly, "The Food Riot as a Form of Political Conflict in France," *Journal of Interdisciplinary History* 2 (1971): 57.

12. Friedrich Melchior Freiherr von Grimm, *Mémoires politiques et anecdotiques inédites de la cour de France pendant les règnes de Louis XV et Louis XVI . . .*, 2 vols. (Paris: Librairie Lerouge-Wolff, 1830), vol. 1, p. 189.

13. Louis de Courcillon, abbé de Dangeau, *Journal du marquis de Dangeau*, 19 vols. (Paris: Firmin Didot frères, 1854–1860), vol. 16, p. 163.

14. Charles Pinot Duclos, *Oeuvres complètes de Duclos*, 9 vols. (Geneva: Slatkine Reprints, 1968), vol. 7, p. 257; Marguerite Jeanne Cordier de Launay, baronne de Staal, *Mémoires de Madame de Staal sur la fin du règne de Louis XIV, la cour de Sceaux, la conspiration de Cellamare, et la Bastille*, 2 vols. (Paris: Alphonse Lemerre, 1877), vol. 1, p. 152.

15. Louis de Rouvroy, duc de Saint-Simon, *Mémoires de Saint-Simon*, 41 vols. (Paris: Librairie Hachette et Cie, 1893), vol. 31, p. 264.

16. Duclos, vol. 6, p. 336.

17. Général de Piépape, "Une princesse conspiratrice," *Revue des deux mondes*, ser. 5, 47 (September-October 1908):598; Saint-Simon, vol. 35, pp. 22-23.

18. *Mémoires de la régence de S.A.R. Mgr. le duc d'Orléans durant la minorité de Louis XV, roi de France*, edited by chevalier de Piossens, 3 vols. (La Haye: Jean van Duren, 1737), vol. 2, pp. 192-193.

19. Pierre Edouard Lémontey, *Oeuvres de P. E. Lémontey*, 2 vols. (Paris: Paulin, 1832), vol. 1, p. 207.

20. *Remontrances du Parlement de Paris au XVIIIe siècle*, edited by Jules Flammermont, 3 vols. (Paris: Imprimerie nationale, 1888), vol. 1, p. 113.

21. Jean Buvat, *Journal de la Régence, 1715-1723*, 2 vols. (Paris: Henri Plon, 1865), vol. 1, p. 342. Discussions of the Cellamare Conspiracy can be found in Emile Bourgeois, *La Diplomatie secrète au XVIIIe siècle, ses débuts: Le Secret de Dubois, cardinal et premier ministre* (Paris: Librairie Colin, n.d.); and W. H. Lewis, *The Sunset of the Splendid Century: The Life and Times of Louis Auguste de Bourbon, duc du Maine, 1670-1736* (London: Eyre and Spottiswoode, 1955).

22. Dangeau, vol. 17, pp. 444-445; Archives de la Bastille, no. 10, 677.

23. Charles Hénault, *Mémoires du président Hénault* (Paris: Librairie Hachette, 1911), p. 129.

24. Mme de Tencin is best known as the mother of d'Alembert and as a well-known *salonnière* and friend of Fontenelle. Jean Sareil, *Les Tencin: Histoire d'une famille au dix-huitième siècle d'après de nombreux documents inédits* (Geneva: Librairie Droz, 1969), p. 38ff.

25. Duclos, vol. 6, p. 386.

26. Duclos. The story is also told in contemporary songs and memoirs. (Bibliothèque Nationale, fonds français 12673, fol. 279.)

27. L. S. Auger, Introduction to Claudine-Alexandrine Guérin de Tencin, *Oeuvres complètes de Mesdames de Lafayette et de Tencin*, 5 vols. (Paris: Imprimerie de Faine Jeune et Cie, 1804), vol. 4, p. 4.

28. Archives de la Bastille, no. 10,947.

29. Mathieu Marais, *Journal et mémoires de Mathieu Marais*, 4 vols. (Paris: Librairie de Firmin Didot frères, 1863), vol. 3, p. 495.

30. Archives des affaires étrangères, mémoires et documents, Rome, vol. 73, fol. 148-149.

31. Pierre Narbonne, *Journal des règnes de Louis XIV et Louis XV de l'année 1701 à l'année 1744* (Paris: A. Durand, 1866), p. 595.

32. Châteauroux to Richelieu, 3 November 1743, in Marie-Angélique Fremyn de Moras, duchesse de Brancas, *Mémoires de la duchesse de Brancas* (Paris: Librairie des Bibliophiles, 1840), p. 123.

33. Frederick II to Châteauroux, 12 May 1744, in *Oeuvres de Frédéric II* (Berlin: Decker, 1854), p. 561. For a good general discussion of Châteauroux, see G. P. Gooch, *Louis XV: The Monarchy in Decline* (London: Longmans, Green, and Company, 1956), p. 98ff.

34. Nicole du Hausset, *The Private Memoirs of Louis XV* (London: H. S. Nichols and Co., 1895), p. 99.

35. Maurepas was also charged with negligence in managing naval affairs.

36. René Louis de Voyer de Paulmy, marquis d'Argenson, *Journal et mémoires du marquis d'Argenson*, 9 vols. (Paris: Mme Vve Jules Renouard, 1865), vol. 7, p. 74.

37. Grimm, vol. 1, p. 138.

38. Starhemberg to Kaunitz, 13 May 1756, quoted in Gooch, p. 165.

39. Jean François Marmontel, *Mémoires de Marmontel*, 3 vols. (Paris: Librairie des Bibliophiles, 1891), vol. 2, pp. 40-41.

40. François-Joachim de Pierre, cardinal de Bernis, *Mémoires et lettres de François-Joachim de Pierre, cardinal de Bernis, 1715-1758*, 2 vols. (Paris: E. Plon et Cie, 1878), vol. 1, p. 372; vol. 2, p. 79.

41. Du Hausset, p. 175.

42. Bernis to Pompadour, 12 September 1758, in Bernis, vol. 2, p. 269.

43. Bernis to Pompadour, 10 October 1758, in ibid., vol. 3, p. 300.

44. Tercier to d'Eon, 27 December 1763, quoted in John Buchan Telfer, *The Strange Career of the Chevalier d'Eon de Beaumont* (London: Longmans, Green, and Company, 1885), p. 137.

45. C. A. Sainte-Beuve, *Causeries du lundi*, 16 vols. (Paris: Garnier frères, 1882), vol. 2, p. 510.

✲ Harriet B. Applewhite and Darline Gay Levy

Women, Democracy, and Revolution in Paris, 1789-1794

WOMEN of the popular classes in Paris made a major contribution to what is most significant, even unique, about the Revolution: its achievement of the most democratically based popular sovereignty in the eighteenth-century western world. Feminist claims for civil and political rights growing out of Enlightenment liberalism never became central to the Revolutionary power struggles and were denied by the Napoleonic Code, but the political activities of nonelite women were at the heart of Revolutionary politics. Traditionally and typically, revolutionary democracy has been studied principally as it affected male populations; yet male leaders of the Revolution themselves remarked upon, exploited, and often attempted to rein in the activism of female revolutionaries. Their observations of women's mass interventions in Revolutionary politics indicate the limits of the first experiences of democracy in France.[1]

Over a century and a half, the processes of monarchical centralization, in combination with economic, demographic, intellectual, political, and administrative change affecting government and people, contributed to the transformation of issues that once had been regional and local into issues with a national focus and impact. Issues traditionally adjudicated in household and parish now were nationally aired and not infrequently resolved centrally. Governors and governed were brought into more frequent contact over matters of general concern, such as tax collecting, the administration of justice, and the regulation of food supplies.[2]

The Enlightenment was one expression of this larger transformative process of nationalization. Enlightenment cultural concerns for legal reform, a national system of education, public health, and better systems of transportation and communication all affected women as well as men, sometimes the same way, sometimes differently. Some

Enlightenment writers urged the extension of monarchical administrative organization to carry out these reforms in areas of education and law where women would be positively affected. Others joined an Enlightenment protest against the consequences of centralization and stressed, instead, the protection of the individual against government expansion. Women writers opposed any government extensions that would threaten the individual's rights to full and free self-expression. Those who spoke from this standpoint often ended up formulating some of the most explicitly feminist demands of the Enlightenment, advocating political and legal equality for women.

The processes of centralization and nationalization had considerable impact in the economic sphere, where the government—vacillating between policies of intervention and traditional regulation, on the one hand, and economic liberty, on the other hand—generated in both the urban and rural populace concerns, anxieties, and uncertainties that affected and eventually transformed their attitudes towards governing authorities. During frequent disturbances growing out of these shifts by the government in its economic policies, women of the people communicated their economic grievances to royal officials. Thus, the tradition of women being centrally involved in subsistence crises and putting pressure on municipal authorities at the Hôtel de Ville developed after the 1760s into a politics of protest against royal ministers and national government and was one attack on the legitimacy of the monarchy.

All these intellectual, social, political, and economic trends had increased the number of people, both men and women, who were aware of the implication of politics for their personal lives. But it was the circumstances of the Revolution itself that allowed Parisian women to stake out the field of their participation, progressively enlarge its scope, and intensify its impact.

These revolutionary circumstances were unique to Paris. Women in the provinces who enjoyed a degree of economic security met in groups during the Revolution, knitted stockings for soldiers, formed clubs to study revolutionary principles, or held ceremonies and gave prizes to children who learned revolutionary slogans and songs. Poor provincial women became, perhaps, the most pathetic victims of the Revolution. For them, a conscript army, a dechristianized republic, a beheaded monarch, and Jacobin rule meant nothing but loss. For these women, unlike the women of Paris, the Revolution did not create institutional networks of local groups in government with direct and visible ties to national institutions offering opportunities for the creation of collective, female political influence.[3]

Paris became the Revolutionary capital, the headquarters of the national legislatures and the central Jacobin Society. Government was no longer centered in the nobility at Versailles but in Paris, in the national legislature, the Commune, and the section assemblies—all of which had galleries open to the public. With such institutions literally in their midst, government could become an immediate daily experience of the women in Paris and, indeed, of the common men as well.

After January 1789, as the hope of regeneration took hold of an entire nation with the electoral process for the Estates General, women in groups joined men in submitting grievance lists, called *cahiers de doléances*, for the deputies to carry to the king at Versailles. These were petitions demanding specific occupational rights for women who were formerly members of guilds; other times, they were general requests for midwifery training, education for women, and other public policies to benefit women.[4]

Olympe de Gouges was a butcher's daughter from Montauban who wrote several plays and pamphlets on the coming Estates General. In her *Les Droits de la femme,* she boldly stated that the "Declaration of the Rights of Man and Citizen" was not being applied to women. She appeared to be demanding the vote for women and a national assembly of women, stressed that men must yield rights to women, and made a strong plea for women's education.[5]

Etta Palm d'Aelders, a Dutch woman who had been in Paris since 1774, made several demands upon radical clubs and the national legislatures. In February 1791, she introduced an ambitious plan to form women's patriotic societies in each section of Paris and in each of the eighty-three departments. She tried unsuccessfully to found a woman's society and later became an ardent advocate of an armed female battalion. In a plea she made to the Legislative Assembly in April, 1792, d'Aelders asked that women be admitted to civilian and military positions, that the education of girls be set up on the same foundations as that of men, that the age of female majority be twenty-one, that there be political liberty and equality of rights for both sexes, and that there be a decree permitting divorce.[6]

These frankly feminist demands, including Condorcet's recommendation of suffrage for women of property, were never debated or seriously discussed by those drawing up Revolutionary legislation.[7] Successive governments after 1795, the Directory and the Napoleonic regime, eroded even those legal and civic gains that women had made in the first six years of the Revolution. The Napoleonic Code did not perpetuate most of the Revolutionary advances in women's legal equality, although it did keep equal inheritance and permit divorce until the Restoration. In general, married women were considered legal minors, were denied legal ownership of property, and were forbidden to make contracts without the consent of fathers or husbands. The double standard of morality was incorporated in private law dealing with divorce, child custody, and alimony.

The most significant dimension of women's Revolutionary achievement was the direct participation in public affairs by women of the
popular classes. These women were active not because they translated
"feminist" demands into revolutionary petitions, riots, and other
popular manifestations but because they claimed that the sovereign
people, male and female, had rights to act on that sovereignty on a
daily basis where government touched their lives.

On September 22, 1789, a Paris newspaper, *Le Petit Gautier*, published
the following anecdote. The morning after the taking of the Bastille,
the editor had seen a mother with her children pulling down a small
wooden toll station on the bridge behind the Arsenal gardens in Paris.
When the editor asked why she was knocking it down, she replied:
"Haven't you ever paid your toll on this bridge? I demolish abuses, and
I am going to make my pot boil with the wood of despotism."[8]
Materially and symbolically, this nameless woman was converting the
supports of monarchy into fuel against it. She can stand for thousands
of women of the popular classes who used the corporate and
institutional supports of the paternalistic Old Regime to boil up a
revolutionary doctrine of popular sovereignty and to create a participa-
tory democracy in which they, along with men of humble rank,
acquired *de facto* citizenship.

The popular classes' claims to the rights of active citizens were put
before lawmakers right from the beginning of the Revolution, after a
century-long shift in attitudes towards the poor. The *philosophes*
especially had seen the strength of the masses as a double-edged
sword. Unsheathed, it was potentially threatening to public order, but
it also could be wielded in combat against despotism.[9]

This view of the people as simultaneously dangerous and useful
produced two radically different interpretations of citizenship in the
first six months of the Revolution. Proponents of a constitutional
monarchy stressed national unity as the cure for despotism, and this
unity became the basis of sovereignty in the Declaration of the Rights
of Man and Citizen. Article III of the Declaration read: "The source of
all sovereignty resides essentially in the nation; no group, no individual
may exercise authority not emanating expressly therefrom."[10]

This concept of perfect unity was quickly abandoned when the
deputies writing the Constitution responded to the tasks of delineating
the rights of citizens by narrowing the male electorate and instituting
indirect elections.

As this progressive and protective narrowing of citizenship and
sovereignty was being codified, the politicized masses, who in part
were provoking the process, were seeing themselves as the sovereign
nation and acting accordingly. Most significant is that women, both
demographically and politically, were a principal force among that

populace. Their tactics included frequent meetings in clubs, popular societies, and section assemblies; surveillance; boycotts; *taxation populaire;* petitions; strikes; denunciations; attendance in the galleries of the Constituent Assembly; popular veto; exercise of the right of recall; open and public deliberations; and democratization of membership in the National Guard.

Thus, two fundamentally different and incompatible concepts of citizenship were being worked out simultaneously: within the committees and sessions of the National Assembly; and outside the legislature in the cafés and arcades of the Palais-Royal, in local clubs and assemblies, and in the streets. On the one hand, constitutional legislation legitimized an abstract nation of passive citizens, who embodied a sovereignty that it in no way acted upon; and on the other hand, singularly aware and active Parisians, men and women, were claiming sovereignty by practicing an almost daily intervention in public affairs.

Rousseau conceptualized an Enlightenment theory of popular sovereignty; the radical journalists shaped its tactics and formulas. Popular sovereignty also can be considered a logical development from the long tradition of collective identity and activities shared by the Parisian *menu peuple:* common interests in security and subsistence; communal daily labor among laundresses or *poissardes* or market women; collective identity fostered by *corps* and *métiers;* parish-based church and charitable activities; and finally participation in festivals, religious processions, and demonstrations.

Women were inextricably bound up in networks of collective experiences common to the nonelites of Paris. It was unthinkable and impossible for authorities and radical men alike to separate them. Modern historians—George Rudé and Richard Cobb, for example— have seen women's activism as part of an insurrectionary tradition in times of dearth and as an indication that women became politically and publicly active only during subsistence crises.[11] But women's activism was much more regular and frequent, and, above all, was based on a broader range of principles, objectives, and tactics than had previously been acknowledged.

Women of the people played central roles in the public space of Paris and Versailles under the Old Regime. Women monopolized certain trades. The *dames de la Halle* ran the stalls of the central markets and the fishwives sold their husbands' catch. Some guilds exclusively for women survived *de facto* after Turgot's official abolition; guild women submitted demands for protections to the Estates General in the spring of 1789. Women participated in religious and seasonal festivals and processions; they instigated insurrectionary protests, like *taxation populaire.* Finally, and most significantly, women had established roles for themselves in key events that legitimized the monarchy. *Poissardes* verified the birth of a royal male heir, corporations of women were part of the celebration of royal birthdays and marriages, and deputations were sent to the king in times of drought and dearth. It was on the base of these traditions that women of the people built their Revolutionary expectations and, in company with male radicals, eventually claimed full sovereignty.

In August and September 1789, Paris was in turmoil over the high cost and scarcity of bread; in Versailles, the National Assembly was struggling to define the fundamental rights of citizens and to place limits on monarchical authority. During these weeks, popular agitation in which women were involved and thirty-four marches of thanksgiving and supplication where they were the principal participants seemed to many contemporary observers ominous portents of social unrest and political upheaval. What is strikingly new is male observers' linkage of traditional festivals with Revolutionary political and military institutions: an elected city government headed by Mayor Bailly and a bourgeois National Guard commanded by Lafayette. Bailly and Lafayette were at the center of a network of political power. As leaders of a municipal revolution, they conspicuously displayed the political strength behind their positions to the deputies and the king at Versailles, but they also were struggling to limit and restrain the passions of an aroused city—hungry, seething with rumor and tension, and heady with doctrines of popular sovereignty discussed in every café and on every corner.[12]

On August 7, a deputation of *dames de la halle* went to Versailles to congratulate the king and queen on the beginnings of the constitution. The traditional connection between royal legitimacy and women's perennial concerns over subsistence takes on a new significance when we reflect that the market women were congratulating the king for acquiescing to a constitution that would limit his powers. They addressed him as "our dear man, our good friend and our father," in that order; they asked the queen to "open your heart to us, as we have opened ours to you." These are hardly phrases of subservient loyalty; they emphasize bonds of affection but, simultaneously, connections of power.[13]

In Paris, the line of march of the thanksgiving processions symbolically linked the protection of Paris by its patron saint (the Église Sainte Geneviève), by the national church (Notre Dame), by its new representative government (the Hôtel de Ville), and by its military force (the National Guard).

Bailly, the mayor, was trying to oversee the policing of these women's processions and deputations, but he was also quite willing to exploit them to demonstrate the political might of Paris to the royal ministers at Versailles. On August 20, he received a reply to his request that the women from the St. Martin market be granted an audience with the king. The minister replied that he had been willing to admit the women from *la halle* but no more. "I ask you to forbid others to come from Paris. You can easily see that such a claim would soon arise in all the markets in Paris, which would create a mob and perhaps generate unrest among the people."[14] Bailly was trying to control and legalize deputations sent to Versailles while at the same time reaffirming (through conspicuous displays) the roles of the market women and popular classes as the principal supports of royal legitimacy and controls on royal authority. The minister, on the other hand, was apprehensive about an organized group of Parisian market women precisely because their encounters with the king could be exploited to expand popular mobilization.

A sense of uneasiness increased among active citizens as the month of September wore on and the women's processions continued. The bookseller Hardy, who initially had dismissed critics of the Parisian processions, was palpably disturbed by a march he described at considerable length on September 14. Hardy reported that there were between one thousand and twelve hundred marchers, a "good portion" of the men and women from the Faubourg Saint Antoine: six or seven hundred girls and women, marching four by four; National Guardsmen; trumpeters and drummers; *vainqueurs de la Bastille*, carrying weapons they had used along with a wooden model of the Bastille; and eleven debtors, whose debts the marchers had paid to secure their release from jail. Hardy found this march both ridiculous and frightening:

> Many people found there was something terrifying in [the procession's] arrangement, composition, and immensity. Sensible people found these public acts which could not be interrupted and of which piety was unfortunately not the full motive, ridiculous. They thought it would have been infinitely wiser for each citizen and each citoyenne to thank the Almighty individually . . . rather than collectively. . . .[15]

The radical journalist Prudhomme was not so apprehensive about the procession of September 14. In fact, he remarked, "if we lack bread and laws, at least we have pageantry and devotions to console us." The march to him was a clear celebration of the conquest of despotism by "the courage and the power of liberty."[16]

Both observers differed radically in their evaluation of the implications of this march but agreed that it signaled the potency of an organized populace. The women marchers were noticed and described, but their presence was not remarked as unusual or especially significant. It was rather the orchestration of different groupings that struck them: girls and women going to pray to the Virgin, the Bastille conquerors, workers from the Faubourg, released debtors, and the armed National Guard—all bearing symbols of hunger and harvest, fallen despotism, and the armed might of a free citizenry.

These two months of ceremony, agitation, and uneasiness set the stage for the second of the great revolutionary *journées*. The October days gave the king further notice of his impotence, reminded the constitution makers in the National Assembly of the debt they owed to popular protest, and taught the nation that its destiny was increasingly in the hands of the people of Paris.

Women's behavior inside the meeting hall of the National Assembly on October 5 was a demonstration of female political power that was of immense significance for the development of popular sovereignty during the Revolution.[17] When the women from Paris swarmed into the meeting hall of the Assembly—not restricting themselves to the galleries but milling about the floor, sitting in deputies' chairs, and, later, in Mounier's absence, even sitting in the president's chair—they were appropriating the tradition of abbeys of misrule, using dramaturgy and farce to ridicule the rule of governing authorities. They shouted, chanted, interrupted debate, and demanded that the deputies discuss subsistence problems in Paris. The *Journal de Paris* noted their odd dress; some wore elegant clothing, but hunting knives or half-swords hung from their skirts. "M. le comte de Mirabeau requested an order from the President to restore liberty and dignity to the National Assembly; but orders are more difficult to execute against women because it is almost impossible to apply force against weakness."[18] When Mounier returned from his audience with the king, the women willingly enough gave back his chair as presiding officer; but they chided him for his support of "this miserable Mister Veto," a reference to the controversy over the royal veto. Mounier, as we might expect, interpreted that as evidence of their stupidity and ignorance; but we can also see these remarks as impromptu farce, festival personification of what was to be ridiculed.[19] Mounier's report coupled the women marchers with the vile low men, both making up a mob of outrageous and menacing *bas peuple* whom he did not know how to handle, except by feeding them like animals: his response to their demands and threats was to order that dinner be brought for them. These riffraff, literally substituting themselves for the nation's rightful representatives by sitting in the president's chair and voting on motions, were for Mounier the ultimate dramatization of Rousseauist doctrine; they administered the shock that propelled him right out of the National Assembly and back to Dauphiné.[20]

The women's goals—a combination of subsistence and new constitutional objectives—seemed clear enough to a trenchant observer like Hardy, although they were obscured by police investigators and, we might add, by modern historians. The women wanted bread, plenty of it at an affordable price, and regular policing of grain transports to assure continued availability. Hardy also reported their announced intention of bringing the king and Assembly to Paris and obtaining the king's consent to the constitution.[21] Prudhomme added their intention to protest and punish the Flanders Royal Regiment's insult to the Revolutionary cockade at a banquet some days earlier.[22]

The reactions of radical journalists and polemicists were ambivalent. They were eager to celebrate another triumph of the Parisians over reactionary and conservative elements, yet uneasy that the sovereign people were bursting out of control. The writers resolved their ambivalence by representing the women as heroines, larger-than-life figures to serve as inspirational symbols, rather than as people with a dangerously loud political voice. The unknown author of a polemic, *Les Héroïnes de Paris*, ascribed to the marchers a sophisticated political objective: to return the king to Paris where he would live under a permanent people's surveillance. He credited them with nerve and energy that had to be reined in: "They must not embark upon any more expeditions which could degrade them." They must become disciplined; they must not drink in excess; and they must not model themselves after charlatans, such as street players, jugglers, magicians, and uncontrollable popular entertainers. Their political roles should be limited to maintaining surveillance over guards at tollgates to prevent rotten fruit and spoiled grain from being imported into Paris. In short, this nervous sympathizer was calling for the women's metamorphosis into *bonnes bourgeoises*.[23]

Radical revolutionaries observing the complex confrontations among the women of Paris, their allies in the National Guard, the monarch, his defenders, and the National Assembly were, in fact, reporting collisions and uneasy collaborations between practitioners of popular sovereignty and defenders of constitutional monarchy. They have taught us to read the evidence from October 1789 from the bottom up, seeing popular politics as a developing phenomenon with roots in traditional popular culture and connections to revolutionary institutional innovations. In the October Days, women were at a transitional moment. There were elements of ritual drama in their actions—playing leader, judging judges, punishing those who escape punishment the rest of the year. But they were not parading through the town square on a holiday; they were invading the palace and the National Assembly on a rainy weekday. They were oddly costumed, and some were even elegantly dressed; but they were armed. Prudhomme, for one, strained to read this behavior as a manifestation of love between the people and their king; he dismissed aristocrats who tried to seduce the women by telling them they would have bread if the king had his full authority.[24]

But Hardy, Prudhomme, most deputies, and probably the whole politically conscious nation knew better. The people of Paris, women prominently in the forefront, had invaded the hall of their representatives, captured their king and queen, and placed them under their permanent and constant surveillance.

The next morning, the royal family was conducted to Paris almost as captives in their carriage. They were surrounded by women with pikes bearing the heads of murdered guards and chanting that they were bringing back "the baker, the baker's wife, and the baker's apprentice," hardly traditional expressions of respect and loyalty to a fatherly monarch. Less than four days later, the king and queen appeared before people gathered in the Tuileries garden in Paris. Hardy's descriptions documented the erosion of royal legitimacy. Many in the crowd refused to bare their heads; no one cried *"vive le roi"*; and there were inarticulate murmurs of gross epithets, which, Hardy added, "signified absolutely nothing."[25] The point is that they signified everything, the shattered trust in the king that would undermine the constitutional monarchy before it was even off the drawing boards.

Within the next weeks, the National Assembly took up residence in Paris and, at the request of the Paris municipality, decreed martial law, which was to be enforced by the National Guard. The precipitating incident was the lynching of a baker by a crowd led by women. The decree stated that, after martial law had been announced, "all assemblages, armed or not, are declared criminal acts, to be dispersed by force." Before dispersing, however, the demonstrators could present a petition containing their grievance in a delegation of six.[26] The people, men and women, had to reduce their very powerful collective demonstrations to six-person delegations or face the guns of the authorities.

In the year and a half that followed, the National Assembly completed its blueprint for a constitutional monarchy and passed a number of laws limiting the rights of citizens: the suffrage decrees, prohibition of collective petitions, and a law prohibiting strikes. What underlay these regulations were particular interpretations of sovereignty, the individual, and the state—interpretations that placed women once again at the center of the debate.

On May 9, 1791, the Assembly took up the issue of collective petitions, which were petitions submitted on behalf of an organization or a group that did not bear individual signatures. Clearly underlying the discussion was the sense that Revolutionary organizations and popular societies had their roots in the corporate underpinnings of unlimited monarchy, rather than in the Enlightenment notion of individualism. The deputy Le Chapelier declared: "in a free government there are but two kinds of rights, those of citizens [and] those of the nation." If popular societies were allowed to publish the results of their deliberations and circulate petitions for signatures, they would become influential and powerful and might undermine the whole authority of representative government. Individual rights would be lost to corporate bodies. The people must speak only through the voices of their representatives.[27]

This view did not go unchallenged. On the second day of debate, the deputy Fréteau stated that the debate so far had omitted "a very worthwhile portion of society—women. I ask whether a widow could be prohibited from presenting a petition to the National Assembly." His remarks were applauded. The wording finally adopted in the law, which allowed only petitions individually signed, was "The right of petition belongs to any individual." One particularly disgruntled deputy, Toulongeon, responded, "You have just extended the right of petition to any citizen, to women, to children, to minors, to foreigners."[28]

We turn to the radical phase of the Revolution, the period of Jacobin ascendancy (beginning in the summer of 1793), and to the activity of the Society of Revolutionary Republican Women, an exclusively female society first officially registered with municipal authorities early in May 1793. The response of Pierre-Joseph-Alexis Roussel and his English guest, Lord Bedford, to a meeting of the society they attended in the fall of 1793 is particularly instructive. Having pictured the Revolutionary Republicans as organized women with a self-conscious awareness of women's proven abilities in military affairs, politics, and administration, Roussel and his English visitor wanted to dismiss, as delusions of "overheated brains," women's plans for expanding the organizational bases of their influence. Yet they had to acknowledge that the society's propositions were dangerous precisely because women already enjoyed in the private sphere a "universal and consequently dangerous ascendancy." Giving women "credit in government" would cause "new discord." In the end, Roussel admitted indirectly that denying women their political rights, including "credit in government," was a last desperate stratagem for preventing their "ascendancy" from overflowing the boundary between the public and the private spheres to find its most effective organized expression in the political arena.[29]

In late October, a brawl involving the Revolutionary Republicans and the market women provided the Jacobins in the Convention with their excuse for a full-blown investigation of the society and a clampdown. This repression came at a point of rupture in relationships between the Parisian working poor, including women of the popular classes, and the Montagnard government. The Montagnards were reluctant to enforce laws decreeing political terror and stringent price controls. They were threatened by radically independent, grass roots politics that the Revolutionary Republicans practiced daily, along with a larger *sans-culotte* population.

Reporting to the Convention for the Committee of General Security on October 30, the deputy Amar recommended outright suppression of all women's clubs and associations. He based this recommendation on openly sexist argumentation. "Should women exercise political rights and meddle in affairs of government?" Lacking in knowledge, attention span, devotion, steadfastness, self-abnegation, self-direction, rhetorical skills, and powers of resistance to oppression— all *sine qua non* conditions for fulfilling public functions—women were constitutionally incapable of governing. "Should women meet in political associations?" The purpose of these associations—unveiling enemy maneuvers, education, and surveillance—were declared incompatible with women's natural roles, "the cares to which nature calls them" and which, interestingly enough, conformed to "the general order of society." Acting on Amar's combined claims that the Revolutionary Republican Women were politically dangerous, and even more fundamentally, were inappropriately and unnaturally political in the first place, the Convention voted to prohibit all women's societies.[30]

Commenting on this decision, Prudhomme wrote in his *Révolutions de Paris,* exhorting the newly silenced women:

> *Citoyennes,* be honest and diligent girls, tender and modest wives, wise mothers, and you will be good patriots. True patriotism consists of fulfilling one's duties and valuing only rights appropriate to each according to sex and age, and not wearing the [liberty] cap and pantaloons and not carrying pike and pistol. Leave those to men who are born to protect you and make you happy. Wear clothing suitable to your morals and occupations; and always punish courageously, as you have just done, any crime which tends to disorganize society by changing sexes or indecently confusing them with anti-civic and perfidious intentions.[31]

On 27 Brumaire, when a deputation of women wearing red caps appeared at an assembly of the Paris Commune, Chaumette, speaking for the municipal legislators, condemned women dressed in this way as "denatured women" and "viragos." They abandoned household cares and the cribs of their children; more fundamentally, they dared transgress the barrier between the public and domestic spaces; and, finally, they were "impudent women who want to become men." Chaumette demanded and secured a vote from the Commune to refuse hearings to deputations of women except by special decree, while permitting them for *citoyennes* as individuals.[32]

From the outset of the Revolution, women of the popular classes were grouped by male authorities with the passive male citizens. They participated as equals in Revolutionary politics, sometimes along with men and sometimes in gender-specific groups, such as the *dames de la halle* or the Society of Revolutionary Republican Women. When men were subject to martial law, limits on petitions, and restrictions on organizations, so were women. It proved impossible to draw a sharp line between the public and domestic spheres and to confine women on the domestic side of that line. Furthermore, the authorities did not try very hard to confine women, since they were accustomed to women's public activities taking place in the public spaces and at times of political manifestations and ceremonies. Women could not hold processions in the rooms where they did their spinning, nor could they verify the dauphin's birth and bear petitions as members of women's guilds without leaving their hearths. Women functioning traditionally within public spaces made it categorically impossible to stop them from remaining there during the Revolution and to stop them from institutionalizing their activities in newly created Revolutionary organizations like popular societies and section assemblies.

The attitudes of the police agents in the fall of 1793 show that there was a current of opinion just waiting to be tapped, a current reinforced by the ambivalences about women's moral and intellectual suitability for public affairs and powerful enough to drown the women's political movement. The charges against the Society of Revolutionary Republican Women were compounded of claims that they were counter-revolutionaries and that they had no business in public forums in the first place, since their natural place and their moral duties were in the home. Chaumette and the Jacobins accomplished in the fall of 1793 what Bailly and Mounier and Le Chapelier and many others before them had been trying to do since the late summer of 1789. They outlawed the collective expression of demands by passive citizens, male and female, for public roles as the sovereign people, as self-determining citizens. They harnessed a power that had been gathering force during four Revolutionary years, that had roots in the organic and communal politics of the Old Regime, and that had gathered a rich variety of new institutional connections in the Revolutionary press, clubs, and sections.

The Jacobins' success against the Revolutionary Republicans meant the triumph of the bourgeois revolution over the popular revolution and, above all, the end of women's serious involvement in political, public life.

Scorned or seduced, maligned or mythologized, condemned or congratulated, women in Revolutionary Paris were seldom understood by historians for what they really were—the sovereign people, inventing with their feet every bit as much as writers with their pens the meaning and function of a new doctrine of legitimacy. There were two political nations in this France, which in 1789 appeared to have embraced the concept of popular sovereignty. The first, which ultimately triumphed, reserved active political influence for a new elite of merit, money, and talent and restricted the passive citizens to an undifferentiated, supported, silent emanation of abstractions. The second was a nation of sovereign people that incorporated female passive citizens along with male, whether by spontaneous *engagement,* exhortation, or passive tolerance. It is this merging of men and women of the popular classes that differentiates the situation of women in Paris from their situation anywhere else in the age of the democratic revolutions. This pattern of alliances with women by radical men occurred whenever and wherever there was overlap in ideologies and interests. When the Jacobins won full control of the Revolutionary political machinery, these ideologies and interests became contradictory. Then, women were legislated out of the political nation, with sex-based arguments thrown in to rationalize the application of a brutal power politics.[33]

NOTES

Portions of this article have been reprinted by permission from Harriet B. Applewhite and Darline Gay Levy, "Responses to the Political Activism of Women of the People in Revolutionary Paris, 1789-1793," in *Women and the Structure of Society: Selected Research from the Fifth Berkshire Conference on the History of Women,* edited by Barbara J. Harris and Jo Ann McNamara. Copyright©1984 by Duke University Press.

1. In recent years a number of essays have appeared in English that depict the roles of women in the Revolution. See Jane Abray, "Feminism in the French Revolution" *American Historical Review* 80 (February 1975):43-62; Margaret George, "The 'World Historical Defeat' of the Républicaines Révolutionnaires," *Science and Society* 40 (1976-77):410-437; Olwen H. Hufton, "Women in the French Revolution" *Past and Present* 53 (1971):90-108; Darline Gay Levy and Harriet B. Applewhite, "Women of the Popular Classes in Revolutionary Paris," in *Women, War and Revolution,* edited by Carol R. Berkin and Clara M. Lovett (New York: Holmes & Meier, 1980); *Women in Revolutionary Paris, 1789-1795,* edited by Darline Gay Levy, Harriet B. Applewhite, and Mary Durham Johnson (Urbana: University of Illinois Press, 1979); Scott Lytle, "The Second Sex (September, 1793)," *Journal of Modern History* 26 (1955):14-26; Leonora Cohen Rosenfield, "The Rights of Women in the French Revolution," *Studies in Eighteenth-Century Culture,* edited by Roseann Runte (Madison: University of Wisconsin Press, 1978).

2. Louise A. Tilly, "The Food Riot as a Form of Political Conflict in France," *Journal of Interdisciplinary History* 2 (1971):23-57; Levy, Applewhite, and Johnson, pp. 3-9.

3. Olwen H. Hufton, "Women and the Family Economy in Eighteenth-Century France," *French Historical Studies* (Spring 1975):1-22; and idem, *The Poor of Eighteenth-Century France, 1750-1789* (New York: Oxford University Press, 1975).

4. *Doléances particulières des marchandes bouquetières, fleuristes, chapelières en fleurs de la ville et faubourgs de Paris* in Charles-Louis Chassin, *Les Elections et les cahiers de Paris en 1789,* 4 vols. (Paris: Jouaust et Sigaux, 1888-1889), vol. 2, pp. 534-537, as

reprinted in translation in Levy, Applewhite, and Johnson, pp. 22-26.

5. Olympe de Gouges, *Les Droits de la femme* (Paris, 1791), as reprinted in translation in Levy, Applewhite, and Johnson, pp. 87-96.

6. Etta Palm d'Aelders, *Adresse des citoyennes françaises à l'Assemblée Nationale* (n.p., n.d. [Summer, 1791]), as reprinted in translation in Levy, Applewhite, and Johnson, pp. 75-77.

7. Condorcet, "Essai sur l'admission des femmes au droit de cité" in *Oeuvres de Condorcet,* edited by A. Condorcet O'Connor and M. F. Arago, 12 vols., (Paris: Firmin Didot Frères, 1847), vol. 10, pp. 119-30.

8. *Journal général de la cour et de la ville, connu sous le nom du "Petit Gautier,"* no. 4 (September 22, 1789):31.

9. Harry C. Payne, *The Philosophes and the People* (New Haven: Yale University Press, 1976).

10. "Declaration of the Rights of Man and Citizen," Article Three, translated in John Hall Stewart, *A Documentary Survey of the French Revolution* (New York: Macmillan, 1951), p. 114.

11. George Rudé, *The Crowd in the French Revolution* (New York: Oxford University Press, 1959); idem, *Paris and London in the Eighteenth Century: Studies in Popular Protest, 1789-1820* (New York: Oxford University Press, 1970); idem, *Reactions to the French Revolution* (New York: Oxford University Press, 1972).

12. Levy and Applewhite, pp. 13, 14. See also Louis-Marie Prudhomme, *Révolutions de Paris, dédiées à la nation et au district des Petits-Augustins* (Paris, 1789).

13. Prudhomme, no. 4, August 7, 1789, p. 39.

14. Jennifer Dunn Westfall, "The Participation of Non-Elite Women in the Parisian Crowd Movements of the Opening Year of the French Revolution," (honors thesis, Mt. Holyoke College, 1976), p. 77, citing Archives Nationales 0'500, fol. 440.

15. Siméon-Prosper Hardy, *Mes Loisirs ou journal d'événements tels qu'ils parviennent à ma connaissance,* Paris, 1764-1789, vol. 8,(September 14, 1789), fol. 475 in Bibliothèque Nationale, MSS, fonds français, no. 6687.

16. Prudhomme, no. 10, September 14, 1789, p. 12.

17. See the fuller discussion and analysis in Levy and Applewhite, pp. 14-16; Levy, Applewhite, and Johnson, chapter 1.

18. *Journal de Paris,* no. 281, October 8, 1789, pp. 1289ff.

19. Jean-Joseph Mounier, *Exposé de la conduite de M. Mounier dans l'Assemblée Nationale, et des motifs de son retour en Dauphiné* (Grenoble, 1789), p. 75; Natalie Zemon Davis, "The Reasons of Misrule: Youth Groups and Charivaris in Sixteenth-Century France," *Past and Present* 50 (1971):41-75. *Le Petit Gautier* cites an alleged conversation among habitués of the Palais-Royal debating various meanings and personifications of Veto, implying that the common man did not fully comprehend the term but nonetheless grasped its political significance. *Journal Général,* no 16, October 4, 1789, 126-127.

20. Mounier, pp. 68-70. For another account, see testimony of one of the twelve women who accompanied Mounier, François Rolin, in *Procédure criminelle, instruite au Châtelet de Paris, sur la dénonciation des faits arrivés à Versailles dans la journée du 6 octobre 1789* (Paris: Assemblée Nationale, Baudouin, 1790), no. 187.

21. Hardy, vol. 8 (October 5, 1789), fol. 501.

22. Prudhomme, no. 8, October 3-10, 1789, p. 5.

23. Anonymous, *Les Héroïnes de Paris ou l'entière liberté de la France, par les femmes . . . polices qu'elles doivent exercer de leur propre autorité. Expulsion des charlatans &c. &c., le 5 octobre 1789* (n.p., n.d.).

24. Prudhomme, no. 8, October 3-10, 1789, p. 15.

25. Hardy, vol. 8, October 9, 1789, fol. 508; Harriet B. Applewhite, "Political Legitimacy in Revolutionary France, 1788-1791," in *Journal of Interdisciplinary History* 9, no. 2, (Autumn 1978):245-273.

26. *Archives parlementaires*, edited by M. E. Laurent and M. E. Clavel, (Paris: Paul Dupont, 1877), ser. 1, vol. 9 (October 21, 1789), p. 475.

27. *Archives parlementaires*, edited by M. J. Mavidal, M. E. Laurent, (Paris: Paul Dupont, 1883) ser. 1, vol. 25 (May 9, 1791), p. 679.

28. Ibid., May 10, 1791, pp. 692-693.

29. Pierre-Joseph-Alexis Roussel, *Le Château des Tuileries*, 2 vols. (Paris, 1802), vol. 2, pp. 34-46, as reprinted in translation in Levy, Applewhite, and Jonhson, pp. 166-171.

30. *Réimpression de L'Ancien Moniteur*, vol. 18, session of 9 Brumaire, Year II, reprinted in translation in Levy, Applewhite, and Johnson, pp. 213-217.

31. Prudhomme, no. 213, 7 Brumaire, Year II, p. 151.

32. *Réimpression de L'Ancien Moniteur*, 18, pp. 450-451, reprinted in translation in Levy, Applewhite, and Johnson, pp. 219-220.

 II

Women and Society

Samia I. Spencer

Women and Education

THERE are few areas in which the critical spirit of the eighteenth century was expressed as vigorously and as profusely as it was in the subject of education, particularly the education of women. Discussion and writing on this topic were not limited to the professional educators (e.g., Rollin, Reballier, abbé de Saint-Pierre, Mme de Genlis, or Mme Campan), to the *philosophes* (e.g., Montesquieu, Voltaire, Rousseau, Diderot, Helvétius, or Condorcet), or even to the novelists (e.g., Restif de La Bretonne, Choderlos de Laclos, Sade, or Bernardin de Saint-Pierre). Rather, the education of women was a central theme in the writings of almost all authors, female and male. It was the subject of debate among the polite society of the Parisian salons and the focus of much broader public attention throughout the country, as demonstrated by the number of *concours* (competitions) on that theme proposed by various provincial academies.[1]

In spite of the volume of material available on the subject, an accurate assessment of actual practices in the education of young women is difficult to obtain. Most of the treatises, pamphlets, brochures, and books dealing with female education in the eighteenth century consist of criticism of the contemporary institutions paralleled by projects for reforms. No systematic study on this subject has ever been published, either in the eighteenth century or subsequently. A thorough bibliography reveals that, in spite of continued interest in this topic, there is a paucity of critical material and not a single full-length volume devoted to it.

In 1698 and again in 1724, government decrees required the appointment by all parishes of male and female teachers. Parents were required to send their children to school until age fourteen, thus establishing, at least in theory, the principle of compulsory education.[2] However, these decrees were never fully enforced, and illiteracy continued to be widespread, even among girls of the upper classes and the bourgeoisie. The famous feminist and political activist Olympe de Gouges dictated all her works to a secretary because she was unable to write. Mme de Genlis was never given instruction in writing; she learned by herself at age twelve. The letters of the well-known author

Mme de Graffigny abound with spelling errors. The most notorious case perhaps is that of the four youngest daughters of Louis XV. After several years at the convent, they were still illiterate; and one of them, Mme Louise, learned to read only at age twelve.[3] In spite of the poor quality of their formal instruction, many women were able to complete their own education independently, some achieving rare prominence in the field of education itself.

Fénelon's *L'Education des filles* (written in 1685 and first published in 1687) and Mme de Maintenon's Maison Royale de Saint Louis à Saint-Cyr (founded in 1686) were viewed by many throughout the first part of the eighteenth century as the ideal in women's education. Both pedagogues rejected the role of the woman as idle social being and proposed a new identity—that of virtuous wife, devoted mother, and knowledgeable homemaker who spreads happiness to those around her. They emphasized the importance of moral virtues and strength— qualities that they believed did not come naturally to women. The role of education, therefore, was to redress the natural *mauvaises inclinations* to *mollesse* and *coquetterie* and to guard women against their evil tendencies and the "natural weaknesses of their sex,"[4] e.g., ruse, guile, dissimulation, and a tendency toward excess. Fénelon and Mme de Maintenon followed different paths to attain these goals.

Although the efforts of Saint-Cyr's founder represent a giant step toward the secularization of education—recruitment of lay teachers and de-emphasis of conventual life as the inevitable destiny of her *demoiselles*—Mme de Maintenon continued to share the seventeenth century's deep distrust for society and a world considered to be impure and unhealthy for the young. For that reason, the *pensionnaires* at Saint-Cyr were totally separated from their families, who were only allowed to pay them a thirty-minute visit every three months. Fénelon, on the other hand, shared the eighteenth-century view favoring home education by the mother or someone trained by her for that specific purpose.

The curriculum at Saint-Cyr excluded more subjects than it included. Mme de Maintenon often stressed the harm of such "taboo" subjects as novels, mythology, physical or natural sciences, ancient philosophy, and even history, except in its most rudimentary form:

> It is appropriate [that girls] have a minor acquaintance [with history] in order not to confuse a Roman emperor with an emperor of China or Japan, a King of Spain or England with a King of Persia or Siam; all this must be accomplished without rules or methods and only so that girls might be no more ignorant than ordinary people.[5]

"Safe" subjects included reading, writing, arithmetic, the lives of the saints, practical crafts, needlework, sewing, and moral and religious theater.

Fénelon's curriculum also stressed domestic and practical skills—the basic principles of law and arithmetic and the art of selecting and managing servants so as to gain their respect and love.[6] Intellectual training was confined to reading, writing, grammar, and spelling. While the study of the French language was considered important, foreign languages, particularly Spanish, were viewed as useless and even "capable of augmenting the weaknesses of women."[7] If a foreign language had to be studied, Latin would be the proper choice, with the restriction that its study be limited to "girls with mature judgement and modest demeanor."[8] Subjects such as literature, music, and art required the utmost care and discretion and the strictest reservations. Artistic talents were tolerated but never encouraged: "If [a girl] has a pleasant voice and an appreciation for the beauty of music, she cannot be made to ignore them forever: prohibition would inflame her passion; it is preferable to allow a moderate flow of this torrent than to attempt to block it."[9] Although Fénelon's ideas were admired and respected, they were not implemented. Even such a modest program remained an ideal.

Our chief source of information on the actual practices and content of women's education in the eighteenth century is the memoirs, letters, and other writings of notable women and famous *salonnières*. While the education of upper-class women is the most thoroughly documented, that of middle-class girls—few of whom became published authors—is less well known. As to the education of girls from poor families, it remains almost a total mystery. Modest statistics giving names, types, and locations of schools are available in various national and departmental archives.[10] These statistics indicate that the quality and scope of education varied widely from one region to another, with Paris ranking at the top of the literacy scale[11] and Brittany at the bottom.[12] In every case, the percentage of literacy among women trailed far behind the same percentage for men.[13] Absent, however, is any information on curriculum, books, level of instruction and achievement, methodology, and other aspects.

Despite mounting criticism against convential education and the increasing awareness by the State of its proper role in educating the citizenry, the Church continued to control and oversee the schools. "The school master is the adjunct of the parish priest. His major responsibility is to train christians. . . . What matters most is not his knowledge . . . but his regular attendance at church functions and the religious teaching that . . . he is capable of giving."[14] Education of girls of all social classes was, then, almost exclusively secured by religious orders.

The early education of the daughters of the upper classes took place at home. Usually, the governess was charged with the basics of reading and religion, while private tutors provided lessons in singing, dancing, and music. Later, girls were sent off to a convent, which they left—still in their teens—to be married.[15] Fontevrault, Panthémont, and La Présentation were among the most exclusive convents reserved for the royal princesses of France and the daughters of the highest-ranking nobility. Families were most anxious to send their daughters to such institutions because they hoped the girls could cultivate the acquaintance of fellow students who would later secure them positions of favor in the intimate circle of a princess or a queen. In general, life for the young ladies was not devoid of pleasant moments. In some instances, the *pensionnaires* were accompanied by their own governess, they were allowed to receive female visitors in their private apartments and often traveling merchants were admitted in the convents to sell their goods to the residents. Social events were not rare; students could entertain each other at tea parties and elegant dinners. Married women often sought temporary or permanent refuge in the convent and were, of course, free to associate with the younger students. According to the Goncourt brothers, these institutions, were in fact miniature courts,[16] which exuded happiness:

> It was, after all, a happy and congenial education that was provided in these convents, constantly enlivened and emancipated with every passing day more and more from the chill and gloom of the cloister, until gradually it inclines almost wholly toward the world, toward everything which makes for the charm and grace of women in society.[17]

This romantic and idealized view, however, is highly retouched and gives neither a complete nor a realistic picture. The impassioned writers neglect to mention the harrowing practices and cruel punishments reported by students:

> In the famous Abbey of Fontevrault, girls were punished by being sent to pray alone in the vaults where the nuns were buried. This practice caused Mme Louise, one of the daughters of Louis XV, to have fits of terror from which she was never able to recover.[18]

These exclusive convents and many others were patterned after Saint-Cyr. Students were divided into four age groups, each of which adopted the color used for that group at Saint-Cyr.[19] The inspiration of the royal institution was quite superficial, though, for the academic and intellectual training did not measure up to the standards of the model. The social function of these convents was undoubtedly its most important one; reading, writing, and catechism occupied a distant second place.

As early as 1718, the duchesse d'Orléans expressed her concern over the quality of conventual education: "It is difficult today to find a convent where children can be well educated."[20] The shocking lack of instruction among teachers was perhaps the main cause of the students' ignorance. In her memoirs, Mme Roland recalls her experience at the Pensionnat des Dames de la Congrégation, one of the most respected and serious institutions of the Paris of 1765. The most competent instructor, the one responsible for the hardest task—the teaching of writing—was a seventy-year-old nun "[who] took pride in being well educated; she still had a beautiful handwriting, did superb embroideries, gave good spelling lessons, and was not a stranger to history."[21] Such outstanding and exceptional skills provoked the envy and jealousy of the less-gifted but numerically more prominent nuns. As for the structure of the school, it was rudimentary; the students ranging in age from six to eighteen, were simply divided into two instructional groups.[22]

Daughters of the *moyenne bourgeoisie* were educated in the same fashion as upper-class girls, with minor differences. Their early education was provided by their mother and close relatives instead of by a governess. Such was the case for Mme Roland, who learned catechism with her mother, drawing with her father, and Latin with an ecclesiastic uncle. She, too, received instruction in writing, geography, dancing, and music through the customary visits of various tutors, all of whom—because of the severe shortage of female teachers—were men. At age ten or twelve, bourgeois girls frequented the convents of teaching orders, such as the Augustines, Bénédictines, Notre Dame, Visitandines, and Bernardines, which provided education not only in Paris but in all major provincial cities as well.[23] However, as the century advanced, the length of time spent at the convent shrank considerably. According to Mme Campan, by 1770, it had been generally reduced to a single year—that preceding the first communion.

Girls from impoverished families would have remained in almost total ignorance had it not been for the charitable efforts of the teaching congregations. Schooling for this social group usually took place in two types of institutions: the *petites écoles* (minor schools), in which pupils learned the elements of religion and housework in addition to reading and writing, or the *écoles de charité* (charity schools), founded by major convents for the benefit of the students unable to afford the cost of conventual education. The programs of the latter schools were strictly practical, consisting mainly of manual skills and crafts.

Education of poor girls in rural areas was even less developed. Although the State required all parishes to establish separate schools for girls and boys, with female and male teachers respectively, many impoverished villages did not have funds for two buildings; therefore, they had only a boys' school. When a female teacher could be recruited to instruct the girls, she would gather them in a small corner of the boys' classroom. Despite the Church's opposition to the principal of coeducation, it was a widespread practice. Classes, in that case, were taught by male teachers, preferably married. The most serious problem facing rural girls' schools was the scarcity of female teachers, who were often recruited from among the close relatives of the parish priest or male instructors. Their role was often that of a "proctor" or a "nursemaid" rather than that of an instructor. In order to encourage more women to become teachers, women were exempted from paying taxes; but despite this incentive, the shortage continued, and some girls' schools were forced to hire male teachers.

The second half of the century saw the recognition of a need to organize vocational and technical education for girls in the provinces. In 1768, a spinning school was founded in Roye. According to the departmental archives of La Somme, the training of the first class of ninety-two students brought about a dramatic development of the textile industry. Similar schools were also established in Bayeux (Normandy) to preserve and promote the art of lacemaking and in Chazelle (Massif Central) to train potential female workers for a recently established cotton mill.[24] Such efforts, however, were few and scattered.

As the century advanced and women extended their roles to all aspects of life—literary, cultural, philosophical, social, artistic, political, and scientific—it became more and more apparent that the education of girls left much to be desired and that reform was necessary. The parties most interested in this struggle were those most acutely aware of the shortcomings of their preparation for life—women themselves. Even the most brilliant among them deplored the education they received and set out to propose more appropriate and more ambitious programs, new methods,[25] and, above all, the development of children's textbooks, which were almost completely lacking.[26] Never did women write so profusely and so passionately as they did in the Age of Enlightenment. They wrote not only to denounce current prejudices and practices but often to communicate with and help other women. Their writings, in most cases, were aimed at a female readership and were intended to fill the gaps of formal education and to contribute to the overall intellectual development of women.

One of the first women to focus attention on female education within the broader context of women's rights and roles was the marquise de Lambert (1647-1733). Like Mme de Maintenon and Fénelon, she agreed that "girls possess an innate and passionate urge to please."[27] Unlike them, however, she did not view this tendency as a proof of their intellectual inferiority. Instead, Mme de Lambert clearly presented the case of women from a woman's vantage point. Society, and men in particular, were the parties responsible for the fate of women: "Since women find the paths to fame and power closed to members of their sex, they achieve these goals via other routes, using their charms as compensation."[28] She deplored the limitations imposed on women, which force them to substitute "debauchery for knowledge."[29] She did not regard woman's condition in society as the inevitable product of her womanhood; instead, she stressed the role of the social and the educational environments, which placed stringent limitations on the humanity of the woman.[30] The most important aspect of education for Mme de Lambert, was moral training—a view she shared with most of her contemporaries, particularly women educators. Although a strong advocate of women's right to education, Mme de Lambert was not an educator in the strict sense of the word. However, she exerted an important influence in the shaping of a new consciousness for women.

The deficiencies of conventual education and of the teachers who provided it were first reported through firsthand experience by Mme de Puisieux (1720-1798). She clearly remembered the five years she spent at the convent, where the substance of her education came not from the efforts of the nuns themselves but from the evenings she spent in the company of a worldly woman who had retired to convent life.[31] The conversations with this woman—rather than formal conventual education—provided the young girl with what practical instruction she received. In this case, the convent provided adequate training quite by accident and was not at all indispensable to it.

Mme de Puisieux's opinion was widely shared by the vast majority of her contemporaries. In fact, the debate about conventual versus domestic—or home—instruction was central to all writings about education in the Age of Enlightenment. Times had changed, a new mentality had arisen, and convents had not kept pace with society. The basic mistrust of the world had been replaced by more optimistic considerations: belief in progress and the basic goodness of man, faith in the future, and an unquenchable thirst for freedom. None of these elements ever pierced the impenetrable walls of convents and monasteries.

The fiercest attacks on monastic education—whether for girls or boys—came from Voltaire; in his opinion, colleges taught "Latin and nonsense."[32] Using similarly harsh language, *L'Encyclopédie* declared that students "usually leave college with an even higher degree of imbecility and ignorance."[33] Why did conventual and monastic education provoke such impassioned attacks? The answers are as varied as the authors who offered them. However, general agreement centered on the following defects:

Irrelevance. With its strict emphasis on the past—antiquity, ancient languages, literature, and history—and its neglect of the present, monastic education provided students with useless information and an outdated mentality, leaving them ignorant of reality and their environment.[34]

Inefficiency. Too much time was wasted on religious studies that failed even to lay the foundations for solid religious principles. *L'Encyclopédie* noted that a young man, after spending ten of the most precious years of his life in a college, left it "with principles of a misunderstood devotion; and more often with such superficial knowledge of religion that it succumbs to the next blasphemous conversation, or the first daring reading."[35]

Inaccuracy of instruction. Values taught in the college or the convent were not those prevailing in the world, thus engendering confusion in young people as they faced real-life situations.

Mediocrity. Designed for the masses, public education did not serve one of the most important groups, the gifted.

Inadequacy of instructors. Inexperienced, out of touch with reality, and ignorant of the world, monks and nuns were incapable of shaping the lives and minds of young people.

Many other arguments raised against religious education were specific to individual authors. Diderot opposed the principle of religious education, which he found irreconcilable with the idea of progress: "The mentality of the catholic clergy, which has always monopolized public instruction, is totally opposed to the progress of Enlightenment and reason."[36] Bernardin de Saint-Pierre opposed conventual education on sentimental grounds; it broke family ties and deprived children of their parents' affection.[37]

Jean-Jacques Rousseau's position on the issue of public versus private education is unclear. In *Emile,* he attacked convents for moral reasons, finding them "veritable schools of coquetry."[38] Elsewhere in the same work, however, he recommended that little girls be separated from their mothers because of the limiting and intimidating influence of the parents on the child's freedom of action:

> Convents . . . are to be preferred to the paternal home, where a delicately nourished daughter, always seated under her mother's eyes, in a closed room, dares not rise, walk, speak, nor breathe, neither does she have a moment of freedom to play, jump, run, shout, or indulge in the liveliness common to her age.[39]

It is somewhat surprising that a man who exalted motherhood and parental love was unable to conceive of a more harmonious or relaxed relationship between mother and daughter.

Private home education was preferred by the majority of the authors. Voltaire's Sophronie summed up the century's position: "I owe to the education that my mother gave me the balance and reason that I enjoy. She did not raise me in a convent, because it was not in a convent that I was destined to live."[40]

Violent attacks were directed at parents who entrusted their children's education to unqualified governesses. *L'Encyclopédie* warned against the influence of lowly and ignorant people on young children: "If you entrust your child's upbringing to a slave, an ancient philosopher said one day to a rich father, you will have not one slave but two."[41] Earlier, Mme de Lambert had also condemned maternal abandonment of children to the care of maids who put "superstition in place of religion."[42] She hoped that, as mothers took an active part in the educational process of their children, they would render "certain virtues hereditary."[43]

Mme d'Epinay (1726-1783), author of the lengthy *Conversations d'Emilie,* acknowledged that reliable governesses could be recruited in other countries, particularly in England, but not in France; therefore, the responsibility of raising children—and daughters particularly— must be assumed by the mother. The relationship between Emilie and her mother was reminiscent of Emile's with his mentor. Although such a strong bond had definite advantages of closeness, trust, and intimacy, it also had serious drawbacks and engendered total dependence in Emilie upon her mother. Nevertheless, Mme d'Epinay's methods deserve to be briefly examined. She stressed the importance of learning through experience and direct observation. Her program of studies included elements of the natural and biological sciences, history, religion, and ethics. Both teacher and child spent long hours reading and discussing books together in order to develop the girl's capacity for careful and critical thinking. At the end of the tenth conversation, Emilie rightly remarked: "It is indeed a difficult task to be a mother."[44] Although in 1783 the French Academy chose Mme d'Epinay's *Les Conversations d'Emilie* over Mme de Genlis' *Adèle et Théodore* for its first *Prix d'utilité* (prize for utility), the twentieth-century reader would probably make the opposite decision.

Mme de Genlis (1746-1830) is probably the eighteenth century's most prominent and outstanding educator. She was the author of more than 140 volumes, a majority of which relate to education in one way or another. Endowed by nature with strong pedagogical inclinations, Caroline-Stéphanie-Félicité du Crest started to teach at age seven, when she would gather the children of her village together to pass on to them what her own instructor had taught her. At age thirty-one, she began a self-imposed retreat in the residence of Bellechasse, where she devoted herself to the education of the children of the duc and duchesse de Chartres. Her dedication and competence made her the only woman ever to receive the title of *Gouverneur des enfants d'Orléans* (Governor to the children of the Orleans family).[45]

The best-known work on education by Mme de Genlis is probably *Adèle et Théodore*, in which she recounts her experiences at Bellechasse. In the preface of the 1804 edition, the author admitted that the baronne d'Almane spoke for her; and, indeed, her *porte-parole* was created in her own image. Like her, the baronne was very much involved in her children's education, a demanding task which prompted her to move to Languedoc, far from the distractions and the social obligations of the capital. In this provincial environment, she devoted herself totally to her children's education, a challenge she could not meet unaided. She engaged and directed an international teaching team consisting of Miss Bridget—hired as tutor of English when Adèle was six months old—and Dainville, an Italian art instructor.

Mme de Genlis' pedagogical insights and intuition were truly remarkable. Two hundred years before their values received pedagogical recognition, she had discovered the importance of visual aids, simulation, role playing, and games. She realized as well the value of impressing the senses to crystallize learning.[46]

Home education—although she was not unaware of its limitations—was highly recommended by Mme de Genlis, for the benefit of both children and mothers. While it provided a solid foundation for the child, it gave the mother a strong sense of identity and made her life happier, more meaningful, and more fulfilled—a sharp contrast with the salon life of Paris.

An ardent Catholic and a staunch advocate of religious education, Mme de Genlis often found herself at odds with the *philosophes*. She deplored the abolition of religious orders; and, in her *Discours sur la suppression des couvents de religieuses et sur l'éducation*, she proposed the creation of new *écoles cloîtrées* (walled schools) patterned after the abolished convents. Although this remarkable educator may not be considered a strong feminist, she believed in the intellectual capacity of women and designed educational programs that would make them active and useful members of society, as well as responsible and respected individuals.

This essay could not be concluded without a brief mention of three other well-known women educators: Mme Le Prince de Beaumont (1711-1780), Mme de Miremont (1735-1811), and Mme Campan (1752-1822).

Mme Le Prince de Beaumont was the enlightened governess of several English families between 1745 and 1762, as well as the author of nearly seventy children's books and textbooks. The lack of appropriate children's readers prompted her to write for the benefit of her young pupils, who were unable to understand the translations of *Télémaque* and *Gil Blas* they were given.[47] Instead of portraying mythological figures or literary characters in *Le Magasin des enfants*,

Mme Le Prince de Beaumont portrayed children who resembled her own pupils and wrote dialogues similar to the ones she must have had with them. *L'Education complète ou abrégé de l'histoire universelle,* designed for more advanced students, is a forerunner of our contemporary textbooks.[48] Each historical event is followed by a commentary, questions, and composition topics on the subject discussed. Although the modern reader would find her books dated, Mme Le Prince de Beaumont was a talented and innovative methodologist in her time.

Mme de Miremont's *Traité de l'éducation des femmes* (published in seven volumes between 1779 and 1789) focused with great detail on teacher training. Although she seemed to favor lay public education, she was confident that with appropriate reforms a new generation of knowledgeable and competent nuns could be trained to improve public education for girls. Her elaborate curriculum for future teachers included an ambitious reading program designed to expose students to the thoughts of the most prominent thinkers, philosophers, and writers, including women authors. Mme de Miremont was a strong believer in Juvenal's phrase "mens sana in corpore sano." She stressed the importance of good body care, balanced diets, regular exercise, exposure to clean, fresh air, and frequent baths.

A successful and respected educator, Mme Campan was also the author of *Mémoires sur la vie privée de Marie-Antoinette reine de France* and *L'Education des femmes.* Out of financial necessity, the former reader to the daughters of Louis XV and lady-in-waiting to Marie-Antoinette founded a school in Saint-Germain-en-Laye, shortly after Robespierre's execution. In less than a year, the number of her students increased from three to one hundred and included such celebrities as Hortense and Emilie de Beauharnais. When asked by the Emperor to direct La Maison de la Légion d'Honneur à Ecouen, an educational institution for the daughters of legionnaires, Mme Campan was able to implement— between 1807 and 1814—some of the reforms proposed by eighteenth-century theorists. At Ecouen, academic subjects were important and were backed by strong practical training. She shared Mme de Miremont's concern for the physical well-being of her students and for their environment. As an educator, Mme Campan's influence was enormous; many of her students became successful teachers themselves, both in public and private girls' schools.

Progress in the education of women in eighteenth-century France was achieved in several areas. The level of literacy among women improved compared to the previous century—moderately in some areas of France and dramatically in others. The need for organized public education for girls and boys was almost universally recognized, and efforts were made to build the foundations of such programs. Women acquired an unspoken right to knowledge and education.

They no longer feared ridicule for being "learned;" they felt free to express their interest in disciplines to which they had had no exposure in the past, such as mathematics, physics, and algebra. In 1786, women were allowed to attend lectures at the prestigious Collège de France, thus giving them an exposure to the ideas of the most respected professors and scientists of the time. Last but not least, women, in increasing numbers, were asking for a voice in shaping their identity and their future. They recognized the critical role of education in their destiny and made invaluable contributions to bringing about a new consciousness and a balanced perspective.

Progress, in the nineteenth century, was slow to come. Women were to wait three-quarters of a century after the Revolution before being allowed to complete their high school education; and at that, Julie Daubié—the first *bachelière*—was reluctantly awarded her diploma in 1864, after the three-year delay that followed her successful completion of the requirements. But in spite of the setbacks brought about by Napoleon, most of the ideas underlying eighteenth-century proposals for the education of women eventually found concrete expression.

NOTES

1. Some of the most informative chapters on the subject of French women's education may be found in Paul Rousselot, *Histoire de l'éducation des femmes en France*, 2 vols. (Paris: Librairie académique Didier, 1883); Léon Abensour, *La Femme et le féminisme avant la révolution* (Paris: Ernest Leroux, 1923); and Georges Snyders, *La Pédagogie en France aux XVIIe et XVIIIe siècles* (Paris: Presses universitaires de France, 1965).

Carolyn C. Lougee, *Le Paradis des Femmes: Women, Salon and Social Stratification in Seventeenth Century France* (Princeton: Princeton University Press, 1976), includes three excellent chapters on the ideas of Fénelon and Mme de Maintenon, which continued to be a major source of inspiration throughout the eighteenth century.

2. Félix Ponteil, *Histoire de l'enseignement en France* (Paris: Sirey, 1966), pp. 12-13.

3. According to Rousselot, they were sent to Fontevrault (vol. 2, p. 97); according to Abensour, they studied at the abbaye de Maubuisson (p. 46).

4. Fénelon, "L'Education des filles," in *Oeuvres* (Paris: Didot, 1843), vol. 2, p. 495. This citation and all subsequent ones are my own translations.

5. Quoted in Rousselot, vol. 2, p. 42.

6. Fénelon warned against letting women become too involved in business matters; widows should seek the advice of men of business (*Oeuvres*, vol. 2, p. 502).

7. Ibid., vol. 2, p. 503.

8. Ibid.

9. Ibid.

10. See Abensour, pp. 49-61.

11. Ruth Graham, "Loaves and Liberty: Women in the French Revolution," in *Becoming Visible: Women in European History*, edited by Renate Bridenthal and Claudia Koonz (Boston: Houghton Mifflin Co., 1977), p. 239.

12. Ponteil, p. 13. Detailed and thorough information on the progress of education in France by region may be found in volume 2 of François Furet and Jacques Ozouf's monumental study, *Lire et écrire* (Paris: Editions de Minuit, 1977).

13. Between 1719 and 1730, a teacher in Landaville, in the Vosges region, asked thirty-six couples to sign the marriage register. While twenty-three men could write their names, thirty-two women out of thirty-six were unable to draw a cross, much less to write their names. Jean Larnac, *Histoire de la littérature féminine en France* (Paris: Kra, 1929), p. 132.

The history of marriage records in France, between 1686 and 1866, has been examined in great detail by Furet and Ozouf, vol. 1, pp. 59-68.

14. Ponteil, p. 10.

15. The legal age for marriage was twelve for girls, fourteen for boys. Engagement could be concluded at age seven for girls and twelve for boys. Georges Snyders cites interesting facts associated with such early commitments: "After marriage is concluded, girls return to the convent where they remain until they are nubile. Saint-Simon reports that the Count of Evreux—having lost his fortune in gambling, and pressed by an urgent need for money—married the twelve-year-old daughter of Crozat. He received a dowry of two millions which he spent while his wife was learning how to read and sing in the convent to which she had been returned on her wedding night" (*La Pédagogie*, pp. 232-233).

16. Edmond and Jules de Goncourt, *The Woman of the Eighteenth Century* (New York: Minton, Balch & Co., 1927), p. 9.

17. Goncourt, pp. 14-15.

18. Rousselot, vol. 2, p. 96.

19. Several Saint-Cyr graduates were recruited to head other institutions (Ibid., vol. 2, pp. 85-86).

20. Quoted by Rousselot, vol. 2, p. 99.

21. Mme Roland, *Mémoires* (Paris: Plon, 1864), p. 31.

22. Ibid., p. 30.

23. For detailed information on the history and geographical distribution of various religious orders throughout France, see "L'éducation des filles," in Roger Chartier, Dominique Julia and Marie-Madeleine Compère's, *L'Education en France du XVIe au XVIIIe siècle* (Paris: Société d'édition d'enseignement supérieur, 1976), pp. 231-247.

24. Abensour, p. 199.

25. A most promising title on this subject, Octave Gréard's *L'Education des femmes par les femmes* (Paris: Hachette, 1907) proved to be disappointing at a closer look. Of seven educators studied, two are men, and one may be curious about Gréard's criteria for selecting the five women discussed. While the inclusion of Mme de Maintenon, Mme de Lambert, and Mme d'Epinay may be understandable, the selection of Mme Roland and Mme Necker is not as clear. Mme Roland simply related her youth as a child prodigy in her *Mémoires*, while Mme Necker intended to write a book on women but never did (p. 296). More startling is the absence of Mme de Genlis, Mme Campan, Mme de Miremont, and Mme Le Prince de Beaumont.

26. The reader may recall that Marie Jeanne Phlipon—the future Mme Roland—was reading Plutarch by age nine and that Mme de Genlis poured over Mlle de Scudéry's novels when she was eight years old. While it is true

that both women were precocious and bright, it is also true that the only books available to them were books intended for adults.

27. Mme de Lambert, *Oeuvres* (Lausanne: Marc-Michel Bousquet, 1747), p. 69.

28. Ibid., pp. 69-70.

29. Ibid., p. 177.

30. Ibid., p. 81.

31. Mme de P[uisieux], *Conseils à une amie* (n.p., 1749), pp. xiii-xiv.

32. Quoted from Voltaire's *Dictionnaire philosophique* in A. F. Théry, *Histoire de l'éducation en France* (Paris: Dezobry, E. Magdeleine et Co., 1858), vol. 3, p. 179.

33. "Collège," *Encyclopédie ou Dictionnaire raisonné des sciences, des arts et des métiers* (Stuttgart-Bad Cannstalt: Friedrich Fommsen Verlag, 1966), vol. 3, p. 635.

34. Voltaire, "The Ignorant Philosopher," *The Best Known Works of Voltaire* (New York: Blue Ribbon Books, 1927), p. 467.

35. "Collège," *Encyclopédie*, vol. 3, p. 635.

36. Diderot, "Plan d'une université pour le gouvernement de Russie ou d'une éducation publique dans les sciences," *Oeuvres complètes* (Paris: Garnier, 1875; Nendeln, Liechtenstein, 1966), vol. 3, p. 415.

37. Bernardin de Saint-Pierre, "Discours sur l'éducation des femmes," *Oeuvres complètes* (Paris: Didier, 1833), vol. 2, p. 360.

38. Jean-Jacques Rousseau, *Emile ou de l'éducation* (Paris: Garnier, 1961), p. 491.

39. Rousseau, p. 457.

40. Voltaire, *Oeuvres complètes* (Paris: Didot, 1827), vol. 2, p. 1934.

41. "Education," *Encyclopédie*, vol. 5, p. 397.

42. Mme de Lambert, p. 56.

43. Ibid.

44. Mme d'Epinay, *Les Conversations d'Emilie* (Paris et Liège: Plombeux, 1784), vol. 1, p. 260.

45. Mme de Genlis elaborated with great detail on the distinction in knowledge, treatment, social status, and salary between a *gouverneur* (governor) and a *gouvernante* (governess). While the former was considered a friend of the family who shared their meals, the latter was counted among the servants and ate at their table. *Discours sur la suppression des couvents* (Paris: Onfrois, 1790), p. 14.

46. For detailed descriptions of Mme de Genlis' ingenious methods and inventions, see *Adèle et Théodore* (Paris: Maradan, 1804), vol. 1, pp. 48-51, 79-80.

47. Mme Le Prince de Beaumont, *Le Magasin des enfants* (Paris: Garnier, n.d.), vol. 1, p. vii.

48. Mme Le Prince de Beaumont, *L'Education complète ou abrégé de l'histoire universelle mêlée de géographie et de chronologie*, 4 vols. (Paris: Billois, 1803).

Cissie Fairchilds

Women and Family

IN FRANCE, the last decades of the eighteenth century saw a revolution in the realm of family life. This revolution was as deep-seated and as far-reaching as the political revolution that would erupt in 1789, and it brought many more changes to the daily lives of women. At the heart of this revolution was the emergence of the modern, affectionate nuclear family, in which the spouses married for love, treated each other with dignity and respect, and worked together to raise their children in an atmosphere of security and indulgence. All this was different from the traditional pattern of family life in France. In the sixteenth, seventeenth, and early eighteenth centuries, families had been patriarchal institutions, in which the husband and father ruled as a monarch ruled his kingdom and God ruled his creation. In the traditional patriarchal family, wives and children were clearly subordinate to their husbands and fathers, who exercised both legal and actual power over their property and their persons. Marriages were arranged with an eye to the economic advantage of the family rather than the personal happiness and fulfillment of the spouses. Within these marriages, relations between husband and wife and between parents and children were cold, distant, and unloving.[1]

Why these traditional patterns of family behavior began to change in the last half of the eighteenth century is at present unclear.[2] What is certain is that change did occur, at both ends of the social scale. In the last decades of the Old Regime, the French nobility began spontaneously to adopt the values of the modern affectionate nuclear family and the domesticity that went with it; at the same time, there were the beginnings of a concerted attempt, which would last through the nineteenth century, to impose these values on the lower classes.[3]

WOMEN IN ARISTOCRATIC FAMILIES: FROM SALONNIÈRE TO WIFE AND MOTHER

On May 31, 1781, the marquise de Bombelles, lady-in-waiting to Mme Elisabeth, great-aunt of King Louis XVI, wrote to her husband, the French ambassador to the Holy Roman Empire:

The court is a dog of a place. I shall long regret the sweet and tranquil life
I led at Ratisbon [Regensburg, where her husband was stationed] and I
feel certain that my lot should have been to be a good wife [*une bonne
femme*] occupied solely with her husband, her children, and her household. For the pleasures of the court, of what is called good taste [*le bon ton*]
have no attraction for me, and I have too bourgeois a way of thinking for
that place.[4]

The marquise was not alone in her dislike for the court and her
preference for the simple joys of family life. Margaret Darrow has
shown that in the late eighteenth century French noblewomen by the
score repudiated their traditional "careers" as court ladies and *salonnières* in favor of the roles of wife and mother.[5] In part, this change
was just one aspect of the general passion for the simple life that swept
the nobility in the 1770s and 1780s. But this change also had deeper
causes: it stemmed from fundamental shifts in attitude toward
marriage and motherhood.

Noblewomen, of course, had always been wives and mothers. In
general, they had married early (in their mid-teens in the seventeenth
century and at seventeen or eighteen in the following one[6]), and their
marriages were arranged by their parents or relatives with an eye to
family advantage rather than to the personal happiness of the spouses.
Their letters and memoirs give the impression that noble wives were
poorly treated by their husbands. At worst, they were bullied and
threatened by everyone in the household from spouse and mother-in-
law to the lowliest servant, as was the seventeenth-century mystic
Mme de La Mothe Guyon; at best, they were simply ignored, like the
poor wife of the libertine comte Dufort de Cheverny, who kindly
taught his boring young bride to play solitaire so that she would have
something to occupy her time while he pursued his own pleasures.[7] It
is not surprising, then, that seventeenth- and early eighteenth-
century noblewomen found little emotional fulfillment in marriage
and that they centered their lives instead around their "careers" as
ladies-in-waiting or *salonnières*.[8]

But by the last half of the eighteenth century, noblewomen began to
expect more out of marriage than a chance to be left alone. The
Enlightenment revolutionized the way people viewed love and marriage. This supremely rational movement popularized the supremely
romantic notion of marriage for love. In the face of centuries of
Christian aestheticism, the Enlightenment propounded the possibility
of individual happiness on earth; in the face of centuries of Christian
disparagement, the Enlightenment rehabilitated the passions, including romantic love and sexual desire, as essential elements in such
happiness.[9] In line with its emphasis on the family as the cradle of
productive citizens, the Enlightenment placed romantic love and

sexual fulfillment, not in illicit relationships (the traditional pattern from medieval courtly love on), but firmly within the marriage bond. Romantic and sexual love became, in the words of Rousseau's Julie, "the greatest matter of life"—and the sole justification for marriage.[10]

Noblewomen of the late eighteenth century were clearly fascinated by the idea of marrying for love. The baronne d'Oberkirch, herself the victim of an unhappy arranged marriage, carefully recorded in her memoirs all the love matches among her friends, and she wondered wistfully if such marriages might work. No, she concluded, "sadly, this happiness of marriages of inclination never lasts because that would be paradise on earth."[11] Teen-aged Laurette de Malboissière agreed that a marriage for love would be paradisical but decided that it was not only possible but also the sort of marriage she wanted. She wrote to her best friend:

> I would wish, if I were married, that my husband occupied himself only with me, that he loved only me . . . that he lived with me forever more like a lover than a husband. . . . When the marriage tie has charm is when [the husband and wife] love each other so tenderly that they look only to give each other new pleasures; when, joining the tender cares of lovers to those of spouses, they know no other happiness than living together.[12]

At least in part, the new expectations that girls like Laurette de Malboissière had of marriage seem to have been fulfilled. In the last half of the eighteenth century, matches among the nobility were still arranged by parents, and family advantage was still their prime consideration. But the young people themselves were allowed to play a greater role in choosing their mates (Mme de La Tour du Pin herself engineered her marriage at age sixteen to the marquis de La Tour du Pin[13]), and the compatibility of the prospective spouses and their possibilities of future happiness together weighed more strongly in all marriage calculations. When, for example, the duc de Croy was looking for a wife for his eighteen-year-old son, "our first object was to make him happy, to give him 'la douceur de la vie'." Therefore, he rejected Mlle d'Enville de La Rochefoucauld, who had a dowry of 800,000-*livres* and the protection of the court but was ugly and bad-tempered, in favor of poorer but prettier and more intelligent Mlle de Salm.[14]

Once the match was made, relationships between the spouses seem to have been warmer and more loving than had previously been the case. A number of noblewomen, including Mme de La Tour du Pin and Laure Junot, wife of the Napoleonic General, maintained in their memoirs that they fell in love with their husbands at first sight when they were introduced to them after the match had been arranged.[15]

This sort of statement is never found in earlier memoirs. Nor do earlier noble couples show the shared delight in domesticity that shines through the letters of M. and Mme d'Albis de Belbèze, noble Toulousan *parlementaires.* Madame wrote to her husband of her problems with the servants and of the clever things their four-year-old daughter had said, and M. d'Albis wrote of his longing to be back in the bosom of his loving family.[16] In the late eighteenth century, noble spouses for the first time used *tu* in their letters and addressed each other with nicknames and endearments. For the first time, they showed their affection by kissing and embracing each other in public.[17] Aristocrats may not yet have married for love, but they behaved after marriage as though they had. Clearly, noble wives were better treated than they had ever been before, and they expected and received more emotional satisfaction from their marriages than they had ever found in the past.

The late eighteenth century saw even more striking changes in noblewomen's role as mother. While the protests of love for their spouses in their letters and memoirs often sound forced, the passages in which noblewomen speak of their love for their children ring true. If the turn toward romantic marriage among the nobility was only half-hearted, the turn toward good mothering was much more complete. Noblewomen, like almost everyone else in the eighteenth century, viewed maternity as the most fulfilling experience a woman could have, "the most sacred and at the same time the sweetest of duties," as one enthusiastic mother, Mme Roland, put it.[18]

It had not always been so. Until the late eighteenth century, it had been considered vulgar for aristocratic mothers to take too great an interest in the dirty and smelly tasks of child rearing. Immediately after birth, babies were handed over to wet nurses, who often starved and neglected them.[19] When they returned home, they passed into the hands of other hired servants, a nursemaid or *gouvernante* until the age of seven and then (for boys, at least) a *précepteur* or tutor. Since parents paid little attention to the process of child raising, these servants were usually equally neglectful of their charges. Mme de La Mothe Guyon summed up many an aristocratic childhood besides her own when she wrote, "My mother . . . neglected me a little, and left me too much to the care of the women [servants], who neglected me also." She was so little supervised that she frequently wandered out into the streets unnoticed; her childhood was full of near-fatal tumbles down airshafts and cellar steps.[20] The servants of the children of prince de Montbarrey neglected to feed their charges, who were so hungry they ate wax; and the parents of the future cardinal de Bernis paid so little attention to him that they did not discover that he had been beaten and tortured by his tutor until his welts began to fester.[21]

But by the last half of the eighteenth century, such horror stories were largely things of the past. Aristocratic mothers took a genuine interest in their children and either raised them themselves or at least closely supervised the servants who did so. In part, they owed this new interest in mothering to the new notions they shared with their society about the uniqueness, preciousness, and fraility of young children.[22] But their interest also stemmed from the fact that in the last half of the eighteenth century motherhood was a much more pleasant experience than it had been. For the first time, birth control was used to limit family size. The average number of children in the families of France's *ducs* and peers dropped from 6.5 in the seventeenth century to 2 in the eighteenth.[23] This meant that noblewomen had to endure fewer painful pregnancies and births, which became less traumatic as doctors rather than midwives began to deliver babies and to substitute medical advances, such as the forceps, for folk practices. Despite the prejudices of modern feminist historians, the intrusion of men into the hitherto female world of childbirth seems to have improved the chances of a mother's survival.[24] At any rate, the presence of a male doctor signified the interest that husbands now took in the process of childbirth. For the first time, aristocratic husbands like the younger duc de Croy watched their children being born.[25] This manifest concern of husbands, their devotion to their children, and the delight they took in playing with them and spending time with them must have reinforced the new satisfaction aristocratic women found in motherhood.

In raising their children, noblewomen followed a cluster of notions propounded by doctors and educators in the late eighteenth century, notions perhaps best summarized as "natural" child raising under the eye of a vigilant mother. The major burden of child rearing manuals in the late eighteenth century was to let nature take its course.[26] Mothers should nurse their own babies; their own mother's milk was the most natural food for infants. Babies should not be swaddled; that restricted the natural movement of their limbs. They should not be forced to learn to walk; they would learn when they were ready to do so. They should not be beaten; they were born good and would grow up good if they were surrounded by a protective environment from which all bad influences were carefully excluded. Key to all of this was the mother. Only she could nurse her child, only she could instinctively anticipate its needs, only she would care enough to exercise the ceaseless vigilance necessary to create the protective environment in which a child could grow and flourish.

Aristocratic mothers interpreted this newly enlarged maternal role in various ways. For most, it meant that they should nurse their own babies. In the 1780s, there was a veritable craze for maternal breast feeding among the highest aristocracy. The marquise de Bombelles nursed her infant son, Bombon, while on duty at court, and even Marie-Antoinette expressed a desire to nurse her children.[27] For a few others, the new child rearing also meant that they should raise their offspring themselves, without the help of servants. Two who attempted to do so were Mme Necker, wife of finance minister Jacques Necker and mother of the future novelist, Germaine de Staël, and Mme Roland, Girondin politician and mother of a daughter, Eudora. Mme Roland's proudest boast was that "the child is not for one hour in a fortnight left to the servants; I never take a step without her." Mme Necker not only cared for Germaine herself but educated her as well, turning her into a child prodigy who knew her catechism before age three and recited long poems in Latin and English at five. Not surprisingly, both of these carefully reared children grew up to hate their mothers.[28]

Perhaps fortunately, most noblewomen did not interpret the new mothering in so strenuous a fashion. They could not really conceive of doing without servants. Therefore, to them, being a good mother did not mean raising a child without help; instead, it meant hiring competent domestics and exercising a constant vigilance to see that they did their jobs properly. The correspondence of aristocratic noblewomen in the 1760s, 1770s, and 1780s reveals an obsession with the child raising process in striking contrast to the silence on this subject in earlier periods. This obsession takes the form of endless worrying over finding and keeping good servants. The marquise de Bombelles wrote constantly about the Swiss nurse, Mme Giles, whom she hired to help raise Bombon. The woman was becoming homesick; could she be persuaded to stay at least until Bombon got over the traumas of weaning?[29] Mme d'Albis de Belbèze was upset by the problem of finding the right *gouvernante* for her four-year-old daughter, Poulou. The current *gouvernante*, Thérèse, beat the child; obviously, she had to go. But was her replacement too lenient?[30] The comtesse de Sabran suffered almost as much as her seven-year-old son, Elzéar, when the boy's nursemaid was replaced with a tutor:

> I am very disturbed right now because of Elzéar; the grief that he feels at being parted from his nurse has upset him so much that he is sick. For the last three days he has neither eaten nor slept and he has a slight fever.... I can't tell you how unhappy this makes me, how worried I am.. . .[31]

Noblewomen like the comtesse clearly took their roles as mothers very seriously. Mothering may have caused them endless trouble and concern, but it also gave them, as the letter of the marquise de Bombelles quoted at the beginning of this section suggests, a satisfaction greater than any that could be derived from their more traditional roles as court ladies and *salonnières*. It was the noblewoman—who had, in modern jargon, more freedom of action and more "options" than any other woman in eighteenth-century France—who most willingly and enthusiastically embraced the new domesticity.[32] In doing so, she made possible the rise in France of the modern, affectionate, child-centered nuclear family.

LOWER-CLASS FAMILIES: THE PERSISTENCE OF THE TRADITIONAL FAMILY ECONOMY

At the other end of the social scale, among the poverty-stricken peasants, who made up some seventy per cent of the French population, and the urban artisans and day laborers, who formed another twenty per cent, family life was very different. In a sense, the lower classes had always had the domesticity that the nobility now sought; they married more or less for love, and they mothered their own children. But working-class domesticity was domesticity with a difference. Overshadowing all other aspects of the lower-class family was its role as an economic unit, a "family economy," dedicated to guaranteeing the sheer physical survival of its members. The contributions of the wife— her work in the fields and her spinning and weaving if she were a peasant's wife, or her labors in the workshop or behind the counter if she were the wife of an urban artisan—were vital to the family budget.[33] It was these economic duties of the lower-class women that shaped their roles as wives and mothers. Thus, "good mothering" in the lower-class context meant a mother's working in the shops or fields so that her children did not go hungry. Lower-class family life did not show a turn toward greater domesticity in the last decades of the Old Regime. Instead, the economic problems of the period—rising prices, especially for food, and population growth, which brought more competition for work and more mouths to feed—meant that the niceties of family life were increasingly sacrificed to the struggle for survival.

Among the lower classes marriage had always been "romantic" in a sense. Young people married not for family or economic advantage but for personal happiness and satisfaction. They generally chose their own mates and carried out the courting process themselves, and they often consummated their love before marriage, since the popular tradition, dating back before the Council of Trent, which considered a betrothal equivalent of marriage, made sex between an engaged couple permissible.[34] Yet this "romantic" view of marriage was always hedged with prudence and respect for community traditions. The lower classes married only when they could afford to do so, when the man had saved enough to buy land or a mastership and the woman had accumulated a substantial dowry to buy the necessary *lit garni* and other household goods. This meant that they married very late; in the eighteenth century, the average age of marriage for women was 25-26 and that of men was 27-28.[35] They usually chose as a spouse someone whose character and background they knew well. In most villages, ninety-five percent of the marriages involved someone who lived within a radius of ten kilometers; in most cities, around half of all the artisans married within their craft.[36] Lower-class courtships were carried out under the supervision of the community, which often subjected couples it thought mismatched to *charivaris*, and marriages and even conceptions were timed according to its age-old rituals. Marriages were usually celebrated on Mondays and Tuesdays, never on Fridays, the day of fasting; marriages and even conceptions were rare during Advent and Lent.[37]

It has been suggested that in the late eighteenth century love and marriage among the lower classes became increasingly more romantic and less prudential. The major evidence for this is the rise in the ratio of illegitimacy, which went from approximately two percent to five percent of all births. This is said to have resulted from an increasing willingness on the part of young people, especially women, to defy family and community mores and have sex without marriage or the promise of one.[38] In fact, this does not seem to have been the case. *Déclarations de grossesse* (statements required by law of unwed mothers detailing the circumstances of their pregnancies) show that the women who bore illegitimate children continued to be marriage-oriented and to hold the traditional mixture of romantic and prudential attitudes in regard to courtship. Most slept with their swains only after marriage was implicitly—and often explicitly—promised. What caused the rise in illegitimacy were the unfavorable economic conditions of the period, which made it increasingly difficult for couples who planned to marry actually to do so.[39] By the late eighteenth century, courting was for lower-class women a gamble that only the lucky won.

We know amazingly little about relationships between husbands and wives once the marriage had taken place. Evidence from popular proverbs ("the hat gives orders to the headdress" and "rich is the man whose wife is dead and horse alive") and folk customs (men who were bossed by their wives were subjected to *charivaris* by the youth of the village) suggest that peasant wives at least were little more than household drudges for their husbands, subject to constant physical abuse and appreciated, if at all, only for the endless work they did.[40] But the glimpses we get of real-life marriages in court records and the like paint a slightly rosier picture. These suggest that while wife beating (often aggravated by alcohol, in which artisans and laborers found relief from the misery of their daily lives) and other forms of abuse were common, wives were often unwilling to accept such treatment as their inevitable lot. They were much less tolerant of their husband's adulteries than noblewomen were. When their husbands beat them or wasted the family patrimony, they fought back, sought refuge with female relatives and neighbors, complained to the police, and even demanded judicial separations or, when they became possible during the Revolution, divorces.[41] Evidently, it was their work and their clearly vital contributions to the family economy that made these women feel entitled to at least a modicum of love and respect. Marie Brunel, wife of a shopkeeper, said in her divorce petition that her husband, Adrien Boullain, was an "angry and hard" man, who subjected her to many insults, threats and beatings, but she deserved better because she had worked hard in the family business, keeping the accounts, paying the workers, selling on the street. "Everyone knows how useful I was to a man who did not know how to read or write; . . . our fortune increased through my efforts and my work."[42]

During their marriages, wives of peasants and artisans had to combine their constant "efforts and work" for the family economy with constant motherhood. The acceptability of premarital sexual intercourse for engaged couples meant that many brides—probably about ten percent—were pregnant at marriage.[43] And if they were not pregnant at the altar, they became so soon after. Birth control was almost unknown among the lower classes before the Revolution.[44] It was not really necessary, for the high age of marriage combined with the high rate of infant and child mortality (only half the children born survived to adulthood) to keep families small. A typical family would have four children, of whom two or three would survive. But the lack of birth control meant that babies arrived at intervals of twenty-five to thirty months as long as the wife remained fertile.[45] Therefore, from the age of twenty-six to forty, a lower-class woman was usually either pregnant or suckling an infant.

Childbirth among the lower classes did not "improve" the way it had for noblewomen during the last decades of the eighteenth century. It was still a female event, pervaded with female folk wisdom. Although the government made efforts to train and license midwives for country districts in the last years of the Old Regime, such women were few and far between. Most peasant and artisan wives still had to rely only on the help of an untrained midwife. Death in childbirth remained a grave risk for lower-class women, while it was lessening for those of the upper classes.[46]

In lower-class households, infant care also remained what it had always been: a compound of folk customs whose primary purpose was to allow the mother to go about her daily chores with a minimum of attention to the newborn child. Swaddling, so deplored by the partisans of the new, natural child raising, was still widely practiced, largely because a swaddled baby could be safely left alone for long periods. Babies were fed on demand because that was easier for a busy mother than trying to keep a schedule, and the custom of washing them only infrequently probably owed as much to the mothers' lack of time as it did to traditional beliefs about the healthiness of dirt.[47] Indeed, the major change in lower-class infant care (and one precisely opposite to the trends among the upper classes) was the spread of wet-nursing, and this was clearly due to the fact that lower-class mothers had to free their time for productive labor. Until the early eighteenth century, the hiring of wet nurses had been confined to the elite, but by the end of the century, the practice spread to the lower reaches of the urban *artisanat*.[48] Any family that could possibly afford to hire a wet nurse did so because the mother's labor was so important to the family economy. Conversely, peasant wives increasingly sought nurslings because that was one more way in which they could supplement the family budget.

These patterns of infant care suggest that the lower-class family simply could not afford the niceties of the new mothering preached by doctors and practiced by the elite. The needs of the new baby had to be sacrificed to the needs of the family as a whole. Care of older children revealed a similar pattern. Children in poor families had to work instead of play. From the age of four, they were considered able to work; and they were set to gathering wood, feeding chickens, or helping to card wool. Unlike noblewomen, lower-class women did not strive to create a secure environment for their children. Instead, they sent them out into the dangerous world of the street to find what work they could.[49] Children left the family at very young ages—nine to twelve—to work as apprentices and servants. At times, children were not just sent out into the world but were also abandoned there. The most striking fact about lower-class family life in the last half of the eighteenth century is the incredible rise in the numbers of children left by their parents in hospitals and charities. In Paris, for example, there were 312 abandoned children in hospitals in 1670; by 1770, the figure was 6,918.[50] Some of these were bastards or orphans, but not all of them were. In the hospital of Aix-en-Provence, for example, only thirty percent of the children admitted were orphans.[51] The rest were legitimate children whose parents could no longer afford to feed them. Child abandonment rose as the price of bread did.[52] It was clearly a last recourse of desperate parents. They sent their children to hospitals when they could not afford to care for them and retrieved them when their family fortunes improved. In 1770, for example, a five-year-old girl was left at the Charité in Aix-en-Provence because her father had died and her mother could not support her; three years later, the mother married a shoemaker and brought her daughter home.[53]

Upper-class observers were appalled by the seeming characteristics of lower-class family life in the late eighteenth century: the increase in illicit sex, the wife beating and abuse, the retrograde infant care and increasing abandonment of children. All of this offended their new-found notions of domesticity. Therefore, they began a campaign, which would grow to epic proportions in the nineteenth century, to impose the new domesticity on the lower classes. Indeed, the story of the working-class family in the nineteenth century is the story of its reshaping, under the twin pressures of industrialization and of this propaganda from doctors, educators, and bureaucrats, to fit the domestic model. But those who attacked the lower-class family misunderstood it. The values of domesticity, romantic marriage, and concerned motherhood were not really foreign to lower-class women; but they were unable to act on them because of economic necessity. Sheer survival had to come first. The experience of women in the family in eighteenth-century France suggests that domesticity was, during that period at least, an upper-class luxury that the lower classes simply could not afford.

NOTES

1. The best description of the emotional climate of the traditional patri-archal family is Lawrence Stone, *The Family, Sex and Marriage in England, 1500-1800* (New York: Harper & Row, 1977), pp. 123-218. This deals primarily with England, but most of what Stone says holds true for France as well.

2. Stone, pp. 257-269.

3. These simultaneous changes are briefly sketched in Jacques Donzelot, *The Policing of Families,* translated by Robert Hurley (New York: Pantheon, 1979), pp. 9-47.

4. Cited in George Sussman, "Three Histories of Infant Nursing in Eighteenth-Century France" (Unpublished paper, Berkshire Conference on Women's History, Northampton, Massachusetts, August 1979), p. 25. An abridged version of this paper appears in George D. Sussman, *Selling Mother's Milk: The Wet-Nursing Business in France, 1715-1914* (Urbana: University of Illinois Press, 1982), pp. 73-97.

5. Margaret Darrow, "French Noblewomen and the New Domesticity, 1750-1850," *Feminist Studies* 5, no. 1 (Spring, 1979): 41-65. Darrow maintains that the change began only during the Revolution, while I think it was already visible during the 1770s.

6. Darrow, p. 59.

7. *La Vie de Mme J. M. B. de La Mothe Guyon, écrite par elle-même* (Cologne: J. de La Pierre, 1720), pp. 54-55, 106-107, 150-151; *Mémoires du comte Dufort de Cheverny,* edited by Robert de Crèvecoeur (Paris: Plon-Nourrit, 1909), pp. 169-185.

8. For the role of *salonnières,* see Carolyn G. Lougee, *Le Paradis des Femmes: Women, Salon and Social Stratification in Seventeenth-Century France* (Princeton: Princeton University Press, 1976), especially pp. 11-55 and 113-170; and Dorothy Anne Liot Backer, *Precious Women* (New York: Basic Books, 1974). For their careers as ladies-in-waiting, see Darrow, pp. 47-48.

9. A good short summary of Enlightenment ideas on love and marriage is James F. Traer, *Marriage and the Family in Eighteenth-Century France* (Ithaca: Cornell University Press, 1980), pp. 48-78. For Enlightenment expectations of happiness on earth, see Robert Mauzi, *L'Idée du bonheur au XVIIIe siècle* (Paris: Armand Colin, 1960), pp. 458-484; for its rehabilitation of sexual passion, see Peter Gay, "Three Stages on Love's Way," in *The Party of Humanity* (New York: Knopf, 1964), pp. 133-161.

10. Mauzi, p. 458.

11. *Mémoires de la baronne d'Oberkirch sur la cour de Louis XVI et la société française avant 1789,* edited by Suzanne Burkard (Paris: Mercure de France, 1970), pp. 208, 369.

12. *Laurette de Malboissière, lettres d'une jeune fille du temps de Louis XV (1761-1766),* edited by marquise de La Grange (Paris: Didier et Cie, 1866), pp. 31-33.

13. *Mémoires de la marquise de La Tour du Pin: Journal d'une femme de cinquante ans, 1778-1815* (Paris: Mercure de France, 1979), p. 62.

14. *Journal inédit du duc de Croy, 1718-84,* edited by vicomte de Grouchy and Paul Cottin (Paris: Flammarion, 1906), vol. 2, pp. 125-127.

15. Mme de La Tour du Pin, pp. 63, 66-67; Laure Junot, duchesse d'Abrantes, *The Home and Court Life of the Emperor Napoleon and his Family* (London: R. Bentley, 1893).

16. *Une famille de parlementaires toulousains à la fin de l'ancien régime,* edited by Auguste Puis (Paris & Toulouse: E. Champion, 1913).

17. For an example, see baronne d'Oberkirch, p. 224.

18. Quoted in Sussman, p. 16.

19. There is a vast literature on wet-nursing. The best short treatments are David Hunt, *Parents and Children in History* (New York: Basic Books, 1970), pp. 100-132; J. Gélis, M. Laget and M.-F. Morel, *Entrer dans la vie* (Paris: Gallimard, 1978), pp. 155-171; and Sussman, *Selling Mother's Milk.*

20. *La Vie de Mme de La Mothe Guyon,* pp. 18, 12.

21. Mme de Créquy, *Souvenirs de la marquise de Créquy de 1710 à 1803* (Paris: Garnier, n.d.), vol. 6, p. 219; Cardinal de Bernis, *Mémoires et lettres de François Joachim Pierre, cardinal de Bernis, 1715-58,* edited by Frédéric Masson (Paris: Plon, 1878), p. 11.

22. Stone, pp. 221-269, 405-480.

23. Claude Lévy and Louis Henry, "Ducs et pairs sous l'ancien régime: caractéristiques démographiques d'une caste," *Population* 4 (1960):820.

24. On the highly controversial point, see Mireille Laget, "Childbirth in Seventeenth and Eighteenth Century France," in *Medicine and Society in France,* edited by Robert Forster and Orest Ranum (Baltimore: Johns Hopkins University Press, 1980), pp. 137-176; and Mireille Laget, *Naissances: L'Accouchement avant l'âge de la clinique* (Paris: Le Seuil, 1982), pp. 201-248.

25. Duc de Croy, vol. 2, pp. 231-232.

26. For late eighteenth-century child raising, see Marie-France Morel, "City and Country in Eighteenth-Century Medical Discussions about Early Childhood," in Forster and Ranum, pp. 48-65; and Donzelot, pp. 9-22.

27. Sussman, pp. 30-31.

28. For Mme Roland, see Sussman, pp. 12-23; and *Mémoires de Mme Roland* (Paris: Baudouin, 1820), vol. 1, p. 292. For Mme Necker, see J. Christopher Herold, *Mistress to an Age: A Life of Madame de Staël* (New York: Bobbs-Merrill, 1958), pp. 22-53.

29. Sussman, pp. 30-31.

30. Puis, pp. 55-56.

31. *Correspondance inédite de la comtesse de Sabran et du chevalier de Bouffliers, 1778-1788* (Paris: Plon, 1875), pp. 75-146.

32. It should be noted that we have said nothing about bourgeois mothers for the simple reason that little is known about the bourgeois family. Modern domesticity may have originated among the bourgeoisie rather than the aristocracy. But the English example (see Stone; and Randolph Trumbach, *The Rise of the Egalitarian Family* [New York: Academic Press, 1978]) suggests that it began at the highest levels of society and filtered down first to the bourgeoisie and later to the lower classes.

33. The best descriptions of the "family economy" of the poor is Louise A. Tilly and Joan W. Scott, *Women, Work and Family* (New York: Holt, Rinehart & Winston, 1978). For the work of peasant women see Martine Segalen, *Love and Power in the Peasant Family,* translated by Sarah Matthews (Chicago: University of Chicago Press, 1983).

34. Beatrice Gottlieb, "The Meaning of Clandestine Marriage," in *Family and Sexuality in French History,* edited by Robert Wheaton and Tamara K. Hareven (Philadelphia: University of Pennsylvania Press, 1980), pp. 49-83.

35. François Lebrun, *La Vie conjugale sous l'ancien régime* (Paris: Armand Colin, 1975), p. 31.

36. Ibid., pp. 27, 26.

37. Ibid., pp. 38-41.

38. This is the (greatly simplified) argument of Edward Shorter, "Female Emancipation, Birth Control and Fertility in European History," *American Historical Review* 87 (1973):605-640; and idem, *The Making of the Modern Family* (New York: Basic Books, 1975).

39. For this argument, see Louise A. Tilly, Joan W. Scott and Miriam Cohen, "Women's Work and European Fertility Patterns," and Cissie Fairchilds, "Female Sexual Attitudes and the Rise of Illegitimacy," both in *Marriage and Fertility: Studies in Interdisciplinary History,* edited by Robert J. Rotberg and Theodore K. Rabb (Princeton: Princeton University Press, 1980), pp. 219-249 and 163-204.

40. Shorter, pp. 73, 58-59. For a more favorable review of marital relations among the peasantry, see Segalen, *Love and Power,* especially pp. 155-161.

41. Roderick Phillips, *Family Breakdown in Late Eighteenth-Century France* (Oxford: Clarendon Press, 1980), pp. 89, 57.

42. Ibid., pp. 134-135.

43. Lebrun, p. 102.

44. Birth control was practiced in scattered areas, both rural and urban, before the Revolution, but these areas are so diverse that historians have not yet discerned a pattern among them that might explain its adoption. See Lebrun, pp. 103-109; and Jean-Louis Flandrin, *Familles, parentés, maison, sexualité dans l'ancienne société* (Paris: Hachette, 1976), pp. 188-192.

45. Flandrin, p. 237; Gélis, Laget, and Morel, p. 185.

46. Laget, pp. 156-167; and *Naissances,* pp. 261-282.

47. Gélis, Laget, and Morel, pp. 115-124; and Françoise Loux, *Le Jeune Enfant et son corps dans la médecine traditionnelle* (Paris: Flammarion, 1978), pp. 123-138, 155-190.

48. Gélis et al., *Entrer dans la vie,* pp. 157-158, and Sussman, *Selling Mother's Milk,* pp. 6-7.

49. The dangers of the street were a major theme of nineteenth-century writings about child care, but parents worried about them in the eighteenth century, too. See Arlette Farge, *Vivre dans la rue* (Paris: Gallimard, 1979).

50. Gélis, Laget, and Morel, p. 173.

51. Cissie Fairchilds, *Poverty and Charity in Aix-en-Provence, 1640-1789* (Baltimore: Johns Hopkins University Press, 1976), p. 85.

52. Flandrin, p. 185.

53. Fairchilds, *Poverty and Charity*, p. 86.

⚅ Elizabeth Fox-Genovese

Women and Work

$\mathbf{W}$ORK constituted the very fabric of the lives of most French women during the eighteenth century. At least ninety percent of them, from about the age of fourteen on, spent most of their waking hours engaged in one or another form of work, which contributed decisively to French economic life as well as to the survival of the majority of French families. But the divisions that crisscrossed French society also crisscross any modern attempt to identify a single model of women's work. If work normally designates hard, physical labor, it also encompasses a variety of tasks and responsibilities that ensure the functioning of the society as a whole. If estate management should be classified as work for men, so must household management be classified for women; if military service is classified as work for men, so must the suckling and rearing of infants be classified for women. Almost everywhere that masculine activity is designated as work, its female counterpart should also be so designated. Only at the very upper echelons, among the court nobility and the wealthy urban classes, do we find some evidence of a sexual division of labor that casts men in performing roles that might properly be labeled work (government or judicial office, banking or other financial and commercial services) while their wives and daughters led lives of genuine leisure.

During the eighteenth century, as previously, the work of women varied according to estate membership, level of income, and urban or rural residence. More dramatically, a woman's work varied according to whether it was performed within and for her family or in what we might call the public sector, for a wage. All of these distinctions and possible criteria for classification remain subject to innumerable exceptions and confusions. The work of a poor noble's wife might closely resemble that of a wealthy peasant's wife; the work of a *moyenne bourgeoise* or of the wife of a comfortable artisan might resemble both in being performed within the familial context while differing from them because of the different female tasks associated with urban and rural residence. The work of all these women would thus differ structurally from that of an urban servant or factory employee in not being performed for a wage; yet, in given regions, the tasks of all such women would likely include some measure of spinning, lace making, or other textile work. In many parts of the countryside, a female servant would perform for a wage tasks that she might have performed gratis for her own family.

In a very general way, it is possible to construct a taxonomy of women's work that identifies tasks, activities, and responsibilities especially associated with the female gender. In its broadest contours, such a taxonomy would delineate the association of women with such forms of work as infant care; food preparation and service; textile work, especially spinning; the washing of clothing and linens; various farm activities, such as poultry raising; and various forms of marketing. Nonetheless, according to region and to the economic structure of the household to which she belonged, a woman could perform any of an enormous range of tasks; the governing structural principle remained the sharp distinction between, and the complementarity of, the labor performed by the two genders.[1] Thus, however important, the associations of culture and practice—encoded in a legion of proverbs and betraying deep assumptions about the appropriate sexual division of labor—do not tell us enough. Throughout the eighteenth century, the heavy hand of tradition continued to govern the patterns of women's work, but the social and economic changes of the "long" eighteenth century that began as early as the 1660s made recognizable inroads in the lives of innumerable French women and their men. None of these changes revolutionized inherited behavior and norms, but, by the 1760s, with the *tournant des mentalités* of which Michel Vovelle writes, they had left a decisive mark on the lives of many. Their combined impact pointed toward those social, economic, and gender relations that would be inscribed in post-Revolutionary society.[2]

It is not yet possible to construct a complete picture of women's work in its remarkable diversity, much less in its variation by region and class. It would be more difficult yet to provide an accurate assessment of the specific contribution of women to French economic development in this period, although it has become inexcusable to neglect the indisputable presence of that contribution. Here, we merely delineate general patterns of change and continuity in the working lives of women in relation to French social and economic change as a whole. The scattered and uneven basic research precludes constructing a single, all-encompassing model; and, in all likelihood, the rich diversity of women's working experience would not lend itself readily to standardization in any case. But the general patterns are clear enough. The more difficult challenge lies in estimating the relations among random variation, quantitative growth, and abiding qualitative change. Did the working lives of any particular group of women change decisively during the century, and, if so, in what ways?

Notoriously, historians love to find traditional society, in all its reassuring stability, in the century that precedes the one they are studying. The tumultuous life of sixteenth- and early seventeenth-century France should protect us against the worst of those illusions. Economic growth did, nonetheless, mark the decades that succeeded the crisis of the late seventeenth century. The long eighteenth century included the eradication of genuinely killing famines and the inauguration of steady population increase. Notwithstanding the absence of precise figures, we can, with some confidence, assert that the twenty million subjects of Louis XIV had expanded to some twenty-six million. Eighteenth-century women may not have been bearing more children than their foremothers—and increasingly some would abandon those they did bear—but they raised more of those they had and kept them to adulthood, just as they were somewhat more likely to share their own adulthood with siblings, spouses, and familiar neighbors.[3]

The secular economic growth and rise in prices that, especially after 1730, accompanied this demographic push brought significant changes in French society as a whole. The persistent rigidity of French social and economic structures ensured a superficial consistency in an increasingly strained organization of French social and economic relations. French women of different social origins and different regions experienced those strains differently. Their working lives cannot be dissociated from the destiny of their regions and families of origin, as well as that of their conjugal families—or from an enforced or chosen unmarried status.

From the point of view of eighteenth-century commentators themselves, the great changes they had witnessed in their lifetimes were the frightening growth of luxury, the accelerated commercial pace, the increase in dangerous urban classes, the degradation of agriculture, the decline in population, the abandonment of traditional rural and familial mores, and the general erosion of an ordered, hierarchical society. These perceptions are more useful as indications of change than as precise descriptions of its character. Population was increasing; estates and even corporations, despite Turgot's edict of abolition (February 1776), remained in place; and, by and large, growth affected the countryside more powerfully than the cities (only Paris, Lyon, Marseilles, and Bordeaux exceeded 100,000 in population; while Nantes, Lille, and Rouen surpassed 50,000, and only fifty others reached the 10,000-50,000 range[4]).

In 1789, France remained an overwhelmingly rural society in which the twenty-one million odd peasants accounted for 85 percent of the total population. Genuine workers, in the sense of those fully dependent upon the buying and selling of their labor power, numbered only 1,200,000, or 4.6 percent of the population. The nobility of the sword and robe together constituted a scant 1.5 percent of the population, or 400,000 individuals, and the secular and regular clergy only 0.5 percent, or 130,000 individuals, of whom 50,000 may have been women. The bourgeoisie, accounting for a modest 8.4 percent of the total, consisted of some 2,300,000 heterogeneous members, but the bourgeoisie did represent society's most dynamic identifiable segment. Everywhere, its numbers were growing and its activities were expanding. The *petite bourgeoisie* grew with particular vigor and, increasingly, formed a distinct layer between the *peuple* and the older, "real" bourgeoisie.[5]

The spectacular growth of external commerce, together with the increasingly rapid pace of internal trade, accounted for much of this dynamism, just as it impressed contemporaries as the carrier of a revolution in behavior and mores. In social life, many were prepared to blame women for—or at least to associate them intimately with—the apparent disorder, much in the manner of those teeth-grinding theorists who today blame feminists for the supposed disaster provoked by a revolt against injustice. Luxury in particular and conspicuous consumption in general were taken to be specifically female failings. Mothers of all social classes were held accountable for their reluctance to nurse their own children. Horrified commentators portrayed the cities, Paris in particular, as dens of female vice and portrayed even convents as seedbeds of future luxury or debauchery. The dramatic increase in abandoned children was ascribed to the license of single women, especially domestic servants. Eager, if hard-pressed, administrators and inspectors of manufactures sought to harness disorderly single women to the discipline of royal manufactures, new factories, and *ateliers de charité*. In short, the representations of women in general and metaphors of rampant female sexuality in particular were repeatedly, if imperfectly, linked to the perception of social and economic change. This emphasis on women at risk, manifested in undisciplined female sexuality and taste for luxury, did at least call attention to important changes that were occurring in the lives of some women, even as it obscured the real character of most women's working lives.[6]

Early modern French prescription and practice identified women's work closely with the family economy operating under the authority of its male head—the woman's father, husband, brother, or son. Among the peasant majority, strong attitudes toward the sexual division of labor prevailed; women in peasant families performed what were taken to be traditional female responsibilities, including infant care, child rearing, food preparation, and the general care of the

dwelling. Normally, they also had their special agricultural responsibilities, most frequently the raising of poultry but also the care of
occasional dairy animals. In most parts of France, women engaged in
spinning for the family's own clothing and, increasingly, for whole-
salers. They might also participate in ribbon making or lace making.
They were ordinarily responsible for doing laundry and for providing
the family with water. All of this work could be, and commonly was,
onerous. Considerable physical labor was required for such tasks as
transporting water to meet the daily needs of families that could
include eight or more members, not to mention *servantes* and *valets*. At
harvest time, if not at other times as well, women could be drawn into
the agricultural labor force. Peasant women could also engage in
marketing the products of their poultry yards, the dairy, and a small
vegetable garden; or they might run a small business of their own,
such as a cabaret, a laundry or dyeing operation, or a butcher shop.[7]

In all instances, the status and economic opportunity of the rural
woman were closely governed by those of her husband. Women's
servile status disappeared with that of their men, but women, like
their men, remained accountable for *lods et ventes, cens, corvées,* and other
obligations that encumbered the holding. In addition, throughout
most of France, by custom and by law, women were strictly subordinated to their husbands. The complex legal network that described their
specific status varied from region to region and deserves extended
study. As a general rule, however, the absolute state had contributed
mightily, when and where it could, to reinforcing the powers of
husbands and fathers. Although in regions such as the Comtat,
Britanny, the Angoumois, and the Ile de France, rural wives might
function and be recognized as *co-fermiers* with their husbands, they
remained virtual servants in many others. The legal and social
institutions that shaped woman's status were particularly important
for her right to, or say in, the disposition of the fruits of her labor. But
even where she retained some legally guaranteed economic rights,
custom might still dictate forms of service and subservience, such as
her serving meals to the men of the household and waiting to eat
herself until they had done. Finally, the importance of the family unit
in rural economic life made it virtually impossible for her to survive on
her own. As in the city, widows inherited going concerns from
husbands and continued on their own; but, even under these
conditions, success normally dictated remarriage or the active collaboration of one or more sons or sons-in-law.[8]

Women's work, in this context, remained highly flexible and
unspecialized, in some instances, almost invisible. The carrying of
water, to keep to the example, was designated as an occupation only in

cities and then seemed to be performed largely by men. The special skills required for spinning, ribbon making, lace making, and the like could be highly complex, but they were normally practiced within the interstices of daily life, rather than as a profession that organized the daily allocation of time. As if in consonance with the informality of the practice, the induction into the skill was passed from mother to daughter as part of the female culture that also included special powers and knowledge associated with childbearing and the medicinal properties of herbs. Girls were, in this sense, slowly inducted into a way of life, rather than receiving an apprenticeship or even specific agricultural training. Even when they, like their brothers, went as servants to a neighboring family, their work would double that of the mistress of the holding in its diffuse character, rather than center on specific tasks. Also, they might occasionally be hired as unspecialized agricultural day laborers. This lack of specialization did not detract from the value of women's work in peasant society; many a proverb reminded young men that the first quality to seek in a prospective bride was her ability to labor.[9]

The work of women in early modern French cities mirrored that of the countryside in its structure, if not in its specific tasks. As Natalie Davis has insisted for the role of women in the *arts mécaniques* in sixteenth-century Lyon, women worked, within the prevailing constraints, "however and wherever they could . . . helping husbands and making anything from pins to gloves." No matter how high the praise they earned for their craft, "it usually remained within the world of their street, their *commérage*, their tavern, their kin—unpublished and unsung."[10] Within the world of corporations and guilds, women enjoyed scarcely greater opportunities for status and independence than they did among the peasantry. As wives and daughters, they retained the customary female responsibilities for the household and the early years of the new generation. In addition to this work, they participated in the crafts of their fathers, husbands, and sons. But they did not normally receive specialized apprenticeships, participate in *compagnonnage*, or receive a formal voice in the deliberations of the corporation. The dominant pattern remained that of a domestic and economic partnership—augmented by the dowry and based on artisanal property, including the man's skill and whatever real estate—in which the man governed and the woman assisted. A similar relationship prevailed among shopkeepers and *marchands*. Custom and law combined to promote asymmetrical relations between men and women within the family, but whatever the subordination of the wife, the work of both partners remained essential to success. The files of the intendant of Bordeaux for the 1770s contain requests from widowers and widows alike for pensions to assist them in caring for the numerous children that their bakery or carpentry shop could not support in the absence of their spouse.[11]

If participation in the family economy characterized the work of most urban women, the city nonetheless offered greater, and more rapidly expanding, opportunities than the country did for women to work outside the family economy. In fact, women's work related to the family economies as a series of gradations, rather than as a stark dichotomy. Women could work as assistants to their men in a single craft; they could work within the household at a different craft, contributing their income to the family pool; they could work outside the household to help support the family; and they could work in or out of the household to support themselves. Only in the last instance did their work contribute primarily to their own economic independence, rather than to the survival or prosperity of their family; and even then, women who lived at home invariably contributed something to the family pool. Girls who worked as employees or servants and retained all, or the major share, of their earnings for themselves normally did so to build a dowry that would permit them to marry. Women's work in the cities could follow any of these patterns, but it was more likely than in the country to offer some element of separation from the working lives of their men—through a different occupation, through the control of earnings, or both.

As a rule, the organized trades or *métiers* did not offer women significantly greater independence or status than did any other arena of French economic life. Women's position in the so-called mixed guilds, those that accepted female as well as male members, never matched that of their male counterparts. Conditions varied from city to city, but women could be found among the drapers, the weavers, the bakers, the fishmongers, the printers, the goldsmiths, the masons, and many others. Their participation in the guild depended upon its particular regulations; but, normally, their entrance depended upon succession from a husband or a father and, even then, did not guarantee them full rights. Printers' widows might continue the work of the shop and even retain journeymen, but they could not inaugurate a new piece of work. The widows of meat roasters and pastry makers did not even have the right to employ an apprentice. Women were not usually represented in the governing councils of the guilds, nor did they participate in the *compagnonnage*, except in the symbolic role of the *mère*, who welcomed and housed the participants in the *Tour de France* during their stay in a particular city.[12]

Some mixed guilds did allow women independent entry. Thus, the drapers and the hostelers of Dijon and the drapers and goldsmiths of Caen, like the grain merchants and fishmongers of Paris, were always referred to as *maîtres et maîtresses, marchands et marchandes, graniers et granières, apprentis et apprentisses*.[13] In these instances, the numbers of female participants seem to have ensured their recognition, if not their full equality. Without detailed local institutional histories, it remains difficult to account for this female presence systematically; but it is safe to assume, at least in the case of Paris and in the case of guilds in which marketing constituted an important element of the activity, that the inclusion of women reflected women's accepted marketing role.[14]

Finally, a few guilds remained purely female guilds. In Paris, only the seamstresses, the spinners, the lingerie makers, and the boutique keepers were of this number; and the same conditions probably existed in the provinces. If some of these female guilds enjoyed long-standing charters and privileges, others were of more recent origins. The seamstresses, for example, received their formal organization in 1675. Organized identically to the male corporations, the female corporations also required apprenticeships and entry fees and tended to restrict the position of *maîtresse* to the daughters of *maîtresses*. Like their male counterparts, these guilds elected juries to protect the integrity of the craft—that is, the monopoly of its exercise. Whatever the difficulties of their position within the guilds, women apparently favored that protection over unfettered economic competition; following Turgot's experiment with freedom, they welcomed the restoration of regulation.[15]

The very complexities of women's position in the corporations during the eighteenth century faithfully reflects their position in the economy and the world of work. That position obeyed the three dominant principles that had governed women's specific roles in the economy since time immemorial: the intimate association of women with a family economy that simultaneously exacted their full participation and their subordination, a gender system that prescribed cultural and social norms and behavior for women in general, and expediency. These principles also governed women's access to other forms of activity and employment within the urban economy.

The city had long offered women special opportunities as midwives, servants, laundresses, prostitutes, and hawkers or market women of various kinds. The services they performed, like the goods they offered for sale, were, in a general way, associated with what were taken to be the appropriate attributes of their sex. Thus, the casual labor, like the more regular wage labor, available to women largely derived from their crude sexuality, their association with clothing and textiles, their responsibility for cleanliness, and their special association with the provision of food. No one has yet advanced a systematic explanation for women's pervasive marketing activities, and space hardly permits one here. Women's market responsibilities in so many disparate societies—for example, those of West Africa and the Caribbean Islands—deeply contravene the tendency to seclude women within the home. Perhaps marketing the basic necessities of life was taken to be a natural extension of the women's domestic responsibilities. In any event, by the beginning of the eighteenth century, women pervaded the tortuous network of the urban market. Trafficking in everything from grain to fish, from flowers to old clothes, they hawked their wares or presided over their stands. Responsible, as consumers, for purveying the subsistence of their families, they came to view the markets in which they also sold as their special preserve. In this respect, the passionate and occasionally violent defense of the so-called moral economy by women in the years preceding and during the Revolution must be understood, at least partially, as an attempt to defend their specific social roles. Their participation in exchange, whatever its apparent independence from traditional constraints, represented merely a transformation of the work that guaranteed their fulfillment of their familial obligations.[16]

These general patterns of female work, which affected a majority of women, persisted throughout the eighteenth century, but economic growth did alter the working lives of significant numbers in a variety of ways. Despite the absence of full-scale agricultural revolution in the countryside and the persistence of weighty seigneurial dues, a long process of consolidation for some and fragmentation for others, including a significant assault on those common lands upon which the survival of so many poorer peasants depended, had been underway since the late seventeenth century. The net effect of these complex changes, including the emergence of commercialized agricultural production in some regions, was to sharpen distinctions of wealth and access to land among the non-noble agricultural classes. In regions like the Nord, so closely studied by Georges Lefebvre, an ever greater number, both absolutely and proportionately, of rural inhabitants could no longer rely upon an agricultural holding to provide secure foundations for the family economy. Under these conditions, women as well as men resorted to wage labor to round out their contribution to family survival. Much of this labor consisted of various forms of agricultural daylabor *(journaliers* and *journalières)* or, for women, of work as servants on wealthier farms. But pure agricultural work, in its manifold variety, could no longer support the growing, and sometimes excessive, rural population.[17]

Throughout the eighteenth century, the tentacles of merchant's capital sank deeper and deeper into the residually seigneurial countryside, binding country and city ever closer together. The results for women varied dramatically, but by the 1760s, it would no longer be possible to draw a sharp line between urban and rural experience. In the still largely isolated Auvergne, for example, holdings that could no longer support a family independently and provide for the dues and taxes it owed required an infusion of cash or, at the very least, additional means of support for some of the family members. Auvergnat men took to the roads to seek work, venturing as far as Paris or northern Spain. Their women remained at home and managed the family holding, in the process taking on most of the agricultural labor traditionally designated as male. The work of the wives of seamen, as in Nantes, held family members and property together during their husbands' long absences. More commonly, women were the first to leave agricultural labor or even the family holding in order to supplement its resources. The growth and transformation of the textile industry, especially the introduction of new fabrics such as cotton and new technology, required the growing participation of nonguild labor. Such labor was entirely consistent with women's long-standing roles as spinners, and many continued to perform piecework in their own homes for pitiful sums. Others, as in Normandy, sought the factories of cities like Rouen and towns like Elbeuf. Sometimes they went as part of a family migration, sometimes on their own.[18]

The intensive commercialization of agriculture, especially viticulture, in the regions around Bordeaux and the remarkable growth of overseas commerce in the city itself combined to produce a soaring growth of the urban population, to which women of the adjacent regions contributed steadily. Commonly migrating as servants, women also went to a wide variety of other urban occupations, in particular those associated with the clothing and food trades. Many ended up as prostitutes; others accumulated sufficient dowries to marry and frequently remained in town as the wives of artisans or shopkeepers. In the 1780s, the *Journal de Guyenne* regularly carried advertisements for positions available and positions sought. Thus, one widow, forty-five years of age, "knowing how to read, write, sew, and iron laundry," sought a job as a governess; another wished to sell wine retail either from her house or from that of the proprietor. And a *modiste* sought to employ a *"demoiselle* who knows how to work in fashion and to whom wages in proportion to her talents would be offered."[19] Cissie Fairchilds has found comparable advertisements for servants in the "Affiches et annonces de Toulouse" in the same period. Nantes, for which Jacques Depauw has found evidence of a steady rise in illegitimate births, and which also experienced the dynamic impact of Atlantic trade, experienced the growth of a working female population, much of it unmarried.[20]

The examples could be multiplied, but, however varied the specific regional patterns, the growth of a female wage-labor force throughout the eighteenth century remains beyond dispute, as does the

importance of the rural roots of urban female employment. The case
of servants in general remains striking. Not merely did the growth of
the urban bourgeoisie create a demand for more urban servants,
perhaps especially the *bonne-à-tout-faire,* but changes in the payment of
servants (wages were increasingly paid rather than noted as due), the
rising cost of male servants, and the growth of urban work for men
combined to promote what we might call the "feminization" of
domestic service. Sometime during the 1760s, it is possible to discern
the outlines of that nineteenth-century experience of domestic service
as a way station for young women between their rural roots and their
urban adulthood. The same period witnessed something of a decline in
the notion of the servant as a member of a patriarchal family and a
rising attempt to define and implement contractual relations between
masters and servants.[21]

The influx of single women into the cities has frequently been held
responsible, albeit with a range of explanations, for the rise in
illegitimate births that characterized the eighteenth century. For
whatever reasons, single women were at risk in the eighteenth-
century urban market; but the coercive bedding of servant girls,
however common, cannot alone account for abandoned children. It is
difficult to apprehend statistically, but the abandonment of children
by married, working parents remains indisputable. And this abandonment itself surely reflected new attitudes towards work and its fruits.
We are glimpsing, in this practice, the beginnings of that dramatic and
precocious control of fertility that would characterize nineteenth-
century France. The link between child rearing and women's work
emerges sharply from the consideration of wet-nursing. Whatever
were taken to be the sins of luxury-seeking, irresponsible, upper-class
women with respect to nursing their own offspring, the most
numerically significant employers of wet nurses were working, urban
mothers. Their labor was necessary to the family economy, and their
occupations did not permit the casual combination of formal work and
domestic responsibilities. Even when married and working for their
families, urban women were increasingly tied to forms of work that
structured the use of their time, rather than fitting into the interstices
of their lives. The same economic growth that provided them with,
and made them dependent upon, such work threw a web around their
rural sisters, who turned to mercenary wet-nursing to supplement
faltering rural family economies.[22]

Throughout the century, the burgeoning textile industry proved a
principal employer of women. In addition to home work and proto-
industrial employment as members of families, women served the
emerging textile factories in considerable numbers. And where unemployed single women threatened to become a charge on public

expenses, convents as well as government and charitable agencies created factory-like employment for them in such forms as the *ateliers de charité*.[23] The growth of the fashion industry provided employment for as many as thirty seamstresses in one place—Rose Bertin's famous dressmaking establishment—and was beginning to provide opportunities for them as shopgirls in fashionable boutiques. The links between such activities and the larger network of the world of fashion are legion, including various levels of prostitution, acting, dancing, modeling for artists, and selling favors with flowers. Sébastien Mercier and Restif de La Bretonne may have overdrawn their pictures of the intertwining of luxury and female sexuality, but they were not entirely wrong. The urban economy was indeed frought with danger for women.[24] But it also offered unprecedented opportunity. Doubtless, few women matched the independent economic success of a Rose Bertin. Even where women, because they were single or widowed, might retain control of their earnings, they normally earned so much less than men that significant economic advancement was precluded. Servants could amass dowries only because their jobs, whatever the hazards, provided lodging and food. Other women increasingly had to provide for themselves. But the city at least offered precarious possibilities that the country did not, for in the cities women could find furnished rooms, lodging houses, and networks of other women, not to mention shops and taverns with prepared food. Women could, in short, live alone and struggle to survive.[25]

The most portentous economic and social changes of the eighteenth century directly marked the working lives of women. For the vast majority of women, their membership in a family economy and the prescribed roles of the dominant gender system continued to govern the work to which they would have access or be obliged to perform, as well as their independent control of the fruits of that labor. Expediency, however, modified these governing principles in any individual case. During the late eighteenth century, women could be found in almost any kind of work, including in such male preserves as the mines and the precarious makeshift activities of scavenging and crime.[26]

As the contours of capitalist France took clear shape during the revolutionary decade, discernible guidelines emerged for the appropriate relation of women to work in a new society. At the lowest social levels, women would continue to work, when and where they could, for the makeshift family economies that would characterize the urban and rural worlds first of the laboring poor and then of the emerging proletariat. At the upper levels of society, women would be discouraged from participation in the extradomestic world of work. Many bourgeoises would work with their husbands in family enterprises ranging from crafts, to shops, to restaurants, to full-scale businesses (we know that in the Nord, at least, women would manage factories); but all of these activities remained closely tied to family life and can be interpreted as an extension of women's role within the domestic economy. As the professions took shape, they would exclude women. The law had always done so; but medicine, which took longer to develop a homogeneous organization, would gradually lop off such female preserves as midwifery, even though the midwives had eagerly pursued their own professionalization throughout the eighteenth century. Education remained a special case, much complicated by the role of the religious orders.[27]

In important respects, the social, economic, and political changes of the eighteenth century resulted not from the experience of the masses of laboring women, which remained governed as much by expediency as by principle, but from the experience of upper-class women. As early as the late seventeenth century, Mme de Maintenon and Fénelon had proposed a new work ethic for the women of the lesser nobility. Their prescriptions had been developed in reaction to the excesses of the *précieuses,* who promoted a mixture of feminism, fashionable gallantry, female learning, luxury, and social mobility. In contrast, Maintenon and Fénelon emphasized modesty, frugality, devotion, domesticity, and, yes, industry. Their vision of the appropriate female role meshed well with older notions of women's role in a family economy, but it broke ground in identifying work and self-conscious domesticity as fitting for upper-class women.[28] The steady rise of luxury and fashionable life throughout the eighteenth century discouraged the general adoption of their program, but the growing sense of a society gone wrong, especially as evinced in the irresponsible behavior of wealthy women, alarmed many.

In the wake of the Revolution, and with the emergence of a unified dominant class of urban and rural capitalist notables, the fears of license and unruly luxury merged with older notions of domestic order to produce a transformed model of domestic economy. This model, like the prototype of Maintenon and Fénelon, emphasized duty and work for women as wives and mothers of families. Buttressed by a capitalist economy and a systematic, bourgeois political economy, it unequivocally identified the domestic sphere as female. In this respect, the new domestic economy proffered a coherent model of women's work still governed by family needs (the paternalism of the *Code Napoléon*) and a dominant gender system, but it was newly recast as a universal model of appropriate female social contribution to which bourgeoises and noblewomen alike could adhere.[29] The model could also be taken to describe the time-honored practices of women in family economies firmly based in artisanal or peasant property and, in fact, owed much to them. In essence, it simply linked women's work to absolute property and male individualism; but in the process, it organized the tremendous variety of women's tasks and contributions under a generalized representation of female identity to which, with the gradual extension of industrialization, increasing numbers of French women could be invited to identify.

NOTES

1. Jean-Marie Gouesse, "Parenté, famille et mariage en Normandie aux XVIIe et XVIIIe siècles. Présentation d'une source et d'une enquête," *Annales: économies, sociétés, civilisations* 27, nos. 4-5, (July-Oct. 1972):1139-1154; François Lebrun, *La Vie conjugale sous l'ancien régime* (Paris: Armand Colin, 1975), esp. pp. 78-84; Yves Castan, *Honnêteté et relations sociales en Languedoc (1750-1780)* (Paris: Plon, 1974), esp. pp. 162-207.

2. Michel Vovelle, "Le tournant des mentalités en France 1750-1789: la 'sensibilité' pré-révolutionnaire," *Social History* 5 (May 1977):605-630.

3. Ernest Labrousse et al., *Histoire économique et sociale de la France*, vol. 2, *Des Derniers Temps de l'âge seigneurial aux préludes de l'âge industriel (1660-1789)* (Paris: Presses universitaires de France, 1970), pp. 23-84; Jean Meuvret, "Les crises de subsistance et la démographie de la France d'ancien régime," in his *Etudes d'histoire économique* (Paris: Armand Colin, 1971), pp. 271-281.

4. Among many, see Victor Riqueti, marquis de Mirabeau, *L'Ami des hommes* (Avignon: n.p., 1756); Chevalier de Cerfvol, *Mémoire sur la population dans lequel on indique le moyen de la rétablir & de se procurer un corps militaire toujours subsistant & peuplant* (London: n.p., 1768; Paris: EDHIS, 1973); Goyon de La Plombanie, *L'Homme en société ou nouvelles vues politiques et économiques pour porter la population au plus haut degré en France,* 2 vols. (Amsterdam: Marc Michel Rey, 1763; Paris: EDHIS, 1970); Edgar Faure, *La Disgrâce de Turgot* (Paris: Gallimard, 1961); Labrousse et al., p. 73; Roland Mousnier, *The Institutions of France under the Absolute Monarchy 1598-1789: Society and the State,* translated by Brian Pierce (Chicago: University of Chicago Press, 1979), pp. 472-473. The edict of August 1776, issued after Turgot's departure, modified but did not rescind his reform.

5. Labrousse et al., p. 607. For a rough estimate of female members of religious orders, see Léon Abensour, *La Femme et le féminisme avant la révolution* (1923, Geneva: Slatkine, 1977), pp. 263-264.

6. Louis Sébastien Mercier, *Tableau de Paris,* 8 vols. (Amsterdam: n.p., 1783); Nicolas Edmé Restif de La Bretonne, *Les Nuits de Paris* (Paris: Aux trois compagnons, 1947), or idem, *Le Paysan perverti* (Lausanne: Editions L'Age d'Homme, 1977); Jean Pierre Gutton, *La Société et les pauvres* (Paris: Editions des Belles Lettres, 1971): esp. pp. 438-466, and idem, *L'Etat et la mendicité dans la première moitié du XVIIIe siècle* (Lyon: Centre d'études foreziennes, 1973): esp. pp. 142-155; Shelby T. McCloy, "Charity Workshops for Women, Paris, 1790-1795," *Social Service Review* 11 (1937):274-284; "Bureaux et ateliers de charité," *Oeuvres de Turgot et documents le concernant,* edited by Gustave Schelle, vol. 3 (Paris: Presses universitaires de France, 1919; Darmstadt: Blaschke & Ducke GmbH, 1972); Camille Bloch, *L'Assistance et l'état en France à la veille de la révolution* (Paris: Librairie Alphonse Picard & Fils, 1980).

7. Olwen Hufton, "Women and the Family Economy in Eighteenth-Century France," *French Historical Studies* 9, no. 1 (Spring 1975):1-22; Restif de La Bretonne, *La Vie de mon père* (Paris: Editions Garnier, 1970). For excellent

general overviews, see Martine Segalen, *Mari et femme dans la société paysanne* (Paris: Flammarion, 1980); and Françoise Zonabend, *La Mémoire longue. Temps et histoire au village* (Paris: Presses universitaires de France, 1980). See also Jean-Louis Flandrin, *Families in Former Times,* translated by Richard Southern (Cambridge: Cambridge University Press, 1979): esp. pp. 85-118.

8. Flandrin, pp. 118-145; Abensour, pp. 238-249; James Traer, *Marriage and the Family in Eighteenth-Century France* (Ithaca: Cornell University Press, 1980). See also Gustave Fagniez, *La Femme et la société française dans la première moitié du dix-septième siècle* (Paris: Librairie universitaire J. Gamber, 1929), esp. pp. 135-203.

9. Gouesse, pp. 1146-1147; Segalen, pp. 23, 30; James L. Lehning, *The Peasants of Marhles* (Chapel Hill: University of North Carolina Press, 1980); Georges Lefebvre, *Les Paysans du nord pendant la révolution française* (Paris: Armand Colin, 1972), p. 277.

10. Natalie Zemon Davis, "Women in the 'Arts mécaniques' of Sixteenth-Century Lyon," *Mélanges Richard Gascon* (Lyon: Presses universitaires de Lyon, 1979).

11. Davis, "'Arts mécaniques.'" Archives départementales de la Gironde, C 66, contains a series of requests mainly from 1774-1775, and C 84 contains a request from Veuve Gougère, *Boulangère,* February 1776. See also Maurice Garden, *Lyon et les Lyonnais au XVIIIe siècle* (Paris: Editions des Belles Lettres, 1970), pp. 275-353; Emile Coornaert, *Les Corporations en France avant 1789,* 2d ed. (Paris: Editions ouvrières, 1968); pp. 184, 190, 206; Madeleine Guilbert and Viviane Isambert-Jamati, *Travail féminin et travail à domicile: Enquête sur le travail à domicile de la confection féminine dans la région parisienne* (Paris: Centre national de recherches scientifiques, 1956), pp. 9-11; Mary Durham Johnson, "Old Wine in New Bottles: The Institutional Changes for Women of the People during the French Revolution," in *Women, War and Revolution,* edited by Carol R. Berkin and Clara M. Lovett (New York: Holmes & Meier, 1980), p. 108.

12. Abensour, pp. 184-191; Coornaert, *Corporations,* and idem, *Les Compagnon-nages en France du moyen âge à nos jours* (Paris: Editions ouvrières, 1966), pp. 178-179.

13. Abensour, p. 189.

14. Johnson, pp. 109-110; Jeffrey Kaplow, *The Names of Kings. The Parisian Laboring Poor in the Eignteenth Century* (New York: Basic Books, 1972), esp. pp. 55-65. On the culture of the marketplace, see A. P. Moore, *The Genre Poissard and the French Stage in the Eighteenth Century* (New York: The Institute of French Studies, Columbia University, 1935). See also Jean Martineau, *Les Halles de Paris des origines à 1789* (Paris: Editions Montchrestien, 1960), esp. pp. 246-248.

15. Abensour, pp. 184-185. On the reaction to Turgot's edicts, see *Histoire générale de Paris: les métiers et corporations de la ville de Paris,* edited by René de Lespinasse and François Bonnardot (Paris: Imprimerie nationale, 1879), vol. 3, pp. 1-34. On male attitudes toward women's participation in corporations, see *Doléances des maîtres-ouvriers fabricants en étoffes d'or, d'argent et de soie de la ville de Lyon adressées au roi et à la nation assemblée,* edited by Fernand Rude (Lyon: Editions Fédérop, 1976), pp. 36-39.

16. Johnson, "Old Wine"; Darline Gay Levy and Harriet B. Applewhite, "Women of the Popular Classes in Revolutionary Paris, 1789-1795," in Berkin and Lovett, pp. 9-36; George Rudé, *The Crowd in the French Revolution* (Oxford: Oxford University Press, 1959); Olwen Hufton, "Women in Revolution, 1789-1796," *Past and Present* 53 (1971):90-108.

17. Olwen Hufton, *The Poor in Eighteenth-Century France* (Oxford: Oxford University Press, 1974), esp. pp. 25-68; Lefebvre, pp. 277-298; Labrousse et al., pp. 487-497.

18. Hufton, *The Poor,* pp. 69-127; Nicole Castan, "La criminalité familiale

dans le ressort du parlement de Toulouse (1690-1730)," in A. Abiateci, et al., *Crimes et criminalité en France sous l'ancien régime (17e-18e siècles)* (Paris: Armand Colin, 1971), p. 95; Gouesse, p. 1148; Jeffrey Kaplow, *Elbeuf during the Revolutionary Period: History and Social Structure* (Baltimore: Johns Hopkins University Press, 1964), pp. 52-99; F. Mendels, "Proto-Industrialization: The First Phase of Industrialization," *Journal of Economic History* 32, no. 1 (March-June 1972):241-261.

19. *Journal de Guyenne*, no. 22 (1787), 86, 87, and no. 25 (1787), 101.

20. Cissie Fairchilds, "Masters and Servants in Eighteenth-Century Toulouse," *Journal of Social History* 12, no. 3 (Spring 1979):368-393, and her *Domestic Enemies: Servants and Their Masters in Old Regime France* (Baltimore: Johns Hopkins University Press, 1984); Jacques Depauw, "Amour illégitime et société à Nantes au XVIIIe siècle," *Annales: économies, sociétés, civilisations* 27, nos. 4-5 (July-Oct. 1972):115-182.

21. Fairchilds, "Masters and Servants." See also Achille Guillaume Le Bègue de Presle, *L'Economie rurale et civile, ou moyens les plus économiques d'administrer et de faire valoir ses biens de campagne et de ville* (Paris: Buisson, 1789), vol. 1, pp. 97-109, on the appropriate contractual relations between masters and mistresses and their servants. Madame Duplessy, corresponding with her newly married daughter, similarly offers advice on dealing with servants as employees (Bibliothèque de la ville de Bordeaux, MS. 1201, letters for the autumn of 1768).

22. See, among many, Claude Delasselle, "Les Enfants abandonnés à Paris au XVIIIe siècle," *Annales: économies, sociétés, civilisations* 30, no. 1, (Jan.-Feb. 1975):187-218; A. Lottin, "Naissances illégitimes et filles mères à Lille au XVIIIe siècle," *Revue d'Histoire Moderne et Contemporaine* 17 (1970):278-322; François Lebrun, "Naissances illégitimes et abandons d'enfants en Anjou au XVIIIe siècle," *Annales: économies, sociétés, civilisations* 27, nos. 4-5 (July-Oct. 1972):1183-1189; Cissie Fairchilds, "Female Sexual Attitudes and the Rise of Illegitimacy: A Case Study," *Journal of Interdisciplinary History* 8 (1978):627-667; George D. Sussman, "The Wet-nursing Business in Nineteenth-Century France," *French Historical Studies* 9, no. 2 (Fall 1975):304-328, esp. 306-308. For an example of a working woman of the artisan class who sent her children to be wet-nursed, see the account of the mother of Pierre Samuel Du Pont de Nemours in *The Memoirs of P. S. Du Pont de Nemours Addressed to His Children*, edited and translated by Elizabeth Fox-Genovese (Wilmington: Scholarly Resources, 1984).

23. See note 6 above and Yvonne Forado-Cuneo, "Les Ateliers de charité de Paris pendant la révolution française 1789-1791," *La Révolution Française*, 86 (1933):317-342, and 87 (1934):29-123.

24. On Rose Bertin, see Abensour, p. 184, and innumerable contemporaneous memoirs such as Henriette Louise, baronne d'Oberkirch, *Mémoires de la baronne d'Oberkirch sur la cour de Louis XVI et la société française avant 1789*, edited by Suzanne Burkard (Paris: Mercure de France, 1970).

25. Roderick Phillips, "Women's Emancipation, the Family and Social Change in Eighteenth-Century France," *Journal of Social History* 12, no. 4 (Summer 1979):553-568.

26. Hufton, *The Poor*; Porphyre Petrovitch, "Recherches sur la criminalité à Paris dans la seconde moitié du XVIII siècle," in Abiateci et al., *Crimes et criminalité*, pp. 187-261; Arlette Farge, *Le Vol d'aliments à Paris au XVIIIe siècle* (Paris: Plon, 1974), esp. pp. 62-69, 116-122; "Filles publiques," Archives municipales de Bordeaux, FF 75.

27. Abensour, pp. 215-221, on the training of midwives and the competitive response of the surgeons; Madame Coutanceau, *Eléments de l'art d'accoucher en faveur des élèves sages-femmes de la généralité de Guyenne* (Bordeaux: M. Racle, 1784); *Une Femme d'affaires au XVIIIe siècle. La Correspondance de madame de Maraise, collaboratrice d'Oberkampf*, edited by Serge Chassagne (Paris: Privat, 1981). For women and education, see the essay by Samia I. Spencer in this volume.

28. Carolyn Lougee, *Le Paradis des Femmes: Women, Salons, and Social Stratification in Seventeenth-Century France* (Princeton: Princeton University Press, 1976), pp. 173-208; J. C. Barnard, *Fénelon on Education* (Cambridge: Cambridge University Press, 1966).

29. Elizabeth Fox-Genovese and Eugene D. Genovese, "The Ideological Bases of Domestic Economy," in *Fruits of Merchant Capital* (New York: Oxford University Press, 1983); Barbara Corrado Pope, "Revolution and Retreat: Upper-Class French Women after 1789," in Berkin and Lovett, *Women, War and Revolution*, pp. 215-236; Margaret H. Darrow, "French Noblewomen and the New Domesticity, 1750-1850," *Feminist Studies* 5, no. 1, (Spring 1979):41-65; Claire de Rémusat, *Essai sur l'éducation des femmes* (Paris: L'Advocat, 1824); Madame Gacon-Dufour, *Manuel de la ménagère à la ville et à la campagne et de la femme de basse-cour* (Paris: Buisson, 1805), and idem, *Manuel complet de la maîtresse de maison et de la parfaite ménagère* (Paris: Roret, 1826).

✨ Ruth Graham

Women versus Clergy,
Women pro Clergy

AT THE BEGINNING of the eighteenth century, men dominated religious life in France; at the end of the century, women were by
far the greater number of the faithful.[1] This feminization of religious
life can be traced not only to events in the Revolution but also to a
resolution of certain conflicts between women and the clergy. To the
dignitaries of the Church, women who meddled in religion during the
eighteenth century were a danger to orthodoxy and to ecclesiastical
discipline. Some noblewomen espoused heretical doctrines; some
women from good families prophesied the downfall of the hierarchy;
and some plebeian women writhed in religious ecstacy. Women clung
to religious traditions whose pagan origins disturbed the enlightened
clergy. Attached to their *bons curés* during the Revolution, some women
resorted to violence to defend the nonjuring priests who had consecrated their existence. After the period of dechristianization, women
flocked to reopen the churches in a Catholic resurgence. It was
women, rather than men, who remained religious in France.

The French hierarchy during the eighteenth century, whether they
owed their position to intrigue at the court of Versailles or they urged
the reforms of the Christian Enlightenment, condemned the "female
theologians" of the upper classes and the "ignorant fanatics" among
plebeian women. The century opened with two shocking scenes that
produced a great outcry. In 1709, Louis XIV, prompted by his religious
advisers, sent two hundred archers to disperse the aging nuns at the
convent of Port-Royal des Champs; and two years later, fearing that
Port-Royal might become a shrine, the king ordered the bodies of the
nuns buried there to be hurled into a common grave.[2] What crime had
these religious women committed? More than a century before, mère
Angélique, not yet thirteen years old and a daughter of the prominent
noble family of Arnauld affiliated with the Parlement of Paris, had
become abbess of Port-Royal. Religious life had been imposed on her,
for she had resisted entering the convent; but after Angélique was
converted to God's purpose, she reorganized the convent according to

the austere rules of Saint Benedict. She enclosed the convent from the outside world, even refusing to receive her father's visit except in a small parlor. As a disciple of the Jansenists, she thought that salvation was possible for only the few who were worthy of God's grace. The mystical nature of the nuns' prayers at Port-Royal came under suspicion. The convent attracted certain *solitaires* to the vicinity to contemplate in solitude God's will. Thus, Angélique made enemies of influential *abbés* and bishops, who perceived the danger to the more worldly church of the cardinal-ministers Richelieu and Mazarin and of the Society of Jesus.[3]

After the death of mère Angélique in 1661, the nuns of Port-Royal refused to sign a formulary that condemned Jansenist propositions as heretical. In 1679, the postulants and pensionaries were ordered expelled from Port-Royal, thus depriving the convent of future generations of nuns. And in 1703 when the aging nuns were asked to sign a formulary and again they refused, the king obtained the pope's permission to suppress the convent.[4]

The Jansenist influence on women did not end with the papal bull *Unigenitus* (1713), which condemned such tenets as salvation proceeded from grace alone and the right of Christians to urge institutional reforms of the Church. Although some bishops and theologians at first opposed the papal condemnation, they eventually bowed to monarchical and episcopal pressure. The resistance of the Jansenist *curés* held firmer in the face of harassment, which deprived some of them of their spiritual functions. The diocese of Paris became the center of religious agitation. Montesquieu noted that Jansenist nuns, in their various ecclesiastical orders, fueled the revolt against the papal bull.[5] A cult, largely but not exclusively of women, developed around the remains of a saint-like Jansenist deacon, François de Pâris, who died in 1727 after a life of chosen poverty and service to the poor. On the day of his burial in the cemetery of the church of Saint Médard, an elderly widow, who was an illiterate woodworker, was cured of paralysis as she approached his bier.

In November 1731, Anne Lefranc, an unmarried woman who suffered from many afflictions, came from her parish in Paris to the tomb of François de Pâris. She was distressed that her *curé* had been dismissed for his Jansenist beliefs. A few days after praying at the tomb, she reported her afflictions cured. This miracle was interpreted by those assembled at the tomb as God's acknowledgment of the truth for which the Jansenists suffered. When the anti-Jansenist archbishop of Paris investigated the miracle, he pronounced Anne Lefranc to be a simple, ignorant girl whose cure was a deception. Protests arose because she had never been allowed to testify on her own behalf. At the advice of the lawyers who supported the Jansenist clergy, Anne Lefranc brought suit against the archbishop. "It is shocking and appalling," wrote the archbishop of Paris to the royal minister, cardinal de Fleury, "that a man of my character and occupying a position of such honor should be exposed to a legal proceeding involving a wretched woman from the dregs of society."[6]

In defiance of the archbishop's order forbidding further observances at the cemetery of Saint Médard, more worshippers surrounded the tomb of François de Pâris. Fashionable people mixed with the very poor; the princesse de Conti, suffering from blindness, appeared at the cemetery. Old women who lived in the parish were hired to say novenas. Convulsions occurred. Aimée Pivert, perhaps an epileptic, experienced spasms when she came to Saint Médard in July 1731; early in August, she went away cured. In mid-August, three women at Saint Médard recovered partially from ailments after experiencing convulsions. More convulsions followed.[7]

In January 1732, the cardinal-minister ordered the police to arrest some convulsionaries at Saint Médard and have them examined by doctors at the Bastille. On January 29, the police closed the cemetery. Unwittingly, their action transformed what happened at the tomb at Saint Médard into a well-organized, popular cult. The convulsionaries, carrying relics of the deacon Pâris, dispersed to hold clandestine meetings in private homes and convents, particularly in the female congregations of Sainte Agathe, the Sisters of the Visitation, the Ursulines, and the Sisters of Sainte Marthe.[8] These conventicles of brothers and sisters, as they were called, met several times a week. The convulsionaries endured physical punishment, sometimes inflicted by *secouristes*, who aided their suffering for Jesus Christ.

According to Robert Kreiser, a modern authority on the convulsionaries, it is not certain how many people experienced these convulsions. One report for the period August 1731 to December 1732 claimed there were 270 convulsionaries in Paris alone, of whom 200 were 'women; other reports give higher figures, with three-fourths of the convulsionaries being women, and higher figures were given to include the convulsionaries in the provinces.[9] The majority of the convulsionaries were of relatively obscure origin, but they were respectably poor and not the dregs of society. Whatever their social rank, they were equals in religion, for, in contrast to the French Church, women participated in the rituals. Jansenist priests were among the brothers of the conventicles. Many years later, the constitutional bishop Grégoire, who admired Jansenist theology but not its popular manifestations, complained that these "mad women" spoke too familiarly to the clergy among them and dared to impose penitences on the priests who knelt before them.[10]

Despite police harassment and the desertion of its more respectable supporters, the cult survived the passing of the decade. The spiritual legacy of Jansenism can be traced throughout the century. In 1770, a Jansenist, Mlle Maillard, wrote to the king to help her friend, Mlle Mote, who claimed she was being mistreated by Jesuits (their order had been recently suppressed in France). "Give us good pastors to purify our souls and bring us, if possible, to the communion table," Mlle Maillard wrote, asking the king to deliver the poor from the persecution of the police, for "whoever persecutes the poor, persecutes Jesus Christ."[11]

Jansenist women were not the only ones to experience religious exaltation. The Visitandines were devoted to the cult of the Sacré-Coeur, founded by one of their members who died in 1690 and then promoted by the Jesuits. Marguerite-Marie Alacoque, while in prayer, saw the Savior, who showed her his heart and said that it was exhausted from his love; he told her to bleed herself when her grief became too heavy to be endured. During the Revolution, the emblem of the Sacré-Coeur became the symbol of Catholic resistance in western France. So did the grave of Jeanne Le Royer, a mystic nun called Sister Nativity who had been expelled from her convent at Fougères in September 1792 to die a fugitive.[12]

That women visionaries elected to suffer for Jesus Christ and promote cults of victims was noted after the end of the eighteenth century by Bishop Grégoire, who did not approve of women's cults. "The devotion of women is often an affair of faction," he wrote. "This devotion holds more to the heart while that of men (holds) to the mind. Men are directed to conviction by reason; women to persuasion by sentiment."[13] Grégoire attributed to women's exquisite sensibilities the fanaticism that turned them into convulsionaries. He then described how, in Lorraine, Jacqueline-Aimée Brohan, daughter of an official, propagated a cult of women who would offer themselves as victims for the triumph of the will of God. Previously, Mlle Brohan had worldly ambitions; she had written articles in journals and novels, and one of them, published in 1755, was entitled *Amans philosophes.* After her life was saved by a miracle, Brohan retired from the world in penitence for having written novels. Writing only devotional works, she predicted in 1774 that God would decimate the earth and choose a new people to do his will. She urged that France recognize twelve female victims who would endure continuous physical punishment so that France would be spared God's calamities, and she offered herself as first victim. The twelve victims, representing the twelve apostles, would start a new mission to propagate Christ's love for his mother, to recognize the fidelity of women to Christ during his mortal life and his passion, and (according to Grégoire) to humiliate the masculine sex, who abused its superiority because men were jealous of the zeal of the weaker sex.[14]

Another woman prophet, Suzette Labrousse, daughter of a noble family in Dordogne, predicted in 1779 that God would choose victims whose sufferings would cause the ecclesiastical hierarchy to be superceded by two great religious societies, one composed of men, the other of women. She also prophesied the devastation of France by brigands and the convocation of the Estates General in 1789. During the Revolution, news of her prophecies created a sensation, but they were dismissed as fanaticism by the enlightened abbé Claude Fauchet, soon to be the constitutional bishop at Bayeux.[15]

The duchess of Bourbon in 1789 made much of Labrousse's prophecies. Unlike Labrousse the duchess did not propagate a cult of victims but a mysticism similar to that of Mme Guyon at the beginning of the century, whose religion of the heart, divested of self-interest in heaven or hell, influenced Fénelon and caused his writings to be condemned by the Church. The Duchess of Bourbon, writing at the end of the century, shared with Mlles Labrousse and Brohan a religious feminism that was highly critical of the clergy. The duchess believed that Adam before his sin was both male and female and that only after his fall could he engender himself. Although the duchess asked God for good pastors, she doubted that the clergy held the keys to the kingdom of heaven; she did not believe in the efficacy of the sacraments, and she preferred to worship in a silent assembly of the faithful, rather than recognize the exterior signs of God's grace. She also doubted that the visible Church, with the pope as head, was the same that Jesus Christ wished to establish.[16]

These were women from privileged families whose mysticism was dangerous to orthodoxy. By and large, women in the eighteenth century clung to traditional religious practices. They also belonged to confraternities, which were laic associations devoted to a particular saint. In the Midi, women belonged to the confraternity of the Rosary, which was dedicated to the Virgin, who was believed to have healing powers and to be the protectress of pregnant women.[17] The festivals for village saints in the Midi allowed girls and boys to meet together in permissible courtship after they had been segregated throughout the year. Other confraternities in Provence channeled women's social life in the service of religion. The youngest brides each summer were chosen as "prioresses" by the confraternity of Sainte Marguerite; it was their responsibility to care for her altar in the churches.[18]

Throughout France, female saints had their special following among women. Sainte Geneviève, patroness of Paris, was the saint to whom all Paris prayed to avert diasters, the saint venerated by female artisans, and the saint to whom the market women of Paris lit a candle at Easter in 1789 to ensure the success of the coming meeting of the Estates General. No wonder Sainte Geneviève had such powers for market women! In the fifth century, during a famine, she had distributed loaves of bread to the people. In times of food shortages in eighteenth-century Paris, processions leading from her church to the cathedral of Notre Dame prayed for her intercession.[19]

In the great ceremonial processions, women had only a secondary role, if any at all; but in the countryside, pilgrimages of the male and female laity to holy places beyond the villages were reputed to be miraculous long before Christianity. Because such pilgrimages rivaled church ceremonies, they were barely tolerated by the clergy and those enlightened priests who deplored the persistent paganism in rural France. Moreover, the clergy who accompanied these processions feared that anything could happen on those long country outings.[20]

Superstitious women in the villages could make trouble for the priest if he displeased them. Witness their treatment in 1759 of a village chaplain in the diocese of Gap who had summoned from the altar a *monitoire* to hear testimony from the parish concerning a recent crime. The women in church screamed and attacked him at the altar, ripping his soutane and beating him with broken bits of the processional crosses. Perhaps they had reasons of their own, but it was thought that the women feared that the *monitoire* would bring hail and thunderstorms to ruin the harvest.[21]

No less a danger to the reformers among the clergy were the women in high places who exerted their influence on hierarchical appointments. Women at Versailles, such as Mme de Maintenon at the beginning of the century and the less respectable Mme du Barry towards the end, could see that a certain younger son of a noble family became an *abbé* or a bishop. The ecclesiastical reformers' aversion toward women as influence peddlers became generalized; all women were considered a source of corruption in ecclesiastical matters. Grégoire perceived woman as temptress when he wrote of "the forbidden fruit toward which the daughters of Eve had always cast looks of greed." Yet he thought that European women owed to Christianity their relatively high position in society, as compared to that of Moslem women or of Jewish women living in eastern France. He denied the truth of the story that a medieval church council in France had debated if women had souls. In 1789, abbé Fauchet assigned to women as sinners a special chapter in his book *De la religion nationale,* in which he proposed workshops to rehabilitate prostitutes and laws to police kept women and to restrict actresses in the theatres.[22]

Perhaps more annoying than fanatical women to the clergy were the women in the towns who had no thought of religion but devoted themselves to their pleasures. Social changes in France during the second half of the eighteenth century had altered the thinking of women as well as men. For the well-being of those concerned, marriages occurred at a more advanced age, and some couples made efforts to limit the size of their families. Such limits on fertility were, of course, a sin. The Gallican Church took a firm stand on the sacred duties of marriage as one of the seven sacraments, and, in 1715, a church conference on marriage pronounced that women must perform their conjugal duties. In the 1770s and 1780s, a sermon on marriage preached by a *curé* of a small parish near Angers informed wives and husbands who prevented the natural effect of the conjugal act that they were guilty of an abomination. Furthermore, the *curé* warned that all conjugal acts were not permitted, that there were rules for moderation expressed by Saint Paul and Saint Augustine that restricted the pleasures of the flesh. In 1782, a *Catéchisme des gens mariés* by Father Féline attributed the limiting of births to the "excessive care shown by husbands for their wives," and he condemned this concern for what he called women's "excessive delicacy."[23] Guilty couples sometimes avoided the confessional, or else the wife went, claiming she was not the active partner in this sin. In the countryside, methods to control fertility could be brutal; a *curé* near Clermont reported that mothers of hungry families accused their men of demanding that their youngest babies die.[24]

The clergy, privileged to hear the secrets of family life, might have chased from the altars the transgressing husbands, leaving their good wives among the faithful. A *de facto* dechristianization of men is also explained by social historians as an alternative sociability, whereby men socialized with men at the bar near the church while women gossiped with each other after church services.[25]

The enlightened clergy in the latter part of the eighteenth century wished to improve female education so that mothers could teach their families the Christian virtues. In 1777, A.-H. Wandelaincourt, principal of the royal college at Verdun and later constitutional bishop at Langres, published his plan of instruction, which included that of girls. He wrote:

> The bad education of women produces more evil than that of men. . . . Women are unfortunately abandoned to themselves. All the cares are for the body; the spirit and heart enter for nothing in the lessons given them. . . . This lively imagination, this precocious spirit, these ingenuous ruses, these tender sentiments which Providence gave women will be bastardized and degenerate if we do not remedy them.[26]

He recommended instructing girls—in French, of course, and not in Latin—in religious history, morality, natural history, the code of laws, drawing, a little arithmetic, and the work of the hands. Wandelaincourt ruled out profane history, geography, and logic, which he thought girls hardly needed; but he must have changed his mind in 1782 when he wrote a book on logic intended for young ladies. As constitutional bishop, Wandelaincourt was later elected to the republican National Convention and served on its Committee for Public Instruction.

The clergy who welcomed the Revolution hailed the regeneration of women as patriots. No longer, said abbé Fauchet in 1790, were women distracted by the frivolous ornaments of slavery; French women had attained from liberty "the perfection of their sex, the simplicity of morals, the primitive graces of the ages of old."[27] The association Fauchet helped found, the Cercle Social des Amis de la Vérité, took the unusual step for that time of admitting women as members and even listening to women orators, such as Mme Palm d'Aelders. Unfortunately for Fauchet, when he became constitutional bishop for Calvados, the women in his diocese were not all patriots. In 1791, he denounced the two hundred drunken women who threw stones at the constitutional priest at Caen, nearly killing him at the altar.[28] After Revolutionary France had confiscated ecclesiastical property and reorganized the Gallican Church so that its ministers were salaried by the nation, many of the clergy refused to take an oath to the new constitution. Fauchet blamed the nonjuring priests for inciting women to violence by denying the efficacy of the sacraments administered by the constitutional clergy. Other constitutional bishops made similar complaints concerning what they called the ridiculous behavior of the weaker sex.[29] There is no doubt that many women, devoted to the nonjuring *curé* who had consecrated their existence and legitimated their children, reacted violently to the juring clergy as "schismatic intruders."

The behavior of some nuns hindered the pastoral missions of the constitutional bishops. Although perpetual vows had been abolished early in the Revolution, nuns could continue to live in community, and female congregations engaged in the work of charity and the education of girls were, for the time being, not suppressed. One young nun, who had left the convent to marry and become a mother, wrote in 1789 that nuns were often the innocent victims of their passions or their families; women who wished to remain in convents should stay there in peace, but those who were forced to enter would thank the National Assembly for their freedom. Post-revolutionary records show the sociocultural isolation of the nuns who left the convent. Compared to their male counterparts in regular orders, a much smaller percentage of nuns married, and most of them sought secular occupations. The Sisters of Charity, after female congregations were suppressed in August 1792, continued to work in Paris as individuals at the request of their republican section committee.[30]

But many of the women who directed convents were aristocrats aligned with the nonjuring and émigré bishops. The constitutional bishops were humiliated on their pastoral visits to these convents. In 1791, one convent begrudgingly opened the gates to Bishop Grégoire, telling him he was not the bishop of Jesus Christ but the bishop of the town hall and the local popular society. Thomas Lindet, constitutional bishop at Evreux, issued a special warning to the nuns in his diocese to shun theological disputes.[31]

The constitutional bishops who remained priests during the dechristianization of the Terror were no friendlier to the women who took advantage of new secularizing laws to rearrange their lives. The right of divorce was an affront to these republican bishops; and to Grégoire, it was even more heinous that of the 5,994 divorces reported within 27 months in Paris alone more than half of them had been initiated by women. Nor did Grégoire approve of the thousands of women who, in 1794, celebrated Robespierre's cult of the Supreme Being by marching in groups segregated according to their status in the family. Grégoire denounced, after the Terror, the goddesses of Reason as prostitutes. In Paris, these women were actresses from the Opera, adhering politically to the leaders of the Commune who campaigned relentlessly (and vainly) to eradicate both religion and prostitution.[32]

Women in the countryside were more hostile to dechristianization than women in the towns, perhaps because dechristianization went hand in hand with the economic Terror of enforcing the Maximum or price controls, which peasants did not favor. Michel Vovelle in his important study of religion and revolution describes the hostility of women to dechristianization in southeastern France and mentions inspirées, prophetesses who led demonstrations to reopen the churches. On the other hand, Grégoire's pastoral letter after the Terror revealed that women at Blois played their part in smashing the images of saints.[33]

It was not until the fall of Robespierre in Thermidor, July 1794, and the decree in February 1795 that separated Church and State that women succeeded in reopening the churches. The Annales de la religion, journal of the republican bishops, reported that the returning émigré clergy had captured the imaginations of the women in Lorraine, who financed their activities; and the journal advised these women, who had become in a metamorphosis doctors of theology, to stay at home and mind their families. Grégoire and his bishops set rigorous requirements for those who wished to receive the sacraments and attributed the success of the royalist priests to questionable religious practices, such as celebrating Easter in the open air with great crowds and distributing tickets guaranteed to heal the sick and to ensure safe childbirth.³⁴ Women who cared not for doctrinal niceties but were hungry for the sacraments—which, willingly or unwillingly, they had done without during the Terror—followed the dissident clergy.

Perhaps women were contrite for their revolutionary sins. A terrible food shortage occurred in 1795 after the price controls set by the Jacobins had been dismantled by the laissez-faire Thermidorians. The failure of the harvest in northern France caused an inflation of open-market prices that brought hunger even to middle-class families. Olwen Hufton, the historian of women of the poor in eighteenth-century France, found evidence in Calvados of women standing in line to have their dying babies baptized and of women who lined up before nonjuring priests to have their tongues scraped from the contaminating masses of the constitutional clergy.³⁵

Who were these women who ran back to the churches to receive the sacraments? The women who had rioted for bread in 1789 and again in 1795? Perhaps. Were they the very women who attended the Festivals of Reason or marched in processions for the cult of the Supreme Being? Unlikely but possible. Whoever they were, they were the women who created a resurgence of Catholicism after the Terror, while the men in some regions stayed away from the churches or, if they attended, neglected to take communion. The Catholic Church in France was no longer the same as in the ancien régime, nor would it ever be the same. The feminization of the body of the faithful had occurred. No longer could the church dignitaries scorn the meddling of women in religious matters, but no longer were women considered dangerous by the male hierarchy.

NOTES

1. Michel Vovelle, *Piété baroque et déchristianisation en Provence au XVIIIe siècle* (Paris: Plon, 1973), pp. 608-609; Bernard Plongeron, *Conscience religieuse en révolution* (Paris: A. & J. Picard, 1969), pp. 170-171; Olwen Hufton, "The French Church," p. 31, and Marc Venard, "Popular Religion in the Eighteenth Century," p. 150, in *Church and Society in Catholic Europe in the Eighteenth Century,* edited by William J. Callahan and David Higgs (Cambridge: Cambridge University Press, 1979).

2. Alexander Sedgwick, *Jansenism in Seventeenth-Century France* (Charlottesville: University Press of Virginia, 1977), p. 189; B. Robert Kreiser, *Miracles, Convulsions, and Ecclesiastical Politics in Early Eighteenth-Century Paris* (Princeton: Princeton University Press, 1978), p. 12.

3. "Abrégé de l'histoire de Port-Royal, seconde partie," in *Oeuvres de Jean Racine* (Paris: Imp. de Momes frères, 1812) vol. 4, pp. 189-258; Sedgwick, pp. 15-16. See *The Political Testament of Cardinal Richelieu,* translated by Henry Bertram Hill (Madison: The University of Wisconsin Press, 1968), pp. 69-70: "Since princes are expected to establish God's true church, they should be very thorough in banishing all false imitations of it, what are so dangerous to the

state. . . . Particularly this is the case in approaching women, since their sex is more given to transports of devotion which is, however, of so little depth that they are vulnerable to such stratagems as they depend less on real substance than upon cunning."

4. Sedgwick, p. 124. Henri-Baptiste Grégoire, *Les Ruines de Port-Royal en 1801* (Paris, n.d.), p. 516: "The nuns were asked to sign five propositions which were condemned in a large Latin book which they could not understand. They resisted. . . . Were these women accused of crimes? No, their house was a school of wisdom." (All translations, unless otherwise stated, are my own.)

5. Montesquieu's *Lettres persanes*, cited by Huguette Cohen, "Jansenism in Diderot's *La Religieuse*," *Studies in Eighteenth-Century Culture* (Madison: University of Wisconsin Press, 1982) vol. 11, p. 79; Sedgwick, pp. 190-191; Kreiser, pp. 14-22, 54, 67, 92; H.-B. Grégoire, *Histoire des sectes religieuses au XVIIIe siècle* (Paris, 1810, publ. 1828) vol. 2, pp. 127-128; Jeffrey Kaplow, *The Name of Kings. The Parisian Laboring Poor in the Eighteenth Century* (New York: Basic Books, 1972), pp. 122-123.

6. Kreiser, pp. 128, 136, 137. Note 144 cites the correspondence of (Archbishop) Vintimille to Fleury, August 5, 1731, Bibliothèque Mazarine, MS. 2357, pp. 465-466.

7. Kreiser, pp. 154-55, 174; Kaplow, p. 124.

8. Kreiser, pp. 250-251, nn. 21, 24, 25. Kreiser also cites testimony of female convulsionaries in Archives Nationales, X-1b, 9690.

9. Kreiser, p. 259, n. 47, cites an unsigned letter dated December 27, 1732, Bibliothèque de l'Arsenal, MS. 5784, fols. 16-17; also, *Lettre d'un docteur de Paris à un ecclésiastique de province concernant les "Nouvelles Ecclésiastiques,"* (1732) and [P.-S. Gourlin] *Recherche de la vérité ou lettres sur l'oeuvre des convulsions* (1733).

10. Grégoire, *Histoire des sectes religieuses,* vol. 2, pp. 130-132, 140, 157-158. Grégoire not only thought these women mad but also sexually aberrant. Kreiser, pp. 253-254, 262, writes that there is no proof that these convulsions substituted for sexual gratification, as the enemies of the convulsionaries claimed.

11. Quoted by Kaplow, pp. 125-126. Mlle Maillard also believed that a *pacte de famine* existed that caused grain to be thrown in the river so that poor people were reduced to great misery. On the survival of the convulsionaries' cult, see Grégoire, *Histoire des sectes religieuses,* vol. 2, pp. 157-158.

12. On Marguerite-Marie Alacoque's cult of the Sacré-Coeur, see Grégoire, *Histoire des sectes religieuses,* vol. 2, pp. 252-272. On Jeanne Le Royer, see Michel Lagrée, "Piété populaire et révolution en Bretagne," in *Voies nouvelles pour l'histoire de la révolution française* (Paris: Bibliothèque Nationale, 1978), p. 269.

13. Grégoire, *Histoire des sectes religieuses,* vol. 2, pp. 26-28.

14. Ibid., pp. 34-44. Among other works, he cites Mlle Brohan's *Réflexions édifiantes,* 2 vols. (Paris: 1791).

15. Ibid., pp. 46-48; Claude Fauchet, *Prophéties de Mlle de Labrousse* (Paris: Imp. de Bonnefoi, n.d.).

16. Grégoire, *Histoire des sectes religieuses,* vol. 2, pp. 72-85. Grégoire also wrote that, though the duchess was a princess of the blood, she wanted no social distinctions recognized, except that of virtues and talents. During the Revolution, she was in exile in Spain, where her work, *Correspondance entre madame de B . . . et M.R., sur leurs opinions religieuses,* was condemned by the Inquisition as obscene. Her other work is *Opuscules ou pensées d'une âme de foi sur la religion chrétienne pratiquée en esprit et en vérité.* On Madame Guyon, see Grégoire, *Histoire des sectes religieuses,* vol. 2, pp. 99-103.

17. Jean Queniart, *Les Hommes, l'église et Dieu dans la France du XVIIIe siècle* (Paris:

Hachette, 1978), pp. 192, 232; Hufton, "The French Church," p. 30; Timothy Tackett, *Priest and Parish in Eighteenth-Century France* (Princeton: Princeton University Press, 1977), pp. 194-196.

18. Lucienne Roubin, "Male Space and Female Space within the Provencal Community," in *Rural Society in France*. Selections from the *Annales: économies, sociétés, civilisations*, edited by Robert Forster and Orest Ranum, translated by Elborg Forster and Patricia M. Ranum (Baltimore: The Johns Hopkins University Press, 1977), pp. 168, 179.

19. Kaplow, p. 120; Steven L. Kaplan, "Religion, Subsistence, and Social Control: The Uses of Sainte Geneviève," *Eighteenth-Century Studies* 13, no. 2 (Winter 1979§1980):142-168; *Cahier des plaintes & doléances des dames de la halle & des marchés de Paris* . . . (Paris, 1789). This *cahier* was hostile to the bishops but not to the *curés*; see my article, "Loaves and Liberty: Women in the French Revolution," in *Becoming Visible. Women in European History*, edited by Renate Bridenthal and Claudia Koonz (Boston: Houghton Mifflin, 1977), p. 239.

20. Michel Vovelle, *Les Métamorphoses de la fête en Provence* (Paris: Aubier/Flammarion, 1976), p. 200; Queniart, pp. 188-189; Hufton, "The French Church," pp. 26-27; Tackett, pp. 199, 204-210; Venard, p. 153.

21. Tackett, pp. 212-213, n. 79.

22. Grégoire, *Histoire des sectes religieuses*, vol. 2, p. 24; idem, *Essai sur la régénération physique, morale et politique des juifs* (Metz: Deville, 1789), p. 157; idem, *L'Influence du christianisme sur la condition des femmes* (Paris, 1821), chapter 1 and p. 14; Claude Fauchet, *De la religion nationale* (Paris: Bailly, 1789), pp. 249-253, 260-261.

23. Queniart, pp. 136, 230-233; *Parole de Dieu et révolution*, edited by François Lebrun (Toulouse: E. Privat, 1979), pp. 74-77; Jean-Louis Flandrin, *Families in Former Times*, translated by Richard Southern (Cambridge: Cambridge University Press, 1979), pp. 236-239. André Burguière, "From Malthus to Max Weber: Belated Marriage and the Spirit of Enterprise," in *Family and Society*. Selections from the *Annales* . . . , edited and translated by Forster and Ranum (Baltimore: The Johns Hopkins University Press, 1976), pp. 239-243, offers Pierre Chaunu's explanation that Jansenists in the eighteenth century were antisacramental and believed that sexuality in marriage was a matter of individual morality.

24. Olwen Hufton, "Women in Revolution, 1789-1796," in *French Society and Revolution*, edited by Douglas Johnson (Cambridge: Cambridge University Press, 1976), p. 151.

25. Vovelle, *Piété baroque*, p. 609, mentions the hypothesis of E. Leroy-Ladurie. Hufton, "The French Church," p. 30, attributes the theory of alternative sociability to Maurice Agulhon in his study of Provence.

26. A.-H. Wandelaincourt, *Plan d'éducation publique* (Paris: Durand, 1777), pp. 137-139, 145.

27. C. Fauchet, *Eloge civique de Benjamin Franklin* . . . *au nom de la commune de Paris*. . . (Paris: J. R. Lerin, 1790), pp. 14-15. *La Bouche de Fer*, vol. 1, nos. 13, 20, 30 (Paris: Le Cercle social, November-December 1790):198, 306-315, 466; vol. 2, no. 23 (February 1791):356.

28. C. Fauchet, *Réplique* . . . *aux objections faites contre son opinion sur les prêtres non-assermentés* (Paris: Imprimerie nationale, 1791), pp. 4-5.

29. H.-B. Grégoire, *Lettre pastorale* (Blois, Paris: Imp. de J.-P.-J. Masson, 1791), pp. 16-17; L.-F. Lalande, *Défense et justification de la lettre pastorale de Luc-François Lalande, évêque du département de la Meurthe* (Nancy: Imprimerie de Vve Bacroi, 1791), p. 90.

30. *Motions addressées à l'Assemblée Nationale en faveur du sexe*, (Paris: chez l'auteur,

rue des Poitevins, no. 20, 1789), pp. 7-9. C. Langlois and T.-J.-A. Le Goff, "Jalons pour une sociologie des prêtres mariés," in *Voies nouvelles* pp. 287, 302; Jean Boussoulade, "Soeurs de charité et comités de bienfaisance des faubourgs Saint-Marcel et Saint-Antoine (septembre 1793-mai 1794)," *Annales Historiques de la Révolution Française* 42 (April 1970):350-356.

31. For the nuns' opposition to constitutional bishops, see A. Gazier, *Etudes sur l'histoire religieuse de la révolution française* (Paris: Armand Colin, 1887), p. 60; V. Dubaret, "Sanadon, évêque constitutionnel des Basses-Pyrénées," *Revue de Béarn et du Pays Basque* (Pau, 1905):529-547; Marc de Seyssel, "Jean-Baptiste Royer, évêque constitutionnel de l'Ain, puis métropolitain de Paris," *Le Bugey* (Belley, 1911) pp. 17, 21-22; R.-T. Lindet, *Lettre aux religieuses des monastères de son diocèse* (Evreux: Ancelle, 1791).

32. Grégoire, *Histoire des sectes religieuses,* vol. 1, pp. 180, 188. See my article, "The Challenge of Secularization to the Sacraments under the First French Republic," *The Catholic Historical Review* 68, no. 1 (1982):13-27.

33. Hufton, "Women in Revolution," pp. 164-165; Michel Vovelle, *Religion et révolution* (Paris: Hachette, 1976), pp. 273-284; idem., *Métamorphoses de la fête,* pp. 202-206; H.-B. Grégoire, *Lettre pastorale . . . 22 ventôse, l'an III* (Blois, Paris: Maradan, 1795), pp. 4-5.

34. *Annales de la religion,* vol. 1 (Paris: Imp.-Librairie chrétienne, 1795), no. 1 (May 2, 1795), p. 23. *Grégoire et l'église constitutionnelle d'Alsace,* edited by P. Ingold (Paris, Colmar: A. Picard, 1894), pp. 101-105, letter of Oct. 27, 1800.

35. Hufton, "Women in Revolution," pp. 165-166.

 III

Women and Culture

❦ Roseann Runte

Women as Muse

I N MYTHOLOGY, the Muses, nine sisters, daughters of Zeus and Mnémosyne, preside over the arts. In literature, as in art, the Muse is the genius of poetic inspiration evoked under the traits of woman. Yet the attempt to establish a correspondence between women and evocations of the Muses in the eighteenth century must be approached with caution, for the word "Muse" was part of a euphemistic tradition. Furetière applies a metonymical definition to the term. A penchant for the Muses, he explains, is an inclination for letters, especially poetry. A poet's lodgings are the abode of the Muses or the Muses' cabinet. The poet himself is the Muses' favorite and his creations are the fruits of the Muses.[1] When Voltaire rues his absence from Parisian cultural life, he writes: "I am at present a poor, provincial soul removed from the sources of wit. It is through you that I want to remain in contact with the Muses."[2] Thus, the reign of the Muses was that of letters. The metonymical employment of the term was such a common linguistic trait that the establishment of an association with actual women would be tenuous at best and would be the result of psycholinguistic analysis.

The word Muse was employed to signify the arts in contrast to the sciences. Voltaire writes to Bernard that "Newton is not making me give up the Muses . . ." (p. 2:300). Again writing about his studies of Newton, which leave him no time for poetry, Voltaire addresses this wish to Mlle Quinault: "Deign write me in order to return me to the Muses . . ." (p. 1:738).

The Muses may be abstract beings who are totally separate from the women as is evident in this verse by Chénier:

> Depart, Muses, depart. Your Art is of no use to me;
> What do your laurels mean to me? You permit Camille to flee.
> Near her I wanted to have your support.
> Depart, Muses, depart, if you can do naught.[3]

In a similar vein, to compliment authors on their writing, one praised their association with the Muses and named them, male and female alike, students of the Muses. Voltaire offers this title to Helvétius, Frederick II and Mme du Châtelet. However, while both sexes could be inspired by the Muses, only female artists took on the trappings of the Muses themselves and were, through the extension of the charms of their works, personified as Muses. Voltaire writes to Mme de Genlis:

> I read your charming work.
> Do you know what is its effect?
> One wants to become more familiar
> With the Muse who created it.[4]

Similarly, a comment on Marie-Geneviève Bouliar's painting identifies her not as a student of the Muses but as a Muse:

> The Greeks, that ingenious people,
> Who knew how to animate nature with diverse beings,
> With nymphs, Muses, and with gods,
> If this charming picture had been known by them,
> Would have called Bouliar Muse of painting.[5]

This identification of woman as Muse follows a tradition of the eighteenth century in which artists painted women in the guise of Muses. Examples include Jean-Marc Nattier's portraits of his wife "dressed in the guise of music" (1737), of Madame*** as Erato (1746), and of Mme Boudrey "as a Muse who sketches" (1753).[6] The representation of women garbed as Muse is not extraordinary considering the popularity of costumes and extravagant guises in eighteenth-century portraiture. What is significant is that they chose to see themselves in this role and to communicate their acceptance of this role to the viewer.

In her role as Muse, the woman could provide inspiration for creative activity or be the object of artistic representations. Woman as Muse may thus be active or passive, and in some cases, she filled both roles simultaneously. Mme de Pompadour, for example, was represented in a portrait by Quentin de La Tour. She was the object of the painter's inspiration. In the painting, she has placed a copy of *De l'esprit des lois* on the table next to her. She was, thus, actively promoting Montesquieu's career at the same time.[7]

The role of women as active instigator of creative activity in the eighteenth century was complex. In general, woman's role as arbiter of public taste was centered in the salons, and it is not an exaggeration to say that literary and artistic fame and fortune depended on the judgment of women.[8] Marmontel wrote in his *Mémoires* that Mme de Tencin advised him to befriend women, "for, it is through women, she used to say, that one obtains what one wishes from men."[9] The role of patroness of the arts was the equivalent of a profession, absorbing the time, energy, talents, and finances of many women. Furthermore, these women wielded considerable power in the Republic of Letters.

Monique Piettre in *La Condition féminine à travers les âges* states that the mythology of friendship by Mlle de Scudéry with the *Carte du tendre* was a mythology of frustration, a fiction into which women, tied by social codes in unsatisfactory and imposed conjugal bonds, could escape without risking the social condemnation following free union. Simultaneously, Piettre notes the growth of new religious orders, which offered careers for women oriented toward external activity in the late eighteenth century. In the eighteenth century, feminine frustration was somewhat released by a change in morality permitting the "consecration" of amorous liaisons by virtue of their longevity and by an increased activity in the sphere of letters, where a new force, public opinion, was mastered by women. This sovereignty was politically insignificant and led "from silken dress to the scaffold."[10]

All of this feminine activity should not be attributed to romantic frustration, and it was not simply an activity undertaken by women to fill their leisure hours to avoid ennui. Voltaire stated that there had been for a long time nine Muses and that healthy criticism should be the tenth.[11] Thus, criticism, debate, and, by extension, aid to the artists whose works one admires could be considered artistic activity. The careers of the eighteenth-century women who ran salons, who acted as the arbiters of public taste, and who professionally supported their protégés as much as they were responsible for the success of their individual productions were the careers of artists. Indeed, Mme de Pompadour wielded a brush herself; and most of these women, in addition to veritable volumes of letters, wrote essays, poetry, plays, and novels.[12] They were the colleagues of the artists they aided, and the reason women had the role of obtaining men's election to the Académie and not vice versa was simply because women could not be elected. If women helped men financially and politically, the reverse is also true. Voltaire was forced to go into hiding under an assumed name for a year after writing a letter in favor of Adrienne Lecouvreur, and he supported Corneille's grandniece. Women also helped women. Catherine II supported the artist Vigée-Lebrun for six years.[13]

The manner in which women performed the role of Muse can be divided into three categories: political support, financial aid, and intellectual assistance. The results of women's political activity are difficult to measure. For example, it is not possible to determine definitively if an academician was actually elected due to the support of women. Other factors may have been involved, including the possibility that different women may have simultaneously acted on behalf of different candidates. The women most commonly noted as responsible for the elections of Montesquieu, Marivaux, d'Alembert, Saurin, Watelet, Suard, Marmontel, Duras, Cicé, La Harpe, Chastellux, and Duclos include Mme de Lambert, Mme de Tencin, Mme du Deffand,

Mme Geoffrin, Mlle de Lespinasse, and Mme de Brancas.[14] Women
such as the duchesse d'Aiguillon protected the *encyclopédistes*, while
others, such as the princesse de Robecq, idled their opponents. Political
aid often came through negative acts. For example, Mme de Pompadour had Dupin's work refuting the *Esprit des lois* withdrawn from
circulation. The political aid offered by women was often in the form
of introductions. Mme Geoffrin recommended Mozart to Prince von
Kaunitz; she also had him play in her salon.[15] The introduction of
artists to other artists and the interested public was an invaluable
source of aid that cannot be measured. Women provided the public
forum in the salon. This public was chosen by them, and the works
introduced as well as their eventual reception was orchestrated by the
women whose generosity was offset by considerable authority and
power.

The financial aid offered creative artists ranges from the ridiculous
to the sublime. Mme d'Herbigny supplied Montesquieu with tea from
England, while Mmes de Pompadour and du Barry with Marie-
Antoinette were responsible for 258 pensions paid to artists and
writers.[16] Among the notable authors aided by Mme de Pompadour
were Marivaux, Rousseau, and Marmontel, for whom she secured a
government office and the editorship of and a pension from the
Mercure. Catherine the Great's aid to Diderot amounted to 60,000
livres, but she also helped others, such as Collot-Falconet, whom she
supported for twelve years. It is impossible not to mention Mme
Geoffrin in this context. Barbara Scott, among others, indicates that
"she was in the habit of visiting artists' homes to see how they were
furnished, trying to find out whether, for example, a clock was needed,
or a desk, and always hunting out a place for some useful piece of
furniture."[17] She refurbished Diderot's study, and this act of generosity, in turn, inspired Diderot to write his 1772 pamphlet, *Regrets sur ma
vieille robe de chambre.* In addition, she purchased sixty-nine paintings and
commissioned five works from Hubert Robert and gave an annuity to
d'Alembert.

The extent of intellectual assistance provided by women to artists is
unfathomable. They were, at times, responsible for the artists' choice
of subject, approach, or style. They provided models. For example,
Marivaux attempted to reproduce images of the salon in his novels and
plays. E. J. H. Greene observes that the salon model in Marivaux's
works extended beyond the replication of character, setting, and style
of conversation to tone: "There is [in *La Voiture embourbée*] an insistence
on the heart which is perhaps an awkward attempt to strike what he
[Marivaux] considered to be the tone of Mme de Lambert."[18] The salon
was also the subject of paintings, such as *L'Assemblée au salon* by
Lavreince and later engraved by Dequevauviller. The same subject

provided a negative inspiration. Gresset's *Le Méchant* mocks Mme de Forcalquier's green chamber.[19] Similarly, women themselves were viewed in differing manners by artists. Mme Geoffrin was painted by both Nattier and Chardin in youth and in maturity. Perhaps a better illustration would be Mme de Tencin, who was "a divine angel" for Montesquieu and "the beautiful and wicked Canoness" for Diderot.[20] Nanette was "beautiful as an angel," according to Diderot, and "a haranguing harpy" in the eyes of Rousseau.[21] It would be impossible to measure the indirect influence of these women on the works of these writers. Even when she was subject, the exact role of the woman is difficult to ascertain. When d'Alembert wrote a book on vaccination, Mlle de Lespinasse, marked by smallpox, is said to have been his inspiration.[22] Diderot's essays on blindness were inspired by the memory of Mélanie, the daughter of Mme de Salignac; however, she died at the age of twenty-two, some sixteen years before Diderot composed the *Additions à la lettre sur les aveugles*.[23] Thus, while surely women did inspire these works and others, it is questionable where memory and imagination begin and where the woman herself played a key role. Indeed, Silvia's performances of Marivaux's roles inspired Marivaux and other authors to write for her and artists to portray her in painting. Yet was it Silvia the woman, Silvia the actress in a role, or the charm of Marivaux's production that inspired the work? The sketch by Watteau de Lille and the engraving by Buquoy of Suzanne sending an answer to Figaro's letter is a concrete extension of this problem; it was the literary character here that was portrayed, not the woman. There are real women and imaginary women. The perception of the woman by the artist may or may not be related to the original. Indeed, the imaginary woman could precede the original. When Rousseau first saw Mme d'Houdetot, he recognized in her the realization of his dream, his Julie. While the identification of the dream with reality appears to be diametrically opposed to the creation of a dream based on reality, the creative process may be similar. In *Les Liaisons dangereuses*, Danceny writes to Mme de Merteuil that he began composing a letter to forget her, to distract himself:

> Unfortunately, when the days are so long, and one is so unoccupied, one dreams, one builds castles in Spain, one creates his own daydream, little by little the imagination becomes exalted: one wishes to beautify his work, one gathers together all which can please, one arrives at last at perfection; and as soon as one achieves it, the portrait leads back to the model, and one is astounded to see that all the time one had only been dreaming of you.[24]

It would seem that dreams take their inspiration from reality and that they therefore represent a composite of all perceptions. Thus, any woman in a novel, poem, play or painting would have a relationship, however indirect, with a real woman, even if her representation were inspired by a painting based on a description found in a novel. Mlle de Scudéry wrote concerning her portrait executed by the artist Nanteuil:

> Nanteuil, on portraying my likeness
> Demonstrated the power of his heavenly art.
> I hate my eyes in my mirror,
> I love them in his painting.[25]

If the women portrayed had trouble recognizing themselves, so did their contemporaries. With the passage of time, the difficulty increases. Robert Shackleton, for example, cannot determine if it was the duchesse d'Aiguillon or Mme Geoffrin who inspired Palissot to create the character of Cydalise in *Les Philosophes*.[26] Similarly, Mlle de Clermont or Mme de Grave might have provided the inspiration for Montesquieu's *Temple de Cnide*. Jeannette Gauffriaud Rosso adds: "Mademoiselle de Charolais, according to Montesquieu himself, is said to have provided the inspiration for *Arsace et Isménie*, that 'novel' of conjugal love in the Orient, to use the author's expression. It is not, on the other hand, impossible to deduce that he wrote it thinking as well of his own wife."[27] Even when a work is dedicated to a woman or when the author leaves an indication of source of inspiration, the information is not always reliable.

While it is often difficult to recognize the woman as source of inspiration from her portrait, it is also perplexing to determine the exact role she played in the creative process. When Montesquieu writes to Mme de Tencin "You are the little mother of my book," what does he mean?[28] What does Voltaire mean when he writes to Mme du Maine?

> My patroness, your protégé must tell your Highness that I followed to the letter all the advice with which she honored me. She will never know how much Cicero and Caesar were thereby improved. Those two gentlemen would have taken your advice if they had lived during your time. I just read *Rome sauvée:* the section [s] which your Most Serene Highness embellished created a prodigious effect.[29]

Was Montesquieu merely grateful to Mme de Tencin for having bought two hundred copies of his work to present at court? Was Voltaire merely purchasing his pardon from Mme du Maine, whom he had angered by inviting 500 people to view *La Prude* when it was performed at her home?

Related to the question of the influence exerted by women on artistic creation is the manner in which they were perceived. Chaulieu gave Mme de Staël the name Doris and Diderot's Mme de La Carlière the name Morphyse. It was a common practice for male authors to give their Muses Greek names, the names of goddesses, and poetic names chosen for their assonance or literary association. Yet, in the eigh-teenth century, these women were also named "mama," "little mother," or "little sister." Tenderness rather than passion is evoked by the attribution of such terms. These names evoke roles in the family, not in society at large. It appears that authors sought the intimacy of the family but were obliged to seek in the family circle names for the roles woman played outside.[30] Men could be associated with a professional occupation, but women had no assigned roles other than those within the family. Therefore, their intimate family role was projected outward to a more public theatre.

This follows the development of eighteenth-century salon life:

> One no longer received guests in the bedroom while one was still in bed, a common practice in the *Grand Siècle* when the bedroom was one of the most important of the house. In its social function the bedroom was replaced by the boudoir, while new rooms were devised for new life: the private study and, later on in the century, the permanent living room.[31]

Paralleling the opening up of the architectural structure came an expansion of women's role. When women left their niche, they brought with them their definition, which was entirely associated with the role they played in the home and no longer appropriate.

Seventeenth-century women mapped out new horizons with the *Carte du tendre*. In turn, these became new confinements. Eighteenth-century women had no map or social guide. No longer were they content to recline gracefully in beds and be described allegorically as flowers. Instead, they pursued activities previously reserved for men. This is reflected in their portraits. They are nearly always active. Even when asleep, the signs of activity are prominent. Mme Greuze, for example, is pictured nodding over an open book, embroidery frame on her feet, glasses and pen on the table.[32] Like their seventeenth-century predecessors, eighteenth-century women were frequently pictured as goddesses but as active goddesses, who were teachers, propagandists of vaccination, participants in social functions, etc.

In the sixteenth century, women were most often portrayed as surrounded by rosy-cheeked cherubs and clouds. In the seventeenth century, they were put on pedestals. In the eighteenth century, however, it was less a case of the woman being deified than one of the goddess being humanized. Goddesses were seen walking among mortals, taking tea, and getting bathed, dressed or otherwise. They were pictured with imperfections. In Watteau's painting, *The Swing*, the woman seated on the moving swing has lost her shoe in the passion of the moment. This activity and humanity coincide with the theory that in a world without sin the distance between man and god was eliminated.[33] Eighteenth-century gardens were liberally sprinkled with statuary representing deities. They were not objects of reverence, rather they were prized for their decorative value. They dotted the walkways as did humans. In Bouilliard and Dupréel's etching of Schall's painting of the bathing lady, it is not certain which figures are statues and which women.[34]All are in the water. Were they in a temple, the deduction would be that the women were deified. Since the goddesses are being treated to the same bath as the women, it would seem that they are being humanized.

This new woman is not easily apprehended nor comprehended by men. Marivaux's heroes are overwhelmed by a foot. Diderot favored hands. Laclos's Valmont viewed women through a keyhole. Women are described through reflection or partially. The whole could not be seized upon or described. The artist attempted to focus on one feature to symbolize the whole. In so doing, he portrayed aspects of incomplete woman.

Another attempt to define the woman, this elusive Muse, was to treat her as a man. Voltaire described Mme du Châtelet to Fawkener as "that lady whom I look upon as a great man. . . . She understands Newton, she despises superstition and in short, she makes me happy." He wrote on another occasion: "I recommend to you Mme du Châtelet and [La Mort de] César; they are two great men."[35] Diderot described Catherine II as "Caesar's soul with all the seductivity of Cleopatra."[36] Marivaux wrote of Mme de Fécour: "[She] had no feminine qualities. It was even one of her graces to not think of having any."[37] Diderot's Sophie was "man and woman, when it so pleases him/her," and he called women in general "creatures as beautiful as Klopstock's seraphim, as terrible as Milton's devils."[38] Piron called Mme de Tencin a "woman above many men . . . in case of need, a statesman / And, if necessary, an Amazon."[39] It is Mme d'Houdetot in a masculine riding costume on horseback who first captures Rousseau's imagination.[40]

To say that a woman was a man was obviously a form of gallantry, a compliment indicating a changing role for women. It signals the recent date of this change, for a vocabulary was not yet at hand to describe the active woman; the best compliment writers could find for her was to call her a man. This reflects a weakening of stereotypical roles, and it is accompanied by the reverse situation, complimenting a male on his feminine qualities. Diderot, for example, admires Grimm because "To the strength of one of the sexes, he adds the grace and delicacy of the other."[41]

Ian Maclean, in his work on feminism in French literature of the seventeenth century traces the image of the heroic woman back to the sixteenth century.[42] I suspect that it could be traced to the origins of literature and that the goddess, Athena, the patroness of the hunt, was a "male woman," as Trousset would have dubbed her. These heroic women, and even Amazons, were androcentric representations as opposed to gynocentric images. These androcentric images were limited to the baroque period. The classical period reverted to the image of woman as the weak sex. Even the strongest of female characters, like Corneille's Pauline, were cognizant of their sex and, therefore, their weaknesses. Writers in the pastoral tradition reversed the roles, making women strong and virtuous and men weak and prone to vice. The *précieuse,* or extension of the *femme-docteur,* was an image separate from either the heroic or the weak woman.

In the eighteenth century, the pastoral, baroque, and classical traditions all persisted in literature. Examples of each type of heroine can be found. The *précieuse,* however, developed into the *femme-philosophe.* Her bedchamber became a salon, a public forum for ideas. She herself became active and took on a masculine role in society. The *femme-philosophe* combined some of the qualities of the heroic woman and the *précieuse.* This fusion can be explained, in part, by the changing definition of vice. When evil was philosophically eliminated, vice was lost as a trait, either male or female. The glorification of the image of mother and family in the latter part of the century responded to the eighteenth-century desire for intimacy. This tendency to extol life in the homes as a new virtue may have also been a reaction to the entrance of women into society. In any case, although women attempted to break out of the family circle, they did not succeed in being cast into new roles. They were adopted by the artists they befriended as mothers, sisters, and daughters. Unfortunately, the newfound virtues of motherhood were not projected into the social arena. Rousseau awarded bracelets not to women who nurtured the arts but to women who nursed their children.

In the eighteenth century, the enigma was a popular word game. A series of clues, often in poetic form, were given, and the auditor had to divine the object, usually an abstract notion such as time. The characteristics of the concept were often puzzling and contradictory. The description of the women who inspired eighteenth-century artists to create works that reflected her image as perceived is similar to the enigma. The different aspects of women may be collected as so many clues. The final response is enigmatic. The word Muse comes from the Greek and means to explain mysteries, according to the *Encyclopédie.* The seemingly elusive nature of the woman and her image, and of the Muse and her personification is due both to the diversity of forms of representation and the varied characters of the individual women and the artists, as well as to the evolving nature of role and image. It is evident authors living in an age of dictionaries and encyclopedias attempted to classify and understand this new woman. They used the vocabulary at hand and described her role in intimate terms. They pictured her in movement. For the execution of the new role, however, they offered her the attributes of virtue, thus of masculinity. Women, in turn, accepted this new role and chose to have themselves portrayed as Muse.

Whether the inspiration provided artists was tangible or intangible, political, financial, or poetic, women played an important role in the arts during the eighteenth century. They were active and their portraits show them engaged in a multitude of occupations. The image of women in art reflects their role in society. The Muse, both woman and her image, was a product of the epoch. The range of her activity, "from silken dress to scaffold," is enormous. That women went from one extreme to the other is perhaps but a reflection of the structure of the society; not only was there no vocabulary to describe women pursuing nontraditional roles in manners transcending stereotypical sex models, but there was no real place for women outside the home. For a brief time, then, and in the limited role of Muse, the eighteenth-century woman was both an anachronism and a product of her time, a social enigma and the inspiration for the many attempts at capturing her essence. Subject of both antifeminist tirades and passages of pure feminine adulation, woman as Muse was generous and powerful. She both inspired and fostered the production of some of the most important works of the century. Woman as Muse was, at once, a literary and artistic image and a political and social reality. Both of these roles were inseparably and symbiotically related. This relationship in an artistic and social environment that was itself in a state of flux produced women such as Mmes du Châtelet, du Deffand, de Lambert, de Tencin and Geoffrin. The list is endless, yet each one deserves the title of artist and Muse.

NOTES

1. A comparison of this entry in Antoine Furetière, *Dictionnaire universel* (1690) with that in the *Encyclopédie* illustrates the thesis of this article. There is no entry under the heading "Muse" in the *Encyclopédie*, but there is an entry under "Muses," in the plural. Each individual Muse is named; and more than the domain (music, tragedy, etc.), her characteristics (melancholy, for example) and the attitude in which she was portrayed are emphasized. The Muses were, in a sense, domesticated, removed from their Olympian mountain, where they were cognizant of past, present, and future and placed in an eighteenth-century present. All quotations in the chapter were translated by the author.

2. François Marie Arouet de Voltaire, *Correspondance*, edited by Th. Besterman (Paris: Gallimard, 1963), vol. 1, p. 489. Further references to this edition of Voltaire's *Correspondance* will be noted in the text.

3. André-Marie Chénier, *Oeuvres*, edited by Jean-Marie Gerbault (Paris: Seghers, 1958), p. 130.

4. Mme la comtesse Stéphanie-Félicité de Genlis, *Mémoires inédits* (Paris: Ladvocat, 1825), 1:154-155. I am indebted to Professor Vivian Cameron, Nova

Scotia College of Art and Design, for sharing this reference and the following one with me.

5. *Explication par ordre de numéro et jugement motivé des ouvrages de peinture, sculpture, architecture et gravure exposés au Palais National des Arts* (Paris: n.d. [1793]), in Bibliothèque Nationale, Département des Estampes, Collection Deloignes, 18:156.

6. Louis Dimier, *Les Peintres français au XVIIe siècle*, vol. 2 (Paris: Editions G. Van Ost, 1930), index. It is noteworthy that the women were more frequently represented as Muses who draw than as Muses of drawing. This indicates their active contributions.

7. Jeannette Geffriaud Rosso, *Montesquieu et la féminité* (Pisa: Libreria Goliardica Editrice, 1977), p. 75.

8. See, for example, Edmond and Jules de Goncourt, *La Femme au XVIIIe siècle* (Paris: Firmin-Didot, 1887), pp. 302-305; Pierre-Maurice Masson, *Une Vie de femme au XVIIIe siècle: Madame de Tencin (1682-1749)* (Genève: Slatkine, 1970), p. 262.

9. Maurice Rat, *Les Femmes de la régence* (Paris: Berger-Levrault, 1961), pp. 116-147.

10. Monique A. Piettre, *La Condition féminine à travers les âges* (Belgium: France-Empire, 1974), pp. 165-183.

11. Voltaire, *Oeuvres complètes*, edited by L. Moland (Paris: Garnier Frères, 1877-1885), vol. 20, p. 222.

12. Albert de La Fizelière, "L'art et les femmes en France," *Gazette des Beaux-Arts* (Paris, 1859), vol. 30.

13. Howard V. and Charlotte B. Evans, "Women Artists in Eighteenth-Century France," (paper read at the Canadian Society for Eighteenth-Century Studies conference, University of Western Ontario, 1980).

14. See Goncourts, p. 304; Jean-Baptiste Capefigue, *La Marquise du Châtelet et les amies des philosophes du XVIIIe siècle* (Genève: Slatkine, 1970), pp. 42ff; Marie Gougy-François, *Les Grands Salons féminins* (Paris: Debresse, 1965); and Roger Picard, *Les Salons littéraires et la société française, 1610-1789* (New York: Brentanos, 1943).

15. Barbara Scott, "Madame Geoffrin: A Patron and Friend of Artists," *Apollo* 85 (January-March 1967), p. 98.

16. John Lough, *An Introduction to Eighteenth-Century France* (London: Longmans, 1961), pp. 241-260.

17. Scott, p. 100.

18. E. J. H. Greene, *Marivaux* (Toronto: University of Toronto Press, 1965), p. 12. See also Marcel Arland, *Marivaux* (Paris: Gallimard, 1950), p. 56 on Silvia; and Ruth Kirby Jamieson, *Marivaux: A Study in Sensibility* (New York: King's Crown, 1941), on dedications.

19. See Goncourts, p. 50. The engraving is also reproduced in the text.

20. Geffriaud Rosso, p. 579.

21. Blandine L. McLaughlin, *Diderot et l'amitié*, in *Studies on Voltaire and the Eighteenth Century*, vol. 100 (Oxford: The Voltaire Foundation, 1973), p. 124.

22. M. Dupont-Chatelain, *Les Encyclopédistes et les femmes* (Genève: Slatkine, 1970), p. 21, n. 1.

23. McLaughlin, p. 130, n. 6.

24. Choderlos de Laclos, *Les Liaisons dangereuses* (Paris: Gallimard, 1958), p. 319.

25. Picard, p. 277.

26. Robert Shackleton, *Montesquieu: une bibliographie critique*, translated by Jean Loiseau (Grenoble: Presses universitaires de Grenoble, 1977), p. 141.

27. Geffriaud Rosso, p. 66.

28. Gougy-François, p. 51.

29. Rat, p. 105.

30. Philippe Aries, *Essais sur l'histoire de la mort en Occident du moyen âge à nos jours* (Paris: Le Seuil, 1975), pp. 451ff; see also Jean-Louis Flandrin, *Familles, parentés, maison, sexualité dans l'ancienne société* (Paris: Hachette, 1976), pp. 17ff.

31. R. G. Saisselin, *Taste in Eighteenth-Century France* (Syracuse: Syracuse University Press, 1965), p. 50.

32. Drawn by Greuze, engraved by Aliamet, this work, entitled "La philosophie endormie," appears in Goncourt.

33. Ronald Paulson, *Emblem and Expression: Meaning in English Art of the Eighteenth Century* (Cambridge, Mass.: Harvard University Press, 1975), p. 95: "It is into the garden into which the old myths go, scattered about in stone."

34. *Aimer en France 1780-1800,* edited by Jean-Paul Bouillon et al. (Clermont-Ferrand: Bibliothèque municipale inter-universitaire, 1977), p. 57.

35. D. J. Adams, *La Femme dans les contes et romans de Voltaire* (Paris: Nizet, 1974), pp. 21-22, 115.

36. McLaughlin, p. 218.

37. Pierre Carlet de Marivaux, *Oeuvres de jeunesse,* edited by Frédéric Deloffre and Claude Rigault (Paris: Gallimard, 1972), pp. 178-180, n. 1.

38. McLaughlin, pp. 134, n. 23, 221.

39. Masson, p. 265.

40. Jean-Jacques Rousseau, *Confessions,* edited by Jean Guéhenno (Paris: Gallimard, 1965), vol. 2, p. 172; Emile Faguet, *Les Amies de Rousseau* (Paris: Société française d'imprimerie et de librairie, 1910), pp. 337ff.

41. McLaughlin, p. 231. Collé also points out Marivaux's feminine qualities; see Gustave Larroumet, *Marivaux: sa vie et ses oeuvres* (Genève: Slatkine, 1970), p. 111; and Emile Faguet, *Dix-Huitième Siècle* (Paris: Boivin, 1890), p. 63.

42. Ian Maclean, *Woman Triumphant: Feminism in French Literature* (Oxford: Clarendon, 1977), pp. 50-169.

🍃 Barbara G. Mittman

Women and the Theatre Arts

It would be difficult, if not impossible, to conceive of the theatre arts in eighteenth-century France—or, for that matter, anywhere in modern western civilization—without the participation of women. Theatre can, indeed readily does, dispense with women as playwrights, directors, producers, designers, etc., but it cannot do without females to interpret female roles. The lame actor Béjart may have created Mme Pernelle in *Tartuffe*, just as in Rameau's *Platée* a tenor traditionally plays the nymph queen of the frogs, but obviously the Rosines and Suzannes and Silvias, and indeed the theatre arts as we know them, would cease to exist without the concurrence of women. But apart from that inevitability, women in eighteenth-century France became more active than ever before in other facets of theatre. The Enlightenment witnessed a noteworthy increase in the number of women playwrights. It also saw the emergence of women as organizers and animators of so-called *théâtres de société*—private salon theatres responsible for some of the most interesting theatrical activity of the century. This chapter will deal with the contributions of women in all three of these areas: as organizers of salon theatre, as performers in public theatres, and as playwrights.

Theatre in eighteenth-century France was first and foremost public theatre. Beaumarchais and Marivaux, Voltaire and Sedaine, all wanted their plays performed at theatres where audiences paid to view the spectacle, the Comédie-Française and the Comédie-Italienne, royal theatres that were later supplemented by a number of commercial Boulevard houses. But some of the liveliest theatrical activity was taking place elsewhere. The innovative, the offbeat, the sharply satirical, and, most of all, the risqué found its outlet not before paying audiences but on private stages in private residences. Because private theatres were not subject to the troublesome censorship that hampered the public stage, they were able to offer the kind of uninhibited fare that most pleased their sophisticated audiences. In that most theatre-oriented of periods, these unofficial playhouses had become all the rage, invading country castles and Paris townhouses as well as the royal court. Virtually every household of social consequence main-

tained a stage and put on plays. In the latter part of the century, some
160 *théâtres de société* could be counted in Paris alone.[1]

Entry to salon theatres, which could accommodate from several
dozen to several hundred spectators, was by invitation only. Their
elite audiences tended to be more receptive and attentive than those in
public theatres, where paid claques were a nuisance and the *parterre*
was generally uproarious. Sometimes attracting more attention than
performances at the Comédie-Française, salon theatre events were
reported on a regular basis, and in generally favorable terms, by the
Correspondance littéraire as well as by other publications. Indeed, so
attractive was the prospect of performing in certain of these little
theatres that actors and actresses sometimes deserted their colleagues
at the Comédie-Française or the Comédie-Italienne in order to appear
on a private stage. During the latter part of the century, this problem
grew so bothersome that special ordinances were promulgated imposing heavy fines on players who were absent from their assigned
performances at the public theatres.[2]

Most of the time, these important little theatres were organized and
animated by women. Among the most celebrated and influential were,
in the early part of the century, those of the duchesse du Maine at
Sceaux and Mme de Pompadour at Versailles and, later on, those of
Marie-Antoinette and Mme de Montesson. These women sometimes
wrote for their own theatre and almost always acted in the plays they
produced, favoring the roles of *soubrette* or peasant girl. In contrast to
the critical attack and moral condemnation to which ordinary female
authors and performers were subjected, these women were treated to
nearly universal approval.

The earliest salon theatre of consequence in the eighteenth century
was presided over by the duchesse du Maine, mistress of the château
de Sceaux.[3] Taking up the social slack left at Versailles by the declining
reign of Louis XIV, the château de Sceaux, with its dinners, balls,
gaming tables, fireworks and theatre, became a nucleus to which
courtiers vied for invitations. Under the direction of the lively, witty,
and fiercely ambitious little duchesse, Sceaux became renowned for
fortnightly galas, at which theatre and theatrical events were the focal
point.[4] Relying at first on such standard salon fare as *La Tarentole*, a
scatalogical comedy-ballet written in 1705 by her friend and mentor,
Nicolas de Malézieu, the duchesse du Maine eventually tired of such
entertainment, titillating though it was. As a replacement, she
instituted the poetic lottery, in which guests would draw lettered lots:
the individual who drew "A" had to present an ariette, "C" meant a
comedy, "O" an opera, and so forth. This conceit was soon replaced
with others meant to stimulate creativity and to respond to the
insatiable quest for gaiety and novelty that seemed to drive the
celebrated *nuits de Sceaux*.

Following the death of Louis XIV and the political setback suffered by the duchesse du Maine, her salon was no longer patronized by the blooded aristocracy that had been its mainstay before but by intellectuals and men of letters.[5] Fontenelle, Marmontel, Montesquieu, and Crébillon became regulars. Voltaire, who took shelter at Sceaux for two months in 1746, both acted in and wrote for her theatre. Despite a falling out caused by a mischevious caper (the *philosophe* had sent out hundreds of unauthorized invitations to one of the duchesse du Maine's *nuits*), he wrote and produced *Rome sauvée* for her in 1750. The author himself played the role of Cicero, accompanied by the celebrated actor Lekain in another role.

Maintaining her salon and its theatre until the end, the duchesse du Maine died in 1753 at the age of seventy-seven.[6] So intense had been her lifelong love of the theatre that Voltaire several months earlier had written to a mutual friend: "She loves theatre and when she is ill, I advise you to administer to her some play instead of extreme unction. One dies as one has lived."[7]

In contrast to the improvisational mode that sometimes prevailed at Sceaux, the theatre established by Mme de Pompadour at Versailles in 1747 was a thoroughly professional operation. As a bride, the tall, well-spoken young woman who was to become Louis XV's official *favorite* had already organized an amateur theatre that, according to one of her guests, was as well-appointed as that of the Opera. At Versailles, able to draw upon the Royal Treasury as well as upon her own talent and intelligence, she created a theatre that was first-rate in every respect. Though players were recruited from suitably exalted social ranks, only those with previous acting experience were accepted. Regarded herself as one of the best salon actresses of the time, Mme de Pompadour saw to it that her troupe was well-rehearsed, sometimes by actresses such as Gaussin and Dumesnil from the Comédie-Française. The players also were well-disciplined; principal roles had understudies, schedules were maintained, and tardiness was not tolerated. The orchestra was top quality, as were costumers, wigmakers and stage decorators. Her staff maintained reserves of costumes, decorations, and stage accessories. Nothing was wanting, and, indeed, nothing should have been, for the king was spending over 230,000 *livres* annually on Mme de Pompadour's theatre.

Named the Théâtre des Petits-Cabinets, her playhouse normally began its season in mid-November, after the court's return to Versailles from Fontainebleau.[8] Attendance was tightly controlled by the king himself, who limited the audience to the most elite and intimate of court society. During the first two years of the theatre's existence, women were not present as spectators, except for those in a special *loge* reserved for actresses who were not part of the performance at hand. Admission to such an exclusive event became much coveted, as did an invitation to play a bit part. Political favors were not infrequently exchanged for an opportunity to penetrate the inner sanctum of the little theatre at Versailles.[9]

Doubtless upset by the lavish expenditures required by the Petits-Cabinets, Louis decreed in 1750 that it be moved from Versailles to Mme de Pompadour's château at Bellevue, where a smaller theatre had recently been built. Despite this gesture towards economy, the very successful production of Rousseau's *Devin du village* given there that year reportedly depleted the Royal Treasury by 50,000 *écus*, at a time when wages to employees of the king's household had been suspended.

Zeal for Mme de Pompadour's theatre eventually diminished. There were fewer performances at Bellevue than there had been at Versailles, and concerts and fireworks began to replace plays as regular fare. The theatre did not reopen after 1753. Having lasted for six years, the Petits-Cabinets had presented plays by Molière, Voltaire, Nivelle de La Chaussée, Dancourt, and Gresset, among others. In all, there had been performances of nineteen plays, thirty-one operas, and ten ballets, several of them given five or six times. Of much shorter duration than the duchesse du Maine's theatre and ending by attrition in the same year, Mme de Pompadour's theatre had greater impact insofar as it represented tangible evidence of keen interest for theatre in the highest of places.

More than twenty years elapsed before resumption of theatrical activity at Versailles. Neither as educated nor as talented as her thespian predecessor, Marie-Antoinette turned to the stage mainly as a distraction in the face of impending disaster. While still dauphine, she took part with her young sisters- and brothers-in-law in a secret little theatre hidden in a corner of the palace, thereby risking the anger of the aging Louis XV, who no longer cared for such entertainments. The youngsters played to an audience of one, namely the dauphin and future Louis XVI. Upon becoming queen, Marie-Antoinette did not immediately establish a salon theatre, for, though Louis XVI adored his wife, he basically disliked theatre, except for burlesque parodies and salacious *parades*. Her fantasies not forgotten, however, the eighteen-year-old queen posed for a portrait in the plumed headdress she affected at the time, causing her scandalized mother, Marie-Thésèse, to lament from Austria that instead of a likeness of the queen of France she had received the portrait of an actress. Louis XVI's taste in entertainment notwithstanding, the Comédie-Française and the Comédie-Italienne were frequently called upon to perform at the court, and after four years, Marie-Antoinette obtained the king's permission to construct a theatre of her own.

Having taken a year to build, at a cost of some 141,000 *livres*—a modest sum compared to some of Mme de Pompadour's ventures—the

Trianon theatre opened in 1779. Decorated in the style of the time, it featured cupids and garlands and much blue velvet. Joining Marie-Antoinette on stage for the opening in Sedaine's *La Gageure imprévue* was an array of nobles, who were, no doubt, bemused to hear their queen, in the role of *soubrette*, proclaim that "we have a complaint, we domestics." Because of the queen's particular fondness for bucolic roles, the Trianon frequently presented little playlets with ariettes, in contrast to the substantial professional pieces that had been the mainstay during Mme de Pompadour's tenure. Initially, the audience at the Trianon theatre was limited to the king, his brother (Monsieur), the royal princesses, and perhaps a few of the queen's ladies—about forty spectators in all. Later, however, tired of playing to empty seats, the troupe enlarged its audience, in one instance extending 263 invitations.

Marie-Antoinette's last attempt at theatre was in April of 1785, when she played the role of Rosine in the *Barbier de Séville*, with Beaumarchais present as special guest. In the midst of the scandal and unrest with which the country was beset, this was viewed as an act of astounding and provocative political *maladresse*.

Mediocre at best, the Trianon theatre suffered by comparison to its rival, the salon theatre presided over by Mme de Montesson. Mistress of the important duc d'Orléans, and later his secret wife, the marquise de Montesson officiated over his private theatre during roughly the same years that Marie-Antoinette's theatre was active. Though according to her niece, Mme de Genlis, Mme de Montesson was not educated, she had a universally acknowledged talent for acting, as well as great self-discipline and the ambition to be a playwright.[10] Her theatre offered two or three performances per week during the winter season, continuing to operate during the Easter closing of the public theatres. The most distinguished people from both town and court made an effort to be admitted. Voltaire himself attended twice in 1778 during his triumphant return to Paris, receiving from the duc d'Orléans' guests the same adulation and homage as he had at the Comédie-Française.

Of a somewhat moralistic bent, Mme de Montesson set aside a special box in her theatre for clergy. She also banned both *parades* and licentious comedies in favor of plays such as Goldoni's *Servante maîtresse* or Carmontelle's *Proverbes dramatiques*, but most of all in favor of her own compositions. Within an eight-year period she wrote some sixteen plays, one of which was performed (and failed) at the Comédie-Française. It was agreed that her plays were consistently mediocre— abundant in sentimentality and moralizing but deficient in plot, style, and good dialogue.[11] The shortcomings of Mme de Montesson's plays, however, did not prevent her theatre from enjoying the greatest

success. The *Correspondance littéraire* consistently found her theatre
"superior to all of the others not only by virtue of the rank of the actors
and the brilliance of the company, but because of the choice of plays
and the manner in which they were acted."[12]

Important as the salon theatres and their organizers were to the
nourishment of theatremania in eighteenth-century France, it was, of
course, as performers on the public stage that women had the most
impact on the theatre arts.

Attitudes towards women performers, however, remained dualistic,
if not downright schizophrenic. Discussed, written about, sought
after, and admired sometimes to the point of adulation, women of the
theatre were nonetheless regarded with sniggering contempt when it
came to moral considerations. While rewarded socially for their
intelligence, gaiety, and wit, actresses were punished legally and
spiritually for their reputed immorality.[13] Regarded by the state as
nonpersons until the Revolution, they could neither inherit property
nor bequeath it. Since actresses were excommunicated by the Catholic
church, they could not legally marry and so, perforce, gave birth to
illegitimate children who could not be baptized. Upon death, church
rites were denied performers who had not abjured their profession in
time.[14]

To be sure, eighteenth-century women of the theatre were frequently every bit as impure as they were given credit for. Because
more often than not female performers received short shrift when it
came to distribution of the profits, they almost always sought
additional means of support for the lavish lifestyle that was expected
of them.[15] Concubinage became the normal mode for most, while, at
the very least, it was routine to offer performance in bed after a
performance at the theatre.[16] These drawbacks notwithstanding, the
glitter and glory of a career on the stage could seem irresistibly
attractive. A young actress, already repudiated by her family, describes
this allure to her sister, the wife of an architect:

> You will never be . . . more than a well-to-do bourgeoise, thoroughly
> nourished, thoroughly bored, confined to the narrow circle of your
> obscure set; . . . [but] a famous actress moves in a brilliant sphere, which
> expands as her talents develop. My name will appear in the public news,
> in gazettes, in the *Mercure*; yours will appear for the first and last time in
> your burial notice.[17]

In any case, French theatre of the eighteenth century did not want for
talented actresses. It was, according to some, France's finest moment
for female performers.

Following the seventeenth century's great Champmeslé, a brilliant
series of actresses upheld tradition at the Comédie-Française until the

Revolution. Of the seventy actresses accepted as permanent members (*sociétaires*) of the Comédie-Française during the course of the century, many were outstanding.[18] Duclos, Dumesnil, Clairon, the sisters Saint-Val, Vestris, Raucourt, and, of course, the great Adrienne Lecouvreur created the best of the tragic roles; while Fanier, Olivier, Joly, Vanhove, de Garcins, Lange, and Contat distinguished themselves in comic roles.

Adrienne Lecouvreur takes her place in the history of French theatre as the first actress to abandon the emphatic, declamatory delivery that was then standard practice.[19] Starting her acting career precociously, Mlle Lecouvreur played Pauline in Corneille's *Polyeucte* in an amateur theatre when she was only fifteen. A born actress, she performed with such success that the Comédie-Française nervously exercised its rights of exclusivity and caused further performances to be banned. Later, upon being invited to join that troupe, she conquered the Paris public with her simple, natural, yet moving acting style, which offered a welcome contrast to the grandiose declamation of the other players. In addition to distinguishing herself in many of the classical roles, most notably Racine's Bérénice, she created a number of new ones. Voltaire, who was a passionate admirer, termed her "an inimitable actress who had almost invented the art of speaking to the heart and of evincing feeling and truth where before there had hardly been more than pomposity and declamation."[20]

She was also a trailblazer socially, having been the first actress to see aristocratic salon doors opened to her. She was painted by Coypel and described by the *Mercure* as "perfectly built, . . . of noble and confident demeanor, . . . with fiery eyes and a beautiful mouth."[21] Her brilliant career, however, was cut short by untimely death in 1730 at the age of thirty-eight, possibly the result of poisoning by a vengeful female rival for the favors of an important admirer, the comte de Saxe. Because she had disdained to abjure her profession before dying, the priest at Saint-Sulpice forbade her burial in his parish. Accompanied by Voltaire, her body was transported to some unused land near the Seine and laid to rest in quicklime. Voltaire, indignant over the ignominious treatment accorded this celebrated actress, immediately composed an inflammatory poem condemning the superstition and backwardness of his countrymen.[22]

Mlle Lecouvreur was eventually replaced as Voltaire's thespian heroine by an actress in the old declamatory style, Claire Josèphe de La Tude, known as Mlle Clairon. Though clearly less talented than her predecessor, Mlle Clairon made several noteworthy contributions to theatrical progress.[23] As the female lead in Voltaire's *Orphelin de la Chine* (1755), she undertook, with the collaboration of her partner, Lekain, to introduce some much needed reform in costuming. Abandoning the elaborate hoopskirts, trains, and plumes that actresses traditionally affected, regardless of the role they were interpreting, she attempted to dress in a style suggestive of the subject at hand, namely China. So delighted was Voltaire with this initiative that he turned over his author's fee to the players to defray the cost of their costumes. Diderot referred to Mlle Clairon appreciatively in that connection as "a courageous actress."[24] Though criticized for her affected, overemphatic acting style (Grimm found her praiseworthy primarily for "the force of her lungs"), she seems to have been the first to attempt a textbook on acting techniques, her *Réflexions sur l'art dramatique*.[25]

In addition, Mlle Clairon proved to be a vigorous champion of actor's rights. As a result of a petty legal dispute, which, in 1765, had pitted the honor of the Comédie-Française against the power of the capricious and disdainful gentlemen of the chamber, Mlle Clairon, along with several fellow actors, was held at the Fort-L'Evêque prison for more than a week.[26] This ordeal was followed by three weeks of house arrest. Upon her release, she sought redress from the king in the form of a declaration in which he would, she hoped, "accord those in the acting profession the rights of citizenship, and abolish, with respect to them, excommunication and the designation of civil dishonor."[27] Unsuccessful in obtaining such an acknowledgment and in poor health, Mlle Clairon retired from the public stage not long afterwards, at the age of forty-four.

As an interpreter of comedy, Louise Contat had the good fortune to be part of the brilliant cast that created the *Mariage de Figaro* in 1784.[28] Taken with the appealing young actress, whose grace and charm overcame a tendency towards plumpness, Beaumarchais reserved for her the role of Suzanne, which she performed to great acclaim. She also proved to be an ideal interpreter of Marivaux, as well as of Molière, her portrayals of Isabelle in *School for Wives*, Elmire in *Tartuffe*, and Célimène in the *Misanthrope* helping to restore the seventeenth-century master to favor. The lifestyle of queenly splendor that success in the *Mariage de Figaro* had permitted Mlle Contat to adopt rendered her particularly vulnerable during the Reign of Terror. She survived, however, and went on to triumph in a number of roles until her retirement from the Comédie-Française at age forty-nine.

Mention should also be made of a contemporary, Mlle Raucourt. During the worst troubles of the Revolution, she opened a theatre that, in 1799, was to become the new Comédie-Française, located then, as it is today, on the rue Richelieu.[29] Noteworthy, in addition, is a distinguished actress at the Comédie-Italienne, Mme Riccoboni, who made her debut in 1734 in Marivaux's *Surprises de l'amour*. Unlike most of her compatriots, Mme Riccoboni eschewed the life of society, preferring instead to compose novels and translate plays from English. A letter to Diderot in 1758 demonstrates that she was also a thoughtful theoretician and proponent of realism in the theatre.[30]

It now seems surprising, in view of then-prevailing attitudes toward women who wrote plays, that the eighteenth century produced even the modest number of female playwrights that it did. Despite the active, if ultimately ineffectual, feminist movement that accompanied the Enlightenment, the intellectual leaders of the *siècle des lumières* were notoriously unreceptive to the notion of females meddling in literature. Nonetheless, the eighteenth century could claim a dozen or more women whose works were performed on the public stages of Paris—a considerable increase over the three or four that the seventeenth century had produced.[31]

The negative attitude toward women inclined to write, and especially to write for the theatre, was neatly, if somewhat viciously, summed up by an article entitled "On Women Authors," which appeared shortly after the close of the century. It is bad enough, the article states, for a woman to abandon both duty and reputation by taking up the writing of novels, but:

> It is far worse when this sex ... places itself at the mercy of tempestuous theatre. . . . If a woman obtains success in the theatre, what happens? . . . Her head is turned; she is intoxicated. . . . But if she experiences the reverses of the theatre . . . , if she is hissed and hissed some more, what will she say? What will she do? In the evening, how will she face her honorable and patient husband, who has tolerated her flight towards immortality, and who, unfortunately finds himself amidst the hoots of the public?[32]

Indeed, the same sentiment had already been expressed by Voltaire several decades earlier, in connection with his niece Marie-Louise Denis' attempt to write a play. "There is a certain dignity attached to the state of womanhood that must not be debased," he wrote to d'Argental. "A woman . . . is indeed degraded when she becomes a playwright and does not succeed."[33]

This kind of thinking was apt to affect women playwrights themselves. Mme de Puisieux, having turned to the theatre, confessed to Voltaire: "Yes, Monsieur, I have had the temerity to undertake a comedy. What will its success be? . . . Perhaps men will have indulgence for a woman who is still of an age to expect it of them."[34] In other words, being a female playwright was fraught with peril, and those who insisted had to recognize that success might depend less on the quality of one's writing than on the quality of one's persona.

Such reluctance to admit women to the ranks of authorship for the theatre was probably related to the matter of literary status. While novels in eighteenth-century France were viewed as frivolous, if not immoral ("fabulous books containing stories of love and chivalry, invented to entertain and occupy the time of idlers"[35]), theatre was considered a serious genre, of high spiritual and moral purpose ("tragedy . . . imitates the beautiful, the great . . . , uplifts the soul and informs the heart"[36]). Men of letters saw in theatre the true test of literary mettle, and those who created for it successfully were rewarded with praise, recognition, and money. Little wonder, then, that women were hardly encouraged to try their hand at this prestigious genre.

Though no female playwright of that era has stood the test of time (apart from Beaumarchais or Marivaux, which eighteenth-century playwright has?), several enjoyed considerable success among their contemporaries. During the early decades, before the thrust toward the *drame,* two women distinguished themselves as playwrights. The first, Marie-Anne Barbier, was the author of four tragedies and a comedy.[37] An admirer of Corneille, Mlle Barbier was a strict adherent to the tenets of classicism. At the same time, she was a feminist who sought to depict in her plays women of outstanding force and character. Drawing the subjects of her verse tragedies largely from Roman history, Mlle Barbier selected material that lent itself to this purpose and generally placed her heroines against a foil of weaker male characters. Though Mlle Barbier's plays were stronger in classical technique than in striking language or character development, they enjoyed success nonetheless. Her first play, *Arrie et Pétus* (1702), the best received of the five, was acted a total of twenty-three times; and another, *Tomyris* (1707), though it did not run long, was sufficiently well attended to yield over four hundred *livres* as the author's share of receipts. There was critical recognition as well. "Mlle Barbier writes verse as powerfully as Corneille," wrote d'Argenson. "She speaks of Romans with great dignity; I know of few women authors who have thought more forcefully."[38]

Mlle Barbier's contemporary, Mme de Gomez, started her career as a playwright several years later. Born into an illustrious family of actors and playwrights (her grandfather and father were the famous actors, Raymond and Paul Poisson respectively), Mme de Gomez turned quite naturally to writing for the theatre.[39] Like Mlle Barbier, she adhered closely to the technical rules of classicism and chose nominally historical subjects. Writing in a romantic, tragi-comic vein, rather than in the Cornelian manner of Mlle Barbier, Mme de Gomez relied heavily on the device of mistaken identity leading to scenes of recognition. Unlike the plays of Mlle Barbier, the works of Mme de Gomez for the theatre do not reflect an interest in feminism.

Her first play, *Habis* (1714), about a young man who as a child had been condemned to death by his father and who had subsequently been rescued from the sea, enjoyed remarkable success. It was performed a total of forty-eight times, making it one of the most frequently seen plays in the early part of the century.[40] Perhaps because her other plays, including a *Sémiramis* that preceded those of Crébillon and Voltaire, were very much less successful, Mme de Gomez subsequently turned her attention to the prose fiction for which she is better remembered.[41]

As the century progressed, the plays of several other women were performed in Paris, most notably *Les Amazones* by Mme du Bocage in 1749. However, none of these playwrights had much impact on theatre prior to Mme de Graffigny. Picking up on the kind of sentimental comedy that was in the air at mid-century (in particular the *comédie larmoyante* of Nivelle de La Chaussée), she wrote a five-act play, *Cénie* (1750), which, because it was in prose rather than verse, helped move French theatre a step farther from the classical mode and a step closer to the *drame*, the new genre that was developing.[42] Well constructed, witty, and offering a satisfying number of sentimental scenes, *Cénie* received fourteen performances at the Comédie-Française. "This play had the greatest success in our theatre," wrote a contemporary critic, "there was a great deal of crying."[43] Though Mme de Graffigny's second work for the public theatre, *La Fille d'Aristide* (1758), was an immediate failure, she had, by her example, influenced authors such as Diderot in the creation of a new prose genre.[44]

The most prolific woman playwright of the century, and certainly the one who staked out the most original territory, was Mme de Genlis.[45] Mistress of the duc de Chartres, she was engaged by that influential personage to educate his children (one of whom later ruled France as Louis-Philippe) and quickly acquired a reputation for her Rousseau-inspired pedagogy. This interest, combined with a genuine love of the theatre, found a natural outlet in the creation of children's plays. Moral tales for children were already quite popular, but no one before Mme de Genlis had written theatre pieces intended for this audience. Generally depicting a virtuous child set in opposition to a wicked child, these plays had titles such as *L'Enfant gâté* and were appealing, despite moralizing speeches, for their fantasy and charm. The first of these, presented about 1775 at the Palais-Royal, elicited the most enthusiastic of responses, as did the four volumes of children's plays she published a few years later (*Théâtre à l'usage des jeunes personnes*, or *Théâtre d'éducation*, 1779-1780). "No one has ever put such rare and amiable talent to better or more interesting use," opined the *Correspondance littéraire*.[46] Others concurred. La Harpe, with whom the author later formed a liaison, was moved to poetry,[47] while Catherine the Great ordered the plays translated into Russian.

This highly successful undertaking was immediately followed by two volumes of equally well received salon plays, the *Théâtre de société* (1781). Nearly as moralizing as the children's plays, her salon theatre seemed aimed at the parents of the children who appreciated her other plays and is of interest now for the occasional vignettes of eighteenth-century life. Surviving the Revolution gracefully, she produced over her lifetime more than one hundred volumes of writings.

Because of the vogue the feminist Olympe de Gouges is currently enjoying, she bears mention in connection with the theatre. Remembered primarily for her revolutionary *Declaration of Women's Rights,* Olympe was also a prolific playwright. The illiterate daughter of a butcher, she dictated some thirty plays, many with revolutionary themes. Noteworthy for her perseverance more than for her talent, she finally persuaded the Comédie-Française to produce *L'Esclavage des nègres* in 1789. Despite the savage reviews and unpleasant personal innuendos it elicited, she subsequently obtained performance of a second play in a boulevard theatre. This work, too, was an immediate and ignominious failure, so vulgar it "caused even revolutionary modesty to blush," according to the *Correspondance littéraire.*[48] After engaging in an unpopular public campaign to have Louis XVI exiled rather than executed, this courageous, energetic, and undauntable patriot died on the scaffold in 1793.

As performers, animators of private theatres, and playwrights, women were intimately involved in the life of the theatre in eighteenth-century France. If no one woman can be singled out as having sharply altered the course of theatre, it is no less true that a number of women made contributions without which the theatre arts would have been much the poorer. The French stage was surely nudged forward in its progress toward realism by the acting style of Adrienne Lecouvreur, the costumes of Mlle Clairon, and the prose of Mme de Graffigny. Mme de Genlis with her children's plays, as well as those grand ladies with their private stages, lent a variety and breadth to the theatre that the public stage alone was incapable of providing. Women had not been of comparable importance to the theatre arts in France in the seventeenth century, nor did they remain so active in the less theatre-oriented nineteenth century. It is perhaps only as our own century draws to a close that women are once again becoming as involved in the theatre arts as they had been during the Age of Enlightenment.

NOTES

1. Grimm, Diderot, et al., *Correspondance littéraire, philosophique et critique,* edited by Maurice Tourneux, 16 vols. (Paris: Garnier, 1877-1882), vol. 1, p. 158. By century's end, there were nearly two hundred such theatres, according to Max Aghion, *Le Théâtre à Paris au XVIIe siècle* (Paris: Librairie de France, 1926), p. 396. My general discussion of salon theatres is based upon

Victor du Bled, *La Comédie de société au XVIIIe siècle* (Paris: Calmann Lévy, 1893); and Adolphe Jullien, *La Comédie à la cour: les théâtres de société royale pendant le siècle dernier* (Paris: Firmin-Didot, n.d.).

2. Aghion, p. 395.

3. Unless otherwise noted, information about individual private theatres and the women who presided over them is drawn from du Bled and Jullien, as well as from Alain Decaux, *Histoire des Françaises*, 2 vols. (Paris: Perrin, 1972).

4. Apparently very attractive despite one atrophied arm, the duchesse du Maine was nicknamed the *poupée de sang* because of her size, reportedly that of a ten-year-old, and her Condé lineage. Married at the age of sixteen to the bastard, but legitimized, son of Louis XIV, her sights were set on nothing less than the throne.

5. Upon the overturn of Louis XIV's last will and testament by supporters of the duc d'Orléans, the duc du Maine's aspirations to the throne were quashed. In the aftermath, the duchesse du Maine was imprisoned until 1720.

6. While the duchesse du Maine was certainly the animating force behind theatrical events at the château de Sceaux, much of the credit for their success was due one of the women of her retinue, Rose de Staal-Delaunay, who assumed the task of principal organizer of the *nuits de Sceaux*. Having proved most helpful and energetic during the political troubles that beset her protector, she later wrote two comedies of her own that were performed in their theatre during its second phase.

7. Cited by Decaux, vol. 2, p. 333.

8. First installed in a gallery adjacent to the Cabinet of Medals, the theatre was named for its location. The operation was later moved to grander quarters in an immense stairwell and was turned into a movable theatre that could be dismantled in fourteen hours and put back together in twenty-four.

9. Highly visible and so close to the heart, Mme de Pompadour's theatre was bound to become a political football as well. Hostile to the favorite's growing influence over the king, the duc de Richelieu, first gentleman of the king's chamber, attempted to refuse her theatre the costumes and accessories it needed. Personally reminded by Louis XV of his previous stays at the Bastille, Richelieu was obliged to beat a retreat and accept Mme de Pompadour as a powerful new presence.

10. In addition to du Bled and Jullien, statements about Mme de Montesson are based on various portions of Grimm's *Correspondance littéraire*, vols. 11-14.

11. They were published in two volumes, entitled *Comédies*, in 1772 and 1777.

12. Grimm, *Correspondance littéraire*, vol. 9, p. 443. Here and throughout, translations are my own.

13. Casting a backward glance, the Goncourt brothers allowed as how, "Singers, dancers and actresses, theatre women . . . with their talents and renown . . . this world of famous *impures* entered society itself, and the highest and best of it." Edmond and Jules de Goncourt, *La Femme au dix-huitième siècle* (Paris: Firmin-Didot, 1887), p. 225.

14. These strictures had applied to members of the Comédie-Française since its inception and were not entirely removed until well into the nineteenth century. In contrast, members of the Comédie-Italienne, whose banishment was ended by the Regency, were spared this kind of treatment. See Henri Lagrave, "La Comédie-Française au XVIIIe siècle ou les contradictions d'un privilège," *Revue d'histoire du théâtre*, no. 2 (1980):129.

15. According to H. C. Lancaster's analysis of account books, "it usually took a woman longer than a man to receive a full share." *The Comédie-Française,*

168 **Women and Culture**

1680-1701: Plays, Actors, Spectators, Finances, Johns Hopkins Studies in Romance Literatures and Languages, ex. vol. 17 (Baltimore: The Johns Hopkins University Press, 1941), p. 13. For an analysis of the discrepancy between an actresses' lifestyle and her income, see Claude Alasseur, *La Comédie-Française au XVIIIe siècle: étude économique* (Paris: Mouton, 1967), pp. 129-132.

16. Grimm, *Correspondance littéraire,* vol. 8, p. 209.

17. Félix Gaiffe, *Le Drame en France au XVIIIe siècle* (Paris: Armand Colin, 1910), pp. 115-116. The actress quoted is Mlle Dangui.

18. The count was obtained from a listing of *sociétaires* by Pierre Dux and Sylvie Chevalley, *La Comédie-Française, trois siècles de gloire* (Paris: Denoël, 1980), pp. 220-221.

19. Information about Adrienne Lecouvreur is drawn from Charles Gueullette, *Acteurs et actrices du temps passé: La Comédie Française* (Paris: Librairie des Bibliophiles, 1881), pp. 169-200; Decaux, vol. 2, pp. 246-251; and Dux and Chevalley.

20. Cited by Dux and Chevalley, p. 61.

21. Cited by Decaux, vol. 2, p. 248.

22. The poem is "La Mort de mademoiselle Lecouvreur, célèbre actrice," 1730.

23. Information about Mlle Clairon is taken from Henry Lyonnet, *Les Comédiennes* (Paris: Marcel Seheur, 1929), pp. 60-67; Dux and Chevalley, and passages throughout the *Correspondance littéraire.*

24. Diderot, "De la poésie dramatique," in *Oeuvres esthétiques,* edited by Paul Vernière (Paris: Garnier, 1959), p. 267.

25. Grimm, *Correspondance littéraire,* vol. 2, p. 265.

26. The actor Dubois, who played a major role in du Belloy's extremely popular *Siège de Calais,* had been incarcerated for defaulting on a debt. Despite repeated orders from the gentlemen of the chamber, the troupe refused to perform du Belloy's play as scheduled.

27. Grimm, *Correspondance littéraire,* vol. 6, pp. 282, 356.

28. Statements about this actress are based on Dux and Chevalley as well as on passages in the *Correspondance littéraire,* vols. 11-14.

29. Dux and Chevalley, pp. 94-95.

30. Diderot, *Correspondance,* edited by Georges Roth (Paris: Editions de Minuit, 1956), vol. 2, pp. 86-89.

31. The number of seventeenth-century women playwrights is based on H. C. Lancaster, *A History of French Dramatic Literature in the Seventeenth Century, Part V, Recapitulation, 1610-1700,* vol. 9 (Baltimore: The Johns Hopkins Press, 1941), pp. 86-87. For the listing of eighteenth-century women playwrights which follows, I culled names from various sources: H. C. Lancaster, *The Comédie-Française, 1701-1774, Transactions of the American Philosophical Society,* vol. 41 (Philadelphia: American Philosophical Society, 1951); René Louis de Voyer de Paulmy, marquis d'Argenson, *Notice sur les oeuvres de théâtre,* edited by Henri Lagrave, *Studies on Voltaire and the Eighteenth Century,* nos. 42 and 43 (Oxford: The Voltaire Foundation, 1966); Bachaumont, *Mémoires secrets pour servir à l'histoire de la république des lettres en France,* 36 vols. (Paris, 1868; Geneva: Slatkine, 1966); and the *Correspondance littéraire.* Only women whose plays were actually produced on the public stage in Paris are included. These women and their plays are: Mlle Barbier, *Arrie et Pétus* (1702), *Cornélie, mère des Gracques* (1703), *Thomyris* (1707), *La Mort de César* (1709), *Le Faucon* (1719); Mme de Beauharnais, *La Fausse Inconstance* (1787); Mme Benoit, *Le Triomphe de la probité* (1768), *La Supercherie réciproque* (1768); Mme du Bocage, *Les Amazones* (1749); Mme de Chaumont, *L'Amour à Tempe* (1773), and in collaboration with Mme de Roxet, *L'Heureuse Rencontre* (1771);

Mme de Genlis, numerous childrens plays published in *Théâtre à l'usage des jeunes personnes*, or *Théâtre d'éducation* (1779-1780); Mme de Gomez, *Habis* (1714), *Sémiramis* (1716), *Cléarque, tyran d'Héraclée* (1717); Olympe de Gouges, *L'Esclavage des noirs ou l'heureux naufrage* (1789); *L'Entrée de Dumouriez à Bruxelles ou les vivandiers* (1790); Mme de Graffigny, *Cénie* (1750), *La Fille d'Aristide* (1758); Mme Hus, *Plutus, rival de l'amour* (1756); Mme de Montesson, *La Comtesse de Chazelle* (1785); Mme Riccoboni, *Le Naufrage* (1726); Mme de Saint-Chamond, *Les Amants sans le savoir* (1771); Mlle de Saint-Léger, *Les Deux Soeurs* (1783).

32. *Le Spectateur français au XIXe siècle* (Paris: Société typographique, 1805), vol. 2, pp. 556-558.

33. Voltaire, *Correspondance, 1704-1778*, edited by Theodore Besterman (Geneva: Institut et musée Voltaire, 1953-1965), vol. 20, p. 315.

34. Ibid., pp. 211-212.

35. Furetière's *Dictionnaire universel* (The Hague, 1690; Geneva: Slatkine, 1970).

36. "Poésie," *L'Encyclopédie, ou dictionnaire raisonné des sciences, des arts et des métiers* (Neufchastel: Samuel Faulche, 1765).

37. Information about Mlle Barbier is drawn from H. C. Lancaster, *Sunset, A History of Parisian Drama in the Last Years of Louis XIV, 1701-1715* (Baltimore: The Johns Hopkins University Press, 1945), pp. 70-79.

38. D'Argenson, p. 316.

39. Material about Mme de Gomez is drawn from Lancaster, *Sunset*, pp. 79-80; and idem, *French Tragedy in the Time of Louis XV and Voltaire* (Baltimore: The Johns Hopkins University Press, 1950), pp. 34-38.

40. According to Aghion, p. 23, a new work that received as many as twenty or twenty-five performances was considered very successful.

41. Her best known works are *Les Journées amusantes* (1723), *La Jeune Alcidiane* (1773), and the frequently reprinted *Cent Nouvelles nouvelles* (1735).

42. Information about this playwright has been drawn from Charles Collé, *Journal et mémoires*, 3 vols. (Paris: Firmin-Didot, 1868); and Grimm, *Correspondance littéraire*, vols. 1-4.

43. D'Argenson, p. 416.

44. Gaiffe, pp. 32-33, 158-159.

45. Much has been written about Mme de Genlis. I have consulted Jacques Truchet, *Théâtre du XVIIIe siècle*, Bibliothèque de la Pléiade (Paris: Gallimard, 1974), vol. 2, pp. 943-969 and 1506-08; Lester G. Krakeur, "Le Théâtre de Mme de Genlis," *Modern Language Review* (April, 1940): 185-192; and *Correspondance littéraire*, vols. 12-16.

46. Grimm, *Correspondance littéraire*, vol. 12, p. 279.

47. La Harpe, "Correspondance littéraire," *Oeuvres* (Paris, 1820-1821; Geneva: Slatkine, 1968), vol. 11, p. 141.

48. Grimm, *Correspondance littéraire*, vol. 16, p. 186. The play was *L'Entrée de Dumouriez à Bruxelles*.

Ursula M. Rempel

Women and Music: Ornament of the Profession?

Mademoiselle Diderot . . . is one of the finest harpsichord-players in Paris, and, for a lady, possessed of an uncommon portion of knowledge in modulation.

Mad. Brillon . . . is one of the greatest lady-players on the harpsichord in Europe. This lady not only plays the most difficult pieces with great precision, taste, and feeling, but is an excellent sight's-woman; of which I was convinced by her manner of executing some of my own music. . . . She likewise composes. . . . She plays on several instruments . . . she likewise draws well and engraves, and is a most accomplished and agreeable woman.[1]

EIGHTEENTH-CENTURY French music reflects the cultural expectations of highly sophisticated and aristocratic tastes; while the dominating genre is opera, others, both sacred and secular, include motets, mass settings, cantatas, trio and solo sonatas, suites, *symphonies concertantes*, ballets, and *chansons*. The period differs from our own in that audiences did not listen to music for the purpose of rehearing standard works; on the contrary, there was a continual hunger for new music, one that could be satisfied since Paris, in particular, had cultural prestige and patrons of financial strength. Surviving pictorial evidence alone gives rich documentation of lavish and extravagant productions throughout Europe, whether large-scale for royalty and, later, the public or small-scale for the salon. Sources such as account books and diaries provide further evidence: "The costs of the wax candles used for lighting the opera house [at Mannheim] for a single performance came to over £ 40, and the expense of mounting a new production approached £ 4,000."[2]

And a few years later we find out that:

The new *salle du Palais-Royal,* three times the size of the old . . . held an audience of two thousand five hundred and had a staff of two hundred and seventy-eight, only five of whom were administrators. There were eighteen solo singers and a chorus of forty, nineteen solo dancers and a *corps de ballet* of seventy-two and an orchestra of sixty-eight as well as choral and ballet masters, accompanists, and a large staff, from designers to stage hands, of thirty-nine.[3]

It is difficult to generalize further about a musical scene that includes Marin Marais' *Le Tableau de l'opération de la taille* (1717) for narrator, viol da gamba, and harpsichord; Salomon's opera *Médée et Jason* (1713); the now vanished keyboard improvisations of Elisabeth-Claude Jacquet de La Guerre (c. 1720); the cantatas of Clérambault (c. 1720); Rameau's *Traité de l'harmonie* (1722); Couperin's *Pièces de clavecin* (c. 1725); Rousseau's *Le Devin du village* (1752); the *Symphonies concertantes* of Gossec (c. 1760); Gluck's *Alceste* (1767); and Grétry's *Richard Coeur de Lion* (1782).[4]

A musical (and political) entrepreneur, Jean-Baptiste Lully (1632-1687), made himself indispensable to Louis XIV. With Louis' support, he came to represent the epitome of French musical taste and, until the mid-eighteenth century, to influence musical styles and genres. As was later the case with Beethoven, Lully's influence vastly exceeded his lifetime, and, like Beethoven's, Lully's successors suffered in comparison with the master. His works were used to support one of the extremes in the eighteenth-century feuds over the esthetic and nationalistic directions of French opera.[5] It was Lully who founded "one of the first schools for the professional woman performer . . . in France. . . . He persuaded Louis XIV to allow girls to dance in the ballets he was composing. . . . The demand for trained singers to take part in opera and oratorios promoted musicians to found special schools for girls."[6]

Roles of women in the eighteenth-century French musical world were governed by the following various, major, and interrelated factors: attitudes towards musicians vis-à-vis the social/class structures; societal trends that influenced changes in musical genres; variations in the venues of musical performance; and the decorum concerning which instrument could properly be played by which sex.

Twentieth-century views about earlier musicians (both female and male) tend to be based on nineteenth-century perceptions of the musician as exalted artist-creator-virtuoso-god. The overwhelming prestige of composers, solo performers, and conductors is a romantic esthetic; the image of a wizard, wand in hand, conjuring up lush orchestral sounds, would have seemed ludicrous to Mozart or Haydn.[7] Nor could they have imagined a Liszt transforming psychic energy into music. Eighteenth-century composers wrote to fulfill commissions and to make money, and performers employed by a court "jobbed it"— often in livery. The musician was seen not as godly creator but as servant or artisan (admittedly, often an upper-class servant), as someone who was often expected to improvise at sight (a skill expected of performers) or to create a new cantata to satisfy a princely whim.

The employment of female instrumentalists in court orchestras was negligible; rather, women musicians were hired by such institutions as the Académie and the Opéra for both solo and ensemble roles as singers and dancers. In the case of singers, a natural and pleasing voice and a talent for the stage were often admission enough to the opera chorus. If the singer were female and attractive, she might find herself in a solo role. Although the training of singers and dancers was more rigorous in the earlier part of the century, resulting in a higher standard of performance, attitudes towards performers tended to remain the same throughout the century. By 1750, professional singers and dancers were not necessarily trained, and the deterioration of performance standards becomes clear when we remember that the Académie "allowed singers to bequeath their roles to their heirs."[8] Professional musicians were no more or less gifted than their amateur counterparts, but they were paid for their services; amateur musicians enjoyed the pleasures of the art without enduring its hardships or social stigma.

The chasms that existed between classes of female musicians (particularly in the earlier part of the century) arose largely from the performance medium chosen, the amateur-professional dichotomy, and ideas concerning public versus private musical consumption. Women musicians who were not opera singers or dancers tended to be daughters of established and prominent musical figures and received their musical education at home—or in some cases, in convents. Such training consisted of performance on an instrument and occasionally instruction in music theory and composition.

For fashionable women, instruction in lute, singing, harp, and harpsichord (later pianoforte) was a social necessity; ladies of quality were expected to entertain at domestic evening entertainments. Lack of talent was apparently not a deterrent. In 1783, Abt Vogler reports:

> Of feminine amateurs who play the keyboard exceedingly well there is an untold number in Paris. There are not a few ladies who can compete with any keyboard professor in playing of a difficult sonata, perhaps even a sonata of his own composition. Scarcely a city in Europe could count so many fair dilettantes who know how to shade their tones so beautifully, so sensitively (they have the temperament for this), with such tender appeal, breathing pleasure, and with such naive deportment.[9]

With more than a little irony, Ancelet writes:

> A timid young lady allows herself to be coaxed for a long time to sing: she is induced to proceed to the harpsichord. After many curtsies, she

proclaims that she has a cold, and finally sings by heart the lesson composed by her teacher. By dint of hastening the tempo, the little song comes to an end and the curtsies begin again.[10]

And a little later in the century, it was believed that "every fine young lady, whether or not she has talent, must learn to play the piano or sing . . . it is the fashion."[11]

But a social grace for one class was quite different from professional training for another. The quotes that open this essay are worth recalling here, and the following passages amplify them:

> Francis, the second of the three [Couperin] brothers . . . had a daughter named Louisa, who sang and played on the harpsichord with admirable grace and skill, and who, notwithstanding her sex, was in the number of the king's musicians, and in that capacity received an annual pension or salary.[12]
>
> . . . The younger Francis [Couperin] died in 1733 . . . , leaving two daughters equally celebrated for their performance on that which appears to have been the favorite instrument of the family; the one a nun in the abbey of Maubuisson; the other is the successor of her father in charge of the harpsichord in the king's chamber, an employment which, except in this instance, was never known to have been conferred on any but men.[13]

Such women as the Couperin daughters achieved significant artistic successes, but their contributions are vastly outnumbered (literally, in terms of volume) by other female music-making activities. Some evidence exists of women writing large-scale sacred works in the early eighteenth century, but the operatic extravaganzas of the same period were mainly the province of male composers.[14] The genres expected of women composers were keyboard suites and solo songs—small-scale works for private audiences. Mid- to late-eighteenth-century tastes for less elaborate modes of opera resulted in some works in this genre by women composers, but the increasing emphasis throughout the century on shorter, secular works matched society's expectations of women as composers of more "frivolous" music. It is true that patronesses of the arts are visible in, for example, the La Pouplinière circle, but women impresarios did not exist. Mounting large-scale productions depended on money, power, business acumen, and public visibility—domains of men.

Partly because of fuller evidence, women composers and performers appear to be more active in the latter half of the century. Together with increasing secularity went a stronger emphasis on solo virtuosi; and solo and ensemble music found venues not only in the traditional academies and salons but also in the entirely new phenomenon of the *concerts spirituels* (founded 1725), the first French example of what was to be a burgeoning platform for musicians, the subscription concert. The *Journal de Paris,* 341, announces a *concert spirituel au château des Tuileries* for December 8, 1789. The program includes:

> [A] Haydn symphony, after which Mlle Rousselois will sing a scene of Cambini . . . [a] Haydn symphony, after which Mlle Rousselois will sing a scene of Méhul—Mlle Candeille will perform a concerto of her own composition on the forte piano, with horn and flute accompaniment performed by Messrs. le Brun and Devienne.

Sex roles determined the instruments women played, and the reasons were not specific to the eighteenth century but were historical. Harpsichords and harps, for example, had been decorated with images of women from the early Renaissance onward, and a symbolic connection between object and player continued in the eighteenth century, both in furniture design and in musical decorum (harp columns were decorated with "Grecian" female heads and surmounted by caryatids). Brass and percussion instruments were closed areas to women—again, for historical reasons: the instruments were scarcely off the battlefield. Nor was it considered flattering to a woman's beauty for her face to be reddened and distorted, lips and cheeks compressed, from playing the oboe, chalumeau, or bassoon—and more breath pressure was needed to sound these instruments than for their present-day equivalents.[15]

Contrary to such potential abandonments of decorum, keyboard instruments, flutes (the flautist's smile), harp, lute, and even voice displayed the female form to full advantage and allowed women to display grace and elegance. All of these factors must be kept in mind when evaluating the roles of women in eighteenth-century French music. It is too easy, from the perspective of the 1980s, to jump to facile conclusions from inadequate evidence; even our knowledge of the barest biographical data is commonly too skimpy for many safe inferences to be drawn.

A preliminary investigation of women active in music from 1715 until the Revolution shows an interesting distribution of women by profession:

Singers:	75
Dancers:	117
Keyboard players:	24
Court musicians:	7
Harpists:	20
Violinists:	2
Teachers:	6
Composers:	57
Publishers:	34

Although every effort has been made to determine the major musical category, some women do appear in more than one.[16] It is immediately apparent from such a classification that the primary function of women musicians was re-creative. Women as performers overwhelmingly dominate the other categories, although in the late part of the century more women appear in music as business and more begin to write—either music or methods. The numbers are somewhat misleading in that they disguise the potential overlap of professions; some singers also danced and vice versa. The relatively minor roles of some women singers would have demanded a certain amount of flexibility; a singer in the chorus may well have been a member of the opera *corps de ballet*, and, unfortunately, too often the *filles de l'Opéra* were also *filles de joie*.[17]

For the most part, however, the overlap here tends to be the result of singers past their vocal prime entering another branch of their profession: teaching, publishing, or composing. The careers of some singers were rather fleeting (three to ten years); and while marriage and/or pregnancy may have intervened in a professional career, Emile Campardon cites other reasons for dismissal or early retirement: seduction, prostitution, scandalous affairs, and theft.[18]

Dual and sometimes multiple instrumental facility was expected of performers. In our age of specialization, when proficiency on one instrument is the norm, it seems alien to accept performers equally adept on several; but even today organists are traditionally harpsichordists as well, since the keyboard techniques are similar. In the eighteenth century, harpists also played harpsichord (later pianoforte), since the age made little distinction between techniques on a horizontal plane (keyboard) and those on a vertical plane (harp). Among harpists, Mme de Genlis is infamous for proposing a five-finger technique that is totally unsuited to their instrument.

Controversy raged throughout the century on the attributes of Italian versus French vocal techniques (Italy had on its side the facts that it had founded the first vocal schools and that its language is conducive to expressive vocal production). According to contemporary sources, France produced great singers, such as Mlle Fel: "She debuted at the opera theater in 1733. For twenty-five years she delighted the public."[19] Rousseau added, "it takes a Fel or a Jélyotte to sing French music, but any voice is good in Italian music, because the beauties of Italian singing are in the music itself, whereas those of French singing, if there are any, are all in the art of the singer."[20]

Burney, however, seems less enthusiastic about French singers. While he disapproves of Italy's "artificial" voices (by which he means *castrati*) and compliments the "natural" female voices in the conservatories of Venice, he is harsh in his condemnation of French singers.

> I arrived at Lyons on my way home ... where, in visiting the theatre, I
> was more disgusted than ever, at hearing French music, after the
> exquisite performances to which I had been accustomed in Italy.
> Eugénie, a pretty comedy, preceded Silvain, an opera by M. Grétry:
> there were many pretty passages in the music, but so ill sung, with so
> false an expression, such screaming, forcing, and trilling, as quite made
> me sick.[21]

On a performance by Mlle Delcambre, Burney remarked that she
"screamed out *Exaudi Deus* with all the power of lungs she could
muster."[22]

Higher on the social ladder than chorus singers—and indeed higher
than many of the solo singers—were court musicians and instrumental
performers, who found a platform in the *concert spirituel;* a number of
them emigrated to England before and during the Revolution. Mme
Krumpholtz, wife of Jean-Baptiste Krumpholtz, the harp composer
and inventor, was the century's most brilliant harpist; renowned in
France, she continued impressing audiences in London during the
Haydn years.[23] There were other contenders for the title: "Madame
Delaval struck out with her 'flying fingers,' such effects from the harp,
as confirming all the poets insist on of the antients [sic] performance
on that noble and sublime instrument."[24]

If the harp was one of the predominantly "female" and important
instruments in the second half of the century (largely due to the
improvements made in its mechanism after 1760), the harpsichord
was the primary vehicle for women in the first half. Here, a number of
important female performers emerges. Loesser reports that "mademoiselle Guyot [d. 1728], the daughter of a barrister of the Supreme
Court, 'combined delicacy and brilliance of touch with perfect science
of composition at the harpsicord' and 'performed all the most difficult
music on the spur of the moment.'"[25]

The female members of the Couperin family were important
enough to yield entries in some of the encyclopedias of their century
and of the next. However, it is Elisabeth-Claude Jacquet de La Guerre
(c. 1668-1729) who emerges as the *première solo virtuosa* of the eighteenth
century. Although even she has not been fully researched, the
scholarship devoted to her exceeds that on any other woman in her
field.[26] She is spoken of as an artist as early as 1725 (in Walther's
Lexikon), and again in 1776, by Hawkins, who gives details of her
capabilities.

> She ... was ... instructed in the practice of the harpsichord and the art of
> composition by her father. She was a very fine performer, and would
> sing and accompany herself with so rich and exquisite a flow of harmony
> as captivated all that heard her. She was also an excellent composer, and,
> in short, possessed such a degree of skill, as well in the science as the

practice of music, that but few of her sex have equalled her. An opera of her composition, entitled Céphale et Procris, was represented in the Royal Academy of Paris in the year 1694, and is extant in print.[27]

Edith Borroff's fine entry in *The New Grove* is an excellent summary of Jacquet de La Guerre's career.[28]

The century's increasing emphasis on secularity—and its concomitant genres—saw a rise both in the number of solo performers and in the amount of music published for specific instruments, including a sudden outpouring of method books. The women who printed, engraved, or published music are related to these trends; it is interesting to note the surprising number of women, many of whom were in business with their husbands. Others appear in documents as widows continuing the family business. By 1770, one could buy not merely violin and keyboard method books but also instructions for the bagpipe and hurdy-gurdy—the latter useful for posturing in an imagined pastoral world.[29]

The teach-yourself-at-home craze caught on swiftly; and, from about 1770 to 1820, women musicians in particular exploited its benefits. No longer was it necessary to make a living merely from concert appearances and teaching; it became possible to cash in on a performer's "hit" by publishing an arrangement of it, and the same monetary advantage became available by implying in a method that the amateur could become as skilled and famous as the author. False advertising is no new invention; numerous eighteenth-century methods feature persuasive title pages that promise to instruct easily, tastefully, and quickly. Mme de Genlis' *Nouvelle méthode pour apprendre à jouer de la harpe* (Paris, 1811) makes the outrageous claim that one can learn to play the instrument "in less than six months of lessons"!

Although we are beginning to redress the balance, history has not dealt kindly with women musicians, and even recent twentieth-century histories of music, at best, make only passing references to them (popular musicians of this century are, of course, an exception). Historians have always filtered their subjects; and music historians, like their allies in literature, art, and architecture may be largely forgiven for not dealing with a specifically feminist aspect of its subject. If one compares the "forgotten" male composers of the eighteenth century in France with those women whose work is not being revived, it becomes clear that the sex of the composer is not necessarily the consideration in the filtering system, but rather the tastes, fashions, esthetics, and new prejudices of a given era. (A Parisian in 1760, hearing the name Bach, would not have thought of J. S., but rather of C. P. E. or, even more likely, of J. C.) Research into women in music in the eighteenth century is still largely embryonic;

although the musical pantheon, like those in other arts, seems established, many Frenchwomen are worthy of being *déterrées* to see whether some of the old marble might begin to crack.

NOTES

1. Charles Burney, *The Present State of Music in France and Italy* (London: T. Becket and Co., 1771), pp. 392, 342.

2. Christopher Hogwood, *Music at Court* (London: Gollancz, 1980), p. 94.

3. Henry Raynor, *A Social History of Music: From the Middle Ages to Beethoven* (New York: Schocken, 1972), p. 237. Raynor's chapter 14 "Music and the French Absolutism," gives further documentation on such matters as production costs, ticket prices, kinds of audiences, and so forth.

4. As beginning references, general histories of music offer sections on the eighteenth century. Useful introductions may be found in Donald J. Grout, *A History of Western Music,* rev. ed. (New York: Norton, 1973); Paul H. Lang, *Music in Western Civilization* (New York: Norton, 1941); Karl H. Wörner, *History of Music,* 5th ed., translated and supplemented by Willis Wager (New York: Free Press, 1973). Works that more explicitly devote themselves to eighteenth-century French music are: James R. Anthony, *French Baroque Music from Beaujoyeulx to Rameau* (London: Batsford, 1973-74); Edith Borroff, *The Music of the Baroque* (Dubuque: William C. Brown, 1970); Manfred Bukofzer, *Music in the Baroque Era* (New York: Norton, 1947); Claude Palisca, *Baroque Music,* 2d ed. (Englewood Cliffs: Prentice-Hall, 1981); Reinhard G. Pauly, *Music in the Classic Period,* 2d ed. (Englewood Cliffs: Prentice-Hall, 1973); and *The Age of Enlightenment: 1745-1790* edited by Egon Wellesz and Frederick Sternfeld, vol. 7, New Oxford History of Music (London: Oxford University Press, 1973).

5. A sampling of texts on the subject can be found in "Operatic Rivalry in France: Pro and Contra Lully," and "Operatic Rivalry in France: The 'Querelle des Bouffons'," in *Source Readings in Music History,* edited by Oliver Strunk (New York: Norton, 1950), pp. 473-507; 619-654.

6. Sophie Drinker, *Music and Women: The Story of Women in Their Relation to Music* (New York: Coward-McCann, 1948), p. 236.

7. Various methods of direction were common in the eighteenth century, depending on the genre and the size of ensemble. In small groups, the harpsichordist gave the necessary cues; and in larger productions—which required a time-beater to keep everyone together—instruments of direction included a heavy stick pounded on the floor and rolled-up white paper flourished in the air.

8. Raynor, p. 241.

9. Arthur Loesser, *Men, Women and Pianos* (London: Gollancz, 1955), p. 318.

10. Ibid., p. 313.

11. *Allgemeine Musikalische Zeitung,* vol. 3 (1800-1801):66.

12. Sir John Hawkins, *A General History of the Science and Practice of Music* (1776; New York: Dover, 1963), p. 779.

13. Ibid., p. 781.

14. Scattered references to women church musicians may be found in Michel Le Moël, "La situation des musiciens d'église en France à la veille de la révolution," *Recherches sur la musique française classique* 15, (1975):191-243; and in Robert Machard, "Les musiciens en France au temps de Jean-Philippe

Rameau," *Recherches* 11 (1971); the whole volume is devoted to the subject. *Recherches* is an annual Parisian publication devoted to "La Vie musicale en France sous les rois Bourbons." Its regular section, "Chroniques," is worth checking; in vol. 15 (1975) is James Anthony's "A Checklist of Research in Progress," an excellent compilation covering books, monographs, dissertations in progress, and editions of music (pp. 262-266). *Recherches* is strong on archival studies; a recent example is Anne Chastel, "Etude sur la vie musicale à Paris à travers la presse pendant le règne de Louis XVI," 16 (1976):37-70. Pages 62-70 comprise a "list [which includes women] of editors, merchants or musicians who sell music."

15. It is a frequent exhortation in eighteenth-century courtesy writings that, while smiling is correct and acceptable, laughing is to be avoided since it makes the potentially divine human countenance look simian; Jonathan Swift is reliably reported to have laughed only twice in his life. For this information I am indebted to Dr. W. John Rempel, Department of English, University of Manitoba.

16. Sources of this information include: Aaron I. Cohen, *International Encyclopedia of Women Composers* (New York: Bowker, 1981); Don L. Hixon and Don Hennessee, *Women in Music: A Biobibliography* (Metuchen, NJ: Scarecrow, 1975); Emile Campardon, *L'Académie royale de musique au XVIIIe siècle* (1884; New York: Da Capo, 1971); Constant Pierre, *Histoire du concert spirituel* (Paris: Société française de musicologie, 1975 [written in 1900]); Jeannie G. Pool, *Women in Music History: A Research Guide* (New York: Pool, 1977).

17. The stigma attached to opera singers, dancers, and actresses was strong indeed. See *The New Grove Dictionary of Music and Musicians*, 1980, s.v. "Laguerre, Marie-Joséphine." Her "early death was apparently the result of loose living."

18. Campardon, p. vi. Working with unedited documents from the National Archives, Campardon lists brief biographical data, dates of debuts, retirements, principal events, theatrical careers, and contemporary opinions of singers and dancers associated with the Academy.

19. Alexandre E. Choron and François J. Fayolle, *Dictionnaire historique des musiciens* (Paris, 1810; Hildesheim: Olms, 1971), s.v. "Fel."

20. Quoted in Strunk, pp. 640-641. An impressive collection of contemporary references to Fel's singing may be found in Mary Cyr's "Eighteenth-Century French and Italian Singing: Rameau's Writing for the Voice," *Music & Letters* 61 (July-October 1980):318-337; the Fel citations are on pp. 320-322.

21. Burney, pp. 387, 388, 389.

22. Ibid., p. 25.

23. For an essay that demonstrates the extreme difficulties in ascertaining *any* verifiable facts about women eighteenth-century musicians from secondary sources, see my "The Perils of Secondary Sources: An Annotated Bibliography of Encyclopedic and Dictionary Sources Relating to the Harpist Members of the Krumpholtz Family," *The American Harp Journal* 7 (Summer 1980):25-30, and especially the "documented" quasi-biography, pp. 28-29.

24. *The Times*, 20 February 1792; quoted in Robbins Landon, *Haydn: Chronicle and Works*, vol. 3 (Bloomington: Indiana University Press, 1976), p. 134.

25. Loesser, p. 310.

26. See Edith Borroff "An Introduction to Elisabeth-Claude Jacquet de La Guerre" (monograph, Brooklyn College, 1966); and Carol Henry Bates, "The Instrumental Music of Elisabeth-Claude Jacquet de La Guerre" (Ph.D. diss., Indiana University, 1979).

27. Hawkins, p. 779.

28. *The New Grove*, s.v. "Jacquet de La Guerre."

29. Lang, p. 732, gives evidence of a parallel shift from publications exclusively for professional musicians to those intended for amateurs: [in Germany] "composers, who formerly addressed themselves exclusively to princes and archbishops, now turned to *Kenner und Liebhaber* ... there was even a periodical, appearing in 1769, entitled 'Der Musikalische Dilettante,' devoted to their service." For a recent article on harp methods see my "Méthodes de Harpe: An Introduction to Eighteenth-Century Tutors," *The American Harp Journal* 8 (Winter 1981).

♨ Linda Gardiner

Women in Science

THE ROLE of women in science in eighteenth-century France is an almost totally unexplored field. Indeed, the topic itself is hardly defined. What to include in addressing it, therefore, is initially unclear. Should one try to reconstruct the scientific training available to French women in the period? Should one look at the "fashions" in science that led some of them to take an interest in various branches of the subject at different times during the century? Should one study the biographies of some specific women who had a more than passing interest in the subject? Or should one actually read the writings of women scientists themselves in order to evaluate their contribution to the field?

All of these options present difficulties for two rather obvious reasons: the lack of much primary research on any of them and the undeniable fact that no matter which of these areas one chooses the number of women one could study is extremely small. It hardly needs to be emphasized that in spite of the relatively greater freedom accorded to women in this period they still encountered intellectual barriers both at the level of access to the normal institutions of learning (which entailed their exclusion from a tradition of problems and research techniques in all disciplines) and at the less formal but equally powerful level of cultural expectations and prohibitions. In the natural sciences, this exclusion had an especially pronounced effect. To be active in science, then as now, required two things in particular: direct access to the people and institutions engaged in significant research and the financial resources for the acquisition of books and laboratory equipment. In France, women were excluded from the schools that prepared for entrance to the universities and, of course, from studying at the universities themselves. This meant that they could not use the normal channels to acquire the essential mathematical knowledge needed to keep up with advances in physics, the major science of the early and mid-century. And even though the schools and universities themselves devoted little time to physics and what they taught was for much of the century the outdated theories of the Cartesians, they still provided a basic training, especially in mathematics, that could easily be supplemented later by a scientifically inclined student. Furthermore, the personal contacts gained in that institutional structure could be continued subsequently by classmates who found that they shared common scientific interests or careers. None of this was available to women.

Even those women who, by the accidents of their upbringing or by force of personality, acquired a measure of scientific knowledge and wished to improve it by becoming part of the scientific community found further obstacles in their way. In an age when scientific advance was in the hands of a very few, those few inevitably tended to band together and to take over, where possible, the prestigious and publicly recognized scientific institutions. In France, this meant primarily the Académie des Sciences, which, through its directly elected members and its network of corresponding and adjunct members from all over Europe, gathered together many of the foremost scientists of the age, especially in the middle part of the century.[1] But women were never admitted to the prestigious Académie (nor, indeed, to the majority of the provincial academies). Their scientific contacts, then, had to be purely on the personal level, dependent on their noninstitutional relationships with practicing male scientists whom they met—again, largely accidentally—and whom they could persuade of their serious interest in the subject. They could not participate in major collaborative research enterprises (such as the French expeditions of the 1730s to Peru and the Arctic Circle, whose purpose was the taking of observations needed to establish the exact shape of the earth). Since laboratory research was still in its infancy and less confined than now to public- or industry-funded institutions, it was possible in principle for a scientifically minded woman to take up smaller-scale research on her own, always assuming that her husband or father was willing to spend money on such eccentric fancies; but the fact remained that only elementary or sporadic projects could be carried out by private individuals. And in any case, then as now, the value of any project required that the researcher be up-to-date with current knowledge and have some idea of what would be worth investigating in the first place. Given these restrictions, women's access to the education and contacts needed for significant research was virtually nonexistent.

These latter points do not bear simply on the role (or absence of role) of women in science; they characterize a more general distinction that gradually came into being during the eighteenth century—that between professionals and amateurs. Although the distinction had not yet become an absolute one, the gap between amateur and professional was widening; it was already extremely difficult to be a practicing amateur, as distinct from those, like many of the *philosophes,* who kept up with the latest information but contributed nothing to it themselves. Women had no choice but to approach science as amateurs; and although many did so, especially in the 1730s and 1740s, those who managed to rise above amateur status to become serious contributors to the field to any degree at all can almost be counted on the fingers of one hand.

Even for this extraordinary handful, we have far less information than we would like, and, in some cases, we know hardly more than their names and a few bare details. Mme du Pierry, Mme Lefrançais de Lalande, Mme Lavoisier, Hortense Lepaute, Sophie Germain, Emilie du Châtelet, all figure in contemporary memoirs or letters and reappear briefly in later histories of mathematics and physics; but beyond the few details of dates and writings (or collaborations), no historian has yet tried to give a more adequate biographical account of these women's careers, let alone tried to evaluate seriously the contributions made by any of them to the advancement of the sciences.[2]

In the light of this massive neglect of the (understandably sparse) contribution of French women to eighteenth-century science, it would seem pointlessly ambitious to attempt within the scope of this brief essay to redress a two hundred-year-old imbalance by means of a hasty biographical or critical analysis of the group of women just listed. It seems equally unhelpful to attempt a generalizing account of "the role of women in science," precisely because the numbers in question are so small. Instead of any of these treatments, I would like to use this essay to focus primarily on a single one of the atypical products, one of the few who transcended mere amateur status to become a "woman in science" rather than an interested onlooker.

The very difficulty of gaining access to the world of science meant that only a tiny sample of women, and a totally abnormal sample at that, is at all relevant. Consequently, rather than seeking the features shared by the few would-be women scientists, I want to argue that we can learn more from a study of any one of them, in all her particularity and atypicality. Even a brief study of the career of such a figure can demonstrate both the potentialities and limitations experienced by women scientists in eighteenth-century France; by seeing just how far one woman could go within the scientific community, we get a vivid sense of the unstable mixture of freedoms and frustrations that fell to the lot of aspiring women scientists in this period.

Of the women mentioned, the only one about whom much contemporary information, as well as a substantial body of original writings (both in and outside science), has survived, is Emilie, the marquise du Châtelet. This fortunate accident makes it possible to use her career as an illustration of the extent to which a sufficiently determined (and privileged) woman could go in gaining acceptance and respect in the scientific community.

Born in 1706 into the Breteuil family, one of the prominent dynasties of the French court, Emilie du Châtelet is all but invisible (except for her marriage in 1726 to the marquis du Châtelet) until 1733. It was then that Emilie encountered Voltaire, already famous as a poet and notorious as the presumptuous critic of French intellectual, religious, and political institutions. At that time, he was one of an intellectually exciting group of playwrights, poets, scientists, and philosophers; and largely through her association with him (a liaison that lasted the rest of her life), Emilie du Châtelet, too, came into contact with what we might call the avant-garde of the French intelligentsia.

During the next fifteen years, living mostly either in Paris or at the du Châtelet estate at Cirey, she wrote and published one book on the metaphysics of natural science (the *Institutions de physique*), an essay on the nature of fire and heat (the *Dissertation sur la nature et propagation du feu*), and two short pieces on the problem of measuring physical force. She also wrote, but did not publish, an essay on optics, a translation of Mandeville's *Fable of the Bees*, a treatise on language, an essay on happiness, and (apparently) a lengthy critical examination of the Bible. She co-authored, anonymously, Voltaire's popularization of Newtonian physics, the *Eléments de la philosophie de Newton*, and she completed a translation of Newton's *Principia mathematica* with a commentary, which was published posthumously and is still the standard French translation of that work. In 1748, while still revising the *Principia* translation, she began an affair with the marquis de Saint-Lambert, which led to an unexpected pregnancy and to her premature death, several days after giving birth, in September 1749. By the time of her death, she was well known not only in French intellectual circles. In Italy she was elected to the Bologna Academy of Sciences and the *Institutions de physique* was published in translation. In Germany, where the *Institutions* was also translated, she was included in a biographical anthology that provided a sort of *Who's Who in Scholarship* of the day, and her work on the nature of force was commented on favorably by the young Kant.

Emilie du Châtelet's childhood education combined typical and abnormal elements. Like the majority of aristocratic and wealthy bourgeois daughters of the time, Emilie attended a convent. In the standard convent education, the basics of literacy that could be expected from a girl of perhaps ten years old would be supplemented by further reading and writing, most often in religious or morally edifying subjects; but the chance of encountering instruction in languages, mathematics beyond basic arithmetic, history other than that to be read in the Bible, or, for that matter, any recent literary or philosophical writings was extremely small. However, at some time in her childhood, she also studied mathematics and Latin—enough of the latter to enable her to translate the *Aeneid.* Her career would have been little different from that of many other intelligent, articulate women who dabbled in philosophy and the sciences during the eighteenth century, but who lacked the basic education in languages and mathematics to carry their interests further, if she had not, at her father's instigation, supplemented her convent education with private tutoring in those vital areas. Knowledge of Latin stood her in good stead in her later scientific and philosophical studies, most of all, of course, in her study and translation of the *Principia;* and although her early mathematical training was more elementary (probably going no further than the elements of Euclidean geometry, to judge by her later difficulties in returning to more serious study of the subject), it still gave her a basis on which to build up the competence necessary to enter the world of international scholarship.

Nevertheless, the form in which she acquired that education differed sharply from that offered to boys of the same class in the same period, and the implications of that fact have real bearing on her later career. The education of boys stressed systematic learning (tedious but still providing a solid foundation in Latin and mathematics especially), which girls had no experience of. Although the Sorbonne had long since ceased to represent the forefront of scholarly excellence, it still provided, for those students who wanted it, a training in traditional scholastic culture that was far more likely to inculcate habits of study, careful reading of tortuous texts, and thorough familiarity with technical, systematic theoretical writings than anything even the most highly educated woman of the same period would be exposed to.

Both the social and institutional character of Emilie du Châtelet's advanced education differed from that of her male peers. No such systematic training supplemented the individual tutoring of a girl living in her family *hôtel,* subject no doubt to a variety of household tasks as well as (from the mid-teens) the endless round of social obligations incurred in the all-important search for a suitable husband. The solitary relation of one pupil with her tutor could never substitute for the school or the university as an institution in which both intellectual and social relationships were formed and in which a variety of skills in social interaction was learned. The restricted model of intellectual behavior that Emilie du Châtelet encountered as an adolescent made it extremely difficult for her to form "normal" professional relationships with those philosophers and scientists she came to know later.

As an adult who had discovered that her true vocation lay in science and philosophy, Emilie du Châtelet had to rely on suitably qualified (and willing) male friends to instruct her so she could acquire the expertise necessary to be taken seriously as a scientist. She had no access in the years after her adolescence and marriage—years in which she came to reject the frivolous amusements of court life in favor of further study—either to privately paid tutors or public institutions, and her repeated attempts to teach herself from the poorly written textbooks of the time soon turned to frustration. She studied with two of the more prominent young Newtonians of the 1730s, Maupertuis and Clairaut; and she encountered on quasi-social occasions (such as the public lectures given by members of the Académie des Sciences) other well-known figures, such as Fontenelle, Réaumur, Buffon, and Diderot, with whom she could discuss topics of current scientific concern. But in the former case, tutoring was intermittent, inevitably interrupted by the primary research interests and frequent visits to other centers of learning of her two teachers. In the latter case, casual discussion and interchange of letters between her and her scientific acquaintances hardly substituted for the sustained, professional, full-time life of the working scientist that they could lead while she could not. It was not until 1738, at the age of thirty-two, that she was able to employ her own tutor, and by then, other family obligations and a variety of fortuitous occurrences (particularly the fact that the tutor, Koenig, supposedly hired to teach her mathematics, turned out to have no interest in so doing and persuaded her to study metaphysics with him instead) continued to hinder her further scientific education.

In short, no matter how determined Emilie du Châtelet was to become a serious scientist, her education both as child and adult could not match that of her male acquaintances for breadth, depth, continuity, or rigor. One obvious result of this, which emerges in her published writing, is that she compensated for these disadvantages by concentrating upon a few clearly delimited areas of scientific investigation; her research on the nature of fire and heat, her contribution to the topical debate over the nature of *force vive* (kinetic energy), and her translation of the *Principia* are all precisely defined projects. Moreover, sufficient expertise to carry them out could be acquired even by the amateur, provided she were determined enough. Indeed, in all three instances, the work she did was, in the estimation both of contemporaries and of subsequent historians, highly competent—not simply "very good for a woman" or "very good for an amateur." But what this sharply focused approach entailed was the impossibility of developing anything like a structured, long-term research program of the kind that more thoroughly trained (and less frequently distracted) scientists could pursue; and so the chances of hitting upon some really valuable new discovery, of becoming a major figure in the history of science, rather than a minor contributor, commentator, and translator, were virtually nonexistent from the start.

A second result of her reliance on occasional tutoring for her advanced scientific education concerns the qualities of intellectual independence and self-confidence that education could instill—qualities almost as crucial to the pursuit of serious research over a lengthy period as formal education itself. The fact that she was unable to travel freely to visit or study under the philosophers and scientists she most admired and was forced to work either with close personal friends like Voltaire or Maupertuis, or else with anyone she could persuade to join her household as an employee, meant that she was inevitably formed intellectually by a small and, in many respects, accidental set of figures, most of whom were already famous for their own work. Her awareness of their much more advanced and important status and her sense of personal indebtedness to them meant that the essential step from pupil to colleague, from tutelage to independence, was one she found very hard to take. The net result is a pattern of expressed self-doubt, self-deprecation, and, in terms of her actual research, tendency to choose safe, "dependent" projects like translation, criticism, and commentary rather than to strike out on her own. All of this was combined with a recurrent sense of frustration and fear that she was perceived as simply a hanger-on or dilettante, tolerated because of her social station or personal charm and not her intellectual abilities, rather than as a real, even if minor, scientist in her own right.

The entire character of her training, from childhood onward, thus displays features of personalization and privatization that produced an unevenly (and fortuitously) educated scientist, unable to participate fully in the formal, public institutions of teaching and research, dependent on the goodwill of more fortunate professional scholars, and, hence, perennially unable to develop a sense of intellectual independence or even be certain that she was welcomed and esteemed, rather than merely tolerated, in the company of those whom she most admired and sought to emulate.

Over and above these constraints, a brief glance at the *other* activities that filled Emilie du Châtelet's life and that, mostly against her will, took up time she would rather have devoted to science and philosophy provides a striking illustration of the way in which the social expectations of the period rendered sustained study and research virtually impossible for women, whatever their social class. As a member of the aristocracy, she was spared the unremitting daily drudgery that effectively barred most women *and* men from intellectual activity of any kind. But although she was privileged, she was not free. With her husband absent on military campaigns through most of their married life, she was obliged to run the various households she and her children lived in. Her responsibilities included, for example, juggling the family finances, planning the extensive renovation of their château, overseeing the farmwork and smithy attached to the château, collecting rents on their properties in Paris, hiring servants, and, most frustratingly for her, managing an elaborate lawsuit over some estates in Belgium, contested by two branches of the family, which could not be entrusted to the efforts of her typically incompetent lawyers. Indeed, this lawsuit occupied the greater part of her time between mid-1739 and 1745, just the years in which, having finally reached a reasonable level of expertise in physics, mathematics, and philosophy, she wanted to make her mark on the world.

Moreover, although she had considerable freedom of action in dealing with these obligations and had the usual degree of social freedom of women in her position under the Old Regime, many decisions still required the consent of her husband. Two in particular made an impact on her own life. First, she was unable to travel either for pleasure or for the sake of meeting fellow scientists unless she had been formally invited to visit some suitable household. The problem was that such invitations, in accordance with the rules of etiquette, had to include her husband; and if he was unwilling or unable to go, she could not accept merely for herself. A lifelong ambition to visit England and make the personal acquaintance of the disciples of Newton never came to anything. Similar plans to visit Italy, Germany, and Switzerland, where the more eclectic forms of Newtonianism that she approved had developed, likewise never materialized; and extensive correspondence with such luminaries as Euler, the Bernouilli family, and Christian Wolff was a poor substitute for direct personal contact.

Another difficulty concerned the hiring of domestic employees, particularly the more expensive ones. Recurrent complications mentioned in her correspondence in connection with the hiring of a tutor for her son were caused chiefly by the fact that M. du Châtelet's consent to all aspects of the arrangement (salary, pension, living expenses, meals, and a host of other details) had to be given before the post was offered. When the question of hiring a tutor for herself arose, the practical objections can readily be imagined. Tutors were not cheap, and the du Châtelets were not wealthy; in the early 1730s at least, M. du Châtelet was apparently not very sympathetic to his wife's eccentric way of life. Only when, by her own admission, she felt too old to learn with great facility was she finally able to hire her own tutor; and when he left her employment after six months or so, she was unable to replace him.

Reconstructing the day-to-day activities of Emilie du Châtelet over any period of time (apart from one four-year period of relatively tranquil and intensive study at Cirey, from 1735 to 1739) from the surviving correspondence makes it abundantly clear why, regardless of the other constraints already described, she could never have led the life of a full-time scientist. Indeed, that she could achieve even as much as she did was due largely to her extraordinary energy and stamina. She could function with four or five hours' sleep a night; and if necessary— for example, when she was racing against time to complete the *Dissertation* in time to submit it to the biennial competition organized by the Académie des Sciences—she could survive on even less, forcing herself to stay awake by dipping her arms in ice water.

Moreover, the continuous round of social obligations, house guests, travel back and forth from Paris and Versailles to Cirey, Belgium, or Lorraine, and an assortment of domestic crises was complicated by Voltaire's demands on her. She acted as his nurse, secretary, advocate at court, and research assistant for most of her adult life, with increasing reluctance but without sufficient strength of will to break off a relationship that, however emotionally rewarding it may have been, was certainly detrimental to her own career.

To take one year, 1734, and trace Emilie du Châtelet's peregrinations through it gives a more concrete idea of the existence she led and of the kind and frequency of interruptions that her then newly-chosen program of scientific study suffered. Between January and early April, she was constantly on the move between her house in Paris, the court at Versailles, her widowed mother's house in the country at Créteil, and the *châteaux* of her society friends around Paris. In April, she went to Autun to celebrate the wedding of her friend Richelieu, staying there almost until the end of June; from then until September, the same social round as before recommenced. During this period, her third child fell ill and died; to a close friend, she wrote complaining of the time his illness had taken up.[3] In October, she went to Cirey, returning to Paris for Christmas, when the same peripatetic existence resumed. Her mathematics lessons with Maupertuis began during the hectic period of January to April but were inevitably interrupted by the trip to Autun. They resumed again on her return to Paris, but at the beginning of September, Maupertuis went with her other mathematician friend, Clairaut, to Basel to visit Jean Bernouilli the elder, patriarch of the famous mathematical dynasty. On returning to France at the end of the year, he went straightaway to the house outside of Paris where he normally took refuge from social distractions to work on his own research, and she saw nothing of him for some time after.

All through that year, Voltaire's welfare occupied Emilie du Châtelet's time and energies more than anything else. Early in the year, he was sick, and she spent much of her time looking after him; then the beginning of May saw the eruption of one of the series of crises in his relations with the authorities. His *Lettres philosophiques*, which had been clandestinely published, were seized, condemned, and publicly burned; and to avoid the danger of imprisonment, he went into hiding at Cirey. Not knowing how real the threat of punishment might be, Emilie du Châtelet was plunged into a state of anxiety that prevented her from pursuing her studies any further.[4] Moreover, she was, for the first of many times, involved in covering Voltaire's tracks, passing on messages to and from friends who could be trusted and asking influential contacts to work for his pardon in return for a promise of good behavior in the future. Throughout the summer of that year, the process of concealing (and reassuring) Voltaire while working for his exculpation was both time-consuming and nerve-racking. The relatively calm, though busy, period of four months or so during which she spent as much time as possible studying with Maupertuis in spite of both their other commitments thus gave way to a period disrupted completely by the Richelieu wedding and Voltaire's flight. The next three months or so in Paris were mostly taken up with Voltaire's case and her son's illness and death. Finally, during three months at Cirey with Voltaire, her mathematical studies were temporarily broken off. They were replaced by the reading of Voltaire's hero, Locke, helping Voltaire by reading and criticizing his current work, and renovating the house. Only at the end of the year, for a frustratingly brief period, could she be in direct contact with Maupertuis again and try to pick up her studies where she had left off several months before.

The process of piecing together the constant upheavals and distractions of such a mode of life makes one realize why Emilie du Châtelet made little attempt, then or subsequently, to carry out large-scale research projects. Her peripatetic existence meant that, purely as a practical matter, schemes requiring the minimum of materials— translations and commentaries that could be worked on with only a few books at a time, for example—were more feasible than long-term, large-scale laboratory research involving the amassing of equipment and a more settled way of life altogether. These considerations, taken together with the kind of psychological and social marginalization she encountered, go very far to explain the limitations of her career as a scientist. She was constantly subject to circumstances beyond her control; and, both in training and self-concept, the disparities between her and the men whose colleague she aspired to be were never more than partially overcome.

But were there any mitigating circumstances at all? Could Emilie du Châtelet derive any benefits from her marginal and precarious status in the scientific world of the mid-eighteenth century?

Although she was bound personally as well as intellectually to a particular group of mentors, she never seems to have felt that she "belonged" fully in the circle of French Newtonians with whom she was chiefly associated. One effect of this was that the often uncritical enthusiasm for Newton's work, which can be found especially in Voltaire but which was shared by the more serious converts to Newtonianism like Maupertuis, as well as by disciples of Newton in England, was not accepted by her. In her work on the nature of force, she early adopted the distinction between *force vive* and *force morte* (kinetic energy as distinct from force in the modern sense of those terms) that Newton had rejected but that Leibniz had insisted was necessary to account for the phenomena of physical impact and the conservation of energy in the universe as a whole. In her *Institutions de physique* and later, she argued that the simple Lockean empiricism of the Newtonians was inadequate as a metaphysical foundation for their physical science and proposed instead to amalgamate elements of the Newtonian system with a version of Leibnizian metaphysics derived from a reading of Leibniz himself and from the works of his successor, Wolff. In sharp contrast to the other French Newtonians, too, she refused to condemn Descartes out of hand, insisting (in the *Dissertation on fire*, for example) that, whatever his particular errors, he played an essential role in the development of modern physics and mathematics. It seems plausible to suggest that the pattern of critical, deliberately eclectic response to the science and metaphysics of the day, which contrasts with the more partisan, almost propagandistic style of the "in-groups" (whether Newtonian, Cartesian or Leibnizian), was available more freely to one who perceived herself as an outsider. Just as Kant, living on the geographical fringes of mainstream culture a generation later, could draw together elements from supposedly incompatible philosophical systems without feeling that he had betrayed allegiance to any one philosophical "party," so Emilie du Châtelet, on the institutional fringe of the French scientific world, could adopt a consciously eclectic and individual position with respect to the competing claims of the three scientific traditions, French, English, and German. Although there is no space here to examine the advantages and defects of the conclusions she developed, her critical, nonpartisan attitude itself must be admitted to be preferable to the blind enthusiasm and often pointless polemic of many among her otherwise more advantaged male peers, in France and elsewhere.

Emilie du Châtelet's career as a scientist, in short, was both constrained and furthered by some factors that were peculiar to her, but also by others that she would have shared with any woman of her class in her time. Before we can do much more than speculate, though, we need to know much more about other women who were, or tried to become, practicing scientists in France in the same period. We do have a few scraps of information; the single best source is Jérôme Lefrançais de Lalande, Director of the Paris Observatory in the mid-eighteenth century, who compiled a *Bibliographie astronomique*. He tells us that one Mme du Pierry was the first woman professor of astronomy in Paris and author of several papers he included in his own works and that Hortense Lepaute, wife of the royal clockmaker, did original work on the oscillations of pendulums of varying lengths that was included in her husband's *Traité d'horlogerie* (1755). Hortense Lepaute was actually hired in 1759 by de Lalande, with Clairaut (the mathematician with whom Emilie du Châtelet had also worked extensively), to calculate the attraction of Jupiter and Saturn on Halley's comet; between then and 1774 she was employed by him to do the computations for *Connaissance des temps*, a handbook of star and planetary locations and movements for the use of astronomers and navigators. Lalande also records that his own niece, Mme Lefrançais de Lalande, carried out a series of valuable astronomical calculations (which he also incorporated into his own works) and published a star catalogue and a set of navigational tables.[5] Toward the end of the century, Mme Lavoisier, wife of the chemist, was studying languages, physics, and chemistry to assist her husband, with whom she collaborated extensively; she made the engravings for his *Traité de chimie* and completed the work he left unfinished at his death.[6]

These bare details tell us nothing about the fabric of the lives led by these extraordinary women, but they do suggest further avenues of exploration. For example, it seems significant that so many of this tiny group were directly related to practicing male scientists. This aspect emphasizes how unavoidable for women scientists was the dependence on personal relationships, and especially on the permission and encouragement of male associates who were themselves in the field. It also implicitly shows how impossible was any sense of solidarity among women scientists themselves; able to pursue their work only through their association with men, they necessarily functioned as "honorary males" and, as such, were inevitably isolated and anomalous as women. The self-doubts expressed by Emilie du Châtelet, we may imagine, were equally felt by her less-documented women contemporaries. Moreover, in collaborating with Voltaire, with her teacher Koenig, and with Clairaut, she had to struggle constantly to gain recognition for what she contributed to the resulting publications— always in the face of the assumption that, as a woman and an amateur, her contribution was bound to be minimal. The recurrence of this "incorporation syndrome" in the cases of these other women is surely significant; their historical invisibility is in large part due simply to the fact that their own work was absorbed into that of their male colleagues.

The combination of practical constraints, lack of autonomy in their studies and research, and almost insuperable difficulty of transcending the personal so as to be recognized—both by their male peers and themselves—as scientists in their own right was an inescapable condition with which any woman scientist of the time had to contend. In that respect at least, we must conclude that for all her privileges, energy, determination, and pure good luck, Emilie du Châtelet's achievement probably represents the maximum possible for French women in science—and not merely in the eighteenth century, but for long after as well.

NOTES

The information on Emilie du Châtelet's career and writings is drawn primarily from *Voltaire's Correspondence*, edited by T. Besterman, 50 vols. (Geneva: Institut Voltaire, 1968-1977). Much of the information appears in a more detailed and thoroughly annotated form in my article, "Searching for the Metaphysics of Science: The Structure and Composition of Mme du Châtelet's *Institutions de physique, 1737-40*," *Studies on Voltaire and the Eighteenth Century*, vol. 201 (Oxford: The Voltaire Foundation, 1981).

1. R. Hahn, *The Anatomy of a Scientific Institution: The Paris Academy of Sciences, 1666-1803* (Berkeley: University of California Press, 1971).

2. For an eighteenth-century source, see H. Montucla, *Histoire des mathématiques*, vol. 3 (Paris: H. Agasse, 1802). For more recent but still outdated treatments, see H. J. Mozans, *Women in Science* (New York: Appleton, 1913); E. Rebière, *Les Femmes dans la science*, 2d ed. (Paris: Nony et Cie, 1897); N. Nielsen, *Géomètres français du dix-huitième siècle* (Copenhagen: Levin and Munksgaard, 1935); Lynn M. Osen, *Women in Mathematics* (Cambridge: MIT Press, 1974).

3. *Voltaire's Correspondence*, letter D782, 6 September 1734, to Sade.

4. *Voltaire's Correspondence*, letter D741, 12 May 1734, to Sade.

5. Joseph Jérôme Lefrançais de Lalande, *Bibliographie astronomique* (Paris: Imprimerie de la république, 1803), pp. 676-687.

6. Cited in Mozans, pp. 214-216.

IV

Creative Women and Women Artists

⚛ Joan Hinde Stewart

The Novelists and Their Fictions

T HE EIGHTEENTH CENTURY was as much inclined as our own to deliberate upon women's roles, their merits and shortcomings, and the traits distinguishing them (for better or for worse) from men. Specifically, the issue of women's writing was much debated. Curious and pertinent assessments of woman's literary talents can be culled from scores of eighteenth-century tracts on morality and society as well as literature. Mme de Lambert takes as point of departure for her *Réflexions nouvelles sur les femmes* (1727) the observation that some fine "novels by ladies," which had recently begun appearing, were ridiculed for no better reason than their female authorship; literary pretensions, she claims, are considered admissible in men but unpardonable in women.[1] Two decades later, in an anti-feminist broadside entitled *L'Année merveilleuse ou les hommes-femmes,* the abbé Coyer—demonstrating both misogyny and misology—pronounced women all flummery and trumpery, all idle talk and gratuitous wit, and hinted in passing that they were no better fit for serious writing than for serious reading.[2] And in 1771, Antoine Thomas, a noted panegyrist of women, nevertheless remarked on the dearth of good contemporary female writers, attributing it in part to women's timidity and to a certain intellectual flightiness; as far as Thomas was concerned, women were characterized by sensitivity and insight but not creative power. He footnotes his observations: "This is not to say that in this century there are not women who have written and who still write with distinction; they are known: but their number diminishes every day, and there are infinitely fewer than there were during the renaissance of letters or even under Louis XIV."[3] Thomas's perceptions notwithstanding, the number of successful women writers had increased markedly as the century advanced. While their inclinations and capacities were endlessly weighed, women continued to write, and they especially wrote novels.[4]

Never separate from the cultural and aesthetic domain, the socioeconomic significance of women's work is nonetheless an especially vital factor in the writing of the eighteenth century. This was, of course, a period when very few professions were open to women. They could become seamstresses, like countless numbers of their impoverished and desperate heroines, or ladies' companions, like Mlle de Lespinasse for a time; but seamstress and companion forfeited both autonomy and a certain amount of dignity. Some won distinction on the stage, like Mme Riccoboni as a young wife, but neither Church nor society considered acting respectable. On the other hand, the financial attraction of the literary profession and the independence it allowed must have been significant inducements, especially when a certain number of commentators were encouraging women precisely to think that their talents peculiarly suited them to novel writing. Female writers of the era constitute one of the earliest significant groups of women to earn an independent living by the exercise of their personal faculties in a domain that led to wide recognition. Mme de Gomez, Mme de Graffigny, Mme Riccoboni, Mme Le Prince de Beaumont, Mme de Montolieu, and numerous others were not women of leisure, writing to while away idle hours; they were independent, middle-aged (and often middle-class) women who wrote to sell.

It was not always easy. Correspondences testify to the obstacles they encountered in bucking the literary establishment and tight-fisted publishers. Mme de Graffigny has documented not only the years of hard labor that went into writing her best-selling novel but also the need of a male agent to represent her interests in the publishing world.[5] Mme Riccoboni continually had difficulties in squeezing payment out of her English publisher, and her career was plagued with the appearance of pirated editions of her works.[6] The Swiss writer Mme de Montolieu, who published her first novel in 1786 and continued writing through the first three decades of the nineteenth century, had chronic trouble getting compensation for tales she placed in the *Mercure de France* and never learned to demand her due with self-assurance and unfeminine assertiveness. "The profession of writer, of translator," she commented, "does not suit a woman far from Paris and who has no one there to look after her interests!"[7] Similar complaints are, of course, voiced by men; but because of woman's status as a social and economic inferior, her professional problems were apparently more acute.

Women's talents, tenacity, and commercial successes nonetheless help define the eighteenth-century French novel. Jean Larnac has remarked that during this period the novel was a "fief of women"; there may be no towering eighteenth-century figure comparable to Mme de Staël in the early years of the nineteenth, but a veritable "army of women novelists" was publishing fiction and achieving extensive renown.[8] Mme de Graffigny's *Lettres d'une Péruvienne* (1747), for example, was phenomenally popular; and in a period of just three years, Mme Riccoboni's first three novels—*Lettres de mistriss Fanni Butlerd* (1757), *Histoire de M. le marquis de Cressy* (1758) and *Lettres de milady Juliette*

Catesby (1759)—catapulted her from relative obscurity to fame. By the century's end, *Lettres de milady Juliette Catesby* alone had appeared in Swedish, Danish, Russian and English, while *History of Lady Julia Mandeville*, by the English writer Mrs. Brooke, was signed "by the translator of Lady Catesby's Letters." A 1765 heroine of Mme Riccoboni, Ernestine, enjoyed such popularity that Marie-Antoinette had a young companion for her daughter rechristened Ernestine. The question of how many of the century's numerous anonymous novels were also in fact written by women will never be resolved, but it is doubtless a considerable number.

Recognition of the sheer numbers of women writing during a period uniquely important to the novel's establishment implies recognition, even if only tacit, of the large measure of female responsibility for making the novel the typical art form of the modern West. Yet the great majority of these novels have not been reissued in well over a century and are, therefore, to be found only in private collections and major research libraries. Partly as a result of this, there is exceedingly little available in the way of sustained critical analysis, except for isolated allusions and monographs on a few of the best known.[9] Even in a vast and erudite tome on the eighteenth-century novel by Pierre Fauchery, we find numerous passing references to the novels of, for example, Mme Le Prince de Beaumont, who was a prolific feminist writer; but we are hard put to locate more than two successive sentences about her work. Like Mme Le Prince de Beaumont, women novelists have, on the whole, been catalogued but not studied. Their major role is seen as vulgarization. Fauchery, indeed, is persuaded that the case of women novelists is not "fundamentally heterogeneous," that the determining myths were of masculine invention and adopted without alteration by women novelists. In his book on "female destiny," only twenty pages out of nine hundred treat the woman writer specifically. For Fauchery, female novelists are not really distinguishable from their male counterparts, except that, on the whole, women are verbose, gauche, only conventionally liberated, most at ease in short fiction, consistently prone to betray the "born moralizer" lurking beneath the "occasional novelist," and inevitably inclined to autobiography; the heroine imagined by the woman novelist is "forever and eternally herself."[10]

Women did without a doubt write within established frameworks and frequently uninteresting fictional conventions. Like male novelists, they wrote letter-novels, memoir-novels and third-person narratives and created both representational and metaphorical heroines, whom they portrayed for the greatest part in relation to men and often struggling with the conflicting demands of virtue and passion. As a group, they treat love, marriage, and abandonment with more or less sensitivity, eloquence, and narrative mastery and tend to avoid the pornographic and the libertine novel, which were flourishing forms. An impressive number were translators as well as novelists and largely responsible for the diffusion in France of English and German fiction. During the second half of the century, they frequently set their novels in England (a country and culture then very much in vogue), although the inspiration for plot often came, undisguised, from their private experience. But this was true of men as well. Like virtually all the period's novelists, they made technical blunders, even as they helped to develop themes and approaches to character that were crucial to the novel and to solve some of the many problems relating to technique in a nascent genre.

Their heroines include, for example, Mme Benoist's Celianne, title character of an ironic 1766 novel, who comes tantalizingly close to making illicit love but is finally "saved" by her husband, as well as the pathetic Fanny in Mme Beccary's *Mémoires de Fanny Spingler* (1781), who is victimized by sexual calumnies and eventually succumbs to her misfortunes. In *L'Aveugle par amour*, a macabre and extravagantly sentimental novel published the same year by Fanny de Beauharnais, protagonist Eugénie blinds herself as an expression of her love for a blind man. The heroine of Mme Daubenton's immensely popular, 900-page *Zélie dans le désert*, on the other hand, is chiefly notable for her prodigious resourcefulness; after her shipwreck on the island of Sumatra, Zélie raises goats and poultry and runs a mill. We do women writers no service to exaggerate either their insights or their skill; but with fantasies and heroines as diverse as these, they offer, at the least, multiple and intense novelistic representations of a classic subject: a temperament in society.

Among the most accomplished not only of women's novels but also of the century's fiction are the early works of Mme de Charrière. Born in Holland, she lived her last thirty-four years in Switzerland, where she published in French, one of her native languages: *Lettres neuchâteloises* (1784), *Lettres de mistriss Henley* (1784), *Lettres écrites de Lausanne* (1785), and *Caliste* (1788). In their portrayal of generational relations, their simplicity of plot, their characteristic refusal to end in any recognizably conventional way, and in the compelling dailiness of their concerns (serving dinner, choosing clothes, avoiding frostbite, finding a husband, earning a living), they encode a fascinating commentary on the position of the "average" European woman in the late eighteenth century.

An early novel by Mme Durand de Bédacier, *La Comtesse de Mortane*, first appeared in 1699, and must have enjoyed considerable popularity, judging from numerous reeditions throughout the eighteenth century. It is a loose weave of standard adventures: a novel about passion, maternal tyranny, disguise and calumny, with several interpolated fairy tales and flashbacks. The strong central alliance—between two women—articulates a peculiarly female kind of bonding, based on confidences and gossip. The reader's attention is further rewarded by a passage like the following, where Mme de Mortane describes her wedding to a hated husband. She notes her "violent" efforts "to avoid making a scene in public," and then:

> I suddenly paled at the end of the ceremony . . . I will not tell you about the horrible pain I felt when they undressed me to put me in the bed; you surely must understand it, provided you are at all capable of hatred and love. Yes, interrupted Madame de Marigue, let us draw the curtain on this adventure; please continue your story.[11]

The paralepsis ("I will not tell you . . .") is, in this case, required by the literally unspeakable significance of the omission. The passage neatly suggests sexual and conjugal coercion and the tensions inherent in their concealment, in the necessity of maintaining both a public and a private self. Stripping away of clothing is the stripping away of social lies. Such themes, which are frequently important in the period's female novel and whose explicit expression is as frequently repressed, strain at the limits of conventionally permitted language, giving unexpected life to words like pain, love, and hatred, which are already in the grip of cliché. The strong sense these words acquire is an example of the way women's use of a convention is simultaneously the convention's renewal.

In spite of shortcomings of style and composition, such novels may be read (especially cumulatively) as compelling and obsessive fictions of the female self, as a kind of writing that maximizes gender differences. Heroines are alternately characterized by compliance with societal expectations or by a (usually moderate) form of defiance, but, in either case, a close reading often suggests that protagonists use and subvert social conventions just as the authors use and subvert literary conventions. These texts are generally bland in appearance. They seem initially not to speak for themselves, only echoing the epoch's familiar language; but they make subliminal statements, sometimes best revealed by interlocking readings. Perhaps no body of work lends itself so little to formal taxonomies and so much demands close and sustained analysis, a willingness to look beneath the surface conventions. In this essay I shall enumerate some of the clues, or cues, to which such an analysis could respond.

A fact of primary significance is this: in a day when women were allowed neither to manage their property nor to dispose of their fortunes, or even of their hand, when they were sometimes sent to convents to preserve intact the inheritance of their brothers, they

wrote for the most part not poetry, or drama, but fiction and produced
a long line of works that, by modern criteria, must be considered best-
sellers. Since the novel is precisely the form that became for Lukacs,
Girard, and Goldmann, among others, the exemplary literary vehicle
for social dissent, we may be at first disappointed to find in these
women only scattered and timorous voices of manifest protest.
Normally, they confine explicit complaint to the spheres of education
and of relations between the sexes. Mme de Graffigny, Mme
Riccoboni, and Mme Elie de Beaumont, for example, all speak out
within their novels against the narrowness and contradictions of the
convent education of girls.

> From the moment when girls begin to be able to receive instruction,
> they are shut up in a convent, to teach them how to behave in society ...
> and we entrust the responsibility for enlightening their minds to people
> in whom it might be considered a crime to possess a mind, and who are
> incapable of molding their hearts, for they do not know the heart.[12]

Mme de Graffigny and Mme Riccoboni also condemn the double
standard, and Mme Riccoboni more than once excoriates men for their
limited sensibility, excessive sensuality, and the dissimulation they
practice on women.

> Look here, you men! What are you? From what source do you derive the
> right to scant toward women the regard that you impose on yourselves
> among one another? What law in nature, what convention in any state
> ever authorized this impudent distinction? What? Your merely given
> word commits you toward the lowest of your kind, and reiterated vows
> do not bind you to the woman friend you have chosen?[13]

Mme Riccoboni suggests here that her contemporaries accepted a
significant gender difference in verbal performance: giving one's word
to a man imposed radically different obligations from giving it to a
woman. My argument is a corollary of that assertion: as the same
word is different when given *to* a man or to a woman, so the same word
may have different senses when coming *from* a man or from a woman.

Women writers also occasionally ride that eighteenth-century
warhorse, the forced vocation; one of the subplots in Mme de Tencin's
Le Siège de Calais (1739) deals with the issue. Mme de Tencin had an
exceptionally intimate acquaintance with the problem, having been
herself forced to take religious vows. But denunciation of this
particular abuse was by no means confined to women, Diderot's *La
Religieuse* (1796) being perhaps the most eloquent example. Indeed, the
most "liberated" of female protagonists by twentieth-century standards
are probably found in novels written by men, Duclos' Mme de Rêtel in

Mémoires pour servir à l'histoire des moeurs du dix-huitième siècle (1751) and Laclos's Mme de Merteuil in *Les Liaisons dangereuses* (1782), for example. Mme Riccoboni, on the other hand, strenuously objected to the character and comportment of Mme de Merteuil and, in a series of letters to Laclos, labeled her an insult to France and womanhood.

But protest in the novel is by definition masked and mediated and, hence, in need of interpretation. If, at first glance, the voices of eighteenth-century French women novelists seem less distinctive than, for example, those of the nineteenth century, we must examine the tensions underlying the earlier era's restricted vocabulary and stylized expression. We should be aware, too, of the extent to which the period was one of linguistic transition. Raymond Williams argues that the eighteenth century saw the beginning of a major new emphasis on language as activity, in close relation to the demystified understanding of society as a set of structures and inventions "made" by human beings. "Language" and "reality" were no longer systematically perceived, as they had been in all previously dominant traditions, as decisively separated.[14] Within a world of mystically withdrawn "things" and (Platonic) ideas, patriarchy could flourish and priests could manipulate the commandments. But with the merging of words and things in the neutral daylight of the eighteenth century, the questions of feminism become possible; the patriarchal repression of words is transparently at issue in the new inquiry into what and how words "mean," what and how they control. Scrutiny of the works of female novelists suggests evidence of just such a move toward language as operative, and certain publications that are marginal to the *genre romanesque*—Mme Le Prince de Beaumont's *Lettre en réponse à L'Année merveilleuse* (1748), for example—challenge male discourse and hierarchies. One discerns in a number of women writers an inchoate realization of the opacity of the signifier and the degree to which everyday speech may sustain patriarchal arrangements—social, political and sexual. Under the pen especially of women writers of the late century, crucial words such as virtue, reason, and happiness slip from their accustomed places, becoming newly functional and acquiring original nuances that embody specifically female vision and desire.

The paradox is that texts that may revise dominant eighteenth-century categories are nonetheless couched in the language of the *poli* and the *agréable*. Important aspects of their nature and significance may thus be elusive. Mme de Montolieu's *Caroline de Lichtfield* (1786), although normally read as a novel of sensibility—André Chénier praises it for "a thousand details full of truth, naïveté, grace and delicacy"[15]—is a startling and funny narrative about female self-concern and sexual anxieties, a retelling of the story of Beauty and the

Beast. Mme de Tencin's *Le Siège de Calais* begins when the hero accidentally finds himself in bed with the heroine, who understandably takes him for her husband. A highly conventional plot element in eighteenth-century fiction involves the notion that, for men, sexual fulfillment signals the end of love; as though reflecting this theme, novels characteristically end where Mme de Tencin's begins, with the lovers' union. But in *Le Siège de Calais*, M. de Canaple is indifferent to Mme de Granson until sex engenders passionate love; he spends the remaining 170 pages trying to win not just her pardon but also her affections. While the novel glorifies sensibility and fidelity and extols the strictest virtue, it also subversively rewrites a standard and essentially male plot; love is not crowned with sex, but sex with love. It seems clear, furthermore, that the use of the historical genre—at which women writers like Mme de Tencin, Mlle de Lussan and Mme Durand de Bédacier excelled—was often a way of displacing discussion of the forbidden, although the "morality" of Mme de Tencin's novels was long the object of critical adulation. Jean Decottignies has demonstrated that while for two hundred years Mme de Tencin's *Mémoires du comte de Comminge* (1735) never shocked the proprieties there lies beneath its familiar figures (parents, lovers, spouse) and episodes (forced marriage, sequestration, convent sojourn) an original work of poetic ambiguity whose "secret meaning" is neither so simple nor nearly so reassuring as La Harpe and other critics preferred to think.[16]

Still another case in point is Mme de Souza's *Adèle de Sénange* (1794), which reminds us of the author's own teen-age marriage to the middle-aged comte de Flahaut: a genial sixteen-year-old is saved from the convent by an apparently grotesque union with a seventy-year-old man, who, at bottom, is as generous as he is gouty and decrepit. Lord Sydenham, a young Englishman, promptly joins them and falls in love with the bride, all the while astounded and somewhat annoyed that she does not quite correspond to his idea of the perfect woman; she is carefree, capricious, and frivolous as well as kind and tender. Sydenham's instincts are so fine that he almost prefers to Adèle's company that of the respectable septuagenarian; but he occasionally wonders, not disinterestedly, how long the old man can survive. M. de Sénange feels some uneasiness about the situation, but he morally adopts both young people and dies leaving them his fortune.

In *Adèle de Sénange*, I read a subtle revision of the idea of the sentimental heroine, accommodating both frivolity and flirtatiousness, as well as an allegory about the ambiguity of virtue, female enclosure and liberation, incest and adultery. This is a text where esthetic concerns (gardens, dress, dance) are translated into psychological and female force. Sainte-Beuve, on the other hand, nostalgically reads only the language of sensibility. He likens Mme de Souza's work to "pure water which can restore our overheated palates." Sainte-Beuve's first-person plural is gender-specific: "our" palates are as masculine as the water is feminine. Mme de Souza, moreover, epitomizes for this critic the very traits he finds lacking in the novels of his own day, the mid-nineteenth century: "that quality of freshness and delicacy, that limpidity of emotion, that sobriety of word, those soft and restful nuances."[17] In 1929, Jean Larnac echoed Sainte-Beuve: the turn-of-the-century novels of Mme de Souza had a "charming finesse;" their style, "correct and moderately embellished, recalled the florid conversations of the old regime."[18] Such comments illustrate the tenacity with which male critics have maintained a cage around the consciousness of eighteenth-century women, benevolently repainting the bars of the cage with the language of decorum and purity.

Adèle de Sénange is written in the form of letters, Lord Sydenham's to his confidant; there are no responses. In fact, during the century's middle and late years, a major fictional form was the epistolary novel, and it was largely popularized by women authors. Late-century letter-novels contemporary with *Adèle de Sénange* were often polyphonic, with an exchange of letters by several correspondents. Laclos's *Liaisons dangereuses* (1782) probably represents the epitome of this form, where a great many letters from different sources are impressively orchestrated. Mme Elie de Beaumont was one of his predecessors; her *Lettres du marquis de Roselle* (1764), with letters by half a dozen principal writers, is a sober and engaging novel about a young man who learns to value the best in woman (intelligence and wit) rather than the worst (dissimulation and dissipation). The majority of the earlier novels written in letter form, however, involve only a single letter writer, usually the heroine. This particular variant of the genre seems historically to be remarkably well suited to the emergence of authentic female voices into an open language. Additionally, the letter form favors a domestic emotional center. When woman's access to the public domain is problematic, the letter form conceals and compensates for her exclusion from history and valorizes her space in life and her private experience of time.

The theme of women writing, of course, is an important one from Molière to Sade and Laclos. Arnolphe's mistake in the *Ecole des femmes* is allowing Agnès to learn to write; Restif de La Bretonne's *Les Gynographes* (1777)—a work whose subtitle enunciates its project to "put women in their place"—specifies that upper-class girls should be taught to read, but even they should not learn to write.[19] Male control depends symbolically on control of words, especially the written word. While eighteenth-century women novelists were using the Word to achieve economic independence, they were also exploiting its symbolism with works in which the epistolary act suggests a way of escape from alienation and fragmentation and allows the heroine to triumph over love and victimization—experiences that tend to be coextensive in the novel.

Among the most widely imitated of such works are the monophonic epistolary novel of Mme de Graffigny and the first of those by Mme Riccoboni, autobiographical and vibrant mid-century portrayals of an otherwise and an elsewhere, narrations of female time and female truth. Zilia, the Inca princess in *Lettres d'une Péruvienne,* is captured by the Spaniards, then falls into the hands of the French. She is brought to Paris where she comments extensively on French manners and morals from the perspective of the naïve foreigner, while she remains faithful to Aza, the brother-lover from whom she was separated. Eventually, he is discovered to be living at the Spanish court, and she is briefly reunited with him, only to learn that he has embraced Christianity with its prohibition of incestuous unions and that he intends to marry a Spanish woman. Still, Zilia refuses the hand of her French rescuer and admirer, the long-suffering Déterville, preferring celibacy, friendship, and the pleasures of nature to those of passion. This final gesture, the rejection of a deserving lover and the decision to live alone in society (Zilia does not withdraw to a convent), is original and courageous; as Déterville's sister explains to her, society looks askance at unmarried and unprotected young women residing alone. English Showalter notes that it is also surprising in terms of conventional fictional endings, for readers' expectations were strongly for marriage either with Aza or with Déterville or, failing that, for Zilia's demise. Socially and psychologically, according to rules both within the fiction and without, Zilia would seem to need a husband in order to survive, but Mme de Graffigny was moving away from obvious linguistic and literary plans.[20]

Mme Riccoboni's first novel, *Lettres de mistriss Fanni Butlerd,* appeared ten years later. Published pseudonymously, it pretended to be a translation from the English, but it was probably a fictionalization of the author's own love affair with the comte de Maillebois. It was one of the very first of a wave of "English" novels in France and was soon recognized as one of the era's most direct and most psychologically satisfying fictions. Lord Alfred, a British peer, swears undying fidelity to Fanni Butlerd, a commoner. They begin an affair; but, predictably, it is almost immediately interrupted when he departs to do his military service, and for a period of close to two months, she writes him impassioned letters. Shortly after Alfred's return, Fanni discovers that he is about to marry someone else, a woman of greater wealth and status. In a final letter—exceptionally eloquent if conventional—Fanni lambasts Alfred in particular and men in general and declares that she will have nothing more to do with them.

Like Zilia, Fanni is victimized by a society complicitous with men and indulgent toward their desires for social status and conquest, on both the battlefield and the bed. Like Zilia, too, Fanni is the novel's sole letter writer, and hers is the only voice the reader hears in this passionate soliloquy. The interest resides, on the one hand, in Fanni's energetic recognition and arrangement of her own sexuality (she does not slip into an affair; she consciously decides to have one) and, on the other, in her lucid effort to anatomize in writing the subtleties, genesis, and growth of female passion. When Zilia and Fanni finally disclaim passion and claim autonomy, they express a forceful symbolic negation of male dominance and conventional sexual and marital categories.

The theme of passionate renunciation that goes back to Mme de Lafayette's *La Princesse de Clèves* was naturally echoed in countless other novels and modulated to express various nuances: not only the anger of a Fanni Butlerd but occasionally the joyful valorization of female alliances. In Mme Robert's *Nicole de Beauvais ou l'amour vaincu par la reconnaissance* (1767), the title character decides that masculine jealousy and excesses are intolerable. As the subtitle suggests, she rejects the Baron, whom she loves and who loves her, in favor of a celibate, happy, and charitable life at the side of her benefactress.

There are, of course, more ways than one of saying no. The narration of the narrowest of female destinies may be symbolically emancipatory. A 1784 heroine of Mme de Charrière, while superficially complying with the demands of husband and society, subversively questions their rationality, their pertinence to a *woman's* life. With Mme de Charrière, the letter-novel realizes its potential as the form best suited to express the control exercised by domestic concerns over female psychology. In the interior domestic spaces she depicts, the donning of an artificial flower or the removal of a portrait from a wall become crucial, determining events. *Lettres de mistriss Henley* is the story of a young woman, orphaned and twenty-five years old, who must marry for financial security. She has two suitors. One is kind and decent, an eminently respectable and universally respected widower who loves the quiet country life. The second, a few years older, is fabulously wealthy, dynamic, a lover of good food and art; the only problem is that some slight suspicion hangs over the Oriental origins of his fortune. The heroine sighs at the prospect of such opulence and pleasure but chooses, as her (female) education has made her feel she must, the course of purity, nobility, sublime and "reasonable" happiness, the simple and decent life. But Mr. Henley turns out to be *too* perfect—a good man but a controlled and endlessly rational one whose very moderation collides with his young wife's vitality, generous impulsiveness, and sensitivity. Realizing his moral and intellectual superiority, she tries to imitate him, but she cannot. Hers is the story of a woman who is inevitably wrong: "Is it possible that he is right, my friend? Is it possible that I am wrong again, always wrong, wrong in everything?"[21] Even the anticipated birth of their child—for Mrs. Henley an event of profound maternal significance, the culmination of hopes and ambitions—occasions only her husband's moralizing response; he thinks his wife perhaps too excitable to nurse the baby. It becomes finally apparent that death is the only alternative to living her husband's version of reason and virtue. Mrs. Henley compellingly figures woman in her status as a social, political, and economic minority. She is oppressed by a society rooted in patriarchy and tradition, where a woman—especially a poor one—cannot survive outside of marriage and a sensitive woman can hardly survive within it.

Contrasting starkly with the work of Mme de Charrière is that of Mme Le Prince de Beaumont, best remembered today for her classic, abridged version of the story of Beauty and the Beast that appeared in 1757 in her *Magasin des enfants* (translated as *The Young Misses' Magazine*). She was an educator and an extraordinarily productive writer, author of educational treatises, novels, fairy tales, and works of Christian inspiration. Her fiction is wordy and long, neither as stylishly written nor as technically successful as the best works of a Mme Riccoboni or a Mme de Charrière and rife with the most outlandish of fictional peripeteia: duels, plague, sequestration, murder, razor-assisted birth, disguise, forged wills. Yet she stands as one of the century's most interesting feminist thinkers; on the one hand, asserting woman's moral and verbal strength and female fitness for literary and scientific study and, on the other, preaching submission to God's will and a morality more severe than what most of her contemporaries espoused in their fiction. In the lengthy *Lettres de madame du Montier* (1756) and *Mémoires de la baronne de Batteville* (1766), the young heroines make, at their parents' behest, marriages of convenience to rich and decent older men. There are indications (though hardly explicit) that their sex lives are wanting. Then, widowed at about the age of thirty, each is sought in marriage by a man to whom she was genuinely sexually attracted. Each refuses, not out of fidelity to the dead husband, but out of a barely articulated fidelity to self and desire for autonomy. They reject the marital and social economy that prescribes sex, procreation, female subservience, and toleration of the double standard. When Mme Le Prince de Beaumont calls this renunciation "virtue," she seems to suggest a new meaning for a much-used word, just as Mme de Charrière implies the bankruptcy of "reason" in the very heart of the Age of Reason.

Virginia Woolf (speaking implicitly of the English novel) reminds us that the eighteenth century was a turning point for female authorship.

Earlier, she is impressed by the "strange intermissions of silence and speech" in women's writing.[22] By the late eighteenth century, fiction by women is *continuous,* deriving its significance partly from its critical mass, partly from the psychological continuities we discern in it, and partly from the transitional use of familiar rhetoric. Women wrote courageously in the face of criticism and ridicule. Restif de La Bretonne has a male protagonist in *La Paysanne pervertie* (1784) put his female correspondent on stern notice: "a woman scientist, or merely a thinking woman, is always ugly—I warn you seriously—and especially a woman author. . . . A woman author transgresses the limits of modesty prescribed for her sex."[23] But women were not deterred by attempts to portray their very female work as emanating from writers who must be by definition unfeminine: ugly and immodest. They went on proving that they *could* write—and write with a difference. Novelists such as Mme de Graffigny, Mme Le Prince de Beaumont, and Mme de Souza reworked the standard marriage plot, imitating male novelists but subtly altering fictional arrangements and making possible new and formative female fictions and discourse. Within the literary systems they used, they were modifying the symbolic order of things. This enormously diverse corpus is reducible neither to a single ideology nor to a few generalizations about theme and form. It stratifies the complexities of convention and originality, vocation and provocation, autobiography and fiction. If we listen closely, we may hear distinctively female voices uttering, in the code of eighteenth-century conventions, things for which no explicit language yet existed.

NOTES

1. Mme de Lambert, *Réflexions nouvelles sur les femmes, par une dame de la cour de France,* nouvelle édition corrigée (Londres: J. P. Coderc, 1730), p. 3. I am in debt to Robert Dawson for lending me a copy of this publication as well as of several other rare and pertinent eighteenth-century editions that he brought to my attention.

2. Gabriel-François Coyer, *L'Année merveilleuse,* in *Bagatelles morales et dissertations,* nouvelle édition (Londres et se vend à Francfort: Knoch et Eslinger, 1755), pp. 30-43.

3. Antoine Thomas, *Essai sur le caractère, les moeurs et l'esprit des femmes dans les différents siècles* (Paris: Persan et Cie., 1823), p. 154. Here and elsewhere, translations from the French are mine.

4. For a seminal discussion of the relation between feminism and the novel in the eighteenth century, see Georges May, "Féminisme et roman," *Le Dilemme du roman au XVIIIe siècle* (New Haven: Yale University Press, and Paris : Presses universitaires de France, 1963).

5. English Showalter discusses this aspect of the novel's genesis in *"Les Lettres d'une Péruvienne:* Composition, Publication, Suites" (paper delivered at the 6th International Congress on Enlightenment, Brussels, July 1983).

6. *Madame Riccoboni's Letters to David Hume, David Garrick and Sir Robert Liston: 1764-1783*, edited by James C. Nicholls (Oxford: The Voltaire Foundation, 1976).

7. Letter quoted in Dorette Berthoud, *Le Général et la romancière* (Neuchâtel: La Baconnière, 1959), p. 326.

8. Jean Larnac, *Histoire de la littérature féminine en France*, 4e édition (Paris: Kra, 1929), p. 251.

9. Given the immensity of the corpus, my essay in no way pretends to deal with all of the important women writers of the eighteenth-century French novel. My selection represents an attempt to strike some balance and suggest avenues for future research, while it is also influenced by personal taste and the basic question of the accessibility of editions.

10. "...la femme qu'elle croit imaginer, c'est encore et toujours elle-même." Pierre Fauchery, *La Destinée féminine dans le roman européen du dix-huitième siècle* (Paris: Armand Colin, 1972), pp. 94 and 111. English Showalter suggested to me that the history of Madame d'Epinay's powerful *Histoire de madame de Montbrillant* is a striking demonstration of the lengths to which the prejudice that the heroine of the woman writer is "eternally herself" can lead readers and editors. Composed in the second half of the eighteenth century, it was published only in the nineteenth century as "memoirs," then labeled "pseudo-memoirs" in the twentieth, and only recently recognized as fiction. The lack of invention, moreover, is a reproach only when directed at women. Has anyone contended that *A la recherche du temps perdu* is inferior because Proust and his narrator share so many experiences and sensations? Proust is just as much "eternally himself."

11. Mme Durand de Bédacier, *La Comtesse de Mortane, par Madame D***, 2 tomes in 1 vol. (Paris: Prault, 1736), p. 36.

12. Mme de Graffigny, *Lettres d'une Péruvienne*, edited by Gianni Nicoletti (Bari: Adriatica Editrice, 1967), p. 290.

13. Mme Riccoboni, *Lettres de mistriss Fanni Butlerd*, edited by Joan Hinde Stewart (Geneva: Droz, 1979), p. 186. For a fuller discussion of this theme in Mme Riccoboni's work, see also my *The Novels of Mme Riccoboni* (Chapel Hill: Studies in the Romance Languages & Literatures, 1976), chapter 5.

14. Raymond Williams, *Marxism and Literature* (Oxford: Oxford University Press, 1977), pp. 21-22.

15. Quoted in Robert L. Dawson, *Baculard d'Arnaud: Life and Prose Fiction*, Studies on Voltaire and the Eighteenth Century, vols. 141-142 (Oxford: The Voltaire Foundation, 1976), p. 676.

16. Jean Decottignies, "Roman et revendication féminine, d'après les *Mémoires du comte de Comminge* de Madame de Tencin," in *Roman et lumières au XVIIIe siècle*, edited by Centre d'études et de recherches marxistes (Paris: Editions sociales, 1970), pp. 311-320.

17. "Notice sur Madame de Souza et ses ouvrages," in *Oeuvres de madame de Souza*, nouvelle édition, précédée d'une notice sur l'auteur et ses ouvrages par M. Sainte-Beuve (Paris: Charpentier, 1840), p. i.

18. Larnac, pp. 169-170.

19. Restif de La Bretonne, *Oeuvres*, edited by Henri Bachelin (Geneva: Slatkine Reprints, 1971) vol. 3, p. 94.

20. Showalter.

21. *Lettres de mistriss Henley publiées par son amie*, in Isabelle de Charrière, Belle de Zuylen, *Oeuvres complètes*, edited by Jean-Daniel Candaux et al. (Amsterdam: G. A. Van Oorschot, 1980-81), vol. 8, p. 111.

22. Virginia Woolf, "Women and Fiction," in *Women and Writing*, edited by Michèle Barrett (New York: Harcourt Brace Jovanovich, 1980), p. 45.

23. Restif de La Bretonne, *La Paysanne pervertie* (Paris: Garnier-Flammarion, 1972), 5e partie, p. 354.

Susan R. Kinsey

The Memorialists

THE MEMOIR, broadly defined as autobiographical literature, is a highly self-conscious text. Somehow it seems more at home
in our century than it does among the mannered, artificial constraints
of eighteenth-century society. Yet the changing social order, culminating with the Revolution, provided a rich milieu for the memoir to
flourish. Georges Gusdorf, whose 1975 article in the *Revue d'histoire
littéraire de la France* is considered seminal to an understanding of
autobiography as a genre, wrote that the author of such a work "tries
hard to discover that center of equilibrium beyond the chaos where
peace can be found even in the midst of war. Thus, autobiography
justifies itself as a compensatory effort during critical periods of
history."[1]

But while autofascination is accepted with curiosity in our time, the
eighteenth century presented a whole range of obstacles to the
memorialist, from the bias against overpersonalization to the question
of credibility. For the women who wrote memoirs, the hurdles were
higher. One's own reputation and the social standing of one's husband
and family could be jeopardized, for instance, by the kind of implicit
criticism of women's lot that many of the memoirs contain. To publish
such a work was, in effect, to defy conventional expectations. It is this
fact that distinguishes women's memoirs from the mainstream of the
tradition and makes them, individually and as a whole, a political act.
This distinction is important because of the part women's memoirs
will play in the definition of women's literature as they cross the
boundaries separating historical from autobiographical writing.

One technical question merits consideration, though, before explor-
ing the implications of the memorialists' act; namely, in what way can
memoir be considered autobiography, and how does it relate to
confessional literature?

In narrowly defined terms, the memoir concerned itself with
history, was often anecdotal, and held the presence of the first person
narrator as a mere formality. Yves Coirault, in an article entitled
"Autobiographies et mémoires (XVIIᵉ-XVIIIᵉ siècles)," proposed the
name *égographie* for this type of writing, which usually emphasized the
author's importance as a politically and socially well-connected man.[2]

Confessions, on the other hand, were intensely personal documents wherein the first person narrator became not only the subject of the book but its object as well, the historical backdrop, a mere curiosity. While Montaigne had offered the public a daringly personal record of his life and thoughts in 1680, the mainstream of confessional literature was pietistic until the publication of Rousseau's *Confessions* in 1782. This work opened up new possibilities for writers of what has now come to be called autobiographical. As Gusdorf explained, "That is the moment at which the autobiography venture rises up to distinguish itself from literature."[3] Inspired by Rousseau, women like Mme d'Epinay and Mme Roland wrote about their lives and the historical events they were part of in a way that joined confessional writing to historical memoir.

But the act of publishing, for an eighteenth-century woman, entailed a great deal of risk. Society was unkind to women who tried to make professional lives for themselves. Memoir writing was particularly problematic, since the personal nature of the work not only exposed the writer to scandal as "writer" but also often laid bare the more intimate details of her life to public scrutiny and rumor. A sample count of the 860-odd memoirs, histories, and correspondences listed in the *Répertoire général des ouvrages modernes relatifs au dix-huitième siècle français (1715-1789)* shows that only about five percent were written by women.[4]

All things considered, therefore, those women who wrote memoirs obviously felt compelled to do so. Why? Two possible motivations emerge: the need for self-justification and a desire to be incorporated in the historical record. It would be unrealistic to polarize the writers between these two considerations, but they do cover the spectrum in varying degrees ranging from, for example, Mme Campan's account of her service to the Revolution to Mme d'Epinay's description of her relationships with the men she loved.

This latter example of memoir writing presents a curious paradox for the author. If her life was already the subject of rumor, explaining her conduct in print might only exacerbate the situation. Women like Mme d'Epinay felt it was a risk worth taking. Her memoirs, not published until 1818 but written much earlier, demonstrate a kind of *sensibilité* that was uniquely eighteenth-century, when a kind of chaste love or worship from afar was the apogée of virtue. But with Mme d'Epinay, one explores a wider expanse of moral terrain, where taking a lover becomes less an issue than one's choice of lover. Of particular importance in Mme d'Epinay's memoirs is the fact that the actual moral dilemma surrounding infidelity is openly debated and virtue is consequently redefined. As one critic put it, "Scandal was thus accepted; but, justified or not, this acceptance did not rule out a debate on the practical considerations of feminine virtue."[5]

Thus, while Mme d'Epinay has prepared a very personal document about her own life choices, she has also provided a defense for the behavior of all women trapped in unhappy lives. To a certain extent, the format of her memoirs, a loosely-constructed novel narrated by a man, her tutor, is perfectly designed to do both. The book's focus is Mme d'Epinay, transparently disguised as Emilie, who evolves and grows from an insecure child-wife into a serene and loving woman. Her first affair, with M. Franceuil, was a stormy one sprinkled throughout with his infidelities.[6] When she finally worked herself out of it, she was several years older and much less impressionable.

Her second liaison, with Grimm, was a more thoughtful one, inspired by respect and admiration rather than by passion. Grimm apparently effected a major change in Mme d'Epinay's personality, which, as she describes it prior to meeting him, was conditioned by the attitudes of self-sacrifice and self-denigration that often characterize women's behavior:

> The only mistake that I made with my friends is to have always thought of them before me, and to have catered to their whims, counting myself as worthless. By virtue of this little system, I had as many masters as friends, and I found the secret of making a source of sorrow from friendship, which is perhaps the single compensation for the misfortunes of the human condition. To have a will of my own seemed a crime to me. . . .[7]

It was through Grimm that Mme d'Epinay finally understood the value of emotional independence. She cites from what Grimm wrote to her in one of his letters: "it is entirely up to you to be the happiest and the most desirable creature on earth, provided that you do not put others' opinions before your own, and that you know how to be self-sufficient."[8]

Her newfound strength must have made it easier, in a sense, for her to deal with Jean-Jacques Rousseau, who came to live at the Hermitage, her country home, in April of 1756 but who left twenty months later under a cloud. Mme d'Epinay may have been infatuated with Rousseau, as some critics have proposed, and her jealousy over his affection for her sister-in-law, Sophie d'Houdetot, may have caused the dissension between them; but considering Rousseau's personality problem—he has been described as a paranoid egomaniac—Mme d'Epinay was probably not at fault. She portrays herself as the unsuspecting victim of his machinations to drive a wedge between herself and Sophie[9] and to disparage her reputation while professing to be her friend.[10] Their quarrel, of course, became public and may have been partly responsible for the composition of these memoirs.

But whether or not the memoirs were an answer to Rousseau's accusations against her, Mme d'Epinay's work serves as a valuable chronicle of one woman's development and as a barometer of many women's dissatisfaction. By the end of her life, Emilie could undoubtedly take pride in thinking that she had educated her daughter, against the objections of her son's tutor, to become a woman of independent spirit satisfied to define her own lifestyle. As Mme d'Epinay put it at the end of her memoirs: "I do not claim that others must imitate me: each does as he or she sees fit, and each is right. What occupies me principally is to know if I have a right to be content with myself; and if I am, I believe that others should also be."[11]

Although Mme d'Epinay certainly was aware that she was to some extent making history, her memoirs lack the historical resonance found in the works of some other eighteenth-century memorialists. These women felt their lives worth telling precisely because of their nearness to or participation in important events. What they wrote were neither objective histories nor memoirs in the *égographie* mode but histories in which they were active participants.

In a society that allowed to women largely passive roles, what these women did could only be called revolutionary. Martin Hall, in an article on women and history, wrote of that period: "History remains above all the privilege of the male; female participation is passive, influencing the course of history only in so far as it provokes male activity. Where this catalytic function is translated into a more active response, it immediately becomes suspect and liable to censure."[12] Against this bias, Mme de Staal-Delaunay, Mme Roland, and Mme Campan rewrote history to include women.

They did face one major structural problem. While these women felt that their lives were worthy of consideration because of their proximity to certain historical events, they did not want to disappear against that backdrop. A balance was needed between the personal story to be told and the broader historical drama. In her memoirs, Mme de Staal-Delaunay cements together the bits and pieces of her own life with fragments from the life of the duchesse du Maine, in whose service she spent many years. She uses the history of the du Maine family as glue to bind the elements of her own story, and the reader is not misled on that score, since she begins her memoirs on a very personal note:

> What happened to me was just the reverse of what one sees in romantic novels, where the heroine, raised as a simple shepherdess, discovers that she is a princess. I was treated in my childhood as a person of distinction; and subsequently, I discovered that I was nothing, and that nothing in the world belonged to me.[13]

She goes on to describe her convent education and her two great loves, the marquis de Silly, an adolescent infatuation, and chevalier de Menil, with whom she fell in love during her confinement in the Bastille. Both men misled and disappointed her.

Between these two unfortunate affairs stands her service in the home of the duchesse du Maine, her involvement in the Cellamare affair, and her subsequent imprisonment. She entered the service of the duchesse as chambermaid in the spring of 1711; and in her memoirs, she details life at the château de Sceaux, which was rivaled only by Versailles for its brilliance. As entertainment, the duchesse created the *grandes nuits* of fireworks, theater, dancing, singing and poetry. There were sixteen of these galas in 1714 and 1715, and Mlle Delaunay supervised the writing of the texts and the presentations themselves: "She was truly the 'soul' of the nuits. She presided over the writing of scripts and the progress of the performance," according to Gérard Doscot in an introduction to the memoirs.[14]

The Cellamare affair, however, was the most important event in Mme de Staal-Delaunay's life. The duchesse du Maine dreamed of seeing her husband's power grow. As a legitimized bastard of Louis XIV and the marquise de Montespan, the duc du Maine was seen as a threat by the duc d'Orléans, who held the presidency of the regency council. After a disagreement between them on the question of the Quadruple Alliance among England, France, Austria and Holland, the duc du Maine was stripped of his privileges.

The duchesse decided that the time had come to call upon the allies of the duc du Maine in Spain in the person of Philippe V, grandson of Louis XIV. Through the intervention of the Spanish ambassador to France, the prince de Cellamare, the duc and duchesse du Maine hoped to see the duc d'Orléans removed from power. But the plot was discovered, and everyone connected with the affair was arrested in December of 1718.

From the Bastille, Rose Delaunay protested her innocence. But what had her role actually been? She admits that she volunteered to monitor the du Maine correspondence with the baron de Walef in Spain and to have his letters written and addressed to her.[15] As a mere accessory to the affair, she insisted that she understood nothing of what was going on: "I shall refrain from explaining their plan, because I never understood what it was all about."[16] It seems a rather questionable defense, though, since Mme de Staal-Delaunay admits she warned the duchesse that her activities might land her in prison.[17] In addition, the author describes a kind of invisible ink with which she was instructed to write between the lines in her letters to Spain.[18] Clearly, she was more informed in the matter than she was prepared to admit in her memoirs. In any event, she ended up spending just over a year in the Bastille for her complicity in the affair.

Married off by the duchesse in 1740 to a prominent military man, Mme de Staal-Delaunay's private life seems strikingly barren. The class system took its toll on her, as it did on others born into the wrong class who considered themselves gifted and intelligent. While writing a memoir was a way of affirming that her life had meaning, she still felt obliged in these same pages to acknowledge her secondary station in life. Consequently, the book ends on a rather sterile note with a tribute to the duc du Maine at his death.

Mme Roland was not subject to the same social forces. She manages to share the spotlight throughout her memoirs with the events of the French Revolution. This she does by bringing together in the book remembrances of her childhood and adolescence, several short portraits of those closest to her in the republican movement, anecdotes, the details of her arrest and interrogation, and her final thoughts before death. All this is contained in several hundred pages written between the time of her arrest in June 1793 and her execution at the age of thirty-nine on November 8 of the same year.

For Mme Roland, imprisoned with the certainty that she was going to die, writing about the past was a way of escaping from the present. A great deal of description of her early years is devoted to a discussion of her "formation" and her passion for the writings of Plutarch. Stanley Loomis, in *Paris in the Terror,* has called her "self-righteous" for the forceful, almost dogmatic, way in which she defends her ideals.[19] But considering the circumstances under which these memoirs were written, it seems understandable that Mme Roland would have wanted to commit the strength of her convictions to posterity.

From the time of her arrival in Paris in February of 1791, Mme Roland opened her home to the diverse group of republicans who would later split apart and try to destroy one another as Girondins and Montagnards. Brissot, Buzot, and Robespierre all frequented her salon. In the part of her memoirs called "Notices historiques," Mme Roland describes the deterioration of relations between her husband, as minister of the interior, and Marat, whom she referred to as a "monster."[20] According to Mme Roland, it was Marat's greed that was at the root of the quarrel.

After Roland's resignation from the post of minister in January 1793 (a post he held from March 1792), he was mercilessly persecuted by the Jacobins led by Marat and Danton, who wanted to silence his accusations of corruption against them. On the evening of May 31, Roland received warning of his imminent arrest and fled the city. His wife, however, chose to remain behind, preferring death to life under what she considered to be a criminal regime: "I prefer to die rather than be witness to the ruin of my country; I shall consider it an honor to be included among the noble victims sacrificed to the murderous fury."[21]

She was arrested, and the charges against her included sedition because of her association with the Bureau de l'esprit public, the propaganda organ of the interior ministry. Mme Roland maintains in her memoirs that she had no part in the work of that "Bureau," but Paul de Roux, in his introduction to the memoirs, assumes otherwise: "The opponents of the Interior Minister were exasperated by the activity of his propaganda arm, the renowned Bureau de l'Esprit Public of which Mme Roland was probably the driving force."[22] In addition, observers such as Lamartine insist that Mme Roland was probably one of the revolution's principal ideologues, through her husband's pen: "After dinner, the Girondins listened to the position papers which Roland, aided by his wife, had written up for the Convention concerning the state of the republic."[23] The fact is that in the record she left to posterity she denied her role as an activist in the events of the Revolution. That denial undoubtedly has more to do with social mores than with political realities.

While Mme Roland was a committed republican, Mme Campan's story of her own life and of the Revolution unfolds in the royal palaces of Versailles and the Tuileries through the eyes of a monarchist—a first lady-in-waiting to Marie-Antoinette. The events she narrates from the life of Marie-Antoinette and the Revolution are not presented chronologically; they are more a series of vignettes laced with anecdotes of life at the court. The book is actually divided into two parts. The first half, for the most part, is devoted to a defense of Marie-Antoinette, her politics, her morality, and her manners. Only in the second part of the book does Mme Campan become more of an active participant in her own story. The point of departure for that change is the insurrection of 1789. As the movements of the royal family became increasingly limited, the king and queen naturally depended more upon their attendants to keep them in touch with the outside world. Mme Campan became indispensable to the queen. The services she rendered to the royal family included such things as taking dictation from the king, making an assassination-proof vest for the king to wear on the anniversary of Bastille Day in 1792, and devising a secret code for the queen's correspondence abroad.

But these memoirs become most interesting as they recount the days leading up to the arrest of the royal family. The extraordinary scene of the mobs storming the Tuileries is memorable as Mme Campan details it: Eight hundred Swiss guards were massacred, bodies were strewn everywhere, and blood stained the hems of the palace ladies' gowns as they ran across the courtyard in an attempt to escape. As she fled down a staircase, chased by a group of men, Mme Campan was seized by one of her pursuers.

> The narrow staircase impeded the assassins, but I had already felt the dreadful pawing of a hand on my back, grabbing my clothing, when a voice called up from the bottom of the stairs: "... we don't kill women."[I]

was on my knees, my executioner let go of me and said: "Get up, tramp; the nation will spare you." The coarseness of these words did not prevent me from feeling suddenly an inexpressible emotion which sprang as much from a love of life as from the idea that I was going to see my son and all that was dear to me once again. One second before, I had been thinking less about death itself than about the pain I would feel from the sword suspended over my head. One rarely sees death so closely without dying.[24]

Mme Campan survived the Revolution to write these memoirs under Napoleon. She founded a school for young ladies at Saint-Germain, which became famous for its educational philosophy and for its roll call of celebrated students, among whom were Hortense de Beauharnais, stepdaughter of Napoleon, and Caroline and Pauline Bonaparte, sisters of the emperor. Later, in 1807, she was named director of a new school at Ecouen established by Napoleon. Her task as outlined by him was to prepare the future mothers of France. She set out to do this by offering a broadly based liberal arts education covering writing, arithmetic, history, language, music (especially religious music), all heavily laced with religious and moral instruction.

With the fall of Bonaparte in 1814 and the restoration of the monarchy, Mme Campan fell irreversibly from favor. The new royalists, as Gabrielle Reval notes in her book on Mme Campan, "never forgave her for having served the Usurper."[25] She lived out the rest of her life, until 1822, in near destitution, isolation, and bitterness.

While a certain amount of independence was available to women of a particular class, what prevailed above all was a profound sense of powerlessness, both social and political. It is true that, to a degree, the institution of the salon offered women a certain control over cultural and literary tastes, but this was actually an illusory power, one of form rather than substance. In fact, eighteenth-century women were at the mercy of male-dominated social institutions such as marriage and the family in much the same way as their sisters before them. One study described their predicament:

> An astonishing contradiction in the eighteenth century juxtaposed a freedom of social behavior with the total dependency that was women's lot. On one hand, there was a greater participation for women in social activities—according to class, obviously—and on the other hand, a very clear oppression of women by men in order to preserve their power.[26]

Marriages were still arranged, and women passed from father to husband through the intercession of the priest. Mme de Staal-Delaunay's description of her own marriage, arranged by the duchesse du Maine, probably reflects how a great many women felt as they were being literally led to the altar: "The contract was drawn up, including the pension which the duc du Maine awarded me upon my release from prison. The duchesse du Maine provided me with the proper clothing. The victim, bound and decorated, was sadly led to the altar. . . ."27

Once married, women were frequently subjected to physical abuse, often beginning the wedding night itself. Mme Roland recalls the shock of her marriage night: "my little trials and tribulations convinced me that I could endure the greatest suffering without crying out. The first night of marriage overturned all pretentions that I had harbored until then. . . ."28 Where physical violence was absent, there were still a husband's infidelities to contend with. Mme d'Epinay was very much in love with her husband when she married, but the reality of his unfaithfulness early in the relationship was extremely difficult for her to bear. She scolded him and was silenced; "I want to be free and no questions asked" was his only response.29 Many women found themselves similarly diminished.

Evolving responses to such institutionalized oppression was no easy matter. The only alternative to marriage itself, for most women, was the convent, and it was a kind of prison. But even a woman as cosmopolitan as Mme Roland admits she found herself so disillusioned with her married life that she often longed for the company of women in a society free of men: "There also predominates a certain something, amiable, ingenuous, graceful, which belongs only to the gentleness of women, to the innocence of their frolicking as they make merry among themselves, far from the company of the opposite sex, which always makes them more somber when it does not make them delirious."30 Divorce was a rare possibility, and becoming a runaway wife was only slightly more feasible. Husbands could appeal to the king for reinstatement of their conjugal rights, making the wife a fugitive from the law. Legal separation, sanctioned by the king, was the only effective alternative, and it was difficult to obtain.

So the issue demanded public debate. The double standard, condoning extramarital affairs for men while prohibiting that same conduct for women, came under attack by Mme d'Epinay. Her memoirs are crisscrossed by women such as her sister-in-law, Mme de Jully, and her friend, Mlle d'Ette, who do not hesitate to discuss their love affairs and to justify them. Mlle d'Ette even advocates that the newly wed Mme d'Epinay take a lover herself to rival her husband's lifestyle. The naïve twenty-three-year-old Mme d'Epinay protests, "people will gossip and my reputation will be ruined."31 To which her friend calmly replies in an expression of the new philosophy, "Where did you get that idea? Firstly, is there a woman about whom people do not gossip? Besides, it is only fickleness, or a bad choice, or as I already told you, indiscretion, which can blacken a woman's reputation."[32] Obviously, discretion and good taste are the keys to this new morality, advocating a kind of limited sexual freedom for women.

Caught in the trap of a bad marriage, a woman who was afraid to test the limits of her freedom might dream that motherhood would satisfy her needs. But for upper- and middle-class eighteenth-century women, child rearing was an unfulfilled and unfulfilling role. It was considered socially unacceptable for a woman of means to nurse her infants and raise her children at home. Wet nurses in neighboring villages were employed to keep the children until they were old enough for some sort of informal schooling. In this way, access to even limited power within the family structure, through influence on the children, was denied to women.

Then, Jean-Jacques Rousseau published *La Nouvelle Héloïse* and *Emile*. To a modern reader, Rousseau's ideas seem sexist. But for the eighteenth-century woman, he represented a break with the past, advocating love rather than autonomous marriage, maternal child rearing rather than wet-nursing, and a broader education for girls destined to mold them as intelligent wives and mothers. His ideas were enormously popular.

No one challenged the fact that women were to be dependent on men, but women such as Mlle d'Espinassy in her 1764 *Essai sur l'éducation des demoiselles* urged a more comprehensive liberal arts education for girls. The trend caught on, and between 1785 and 1791, about 150 volumes appeared, directed at the new market of home education for women; books on travel, history, morality, astronomy, the arts, and domestic medicine abounded. Mme Campan played a significant role in the movement to institutionalize these educational innovations through her school for girls at Saint-Germain, which opened in 1794. The curriculum consisted of religion, history, literature, grammar, mathematics, natural science, astronomy, physics and chemistry. As progressive as this program may appear to have been, it should be remembered that these girls were being groomed for a traditional role. As one critic wrote: "The originality of this education is that while appealing to strict methods and a rigorous discipline, it never loses sight of its objective, which is to turn out seductive women."[33]

Naturally, the limitations of that role became less and less acceptable to women as their access to power increased; but in the eighteenth century, expressions of dissatisfaction were still restricted. The basic problem for women was a political one, in that the preservation of the monarchy and, with it, the existing social order went hand in hand with women's oppression. Restif de La Bretonne, who admired the discipline of an autocracy, characterized the political situation with the following analogy: "The Royalty, which, whatever else one might say, was conceived on the model of a patriarchal family, is nothing other than an artificial marriage of the nation and the Ruler to whom she submits, not as a slave, but as a legitimate wife."[34] Mme Roland saw women's problems in political terms, and when the Académie de Besançon proposed a paper entitled "Comment l'éducation des femmes pouvait contribuer à rendre les hommes meilleurs," she introduced into it her ideas on the need for massive social change.

> I recall that in wanting to treat this subject, I felt that it was absurd to establish a mode of education bearing no relationship to the general morality, which depended upon the government; and that it would not do to claim the reform of one sex by the other. Rather, it would be better to improve everyone's lot with good laws. Thus, I explained how, it seemed to me, women ought to be; but I added that they could not become that way until things changed.[35]

Among the women discussed here, class discrimination probably touched no one more directly than Mme de Staal-Delaunay, who spent much of her life in the service of the duchesse du Maine. She had a strong sense of her own worth and no satisfaction at all in the fact that she was destined for servitude. A verbal self-portrait she composed for Mme du Deffand expresses her unhappiness: "Love of liberty is her dominant passion; and a very unfortunate one for her, since the greater part of her life has been spent in servitude: in fact, her condition has always been intolerable for her, despite its unexpected benefits."[36] In the works of both Mme de Staal-Delaunay and Mme Roland, there is an acknowledgment, but never an acceptance, of the superior position of the upper classes. Even in her teen-age years, Mme Roland resented society's complete disregard for merit in favor of birth: "I could not hide the fact that I was more worthy than Mlle d'Hannaches whose forty years and bloodline did not convey the aptitude to write a common-sense letter which was readable; I considered the world unfair and all social institutions unjust."[37]

To this oppression, society's answer as a whole was the Revolution itself. Women began to see the possibility of more freedom within the new order. On the eve of the Revolution, women's rights, in the broadest sense, first became an issue. It was a time of enthusiasm, and many liberal thinkers among the *philosophes* put forward programs for incorporating women into the ruling establishment. Condorcet, for example, in 1787, in his *Essai sur les assemblées provinciales,* "clearly demanded the right, for a woman who held property, to have a seat in these assemblies."[38] And so it continued up through the famous insurrection of July 14, 1789, when women fought alongside men. On October 5, 1789, four thousand women marched on the National Assembly. But as Maïté Albistur wrote in *Histoire du féminisme français:* "these insurrections do not prove advantageous for them. To the contrary, the picture of these fighting women will imprint itself on 'the collective imagination' and, by inspiring fear, will provoke a male reaction."[39] And the reaction did come. On October 20, 1793, by order of the Convention, all women's clubs were shut down. By 1795, the Convention had forbid housewives from gathering in the streets in groups of more than five.[40] The years of exuberance were over and women found themselves deceived and disappointed.

What was the nature of the force at work to undo what the Revolution had promised women? Men's unique and private access to history had been breached by women. Now, that chasm had to be reopened and women distanced once and for all. *Gloire* was the code word. A woman's reputation or *gloire* depended on her anonymity. As Patricia Meyer Spacks explains, *gloire* for men was palpable triumph by courage, inventiveness, enterprise, and intelligence; for women, it was a sort of triumph by being "good," which was undramatic and passive.[41] Therefore, any woman who chose to become a public figure was a pariah in her own time and had to trust posterity to vindicate her. Mme Roland understood the pressures and wrote in 1793:

> Never did I have the slightest temptation to become a writer; I saw very early that a woman who won this title lost a lot more than she gained. Men do not respect her at all and other women criticize her; if her works are bad, she is made fun of, and rightly so; if they are good, the credit is taken from her. If society is forced to acknowledge that she is, in fact, the author, it so dissects her character, her morals, her conduct and her talents that her intellectual prowess is diminished by the dazzle of her defects.[42]

Yet Mme Roland did write, and what is clear from her memoirs is that she, like most other women of her time, felt strictly bound by a role that was considered "appropriate" behavior. During her trial, she insisted in the *Projet de défense au tribunal* that she acted within these boundaries: "I followed the progress of the Revolution with fervor, but I never exceeded the limits imposed upon me by gender."[43]

Broadly speaking, enforced anonymity for women was another way that men controlled the political and social hierarchy. The penalty for violating this code of conduct could be violent. Eugène Crépet suggests that Mme Roland was executed not for her politics but for her visibility: "Mme Roland's irremissible crime is that of confronting head-on by her example one of the most stubborn prejudices in the French psyche—that stupid and deadly prejudice which precludes for women all ideas and attitudes having to do with public service."[44]

To exercise control over one's private life, to cultivate a public persona, both of these avenues were blocked for the eighteenth-century woman. Writing became a way of satisfying the need for power on several levels. Psychologically, it promoted a sense of sisterhood in the face of fear, isolation, and feelings of inferiority and hopelessness. Channels of communication were opened in which the act of writing itself took on a special significance, according to Patricia Meyer Spacks: "What is striking in the work of virtually all women writing about themselves, in the present and in the past, is the degree to which writing is itself a solution to their most pressing problems. . . . Writing for publication, at once a private and a public act, demands self-expression and implies communication."[45]

On an equally important level, writing offered a world of experiences that could be ordered, even manipulated, by women who lacked that power in their daily lives—a kind of vicarious powerbrokering that must have been satisfying for both writer and reader. As Spacks explains it, "writing, moreover, declares the possibility of at least retrospective control over experience—that control which women in their lives so often lack."[46] Within the framework of this last observation, the memoir assumes particular importance. As a quasi-historical document, involving real people and real events, it gives its authors control, not over a fictitious world, but over real life, albeit retrospectively.

Finally, on a philosophical level, the memoir provided as rich a ground as possible at the time for the subtle advocacy of social and political reform. These women writers were not banner wavers, nor were they, or could they have been, overtly championing women's issues. That language, not to mention that concept, is the product of a later time. What they did do, however, is risk public censure to describe their own lives. And it is between the lines of the memoirs that their frustrations and their dreams can be read.

NOTES

1. Georges Gusdorf, "De l'autobiographie initiatique à l'autobiographie genre littéraire," *Revue d'histoire littéraire de la France* 2 (1975): 972.

2. Yves Coirault, "Autobiographies et mémoires (XVIIe-XVIIIe siècles) ou existence et naissance de l'autobiographie," *Revue d'histoire littéraire de la France* 75 (November-December 1975): 950.

3. Gusdorf, p. 998.

4. Vicomte Charles du Peloux, *Répertoire général des ouvrages modernes relatifs au dix-huitième siècle français (1715-1789)*, (Paris: Ernest Grund, 1927).

5. René Démoris, *Le Roman à la première personne* (Paris: Armand Colin, 1975), p. 282.

6. According to Eugène Despois, in an article entitled "Les Mémoires de Madame d'Epinay," an illegitimate son born from this affair became the bishop of Soissons under Napoleon *(Revue nationale et étrangère*, 13,[1863]:171-181).

7. Louise-Florence-Pétronille Tardieu d'Epinay, *Mémoires et correspondance* (Paris: Brunet, 1818), vol. 3, pp. 123-125.

8. Ibid., p. 12
9. Ibid., pp. 84-85.
10. Ibid., pp. 145-146.
11. Ibid., pp. 123-125.
12. P. M. Hall, "Duclos's *Histoire de madame de Luz:* Woman and History," in *Woman and Society in Eighteenth-Century France, Essays in Honour of John Stephenson Spink* (London: The Athlone Press, 1979), p. 143.
13. Mme de Staal-Delaunay, née Marguerite Jeanne Cordier, *Mémoires* (Paris: Mercure de France, 1970), p. 29.
14. Ibid., p. 15.
15. Ibid., p. 114.
16. Ibid., p. 115.
17. Ibid., p. 116.
18. Ibid., p. 114.
19. Stanley Loomis, *Paris in the Terror, June 1793-July 1794* (London: Jonathan Cape, 1964), p. 177.
20. Marie-Jeanne Roland, *Mémoires* (Paris: Mercure de France, 1966), p. 90.
21. Ibid., p. 42.
22. Ibid., p. 21.
23. Alphonse Marie Louis de Lamartine, *Histoire des Girondins,* 5th ed. (Brussels: Joseph Baer, 1851), vol. 2, p. 295.
24. Jeanne Louise Henriette Campan, *Mémoires* (Paris: Ramsay, 1979), p. 255.
25. Gabrielle Reval, *Madame Campan assistante de Napoléon* (Paris: Albin Michel, 1931), p. 303.
26. Maïté Albistur and Daniel Armogathe, *Histoire du féminisme français du moyen âge à nos jours* (Paris: Editions des femmes, 1977), p. 175.
27. Mme de Staal-Delaunay, p. 230.
28. Mme Roland, p. 256.
29. Mme d'Epinay, vol. 1, p. 16.
30. Mme Roland, p. 247.
31. Mme d'Epinay, vol 1, p. 127.
32. Ibid.
33. Reval, p. 188.
34. Nicolas-Edmé Restif de La Bretonne, *Les Gynographes* (The Hague: Gosse et Pinet, 1777), pp. 57-58.
35. Mme Roland, p. 327.
36. Mme de Staal-Delaunay, p. 221.
37. Mme Roland, p. 246.
38. Léon Abensour, *Le Problème féministe* (Paris: Radot, 1927), p. 69.
39. Albistur and Armogathe, p. 227.
40. Abensour, p. 84.
41. Patricia Meyer Spacks, "Reflecting Women," *The Yale Review* 63 (October 1973): 27.
42. Mme Roland, p. 304.
43. Mme Roland, p. 371.
44. Eugène Crépet, "La vertu féminine au XVIII siècle," *La Revue moderne* 40 (1867): 103.
45. Spacks, "Reflecting Women," p. 39.
46. Patricia Meyer Spacks, "Women's Stories, Women's Selves," *Hudson Review* 30 (1977): 46.

✥ Judith Curtis

The Epistolières

THE SIX WOMEN in this essay were not chosen primarily for the literary merit of their letters nor because they all led lives of conspicuous and lasting accomplishment; one or the other of these criteria, strictly applied, could well eliminate most of them. They were chosen in the first place because each led a life that was in some way exceptional and worthy of study and left us essential materials for that study in her correspondence and, secondly, because some at least of that correspondence is reasonably accessible and still highly readable. Sometimes these letters need to be seen in the context of other works: Mme du Châtelet's *Discours sur le bonheur*, for example, or Mlle Delaunay's *Mémoires*. Sometimes they are themselves the sum total of their author's written legacy.

This kind of selection, obviously, does not exhaust the possibilities of the topic. Other collections exist that more usefully convey the flavor of everyday life among the unremarkable majority (at a certain level, of course, of literacy and ease). However, our six *épistolières* all have something to tell us about their experience that goes beyond, while it may still include, the mere daily record.

MLLE DELAUNAY

It is a notable fact that although most of the surviving correspondence of Mlle Delaunay (Marguerite Jeanne Cordier, 1683-1750) is addressed to men her life was almost entirely shaped by other women: the mother who left her to be brought up in a Rouen convent and whose family name she adopted;[1] the abbess of the convent, a well-born "godmother" to whose patronage she owed her pampered childhood and unusually sound education and whose death left her suddenly destitute; the duchesse who bungled her entry into the service of Mme du Maine, so that it was as a mere chambermaid, rather than as the governess she was qualified to be; and, above all, the duchesse du Maine herself, whom she served as maid, secretary, and companion for over forty years. It was out of loyalty to her haughty mistress that Mlle Delaunay spent many months in the Bastille after the rout of the Cellamare conspiracy; it was for her that she turned poet and playwright, supplying texts for the famous entertainments known as the *nuits de Sceaux*;[2] and it was at her behest that she eventually made a "convenient" marriage to a minor officer in the ducal household, the baron de Staal. Mme du Maine seems to have filled the place in her life that a shadowy mother and sister never occupied. While she chafed under the authority of the duchesse, her memoirs are colored by a grudging admiration and a surprisingly hardy desire to earn the other's approbation.

Best known for the *Mémoires* in which she relates all these events, Mlle Delaunay also left letters that illuminate that often reticent, prematurely terminated work. Letters not only mark important events in her life but were often causes. It was a witty note written to the philosopher Fontenelle that first brought her to the attention of the duchess and of salon society as a whole. Her singular three-year correspondence with the chevalier de Menil, her fellow prisoner in the Bastille, is the minute revelation of a woman actually writing herself into a state of romantic obsession, then, by degrees, coming to terms with her partner's defection. Not the least interesting thing about this correspondence is that it should have survived at all among the papers of someone notoriously discreet about many sides of her experience; but it is characteristic of her, even in the memoirs, to blend vanity with an often painful frankness about her misadventures. She also preserved the faintly grotesque letters of her septuagenarian admirer, the abbé de Chaulieu, and the texts of those she wrote to and on behalf of her first idol, the marquis de Silly, when he called on her skills to help extricate him from involvement with another woman. Reflecting as they do the sentimental and stormy passages in her life, these pages are a corrective to the impression often left by the exquisite reserve of the memoirs, a reserve that has led some critics to see in her a "cold and unpoetical personage."[3] Not coldness but discipline and elegance of expression, a piquant counterpoint to the underlying emotion, are the marks of everything she wrote. A modern, properly authenticated edition of the correspondence is needed to make it available to a wider public.

The last important collection of Mlle Delaunay's letters, and one that is fairly easy to come by, is that written in 1747 to the marquise du Deffand, a confidante who inspired some of her most spontaneous pages.[4] This small collection is recommended not only for its much quoted account of a visit paid to the ducal court by Voltaire and Mme du Châtelet but especially because it presents the essential Delaunay: superb stylist, relentless analyst of herself and of the society around her, wistful seeker after patience and repose, affectionate friend.

Delaunay indeed had many friends among the eminent and well-born; the fundamental tension of her story lies in the fact that, lacking birth and fortune, she remained in spite of her gifts "in service" until her death. Like Julie de Lespinasse, she won a certain prominence by her intellect and charm but never escaped the rules of the hierarchy. She herself, in the first lines of her memoirs, invites the reader to see in her life the disadvantages of being "educated above one's station."[5] Rather than emerging as a rebel against the definitions of appropriate behavior for her sex and her class (she had the makings of a splendid satirist, and "libertine" was Chaulieu's favorite term for her in her youth), she retreated into strict outward decorum and self-censorship. Nonetheless, the famous irony she directed so often against herself and the detachment she cultivated barely mask the frustration and the countless disappointments of a woman who saw her abilities trivialized and her lonely fidelities taken for granted. Let it be said on the positive side that she managed to leave the record of a finely-trained mind and a spirit that was to a remarkable degree both sensitive and resilient.

MLLE AÏSSÉ

If there were not independent evidence for the existence of Mlle Aïssé (1694-1733) and her liaison with the chevalier d'Aydie, we would have to regard her as a clever fiction from the school of Guilleragues or abbé Prévost, so strikingly does her story correspond to the myths of female destiny that typify the eighteenth-century novel.[6] Bought as a child in a slave market in Constantinople, persecuted by a lecherous guardian and a corrupt foster mother, adored by a young nobleman she could not (or would not) marry and to whom she secretly bore a child, the reputedly beautiful, high-minded "Circassian princess" was bound to inspire the writers of lachrymose drama and romanced history.[7] But what made her tale so irresistible, what made her "conversion" and early death not merely touching but somehow exemplary and aesthetically satisfying, was the spiritual conflict depicted in her letters. A few years after the beginning of her affair, Aïssé was befriended by one Julie Calandrini (1668-1754), a resident of Geneva, who did not share the common respect for her discreet and loyal passion and who apparently made their friendship conditional on Aïssé's either marrying or renouncing her lover. Accepting the older woman's moral authority— "if only you had been my foster mother," she sighs on page after page— Aïssé embraced the dilemma, expressing her anguish in a seven-year correspondence that seemingly takes us to within days of her death. The nineteenth century termed her a martyr to the conflict of love and sacred duty; we are more likely to speak of a social code that stood in the way of the desired marriage and a definition of virtue rigidly applied, neither of which Aïssé was able to reject.

The letters to Mme Calandrini were first published in 1787 by Calandrini's granddaughter, along with notes by Voltaire and a highly sentimental biography that has contributed at least as much as the letters to the enduring legend. Many of its details are impossible to confirm. Eugène Ritter casts doubt on the standard arrangement of the letters, suggesting that sections have been shifted from their proper place in the sequence and reminding us of the possibility of other sorts of tampering as well.[98] Thus, while we can easily recognize the earliest letters and the last, we cannot use the main body as evidence of the sequence of events or the writer's evolution. An argument that might be used for the overall authenticity of the correspondence is the revelation, within these pages, of a side of the writer that makes a pointed contrast with the idealized figure first presented in the 1787 biography.[9] Certainly the "tender" Aïssé is there, breaking her heart over her two incompatible yearnings; but before that aspect fully emerges, there is also an Aïssé who is gossipy, practical, outspoken, smug about her own moral delicacy, and much less ingenuous than the commentators would lead us to believe. She has a taste for the bizarre and the horrific: the tale of Isez and the figure in white (Letter VI) and the popular version of the "murder" of Adrienne Lecouvreur (Letter XXVI). She can be as merciless and incisive as Mme du Deffand in her portraits. Publication of the letters brought protests from the relatives of her foster mother, Mme de Ferriol, who appears in these pages as a bloated harpy despite Aïssé's declared resolve to be charitable. And as much as Calandrini may be said to "manipulate" her, Aïssé, in turn, seeks to impose on her reader an ingratiating self-image, the meek, noble, pitiable image of the legend.

In short, there is in these thirty-three letters a personality that is stronger, more complex, and more interesting than the novelesque heroine generally invoked. They deserve to be examined again, once perhaps with an eye misted by tears, but at least once without.

MME DU CHÂTELET

Emilie du Châtelet (1706-1749) has almost always been studied purely within her relationship with Voltaire. When, after two centuries, her surviving letters were finally given a full edition, it was as a result of Besterman's vast labors on the Voltaire correspondence (although her exchange with Voltaire has not come down to us). The idea of such an edition would have surprised her; one's letters, she once observed, taking rather a minority view for her times, are not written carefully enough to be put on public view.[10] When she picked up her pen, it was not to compose for a salon audience but to transact business, consult a colleague, ask a favor, or pour out her love and anxiety, impressing on the page all the vigor of her nature and all the fierce commitment she brought to her studies and to her attachments. Missing are the gossip, the concern for style, and the small essays in *philosophie* or self-analysis that we take for granted in most letters of the period.

Mme du Châtelet's other works being in the fields of treatise or translation, only in the letters and in her brief *Discourse on Happiness* does she reveal herself to us directly. What the latter works give us are the keys to behavior that others have judged eccentric or grotesque: her protectiveness towards Voltaire; her plain, unstudied disregard for the proprieties; her sublime self-absorption; and the fact that, for her, passions and intellectual pursuits together made up an uncompartmentalized whole. It is in the letters that we find her extravagant devotion to the insipid Saint-Lambert. It is also there that we see her delaying until dangerously late in her pregnancy the journey that would reunite them, so as to complete her translation of Newton before the confinement she rightly feared would end her life. The last item in the Besterman collection is the covering letter she wrote when sending her manuscript to the royal library days before her death.

The question of how contemporary and later generations judged our *épistolières* is one that deserves some exploration. Mme du Châtelet, so visibly unconventional, is an informative case (the exception to the usual pattern being Mlle Aïssé, untouched by taint of intellectualism or multiple amours, who became the nineteenth century's *hermine humaine*,[11] a Clarissa among her libertine sisters). While many who were in a position to judge—Voltaire, Clairaut, Luynes, Maupertuis— paid tribute to her qualities of mind and heart, we do not have to look further than the works of some other letter writers to see her activities disparaged and dismissed. Mlle Delaunay, whom one might expect both to understand Emilie's pursuits and to envy her independence, professed to see in them only affectation and bad manners, making of her an object of satire.[12] (Emilie, one infers, treated Delaunay not as an intellectual equal but as a social inferior, a mere *dame de campagnie*.) Mme du Deffand acknowledged her intellect but accused her of striving for "singularity," for a reprehensible air of superiority to others of her sex.[13] Traditional in most of her views, Deffand felt that learning in a woman (and men as well) should be lightly borne in society. Society, as a whole, was even quicker to find something freakish in the way Emilie conducted her studies and her affairs.

In the nineteenth century, Mme du Châtelet was variously presented as a *belle pécheresse,* an exemplary victim of Voltaire's irreligion and the age's immorality (strangely enough, Delaunay was also identified with "Voltaire's coven"[14]) and a repellant oddity whose interest in science and mathematics and whose frankness in sexual matters cast doubt on her very femininity.[15] We are only now seeing fulfillment of the hope expressed by Louise Colet in 1845, in the first important essay on the letters of Emilie, that she would one day emerge to be assessed in her own right.[16] The serious reevaluation began with such works as Ira Wade's;[17] Besterman and Mauzi have provided us with authoritative modern editions of the letters and the *Discours sur le bonheur;*[18] and René Vaillot's recent biography,[19] which makes of her life a coherent whole, suggests the kind of comprehension that the late twentieth century may be peculiarly fitted to bring. In the most prosaic of her letters—and perhaps by that very quality—Emilie du Châtelet speaks to us in the most immediate and recognizable terms.

MME DU DEFFAND

The marquise du Deffand (1697-1780) is the best-known, most quoted woman letter writer of her century, the one most conscious of the example of Mme de Sévigné. This brief survey of her correspondence will emphasize content rather than form; but it is satisfying to note that critical attention has begun to address her sheer skill in the field of composition.[20]

Her letters, it has sometimes been observed, were very much an extension of the conversation she directed in her salon. Blind spider at the center of a vast web, for thirty years she commanded a tribute of words and ideas, from Voltaire at Ferney, from the duc de Choiseul and even more from the duchess in their country exile, from Horace Walpole across the Channel. The Lescure edition, which represents all her correspondents in a chronological ordering, gives us some sense of her restless mental activity and of the amount of time spent framing and dictating those models of structure and expression that often struck an answering fire from her friends.[21] The correspondence with Mlle de Lespinasse captures both the cordiality of their early relations and unconscious hints of the rupture that lay ahead. The Choiseul letters are a remarkable record of the long friendship between the old marquise and the young woman she called *grand'maman*. In those written to Walpole, the brilliant style of the *lettre galante*, or the social gazette, is set against the frank display of her admiration for a reluctant idol. The correspondence with Voltaire produced the well-known exchange on the subject of *l'ennui*, which—with its recurrent themes, deeply felt imagery (boredom is *le ver solitaire*, the worm that saps the vitality of its host), and trenchant style—constitutes on its own something like a unified work of art and shows how easily the letter enters the realm of the personal essay or even of the dramatic monologue. The intensity of Mme du Deffand's thought in these pages, the rigor of her examination of existential questions, far outstrips anything in Voltaire's somewhat patronizing replies.

Commentators have now and then expressed surprise that so many gifted women of the Enlightenment (Julie de Lespinasse being another example) left no written works apart from their personal letters. The observation springs from the assumption that the letter is a negligible genre and often leads to the conclusion, or at least the implication, that these women lacked the discipline or the mental toughness required for real authorship, their energies being dissipated to the salon air. Given the social standing and the rather conventional views of a Mme du Deffand, the letter is quite simply the only logical form. She had no taste for fiction, detested anything that her hypersensitive ear found pedantic or pretentious, and, with all her critical talents, would have recoiled from any activity resembling journalism, like most women of her rank. The letter—a respected form, something to be read aloud in company, passed from hand to hand, and preserved—was for her a natural outlet and perfectly served her impulse to involve others in continuous social discourse. On a deeper level, it is probable that letter writing, which encourages both introspection and the urge to display, not only expressed but, in fact, fostered her tendency to analyze herself and all around her with an impressive but unforgiving lucidity. In this light, the letter may be seen not simply as a pastime for someone living in enforced darkness and inactivity but as a factor in the evolution of a personality. For the marquise, it was an intensely reflexive exercise, aggravating rather than relieving her sense of being trapped within her own consciousness.

MME DE GRAFFIGNY

"I no longer care about anything, and the end of my life is all I wish for."[22] It is pleasant to discover that the woman who wrote this line on her arrival in Paris in 1739—a frightened provincial, finances and love life in disarray, suffering from "vapors," depression, and desperate uncertainty about her future—was to be, only a few years later, the "reigning queen" of French literary circles.[23] Further, from the point of view of women's history, her correspondence is perhaps the most valuable of all, being a candid and highly inclusive record of daily life over a period of twenty years. Several times a week, for much of this time, Mme de Graffigny (1695-1758) addressed to her chief correspondent in Lunéville, François-Etienne Devaux, voluminous accounts of the activities both of her salon and of the long list of *litterati* and prominent figures she knew or knew of in Paris and Lorraine, as well as a running commentary on every aspect of her private life—financial, medical, sexual, professional, and domestic. Some twenty-five hundred of these letters survived in manuscript, thanks to Devaux, who also preserved most of his own replies. This huge body of material, largely passed over by scholarship, permits an especially immediate contact with the texture of a life very little obscured by previous interpretations or editorial "corrections." To the self-censorship practiced by many letter writers, Graffigny preferred an elaborate system of pseudonyms and coded expressions, which meant that few topics were denied her.

Mme de Graffigny brought to Paris a fervent interest in literary and intellectual trends, the informal but intense education of her years at the court of Lorraine, and a need to find some way of increasing her income. A widow, she was relatively unencumbered; and she seems to have clung with tenacity to an ideal of independence, declaring to Devaux that she would rather subsist on bread than live by thanks and compliments in someone else's establishment.[24] She escaped permanent installation either as a convent pensioner or as a companion to a woman of higher rank, the only two fates that seemed open to someone in her circumstances; and she declined to remarry when the occasion offered. When in the end she managed to set up her own household and salon, it was by cultivating her contacts and making for herself a place in the worlds of authorship and of influence peddling, skirting the social barriers that discouraged her direct entry into the writing profession.[25] Public acclaim followed the appearance of her novel, *Les Lettres péruviennes* (1747), and her play, in the *genre larmoyant*, *Cénie* (1750). Both works, after immense popularity, were soon forgotten, but the former in particular is noteworthy as a rather "philosophical" variant on the so-called Portuguese model of the epistolary novel; within a sentimental framework, Graffigny writes a commentary on French mores reminiscent of the *Lettres persanes*, and she compensates her heroine for lost love with a life eased by wealth and devoted to "the pure and peaceful joys of friendship." The novel's remarks on the education and treatment of European women and its protest against the abusive, cynical male behavior sanctioned by French law (an echo of the author's own unhappy marriage) constitute the strongest feminist statement made by any of our *épistolières.*

Graffigny, not closely connected with any of the century's great men (only her letters describing a visit to Voltaire at Cirey were previously published[26]), has seemed to history a very modest figure; yet, in some ways, she might stand for Enlightenment woman in her most positive aspect. However tremulous her approach to the challenges, however precarious and qualified her independence, she was free of many of the prejudices and constraints still visible in the lives of her contemporaries; and she seems to have taken advantage of every small toehold offered by society in order to pursue her own notions of liberty and accomplishment.

MLLE DE LESPINASSE

The letters of Julie de Lespinasse (1732-1776) are another reminder, if one were needed, that whatever may survive of a woman's private papers it is those reflecting her love life that are most likely to make their way into print and to determine what succeeding generations know of her. For Robert Mauzi, she represents *la vocation du malheur*—a woman whose very sense of self was contingent on suffering.[27] Jean Duché uses her as an example of female masochism working against the "libertine" equality of the sexes that typified her social group.[28] For others, she was "the Sappho, the Héloïse, the Elizabeth Barrett Browning" of her century.[29]

Apart from a small number of letters to Mme du Deffand, all of her surviving correspondence dates from the period of her salon. Regrettably, the practical, sober pages written to her young half brother, as well as those reflecting her friendships with Suard, Shelburne, and Hume, full of her ardent political views, still gather dust in archives, quoted by a rare scholar.[30] We have only a slim, outdated edition of letters to such intimates as Condorcet to give us some glimpse of the alert, charming hostess portrayed by Diderot in *Le Rêve de d'Alembert* and of her long, close association with such prominent figures as these prime movers of the *Encyclopédie.*[31] Yet, at the same time, established by the generosity of friends in her own premises, Lespinasse is known to have led a brilliant public life, having scored no small victory by taking with her in the rupture with Mme du Deffand many of the fashionable and intellectual elite of the latter's circle. As an *épistolière,* however, she is likely always to be known for the letters to the comte de Guibert, first published in 1809 on the instructions of his widow (with the sorts of omissions one can imagine). What these letters unfold is a private drama of illness, passion, and confusion, four years in which the public life was a tiring distraction. And it may be that Lespinasse would have approved of posterity's seeing only this partial reflection of her experience.

Julie herself, in her letters, traced the roots of her chronic morbidity to the shocks and deprivations of her youth, when, illegitimate and orphaned, she was exploited by relatives. Suicidal tendencies and repressed anger had already flared in her relations with Mme du Deffand. Her dependence on opium aggravated a physical decline derived from nervous, respiratory, and digestive complaints that can readily be traced in her correspondence. Even in the first period of success and independence, she had confided to Condorcet that her gaiety was only a mask: "In almost every case I ask myself before I act: *what is the use?* and I find no answer . . . My soul is dead to any form of enjoyment."[32] To another friend, she wrote enviously of a woman destroyed in a doomed love affair—enviously, for a great love is "rare . . . sublime . . . to be honored like virtue" and death merely a release from pain.[33] The "Muse of the Encyclopaedia," as has often been remarked, was also an authentic carrier of the sensibility that was then sweeping Europe and that would be labeled pre-romantic.

In her last years, Lespinasse filled the emotional void with two tragic affairs: the young marquis de Mora, snatched away by disapproving relatives and then by tuberculosis, and the charismatic Guibert, for whom she "betrayed" Mora even before his death. Death and longing, exaltation and remorse, pain in the midst of pleasure, pleasure in pain—these are her themes in the letters. What is harrowing about them is that they are genuine and suggest in one of the most admired women of the century an abdication of potential, a kind of moral suicide that seems to justify the popular biographers in the choice of such subtitles as *mourir d'amour*.[34] The strength of the letters is that they are fine, intense analyses of human feeling and eloquently composed, evidence of what may justly be called a literary gift. If certain details of Lespinasse's biography remind us of Delaunay's, the Guibert letters take us back to the "novel" of Aïssé, to an impression of a self-conscious heroine in an adventure that conforms to aesthetic rules. Susan Lee Carrell has suggested a provocative response to those who would leave the letter writers on the backstairs of social history.[35] She treats Mlle de Lespinasse as a *romancière,* instinctively making of real life, even as she lived it, the stuff of a work whose nearest analogues are fictional rather than documentary. In the light of Carrell's study, not only the letters of Lespinasse but also those of Aïssé, many of Delaunay's, perhaps even some of Deffand's to Walpole, may be seen to require an analytical approach that takes into account the conventions of the epistolary novel.

Although our six *épistolières* come from only a narrow range of social strata, their letters do shed light on the moral and material conditions and the boundaries within which many of the women of eighteenth-century France lived their lives. Ill health, for example, is one of their most persistent themes; three of the six wrote their deathbed letters before reaching the age of forty-five, and the others suffered long, limiting infirmities. On the other hand, certain subjects are less frequently treated than the researcher might expect; these include the great public events and ideological debates of the age, although there is good evidence that these women were keenly alive to the intellectual and political climate. In many cases, their silence is attributable to discretion, to the fact that letters were notoriously apt to fall into the wrong hands. We also learn little here of domestic life or of real family relationships. Children are only notable by their absence: Graffigny's dead in infancy, Aïssé's daughter hidden away in a convent, Châtelet's offspring occupying very little of her attention. Parental figures are, at most, surrogates in uneasy relationships created by women literally or spiritually orphaned. One thinks of Aïssé and Mme Calandrini; of Lespinasse's explosive association with her patroness and probable aunt, Mme du Deffand; and of Deffand herself casting one after another of her friends as *tuteur*, grandparent, model, or counsellor. Marriage, its joys or its duties, is not a theme; Emilie du Châtelet, once again, might be as much a widow or a spinster as all the others. Gender, whether as a matter of sexuality or as a concern with appropriate female behavior, is only occasionally and obliquely an issue, a muted subtext in spite of the period's marked interest in defining the specifics of male and female physiology and social roles. It is as though these women simply took for granted either their conformity to the norms or their right to flout them.

At the same time, every one of these correspondences contains the evidence of at least one major love affair: Delaunay to Menil and to Silly, Châtelet to Saint-Lambert, Lespinasse to Guibert, even Deffand to Walpole. So many Héloïses, they plead for warmth and reassurance, each addressing an Abélard in the end unwilling or unable to make a satisfying response. (The pattern is repeated most vividly in Graffigny's epistolary novel.) Far from offering support for the common idea that *l'amour-plaisir*, lightly taken up and as lightly abandoned, was the prevailing notion in eighteenth-century life as in much of its literature,[36] our letter writers, rather, shared a tendency to drape the mantle of a grand passion on shoulders it did not fit. Traditional commentary has naturally emphasized these love stories; but if the central theme in the writings of these women, no less than in the works of any philosopher of the age, is the definition and pursuit of *le bonheur*, it is a fact that nearly all of them saw happiness as having as much to do with finding worthwhile employment for one's energies and a measure of material independence as with the transports of the heart.

The letters do tell us—and they are an imposing body of evidence—about a network of long-term loyalties, of friendships linking women to women and women to men (despite the commonplace then current that such bonds were impossible[37]), in which the regular exchange of confidences, support, and encouragement was clearly very valuable to those concerned. What Hénault said of Mme du Deffand—"Friendship was in her a passion"[38]—could be said of most others in the group. This, of course, was an aspect of the period's sensibility, and the letters are an important source for the study of the evolution of attitudes on an intimate scale. An evolution can in fact be roughly traced, beginning with a "first generation," Delaunay and Deffand, who show most strongly the influence of a classical ideal, skeptical and Epicurean, of repose, self-possession and even self-perfectability. They share, at the outset, a mistrust of the passions and of all that the marquise called *"le roman."* Delaunay's pages reveal an immense struggle to subdue her own impulses, to achieve a rational, radical detachment: "To be truly at peace, one must care neither for oneself nor for others...."[39] Deffand, most acutely of all, knew the century's *mal de vivre*,[40] the hollowness at the center of all experience, and, by the end of her long life, was asserting the claims of feeling, not reason: *"Sentiment!* to you the word seems ridiculous; but for my part, I maintain that without feeling, the mind is nothing but a vapor, a smoke . . . ; only the passions make us think."[41] In the meantime, Mme du Châtelet, in the *Discourse on Happiness,* was working out a practical philosophy that would recognize the value of our passions and even our illusions, while reconciling them with a more traditional form of *sagesse.* Spiritually, Mme de Graffigny is another bridge between generations, her dramatic works perfectly expressing the earnest sentimentality of the mid-century. By the 1770s, the emphatic creed of Mlle de Lespinasse, "to love, to suffer, heaven and hell,"[42] is at the opposite pole from the sober ideal of Delaunay, although its roots are there in the latter's habit of preserving the record of her most private defeats, as though her pain had hallowed them and made them fit for display. From a thing to be avoided, suffering becomes by degrees something to be explored and proclaimed.

Finally, the question of how these women, explicitly or by inference, defined their understanding of happiness brings us back to the essential common theme of independence. Expressions of this theme range from Delaunay's rueful admission of her own "insuperable love of freedom and peace of mind"[43] and Châtelet's insistence that we must never "place our happiness entirely in the hands of another"[44] to

Graffigny's complaints about the rubs of living under another person's roof. Delaunay claimed to have come closest to her ideal of liberty only in prison, for the prisoner is at least not obliged to serve the whims of others.[45] Aïssé too reveals the plight of the *déclassée*, the unpaid companion to a woman of rank, unmarriageable for lack of income or pedigree. (It is possible that the calm satisfaction with which she explains her refusal to agree to a misalliance with her chevalier is largely that of someone exercising, for once, the right to decide her own fate.) Lespinasse, illegitimate and penniless, was in a similar position. Her letters to Deffand breathe the effusive humility of the female dependent, while the letters to Guibert offer glimpses of the anguish of the years spent at the mercy of her relatives. She replaced a material with an emotional dependence in the last years of her life and, like Delaunay, found implacable social barriers between herself and the satisfaction of her strongest impulses.

Emilie du Châtelet, by virtue of wealth, rank, and temperament, emerges as the one of our group best able to follow her own bent and suffer little from the resentment and disapproval that this aroused. Not surprisingly, she appears to us now the least constrained by social and moral codes and the one with the most robust sense of her own worth. At the opposite end of the scale in this regard stands Mme du Deffand, in spite of similar rank, means, and mental vitality. Deffand was the prisoner not only of her blindness and her adherence to largely conventional standards of judgment and behavior but also of her fine critical intelligence, which, lacking an object, like Delaunay's, became in the end self-devouring and self-limiting. Her incessant need for displays of regard from her friends suggests less the "appetite for absolutes" referred to by Mauzi than a fundamental lack of self-esteem.[46] Mme de Graffigny, whose activities seem to have been beneath the notice of Deffand, offers the most unexpected success story of all, a story it will be possible to analyze in proper detail once her letters can more easily be consulted.

In this study, letters have been treated mainly as a means of access to the attitudes and experience of their writers; their documentary value, for any attempt to understand how Enlightenment women saw themselves and their society, can hardly be overstated. But it seems worth emphasizing that long contact with these correspondences leads, on the one hand, to a conviction that the letter, for all its documentary nature, needs to be placed more often than it has been alongside the generally accepted literary forms (is a piece of writing literature only when the *destinataire* is not specified?) and, on the other, to a sense that letter writing, when a constant activity, should be viewed as something that not only expresses but actually helps to shape experience and thought. This would appear to be the case first because of the egocentrism, the habits of reflection and self-analysis, that the exercise encourages and, secondly and most especially, because of the letter's strong associations with popular fiction in an age familiar with the Portuguese nun, Clarissa, *La Nouvelle Héloïse*, and dozens of their less famous sisters. Reading these real letters, one is often reminded that in the epistolary novel, too, the heroine's typical progress is merely towards resignation in the face of loss, frustration, and constraint.

NOTES

1. She was known in society as Rose de Launay or Delaunay. In many catalogues, she appears under her married name, baronne de Staal.

2. *L'Egarement* and *La Mode*, three-act prose comedies, appeared in the 1756 Amsterdam edition of her *Mémoires*. Clarence D. Brenner, *A Bibliographical List of Plays in the French Language, 1700-1789* (Berkeley, 1947) also lists two unpublished verse playlets.

3. Julia Kavanagh, *Women in France during the Eighteenth Century* (London: Putnam's, 1893), vol. 1, p. 58.

4. See Mme du Deffand, *Correspondance complète*, edited by M. F. A. de Lescure (Paris: Plon, 1865), vol. 1.

5. Marguerite Jeanne Cordier, *Mémoires*, edited by G. Doscot (Paris: Mercure de France, 1970), p. 29: "Mon âme, n'ayant pas pris d'abord le pli que lui devait donner la mauvaise fortune, a toujours résisté à l'abaissement et à la sujétion où je me suis trouvée: c'est là l'origine du malheur de ma vie." (My soul, not having acquired in the beginning the bent that an ill fortune was to impose on it, has always resisted the humble and subordinate position in which I have found myself: therein lies the source of all my unhappiness.)

6. See, for example, Pierre Fauchery, *La Destinée féminine dans le roman européen du dix-huitième siècle* (Paris: A. Colin, 1972).

7. One of Prévost's romances was inspired by her story: see E. Bouvier's "La Genèse de *L'Histoire d'une Grecque moderne*" in *Revue d'histoire littéraire* 48(1948):113-130. The nineteenth century produced two dramas based on her life (*Mademoiselle Aïssé* by Lavergne and Fouche, 1854, and *Aïssé* by L. Bouilhet, 1872), and the 1930s saw a revival of interest: for example, M. Aimery de Pierrebourg, *Mademoiselle Aïssé et son tendre chevalier* (Paris: Fayard, 1930).

8. Eugène Ritter, "Note sur les *Lettres* de Mlle Aïssé," in *Mélanges offerts . . . à Gustave Lanson* (Paris: Hachette, 1922), pp. 313-318.

9. The argument falters, of course, if one supposes that a friend of Aïssé (she had many, including Mme du Deffand, with the necessary skills and knowledge) elaborated a set of letters, perhaps on the basis of a few genuine ones. There is cause for some wariness in the number of faked correspondences and memoirs produced in the late eighteenth and early nineteenth centuries. The authenticity of the Aïssé letters was challenged when they first appeared.

10. *Lettres de la marquise du Châtelet*, edited by T. Besterman (Genève: Voltaire Foundation, 1958), no. 279.

11. M. F. A. de Lescure, Introduction to *Correspondance complète*, vol. 1, p. xxxiii, n. 4.

12. See Mlle Delaunay's letters to Mme du Deffand in the latter's *Correspondance complète*, vol. 1.

13. Ibid., vol. 2, appendice xxviii.

14. M. F. A. de Lescure, *Les Femmes philosophes* (Paris: Dentu, 1881).

15. See V. Fournel, "Les Epistolières," in *De J.-B. Rousseau à André Chénier* (Paris: Firmin-Didot, 1886), p. 188; or E. Henriot, *Epistoliers et mémorialistes* (Paris: La Nouvelle Revue Critique, 1931), p. 140.

16. Louise Colet, "Madame du Châtelet: Lettres inédites," *Revue des Deux Mondes* 11 (1845):1011-1053.

17. Ira Wade, *Voltaire and Mme du Châtelet: An Essay on the Intellectual Activity at Cirey* (Princeton: Princeton University Press, 1941).

18. Emilie du Châtelet, *Discours sur le bonheur,* edited by R. Mauzi (Paris: Les Belles Lettres, 1961).

19. René Vaillot, *Madame du Châtelet* (Paris: Albin Michel, 1978).

20. For example, Lionel Duisit's *Madame du Deffand épistolière* (Genève: Droz, 1963).

21. *Correspondance complète* (note 4).

22. Unpublished letter of 18 February 1739; *Yale Graffigny Papers,* 8:13-18.

23. English Showalter, Jr., "Diderot and Mme de Graffigny's *Cénie,*" *The French Review* 39 (December 1965):394-397.

24. Madame de Graffigny to Devaux, 22 February 1739; *Yale Graffigny Papers,* 8:33-36.

25. See English Showalter, Jr., "The Beginnings of Madame de Graffigny's Literary Career," in *Essays on the Age of Enlightenment in Honor of Ira O. Wade* (Genève: Droz, 1977).

26. In collections such as E. Asse's *Lettres de Mme de Graffigny, suivies de celles de Mmes de Staal, d'Epinay* . . . (Paris: Charpentier, 1879) and in the Besterman editions of Voltaire's correspondence. As I write, the entire Graffigny correspondence is being prepared for publication (Oxford: Voltaire Foundation) by a group of editors, of which I am a member, headed by Professors J. A. Dainard (Toronto) and English Showalter (Rutgers).

27. Robert Mauzi, *L'Idée du bonheur dans la littérature et la pensée françaises au XVIIIe siècle* (Paris: Colin, 1960), p. 25.

28. Jean Duché, *Le Premier Sexe* (Paris: Laffont, 1972), p. 331.

29. Julie de Lespinasse, *Lettres inédites,* edited by Charles Henry (Paris: Dentu, 1887), p. 34; N. Royde-Smith, *The Double Heart* (New York and London: Harper, n. d.), p. 154.

30. P. de Ségur, *Julie de Lespinasse* (Paris: Calmann-Lévy, 1906; London, 1906).

31. *Lettres inédites.*

32. Ibid., 9.

33. Ibid., 20.

34. J. Lacouture and M.-C. d'Aragon, *Julie de Lespinasse* (Paris: Ramsay, 1980).

35. Susan Lee Carrell, *Le Soliloque de la passion féminine ou le dialogue illusoire* (Tubingen: Gunter Narr; Paris: Jean-Michel Place, 1982).

36. Philip Stewart, *Le Masque et la parole* (Paris: José Corti, 1973).

37. Frederick Gerson, *L'Amitié au XVIIIe siècle* (Paris: La Pensée universelle, 1974).

38. "Portrait de Madame la marquise du Deffand par M. le président Hénault," in *Correspondance complète,* vol.2, p. 752.

39. Delaunay to Deffand, 10 September 1747.

40. See Mauzi, *L'Idée du bonheur,* introduction.

41. Deffand to Walpole, 23 October 1769 and 11 June 1769 (nos. 306 and 294 in the Lescure edition).

42. Lespinasse to Guibert, [mardi, onze heures du soir] 1775: "To love and to

suffer—Heaven and Hell—to that I would vow myself . . . That is the climate I
wish to inhabit, and not the temperate zone in which live all the fools and all
the automatons by whom we are surrounded." *Letters of Mlle de Lespinasse,*
translated by K. P. Wormeley (Boston: Hardy, Pratt & Co., 1902), p. 216.

43. *Mémoires,* p. 209.

44. *Discours sur le bonheur,* p. 35.

45. *Mémoires,* p. 144.

46. Robert Mauzi, "Les Maladies de l'âme au XVIIIe siècle", *Revue des sciences
humaines* (1960):459-493; 464.

✂ Danielle Rice

Women and the Visual Arts

French art during the eighteenth century is generally divided into two phases. The rococo dominates the first half of the century, and the latter half is characterized by subjects and forms modeled on antiquity and by a strong reaction against the decorative excesses of the earlier style. A scholarly tradition established in the nineteenth century by the Goncourt brothers attributes to the ascendancy of women the existence of the rococo and the essence of eighteenth-century art.[1] But, in fact, the actual influence of women and of women artists upon this supposedly feminine aesthetic has as yet to be properly distilled from myth and prejudice.

Economic and political factors, rather than women, determined most of the changes that occurred during the first two decades of the eighteenth century. The depleted finances of the crown curtailed the money spent by the Direction Générale des Bâtiments du Roi on large public commissions during the last few years of the reign of Louis XIV.[2] In addition, after Louis XIV's death in 1715, the Regent Philippe, duc d'Orléans, moved the court from Versailles to the Palais-Royal in Paris. This meant that many nobles previously housed at Versailles moved back to their private hotels in Paris. As they sought to redecorate their salons, these aristocrats developed a taste for intimacy and sumptuous decorative details. The art they popularized was radically different in scale, form, and content from the art produced for the ceremonious grandeur of the apartments at Versailles.[3]

The painter whose name is most closely linked with this period is Antoine Watteau (1684-1721). His small, brilliantly colored depictions of richly clad Parisians enjoying the pleasures of breezy parks and enchanted isles guaranteed his popularity at a young age. Watteau's fame was such that in 1717 the Académie Royale de Peinture et Sculpture created a new category especially for him, admitting him as painter of *fêtes galantes*. Watteau's victory was preceded and partly determined by the victory in the same academy of the *rubénistes*, the proponents of color, over the *poussinistes*, or upholders of the baroque classical ideal.[4] These events mark the beginnings of the rococo style in painting.

One woman artist played a particularly important role at this time. Like Watteau, whose portrait she drew during her brief stay in Paris in 1720, the Italian pastelist and painter Rosalba Carriera (1675-1757) had a seminal influence on the development of the rococo aesthetic in France and throughout Europe.[5] The Venetian-born artist enjoyed tremendous success and had an unparalleled international reputation during her lifetime. She was the first artist to master the painterly, expressive qualities of the pastel medium. Instead of colored drawings, she produced richly textured, airy, subtly colored pastel paintings. Her technique opened up unforeseen possibilities for virtuoso handling not only of pastels but also of oils. She was known, too, for her sensitive appreciation of the characters of her sitters.

The Académie Royale admitted Carriera to its ranks in 1720, ignoring a policy made in 1706 that no more women would be allowed entrance. This was significant since a French artist's success at the time was contingent upon membership and rank in the Académie. The Académie had been founded in 1648 for the express purpose of enhancing the image and power of the king through a monopoly of art patronage.[6] It was first of all an art school that placed most of its emphasis on drawing from the male nude. It also assisted in the selection and promotion of artists. In addition, the academy not only provided artists with access to royal patronage but also gave them an opportunity to exhibit their work publicly in the Salons.

The number of academicians varied but generally comprised about one hundred members. There were several ranks of membership. Agréé, or apprentice, was the rank given to students who had passed the first requirements and generally had spent some time studying in Rome. The artist would be received into full membership upon presentation of a *morceau de réception,* the subject of which was determined by the academy. Once a full academician, the artist could rise to the status of assistant professor, professor, supervisor, right on up to the much-coveted position of *premier peintre du roi,* much in the same way that one makes one's way up the academic ladder in a present-day university.

The academy also defined the hierarchy of genres, a necessary scale of values by which to judge a work of art. Paintings were divided into categories according to their subject matter. History painting, the *grand genre,* was the most important category, followed in importance by portraiture, genre painting, still life, and landscape painting.

At its foundation, the academy had fairly liberal intentions toward women, and by 1682, seven women had been admitted.[7] However, women were never allowed to participate in the all-important life classes, nor could they compete for the sought-after Prix de Rome, which was predicated on the submission of complex figurative compositions. Without these avenues, the *grand genre* of history painting and, with it, the ladder to academic success were inaccessible to women from the very beginning. The women members of the academy were at best honorary, members in title only.

In 1706, the academy reversed its original policy and closed its doors to women. This decision, made at a time when several women had just applied to become academicians, probably reflects the fears of the male members that the prestige and professionalism of their institution would be threatened by the presence of females.[8] Fortunately, exceptions to this policy were made throughout the eighteenth century. After Rosalba Carriera, two more foreign women, the Dutch flower painter Margaretta Haverman (1693-after 1750) and the German portraitist Anna Dorothea Lisiewska-Therbusch (1721-1782), and five French women were admitted before the academy's demise during the Revolution.

We shall return to the French women academicians in a moment, but before we do, we should examine briefly the career of a woman whose direct influence on the academy and on artistic production shaped the art of the mid-eighteenth century. This woman was Jeanne Antoinette Poisson (1721-1764), better known as the marquise de Pompadour.[9] Poisson, whose father had been exiled at the time of her birth, owed most of her education and her rise to power to Lenormant de Tournehem, a friend of her mother's, a nobleman with a good position in society. Jeanne Antoinette and her younger brother, Abel, were brought up in Paris in a cosmopolitan world where art, music, literature, and dance were mastered and displayed in the company of the educated men and women who gathered in the salons to discuss the latest intellectual and artistic events. Jeanne's acquaintances in Paris included such men as Voltaire, Marmontel, and Fontenelle, among the foremost writers of the day.

In 1741, Lenormant de Tournehem married his own nephew, Lenormant d'Etoiles, to Jeanne Poisson, but it is obvious that he had even higher aspirations. In 1745, a meeting was arranged between Jeanne d'Etoiles and the king, and she became the king's mistress. In spite of great opposition to her presentation at court because she had not been nobly born, in the fall of 1745, Jeanne d'Etoiles, named marquise de Pompadour, attained the position of official royal favorite. It is not coincidental that in December of the same year, Lenormant de Tournehem was appointed Surintendant de Bâtiments du Roi.[10]

The position of Surintendant gave de Tournehem total power over artistic production in France. The Académie Royale, along with the academy of architecture, the royal tapestry works, and the manufacture of porcelain, all came under his jurisdiction. A month following his own appointment, in January of 1746, Lenormant de Tournehem named as successor for his position the younger brother of Mme de Pompadour, Abel Poisson, later known as the marquis de Vandières, de Marigny, and de Ménars.

Tournehem and Pompadour arranged for Abel Poisson's training by sending him to Rome in 1750 in the company of young artists and architects.[11] In 1751, at Tournehem's death, the marquis de Marigny was thus perfectly equipped to undertake his new responsibilities as Surintendant des Bâtiments, a post he held until 1773. Pompadour's influence both on Lenormant de Tournehem and on her brother has never been properly studied, but it is evident that through the two men and through her own extensive private and public building programs her power over the arts from 1745 to her death in 1764, and indirectly right on up to 1773, was extensive and far-reaching.

Unfortunately, the royal favorite's name, paired with that of François Boucher (1703-1770), her preferred painter, retains even today some of the negative connotations it acquired during the Revolution. In the 1790s, Pompadour was synonymous with all the decadence of the ancien régime. During the nineteenth century, several historians, including the Goncourt brothers, did a great deal to restore some of Pompadour's power. But most of them insisted on the essentially frivolous nature of the art associated with her and found it necessary to apologize for the "courtisanesque" aesthetic she inspired.[12]

The Goncourt brothers openly challenged the argument that Pompadour had had anything to do with the nascent interest in classical art.[13] But there are numerous indications that Mme de Pompadour was not only aware of the changes taking place in art at mid-century but also encouraged these changes. Her decision to send her brother to Rome for his education indicates her recognition of the importance of Italian baroque and ancient Roman art. She was also instrumental in appointing the painter Jean-Jacques Bachelier (1724-1806) as the artistic director of the royal porcelain factories at Vincennes and Sèvres.[14] Bachelier invented the bisque technique, and he introduced simple, new designs modeled on ancient vases. He educated the porcelain workers away from the overly imaginative, abstract rococo shapes and patterns by enforcing the study of geometry and design. In addition to her influence over porcelain manufacture, Pompadour encouraged classical forms in architecture. She supported the architect Jacques-Ange Gabriel and admired his designs for the Ecole Militaire and the Petit Trianon.[15] In-depth scholarship on Pompadour's relationship to the arts would probably reveal many more examples of this kind.

Scholars today, however, are apt to refer to Pompadour with sweeping generalizations. Some attribute to her an exaggerated influence, while others fail to consider her role in the light of new discoveries about the period. L. D. Ettlinger admits that Mme de Pompadour "became the most influential arbiter of taste" in her time but saddles her also with the responsibility for the change from a male to a female sensibility and with the transfer of the arts from the public to a private sphere.[16] Thus, Pompadour is indirectly and unreasonably associated with changes that had occurred before her birth during the Régence. On the other end of the spectrum, the important research published recently by Pierre Rosenburg emphasizes the fact that there is more to French painting during this period than Watteau, Boucher, and Fragonard.[17] Rosenberg places the stress on art commissioned not for the court but for the church and for public buildings. In all of this new literature, Mme de Pompadour is mentioned only in passing. Most of the credit is given to her uncle, Lenormant de Tournehem, and to her brother, the marquis de Marigny.

It is not really surprising that art historians are reluctant to treat Mme de Pompadour seriously and to re-evaluate the period of her most prominent influence in terms that include her. Art history traces the progress of great individual achievements. In contrast, the history of mid-eighteenth century art is the history of collaborative efforts where the distinctions between the "minor" and the "fine" arts are far from clear. The artists patronized by Mme de Pompadour worked collaboratively on architecture, designs for interiors, tapestries, porcelains, and painted decorations. Descriptions of the total environments conceived by Pompadour and executed with the help of teams of artists at the château de Bellevue and her other residences almost defy the imagination. These palaces were comprehensive works of art. At Bellevue, even the livery of the servants was planned to harmonize with the total aesthetic balance of the environment.[18] Until art historians are able to accept such examples of collaboration as valid works of art, the evaluation of periods like the mid-eighteenth century will remain incomplete.

Another problematic aspect of Mme de Pompadour's participation in the arts is the fact that she herself was an accomplished amateur artist. Her talents were often praised by her contemporaries. Voltaire, for example, wrote gallantly of her drawings:

> Pompadour ton crayon divin
> Devrait dessiner ton visage
> Jamais une plus belle main
> N'aurait fait un plus bel ouvrage.[19]

Pompadour also organized performances, designed costumes, acted, sang, and encouraged the active participation of all the members of the court. It is probably due to her example that drawing and painting became so fashionable with the ladies of the court. Queen Marie Leczynska's artistic ventures were often praised along with those of Mme de Pompadour by contemporary critics.[20]

Although Mme de Pompadour herself readily admitted that drawing was meant to be an amusement and not an occupation for well-bred ladies, there are indications that the spread of amateurism was generally beneficial for aspiring women artists. Several women were able to make a living teaching painting and drawing either privately or in the convents. A number of women attempted to elevate themselves from the rank of amateur by participating in the exhibitions of the less exclusive Académie de Saint Luc and also in the Salons de la Correspondance organized by Pahin de La Blancherie.[21] But for the most part, these women were not recognized by their contemporaries as professionals.

Mme de Pompadour did not patronize any women artists herself, and only one gained admission to the Académie Royale during her lifetime. This was the flower painter and miniaturist Marie-Thérèse Reboul (1728-1805), accepted in 1757. That same year, Reboul married the painter Joseph-Marie Vien (1716-1809), and it is to his influence that her admission is often attributed.[22] Reboul exhibited regularly at the Salons and assisted her husband by engraving several of his designs. Her Salon entries were usually well received by the critics but treated with gallant condescension. Writing of Reboul's work in the Salon of 1763, one critic remarked that even women had viewed her paintings with pleasure. The implication here is obviously that women would normally be offended by another woman's success. The critics were very conscious of the unique position Reboul enjoyed in being the only female academician at the time. One journal praised her works by saying that they continued to justify the honors which Reboul had already received. Denis Diderot offered words of praise for the "elegance and good taste" of her flower paintings.[23]

In 1770, two more French women were received into the Académie Royale. They were Marie-Suzanne Giroust (1734-1772) and Anne Vallayer-Coster (1744-1818). Giroust was the wife of the Swedish-born portrait painter Alexandre Roslin and a close acquaintance of the Vien family.[24] Giroust worked with pastels in the tradition of Rosalba Carriera. She studied with the well-known pastelist Maurice Quentin de La Tour, and she is reputed to have been one of the finest women pastelists of the late eighteenth century. She was particularly well respected for her portraits of family members and friends. Unfortunately, her success was short-lived, for she died of breast cancer in 1772 at the age of 38.

The still-life painter Anne Vallayer-Coster, who was received into the Académie the same year as Giroust, is the best known and most studied of the three French artists we have just discussed. Although her early training remains a mystery, her work has been compared to that of the two most important still-life painters of the period, Jean-Baptiste Oudry (1686-1755) and Jean-Baptiste-Siméon Chardin (1699-1779). The engraver J. G. Wille (1715-1808) remarked in his journal at the time of Coster's admission that her talent "is truly that of a man perfected in this genre of painting representing still life."[25]

Vallayer-Coster was the daughter of a goldsmith, who was employed at the Gobelins tapestry works; she married a lawyer, who was also a wealthy and influential member of Parliament. Her father's connections with the Premier Peintre du Roi Jean-Baptiste-Marie Pierre (1714-1789) and her husband's wealth and position probably played a part in ensuring her success, but the critical acclaim her paintings commanded during the height of her productivity between 1769 and 1787 was due to her talent and labor alone.

Reboul, Giroust, and Vallayer-Coster all had connections with male artists either through marriage or birth; these kinds of family ties are generally the rule for women artists. There are a number of women related to male artists who, although they did not gain admission to the Académie, nevertheless achieved some renown and should be mentioned briefly. Marie Anne Loir (1715-c.1769) was the sister of pastelist and sculptor Alexis Loir (1712-1785) and a student of Jean-François de Troy (1679-1752), whom she accompanied to Rome in 1738. She was elected to the Académie de Marseilles and was often praised for her portraits. Françoise Duparc (1762-1788), the daughter of the sculptor Antoine Duparc, became particularly well known for her original depictions of working-class people. Like Loir, Duparc was recognized by the Académie de Marseilles.[26]

Marie Anne Collot (1748-1821) entered the studio of the sculptor Etienne Maurice Falconet (1716-1791) at the age of fifteen. She became Falconet's daughter-in-law by marrying Pierre-Etienne, a painter in his own right, in 1777; but her reputation was tainted by rumors that she had also been the mistress of the father. From an early stage in Collot's career, the sculptor Falconet, who "nursed an almost morbid aversion toward bust portraiture," relinquished most of the portrait commissions to Collot.[27] She accompanied Falconet to Russia in 1766 and remained there with him until 1778, executing a large number of works. She was appointed official portrait sculptor to Catherine the Great, from whom she received numerous commissions. In 1783, the date of Collot's last known sculpture, Falconet became ill, and she devoted herself entirely to his care, neglecting her art. After both Falconet and his son died in 1791, Collot retired in Lorraine for the remaining thirty years of her life.

Like Marie Anne Collot, Marguerite Gérard (1761-1837) was also raised in the ménage of an artist and devoted a large portion of her time to family matters.²⁸ When her sister married the brother of Jean Honoré Fragonard (1732-1806), Marguerite Gérard was invited to join the extended family of the artist. She thus had the opportunity to study with Fragonard and to see many private art collections accessible only to artists. She was the first French woman to achieve professional success as a genre painter. Her style is carefully distilled from the precious genre paintings of the Dutch masters and Fragonard's techniques. Unfortunately, she was accused of being Fragonard's mistress and of having her canvasses finished by the master. As we have seen, women artists have always attracted such slander; none of these claims have ever been substantiated, and her style and choice of subjects have been shown to be distinctive and original. Although Gérard was never an academician, after the Salon was open to women in the 1790s, she exhibited regularly and was very successful during her lifetime.

Marguerite Gérard was the youngest of the four women artists who, on the eve of the Revolution, achieved a degree of fame that not only equaled that of male contemporaries but has also insured them a place in history. We have already mentioned the still-life painter Anne Vallayer-Coster; the other two artists are considered even more significant than either Gérard or Vallayer-Coster. In fact, Adélaïde Labille-Guiard (1749-1803) and Elisabeth Vigée-Lebrun (1755-1842) may be said to have been two of the most celebrated women artists of their time.²⁹ They reached the peaks of their respective careers in 1783, when they became the last two women to be accepted into the Académie Royale before this institution was abolished in the 1790s.

Labille-Guiard and Vigée-Lebrun differ from all their female predecessors in several respects. They practiced portraiture; but they did so on a very large scale, and they even experimented with history painting. They achieved more recognition as artists and thus helped to pave the way for the many women artists who followed. In spite of this, they were not able to escape slander and notoriety. From the very beginnings of their public success, they were typecast by their critics— Labille-Guiard's style was seen as stiff and masculine while Vigée-Lebrun's technique was challenged for being too soft and superficial— and pitted against one another as rivals.³⁰ Although it is true that some degree of rivalry must have existed when the stakes and patrons were as high as they were, the extent of this antagonism has never been fully documented. What is certain is the fact that the two artists not only had clearly distinct styles but also vastly different personal lives and political sentiments.

Adélaïde Labille-Guiard was Vigée-Lebrun's senior by five years. She came from a humble background and received her first artistic instruction with the miniaturist François Elie Vincent (1708-1816).

Vincent's son, the painter François André Vincent (1746-1816), became Labille's close advisor and her second husband. Between 1769 and 1774, Labille-Guiard studied with Maurice Quentin de La Tour and, under his guidance, became a skilled pastelist and perceptive portraitist. She exhibited in the exhibitions of the Académie de Saint-Luc and at the Salon de la Correspondance. She worked her way into the Académie Royale primarily by painting portraits of the academy's members, thereby acquainting these artists with her skills.

In addition to the patronage of artists, Labille-Guiard also secured the patronage of members of the royal family. She was given the title *peintre de mesdames*. In spite of this association with the court of Louis XVI, Labille-Guiard weathered the tides of the Revolution without much difficulty because her sentiments were clearly with the revolutionaries; in 1791, she exhibited eight portraits of the deputies of the National Assembly. She was also instrumental in planning the reconstruction of the old Académie Royale. She asked that the academy eliminate its limitation on the number of women members, and she suggested that since women would not be allowed to teach or hold office an unlimited number of women artists should be accepted with the honorary rank of *conseilleur*. The only privilege attached to this rank was that of exhibiting at the Salon, which admittedly was of very high practical value. Unfortunately, the loss of the rank of academician made official the view that women could not really compete with men to become great artists.[31]

Elisabeth Vigée-Lebrun outlived Adélaïde Labille-Guiard by nearly forty years, which may be the reason why she appears to overshadow her contemporary. Elisabeth Vigée-Lebrun was more precocious and also more concerned with glamor than Adélaïde Labille-Guiard. She was the daughter of the pastelist Louis Vigée, a member of the Académie de Saint-Luc. She studied with a number of her father's friends, including Gabriel François Doyen (1726-1806) and Joseph Vernet (1714-1789). In 1779, she completed her first of many portraits of Marie-Antoinette, whose favorite painter she rapidly became. Throughout her life, Vigée-Lebrun was patronized by the aristocracy and by royalty all over Europe. She was a brilliant hostess and felt comfortable in social situations with the nobility who formed the core of her clientele. Her salon attracted the celebrities of the period and her evening parties, often designed with original themes, were celebrated throughout the continent.

In 1789, with the coming of the Revolution and endangered by her ties to the royal family, Vigée-Lebrun fled to Italy. She was accepted into the academies of Rome, Parma, and Bologna. She continued her travels and visited Naples, Vienna, Dresden, St. Petersburg, Moscow, London, and Geneva. Everywhere she went, she was warmly greeted and deluged with well-paid commissions. When the Bourbons were restored to power in France, she returned and regained the favor of the court. Even though she was over sixty at the time, she continued to paint; and she exhibited until 1824, when she began to spend her time writing and compiling her memoirs.[32]

A number of women artists born in the 1760s profited from the success of Adélaïde Labille-Guiard and Elisabeth Vigée-Lebrun and from the increased access to Salon exhibitions that Labille-Guiard's reforms had brought about. Many of these artists are known chiefly because their names appeared regularly in the Salon *livrets*. For example, Marie-Geneviève Bouliar (1762-1825) exhibited over forty paintings between 1791 and 1817, but few of these works can be traced today.[33]

Several other women of the 1760 generation deserve to be mentioned. Gabrielle Capet (1761-1817) was Labille-Guiard's student, living with her teacher and caring for her until her death. Capet specialized in portrait miniatures. Jeanne-Elisabeth Chaudet (1767-1832) studied with Vigée-Lebrun and exhibited at the Salon between 1798 and 1817. She painted children and animals in antique bas-relief-like profiles. Marie-Guillemine Benoist (1768-1828) studied with Vigée-Lebrun and Jacques Louis David (1748-1825). She exhibited regularly in the Expositions de la Jeunesse from 1784 to 1788 and, after 1790, in the Salons. Unfortunately, nothing is known about her project for a studio for women artists.[34]

Another of David's students was Constance Marie Charpentier (born Blondelu, 1767-1849), who exhibited between 1798 and 1819. She executed ambitious mythological and allegorical scenes in addition to portraits and genre work, but only three of her paintings are known. Of these three, the portrait of Charlotte du Val d'Ognes in the Metropolitan Museum, New York, has had an infamous history of attributions. Originally given to Jacques Louis David, the portrait was credited to Charpentier in 1951. At present, its authorship is again being challenged.[35]

The problem of identifying extant works by women artists plagues the study of this subject. It is quite probable that many paintings by women are presently masquerading as the work of the more famous male teachers. Charpentier's case is only one example. Her contemporary, Jeanne Philibert Ledoux (1767-1840), suffers from the same fate as Charpentier. Ledoux's paintings are often confused with those of her teacher Jean-Baptiste Greuze (1725-1805).[36]

In closing, we should refer to the tragic career of Constance Mayer (1775 or 1778-1821), who studied first with Greuze and, after Greuze's death, with Pierre Paul Prud'hon (1750-1823). She began exhibiting in 1796, but her greatest success came after 1804 when she adopted Prud'hon's style. Throughout her life, she was apparently haunted by periods of depression and self-doubt. In one of these moments, she committed suicide, leaving Prud'hon, whose affection for her is recorded in his letters, to mourn her death.[37]

The number of women artists working during the last two decades of the eighteenth century is quite impressive. It indicates that women did indeed achieve a degree of acceptance as artists at this time. Interestingly, they did so at a time when the dominant style was the neoclassicism of Jacques Louis David. With its restrained brushwork and moral, classical subjects, the art of David expressed a new masculine aesthetic that consciously rejected the soft, sensuous, feminine qualities of the rococo.

Perhaps the names of individual women are more prominent in the latter part of the century simply because the ideal of the individual master became more pronounced at this time. As we have noted, the first part of the century deserves to be studied in terms of collaborative efforts involving all the arts. Research into engraving, porcelain painting, dressmaking and design, all fields that were open to women, would probably reveal that a large number of women artists were involved even at the beginning of the century.

More attention should also be devoted to the function of amateurs and patrons at this time. The position of artists in society was challenged in the eighteenth century with the advent of art critics. With increased published information about the techniques and methods for making art, amateur painters as well as amateur collectors of both sexes flourished. The image of the Romantic artist, alienated from society and inaccessible to it, developed partly in reaction to this invasion of the art world by well-educated amateurs.

We can safely conclude that women did indeed play a part in eighteenth-century art, both through their patronage and through their own creative endeavors. We can even argue that they played a more important role than in preceding centuries. But the understanding of their function is far from complete. A detailed analysis would perhaps reveal many important facts regarding the complex, changing relationship between artists and society at this time. Such a study would be well worth the effort.

NOTES

1. E. and J. de Goncourt, *The Woman of the Eighteenth Century*, translated by J. Le Clerq and R. Roeder (New York: Minton, Balch and Company, 1927), pp. 243-266.

2. J. Locquin, *La Peinture d'histoire en France de 1747 à 1785* (1912; Paris: Arthena, 1978), pp. 1-3.

3. On the decorative art of this period and its roots, see F. Kimball, *The Creation of the Rococo* (Philadelphia: Philadelphia Museum of Art, 1943).

4. For a discussion of these academic debates, see A. Fontaine, *Les Doctrines d'art en France de Poussin à Diderot* (1909; Geneva: Slatkine, 1970). Fontaine also published the original records of the famous quarrel in *Conférences inédites de l'Académie Royale de Peinture et de Sculpture* (Paris: A. Fontemoing, 1903).

5. The standard source on Carriera is V. Malamani, *Rosalba Carriera* (Bergamo: Institute Italiano d'Arti Grafice, 1910). See also *Rosalba Carriera: Journal pendant son séjour à Paris en 1720-1721*, translated by A. Sensier (Paris: J. Techener, 1865) and the entry on Carriera in A. S. Harris and L. Nochlin, *Women Artists: 1550-1950* (New York: Alfred A. Knopf, 1976), pp. 161-164. For additional bibliography on Carriera and the other women artists in this essay, see D. G. Bachmann and S. Piland, *Women Artists: An Historical, Contemporary and Feminist Bibliography* (Metuchen, NJ: Scarecrow Press, 1978).

6. For the history of the French academy and its context, see N. Pevsner, *Academies of Art, Past and Present* (Cambridge: Cambridge University Press, 1940).

7. A. S. Harris, "Women Artists and the Academies of the Eighteenth Century," in Harris and Nochlin, pp. 36-38, provides an excellent overview of the subject.

8. A. de Montaiglon, *Procès-verbaux de l'Académie Royale de Peinture et de Sculpture 1648-1793* (Paris: Charavay Frères, 1881), vol. 4, pp. 33-34.

9. The bibliography on Pompadour, if out-of-date, is extensive. The following sources are appropriate to Pompadour's involvement in the arts: E. Campardon, *Madame de Pompadour et la cour de Louis XV au milieu du dix-huitième siècle* (Paris: H. Plon, 1867); A. de La Fizilière, "L'art et les femmes en France: Mme de Pompadour," *Gazette des Beaux Arts* 3, (1859): 129-152, 210-211, 292-314; E. de Goncourt, *Madame de Pompadour* (Paris: Firmin-Didot et Cie, 1888); K. Gordon, "Madame de Pompadour, Pigalle and the Iconography of Friendship," *Art Bulletin* 50 (1968): 249-262; P. de Nolhac, "Madame de Pompadour et les arts," *L'Art* 5 (1902-1903).

10. Locquin, pp. 1-13.

11. Ibid., pp. 14-40.

12. Fizilière, p. 228.

13. Goncourt, *Madame de Pompadour*, p. 327, n. 1.

14. J. Terrasson, *Madame de Pompadour et la création de la porcelaine en France* (Paris: Bibliothèque des Arts, 1969). Unfortunately, this source is much too general to be of any real value for a scholar wishing to study the extent of Pompadour's interraction with artists. See also J.-J. Bachelier, *Mémoire historique de l'origine du régime et des progrès de la Manufacture Nationale de porcelaine de France* (Paris: Delance, 1781); and G. Lechevalier Chevignard, *La Manufacture de Porcelaine de Sèvres*, 2 vols. (Paris: Renouard et Laurens, 1908), especially vol. 1, pp. 28-114.

15. Mme de Pompadour funded the cost of much of the construction of the Ecole Militaire out of her own pocket. For a description of this and other projects see Goncourt, *Madame de Pompadour*.

16. L. D. Ettlinger, "Taste and Patronage: The Role of the Artists in Society," in *The Eighteenth Century*, edited by A. Cobban (London: McGraw-Hill Book Company, 1969). p. 250.

17. P. Rosenberg, *The Age of Louis XV: French Painting 1710-1774* (Toledo, Ohio: The Toledo Museum of Art, 1975). Rosenberg has published extensively on eighteenth-century art and organized numerous exhibitions. He is almost singlehandedly responsible for the recent revival of scholarly interest in this period. He was also instrumental in the republication of Locquin's important monograph, *La Peinture d'histoire en France de 1747 à 1785*.

18. On Bellevue and other of Pompadour's châteaux, see Goncourt, *Madame de Pompadour*. Also interesting is the "Relevé des dépenses de Mme de Pompadour," published by J. A. Leroi, *Curiosités historiques* (Paris: H. Plon, 1864), providing a breakdown of the expenses incurred by the royal favorite for art as well as for charities and personal goods.

19. "Pompadour, your pencil divine/ Should your own features draw./ Never would a prettier hand/ Make a prettier work" [my own translation]. Cited by K. Gordon, p ?54. On Mme de Pompadour as an artist, see also P. Gusman, "Madame de   padour, artiste et graveur," *Byblis* (1925-1926): 18-19.

20. Harris and Nochlin, p. 41, nn. 147, 148.

21. See the list compiled by E. Bellier de La Chavignerie, "Les Artistes français du XVIIIe siècle oubliés ou dédaignés," *Revue universelle des arts* 19-21 (1865). See also J. Guiffrey, "Histoire de l'Académie de St. Luc," *Archives de l'art français*, nouv. per. 9 (1915):1-516.

22. Harris and Nochlin, p. 36. This is misleading however. Vien, who was later to become extremely important—he is one of the artists credited with the introduction of the *style antique* in painting—had only been an academician for three years. It is more likely that Reboul owes her acceptance not to Vien but to a mutual benefactor and a very influential collector, the comte de Caylus. It was Caylus who supported Vien's own admission to the academy against strong opposition and who, in 1757, arranged the marriage between Reboul and Vien (Locquin, p. 193, n. 3). On the relationship between Vien and Caylus, see my unpublished dissertation, "The Fire of the Ancients: The Encaustic Revival, 1755 to 1812" (Yale University, 1979), pp. 57-93.

23. *Diderot: Salons*, edited by J. Seznec and J. Adhemar, 2d ed. (Oxford: Oxford University Press, 1975), vol. 1, pp. 177, 231.

24. Harris and Nochlin, p. 39; G. W. Lundberg, *Roslin Liv och Werk* (Malmo: Allhems Forlag, 1957), vol. 1, pp. 79, 80, 102, 125ff., and 305 for references to Giroust.

25. Cited in Harris and Nochlin, p. 179. The standard monograph is M. Rolland Michel's *Anne Vallayer-Coster* (Paris: Comptoir international du livre, 1970).

26. Harris and Nochlin, pp. 167-168 for Loir; pp. 171-173 for Duparc.

27. G. Levitine, *The Sculpture of Falconet* (Greenwich, Connecticut: New York Graphic Society, 1972), pp. 18-21 for references to Collot. Also, Charles Cournault, "Etienne-Maurice Falconnet et Marie-Anne Collot," *Gazette des Beaux Arts*, ser. 2 (1869):117-144; L. Reau, "Une femme-sculpteur française au dix-huitième siècle, Marie-Anne Collot (Madame Falconet)," *L'Art et les artistes* (February 1923):165-171.

28. Harris and Nochlin, pp. 197-201. A monograph on Gerard by Sally Wells-Robertson is forthcoming. See also C. Duncan, "Happy Mothers and Other New Ideas in French Art," *Art Bulletin* (December 1973): 570-583, for an interesting discussion of Gerard's preferred subjects.

29. For complete bibliographies of these two artists, refer to Bachman and Pilland. See also Harris and Nochlin, pp. 185-187 for Labille-Guiard; pp. 190-194 for Vigée-Lebrun. The standard monograph on Labille-Guiard is by A.-M. Passez, *Adélaïde Labille-Guiard, 1749-1803* (Paris: Arts et métiers graphiques, 1973); for Vigée-Lebrun, see her own *Souvenirs de Mme Louise-Elisabeth Vigée-Lebrun*, 3 vols. (Paris: G. Charpentier, 1835-37); the monograph by L. Hautecoeur, *Madame Vigée-Lebrun; étude critique* (Paris: H. Laurens, 1917); and J. Baillio, *Elisabeth Louise Vigée-Lebrun 1755-1842* (Fort Worth: Kimbell Art Museum, 1982).

30. C. Oulmont, *Les Femmes peintres du XVIIIe siècle* (Paris: Editions Rieder, 1928), pp. 23-30, is a good review of some of the contemporary aspects of the rivalry.

31. Harris and Nochlin, p. 37.

32. Vigée-Lebrun, *Souvenirs*.

33. Harris and Nochlin, pp. 202-204.

34. Ibid., pp. 195-196 for Capet; pp. 46-47 for Chaudet; pp. 209-210 for Benoist.

35. Ibid., pp. 207-208. For the attribution of the Metropolitan's portrait, see C. Sterling, "A Fine 'David' Reattributed," *The Metropolitan Museum of Art Bulletin* 9, no. 5 (1951): 121-132. Currently, the portrait is labeled as by an unknown artist of David's school.

36. Harris and Nochlin, pp. 205-206.

37. Ibid., pp. 213-214.

 V

The Philosophes:
Feminism and/or
Antifeminism?

✵ Sara Ellen Procious Malueg

Women and the Encyclopédie

To DISCUSS WOMEN and the *Encyclopédie* thoroughly is not possible in an essay such as this.[1] We would need to consider the role of women in the publishing enterprise, from conception and preparation to publication, distribution, and subscription. At the same time, we would have to assemble, organize, analyze, and synthesize all references to women in the seventeen volumes of text and eleven volumes of plates.

My aims are far more modest, in keeping with the goals of this collection. I intend to touch briefly on some of the ways in which women were important or unimportant to the publishing enterprise, to give an introduction to the diverse views of women presented in *Encyclopédie* articles and plates, and to suggest some of the research still to be done.

Women have not been linked to the conception of the project or to the printing and dissemination of the volumes, though there may be unsung heroines who will still receive their due. Yet, in their own way, women lent their support. Who has not heard of the clever action of Mme de Pompadour to defend the *Encyclopédie* in 1759, when the Parlement and government had taken action against it. Nancy Mitford describes the scene:

> Soon after the *Encyclopédie* had been confiscated there was a supper party at Trianon. The duc de La Vallière happened to say he wondered what gunpowder was made of. "It seems so funny that we spend our time killing partridges, and being killed ourselves on the frontier, and really we have no idea how it happens." Madame de Pompadour, seeing her opportunity, quickly went on: "Yes, and face powder? What is that made of? Now if you had not confiscated the *Encyclopédie*, Sire, we could have found out in a moment." The King sent to his library for a copy, and presently footmen staggered in under the heavy volumes; the party was kept amused for the rest of the evening looking up gunpowder, rouge and so on. After this subscribers were allowed to have their copies, though it was still not on sale in the bookshops.[2]

Nor can one forget the influential women of the Parisian salons. There were champions, such as Mme Geoffrin, hostess, *protectrice*, and

"Maecenas" of the encyclopedists,[3] who contributed not just moral support but two hundred thousand *livres* to the enterprise.[4] And not to be forgotten is the "Muse of the *Encyclopédie*," Mlle de Lespinasse, whose salon has been called the "laboratory of the *Encyclopédie*."[5] At the same time, there were adversaries among the salonkeepers, one of whom was, ironically, Mme Geoffrin's daughter, Mme de La Ferté-Imbault, who welcomed enemies of the *Encyclopédie* to her salon.[6]

Women were also among those who read and reacted to the *Encyclopédie*. Although there is no indication that any of the subscribers were women,[7] some women obviously had access to the work. Mme de Pompadour, of course, read the work and found it useful. Palissot tells us of one woman whose response to a long article on "soul" was that of dissatisfaction.[8] And there was the reaction of Mme de Genlis, who, having read the *Encyclopédie* twice, and feeling that people could never get along without this work, conceived the impractical (at her age of seventy-five) project of "redoing" the *Encyclopédie* in order to "purify and abridge this incoherent and dangerous compilation."[9]

Yet to be done is a detailed study of the reactions of women readers to the *Encyclopédie*. They are not to be found in the most widely read publications of the day,[10] for, as Edmond and Jules de Goncourt tell us, "Books in this age were but a chance manifestation of feminine genius. . . . The woman of the eighteenth century reveals herself above all in her conversation."[11] Therefore, to learn the full range of reaction of contemporary women to the *Encyclopédie*, one would have to examine memoirs, letters, recorded conversations, and the like. In all likelihood, feminine commentary ranges from very favorable to very critical.

As to the *Encyclopédie* itself, the findings on women's contributions are disappointing. There are only two recognized women contributors, and, of the two, only one is known by name. This is a Mme Delusse, identified in Jacques Proust's list of collaborators to the *Encyclopédie* as wife or sister of the Delusse who contributed "lutherie" to the fifth volume of plates (vol. 22).[12] Mme Delusse was presumably of the same circle as her husband or brother, belonging to a class of workers who practiced an art that required as much intelligence as skill. Her contribution is probably representative of the woman artisan who was as capable as her husband or brother. The entries attributed to Mme Delusse are in volumes 22 and 24. They are straightforward explanations of plates on a subject of which she obviously had command. They do not include history or personal observations.

The other contributor, an anonymous female, is acknowledged in the introduction to volume 6 (p. vi): "A woman whom we do not have the honor of knowing has sent us the articles FALBALA, FONTANGE, and others." John Lough suggests that this anonymous woman was probably Suzanne Marie de Vivens, marquise de Jaucourt, the chevalier's sister-in-law.[13]

The articles "Falbala" and "Fontange" are of limited interest. "Falbala" (6:387, col. 2) consists of thirty-seven lines of text about bands of material that were applied to women's dresses and skirts. There are a definition, an anecdote about the etymology of the word, its history in fashion, and commentary on the importance of fashion to women who "more easily renounce the pleasure of loving than the desire to please." The article is light, witty, and superficial, apparently by a worldly woman writing on a topic of interest to her equals, one on which women were considered to be authorities.

As concerns the article "Fontange" (6:105, col. 2-6:106, col. 1), Lough seems to suggest that the female contributor submitted only a few fragments of the article.[14] Yet the whole article gives the impression of having been written by one person *je*, a point of view not expressed in "Falbala." Again, the author, or authors, gives the historical sense of the word before describing its contemporary meaning of tied ribbons that complement a hairdo.

A cross-reference in the article "Fontange" to "Palatine," another term of fashion, is not helpful in identifying the woman contributor or locating "other articles" because the tone and content of "Palatine" do not resemble those in the aforementioned two articles. To date, there has been no determination of the "other articles" this unnamed woman contributor may have sent to the editors or whether the other articles were even printed.

When these few women and brief articles are measured against the hundred-plus contributors and thousands of pages making up the *Encyclopédie*, we are forced to conclude that women's contributions were neither very numerous nor of much impact. Nor are statistics likely to change significantly. About sixty percent of the articles have been attributed, with the authors of the remainder not likely to be identified.[15]

Of perhaps more significance to us is the absence of any expression of awareness that the situation should have differed in any way. Contributors were drawn primarily from a cross section of the professional and upper-class men of France during the 1750s and early 1760s. Even foreign men seem to have written more articles than French women; Lough lists a number of Swiss, a Berliner, a Lithuanian, and a Portuguese.[16] Might the paucity of women authors be explained by the fact that few women were held in high esteem for their writings or recognized as authorities in fields other than fashion and society? If so, the predominance of male contributors is a reflection of society rather than a conscious exclusion of women by the editors.

Until fairly recently, it was common to draw conclusions on how women fare in the *Encyclopédie* from one or two of the major entries entitled "Femme," in particular "Femme" (*Morale*) by Desmahis and "Femme" (*Droit nat.*) by Jaucourt. But there are four principal entries for "Femme" in the *Encyclopédie*, as well as twenty-seven entries whose titles begin with the word "femme." All of these cover a little more than thirteen folio pages. To use only one or two of the articles might be misleading.

Jaucourt's article, about two columns in length, is a clear statement of the equality of the sexes in marriage and a recognition that custom and temporal laws have often obscured this equality. "Marriage is by its nature a contract and the reciprocal rights, beyond those dictated by natural law, to be determined by the man and woman agreeing to the contract," says Jaucourt (6:471, col. 2). His even longer article, "Femme en couche," (*Med.*), over five columns in length, is equally sympathetic, giving testimony to Jaucourt's understanding and appreciation of women's "precious token of their love" during childbirth (6:479, col. 1-6:481, col. 2). It is easy to understand why, on the strength of such articles, Vera Lee, le comte de Luppé, and others consider Jaucourt a strong voice for women.[17]

Desmahis's article, about 6½ columns in length and the longest of the four entries entitled "Femme," for the most part contradicts the idea of equality advanced by Jaucourt. The bulk of the article is an exaggerated painting of one type of contemporary woman about whom the author has little good to say. To Desmahis, women are weak, timid, shrewd, false, less capable of attention than men, vicious, vindictive, equivocable, cruel, curious, less capable of friendship with their own sex, living a continual lie called coquetry, vain, superficial, deceitful, inconstant, etc. With such obvious disdain for the fair sex and such one-sided reporting on the part of Desmahis, it is no wonder that this article infuriated broad thinkers of the period like Voltaire, and even his archenemy, Fréron.[18]

The kindest thing Desmahis can say about woman is that society contributes to her problems. He shakes his head in disbelief over the relative lack of education for women and its results: "We must be surprised that such untutored souls can produce so many virtues, that there are not more vices germinating in them." The problems of education are numerous: it is in the hands of women who have renounced the world, it does not prepare woman for what she meets when she enters society, and its focus is on beauty and the artificial means of augmenting it rather than on character and thinking ability (6:472, col. 2).

Barthez in "Femme" (*Anthropologie*) broaches the subject that woman is to a certain extent *un homme manqué* (an imperfect man). Yet, elsewhere, he recognizes woman's equality and creativity and also discusses education. He mentions Marie de Schurman, a feminist advocating universal education for Christian women. Although he questions her assertion that the study of letters enlightens and gives a wisdom not to be bought by the dangerous help of experience, he affirms that "it appears certain that this study causes distractions that weaken tendencies toward vice" (6:469, col. 2).

After an historical and geographical survey, including past accusations that women are at the origin of superstition and sorcery, he comes out with an explanation that places him among women's allies: perhaps such accusations were made because "people recognized that women had more resources of the mind than they were willing to grant them" (6:470, col. 1).

Boucher d'Argis's article "Femme" (*Jurisp.*) is a compendium of pronouncements on the legal *état présent* of women in France, often with a notation of how laws differ in other times or countries. He reports that women, because of the fragility of their sex and their natural delicacy, are excluded from some offices and incapable of certain appointments: ecclesiastical, monarchial, military, and others (6:475, cols. 1-2). He describes contemporary practice that women cannot be witnesses in wills or before notary publics but can give depositions, though it is commonly said, and to a certain extent he seems to agree with the practice, that it takes *two* women to make *one* witness (6:476, col. 1).

Yet he does recognize that women have distinguished themselves by receiving the doctor's degree in foreign academies: Hélène-Lucrèce Piscopia Cornara in philosophy at Padua in 1678; la demoiselle Patin, the same in 1732; Laure Bassi in medicine at Bologna; the Signora Maria-Gaetana Agnesi, in mathematics at Bologna in 1750. And although he goes no farther, he may be planting the idea that women's access to education should be more commonplace in his own country as well as elsewhere.

While there is no way to mention here all the aspects of women found in the entries on "Femme," perhaps enough has been included to illustrate that approach and content differ greatly from article to article. Anyone who reads a few pages of the work cannot help but realize that content is not predictable, that uniformity was not an aim of the work, and that to fully understand any question one cannot go to any one article and expect to see the full picture.

Unfortunately, this was not understood by one recent writer who judged that "the presence of four articles on women in the *Encyclopédie* clearly indicates the ambivalence of Enlightenment ideas on the subject of equality of men and women."[19] The ambivalence that exists has nothing to do with the number of entries. To so explain the number is to fail to acknowledge how the *Encyclopédie* was composed. It was not at all unusual for the editors to have a number of authors contribute an entry dealing primarily with one aspect of a broader topic.

Nor should the sometimes opposing views of contributors surprise us; each contributor was given license to choose what he would say. As far as we know, there was no editorial policy set for the subject of women, for example. Rather, it was up to each contributor to approach a topic as his background or interest dictated. This naturally encouraged a divergence of views.

As to the subject of equality, it could be risky to say that the encyclopedists were ambivalent on this matter on the basis of only four entries among the thousands. It would be almost as dangerous to judge the encyclopedists as ambivalent because the figure represented in the frontispiece of the volumes alternates between Apollo and Minerva. However, the more entries we read, the more frequently we find contradictory opinions. Therefore, we can say that there is ambivalence when we consider the contributors as a whole. More research is needed to determine the extent to which individual authors expressed this ambivalence.

At least one scholar, P. Charbonnel, has suggested that the apparent contradictions, the ambivalence on the matter of equality for women, were deliberate. While Charbonnel realizes that one can examine the overall picture of women in the *Encyclopédie* and conclude that the encyclopedists confirmed the servitude and humiliation of women rather than contesting them, she questions this interpretation by asking whether the seeming conformity might only be dust cast into the eyes of credulous readers and inattentive censors.[20] The disconnected remarks, far from being innocent, could correspond to the ambition spread throughout the *Encyclopédie* of inciting readers to consider the Holy Scriptures and certain customs as sacred no longer. She feels that Barthez, Desmahis, and Jaucourt all wished to see prejudices changed. And she suggests we can read into Barthez an intention to cast doubt on the idea of male supremacy when he points out that autopsies reveal indifferentiation of sexes in the fetus at four months, raising questions about the androgynous nature of humans and suggesting that rather than woman being "an imperfect being" or "an imperfect man" man might be "an imperfect woman."

But does Charbonnel's thesis that "Femme" is representative of the avant-garde nature of the work that attempts to bring change by hiding revolutionary statements among traditional and openly misogynist assertions hold up other than in the four articles on "Femme"? Isolated but similar remarks throughout the *Encyclopédie* lend support to Charbonnel's interpretation. In an article that would certainly not be the first place we would look for ideas on women, in one of the entries on "Man"—"Homme" (*Morale*)—the author Le Roi blames jealous men for depriving women of the chance to develop fully. From childhood, women are prepared for what Le Roi calls "slavery"; they are focused on bagatelles, falsities, a limited circle of objects, rather than on noble and generous qualities and virtues. The very fact that they have learned their lessons well dooms them to be victims of frivolity, a state Le Roi, for one, finds abhorrent (8:278, cols. 1-2). Though this is more awareness of a problem than a plea for change, it is the type of passage that might lead to generalizations about the encyclopedists' recognition that change was necessary, which is after all the first step in effecting change.

On the other hand, other isolated remarks occur in equally unlikely places and seemingly contradict each other. In "Imagination des femmes enceintes sur le foetus, pouvoir de l'" (8:563, col. 1), the contributor gives many examples of the power of a pregnant woman on her fetus but then tells us that these cases ought more reasonably to be attributed to the imagination of the person who believes he sees this influence than to the mother who really has no such power. However, in "Enfans (maladies des)" (5:659, col. 2), the contributor flatly states that hereditary vices come especially from the mother. What are we to make of such contradictory remarks?

The only way to be sure that we can clearly see all the threads woven into the tapestry representing women in the *Encyclopédie* is to read the entire seventeen volumes of text and eleven volumes of plates. For the volumes of text, this has been done by Terry S. Dock, who identifies the articles that treat women and organizes the materials into three sections: woman as a physical being, woman as a psychological being, and woman as a social being.[21] In the first case, woman is seen as *un homme manqué,* weak and delicate, but sympathetically viewed during puerperium, admired for risking her life to insure the continuation of the species, and recognized for her female pulchritude. But Dock admits that despite some advanced notions from the encyclopedists, "they do nothing . . . to modify radically the traditional concept of the weak, delicate woman."[22]

As for woman as psychological being, she is seen as having a lively imagination, strong passions, timidity, and modesty. Yet, at the same time, the question is posed as to whether woman's weakness and inferiority might be socially induced. Dock points out that within the "curious mixture of traditional and enlightened thought . . . any major discussion of women is left to the minor contributors" and that, unfortunately, there is no program designed for educating women.[23]

As regards the social role of woman, i.e., daughter, wife, and mother, the most noble and important function for the encyclopedists, in Dock's view, is that of mother. Laws reinforce and sanction the notion of woman's inferiority and exclude her from the power professions, no matter that she is as capable as man, for example, in ruling the family. But she does have a role to play in raising children, in supporting mankind, hardly an avant-garde notion!

In addition to analyzing references to women in the *Encyclopédie*, Dock draws attention to notable absences, not just of women contributors but also of specific topics. For one thing, as she points out, the encyclopedists "omit any reference to the salons in which women exercised such power and influence." This "conspiracy of silence" may have been a deliberate attempt to reduce the threat to "the stability of the bourgeois social structure."[24] But, again, we have no proof of an editorial policy.

Her conclusion, based upon many references to women throughout the *Encyclopédie*, is in some ways similar to Charbonnel's, which grew out of a study of the four main entries "Femme." But for Dock, the encyclopedists did not necessarily have the master plan to improve the lot of women, such as implied by Charbonnel; rather, with some of them debunking traditional notions of women and extending dignity to women, they may unwittingly have brought about subsequent changes in women's condition, changes which none of them could have imagined.

And how did the encyclopedists extend dignity to women, whether deliberately or not? Certainly by favorable remarks scattered through-out the seventeen volumes of text. But likewise by according working women the same recognition as working men, by faithfully recording their labors and instruments of labor, as they sought to portray all facets of human existence, not only in the text but also in the eleven volumes of plates.

To date, there has been little attention paid to women as they are pictured in the plates. Yet we know from Diderot that "the volumes of text and the volumes of plates shed light on each other, correct each other, and complete each other reciprocally."[25]

While one ideal of the emerging Enlightenment, under the impetus of Rousseau's glorification of the nurturing female, was the woman who stayed home to care for husband and children, this was not the reality for contemporaries of the *Encyclopédie*. Lower- and middle-class women were needed in the work force. They took their places alongside men in shops, factories, and fields. Rarely leading or controlling but rather filling support roles, they were often given less physically demanding tasks, sometimes allowed to use their creativity, and sometimes replaced men. Women had their own exclusively female corporations. They also belonged to mixed corporations, where they were ordinarily hired into lower positions with lower pay.[26]

The volumes of plates better than the volumes of text show working women. Although the first seventeen volumes of text usually describe occupations in general terms without referring to women at all, the volumes of plates recognize their importance in the work force and present them pictorially. In a way not possible to exploit in the realm of painting, where subjects had to be noble, heroic, pastoral, etc., where a Chardin was criticized for painting scenes of everyday life, the engravers of the *Encyclopédie* could portray life as it was.

When analyzing women as represented in the plates of the *Encyclopédie*, we realize immediately that we are not dealing with representation in great numbers. Many subject entries have no scenes or figures containing people at all. In the section "Architecture," for example, the plates are of parts of buildings only. The subdivisions of "Histoire naturelle" have pages and pages of fish, insects, amphibians, etc., but no people.

It was, however, usual to include a vignette representing the studio or workshop for each industry or commercial occupation pictured. Even though women are definitely in the minority in the plates, some of them give us a most vivid idea of women at work. To understand the predominance of males, consider that in "Manufacture des glaces" (vol. 21), twenty-four plates show no women but 171 males working. A representative list of occupations where no women are pictured includes the following:

basketmakers	grain threshers	shoemakers
blacksmiths	locksmiths	silk worm cultivators
canon makers	masons	tailors
cider pressers	military	tanners
clockmakers	miners	tile layers
foundry workers	roofers	tool makers
glassblowers	sculptors	

Not surprisingly, women predominate and outnumber men in plates and figures of occupations traditionally considered "women's work":

> making butter in a churn (18,"Œconomie Rustique, Laiterie,"fig. 1)
> working on bonnets (18, "Aiguillier-Bonnetier," pl. 3, figs. 2, 4, 5, and 6)
> embroidering (19, "Brodeur," pl. 1, fig. 2)
> cutting material to form a cloche (20, "Découpeur et Gaufreur," pl. 1, fig. 1)
> making lace (20, "Dentelle," pl. 1, figs. 1 and 2)
> making false pearls (21, "Emailleur à la Lampe, Perles Fausses," pl. 2, fig. 3 and pl. 3, figs. 1-6)
> cutting, rounding, stretching, gluing, painting, and mounting fans (21, "Eventailliste," pl. 1, "Colage et Préparation des Papiers"; pl. 2. "Peinture des Feuilles"; pl. 3. "Monture des Eventails")
> spinning and unwinding thread and wool (21, "Fil, Roüet, Dévidoirs,"

pls. 1-2) or spinning and weaving (26, "Tapis de Turquie, Division des Fils et autres Opérations," pl. 5, figs. 4 and 5)

making artificial flowers (21, "Fleuriste artificiel," pl. 1)

washing, smoking, and salting sardines and herring (25, "Pesches de Mer," pl. 12, figs. 1 and 2 and pl. 13, fig. 1)

sewing, arranging, adjusting feathers on hats and dresses for noble men and women and on adornments for horses' heads (25, "Plumassier Panachier," pl. 1 and pl. 2)

making silk cloth and stockings (28, "Soierie," pls. 1, 23, 28, and 123).

Even within industries usually associated with men, women can be seen at their "womanly" work or at the lightest tasks:

tending the fire and separating hemp fibers from bark while men are occupied with more physically demanding tasks (28,"Œconomie Rustique, Culture et Travail du Chanvre," pl. 1, 1re et 2me Division)

sewing gut while men do nonsewing tasks (19, "Boyaudier," fig. 3)

carrying sheets of cards to the cutter while men cut, paste, etc. (19, "Cartier," pl. 1, fig. 5)

finishing the print characters the man had cast, by breaking letters apart and polishing them (19, "Fonderie en Caractères," pl. 1, figs. 1 and 2)

preparing the material for the men who are making it into the finished product (20, "Cirier, en Cire à Cacheter," pl. 1, figs. 1 and 2)

cutting material that a male worker is using to line a case (21, "Gainier," pl. 1, fig. 3)

cutting rags from which to make paper and hanging paper on drying lines (22, "Papetterie, Délissage," pl. 1. Bis, figs. 1 and 2; "Papetterie, Etendage," pl. 12, figs. 2 and 3; "Papetterie, La Salle," pl. 13, figs. 1-4)

whitening sheets of tin (23, "Métallurgie, Fer Blanc," pl. 2)

braiding (25, "Perruquier, Barbier," pl. 1, fig. c)

stitching a book, while men hammer, cut, or press bindings (25, "Relieur," pl. 1, fig. b)

sewing on drapes (26, "Tapissier, Intérieur d'une Boutique et différens Ouvrages," pl. 1, fig. 1)

spinning, while men are at other tasks (26, "Tapisserie de Haute Lisse des Gobelins, Plan et Perspective de l'Attelier, des Métiers, et différentes Opérations," pl. 1, fig. o)

dragging glass across the workshop, while men are shown blowing glass and working with machines (27, "Verrerie en bois," second series, pl. 18, fig. 2).

At times women did not do the actual work of a trade or industry but contributed to the business in other ways. As wives or daughters, they ran the shop for husband or father; as widows, they inherited businesses that they then managed. Plates show:

a merchantwoman sorting corks (19, "Bouchonnier," fig. 3)

the mistress arranging products (20, "Coutelier," pl. 1, fig. 6)

a woman making a sale (21, "Ferblantier," pl. 1)

two women behind the counter, selling furs (21, "Fourreur, Outils,"
pl. 5)

the mistress at the counter weighing and selling jewelry (25, "Orfèvre
Bijoutier," pl. 1, fig. f)

a woman selling pastries to a male and a female client (25, "Pâtissier,
Tour à Pate, . . . ," pl. 1ere).

We also find women working at less traditional tasks:

removing sheets of gold from the pounding board (19, "Batteur d'Or,"
pl. 1, fig. 3)

engraving silver (18, "Argenteur," pl. 1, fig. 1)

composing with letters cast in the shop (19, "Fonderie en Caractères,"
pl. 3, fig. 1)

turning a drum (20, "Blanchissage des Cires," pl. 2, fig. 1)

making pin heads of round points (20, "Cloutier d'Epingles," pl. 1, fig.
3)

inlaying gold or silver strands to give artistic designs that are
successful or not according to the "genius of the artist." Such a reference
to women's creativity is rare in the volumes of plates. (26, "Piqueur et
Incrusteur de Tabatière, Ouvrages et Outils," pl. 1, figs. a and e)

breaking old pottery to recover the glass in them (27, "Verrerie en
bois, l'Opération de briser les vieux pots . . . ," pl. 8, fig. 3)

dragging glass across the workshop floor (27, "Verrerie en bois, Vue
Intérieure du Four . . . ," pl. 18, fig. 2).

From the foregoing description of women in the volumes of plates,
we can see that women had an important role in the rural and urban
labor force. The plates give recognition to the working people making
up this force, women included. Without the plates, an important facet
of the lives of eighteenth-century women would have remained
largely unrepresented to readers of the *Encyclopédie.*

To consider women and the *Encyclopédie* is to examine women in
eighteenth-century France—as they are important to the endeavor of
the *Encyclopédie,* as they are viewed by the encyclopedists, as they are
represented in their everyday pursuits: a vast and fascinating topic.
While the encyclopedists in their treatment of women are often guilty
of common forms of bias—invisibility, stereotyping, imbalance and
selectivity, unreality, fragmentation—the *Encyclopédie* nonetheless presents the other side of the coin as well. The good and the bad, the
profound and the superficial, the complimentary and uncomplimentary
coexist. Underlying everything, there is always the possibility for
progress, hope for a better future. And if we agree with interpretations
such as Charbonnel's and Dock's, the *Encyclopédie* is one of the works
that prepared the climate of change and the actions that have more
recently moved women closer to the goal of equality in France and
elsewhere.

NOTES

1. The title *Encyclopédie* used throughout this essay refers to the *Encyclopédie ou dictionnaire raisonné des sciences, des arts et des métiers, par une société de gens de lettres*, edited by Denis Diderot and Jean Le Rond d'Alembert, 17 vols. (Paris: Briasson et al., 1751-1765) and the *Recueil de planches sur les sciences, les arts libéraux et les arts méchaniques, avec leur explication*, 11 vols. (Paris: Briasson et al., 1762-1772).

For this essay, I consulted the Oregon State University edition of the *Encyclopédie*, which has the following publishers and dates: vols. 1-3, 9 (Genève: Chez Cramer l'aîné, et Cie., 1772); vols. 4-7 (Paris: Chez Briasson et al., 1754-1757); vols. 8, 10-17 (Neufchastel: S. Faulche & compagnie, 1765); vols. 18-28 (Paris: Chez Briasson et al., 1762-1772).

All further references to this work appear in the text; references to the first seventeen volumes of text include volume, page, and column notation; references to the eleven volumes of plates are to volume, plate title and number, and figure notation where pertinent.

2. Nancy Mitford, *Madame de Pompadour* (New York: Random House, 1953), pp. 166-167. A similar, slightly fuller account is given in Casimir Stryienski, *The National History of France: The Eighteenth Century*, translated by H. N. Dickinson (New York: G. Putnam's Sons, n.d.), pp. 314-315.

3. Fernand Nozière, "Le Salon de madame Geoffrin," in *Les Grands Salons littéraires (XVIIe et XVIIIe siècles): Conférences du musée Carnavalet (1927)*, edited by Fernand Nozière (Paris: Payot, 1928), p. 110.

4. Louis R. Gottschalk, *The Era of the French Revolution, 1715-1815* (Boston: Houghton Mifflin Company, 1929), p. 82.

5. Nozière, p. 135.

6. Nozière, p. 139.

7. John Lough, *The Encyclopédie* (New York: David McKay Company, Inc., 1971), pp. 59-60.

8. See the excerpt from Palissot's *Petites lettres sur de grands philosophes* (Paris, 1757), pp. 91-92, quoted by John Lough, *Essays on the Encyclopédie of Diderot and D'Alembert* (London: Oxford University Press, 1968), p. 275.

9. Stéphanie Félicité Ducrest de Saint Aubin, comtesse de Genlis, *Mémoires inédits . . . sur le dix-huitième siècle et la révolution française* (Bruxelles: P. J. de Mat, 1825), vol. 7, p. 81 and vol. 6, p. 197. Translations from the French works cited in the notes are my own.

10. Lough in his survey of the periodical press and of polemical writings on the *Encyclopédie* mentions not one woman's reaction. *Essays*, pp. 252-423.

11. Edmond and Jules de Goncourt, *The Woman of the Eighteenth Century: Her Life, from Birth to Death, Her Love and Her Philosophy in the Worlds of Salon, Shop and Street*, translated by Jacques Le Clerq and Ralph Roeder (New York: Minton, Balch & Company, 1927), p. 258.

12. Jacques Proust, *Diderot et L'Encyclopédie* (Paris: Armand Colin, 1967), p. 529.

13. Lough, p. 479.

14. Ibid., p. 479.

15. Robert Darnton, *The Business of Enlightenment: A Publishing History of the Encyclopédie 1775-1800* (Cambridge: The Belknap Press of Harvard University Press, 1979), p. 15.

16. Lough, pp. 52-54.

17. Vera Lee, *The Reign of Women in Eighteenth-Century France* (Cambridge, Mass.: Schenkman Publishing Company, 1975), pp. 48, 50; Albert Marie

Pierre, comte de Luppé, *Les Jeunes Filles à la fin du XVIIIe siècle* (Paris: Librairie ancienne Edouard Champion, 1925), pp. 7, 10.

18. Lough, p. 386.

19. Abby R. Kleinbaum, "Women in the Age of Light," in *Becoming Visible: Women in European History,* edited by Renate Bridenthal and Claudia Koonz (Boston: Houghton Mifflin, 1977), p. 223.

20. P. Charbonnel, "Repères pour une étude du statut de la femme dans quelques écrits théoriques des 'philosophes'," *Etudes sur le XVIIIe siècle* 3 (1976): 93-110.

21. Terry Smiley Dock, "Woman in the *Encyclopédie*" (Ph.D. diss., Vanderbilt University, 1979), pp. 228-229.

22. Dock, p. 102.

23. Ibid., pp. 153-154.

24. Ibid., p. 228.

25. Denis Diderot, *Correspondance,* edited by Georges Roth (Paris: Les Editions de Minuit, 1961), p. 5:83.

26. Léon Abensour, *La Femme et le féminisme avant la révolution* (Paris, 1923; Genève: Slatkine-Megariotis Reprints, 1977), pp. 184, 195.

Pauline Kra

Montesquieu and Women

Montesquieu in his writing on women brought to the forefront the empiricism, relativism, pragmatism, and breadth of vision that are characteristic of his thought. Discarding the notion of the natural inferiority of woman, he explored the multiplicity of factors that affect her condition and studied the effect of circumstances on feminine character and behavior. The scope of his inquiry embraced women from ancient Persia, Greece, and Rome to contemporary Europe, from the Oriental seraglio to the French court. In this broad historical and geographic perspective, he examined the variety of customs and institutions that regulate the relationships between the sexes and the many forms of interaction, from the harmony that may exist in an incestuous union to the alienation that may result from the indissoluble Catholic marriage. Relativism and pragmatism account for the complexity of his position and for the apparent inconsistencies that have given rise to widely divergent assessments of his attitude. He has been traditionally considered a feminist[1] but has also been branded a misogynist[2] and antifeminist.[3] He placed himself outside the theoretical debate on the equality of the sexes when he attributed to a "gallant philosopher" the feminist arguments derived from Poulain de La Barre. Yet his own analysis of customs and institutions gave empirical support to the feminist ideas and to the demands for the improvement of the status of women.[4]

Women figure prominently in his works as he explored their condition through fiction, satire, and sociological and political analysis. The *Lettres persanes* are, among other things, a feminist manifesto that depicts the forms of subordination and abuse and traces the path to liberation. The *Esprit des lois* offers an analytical study of the status of women, its causes, its consequences, and necessary reforms. He applied the full range of possibilities offered by the structure of the *Lettres persanes* to the subject of women. The fiction of the Oriental traveler allows him to describe women in the Orient and in Europe and to draw parallels between their circumstances. Stories within the letters provide the means for depicting an ideal in contrast with reality. The fiction of the seraglio presents the condition of women as an unfolding drama. The epistolary form enables him to represent a multiplicity of views and roles assumed in personal interactions. Women are portrayed as they are seen through the eyes of two Persians, of eunuchs, and of Europeans. Persian and European women express their feelings and depict their plight. The manner in which the men and women address each other offers a study of the relationships between the sexes.

The central image of the *Lettres persanes* and the one that frames the work is that of the seraglio, where women are held as prisoners. The harem intrigue is a study of the conditions of polygamy and of their effect on the women, the eunuchs, and the master. But beyond the exploration of polygamy, the plot has broad universal implications as a picture of feminine subordination and revolt. Enslaved and submissive to male ideology at the beginning, women express their own views of their nature and attempt to shape their own destiny in the end. The condition of women is itself a case study in despotism, irrational authority, ideologies, religious dogmas, and moral codes.

The very first paragraph of the *Lettres persanes* introduces women as an object of irrational and contradictory attitudes. The travelers spent a day at Kuom where they paid their respects at the tomb of Fatima, the virgin mother of twelve prophets. Woman is seen idolized, revered simultaneously for her chastity, her virginity, and her motherhood. While the prophets attained their rank independently, Fatima's status in the Islamic pantheon stems from being their mother. Moreover, this view of woman is presented within the matrix of religious dogma common to Christianity and Islam.[5] The simultaneous exaltation and humiliation continues in the second letter addressed to the eunuch, the "faithful guardian of the most beautiful women of Persia." The same ambivalent attitude is expressed later in Usbek's aspirations for Zelis's daughter (L.P. 71).[6]

The prison of the harem is both physical and ideological. The early part of the seraglio correspondence reveals the ideology on which the system is based, the manner in which it is enforced, and the psychological and behavioral reactions to it. The regime is shown to rest on mutual deception. The master imposes on the women a view of their function and relation to him, and they, in turn, deceive him into believing that they accept and believe the male definition. Writing to the eunuch, Usbek expresses the ideal conception of the harem, which he professes to hold and wishes to impose. To warrant the system, he pretends to love the women and to have total confidence in the eunuch's loyalty (L.P. 2). But in his letter to Nessir, he admits that he feels neither love nor desire for his wives and has no faith in their guardians. The women must be deceived to prevent their tears if they love him and their independence if they don't (L.P. 6). Montesquieu explained in the *Esprit des lois* that there are two types of jealousy: one which stems from love and another brought on by customs, tradition, and religion (E.L. XVI, 13). Usbek's jealousy is clearly of the latter type.

Writing to his wives, Usbek justifies the harem system by his love and by an exalted idea of purity. He calls the seraglio a holy temple that protects the weaker sex from the temptation of vice (L.P. 20). To the fiction of love and purity, the letter addressed to Roxane adds the illusion of happiness. Usbek seeks to persuade her that she loves him, that she is happy in the seraglio, and that all her actions are aimed at pleasing him (L.P. 26).

In their state of extreme dependency, the women cooperate to maintain the fiction by assuming postures that are in accordance with their perception of male expectations. Zachi and Fatmé express attitudes that conform with the ideal image of a harem concubine. Repeatedly reassuring Usbek about the system of vigilance, Zachi represents herself as a fervent, sensual lover and him as passionately attracted to all his wives (L.P. 3, 47). Fatmé similarly plays the role of passion and desire as she describes her efforts to please Usbek and her memories of his embrace. But while playing the expected part, she allows herself to utter an indictment of the system that frustrates women's desires, turns them into useless ornaments of a seraglio, and makes them respond not through love but through the despair of the senses (L.P. 7). The reason for the continued deception is apparent from the letter of Zélis, who, desperate because she has been separated from her female slave, Zélide, protests her love for Usbek in order to counter the eunuch's accusations of lesbianism. The women foster the pretense of love to protect themselves against the tyranny of the eunuch (L.P. 4).

As the plot progresses, Zélis still voices acceptance of the system and willingness to transmit its values to the next generation by placing her daughter within the walls, but she expresses at the same time her inner resistance to the regime and her awareness of its flaws. If women belong to one man, it is not out of personal choice but because laws separate them from all others. She complains that they are used to satisfy male desires but are never fully satisfied themselves. She shatters the myth of masculine power and independence as she proclaims her own spiritual freedom and interprets Usbek's jealousy and vigilance as signs of his dependency (L.P. 62).

In the ideal situation, the master hides behind the facade of husband and lover (L.P. 65). During the final revolt, however, Usbek abandons the mask and shows clearly that his only motivation is desire for revenge and restoration of order. While he openly exercises his tyrannical power, he reveals to Nessir his anguish, weakness, confusion, and despair (L.P. 155). To keep the women captive in the seraglio, men have become prisoners themselves.

The seraglio revolt marks the rejection of the harem rules, the repudiation of the mask, and the liberation from the male concept of the woman's role. Zélis throws off the symbolic veil, Zachi is found in bed with one of her female slaves, the wives communicate through letters with the outside world, and men are introduced within the walls. The women gradually abandon the pretense (L.P. 157, 158). Roxane, the most independent of all, hides the longest under the veil of modesty. Only after the brutal death of her lover and her own tragic determination to die does she proclaim intellectual liberation. The essence of her concluding letter is that the system under which she had been made to live was founded on deception. Usbek had tried to deceive her, and she had deceived Usbek into believing that she was deceived (L.P. 161).

Ironically, the one male who expresses sexual desire for the women is the eunuch, and he is the only one who believed the fiction of the master's happiness. He is the one to state the idea that men are born to command over the weaker sex, whom he calls eternal victims of shame and *pudeur*, created to ignore their senses and to be irritated by their desires (L.P. 9, 160). Thus, Montesquieu uses a mutilated male to state the notion of feminine inferiority.

The ongoing debate on the nature and treatment of women is reported in two letters that by their place in the work reflect the progressive intellectual liberation in the seraglio. Letter 38 presents the various opinions held by men, while Letter 141, is the feminine counterpart, in which women speaking to women judge their status and express their own perception of their nature and aspirations. Letter 38 is a summary of various opinions and a satire on the ways in which the subject had been argued. In the controversy between Orientals and Europeans about the degree of freedom that should be granted to women, Montesquieu shows that both sides assume that they have a natural authority over women and that the opposing views are both calculated to serve the greatest convenience of men. Feminist theories in the tradition of Poulain de La Barre on the equality between the sexes are attributed to a "gallant philosopher" and qualified by Rica as paradoxical. Montesquieu shared the notions that beauty gave women a source of natural ascendancy, that their talents have been repressed by lack of education, and that men exercised over women a tyrannical power established by force. But he objected to the theoretical approach and to the polemical exaggeration of the "gallant philosopher." His own empirical method, which lends support to the feminist ideas, is announced by the historical examples of the Egyptians and the Babylonians, who gave women authority over their husbands. The concluding quotation from the Koran proclaims reciprocity between the spouses with a slight advantage to the man, which is consistent with Montesquieu's concept of the optimal family structure; but Rica's unquestioning submission to the Prophet's teaching is again satirical. The letter is equally critical of male chauvinism, feminist exaggerations, and absolute religious precepts.

Letter 141 presents a tale told to women by a woman within a Persian story sent by Rica to a French lady and, only in this indirect form, communicated to Usbek. The structure of the letter, the use of third-level discourse, indicates to what extent the truth about women's feelings and sexuality had been suppressed. At the very beginning of the letter, there is a clash between a man's view of woman's role and her own aspirations. Impressed by the lady's beauty, Rica judges her worthy of occupying an exalted rank in the royal seraglio. She, on the other hand, expressing a European woman's opinion of polygamy, finds repugnant the way of life in which one man is shared by ten or twelve women. Zulema, who tells the story within the story, in what would be called today a "consciousness-raising session," is an expert theologian who knows the entire Koran by heart and all the commentaries. Her vast learning without pedantry exemplifies the intellectual potential of women, while she is also a paradigm of the *philosophe* who brings instruction through Persian tales. She repudiates the religious teachings on feminine inferiority and traces their origin back to the Hebrew scriptures. Her story shows the dangers of sincerity because Anaïs is put to death for speaking the truth to her jealous husband. The celestial seraglio Anaïs receives as her reward is a fantasy that expresses a woman's perception of her sexual capacity. The developments in Ibrahim's earthly harem, to which Anaïs sends one of her heavenly lovers, suggest that polygamy is viable only with a master endowed with supernatural powers. The final outcome is a commentary on female fertility, which cannot be realized under the normal conditions of polygamy; in the company of the celestial Ibrahim, the eleven women gave birth to thirty-six children in the course of three years. The reforms introduced by Ibrahim represent the dream of freedom of Oriental women, a dream that had to be relegated to the realm of fiction. The French lady's reaction to polygamy is consistent with Zulema's story and gives universality to the fantasy.

In spite of differences of manners and customs, the condition of European women is shown to have many similarities to that of the Oriental. In imitations of the *Lettres persanes,* comparisons to Oriental polygamy are made explicitly in order to bring out the corruption of European morals and the subordinate status of women. In Montesquieu's work, the parallels are implied but nonetheless clear in their intent. The very first letter written from Europe brings out the pervasiveness of the veil; the Italian women wear only one veil, while the Oriental women wear four. The irony of Usbek's statement that the former enjoy great freedom is apparent from the enumeration of things they are allowed to do: they may look at men through blinds, go out chaperoned, and meet men of their immediate family provided their husband does not object. Behind the symbolic blinds, women see unseen (L.P. 23). The first letter from Paris points out the universal religious humiliation of women. The French women are in revolt against the *Bull Unigenitus,* which prevents them from reading the Bible. Rica finds that the pope's decision is in agreement with the Islamic view that women are inferior creatures who will not enter paradise (L.P. 24). There are also implied analogies between the harem and the Catholic convent, where nuns are sequestered and subjected to austere rules as the spiritual spouses of a distant male image.

The only two letters written by European women express dependency and distress. They begin with the statements "I am the most miserable girl in the world" and "I am the most miserable woman in the world!" (L.P. 28, 51). The first woman is a dancer of the opera who has been seduced by an *abbé* and who, pregnant and no longer able to appear on the stage, seeks Rica's protection to obtain a job in Persia. The symbolic white veil of a priestess of Diana did not protect her even from a member of the clergy, yet she must once again pretend to be pure in her appeal to Rica. The second woman is an unhappy Russian wife who complains that her husband does not beat her and, thus, fails to show interest in her.

The description of French women is critical and satirical, but their weaknesses and negative traits are explained by their subordinate status and the abuse to which they are subjected. The broad panorama of French types whom Usbek meets at the country estate of a happily married couple includes examples of seducers and Don Juans: ecclesiastics or spiritual directors who take advantage of women in their solitude and ladies men who make a game of conquest and abandonment to the despair of women, their husbands, and their fathers (L.P. 48, 78, 79).

In a society in which status and respect depend on youth and even the husband's affection is contingent on the wife's beauty, women are the greatest victims of time. The old coquettes who try to disguise their age through cosmetics and lies are ridiculed but justified in their desire to conceal from others and from themselves the tragic truth (L.P. 52, 55, 59). In a city where libertines support a countless number of prostitutes, these women also lie about virginity and youth (L.P. 58). Gambling is a major vice engaged in by women, but Montesquieu treats it as a passion to which they resort in old age to fill the void when they are deprived of other interests (L.P. 56). Others turn to piety in order to find among the *dévots* the acceptance and respect that they no longer obtain elsewhere.

In his highly critical picture of the corruption of French morals, Montesquieu blamed the husbands as much as the wives (L.P. 55, 86; P. 283). The ideal counterpart of polygamy and of the divided French marriages is depicted in the fable of the Troglodytes and in the story of Aphéridon and Astarté (L.P. 12, 67). Among Montesquieu's minor fictional works, *Histoire véritable* continues the satire on the corruption of European morals and the evils of polygamy, while *Arsace et Isménie* presents an idealized romantic image of happiness found in faithful reciprocal love.

In the *Esprit des lois* and in the *Pensées*, Montesquieu examines the influence of physical, moral, economic, social, and political factors on the potential of women, their role in society, and types of family structure. He rejects absolute norms based on a universal concept of the nature of woman, but in evaluating existing institutions, he gives preference to those that provide the greatest degree of freedom and equality for women. In every case where he states a general practice based on reason and experience, he mentions also exceptions and alternative forms. The subject of women figures prominently in the books on morals and sumptuary laws under the various forms of government (E.L. VII), domestic slavery in relation to climate (E.L. XVI), the national character (E.L. XIX), population (E.L. XXIII), religion (E.L. XXIV), and jurisprudence (E.L. XXVI).

Montesquieu considered the feminine character to be a function of physiology, physical environment, and social conditioning. In the *Essai sur les causes qui peuvent affecter les esprits et les caractères*, he stated that physiological differences between the sexes result in differences of character. The menstrual cycle produces changes in mood and because of different anatomical configuration and hormonal balance, the fibers of women are softer, more delicate, and more flexible than those of men. Yet, unlike Malebranche and others he did not conclude that the organic differences result in inferior aptitudes.[7]

He regarded beauty as an essential feminine attribute, but he pointed out that the ascendancy it gives depends on climate and that appearance is modified by environment (L.P. 34; P. 1011, 840). The degree of power that women derive from beauty depends on its chronological coincidence with the development of reason (P. 757; E. L. XVI, 2). Though he recognized empirically the importance of beauty, Montesquieu was aware that its criteria are imaginary and relative to country and time (Sp. 113). In the present state of affairs, he remarked, women do well to be as pretty as possible, but it would be good if they were all equally beautiful or equally ugly to do away with the pride of beauty and the despair of ugliness (P. 2094).

He explains various negative personality traits as the result of conditioning. Not unlike the "gallant philosopher" of the *Lettres persanes*, he notes that male domination stifles the talents of women (P. 596). Similarly, the falsehood of women is due to their dependent status. The greater the dependence, the greater the falsehood, just as higher taxes increase the amount of smuggling (P. 276). Greed is a sign of weakness, but women are often greedy out of vanity and desire to show that money is spent on them (P. 904, 456). Women talk more than men because they lack serious occupation (P. 307). The silly behavior of girls and their eagerness to marry are clearly stated to be the result of the way they are treated; constrained and condemned to triviality, they do not dare use their faculties, and marriage alone gives women freedom and access to pleasures (E.L. XXIII, 9; P. 233).

The attraction between the sexes, Montesquieu maintained, is a fundamental law of nature (E.L. I, 2), but it is variously modified in humans by ways of thinking, character, passions, concern for beauty, and fear of pregnancy or of a large family (E.L. XXIII, 1). The relative importance attached to the physical and emotional aspects of love varies also with time and place (E.L. XXVIII, 22).

Rejecting universal norms, he showed that marriage customs as well depend on a variety of factors; they are developed in ways that are not always natural or reasonable, and there is nothing in the nature of woman that relegates her permanently to a subordinate position. In primitive families, men had authority over their children but not over their wives. It was indeed the incompatibility between the obedience that a daughter owed her father and the equal status held by the wife that gave rise to the repugnance for incestuous marriages (P. 205).[8] The Egyptians submitted to the authority of their wives in honor of the goddess Isis and enjoyed the servitude so much that they took care of the house and left outside affairs to women. Scythian women revolted against marriage as slavery and founded the Amazon empire. If the Amazons or the Egyptians had continued their conquests, men would live in submission and one would have to be a philosopher to maintain that another arrangement was more natural. If, on the other hand, Islam had conquered the earth, women would be everywhere behind bars (P. 1622).

An essential idea in Montesquieu's analysis of the relationships between the sexes is that their relative ascendancy depends on physical causes determined by climate. Nature gave man physical strength and reason; it endowed woman with beauty and reason. Women are weakest in hot climates, where their beauty wanes before their rational faculties are fully developed. Their dependence makes it easy for men to move from one woman to another and leads to the institution of polygamy. In temperate climates, on the other hand, there is greater equality between the sexes because women mature later, their beauty lasts longer, and they have more reason and knowledge at the time they marry. In cold climates, women have the additional advantage of superior reasoning because unlike men they do not drink. The monogamous marriage, which represents "a kind of equality between the sexes," prevails therefore in the colder climates (P. 757, 1069; E.L. XVI, 2).

He discarded universal norms of family structure and the traditional notion that the wife must by nature be subordinate to her husband. It is unnatural, he wrote, for women to rule over the household, as they did among the Egyptians; but he did not deny the possibility of equal sharing of authority. In a major departure from traditional views, he argued vigorously against the exclusion of women from political life and succession to the throne. It had been contended in the Aristotelian tradition that because of her weakness woman should not take any part in the running of the state. Montesquieu declared that, on the contrary, her very weakness may be a source of political virtues of gentleness and moderation needed for good government. While successful women rulers had been viewed before him as exceptions, he puts forth the reigns of Elizabeth I and Catherine II as proof of woman's ability to govern in a variety of political systems (E.L. VII, 17). Significantly, the chapter on feminine rule is placed at the end of a book that examines the forms of legal subjection imposed on women under the various regimes. He interpreted the salic law as a measure adopted for economic reasons, rather than out of discrimination against women (E.L. XVIII, 22). Yet he admired women who placed devotion to their husbands above political ambition. He praised the greatness of Queen Ulrica Leonora of Sweden who abdicated in favor of her husband (L.P. 139); and in *Arsace et Isménie,* the heroine steps down from the throne, entreating her subjects to accept the man she loves as their master.

Montesquieu's view of marriage is pragmatic and independent of the theological definition he satirized in the *Lettres persanes* (L.P. 116). In his analysis, matrimony is simply the basic social structure necessary for procreation and the survival of the species. Unlike in animals, where the female suffices to assure the survival of the young, the more prolonged physical and moral nurturing in humans requires the efforts of both parents. Marriage is the convention that designates the father. But though matrimony is the prevailing institution among civilized peoples, he notes at the outset that there are other ways of assigning parental responsibility; among the Garamantes, a nomad people of Africa, the father was designated on the basis of resemblance. He condemned illegitimate relations on the pragmatic grounds that they do not contribute to propagation, because the father does not fulfill his natural obligation and the unwed mother finds too many obstacles to bringing up the children alone (E.L. XXIII, 2).

The extensive study of polygamy is part of his analysis of the effect of climate on social and political institutions. He demonstrates that hot climate promotes conditions favorable to polygamy and to the sequestration of women, but he is critical of the manner in which one sex takes advantage of physical circumstances to enslave the other. There is every reason to believe his claim that he explained the reasons for the practice of polygamy but did not approve of it (E.L. XVI, 4). Through numerous statements and arguments, he condemned the plurality of wives (E.L. XV, 12, 19; XVI, 1-6, 8, 10, 14; XXIII, 5; L.P. 114) and parodied the opinion that the treatment of women should be determined by climate. In an ironic chapter, he enumerates, on the one hand, the crimes, horrors, poisonings, and assassinations perpetrated under the effect of hot climate by the women of Goa; and on the other, he portrays with equal exaggeration the moderation and purity of morals in temperate climates (E.L. XVI, 11). He parodies also the oriental contention that women have so many duties to fulfill in the family that they must be sheltered from all outside concerns (E.L. XVI, 10).

The one traditional universal norm Montesquieu upheld is that of the chastity of women. Feminine continence, he maintained, is a law of nature reflected in the scorn that all nations attach to incontinence. The loss of virtue in a woman is a major flaw that entails overall psychological degradation and corruption (E.L. VII, 8; XXVI, 8). Moreover, public incontinence is harmful to society because it does not contribute to propagation and weakens the stability of marriages; the decline in the number of marriages reduces the fidelity of those who have been contracted (E.L. XXIII, 2, 21).

The distinctive aspect of Montesquieu's writing on women is his extensive analysis of the relationships between their condition and the political, social, religious, and economic structures. He demonstrated that the status of women and their morals are closely linked to the political regime. They have least freedom under the two extremes of despotism and republic. Under despotism, the protection of morals is entrusted to harem walls and the enslavement of women is part of the general climate of servitude (E.L. VII, 9; XVI, 9; XIX, 12, 15). In the republic, women are free under the law but captives of austere moral restraints (E.L. V, 7; VII, 9-13; XIX, 27; P. 491). It is the monarchy that allows the greatest degree of freedom for women and requires least purity of morals (E.L. V, 7). Noting the disadvantages of extreme moral rigor of ancient republics, he showed a clear preference for the relative freedom prevailing under monarchy. In Greek republics, he observed, the effective preservation of feminine chastity was accompanied by rampant homosexuality (E.L. VII, 9). In England, leading separate lives, women are modest and timid, while men throw themselves into debauchery (E.L. XIX, 27). The decline of virtue under the corrupting influence of court is regrettable, but it is compensated for by the positive influence of women.

In the chains of causality that characterize the *Esprit des lois*, feminine behavior appears as the result of conditions imposed by climate, political regime, customs, and laws. The one book in which woman's traits and behavior appear as a cause at the beginning of the chain is Book XIX on the *esprit général*. The book demonstrates that where woman acts within a parameter of freedom her role has positive effects on the development of national character, the arts, the economy, and political institutions. The French monarchy is used in this context as a case study for the demonstration of the benefits that result from free association between the sexes. Men and women, Montesquieu contended, realize their potential best in an atmosphere of freedom for both sexes. Allowed to extend their activities outside the home, women make a major contribution to the development of sociability, manners, and politeness. They promote the refinement of taste and the progress of arts, commerce, and industry. The positive civilizing influence of women is brought out also by the example of Russia, where reforms were resisted so long as women were kept in seclusion but European customs and manners were eagerly adopted when Peter I liberated the Russian women and brought them to court. Feminine vanity, tastes, and passions provided the necessary impetus for change.

The Russian example serves to show, in addition, that the liberation of women leads to greater political freedom. It is the absence of women from public life in despotic countries that safeguards the tranquillity and the stagnation that are essential for the preservation of the regime (E.L. IV, 3). The free interaction between the sexes, on the other hand, produces social ferment that disrupts despotic rule (E.L. XVI, 9). Montesquieu deplored the corruption of morals, the loss of gravity, and the folly (P. 1062); but he viewed the overall effect of women's participation as favorable to political freedom and progress of civilization (E.L. XIX, 5-15).

In his appraisal of civil laws regarding marriage, divorce, adultery, and abortion, he advocated measures that would give greater freedom and equality to women (E.L. VII, 15; XXIII, 7-9). He regarded marriage as a contract that is intended to serve the good of society and that should fall, therefore, under the jurisdiction of civil rather than canon law (E.L. XXVI, 13). The Catholic prohibition of divorce is, in his opinion, harmful to both sexes, to growth of population, and to the institution of marriage itself (L.P. 116). Divorce, on the other hand, is generally useful to the state and to the spouses, though it does not always serve the best interests of the children (E.L. XVI, 15). Mutual incompatibility, he maintained, is the most compelling and sufficient reason for divorce (E.L. XVI, 16). He judged tyrannical the law that gave the right of repudiation to the husband but not to the wife, and he even suggested that under polygamy the right of repudiation should be given only to the woman in order to counteract the man's authority within the household (E.L. XVI, 15). The chapters on repudiation and divorce are placed significantly at the end of the book on polygamy, just as the chapters on the liberation of slaves conclude the book on slavery.

He condemned as contrary to natural law a series of civil statutes that tyrannized women (E.L. XXVI, 3, 4, 9). Yet, in dealing with adultery, he denied women the equality granted to them by the church. While the church demanded fidelity equally from both spouses, Montesquieu followed the spirit of contemporary jurists who punished the infidelity of the wife but condoned it in the husband (E.L. XXVI, 8). He criticized, however, excessively severe punishment of adultery (E.L. XIV, 15; XXVI, 19). As a counterpart to marriages of convenience, he recalled with admiration the custom of the Samnites that assorted young people on the basis of their courage, beauty, and virtue (E.L. VII, 15, 16).

Since depopulation was one of his major concerns, he cited at great length Roman laws designed to increase the number of marriages and children, and he suggested that similar laws were necessary again in Europe (E.L. XXIII, 21, 26; XXVI, 18). His approach to abortion was equally pragmatic. He deplored as harmful to population the practice of abortion for cosmetic reasons among savages (L.P. 120), but he considered abortion a legitimate means of population control in areas of inadequate food supply. In support of this measure, he referred to Aristotle who recommended induced miscarriage for population control.[9] He also recalled that on the American continent Indian women resorted to abortion as a protest against the cruelty of the colonizers (E.L. XXIII, 11, 17).

One of the logical outcomes of Montesquieu's vast analysis of relationships among physical, moral, and political factors is the total rejection of fundamental traditional notions about woman: that she is, by nature, physically and mentally inferior and that she should, therefore, have subordinate status in the family, be relegated to the home, and be excluded from public office. He recognized differences between the sexes but did not conclude that woman's physiology results in inferior psychology. He also objected to the principle that woman's participation in society and the qualities that she developed were inexorably limited by her physical traits. He maintained that the distinctive characteristics of the sexes are enhanced by separation but become flexible in civilized society when men and women interact freely and women participate in life outside the home (E.L. XIX, 12). There are statements in his work on women's weaknesses and vices that, taken out of context, may be construed as antifeminist, but the negative characteristics are never presented as inherent in the nature of women or as traits that cannot be overcome. The *Lettres persanes* argue clearly against enslavement, subordination, and ideological humiliation. They proclaim feminine intellectual independence and liberation from the walls, the veil, and the male conception of women's role. The *Esprit des lois* continues to expose the irrationality of male views and the injustice and destructiveness of conditions imposed on women. Montesquieu vindicated woman's right to political rule and advocated legal reforms in her favor. Through the study of polygamy, he attacked servitude motivated by climate, politics, and male selfishness. His strongest defense of women is the book on the national character (E.L. XIX), which demonstrates the social, cultural, economic, and political benefits of women's freedom. He agreed with contemporary feminists that feminine potential and its fulfillment depend on opportunity, and he enriched their arguments with his own empirical approach. Ahead of his time, Montesquieu created an awareness of the complexity of the factors that modify the relationships between the sexes, of the many forms they may take, and of their ongoing evolution.

NOTES

1. Léon Abensour, *La Femme et le féminisme avant la révolution* (Paris: Leroux, 1923).
2. Jeannette Geffriaud Rosso, *Montesquieu et la féminité* (Pisa: Libreria Goliardica, 1977), p. 480.
3. Robert F. O'Reilly, "Montesquieu: Anti-feminist," *Studies on Voltaire and the Eighteenth Century*, vol. 102 (Oxford: The Voltaire Foundation, 1973), pp. 143-156.
4. For biographical information on Montesquieu's relations with women, see Rosso, pp. 27-147.
5. A pun has been noticed in the name Com.
6. References to Montesquieu are from the following editions: *Lettres persanes*, edited by Paul Vernière (Paris: Garnier, 1975); *De L'esprit des lois*, edited by Robert Derathe, 2 vols. (Paris: Garnier, 1973); *Pensées* and *Le Spicilège* in *Oeuvres complètes de Montesquieu*, edited by André Masson, vol. 2 (Paris: Nagel, 1950-1955). They are abbreviated in the text as: L.P.; E.L.; P.; Sp.
7. See Paul Hoffmann, *Le Femme dans la pensée des lumières* (Paris: Ophrys, 1977), pp. 60, 67, 95-97.
8. For an anthropological explanation of the taboo of incest, see E.L. XXVI, 14.
9. Aristotle, *Politics*, bk. 7, ch. 16, no. 15.

✒ Gloria M. Russo

Voltaire and Women

From NINON DE LENCLOS, who encouraged the young boy, to Marie-Louise Denis, who cheered the old man, women were vital to the happy existence of Voltaire.[1] As a young man, he traveled in the aristocratic and intellectual circles dominated by the women of eighteenth-century Parisian society. Charmed by his wit, elegance, brilliant conversation, and verve, they invited him to adorn their gatherings of the politically and intellectually powerful.

Disappointed in his first youthful love affair, Voltaire slipped easily from one romantic involvement to the next until finally he met the "divine Emilie," Mme du Châtelet. Mutually fascinated by their intellectual pursuits, the self-taught scientist and the well-known *philosophe* formed a liaison that endured until her death, a period of over sixteen years. In the company of his unfailingly stimulating intellectual companion, Voltaire's literary production was prodigious; plays, poems, intensive work on the histories, short stories, philosophical and scientific treatises, as well as the semisecret work on *La Pucelle,* all flowed from his pen while at Cirey.

The next woman in his life, his niece Marie-Louise Denis, offered him much less in the way of mental stimulation, but she did reawaken his sexual appetite. Long before Mme du Châtelet's death, uncle and niece had become lovers. Voltaire spent the remaining twenty years of his life with "mia carissima" at Ferney. Stimulated by her flesh but not her mind, he continually sought to educate her and to encourage her to write plays. The contrast between his two mistresses of such long duration, revealed in his and his acquaintances' correspondence, is striking.

His interest in women who are both intellectually and sexually stimulating, with heavy emphasis on the former, is equally evident in his literature.[2] In this brief essay, we shall examine his theater and short stories in order to demonstrate his predilection for strong, almost virile women, but especially those women in whom this quality is tempered or offset by a sensual, loving nature. We shall also consider the women who figure in *La Pucelle,* the single work that allows us to glimpse our author and, hence, his viewpoints directly without the barriers of literary convention.

Voltaire's dramatic outpouring includes some twenty tragedies, as well as several comedies and operas. The tragedies, being of superior quality, merit our attention. These works give clear evidence of Voltaire's often stated preference for and adherence to the classical structure of a play: verse rather than prose, observance of the *bienséances*, respect of the aristotelian rules of time, place, and action. In imitation of his acknowledged model, Racine, Voltaire's heroes, male or female, pursue with vigor *la gloire*, relegating all other considerations to an inferior level of desire and intensity of need.[3] Hence, many of these characters exhibit a drive or relentlessness that brooks no obstacle and that may thus earn them a qualification as cruel, egomaniacal, faithless. However, these descriptions apply equally or more aptly to the male figures in the tragedies. Although frequently torn between love and duty—the classic dilemma—the women demonstrate a gentler nature, one in which their grandeur, a natural correlative of *la gloire*, is tempered by their love, whether maternal or passionate.

The vocabulary of Voltaire's tragic heroines is heavy with references to *la gloire, l'honneur, le devoir, la vertu.* Jocaste (*Oedipe*, 1718), even in the face of the horror of her personal situation, is able to state: "I have lived virtuously"(5.6). Mariamne (*Mariamne*, 1725) declares to her husband that she possesses a heart "which will preserve its virtue to the tomb" (4.4). Even Eriphyle (*Eriphyle*, 1732), whose murder of her husband would seem to exclude her from those who can claim pure lives, purifies herself to the point where her subjects proclaim "our grateful hearts bear witness to her virtue" (5.4).

Le devoir is another leitmotif of these heroines, one that begins with Voltaire's earliest tragedies and persists throughout the entire series. Artemire, heroine of the play bearing her name (1720), which exists only in fragments, remains faithful to a hated husband, thus preserving *la gloire* and enabling her to state with equanimity "My duty is enough for me" (1). Eriphyle, in the presence of her long-absent son and touched by a reawakening maternal love, calls upon her innate sense of *la gloire* to reestablish her values: ". . . love of my duty, resume your absolute power over my soul" (2.4). Zulime (*Zulime*, 1739) also speaks frequently of *la gloire* in association with *le devoir* in trying to explain or justify her forbidden love of Ramire. At the moment of her death she too can state: ". . . I have fulfilled my duty" (5.3). Alzire (*Alzire*, 1734) is always pushed to act by *le devoir*, although she seems more susceptible to love than the other heroines.

Another facet of *la gloire* is *l'honneur*, a mobile that directs the actions of such heroines as Zaïre (*Zaïre*, 1733), Adélaïde (*Adélaïde du Guesclin*, 1734), Alzire, Zulime, Palmire (*Mahomet*, 1741), and Mérope (*Mérope*, 1743). Accused by Orosmane, the sultan and master of the harem, of

loving another, Zaïre insists upon her innocence by replying "honor
... is engraved in my heart" (4.6). Guided by her unfailing sense of
l'honneur, Adélaïde agrees to marry one brother in order to save the life
of the other, whom she deeply loves. Alzire seeks to free her lover
from imprisonment by her husband after a war battle, and Zulime
ceases to persecute two lovers on the basis of each character's sense of
l'honneur. The same is true of Palmire and Mérope. *L'honneur* saves
Palmire from the extremes of anguish when she discovers the ugly
side of her idolized Mahomet's fanaticism. Mérope also speaks the
language of *la gloire* and *l'honneur* while, at the same time, exhibiting
maternal love and protection toward her rediscovered son.

And how many of these tragic heroines die, in the classic tradition,
to preserve their *gloire?* To mention only a few, Jocaste, Tullie (*Brutus,*
1730), Zulime, and Palmire all commit suicide as a purificatory act that
assures them of the restoration or retention of *la gloire,* whether this be
in the guise of *l'honneur, la vertu,* or *le devoir.* Sémiramis (*Sémiramis,* 1732)
and Eriphyle, both guilty of their husband's deaths, die by accident at
the hands of their sons, thus purified and once again fully clothed in *la
gloire.*

And so the procession of grandiose heroines winds its way across
the tapestry of Voltaire's tragedies. The common thread of *la gloire,*
variously disguised as *l'honneur, le devoir, la vertu,* weaves them all
together with an occasional thread of an entirely different hue,
maternal love, a heart that responds on the basis of love alone. Strong-
willed, single-minded, indomitably dedicated to the pursuit of a given
goal, Jocaste and the many other women who follow her parade before
us creating the image of a strong, almost inflexible female, yet one
whose heart responds readily to the voice of the beloved but never at
the expense of *la gloire.* In the tragedies, the women do not so much
inspire love as respect. If they are loved—and they are—there are no
great outpourings of passionate desire from their men. Their sensuality
is not so much hidden as simply ignored. The opposite holds true in the
short stories. The women who people these tales exude an aura of
desirability, of personal attraction, that bears no relation to their other
traits of characters. Vicious or meek, intelligent or foolish, conniving
or forthright, these women inspire a passion capable of driving their
lovers to any lengths.

Astarté (*Zadig,* 1748), strong, honorable, virtuous, moves Zadig so
strongly that he "left her presence bewildered and wild with joy, his
heart weighted by a burden he could no longer bear" (p. 20). The
strength of this love impels an eager but certainly not faithful Zadig
through the rest of the tale in search of his beloved from whom he is
suddenly separated. His infidelities during his quest as well as his
previous amorous attachments to Sémire and Azora, his wife, bear

witness not only to his weakness but also to the sensuous nature of each of these women.

In the same story, Zadig is not alone in his enchantment. Moabdar, Astarté's jealous husband, falls under the spell of Missouf, a woman who attracts men without effort and who delights in their attentions. Preoccupied with her and her pleasure, Moabdar "seemed to have drowned his sense of virtue in his prodigious love for the beautiful wench" (p. 45). Consumed by their passion, Moabdar loses his kingdom and his sanity. Missouf certainly will have little difficulty in finding a new lover.

Le Monde comme il va (1748) presents women with the same sensuality, the same ability to inflame men. Early in the story, the women of Persepolis are found in the temple pretending to stare directly ahead, but they are in reality watching the men out of the corner of their eyes (p. 69). Immediately on the heels of this scene follows another one in which two women give ample evidence of their desire and desirability. The first is a young widow whose sensuality leaps from the page. She luxuriates in contact with not one but two men: "[she] had one hand around the magistrate's neck while holding out the other to a handsome and modest young citizen of the city." Meanwhile, this same magistrate's wife slips away with her "advisor" and returns from their rendezvous with "her eyes moist, her cheeks flaming, her step ill-assured, her voice trembling" (p. 70).

One woman stands out in contrast to the female cast of characters in *Le Monde comme il va:* Téone. She, indeed, has a lover, totally devoted to her, whose actions are dictated by the desire to merit Téone's "esteem." She herself wins Voltaire's highest recognition; he awards her the worth of an "honnête homme" (gentleman). Thus, this heroine resembles more closely those of Voltaire's tragedies than her sister characters in *Le Monde comme il va.*

Cosi-Sancta (*Cosi-Sancta*, written in 1746-1747, published in 1784) combines qualities from both Astarté (*Zadig*) and Téone (*Le Monde comme il va*). Cosi-Sancta attracts men with the same ease as her two predecessors, inspires them with passionate devotion, and saves them from death. However, unlike the other two, Cosi-Sancta is forced to surrender herself physically in order to prevent her husband's execution. Unwilling at first, she concedes at her husband's direction: "Impelled by charity, she saved his life; this was the first of three times" (p. 612). She saves her brother and son in the same manner and is canonized after her death "for having done so much good for her family by humbling herself . . ." (p. 613).

Woman's seductive nature is again vigorously underscored in *Memnon ou la sagesse humaine* (1749). Memnon, who has vowed never to love a woman, immediately falls under the spell of a young woman seen from his window: "young, pretty ... she was sighing and weeping which only added to her charm." Completely taken in both by her beauty and her false story of persecution, Memnon becomes more and more captivated until "they no longer knew where they were" (p. 82). The young Ninivien succeeds not only in captivating the wise Memnon but also in relieving him of a considerable sum of money.

In *Les Deux Consolés* (1756), an historic parade of women passes before the reader's eyes: Henriette-Marie de France, Marie Stuart et Elisabeth I d'Angleterre, Jeanne de Naples, Hécube, Niobé. The historic trials and tribulations of these women are not the topic but rather their love affairs and their suffering at the loss of the beloved, thus underscoring their sensuality as being of fundamental importance.

This desire for pleasure is transformed into the principal mobile of the existence of Cunégonde (*Candide*, 1759). This one-dimensional character sets out on the road of bodily pleasure at the age of seventeen and follows it vigorously to the story's final line. In the opening pages, the naïve girl watches the lovemaking of Pangloss, her philosophy teacher, and Paquette, her maid; she returns home "yearning for knowledge and dreaming that she might be the sufficient reason of young Candide—who might also be hers" (p. 2). The leitmotif is set, and Cunégonde begins her weary journey from rapist to lover after lover (on two continents and in countless countries) to finally end her days with Candide. Throughout her odyssey, Cunégonde seems to delight in physical sensation and accepts as a matter of course her ability to attract men. That she delights in physical pleasure becomes amply evident in her descriptions of her lovers' bodies: "I won't deny that he [the Bulgarian captain] was a handsome fellow, with a smooth white skin" (p. 15). Her description of Candide is equally sensual: "I saw you stripped for the lash ... I may tell you, by the way, that your skin is even whiter and more delicate than that of my Bulgarian captain. Seeing you, then redoubled the torments which were already overwhelming me" (p. 16).

Her desire for Candide remains steadfast throughout the entire tale. Unaware at the end that her ravishing beauty has vanished, "she reminded Candide of his promises in so firm a tone that the good Candide did not dare to refuse her" (p. 73). Once married, however, Cunégonde "growing every day more ugly, became sour-tempered and insupportable" (p. 74). Clearly her bad temper and ugliness are linked; her physical unattractiveness has become a barrier to her sensual pleasure. Candide married her but offers little satisfaction to Cunégonde's sensual nature.

Mlle de St. Yves (*L'Ingénu*, 1767) presents a sharp contrast to Cunégonde. This young woman is the warmest, most touching heroine of Voltaire's short stories. Like Cunégonde, her sensuality awakens early in the story but is always surrounded by an aura of simplicity, charm, and naïveté far removed from the sometimes lascivious interest of the characters in other short stories. Without innuendo, she asks "how people made love in the land of the Hurons" (p. 109). To the Ingénu's reply, "They do fine deeds so as to give pleasure to people who look like you" (p. 109), la St. Yves blushes with delight. The combination of blushing and taking pleasure in his appreciation of her person underscores both native modesty and her already nascent desire. The latter is made clearer still by her observation through the keyhole of l'Ingénu under the pretext of wanting to know "how a Huron slept;" she finds him sleeping, to her evident pleasure, "in the most graceful attitude in the world" (p. 111). There is no doubt of the pleasure she derives, several scenes later, from watching him "in midstream a tall pale figure." Her first instinct is to turn away but her senses triumph and draw her back to hide in the bushes in order to see "what it was all about" (p. 119). When, finally, l'Ingénu bursts into her room intending to "marry" her, la St. Yves' sense of probity forces her to refuse him and to force him to leave. Significantly, however, his departure leaves her deeply troubled.

Unlike Cunégonde, or even Cosi-Sancta, she is unable to reconcile her love of l'Ingénu and any infidelity to him. Faced with the choice of either leaving her beloved in prison or freeing him "at the price of her most precious possession, which should belong only to the unfortunate lover" (p. 169), she prefers death. Dissuaded by her companion, who explains that most men owe their positions and fortunes to their wives ("it is a sacred duty which you are bound to carry out," p. 170), la belle St. Yves finally allows herself to be led to the rendezvous with l'Ingénu's liberator and pays the price of his freedom.

In a moving and almost lyrical passage, Voltaire describes her flight to the prison, armed with the order to free l'Ingénu:

> It is difficult to describe what she felt during the journey. Imagine a noble and virtuous woman, humiliated by her disgrace, yet intoxicated with tenderness, torn with remorse at having betrayed her lover, yet radiant with pleasure at the prospect of rescuing the man she adored. Her bitter experiences, her struggles, her success, all these were mingled in her reflections. She was no longer the simple girl with her ideas restricted by her provincial upbringing. Love and misfortune had formed her character (p. 173).

Her contradictory emotions, her pain and confusion, all render her eminently human and believable. No longer simple and naïve but still clinging to her innate nobility and sense of *la gloire*, la belle St. Yves, at once "elated and heartbroken" (p. 175), falls ill from shame and distress, "her soul . . . destroying her body" (p. 184). Her death follows quickly upon her recital of her painful adventure, her memory purified by the nobility and depth of her love of l'Ingénu.

Mlle de St. Yves perhaps comes closest to approximating a flesh-and-blood creature in both the tragedies and the short stories of Voltaire. She incarnates strength and weakness, wisdom and folly, self-control and sensuality on a human scale. She is a sympathetic character who lives and dies, figuratively and literally, for her beloved. The reader senses a certain affection for her from Voltaire that is lacking in the other female characters created by his prolific pen in the two genres thus far examined.

Affection for a character, or group of characters, women all, is, however, apparent in one of his lesser read works, *La Pucelle* (1730-1761). This burlesque mock epic, originally intended only for private consumption and not publication, was written and rewritten over a lengthy period that corresponds to a very fertile era in Voltaire's production of the tragedies and short stories. Voltaire lavishes great attention upon four female characters, Jeanne (*La Pucelle*), Judith, Agnès, and Dorothée. These women form two distinct couples, Judith and Dorothée serving as the alter egos of their counterparts, Jeanne and Agnès; each one exhibits characteristics common to the female cast of characters of the tragedies and short stories.

In order to situate this tale, based very loosely on the story of Jeanne d'Arc, suffice it to say that the preservation of France depends entirely on the preservation of Jeanne's virginity:

> The greatest of her rare exploits
> was to preserve her virginity for a year
>
> (1.17-18)

> . . . she bore beneath her short skirt
> the entire destiny of England and France
>
> (2.93-94)

War with England is only secondary and symbolic. The main story line involves the sexual adventures of all the characters, the four women obviously in the forefront.

Their sensuality is, therefore, heavily underscored. Examples abound throughout the epic, especially in reference to Agnès. The two lovers, Agnès and Charles VII, mutually share the fire of their passion:

> Our two lovers filled with trouble and joy,
> drunk with love, exchanged bewitching glances,
> the fiery forerunners of their pleasure
>
> (1.68-71)

A single verse most fully captures the full extent of her inebriation from and dedication to the pursuit of physical pleasure: "I am Agnès; long live France and love" (3.327).

For her, love and sensual gratification are the mobiles of existence; little else matters, even fidelity to Charles. Thrown from her mount, while seeking Charles, she is helped by the young English page Monrose:

> The beautiful Agnès blushing without anger did not
> find his hand too daring and looked at him invitingly without
> knowing precisely why, swearing meanwhile to be faithful
> to the king.

> (6.230-233)

Needless to say, her fidelity is extremely short-lived. She continues her search but now in the company of her young lover.

Dorothée, her mirror-image, possesses an equally sensuous nature. She describes the "delectable moment" of her first encounter with La Trémouille:

> Ah! overcome I could neither speak nor see. My
> blood burned with an unknown fire; I was unaware
> of the dangers of tender love and from sheer
> pleasure I could not eat.

> (7.69-72)

Unlike Agnès, however, she does remain faithful to her lover and almost pays with her life for this fidelity.

Her brush with death does not strengthen Dorothée; she remains weak and frightened even in the company of the extraordinary Judith de Rosamore. The boastings of Judith's lover give ample proof of her sensual nature, but she is more notable for her spirit and unflinching sense of *la gloire*. Forced to protect not only herself but also the hapless Dorothée from the unveiled demands of their captor, she states unequivocally:

> I intend to give him something quite other . . . .
> we shall see what I dare to do. I know how to
> avenge my honor and my charms. I am
> faithful to the knight I love.

> (9.100-103)

And, like her biblical namesake, she beheads her captor and saves herself and her companion. "Speaking little, but beautiful and shapely, tender by night, insolent by day, capricious at table and in bed," Judith de Rosamore is, indeed, the opposite in everything to Dorothée (8.229-232).

Yet, Dorothée does find the strength to save La Trémouille's life in a duel by placing herself between the combatants. The unhappy result of this attempt to be more than passive is her own death at the hand of her beloved, who then kills himself in grief (19.150-241). Judith, on the other hand, fights side-by-side on the battlefield with her lover. At the sight of his body transpierced with a spear—"Not a single sigh, she shouted revenge" (16.305)—she grievously wounds one attacker before she is killed by another. Judith dies in full possession of *la gloire*, clothed as a warrior, at the side of her lover:

> One would think to see the superb Pallas
> abandoning her needle in order to plunge
> into battle, or Bradamant, or even Jeanne herself.
>
> (16.383-385)

The characteristics that Jeanne and Judith share include a combination of sensuality and strength of character—as well as physical strength—unknown to the other two women in *La Pucelle*. These two aspects of Jeanne's personality are well-reflected in her reaction to the impending deaths of herself and Dunois, her lover, by impalement:

> Jeanne, impervious as always to danger, languidly
> gazed upon the handsome bastard, and for him alone
> her heart groaned. Their nakedness, their
> beauty, their youth, in spite of them awakened
> their tenderness.
>
> (4.468-472)

Even in the midst of the most extreme danger, she, unafraid, derives pleasure from the sight of Dunois' naked body.

Voltaire, himself, best summarizes these dual qualities in the opening lines of the first poem:

> Jeanne demonstrated the vigorous courage
> of a true Roland hidden behind a woman's
> face, behind a corset and a petticoat.
> I should prefer for my own use in the evening
> a beauty gentle as a sheep; but Jeanne d'Arc
> had a lion's heart; you will see this if
> you read this work.
>
> (1.9-15)

It would seem, then, that the author prefers Agnès or Dorothée, who, during the course of the epic, are referred to as a "lamb" or "sheep." Yet he describes Judith de Rosamore with such obvious affection and in such glowing terms that it hardly seems possible.

The key, of course, lies in his allusion to Judith as "tender by night" (8.230) and in the closing lines of the final poem.

> The king, ranked among the conquerors, dined
> with Agnès in Orléans. That same night
> the proud and tender Jeanne . . . kept
> her word to her friend Dunois.
>
> (21.455-460)

Judith's counterpart and the burlesque epic's principal character, Jeanne, also possesses the same traits. She is "proud" and "tender" but forced by her own naïveté and the necessity of preserving her virginity not to develop the latter to its full potential. Judith is the promise of Jeanne's continuing metamorphosis into a woman capable of balancing both aspects of her personality. Significantly, Agnès is dismissed by the author without a backward glance, but Jeanne is led into the future of shared passion, shared pursuit of *la gloire* with her beloved.

Thus, within the context of the twenty-one poems of *La Pucelle,* Voltaire does not radically change his portrait or preference of his ideal woman. He simply adds to his choice of "a beauty as gentle as a sheep" a desire for an intelligent, sympathetic companion conscious of her personal *gloire.* Humorously epitomized in Judith and Jeanne, particularly the wiser Jeanne of the future, are the qualities of the heroines of Voltaire's tragedies: *la gloire, l'honneur, la vertu, le devoir.* They also reflect the characteristics of the sensually alive and aware women who people the short stories. They most closely resemble Mlle de St. Yves, or perhaps it would be more exact to say that she resembles them, since *L'Ingénu* followed publication of *La Pucelle.* Agnès and Dorothée certainly show no similarity to the women of the tragedies but a great affinity to those of the short stories.

There can be no doubt that in *La Pucelle* Voltaire presents the composite of his perception of the ideal female, aspects of which appear in the two other genres examined. Realization of the importance of the role this mock epic plays in the free expression of Voltaire's thought erases the confusion concerning his position on women. He is not ambivalent in his other works; he simply presents one aspect only in each, either constrained by literary conventions, or, possibly, length or philosophical intent.

It is equally clear that the "divine Emilie" and the "mia carissima" of Voltaire's personal life appear in various guises in both his plays and short stories. In *La Pucelle,* his cherished mock epic written for the most part at Cirey and completed at Ferney, these two women who dominated his life reappear. Mercilessly but ever so lovingly burlesqued, the force and energy of Mme du Châtelet echo in the virile but vulnerable Jeanne (Voltaire refers to each of them as "a man"); hapless Agnès and Dorothée, the objects of every man's sexual desire, strongly resemble Mme Denis, who knew how to awaken passion but showed little other aptitude. In Judith de Rosamore, Jeanne's exciting counterpart, the characteristics of the two women merge, and Voltaire's ideal woman is revealed: she equals her lover on all planes—intellectual, moral, physical, sexual—and her strength and intelligence are enhanced by a sensual, loving nature. She is the woman who was Mme du Châtelet during the happiest period of their liaison and the one he continually tried to make of Mme Denis.

NOTES

1. Voltaire, *Théâtre* (Paris: Librairie de Firmin Didot Frères, 1843); idem, *Romans et Contes*, edited by Henri Bénac (Paris: Editions Garnier frères, 1960); idem, *La Pucelle*, edited by Jeroom Vercruysse (Genève: Institut et Musée Voltaire: 1970). Translations of the works found in the text are taken from the following sources. Voltaire, *Candide or Optimism*, translated by R. M. Adams (New York: W. W. Norton and Co., 1966); idem, *Zadig-L'Ingénu*, translated by J. Butts (Baltimore: Penguin Books, 1964). All other translations are those of the author. References for plays in the text are to act and scene. References for *La Pucelle* are to chant and line.

2. Madeleine R. Raaphorst, "Voltaire et féminisme: Un examen du théâtre et des contes," *Studies on Voltaire and the Eighteenth Century*, vol. 39 (Oxford: The Voltaire Foundation, 1972), pp. 1325-1335 and D. J. Adams, *La Femme dans les contes et les romans de Voltaire* (Paris: A. G. Nizet, 1974), both give clear indications of this preference, without ever crystallizing the inference.

3. The terms *la gloire, l'honneur, le devoir*, and *la vertu* are used throughout the text. They all approximate the English "duty" but with varying nuances. *La gloire* is an innate sense of one's self-worth or renown. *L'honneur* is esteem based on self-worth. *Le devoir* is obligation based on self-knowledge as well as public responsibility. *La vertu* is an unfailing inclination toward virtue.

🐚 Blandine L. McLaughlin

Diderot and Women

WHILE THERE EXISTS in the eighteenth century an impressive body of writing on women, apologies along Petrachist lines and traditional treatises on the relative excellence of the sexes and their equality or inequality remain far more numerous than those containing new and revolutionary ideas. Furthermore, the *querelle des dames*, in great part the work of men, is little conducive to the birth of an authentic and autonomous feminism. That "great revolution," which Laclos declares only women can bring about, does not appear imminent.

The *philosophe* and encyclopedist, Denis Diderot, whose fictional writings contain some extraordinary feminine characters, was always fascinated by the woman. His deep personal involvement with women —his wife, his daughter, his mistress and her sisters, as well as their mother, among others, made the woman a constantly felt presence in his life and a frequent object of his reflection. Such fictional characters as Suzanne Simonin and Mlle de La Chaux not only give evidence of Diderot's sympathetic attitude toward women but also register a firm protest against the demeaning position of women in eighteenth-century French society. Suzanne Simonin, the heroine of his famous novel *La Religieuse*, is a young woman of courage, sensitivity, lucidity, and determination. Her struggle against repressive civil and religious law, family authority, and social tradition is calculated to evoke a strong response and to draw attention to the plight of so many unfortunates of her sex. Diderot often encouraged women of talent, such as Mlle Jodin, an aspiring actress, and Mlle Collot, Falconet's nineteen-year-old protégée and assistant; and he took particular interest and delight in the education of his daughter.

But if Diderot had a genuine interest in women, their well-being, their education, and creative powers, he was not one of those who, following the example of Poulain de La Barre, attempted to eliminate the distinctions traditionally maintained between the sexes. In fact, in many respects, Diderot shared the more traditional view of women of many of his contemporaries. This view, which had not substantially changed since Montaigne, is succinctly expressed by Mme Thiroux d'Arçonville in her treatise *De l'amitié*, published in 1761:

Friendship which requires firmness of spirit, right conduct, and discernment of choice, is very little suited to a sex which is weak by nature, frivolous by education, scatter-brained by pretension, coquette by vanity, & inconstant for want of occupation. Women are thus capable of friendship only to the degree that they depart from their essence, & that they are more disposed to those male virtues which characterize superior men.[1]

Numerous passages in his works and correspondence attest that Diderot subscribed to this perception of women. In his *Réfutation d'Helvétius,* Diderot remarks, "Nothing is so rare as logic: an infinite number of men lack it, nearly all women have none."[2] The same idea is repeated in the *Neveu de Rameau,* in reference to sound reasoning, which Diderot describes as "a thing so uncommon among men, and still rarer among women."[3] Again, in *La Religieuse,* Suzanne, having described the suffering she has undergone, comments: "life is a burden to me; I am a woman; I have a weak mind as do those of my sex."[4] A letter to Sophie Volland provides another illustration: "How essential it is that a woman annex to herself a man of sense! You are for the most part only what we wish you to be."[5] Those rare women not characterized by these traits are seen as deviating from their essence when they embody those qualities that are considered the prerogative of superior men. "There are women who are men, and men who are women. . . ."[6] Of Sophie, his mistress, he says that she is "man and woman, as she pleases";[7] and in another instance, he means to compliment her when he says "you are scarcely a woman."[8] While Diderot concedes that women could be better educated than they are, he disagrees with Helvétius that women are capable of the same education as men.[9] Furthermore, from the acknowledged genius of a few women, he denies that one can infer an equal aptitude to genius in both sexes: "The Saphos, the Hypatias, the Catherines were women of genius. . . . And from this small number I am to conclude equal aptitude to genius in one and the other sex, and that one swallow makes a summer."[10]

Such examples are readily found in Diderot's works, but one must look further to get at the basis of his thought about women. "When one writes of women," says Diderot in his essay *Sur les femmes,* "one must dip his pen into the rainbow and sprinkle over the lines the dust of butterfly wings."[11] Such a remark may well give the impression that this work is little more than a stylistic exercise. Yet, without being a systematic exposition of Diderot's ideas on women, it nevertheless contains a number of ideas fundamental to his perception of women as expressed in his philosophical works and vividly illustrated in his fictional works. Ruled by her passions, the woman emerges in this essay as a creature of excesses; she experiences love, anger, jealousy, and superstition to a degree never experienced by men.[12] Her singular behavior is explained by "the organ proper to her sex,"[13] which exerts a powerful influence upon her. The idle and frivolous life imposed upon her by society only intensifies this influence. While a full and active life distracts the man from his passions, this is not so of the woman: "The woman incubates hers: they are a fixed point to which the idleness or the frivolity of her occupations keep her gaze ceaselessly attached."[14] This physiological explanation of the woman's character is entirely in accord with the ideas expressed in Diderot's *Rêve de d'Alembert* and *Eléments de physiologie,* in which he stresses the relationship between the psychic and the physiological. The sexual organs, like all the organs, have a life of their own: "All of our organs ... are but distinct animals which the law of continuity maintains in sympathy, unity, general identity."[15] The sense of identity the person has is the translation of the unity the body has realized among its different parts, each of which has a *will* of its own. This unity may, at any time, be disrupted, and the life of the body be reduced to fragmentary and anarchical determinations. Vapors, to which women of the eighteenth century were often subject, are symptoms, according to Diderot, of this *anarchy* of the organs, of their insubordination to the brain.[16] It is in the brain that sensorial impressions are synthesized, according to laws that Diderot describes as analogous to the laws of acoustics.[17] The brain is a resonance center and, by means of mental representations, can give to a desire or need, a decisive influence over the whole body. A passionate love can thus become a force capable of restoring the organic order perturbed by accidental or morbid causes.[18] In the *Rêve de d'Alembert*, Bordeu relates the incident of a woman who, perceiving that her lover was losing interest in her because of her illness, cured herself of a nervous malady through the power of her will.[19] "She resolved to be cured. . . . There arose within her a civil war in which it was first the master who prevailed, then the subjects."[20] (p. 348) Several instances of the same type are mentioned in *Sur les femmes.*[21] Passion is perceived by Diderot, not as a primitive tendency of the body, but as the exacerbation of certain internal movements or organic *wills* that are thwarted or obstructed.[22] It is a pathological state. As Hoffmann explains it, the great passions—delirium, fanaticism, ecstasy—have their source in man's condition as a social being, wherein he experiences the presence of the other as an obstacle to his happiness. The ideas and feelings of the passionate man compose a mental structure whose relation to reality is falsified. This is explained by his imperious need to give meaning to a reality that is disappointing to him and results in his inventing a new and fictitious world in which he can be happy. Madness, an extreme form of passion, is, for Diderot, the breaking of the link between the real and the mental. Imagination, like madness, of which it is a moderate form, is a distraction from reality, an indifference to its order. The sensitive being, and the woman above all, is subject to the determinism of her organs, and her behavior is the result of this sensitivity and of social taboos. When such a tendency is aggravated by a life of reclusion, the result can be a total loss of touch with reality, and madness.[23] This is vividly illustrated in Diderot's *La Religieuse*. The mysticism, cruelty, and lesbianism of the superiors of the three convents to which Suzanne Simonin is successively sent derive from the same cause, i.e., hysteria, which Diderot considers an intrinsic part of the feminine character. However, in the case of the superior of St. Eutrope, as Hoffmann notes,[24] the problem occurs when she internalizes the taboo and perceives her behavior and her irrepressible desire as sinful. Her delirium is filled with terrifying images by which she punishes herself. Since she is unable to be happy, she bans her desire in order to give meaning to her suffering. Her lesbianism is, thus, a form of organic madness; and her delirium is a result of the excessive authority accorded the childish prejudices instilled in her, a kind of conspiracy of sensuality and sacred terror. The exaltation of Mme de La Carlière, her theatrical actions, and her solemn and dignified bearing as well as the single-minded relentlessness with which Mme de La Pommeraye pursues her revenge against the marquis des Arcis are further illustrations of this natural inclination to hysteria. "Impenetrable in dissimulation, cruel in vengeance, constant in their projects, without scruples as to the means of succeeding. . . . ," Diderot writes in *Sur les femmes*.[25] But the great poetic vision he ascribes to woman originates from the same "ferocious beast" that she carries within herself. "It is from the organ proper to her sex that all of these extraordinary ideas proceed."[26] Only a woman, he says, is suited for the role of Pythia.[27] "Only the head of a woman could become exalted to the point of divining seriously the approach of a god. . . ."[28] Here again, one is reminded of *La Religieuse* and Mme de Moni, the superior of the first convent, whose moments of great exaltation, eloquence, and inspiration Suzanne witnesses: "In truth," she says, "this woman was born to be a prophetess. . . ."[29] Woman, as described in *Sur les femmes*, retains the great energy of primitive nature that manifests itself as readily in Machiavellianism as in mysticism. As for her intellectual powers, as noted in other works, Diderot judges them to be weak: "For lack of reflection and of principles, nothing penetrates beyond a certain degree of conviction in the understanding of women."[30] Women's pride and self-interest, however, retain all of their primitive force. At heart, women remain "real savages."[31]

If, in this essay, Diderot dwells considerably upon the bizarre, the violent, and the spectacular aspects of the feminine temperament, in which one can readily recognize many of his own literary creations, he also speaks with compassion of the unhappy condition of women and of the injustices that have always been their lot. "In nearly all countries, the cruelty of civil laws has been joined with the cruelty of nature against women."[32] Woman's unhappy fate in society, he points out, is due primarily to her biological vocation. It is her body that determines her relationship to the world; and while fulfilling the destiny prepared for her by her body and imposed on her by its mechanisms—the instinct and the imagination—the woman encounters suffering and disillusionment. From dependence upon her parents, she goes to dependence upon her husband. Her anticipation of freedom through marriage is short-lived:

> Her imagination opens upon a future filled with chimera; her heart swims in a secret joy. . . . A husband is chosen for her. She becomes a mother. . . . It is in pain, in peril of their lives, at the expense of their charms and often to the detriment of their health, that they give birth. . . The years pass; beauty fades; the years of abandonment arrive. . . ."[33]

Having lost her beauty, and her capacity to bear children, she no longer has a role in society: "What, then, is a woman? Neglected by her husband, deserted by her children, a mere cipher in society. . . ." Her only recourse, he adds, is "to take to religion."[34]

The woman, as perceived by Diderot, is doubly a victim: she is subject to time because she is dependent upon the body, and she exemplifies the fragility of a happiness based on the imagination. The woman constantly imagines her happiness as if to compensate in advance for a destiny of suffering that she cannot escape. Her happiness is both carnal and laden with fiction, rooted in the body and threatened by it. The happiness she dreams of is soon belied by illness and suffering. Her life ceases to be perilous only to become insignificant.[35]

Does Diderot then see no solution to the problem of the woman? In *Sur les femmes,* he has little to offer them but pity: "Women, how I pity you! . . . had I been a legislator . . . , freed from your servitude, you would have been sacred in whatever place you may have appeared."[36] But the question was never far from Diderot's mind, and in his correspondence, he proposes to his mistress and her sister certain *cas de conscience* (points of conscience) that would seem to propose alternatives to this unhappy situation of the woman. One case involves a young woman who wished to have a child but who had, in Diderot's words, "sense enough to perceive that marriage is a stupid and troublesome state."[37] She justifies her action on the grounds of her courage in accepting the physical risks involved in childbirth and in facing public reprobation. She further claims that she is capable and desirous of instilling in the child principles of honor and of justice and of providing society with a good citizen. It is not difficult to discern here what Diderot is suggesting. Outside the institution of marriage, the woman can hope to escape the contradiction between the natural inconstancy of the human heart and the indissolubility of marriage. The solution chosen by the young woman, in fact, gets rid of the dilemma at the heart of Diderot's psychology. On the one hand, she will obey the dictates of nature that demand that she be fruitful, since it did not make her sterile;[38] on the other hand, she will escape the fatality of inconstance.[39]

In another instance, Diderot does not scruple to approve the actions of a mother of six children and of little means who proposes to "give one night" to a man in consideration of which he will assure her husband an important position. "Only one night is asked of her. Shall she refuse a quarter hour of pleasure to the one who offers in exchange ease for her husband, education for her children, a suitable condition for herself?"[40] Diderot's judgment here is based on the demands of nature, and nature, he says, is not concerned with morality. "It is entirely engaged in two pursuits: the preservation of the individual, the propagation of the species."[41] In the name of a utilitarian morality, Diderot reduces sexuality to a mere mechanical function having no moral significance. In the *Suite du rêve de d'Alembert,* pleasure becomes the sole value, and anything that promotes it is legitimate.

Ultimately, what Diderot wishes to do is to free the relationship between men and women of all the constraints that civil and moral authority have placed upon it. As noted before, marriage for Diderot is "a stupid and troublesome state." His own unhappy marital experience certainly influenced his perception of this institution as not only unhappy for both partners but also contrary to nature. Man's natural inconstancy, he maintained, is incompatible with a lifelong commitment. "The vow of indissoluble marriage makes and must make almost as many unhappy people as there are spouses."[42] Diderot's attitude toward marriage, while in keeping with his materialistic philosophy, also reflects the mores of the society in which he lived. Eighteenth-century society viewed marriage as an institution whose essential objects were to maintain the family and transmit property.[43] It was primarily a juridical institution. If the immutable character of marriage was widely upheld, it was far more from a desire to insure that the terms of the contract would be maintained than to be faithful to sacred vows. Diderot was one of the rare men of his day, and of his milieu, to believe, at least for a time, that love and marriage were compatible. When he decided, against his father's wishes, to marry Antoinette Champion, he firmly believed in love as the basis for marriage. "What makes the happiness of the spouses," he wrote to his fiancée, "is their mutual tenderness."[44] The same philosophy is evident in his *Père de famille*, even though by that time (1758) he had long lost his illusions about his own marriage. In May 1765, he writes:

> One of the great disadvantages of the state of society, is the multitude of occupations, and especially the casualness with which one takes on obligations which dispose of all happiness. One marries; takes on an occupation; one has a wife, children, before having common sense. Ah! If it were to do over![45]

Sentimentally, the marriages of those of whom he speaks in his correspondence were hardly better than his; however, they were far more socially and economically stable than his own.[46] The majority of the time, husband and wife lived separate lives, once descendants were provided; and so long as outward appearances were maintained, each arranged his sentimental life as he saw fit, without objection from either partner. For Diderot, the real couple is joined by mutual tenderness, and to oblige two people who biologically change constantly to promise eternal fidelity is against nature. "Marriage is an *indissoluble* engagement," he writes in the *Encyclopédie*. "The wise man shudders at the very idea of an *indissoluble* engagement. The legislators who prepared for men indissoluble ties were little aware of his natural inconstancy. How many criminals and unhappy people have they created!"[47] His story of Mme de La Carlière, linked both genetically and ideologically with the *Supplément au voyage de Bougainville*,[48] illustrates society's view of marriage as an indissoluble union and its condemnation of infidelity, or what Diderot ironically calls "consequences of our absurd legislation."[49] Mme de La Carlière combines the poetic and the pathetic aspects of the woman whose exalted image of love inevitably leads to disillusionment and unhappiness. She insists upon absolute fidelity; and when she learns that her husband, Desroches, has once been unfaithful, she condemns him without appeal. The account of the relationship between Mlle de La Chaux and Gardeil in *Ceci n'est pas un conte* makes the same point with respect to the inconstancy of the human heart and the folly of eternal vows.

In Diderot's *Supplément*, Orou, native of Tahiti, defines marriage in Tahiti as "the agreement to occupy the same cabin and to sleep in the same bed, so long as we find this agreeable."[50] While Diderot does not propose this as an alternative to marriage, he attempts in this work to find a basis for individual morality in the laws governing the development of the species, rather than in the interdictions of religion.[51] As Gilbert Chinard remarks: "To the sublime mummery of Mme de La Carlière . . . Diderot means to oppose good natural law such as it is found among the natives of Tahiti."[52] But if Diderot felt that "one can be inconstant in love, even pride himself in having little religion with respect to women, without being bereft of honor and probity," he was not a proponent of total sexual freedom.[53] Even in Tahiti, a whole network of laws surrounds the reproductive act. As Michèle Duchet remarks: "Nothing, however, is less anarchical than this Tahitian paradise. . . ."[54] Diderot was compelled to introduce detailed laws in Tahiti in order to reconcile the inhuman order of the body with the obligatory political order.

One of the arguments Orou makes against marriage is that it transforms the person into an object to be possessed. However, it soon becomes evident that in the state of nature, such as it exists in Tahiti, the man and woman are even more transformed into objects and means because sexual relations are totally subordinated to the continuance of the race and the public interest.[55] As Herbert Dieckmann points out, the only argument of the *Supplément* that might have served as a basis for reform was the one that condemned the will to possess in love and the transformation of a thinking, feeling, and free being into an object. But Diderot did not pursue this argument beyond an eloquent protest. Had he further developed his idea of the freedom and dignity of the person who loves, he would have observed, suggests Dieckmann, that this idea, far from removing moral ideas from "certain actions," would rather have increased their number.[56]

Despite his frequent assertions that marriage is contrary to nature and his apparent approval of alternatives to marriage, there was never any question in Diderot's mind as to *alternatives* for his own daughter. The man whom she ultimately married had been chosen for her when she was little more than a year old,[57] and Diderot's preoccupation with her dowry fills many pages of his correspondence. It was only a month before he wrote his *Supplément,* in which marriage is judged as contrary to nature and to the dignity of the person, that Diderot's daughter, Angélique, was married. In the letter Diderot wrote her on that occasion, one hardly recognizes the author of the *Supplément.* His advice to her is not unlike that found in the most traditional marriage manuals of the day. His authority over her, he says, now belongs to her husband, and her happiness also is bound up entirely with his. "Your happiness is inseparable from that of your spouse. . . . Have for [him] all the condescension imaginable."[58] He counsels her against anything that might be interpreted as improper behavior, for "One has the right to judge women on appearances. . . ." Her life must now revolve entirely around that of her husband; she must receive all those whom he desires her to meet, but her own associations must be restricted as much as possible. "Restrict, restrict again your society. Where there are many people, there is much vice."[59] In *Sur les femmes,* Diderot condemns the idleness and frivolity of the lives of women and attributes to this form of life much of their instability. The antidote for this, he believes, is in occupying women with household duties. "Rise early; give to your domestic occupations of all kinds the first hours of your morning; perhaps your entire morning. Fortify your soul.."[60] However, he stresses equally his daughter's need to improve her mind by reading and improving her talents. He advises Angélique to retain her teacher, if only to motivate her to work; and he cautions her against dissipation: "Fear dissipation. It is the symptom of boredom and of distaste for all solid occupations."[61] As to the roles of husband and wife: "Exterior affairs are his; those of the interior are yours."[62]

In reminding his daughter that her happiness was inseparable from that of her husband, Diderot undoubtedly believed this to be true ideally; however, such had not been the case with respect to his own wife, whose existence he recognized as futile and unhappy: "And whose is the health which could withstand the life which she leads? Never going out, working constantly; living on nothing; and screaming from morning until night. Bronze would not withstand it."[63]

The inconsistency in Diderot's views on marriage, as expressed in the *Supplément* and in his letter to his daughter, may be explained in part by nostalgia for the simple life, uncomplicated by the interdictions of religion and society. Dieckmann puts it very well when he says:

> For those who suffer from deep-seated conflicts caused by the passions and the distressing confusion of emotions repressed by an interior resistance or by exterior obstacles; for those who are trapped in the contradictions of love and desire, the simple unequivocal appetite and its satisfaction take on curiously an almost ideal signification.[64]

In the conclusion of the *Supplément*, however, Diderot's position is not so far removed from that in his letter to his daughter. While persisting in the view that certain actions are wrongly judged by religion and society, he nevertheless advises against committing such actions; and he adds, "We will speak against senseless laws until they are reformed; and, meanwhile, we shall submit to them. . . . There are fewer disadvantages in being mad with the madmen, than in being wise all alone."[65]

In Diderot's philosophical works, the woman is perceived as a body; but he is aware that the body, by itself, cannot be a source of happiness, and must be reinvented by the imagination. This contradiction in Diderot's thought, says Hoffmann, made it impossible for him to come to terms with the question of love.[66] The right to inconstancy is one of the principle ideas of the *Supplément* that renders love insignificant in all its forms: conjugal, paternal, maternal, and filial. If love is protected from all suffering, it is also deprived of all joy. Diderot thus oscillates between a naturalistic interpretation in the *Rêve de d'Alembert* and in the *Supplément* and a poetic vision in the story of Mme de La Carlière and in the *Réfutation*.[67]

The illusion of eighteenth-century philosophy was to discover rational models of society by which might be reconciled order and happiness, the body and the law.[68] The *Supplément* was Diderot's attempt to do this; it was his utopia, wherein he attempted to construct a primitive state in which happiness existed and the body determined the nature of the institutions. But in confusing the mythical order with the political order, he transformed the state of nature into a *machine-society*, wherein all conflict was abolished, but with it, too, all freedom.[69] In other works, however, such as *Sur les femmes* and the *Réfutation*, Diderot devaluates the state of nature. He notes the miserable condition of savage women, brutally oppressed by men: "The woman, unhappy in the cities, is even more unhappy in the depths of the forests."[70] These contradictions, says Hoffmann, are the result of a dual view of nature, one patterned after Hobbes, the other after Rousseau; and Diderot alternates between the two.[71] The savage woman of the Orenoque, described in *Sur les femmes*, and Polly Baker in the *Supplément* together seem to symbolize the woman: the first is a victim of brute nature, devoid of all feelings of pity and humanity; the second, a victim of a society ruled by prejudice.[72]

In the chapter "Morale" of the *Histoire des deux Indes*, Diderot clearly modifies the ideas expressed in the *Supplément*. He admits the failure of the Tahitian utopia; no social order can be founded on total sexual freedom. It is the value man assigns to behavior and binds himself to respect that constitutes morality. Thus, if infidelity is, in itself, an indifferent act, it is an immoral act, because it goes against established law. The sexual act also entails a moral sense from that time when social life has developed prejudices in man. Accepted opinion, however unreasonable, is legitimate insomuch as it has received a value status. Henceforth, a certain idea of continence and of modesty is linked in the mind of the woman to her sense of dignity and of morality. Without this constraint, Diderot says, the woman would yield to the excesses of her nature.[73] Nature, in the state of civilization, thus seems to have lost its normative sense. Opinion, here, takes the place that the law had in the Hobbesian dialectic and value had in Rousseau's thought. Deference to opinion is not only the fundamental structure of all social life, but the prejudice that imposes fidelity in marriage and modesty on women is identified with the law of reason itself.[74] If nature appears first as a norm then as excess and prejudice and modesty first appear as signs of a weakness of mind then as values essential to all familial and social life, this contradiction, says Dieckmann, reflects Diderot's attempt to rationalize love. "Bourgeois marriage and the free union are two attempts made to rationalize love."[75]

In the final analysis, women remain for Diderot mysterious beings, "most extraordinary children."[76] On the one hand, he declares that if women are "real savages" and "entirely machiavelic,"[77] this is due to a society that rules by prejudice and represses the instinct; on the other hand, he seems to imply that the constraints of society are necessary to restrain the energy peculiar to a creature determined by "the organ proper to her sex."[78]

By temperament—warm, enthusiastic, and capable of remarkable flights of fancy—Diderot was naturally disposed to great sympathy for those whom he describes as "beautiful as the seraphins of Klopstock, terrible as the devils of Milton."[79] However, his fascination with all that proclaimed the uniqueness of the individual inclined him more to an interest in woman's psychological condition than in her social condition. He condemned the idle and frivolous life society imposed upon women and encouraged those who were able to rise above this condition, but he viewed the role of women as essentially different from that of men. If he perceived the woman as an extraordinary and poetic being, endowed with all the energy of primitive nature, he saw her no less as the ideal companion of man, whose happiness and fulfillment are intimately bound up with hers.

> Oh! how many true, touching and tender things are there to say about the inclination of the man toward the woman . . . woman, the being in nature who most resembles the man, the single worthy companion of his life, the source of his most delightful thoughts . . . the mother of his children . . . , the unique individual beneath heaven to feel his caresses and whose soul fully responds to his. He who does not love the woman is a kind of monster; he who seeks her out only when prompted by need, departs from his kind and places himself alongside the brute.[80]

To categorize Diderot as feminist or antifeminist would be an oversimplification. As Hoffmann points out, the terms feminism and antifeminism are inadequate to describe the main currents of thought that prevailed throughout the eighteenth century. He links Diderot (the Diderot of the last part of his life) with Montesquieu and states that both

> inscribed into history the search for values; but, following Locke, they accepted the rational structure of the mind, which, in their eyes, is justified by man's sociability, which is unquestionably his destiny. They saw a meaning, a tension in history, an effort toward the founding of social and political conditions which would be more and more in accord with the fundamental demands of reason.[81]

NOTES

1. Mme Thiroux d'Arçonville, *De l'amitié* (Amsterdam, 1761), pp. 78-79.
2. Diderot, *Oeuvres philosophiques*, edited by Paul Vernière (Paris: Garnier frères, 1961), p. 593. Subsequent references to the *Réfutation*, to the *Rêve de*

d'Alembert, and to the *Supplément au Voyage de Bougainville* will be from this edition.

3. Diderot, *Le Neveu de Rameau*, edited by Jean Fabre (Genève: Droz, 1963), p. 30.

4. Diderot, *La Religieuse*, edited by Jacques Proust (Paris: Librairie générale française, 1972), p. 109.

5. Diderot, *Correspondance*, edited by Georges Roth and Jean Varloot, 16 vols. (Paris: Les Editions de Minuit, 1955-1970), vol. 5. p. 90. Subsequent references to this work will be indicated as *Corr.*, with volume and page number.

6. Diderot, *Sur les femmes*, in *Oeuvres*, edited by André Billy (Paris: Gallimard, 1951), p. 987. Subsequent references to this work will be from this edition.

7. *Corr.* 2.136.

8. Ibid., 4.54.

9. *Réfutation*, pp. 601-602.

10. Ibid., p. 606.

11. *Sur les femmes*, p. 986.

12. Ibid., p. 979.

13. Ibid., p. 982.

14. Ibid., p. 980.

15. *Oeuvres philosophiques*, p. 293.

16. See Paul Hoffmann, *La Femme dans la pensée des lumières* (Association des publications près les universités de Strasbourg; Paris: Editions Ophrys, 1980), p. 496.

17. *Rêve de d'Alembert*, pp. 271-272.

18. Hoffmann, pp. 496-497.

19. "Always, the body is the origin of the will . . .", ibid., p. 497.

20. *Rêve de d'Alembert*, p. 348.

21. "A physician says to the women of Bordeaux, tormented with frightful vapors, that they are threatened with epilepsy; and thereupon they are cured." *Sur les femmes*, p. 984.

22. Hoffmann, pp. 498-499.

23. "[T]he passionate woman would need only the complete solitude which she seeks." *Sur les femmes*, p. 980.

24. Hoffmann, p. 503.

25. *Sur les femmes*, p. 980.

26. Ibid., p. 982.

27. In Greek mythology, Pythia is the priestess of Apollo at Delphi who delivered the oracles.

28. *Sur les femmes*, p. 980.

29. Diderot, *La Religieuse*, p. 42.

30. *Sur les femmes*, p. 986.

31. Ibid., p. 987.

32. Ibid., p. 985.

33. Ibid.

34. Ibid.

35. Hoffmann, pp. 532-533.

36. *Sur les femmes*, p. 986.

37. *Corr.* 4.121-122.

38. Ibid., 123.

39. Hoffmann, p. 489. See also pp. 488-491, in which Hoffmann points out the contradictions inherent in this and the second *cas de conscience* presented in another letter to S.V., *Corr.* 4.84.

40. *Corr.* 4.84.

41. *Corr.* 4.85. Also: "What connection is there between a just or generous action and the voluptuous loss of a few drops of a fluid?", ibid.

42. Ibid., 5.134.

43. Jacques Proust, *Diderot et l'Encyclopédie* (Paris: Armand Colin, 1962), p. 333.

44. *Corr.* 1.46.

45. Ibid., 5.37.

46. Ibid.

47. Diderot, *Oeuvres complètes*, edited by Assezat and Tourneux, 20 vols. (Paris, 1875-1877), vol. 15, p. 205.

48. Hereinafter referred to as *Supplément*.

49. *Sur l'inconséquence du jugement public*, in *Oeuvres*, p. 825.

50. *Oeuvres philosophiques*, p. 484.

51. Michèle Duchet, "Le Primitivisme de Diderot," *Europe* (janvier-février 1963):127.

52. *Supplément*, edited by Gilbert Chinard (Paris: Droz, 1935), p. 47.

53. *Ceci n'est pas un conte*, in *Oeuvres*, p. 802.

54. Duchet, p. 133.

55. See *Supplément*, edited by Herbert Dieckmann (Genève: Droz, 1955), pp. xlii-xliii.

56. Ibid., p. lxvi.

57. See *Corr.* 1.190.

58. Ibid., 12.123.

59. Ibid., 125.

60. Ibid., 126.

61. Ibid.

62. Ibid., 124.

63. Ibid., 3.124.

64. Dieckmann, *Supplément*, p. xlviii.

65. Ibid., p. 515.

66. Hoffmann, p. 535.

67. Ibid.

68. Ibid.

69. Ibid.

70. *Sur les femmes*, p. 985.

71. Hoffmann, p. 535.

72. Ibid., p. 520.

73. Ibid., p. 529.

74. Ibid., pp. 530-531.

75. Herbert Dieckmann, *Romanische Forschungen*, 1936, pp. 246-248, cited in Hoffmann, p. 532.

76. *Sur les femmes*, p. 984.

77. Ibid., p. 987.

78. Ibid., p. 982.

79. Ibid., p. 979.

80. Assezat and Tourneux, vol. 4, p. 95.

81. Hoffmann, p. 22.

✦ Gita May

Rousseau's "Antifeminism"
Reconsidered

As MOST OF US have come to realize, feminist revisionist criticism has demonstrated impressive vitality in the last decade and at least as much validity as a mode of inquiry as structuralism, marxism, and psychoanalysis.

When one approaches the eighteenth century, one encounters the two main vexing problems facing the condition of womanhood: the angel-devil images and stereotypes already described in Simone de Beauvoir's *Second Sex* and the entrapment of woman within prison-like spaces (the home, marriage, the convent).

The all-too-rosy picture the Goncourt brothers painted of the eighteenth century as one that consecrated the reign of women, by now, has been largely superseded by feminist criticism. Yet the traditional clichés of the eighteenth-century woman as dominating court life and politics, as well as the intellectual and artistic salons of the day, are far from dead.

That women under the Old Regime were imprisoned in one way or another since birth was an existential given widely, if covertly, recognized even then. No wonder, therefore, that the family, the convent, marriage, and even the exotic metaphor of the harem are so prevalent in the eighteenth-century novel as literary representations of the sequestered young woman. The toil that went into household duties was, of course, backbreaking (even with the help of servants); but childbearing, with its attendant risks and burdens, contributed most heavily to the subjection of women. Education for women was, of course, nonexistent, or extremely perfunctory at best. Those women who, under such unpropitious circumstances, succeeded in cultivating their minds and in taking an active part in the intellectual and artistic circles of the time were looked upon with condescending benevolence, curious amusement, or outright hostility.

That women were regarded by even the most enlightened men as inferior in intellect, as weaker vessels that had to be both disciplined and protected, will be illustrated by Rousseau's ambivalent stance.

Rousseau's attitude toward women and his theoretical, fictional, as well as autobiographical treatment of the subject present a rather provocative paradox. On the one hand, some critics and commentators have stressed what they viewed as the antifeminist features that, at least from their vantage point, seem to pervade his thinking on the role of women in the home, in society, and in public affairs and the arts.[1] Yet some of the most independent-minded women who played a leading part in revolutionary politics and on the European literary stage—the names of Mme de Staël, Mme Roland, and George Sand come readily to mind—remained loyally steadfast disciples and admirers of Rousseau throughout their turbulent lives, which, in so many ways, belied the model of perfect womanhood that constituted his legacy to the members of the "second sex."[2]

Why did such highly intelligent and strong-willed women respond to Rousseau with uncritical fervor? What was it in Rousseau's writings that carried such a special meaning for these and other women? There is no doubt that, for several generations of women readers, the personality and works of Rousseau afforded an unparalleled opportunity for self-revelation.[3] Rousseau somehow assumed the guise of a magician capable of throwing a blazing light on their hidden malaise and discontent. After reading his writings, they dared expect something more from life than self-abnegation in the performance of their duties as wives and mothers. Already before the Revolution, Rousseau came to be regarded by countless women readers as that rare, sensitive soul capable of comprehending their innermost needs and aspirations. To twentieth-century feminists, however, Rousseau's ideas regarding the status, education, and role of women appear considerably less liberal and enlightened than those of such *philosophes* as Montesquieu, Diderot, Helvétius and Condorcet.[4]

Yet it was to Rousseau that the most remarkable women of the eighteenth and even the nineteenth centuries turned for inspiration, encouragement, and reassurance. That the author of the Enlightenment who explicitly exhorted women to seek their personal fulfillment as chaste and virtuous wives and mothers, especially in the fifth book of the *Emile,* should have been singled out as a spiritual guide by women whose own unconventional conduct and political and literary activities would have undoubtedly baffled and displeased him constitutes a unique case of influence through subjectively perceived affinities. Rousseau fired the hearts of these women because they saw in him the victim and the outcast, and it is precisely what Simone de Beauvoir has defined as the "otherness" of the "second sex," the profound sense of alienation that is the hallmark of the female condition in society, that caused this transfiguration of Rousseau's own persona into a privileged symbol and an ever-ready spring of spiritual renewal and moral regeneration.[5]

That readers of Rousseau of both sexes have generally found in his works what they were looking for and have all too often interpreted them to suit their subjective needs, rather than to seek an objective understanding of his own ideas, cannot be denied. This is especially the case with women readers such as Mme de Staël, Mme Roland, and George Sand when they reverently turned the pages of the *Emile, La Nouvelle Héloïse,* and the *Confessions.* The powerful appeal of these books was largely due to the fact that they reflected, on an existential rather than theoretical or intellectual level, the deepest concerns and yearnings of these women.

While present-day feminists may balk at Rousseau's portrayal of a Julie or especially a Sophie as rather pliable, docile, and passive creatures, earlier women readers thought them admirable, moving characters, capable of ennobling their lives and of endowing courtship, marriage, and motherhood with a new moral seriousness and dignity. Although Rousseau had hardly advocated equal rights for women, he had painted an extremely appealing picture, through Julie in the hugely popular *La Nouvelle Héloïse,* of a beloved and highly respected companion, wife, and mother. And it is mainly through this novel, with its potent combination of passion and didacticism, that women readers had their first, unforgettable intimations of the happiness and status to which they were entitled to aspire. If nature did not destine them to be the intellectual equals of men, it conferred on them the more precious privilege of exerting a moral ascendancy over the family by their innate aptitude for love and unselfish devotion. Thus, their sphere of influence would be far greater than if they attempted to compete with men and to arrogate some of their authority. That they were necessary for the happiness of men made them their indispensable mates and trusted friends rather than their subservient vassals. Those women who sought personal achievement through involvement in social or political activities or in a personal career in the arts or letters did so at the cost of their most sacred trust. A woman's fulfillment could only be found in her role as guardian of the home and hearth, since the natural order of things has preordained her, both physically and mentally, for this place in society.

It is hardly necessary to review Rousseau's arguments and examples in support of his theory. Suffice it to say that, for him, nature had fashioned woman to be dependent upon her male companion; hence, the importance of those agreeable qualities in woman that will please man. Women who swerved from their essential calling as wives and mothers and strove to compete with men in the community and public affairs betrayed their very nature.

It is not my purpose to reexamine Rousseau's conception of womanhood, either through a reassessment of his theoretical and philosophical ideas, as they are especially set forth in the fifth book of the *Emile*, or through an analysis of his portrayals in the *Confessions* of the real women who entered his life or of the ideal one he so lovingly created for *La Nouvelle Héloïse*. Be it mentioned in passing, however, that, as Jean-Louis Lecercle has convincingly shown, a more sympathetic, less "sexist" image of woman emerges from Mme de Warens and Julie than from Sophie.[6] This is probably because, in his educational treatise, Rousseau conceived in Sophie the theoretical embodiment of a philosophical model, whereas Julie was brought into being by his imagination and sensibilities as a writer and dreamer and Mme de Warens is particularly compelling because she represents a real human being. Her femininity is all the more appealing because little idealization or theorizing has gone into her depiction.

The purpose of determining whether the charge of "sexism" so frequently leveled by modern feminists against Rousseau is a fair one would be better served by scrutinizing the impact he had on earlier women readers. To this effect, the reactions of the three women already cited in this essay, Mme de Staël, Mme Roland and George Sand, can serve as useful examples. As highly perceptive, articulate readers, they have left us a detailed record of the thoughts and feelings they experienced when, as independent-minded yet impressionable young women, they first came across Rousseau's controversial writings. Curiously enough, these exceptionally intelligent women obediently and unquestioningly subscribed to those views of Rousseau that no modern feminist in her right mind would endorse. Touchingly loyal in their admiration and affection for the one writer who had unlocked the door to their inner selves, they would refuse to acknowledge the discrepancy between their avowed espousal of Rousseau's conception of womanhood and some of their most irrepressible aspirations as women who yearned to play a significant part on the stage of the world. Even when it was too late to change the course of their lives, they continued to evoke Rousseau's principles on how women could achieve happiness. They sighed for the inner peace and tranquillity of mind that domesticity, depicted in such enticing colors in *La Nouvelle Héloïse*, could not fail to bring them, yet they could not resist the powerful urgings of their literary, social, and political ambitions. Finding themselves in the limelight, they hankered for a more private, hidden existence and blamed circumstances, rather than their own doings, for their controversial celebrity. Their Rousseauistic fervor would not permit these women to recognize that theirs was a nature that needed a broader sphere of activity than the one their master had prescribed for members of their sex, thus making matters more difficult for themselves by creating a conflict—of which most of the time they could not even be consciously aware—between their beliefs and their actions.

Of the three women, Mme Roland is the one who followed most unswervingly Rousseau's restrictive views on women. Manon Phlipon (the future Mme Roland) had the revelation of Jean-Jacques in 1776, a relatively late date, for by then she was in her early twenties and had already read a vast number of books, including the major works of such authors as Locke, Montesquieu, Voltaire and Helvétius.[7] At a time of stress and crisis in her own life, when she had practically given up the hope of finding a suitable husband because of her modest personal circumstances, Rousseau renewed her faith in mankind by depicting in *La Nouvelle Héloïse* the conjugal and domestic happiness to which a virtuous woman was entitled. In a passionate, eloquent language to which she responded with her whole thinking and sentient being, Rousseau gave full expression to those painfully repressed longings and resentments Mme Roland had thus far secretly harbored both as a woman and as a member of the struggling petty bourgeoisie. At last, she had found a kindred soul who knew how to speak directly to anguished, sincere women; and to Sophie Cannet, her confidante, she wrote, "Rousseau is the friend of humanity, its benefactor and mine. . . . I fully realize that I owe him the best part of myself. His genius has warmed me, I have felt elevated and ennobled by him. . . . His *Héloïse* is a masterpiece of sentiment."[8] Going further than her master, Manon Phlipon fervently upheld the moral usefulness of the novel against the author's stern warning that the book should not be allowed into the hands of innocent young girls lest it kindle their imagination and senses: "The woman who has read it without becoming a better person, or at least without having that desire, has a soul of mud and a listless spirit. She will never rise above the common level."[9] In her own quest for happiness through marriage and motherhood, she subconsciously patterned her behavior after that of Julie by choosing as her husband an older, more world-wise man, Roland de La Platière, rather than an impetuous young lover. Passionate love would eventually triumph in tragic circumstances that would leave Mme Roland no other option than heroic self-sacrifice and a glorious martyrdom.

While in prison and awaiting her execution, Mme Roland came to the realization that absolute, fearless candor and straightforwardness had been among the qualities she had most admired in Rousseau's *Confessions*. She would prove a worthy disciple. She would not even allow traditional scruples of feminine *pudeur* to prevent her from revealing her inmost self, even in the most embarrassing situations.

As a result, her blunt frankness, especially on matters of a sexual nature, shocked some of her nineteenth-century admirers, especially Sainte-Beuve, who found some of her revelations most unladylike.[10] Mme Roland's untimely death enabled her to keep intact her Rousseauistic ideals. The guillotine spared her the confrontation with the bittersweet lessons of experience and allowed her to preserve until the end her faith in Rousseau as the best friend of women and their most sincere spokesman. The self she had so patiently elaborated was essentially a private one and a scrupulous duplication of Rousseau's image of ideal womanhood. It is indeed one of the ironies of history that, despite her desperate efforts to preserve the privacy of her inner world, she ended up playing a notoriously political and public role during the Revolution.

Already as a young girl, Manon Phlipon liked to take refuge in the protective, enclosed area of a recess in her parents' parlor. She became especially fond of what she liked to refer to as her "cell," which had been converted into a small separate room for her convenience. The furniture of this cubicle was the simplest: a bed, a chair, a writing tablet, and a few bookshelves. Manon's "cell" was to become the center of her private, secret world.

At the age of eleven, Manon felt irresistibly attracted to a religious vocation. The silence and serenity of monastic life assumed the most seductive colors, and she fondly pictured herself spending the rest of her days in a convent. In 1793, when awaiting the guillotine, her memories of this episode in her life were made all the more poignant by the fact that she found herself confined in a prison only a few streets away from the convent that had been selected for her as a young girl.

Women who dared interfere in revolutionary politics paid a heavy price for their activism. Soon, Mme Roland, who greeted the Revolution with unbounded enthusiasm, found herself in prison in the company of counterrevolutionaries, common criminals, actresses, and prostitutes. Yet, as her memoirs and letters attest, it was in prison that she at last found a measure of serenity and peace of mind. Once more an enclosed area became a refuge from the stresses and strifes of life, a means of transcending her physical limitations. Taking her cue from Rousseau's *Confessions,* she sought a better understanding of herself by retracing her life from her girlhood to her eventual involvement in revolutionary politics.

Germaine Necker, the future Mme de Staël, published in 1788 an essay, *Lettres sur les ouvrages et le caractère de J. J. Rousseau,* which gives clear evidence of her enthusiastic admiration.[11] Despite the fervent, hyperbolic tone of this youthful work, however, one senses a less uncritical stance than in the case of Mme Roland. A strong personality, endowed with a powerful intellect, is obviously asserting itself in this perfervid panegyric.

Yet Germaine Necker had this in common with Manon Phlipon: books had largely conditioned her intellectual outlook; and she, too, would, despite her own independence of mind about the conventions attached to her sex, reveal a rather surprising conservatism and ambivalence in her views on the role of women in society. Like Mme Roland, she espoused Rousseau's endorsement of masculine superiority in the intellectual and creative realm. In her own novels, *Delphine* and *Corinne,* she does not concern herself with the rights of women in general but pleads the case of the exceptional woman whose talents and genius set her apart from the other members of her sex while exposing her to the hostility and incomprehension of men.[12] Thus, she would always look upon Jean-Jacques as a kindred spirit, for he, too, had been a misunderstood and persecuted genius.

Mme de Staël was far less reluctant than Mme Roland to take on a political battle or a literary controversy if her sense of justice or her active intellect was sufficiently aroused. Rather than seeking excuses for her activism, she welcomed, indeed thrived on, conflict and controversy. A loyal, fearlessly outspoken disciple of the liberal, melioristic principles of the *philosophes,* she continued to uphold them through tumultuous, dangerous times; and she fulfilled her difficult roles as inheritor of the spirit of the Enlightenment and as prophetess and spokeswoman of the Age of Romanticism.

When the young Aurore Dupin, the future George Sand, came across Rousseau's works, this discovery turned out to be the high point of her restless intellectual and spiritual quest.[13] Like Mme Roland and Mme de Staël before her, she had been a voracious reader; but the revelation of Rousseau marked, in her own words, the end of her search. Henceforth, she would always consider herself a spiritual daughter of Jean-Jacques, in her political and moral philosophy, as well as in her religious beliefs. And like her predecessors, she never missed an opportunity to justify his personality and character against his posthumous adversaries, who continued to be as numerous and as vociferous as in his own lifetime.[14] She viewed him as a man of passion and sensibility and as a dreamer, and she was fond of associating him with her own ecstasies and euphoric moods when beholding the beauties of nature.

For George Sand, Rousseau played a catalytic role as the author of the *Confessions* when she undertook to write the story of her own life; instead of following his example as obediently as a Mme Roland, she boldly challenged his concept of sincerity, for as a woman autobiographer she felt with special acuteness the responsibilities and limitations of her prerogatives. Rousseau was wrong, she proclaimed, in believing that the autobiographer's essential duty was to tell all.[15] Integral truth can be harmful to others; and a woman, who is especially vulnerable to the libelous and defamatory interpretations of scandalmongers, must be on her guard. Hence, George Sand was determined to avoid at all cost sensational revelations about her celebrated love life, and she did not hesitate to give stern and clear warnings to those of her readers who would be looking for titillating disclosures that her book was bound to be a great disappointment to them.[16]

Whatever reservations Mme Roland, Mme de Staël, and George Sand ultimately came to express about Rousseau's personality and works, it is highly significant that at no time did they feel compelled to question his views on the "second sex."

NOTES

1. See Richard A. Brooks, "Rousseau's Antifeminism in the *Lettre à d'Alembert* and *Emile*," in *Literature and History in the Age of Ideas*, edited by Charles G. S. Williams (Columbus: Ohio State University Press, 1975), pp. 209-227.

2. See Madelyn Gutwirth, "Madame de Staël, Rousseau, and the Woman Question," *Publications of the Modern Language Association of America* (January 1971):100-109; Gita May, *De Jean-Jacques Rousseau à madame Roland: essai sur la sensibilité préromantique et révolutionnaire* (Geneva: Droz, 1964); idem, *Madame Roland and the Age of Revolution* (New York: Columbia University Press, 1970); idem, "Des *Confessions* à l'*Histoire de ma vie*: Deux auteurs à la recherche de leur moi," *Présence de George Sand* (May 1980):40-47.

3. For Rousseau's impact on women of the French Revolution, see Ruth Graham "Rousseau's Sexism Revolutionized," in *Woman in the Eighteenth Century*, edited by Paul Fritz and Richard Morton (Toronto: Samuel Stevens, Happert and Co., 1976), pp. 127-139. Also see G. D. Kelly, "Godwin, Wollstonecraft, and Rousseau," *Women and Literature* (Fall 1975):21-26.

4. See Paul Hoffmann, *La Femme dans la pensée des Lumières* (Paris: Editions Ophrys, 1977); Jeannette Geffriaud Rosso, *Montesquieu et la féminité* (Pisa: Libreria Goliardica Editrice, 1977); and Arthur M. Wilson, "Treated like Imbecile Children (Diderot)," in Fritz and Morton, pp. 89-104.

5. For three portrayals of women in the *Emile*, *La Nouvelle Héloïse*, and the *Confessions*, see Jean-Louis Lecercle, "La Femme selon Rousseau," in *Jean-Jacques Rousseau: Quatre Études*, by Jean Starobinski, et al. (Neuchâtel: A la Baconnière, 1978).

6. Lecercle, "La Femme selon Rousseau."

7. May, *De Jean-Jacques Rousseau à Madame Roland;* see also *Madame Roland and the Age of Revolution*.

8. *Lettres de Mme Roland*, nouvelle série (Paris: Imprimerie nationale, 1913-1915), vol. 1, p. 392. Translated quotations are my own.

9. Ibid. See Rousseau's famous preface for the warning that his novel should not be placed within reach of chaste young girls.

10. See Charles-Augustin Sainte-Beuve, "Madame Roland," in *Nouveaux Lundis* (Paris: Calmann-Lévy, 1896), vol. 8, pp. 198-200.

11. Madelyn Gutwirth, "Mme de Staël, Rousseau and the Woman Question." See also Jean Roussel, *Jean-Jacques Rousseau en France après la révolution; 1795-1830* (Paris: Colin, 1972), pp. 315-358; Raymond Trousson, *Rousseau et sa fortune littéraire* (Paris: Nizet, 1977); and Paul de Man, "Madame de Staël et J. J. Rousseau," *Preuves* (December 1966):35-40.

12. Madelyn Gutwirth, *Madame de Staël, Novelist* (Urbana: University of Illinois Press, 1978). See also Gita May, "Le Staëlisme de Corinne," *Symposium* (Spring-Fall 1958):168-177; and idem, "Madame de Staël and Stendhal: A Case of Grudging Recognition," *Women and Literature* (Fall 1978):14-24.

13. George Sand, *Histoire de ma vie*, in *Oeuvres autobiographiques*, edited by Georges Lubin (Paris: Bibliothèque de la Pléïade, 1970), vol. 1. p. 1061. See also May, "Des *Confessions* à l'*Histoire de ma vie*," pp. 40-47.

14. Raymond Trousson, "Les Confessions devant la critique et l'histoire littéraires au XIXe siècle," in *Oeuvres et critiques*, edited by Roland Desné (Paris: Jean-Michel Place, 1978), pp. 51-62.

15. See Sand, vol. 1, pp. 10, 12.

16. Ibid., pp. 13, 15.

 **VI**

Portrayal of Women
in French Literature

Ruth P. Thomas

The Death of an Ideal: Female Suicides in the Eighteenth-Century French Novel

EVER SINCE *Tristan et Iseut* and its narrator's promise to tell a tale *d'amour et de mort*, love and death have been linked in French fiction. Happy love, as Denis de Rougemont remarked, has no story, so it is not surprising that almost all the great eighteenth-century French novels in which sentiment is crucial end tragically, with one or more of the principal characters dying. Given the stereotype of the female as the weaker and more vulnerable of the two sexes and the conventional notion of the woman who lives and dies for love, the tragic destiny usually, and not unexpectedly, befalls her. More noteworthy, however, is that most of the heroines' deaths could be termed suicides. If Roxanne is the only heroine who actually commits the fatal act, Manon, Julie, Mlle de St. Yves, Mme de Tourvel, and Virginie will their own deaths and contribute to them.[1] They too are stereotypes, but they are victims not of men's scorn but of their illusion. Idealized and even idolized by men, they internalize male values and then are unable to reconcile the demands of the real world with their idealized image of themselves.

The gallery of portraits in the eighteenth-century French novel escapes easy classification. The semi-comic Mlle de St. Yves, through whom Voltaire satirizes the practices and personages of the Church, is totally unlike the evasive and elusive Manon. Neither has much in common with the virtuously simple Virginie, depicted in the Bible-like setting of the pastoral. And while Mme de Tourvel, Mlle de St. Yves, and Virginie were all modeled in some measure after Julie, the differences outnumber the similarities. But whoever the heroine and whatever the setting—Paris, Persia, the provinces, or "Paradise"—the woman's ideal is essentially the same. Virtue is purity and chastity and marital fidelity. The life of the woman is often summarized by the clichés of virgin bride and faithful wife. Nor does fidelity stop with marriage. When the husband of Mme de Merteuil dies, she is expected to enter a convent. Other virtues, to be sure, are prized—Julie and Virginie, for example, are loved and admired for their *bienfaisance*—but virtue is never far from the notion of female purity.[2]

The conception of the virtuous woman denies the female her sexuality and heightens the distance between men and women. For the man, even the libertine Valmont, the "pure" woman appears inaccessible and unattainable. As *ange* and *divinité*—the terms come up in almost all the novels—she is stripped of her earthly reality. This image of the woman, which denies her sexuality, paradoxically reduces her to a sexual object, for the ideal of the virtuous woman springs from the traditional male conception that the female is his possession or chattel. In either case—angel or sexual object—such a notion negates the real, spontaneous, emotional needs of the woman as a person and runs counter to the Enlightenment's ideal of self-fulfillment.

That such virtue is the lot only of women and that the male is judged by a totally different and even opposite standard are the stuff of these novels, but illustrated most amusingly in *L'Ingénu*. The hero, according to the narrator, has a "virtue" that is "male and intrepid, worthy of his patron Hercules," who had changed "fifty girls into women in a single night."[3] Although Voltaire shows the comic aspect, the situation of the woman is serious. Through its various institutions, society conspires to perpetuate the feminine ideal and to punish deviations.[4] The family arranges loveless marriages based on money or social status for Julie, Mme de Tourvel, and Mlle de St. Yves. Virginie's mother is rejected by her family for marrying beneath her, and Julie's father threatens Julie with death should he find that Saint-Preux is her lover. The Church allies itself with and becomes the instrument of the family: when des Grieux meets Manon for the first time, she is on her way to a convent "to check . . . her bent for pleasure."[5] And Mlle de St. Yves is locked up in a convent to prevent the Ingénu's advances. The existence of the harem shows the prevalence of such principles in a non-European society. To preserve feminine virtue, the State joins with the family and the Church. Manon is deported for prostitution, while Virginie is shipped off to France at the first sign of her nascent sexuality on the recommendations of the priest and the governor.

Simply then, the dictates of the woman's own nature are in conflict with the rules and conventions of society. But that is not the entire story. For the conflict is complicated by the woman's ambiguous and paradoxical position in a society whose demands upon her are mutually exclusive. At the same time, she must be virgin and whore. Noting that "the heroine of the masculine imagination is always essentially a double figure," Nancy Miller quotes Simone de Beauvoir:

"In the figures of the Virgin Mary and Beatrice, Eve and Circe still exist."[6] Chastity is required, promiscuity rewarded. At the least, the giving of sexual favors is socially acceptable. Des Grieux tells his father: "I live with a mistress . . . two thirds of France's good society pride themselves on having one" (*ML*, p. 163). As a corollary to this, few entirely virtuous women remain. Mme de Merteuil informs Valmont that Gercourt, determined to marry a virgin, is foolish enough to believe that "he will avoid the inevitable fate" (*LD*, p. 10). Sexuality is, as Manon discovers, financially profitable. To her chagrin, Mlle de St. Yves finds it offers other advantages since it has an exchange value. According to her friend,

> The most mediocre and the most important positions have often been given only at the price that is being exacted of you. . . . Do you think that all those who have headed provinces or even armies, have owed their honors and their good fortune simply to their services? There are some who are indebted to those good ladies their wives (*I*, p. 267).

Sexuality even provides the basis for marriage. Julie seeks expressly to have a child so that her parents will accept her union with Saint-Preux. Institutions like the Church, which publicly condemn sexuality, privately condone it. des Grieux assures Tiberge (and Mlle de St. Yves discovers, too) that there are many prelates who can "perfectly well reconcile a mistress with a benefice" (*ML*, p. 65). So beset by conflicting voices, the woman finds her position untenable.

Mlle de St. Yves' case is classically straightforward. Her death is self-imposed: "The sad St. Yves contributed even more than her doctor to make her illness dangerous. Her soul was killing her body. The swarm of thoughts which agitated her sent into her veins a poison more dangerous than that of the most burning fever" (*I*, p. 277). It is the extreme but inevitable solution—the woman who has lost her virginity can no longer live with herself. That her fall is due to *un excès de vertu* (*I*, p. 267), that she has betrayed her lover in order to save him, that it is the Church itself that is responsible for her fall—none of these attenuates the "crime" of the idealistic Mlle de St. Yves. She concludes: "I am dying, and I deserve it" (*I*, p. 278).

Although Mlle de St. Yves is a martyr in the name of chastity, she is not a person of extremely difficult virtue. Sensual and highly sexed, she has a more than casual interest in things erotic. She is curious to know "how they made love in the land of the Hurons" (*I*, p. 226); she peeks through keyholes and peers through the rushes of the river where the Huron would be "baptized" in order to gaze at the young man in the nude. If chastity is the supreme female virtue for Mlle de St. Yves, brought up with the traditions and prejudices of Basse-Bretagne, the Ingénu has no such ideal. He is the natural man; his first mistress, after all, preferred him to her other lovers. Thus the image of the virtuous (i.e., virginal) woman is the heroine's creation. The death of Mlle de St. Yves, which is the sign of subservience to the male ideal and of her dependency on male values, is paradoxically her freedom from them. Through death, she escapes the laws to which her sex is subject in this world. As her friend tells her, "We poor women need a man to guide us" (I, p. 265). Only by choosing death—or, in the case of Mlle de St. Yves, by not refusing it—can the woman gain her autonomy.

Mlle de St. Yves dies because she cannot live up to the male ideal of woman; Manon and Virginie, because they have conformed to it. They become the personification of the masculine dream. In the angelizing process that strips the heroine of her physical and social reality, each is raised to a legend or myth. The female dies so that the hero can preserve his dream. In *Manon Lescaut*, des Grieux creates for Manon a *persona*. He calls her "another me" (*ML*, p. 77), and she corresponds to the image he has of himself. As des Grieux is more "sensitive" than "the ordinary man," one of those persons who can "receive ideas and sensations that transcend the ordinary bounds of nature" (*ML*, p. 81), so Manon belongs to another and higher level of reality. des Grieux imagines her as the companion in his "simple and Christian," "peaceful and solitary" life (*ML*, p. 40), the "charming girl" whom his father "would himself have cherished," "only too worthy of being his son's wife" (*ML*, p. 72), the "idol of [his] heart" (*ML*, p. 101), "too adorable to be a mere human being" (*ML*, p. 46). As Herbert Josephs has pointed out, des Grieux's "various attempts to deal with the unfamiliar reality symbolized by Manon are all characterized by a single, constant process of spiritualization."[7] Manon is des Grieux's literary creation— the simple life he imagines with her has, it has been noted, Horatian overtones.[8] But it is more than that. Des Grieux suggests the literary quality of their relationship when he revealingly remarks that "it was a heart such as mine that the faithful Dido needed" (*ML*, p. 38). This mythical Manon is light years away from the pleasure-seeking and pragmatic character the reader perceives directly by her letters, words, and acts. Through his mythical creation, des Grieux figurative- ly cuts Manon from the ties of society, symbolically represented as they fly from the corrupt, civilized world of Europe to the new natural world of America. But the presence of Manon belies des Grieux's dream. Flesh, Manon is desired by the Governor's nephew. As long as Manon retains her body, she will be desired, soiled, and degraded. She can never be the image of perfection—"the most perfect thing it [the earth] had ever borne" (*ML*, p. 200), des Grieux says significantly as he buries her—that he seeks. In the Old World Manon separated *coeur* and *corps;* in the New World des Grieux and Manon are themselves separated and cannot marry. By freeing Manon from society, des Grieux has bound his mistress more completely to himself and created in her a new dependency. He is the "master of Manon's heart" (*ML*, p. 180); she has no will but his. Because, in a sense, she has nothing else to live for, Manon abandons herself totally to des Grieux. Giving up her autonomy and independence, she has died to herself. On the boat to America, she pleads, "Let us die at Le Havre, my dear chevalier. Let death finish our miseries with a single blow!... Let us die... or at least kill me" (*ML*, p. 182). Des Grieux has given up everything to follow his mistress to America. The enormity of his sacrifice is a mirror for her own. So Manon, whose relationship with des Grieux has already been marked by passivity and submissiveness ("Manon was ... complacency itself" [*ML*, p. 49]), controls her destiny by giving up her life. Her death—she becomes weak as she flees with des Grieux into the desert—is inexplicable except in terms of suicide. Since Manon has survived on the streets of Paris, she should be able to thrive in the hardships of the New World, much more so than the aristocratic des Grieux, accustomed to the "sweetness of [his] father's house" (*ML*, p. 70).[9] Like Mlle de St. Yves', Manon's death has its ironies and paradoxes. The victim becomes the executioner as Manon destroys not only herself but also des Grieux for denying her real self. The hero calls his mistress' death "a misfortune without precedent" and relates that the rest of his life is "destined to mourn it" (*ML*, p. 199). Manon is the victim of des Grieux's illusion, but no less than des Grieux himself. In death, Manon, like Mlle de St. Yves, takes her revenge on society, destroying the body that society demanded of her.

Virginie also sheds her earthly trappings to become a pure spirit, but her process begins almost at birth. In the Arcadian paradise of her childhood, all that is carnal (and natural) is denied ("Madame de La Tour understood very well the cause of her daughter's malady [her awakening sensuality], but she didn't dare speak to her about it") or sublimated ("it was only when the embers of a former passion keener than friendship were rekindled in their hearts, that a pure religion, aided by innocence, directed them towards another life").[10] At best, sexuality is a vice or a crime: Marguerite, seduced and pregnant by a gentleman, believes, like Mlle de St. Yves, "I deserved my fate" (*P&V*, p. 83); "I only came to know misfortune when I strayed from virtue" (*P&V*, p. 85). At worst, it is a curse of God. Mme de La Tour tells her daughter who has reached sexual puberty, "pray to God. . . . He is testing you today to reward you tomorrow" (*P&V*, p. 135). For Virginie, as for Manon, the model is a literary one. Bernardin de Saint-Pierre called his novel a *pastorale;* and Florian, who defined the genre in the eighteenth century, noted, "the primary attraction of the most beautiful of shepherdesses is her modesty."[11] The characters pattern their existence after the natural rhythms and cycles of the Bible. Their pantomime of biblical scenes, the old man declares, was rendered "with so much truth that you would think yourself transported to the fields of Syria or Palestine" (*P&V*, p. 126). Paul is compared to Adam, and Virginie is "gentle, modest, and trusting, just like Eve" (*P&V*, p. 130). When Paul learns to read, he sees in Virginie the traits of the characters of the *Télémaque* (*P&V*, p. 159). As Manon is des Grieux's idol, so Paul tells the old man that without Virginie, "I have nothing; with her I would have everything. She alone is my birth, my glory and my fortune" (*P&V*, p. 179). Bernardin de Saint-Pierre, moreover, underscores this notion of illusion by having Virginie wear around her neck a little portrait of Saint Paul that Paul has given her and with which she dies. She is not faithful to Paul but to his image. Like Manon's, the adventures of Virginie take her to the Old and New Worlds (although her journey is in reverse), and she too finds the same traditions and prejudices. To keep her body from being seen by men's eyes, she refuses to disrobe aboard the Saint-Géran and swim to safety, and that costs her her life. Apparently the product of her European conditioning, this modesty is not very different from what her mother instills in her. Mme de La Tour instructs her daughter not to show her erotic feelings to Paul: "Hide your love from Paul. When a girl's heart is captured, her lover has nothing more to ask of her" (*P&V*, p. 144). So that Paul may forever keep the pure image of herself, Virginie dies, a martyr to virginity, "faithful to the laws . . . of virtue," preferring to die rather than "violate modesty" (*P&V*, p. 221). Death saves Virginie from the torments of Mlle de St. Yves and spares Paul the suffering of des Grieux in America. The old man explains that had Virginie lived she might very well have been forced one day to seek the help of "officials without principles and morals" and "to pay court to them." "Because of her beauty and virtue," the young woman would have been as desirable and desired as Manon, and Paul would have been "persecuted by those very persons from whom [he] expect[ed] protection" (*P&V*, p. 217). Death is just one of Virginie's sacrifices to Paul. As a child, she "hid . . . her pain so as not to cause him suffering" (*P&V*, p. 89), and when she leaves for France, after Paul has refused to go seek their fortune, it is for him: "I am going for you" (*P&V*, p. 152). In death, Virginie becomes a purely spiritual being: "Virginie, seeing death inevitable, . . . seemed to be an angel on her way to heaven" (*P&V*, p. 203). She is revered as a saint. The old man relates her words from beyond the grave: "I am pure and inalterable like a ray of light" (*P&V*, p. 221). Like des Grieux, Paul preserves his dream, but he too must pay the price. In death Virginie destroys the entire community; the deaths of Paul, his mother, and her mother follow Virginie's own.[12]

A victim of illusion, Julie is also a victim of self-delusion. For Mlle de St. Yves, the real (sexual) consequences involved in releasing the Ingénu from prison subsume and destroy her ideal. For Manon and Virginie, the ideal myth has replaced the real self. For these three heroines, there is no open conflict or internal struggle as each accepts her role and submits passively to her destiny. Julie, however, believes that she can harmonize the real world and the ideal within her life. Rousseau fashioned his heroine to embody both passion and duty ("a young person born with a heart as tender as it is honorable lets herself be conquered by love as a girl, and finds as a woman the strength to conquer it in turn and once again become virtuous"), just as he created Clarens to combine nature and society, and the novel to reconcile *chrétiens* and *philosophes*.[13] With Julie's death comes the confession of her failure: "For a long time I have deceived myself" (*NH*, p. 740). But her death itself is the expression of her failure, for Julie is a suicide. If her death is not self-imposed (she dies after rescuing her son from the water), it is surely self-willed. In her quest for the ideal—"the land of chimeras" (*NH*, p. 693)—Julie has constantly denied and refused her real and human self. Of all the heroines she is the most explicitly and perhaps consciously spiritualized, one of those "people of the other world" (*NH*, p. 12) with whom Rousseau peopled his novel. The already inaccessible Petrarchian figure of the first books is transformed into the ethereal being of the novel's second half. But the real person, which Julie denies, returns to reassert its dominance and finally claim its victory. In the *bosquet* at Clarens, Julie finds that she has been wrong in believing that her "senses have no need of a lover" (*NH*, p. 51). At Meillerie, in her boating excursion with Saint-Preux, she discovers she was mistaken in thinking, as she did at her marriage, that she has really changed and that her "conscience and senses were tranquil" (*NH*, p. 355). The obstacles that, in the tradition of courtly love, separate the lovers and enable them to preserve their passion, permit Julie to preserve her virtue.[14] With the return of Saint-Preux to Clarens, her fall becomes inevitable. As Julie says, "One more day, perhaps, and I would have been guilty!" (*NH*, p. 741), and so she dies with joy, happy that she has been able to live up to her image of herself. She is proud that "I did what I had to do; my virtue remains unsullied, and love has remained without remorse" (*NH*, p. 741). In dying for her son, Julie gives concrete form to the sacrifice that has marked her life, and for her, "it is just dying one more time" (*NH*, p. 741). Like Manon, Julie has already died to herself. Rousseau associates love and death not just metaphysically—only death assures love's permanence—but also because the death of the self can be concretized as an "alienation of the individual," and this is one of the dangers of love.[15] For Julie, loss of virginity is loss of self. When she yielded to Saint-Preux, Julie figuratively committed suicide: "I had to put . . . myself to death" (*NH*, p. 96).[16] Unlike Mlle de St. Yves, Julie survives her fall but only because redemption is possible: Saint-Preux's virtue (masculine and, therefore, intact) will replace her own, and she will live through him. She tells her lover: "Let your worth erase my shame; through your virtue make the loss of mine excusable. Be my entire self, now that I am no longer anything" (*NH*, p. 103). Julie belongs so totally to Saint-Preux that he must release her before she can marry Wolmar, and she requests of him: "Give me back . . . the liberty I entrusted to you" (*NH*, p. 325). But the bonds are loosened only to be tied—by Julie's father—even more tightly. Julie, married to Wolmar, is "linked to the destiny of a husband, or rather to the wishes of a father by an indissoluble chain" (*NH*, p. 340). For Julie, as a daughter, mistress, wife, and mother, her life and death are determined by male values. With her death comes the end of another illusion, as the ideal community of Clarens begins to fall apart. No one remains unscathed when the inhuman ideal is imposed upon the real world.

Death precedes and prevents adultery for Julie, but not so for Roxanne and Mme de Tourvel. By choosing lovers, after having been faithful wives, these heroines opt for the real world over the ideal and seem to escape the female destiny. But the conflict is merely restated in different terms. Through the constraints of marriage—moral for Mme de Tourvel, and moral and physical for Roxanne, since the harem is a prison—the social ideal of the virtuous woman has become the reality, and the real emotional and human needs that cannot readily be fulfilled have become the ideal. Both women are desirable because for the male they embody the female ideal of purity and chastity. Not only is chastity the *sine qua non* of the harem (the husband who finds his bride is not the virgin he expected can maim her before sending her back to her parents), but the well-brought up Persian bride is expected to delay consummating her marriage, for "it seems like debauchery to give the ultimate favor so soon."[17] Valmont pursues Mme de Tourvel as, what he calls, "the enemy worthy of me," because of "her conjugal love, her austere principles" (*LD*, p. 13). Ironically, the virtue of Roxanne and Mme de Tourvel is not as pure as it seems. Roxanne's "chaste" resistance to Usbek—it is two months before she yields—masks her hatred, and Mme de Tourvel's virtue, like that of the princesse de Clèves, hides her fear of passion and is a function of her pride. Both heroines are forced into a virtue that is not natural to them. Along with the constraints it imposes, marriage deprives Roxanne and Mme de Tourvel of their autonomy. Roxanne is just another harem wife, while Mme de Tourvel is *la présidente*, an extension of her husband. Adultery finally offers the satisfaction of sexual needs (more acute since both husbands are absent), identity, importance, and self. Roxanne can change the very nature of the harem and make it "a place of delight and pleasure" (*LP*, p. 333). For Mme de Tourvel, life takes on new meaning and purpose when she finds that Valmont needs her to make him happy ("Who knows . . . if this happiness was not reserved for me, to be necessary for his?" [*LD*, p. 314]). But the self is discovered only to be lost once again. Replacing the husband, the lover exacts the same sacrifice and commitment as did Usbek and M. de Tourvel. Mme de Tourvel writes to Mme de Rosemonde that Valmont has become "the single center of my thoughts, my feelings, my actions" (*LD*, p. 305), and Roxanne takes her life because, as she asks, "what would I do here, since the only man who held me to life is no more?" (*LP*, p. 334). Mme de Tourvel dies, significantly, not when Valmont has betrayed her, but only when she learns of his death. Her prayer to God is "I submit to your justice; but pardon Valmont" (*LD*, p. 374). Moreover, the feminine ideal both have refused through adultery still determines their lives. Roxanne pays lip service to the notion of female purity by taking a lover within the walls of the harem and keeping up the appearance of the virtuous wife. She commits suicide also to avoid the revenge of her jealous husband. Mme de Tourvel is tortured by guilt. Delirious, she calls out to her husband to punish her: "Come punish an unfaithful wife. Let me suffer at last the torments I have deserved" (*LD*, p. 369). She is perhaps the most tragic of all the heroines, caught between not only what is and what might be but what has been as well. Her folly, which precedes her death, could be a metaphor for the position of the woman. Manon, Virginie, and Julie refuse to compromise and die to avoid corruption; Mlle de St. Yves, Roxanne, and Mme de Tourvel compromise, are corrupted, and die. The reasons for their deaths differ, but the ideal is the same.

The essence of the novel is the incompatibility between the real world and the ideal. It reaches its high point in the nineteenth century with *Mme Bovary*, whose heroine also is a suicide. The male protagonists of later novels also suffer from social alienation: for example, Julien Sorel, Eugène de Rastignac, and Meursault. But in the eighteenth century, this incompatibility is stated in purely sexual terms, with the real constraints placed on the woman's ideal. The victim is necessarily a woman, for eighteenth-century society defines social relationships in terms of the erotic yet, at the same time, distrusts passion and demands that marriage be based on a more stable and rational foundation. Chastity and fidelity are not considered masculine virtues. The innocent and pure hero is naïve, like Jacob or Melcour, and his adventures are recorded in a comic novel. Even the pure Saint-Preux, who was to commit suicide with Julie at Meillerie in the original version of the novel, is allowed to survive. So it is the woman, trapped in an irreconcilable dilemma, whose tragic destiny forms the story of love and death that is the eighteenth-century French novel. But, of course, there are no real suicides in the novel. Death for the character is murder by the author's hand. It is banal to suggest that the author is the creator and destroyer of the character who dies, but this banality takes on curious overtones in these novels. The authors were men after all; and in murdering their heroines, they were, wittingly or not, re-enacting the social drama taking place on a larger stage in the eighteenth century.

Then especially, fiction served reality, and these male writers believed that chastity and fidelity, lying at the heart of the family and the community, ensured the stability of the entire social structure. The woman, like Manon or Virginie or Julie, was the cohesive force. While the Enlightenment recognized the woman's natural (that is, physical) needs and attacked the unreasonable demands made on her through marriages of convenience and the like, it stopped short of granting her what men had—complete autonomy. Male dominance survived but only through the woman's death.

NOTES

1. Mlle de St. Yves is included among the heroines of eighteenth-century French novels even though *L'Ingénu* is not, strictly speaking, a novel. Although it begins like a *conte philosophique*, it does have a number of the characteristics of the novel. For a discussion of this, see English Showalter, Jr., *The Evolution of the French Novel, 1641-1782* (Princeton: Princeton University Press, 1972), p. 330.

2. Julie says, "I want to be chaste, for it is the primary virtue which fosters all the others." Jean-Jacques Rousseau, *La Nouvelle Héloïse*, edited by Henri Coulet and Bernard Guyon, in *Oeuvres complètes*, Bibliothèque de la Pléïade (Paris: Editions Gallimard, 1964), vol. 2, p. 357. Subsequent references to *La Nouvelle Héloïse* are all to this edition and are abbreviated as *NH*. All translations from the French are my own.

3. Voltaire, *L'Ingénu*, in *Romans et contes*, edited by Henri Benac (Paris: Garnier frères, 1960), pp. 239, 236. Subsequent references to *L'Ingénu* are all to this edition and are abbreviated as *I*.

4. Certainly the institution of marriage in the eighteenth century reinforces the paradoxical situation of the woman. Even lifelong alliances are not based on sexual desire or need. When Mme de Merteuil advises Mme de Volanges not to let Cécile marry Danceny, she says, "I don't see how an inclination, born one moment and dead the next, can have more force than the inalterable principles of decency, honor, and modesty." She would have Mme de Volanges believe that "it is not for a momentary illusion to determine the choice of our whole life." Choderlos de Laclos, *Les Liaisons dangereuses*, edited by Yves Le Hir (Paris: Garnier frères, 1961), pp. 240, 242. Subsequent references to *Les Liaisons dangereuses* are all to this edition and are abbreviated as *LD*.

5. Abbé Prévost, *Histoire du chevalier des Grieux et de Manon Lescaut*, edited by Frédéric Deloffre and Raymond Picard (Paris: Garnier frères, 1965), p. 20. Subsequent references to *Manon Lescaut* are all to this edition and are abbreviated as *ML*.

6. Nancy K. Miller, *The Heroine's Text: Readings in the French and English Novel, 1722-1782* (New York: Columbia University Press, 1980), p. 74.

7. Herbert Josephs, "*Manon Lescaut:* A Rhetoric of Intellectual Evasion," *The Romanic Review* 59 (1968):188-189.

8. Prévost, p. 41, n. 1.

9. In their introduction to *Manon Lescaut,* Deloffre and Picard offer a different interpretation of Manon's death: "In fact she lets herself die for her lover. But she doesn't have the strength to live for him. Along with the frivolities of Paris, her real reasons for living have been snatched away from her. . . . Yes, this delicate and fragile creature cannot bear transplantation; but perhaps just as much as discomfort and fear, it is the deprivation of frivolous pleasures and the gravity of a great love that kill her" (p. cl).

10. Bernardin de Saint-Pierre, *Paul et Virginie,* edited by Pierre Trahard (Paris: Garnier frères, 1964), pp. 134, 88. Subsequent references to *Paul et Virginie* are all to this edition and are abbreviated as *P&V.*

11. Florian, *Essai sur la pastorale* (1787), quoted in Vivienne Mylne, *The Eighteenth-Century French Novel: Techniques of Illusion* (Manchester: Manchester University Press, 1965), p. 250.

12. In "*Paul et Virginie* and the Myths of Death," *Publications of the Modern Language Association* 90 (1975):247-255, Clifton Cherpack speaks of the deep strain of pessimism in the novel, where death is valued more than life, and he considers the work a version of the Tristan myth. For him, "Virginie is not a girl who, through innate modesty, dies rather than show her body [but] the world-renouncer who, by giving up the world and embracing death, resembles the redeemer who must crucify himself in order to avoid corruption" (p. 254). From the perspective of the novel, however, Virginie's notion of purity is the result of her social conditioning, and while her values are presented in an exaggerated form, they do not differ radically from those of the other heroines.

13. Jean-Jacques Rousseau, *Les Confessions,* edited by Bernard Gagnebin and Marcel Raymond, in *Oeuvres complètes,* Bibliothèque de la Pléiade (Paris: Editions Gallimard, 1959), vol. 1, p. 435.

14. Since obstacles ensure the preservation of passion, then Julie's death, the ultimate obstacle, can also be viewed as the triumph of her love for Saint-Preux. Aram Vartanian makes this point in "The Death of Julie: A Psychological Post-mortem," *L'Esprit Créateur* 6 (1966): 77-84. According to him, "we understand that death was so attractive to Julie because it had become for her, involuntarily, an *affirmation of desire,* which was no longer possible under the self-imposed conditions of her virtuous life" (p. 82). "Erotic passion, checked in life, triumphs in and through death, the only way left open to it" (p. 83).

15. See Rousseau, p. 1357, n. 2.

16. Nancy Miller points out that Julie succumbs "to an irrational act of love, an irresponsible impulse that commits the 'je' of the daughter to death, to eternal dishonor" (p. 102).

17. *Lettres persanes,* by Montesquieu, edited by Paul Vernière (Paris: Garnier frères, 1960), p. 60, n. 1. The quote is taken from Chardin's *Voyages en Perse.* Subsequent references to the *Lettres persanes* are all to this edition and are abbreviated as *LP.*

❧ Alice M. Laborde

The Problem of Sexual Equality in Sadean Prose

THE GROWING INTEREST in the marquis de Sade's works has brought out a wealth of new interpretations and interesting ideas. The past decade has been particularly prolific in this respect. A glance at the bibliography offered by Françoise Rosart serves as a point of reference.[1] The critical bibliography compiled by Michel Delon for the years 1968-1978 proves the fecundity of these critical studies.[2] It illustrates the renewed appeal of Sade's works for an ever-larger audience. One will also note a new phenomenon: the participation of women critics in a field that, for two centuries, had been almost exclusively the domain of male scholarship. The lack of participation by women in publications such as the Sade special issue of *Yale French Studies* in 1965,[3] in the proceedings of the 1966 Colloquium of Aix-en-Provence,[4] or in a 1967 issue of *Tel Quel*[5] was a phenomenon to be noted since these publications were main events for Sade specialists and, as such, appropriately reflect a trend in the 1960s. In contrast, the October 1972 issue of *Europe* dedicated to Sade indicates a new trend; women scholars are now represented.[6] The Sade issue of *L'Esprit créateur* in 1975, with the exception of one article co-authored by Otis Fellows and Jenny Batley, is even exclusively written by women scholars.[7] The 1977-78 issue of *Obliques,* devoted to Sade studies, is also representative of a continuing female interest in Sade's works.[8]

Furthermore, for the first time in the history of Sade scholarship one can observe, as does Michel Delon, that the diversity, the scope, and the wealth of critical studies related to the marquis' works are becoming comparable in variety and volume to those devoted to any other philosopher of the period. "Among the most-researched French authors of the eighteenth century, Sade takes the sixth position after Voltaire, Rousseau and Diderot *ex aequo,* Marivaux, Montesquieu and Prévost [in order]," declares Delon.[9] These observations clearly show a kind of revolution in the habits of scholars who, until recently, confined their studies in that field to somewhat restricted investigations involving, almost exclusively, ethical problems (Klossowski is a good example of this tendency), while new and fruitful avenues of knowledge borrowed from anthropology, medicine, physio-psychology, linguistics, aesthetics, politics, and other fields have recently been largely responsible for a wider range of critical approaches.[10]

Have literary critics today reached a consensus on how to approach and evaluate sadean prose? Far from it and rightly so, for its readers remain baffled by its contradictions, by its ambiguities, and, above all, by the instinctive repulsion they feel at its very style. Many authors before Sade had been determined atheists, many had written pornographic material, and others had indulged in scenes of extreme cruelty; but no one had ever done so in such an outré style. The gargantuesque exploitation of women by the sadistic libertines is, indeed, one of the most striking characteristics of this production. This aspect is already obvious in *Justine;* it becomes predominant in *La Nouvelle Justine, L'Histoire de Juliette,* and *La Philosophie dans le boudoir.* No wonder that the majority of women readers have reacted violently against such a text—and they are not all declared feminists. A majority of their male counterparts have shared their criticisms and often initiated them. One will read with interest the work published by Jane Gallop, who denounces in Freudian terms the scandalous posture taken by sadistic libertines toward their female victims.[11] The studies done by Béatrice Didier, Nancy Miller, Anne Lacombe, Angela Carter, and Beatrice Fink, to cite only a few, are testimonies to these critics' sensitivity to this aspect of sadean prose.[12]

Was Sade an antifeminist? Did he try to avenge himself of the tortures imposed on him by his family, especially his mother-in-law? Or was he trying to point out certain of his convictions in the context of a particular historical, demographical, economical, social, political, and psychological makeup? As to his desire for revenge, we can emphatically answer no, for we know from the work done by his biographer Gilbert Lely that Sade the "Republican" had ample opportunity to send his mother-in-law and her whole family to the guillotine while he was in charge of the Section des Piques in Paris after 1789. To the contrary, he chose to destroy the proof of his family's emigration from France, an act of the highest gravity in the eyes of the Republicans of Paris.

In order to understand Sade's concept of relationships between men and women, one has to take into account his firm belief, years before Malthus, in the dangers of overpopulation and his conviction that France's problems were due to the incompetence of the king and to overpopulation. Indeed, in 1789 France was the most populated of European states. Sade's interest in contraceptive methods was not purely selfish but directly linked to his patriotic intention. The emphasis put by his libertines on unorthodox sexual practices can be partially explained in this context.

Sade was not a religious man, and he expressed his anticlerical views in a loud voice. His position was subversive from a religious standpoint, and it had far-reaching implications on the political scene. He saw the Church of France as a dangerous political force exploiting an incompetent king. At the time, the concept of the "divine right of kings" gave the Catholic church a powerful hand at the highest levels of French politics until the removal of Louis XVI. Sade also knew, as we do today from the work of sociologists such as Jean Portemer,[13] that certain institutions—convents and even prisons—were exploited in most instances not by the king and his police but by families for their own reasons (often financial, sometimes educational or correctional). Private citizens had the right to use such institutions in a manner well received by the Church and society for getting rid of their troublesome children or their enemies. Sade himself was a victim of such a practice for some thirty years of his adult life. He was not sent to prison under the king's order but at the request of his own family, who regularly paid the king a pension to keep Donatien in prison. Who were the most likely victims of such a practice? Women certainly were, since they depended more exclusively on their families for subsistence than men did. Here, we see a real and important link between Sade's own situation and the predicaments endured by his heroines. He saw himself as a victim of the Montreuil family, just as women were at the mercy of their own families. His letters to his wife, Renée, are an eloquent testimony of his state of mind.

However, such circumstantial evidence does not explain the form Sade gave to his own writing. In order to understand his intentions as a writer, we have to turn to his *Idée sur les romans,* a theoretical essay in which the writing of a novel is viewed as an indispensable study done to complete the work of the historian. The role played by the imagination in the writing of a novel is well emphasized, and the freedom of the writer is viewed as a nonnegotiable matter. On the other hand, Sade's sharp criticism of some of the best-known pornographic works of the time, Restif's production, for example, might surprise most readers, in view of what Sade himself was capable of writing in the same vein. What, then, were Sade's arguments in distinguishing his writings from the pornographic production of others? He viewed himself as a philosopher. He pretended to show the very matrix of the human soul, as well as the way society, with its hypocrisy and disguise, had transformed it for the worse. Among the natural fibers of human beings, he gave priority to a few *signs;* desire for power, cruelty, sexual impulse, and, last but not least, imaginative power. Sexual drive was not viewed as the main human attribute but one to reckon with, since it was at the level of sexual experience between individuals that the desire for power, cruelty, and imagination could best be exploited and given full rein. Is this concept a sufficient argument for explaining the endless injection of recurrent orgy scenes? Yes, to a certain extent, since sexual activity was understood by Sade as the unique human activity capable of enhancing the intrinsic motives for human behavior. Did such a concept excuse the scandalous cruelty of libertines toward their victims? Yes, in the limits of Sade's understanding that the natural physical phenomena were bound to the process of destruction/ creation with complete disregard for the sensitivity of the matter victimized by these natural phenomena.

However, Sade did not limit his ambitions to this pseudophilosophical explanation of his understanding of human signs. He also had ambitions as a novelist. He conceived a complex analogy between natural phenomena as he understood them after his reading of Lucretius' *De Rerum Natura* and the works of more recent materialist thinkers, whom he copied without shame. Jean Deprun has shown in a detailed analysis Sade's extensive borrowing from Voltaire, Fréret, and d'Holbach.[14] In the name of the "destructions" and the "transmutations" these authors observed in the physical world, Sade achieved a succession of narrative sequences exploiting these phenomena at the level of semantic manipulations. The result was not *Justine,* which was still in the manner of a mimesis and, for this reason, always rejected by Sade as an indecent piece of literature, as were, for the same reason, Restif's novels. However, *La Nouvelle Justine* and *L'Histoire de Juliette,* taken in their totality, were not representative of a commemoration of historical events but were merely imaginative creations in which the unit of gesture was reproduced *ad infinitum* in order to suggest the multiplicity of options for action and also to reveal the accelerated cadence of the options in a manner analogical to the movement of the incessant "destructions" and "transmutations" observed at the level of atomic elements. If this assessment is correct, classifying sadean prose as a mere pornographic exercise is difficult. Passages of *La Nouvelle Justine* and *L'Histoire de Juliette,* taken out of context, would indeed be pornographic; but the complex intentions of the author, as expressed in his complete novels and the semiosis he achieved, seem to call for a different evaluation. To reinforce this conclusion, one would want to consider the profound evolution of the libertines' attitude toward their female victims. Justine is, and will forever stay, a victim; but Juliette evolves from the role of victim to that of equal partner of her libertine educator. The historical objection will be that one was a virtuous woman while the other was without morality. Sade would answer this objection, as did Diderot in his essay on sexual morality entitled *Supplément au voyage de Bougainville,* by saying that sexual activity is not a moral activity per se. It is, first of all, a physical activity decided by specific chemical and physiological conditions that, in turn, have far-reaching demographical implications and considerable political consequences. Sade would not deny the ethical implications of a given sexual conduct; but he would view it within a particular sociological and moral context, and, as such, he would consider it relative.

Sade did not reach these conclusions right away. His work shows a slow evolution; his "system" was offered little by little. At a certain point the absurdity of the partial or total destruction of all victims by the libertines became so evident to him that the "philosopher" had to find a solution to this dilemma. It is at this point that the concept of "apathy" became prevalent and the notion of an equal partnership between male libertines and women victims took the form that is presented explicitly in *L'Histoire de Juliette* and, more theoretically, in *La Philosophie dans le boudoir.*[15]

The French poet Guillaume Apollinaire, who read Sade attentively, was one of the first to point out, as early as the beginning of our century, the importance of *La Philosophie dans le boudoir* to our understanding of Sade's position toward women's rights. Maurice Tourné in 1972[16] and Béatrice Didier in 1977 offered a view of Sade's concept of women based on a reading of his works that corroborated Apollinaire's observations. However, these critics did not address themselves specifically to the study of *La Philosophie dans le boudoir,* which represents the cornerstone of Sade's interpretation of nature and human relations. In a note in his Introduction to *L'Oeuvre du marquis de Sade,* Apollinaire suggested that this novel is capital, that it is the *sadicum opus* par excellence:

> The Marquis de Sade, the freest spirit who ever existed, had, on the subject of woman, some particular ideas and wanted her as free as man. Those ideas, which will someday be brought out, gave birth to a double novel: *Justine* and *Juliette.* It is no accident that the Marquis chose heroines, and not heroes. Justine is the woman of the past, enslaved, miserable, and less than human; Juliette, to the contrary, represents the new woman that he envisioned, a being not yet conceived, who emanates from humanity, who will have wings and who will renew the universe.[17]

The importance of such a judgment is not shared by all, even today. The Sade specialist Gilbert Lely contradicts this critical judgment. Speaking about Sade's pamphlet *Français, encore un effort si vous voulez être républicains* and evidently negating the relationship between this text and the rest of the novel, Lely declared:

> This long pamphlet, *arbitrarily* [my emphasis] inserted in an exquisitely constructed whole, is not without jeopardizing the harmony of *La*

> *Philosophie dans le boudoir.* . . . It is possible that Sade, having at first destined it to be a separate publication, felt that he must include it in his work, in order to rejuvenate both its fiction and morals, already excessively perfumed with the fragrance of the Old Regime.[18]

Gilbert Lely has quite evidently not perceived the political and feminist implications of *La Philosophie dans le boudoir,* but it cannot be explained as only a frivolous *passe-temps* or a pedagogical essay. It represents an authentic call to a rebellious act of subversion against a particular political and economic status quo.

The ambiguity of the message suggested by Sade in this novel is indicated by the author himself, who, first in his introduction, directs his appeal to the lewdness of the libertines and proclaims that his novel will, in many ways, delight, refresh, and tease their own needs for lewdness. On the opposite page, however, Sade took the time to suggest another aspect of the novel when he wrote, "Reading to be prescribed by the mother to her daughter." This formula suggests that the book should be considered not only as a pedagogical essay but also as an occasion for concerted efforts on the part of women, because the author implies that mother and daughter, as women, share certain particular concerns about life, concerns that are typically feminine.

La Philosophie dans le boudoir can be viewed as a three-part discussion of the question of woman's right to equality. In the first part, the author offers the details of the problem regarding the rights and duties of the married woman, and in the last part, he attempts to expose the rights and duties of the young girl toward her parents. These two parts are linked by the theoretical interlude of *Français, encore un effort si vous voulez être républicains,* which serves as an exposé of the philosophical, ethical, and political background susceptible to justifying the claims of women to a status of equality with men.

In view of the status of women in eighteenth-century France, it is understandable that Sade's most important political attacks are against the institution of marriage as it then existed and against the unchallenged authority of parents over their children. Sade denounces marriage as a means (morally approved and legally ratified by the laws of the country) to achieve the parents' own ambition and, often, to satisfy their own personal greed. Marriage then was based on the dowry brought by the bride and too often became a kind of business contract between two families without the consent of the children. Most of the time, the bridal couple had no knowledge of the details of the transaction, and the future bride, especially, was judged unprepared to understand the subtleties of such an arrangement. Sade's presentation and criticism of the facts are in no way contrary to what historians of the period report. In fact, he had firsthand knowledge of this kind of transaction since his own marriage to Renée de Montreuil was negotiated by his father—against Donatien's will—for reasons that were financially convenient to the elder Sade. What the marquis suggests here, and with good reason, is that too many marriages were the occasion for exploitation of children by their own parents. He then denounces the fact that, in marrying, the young girl does not gain freedom of expression or the right to become a first-class citizen in her own right (like her husband). Instead, she exchanges one form of servitude and tutelage for another—a fact duly recorded by sociologist Jean Portemer. Sade's criticism is definitely expressed in terms of the respect due to the sensibility and intellectual capacity of woman. Her condition as a young girl or a married woman should not negate her natural privilege, which is to develop and fully exercise her sensibility and her intellectual potential (*P.B.*, p. 67).

La Philosophie dans le boudoir is also Sade's version of a ready reference for the many practical uses (orthodox or unorthodox) of certain well-circumscribed anatomical organs; Sade mentions the names and functions he knows as accurately as he can. In this sense, he believes he is making a scientific contribution to the question of sexuality and human reproduction. In terms of twentieth-century scientific knowledge, his efforts are not always accurate; but in the context of eighteenth-century scientific knowledge, he is certainly more in tune with the reality of the time than was Diderot. The latter gave detailed descriptions of the organs involved, but his limitations were evident when it came to what was known, at the end of the century, as the problem of generation. However, both authors imparted the same role to woman in procreation, and it is definitely secondary to that of the man, since they expressed the belief that woman fed the fetus while man provided the origin of life. Diderot gave the last and best account of what he understood of this phenomenon in his *Eléments de physiologie*, written between 1782 and 1784.[19] Sade offered his own account of this complex question in *La Philosophie dans le boudoir*, published for the first time in 1795.

The marquis' understanding of the role of woman in procreation is most enlightening since it perfectly explains his own attitude toward motherhood, which Sade so violently attacks in one of the most indigestible parts of *La Philosophie dans le boudoir*. Since the mother does not give life but supports it by feeding the embryo and then the fetus, Sade considers her solely responsible for perpetuating life in bringing the embryo to maturity. For Sade, this female physiological function is the most "unpatriotic" of all, since he is firmly convinced that France and all of Europe are overpopulated and always have been so. (The *disettes* and famines that plagued Europe at regular intervals might be considered the origin of such a view.[20])

Indeed, it makes one shiver to think of the horrible massacre performed by Sade's libertines on fertile women. We have a typical example of cruelty toward motherhood in *La Philosophie dans le boudoir*, when Mme de Mistival is outrageously attacked by her own daughter, Eugénie. From Sade's perspective, this attack is a symbolic gesture against all the virtues and principles that Mme de Mistival stands for and respects. The essence of patriotism, which, for a woman, is to ensure the perpetuation of the race, is mocked. Obedience and submission to men and particularly to her husband, virtues diligently practiced by the heroine, are ridiculed. Her negation of her own sexuality and of her own desires is exposed as contrary to her natural interests. Her concern for the respect of moral principles established by the society to which she belongs is also ridiculed. In the same vein, the symbolism of love, generosity, purity, and fecundity represented by Mary, the mother of Christ, is, under these circumstances, another bastion of hope that Sade was determined to destroy.

That explains his incredible attack on any woman exemplifying these traits, but it does not mean that Sade was not interested in the fate of women. While Diderot expressed a sort of discouragement in the face of women's destiny and could offer, as sole hope, what he perceived as the concomitant evolution of economics and politics with that of female status in his essay *Sur les femmes* (1772), Sade built a case for women's liberation. That definitely took place in the works he wrote after 1791, for it was then that his most important production and his philosophical system, as such, were conceived. We can see *120 Journées de Sodome*, written in the Bastille before 1789, as a stepping stone, as was *Justine*, published in June 1791, but in no way are they their author's last word.

The years after 1789 are important in Sade's life, for many reasons. First he was freed; then he engaged in active political life and became an energetic champion of social reforms̃new responsibilities that tested his humanitarian nature. It was also a time to test his own moral principles. Confronted with the extraordinary opportunity to destroy, *en bloc*, those who had made him suffer for so long, mainly his wife's family, he chose to protect them and spare them the ultimate punishment reserved for *ci-devants* who had emigrated. He could even have sought revenge against his wife, who had obviously abandoned him after July 14, 1789 and refused to consult with him on the painful question of his mother's estate; but he did not do so. Some would say that he was suddenly redeemed by the love of a simple and shy woman, Marie-Constance Quesnet, a former actress whom he had met in 1790. That would be a simplistic explanation for a long-term attitude toward the humanitarian problems that would confront Sade as a member of the Section des Piques in Paris, in 1793. The companionship and the understanding of Marie-Constance Quesnet certainly played a role in the productive life of Sade, but he was also then, at 50, a more mature man, who had time to reflect on human nature as well as his own. He did not settle for a method of expression that would conform with the norm *en vigueur*, but the very style Sade chose has misled many of his critics until today.[21] To a certain extent, that is unfortunate because it has often deemphasized or overshadowed some of the implications of Sade's works with regard to political and humanitarian problems. The reading of the marquis' works is a difficult enterprise; the obvious, in this case, is only part of the message. This difficulty explains the profusion of interpretations as well as the reader's confusion. Sade is a man of the eighteenth century and, as such, practiced mystification with delight. However, his unique style should not blind us when it comes to appreciating the humanitarian and political implications of his text.

The political allusion is particularly obvious, for example, when Sade demands (*P.B.*, p. 67) that at the age of seven (called in France, even today, *l'âge de raison*) girls be relieved of paternal dependence and receive a national education, the same education for all girls—peasant, bourgeois, and noble alike. A revolutionary idea for its time, it would have involved a deep cultural change coupled with a complex economic revolution, because it would have eliminated child labor, particularly in the rural areas. Sade also advocated a form of public education rather than the private one that was often the case in the eighteenth century, especially for girls. Public funds would provide the means of implementing such an education. Women would receive their education from age seven to fifteen, an enormous span of time for a population whose longevity was considerably shorter than ours. The period would cut short the time of maternity for young women, but Sade is consistent because his goal, in the long run, is to limit the number of births.

In order to understand the full implications of Sade's plea for liberated sexual activity for women, one should consider the position of woman in eighteenth-century France in the light of the treatment imposed upon Manon Lescaut, for example. For her sexual adventures with a certain number of well-known government officials, her society sent Manon first to prison, then to the hospital with prostitutes, and, finally, to Louisiana in exile. Manon was not a prostitute, in the strict meaning of the term, but she received the treatment reserved for prostitutes at that time. Des Grieux, who had shared in Manon's larceny and was himself responsible for the death of a man, promptly recovered his freedom when his father decided, at last, to come to his son's rescue in Paris. Such evidently discriminatory treatment of women is, for Sade, the occasion to encourage women to rebel openly or, at least, to learn ways to hide their own deeds. While Diderot was shocked and bewildered by the proclivity of women to hide, lie, and cheat, Sade felt that these means were a form of self-protection for individuals unprotected by laws and exploited by society.

The long diatribe against marriage in *La Philosophie dans le boudoir* was then born of Sade's complex intentions, first, toward the question of demography, and, second, toward the question of male-female sexual equality, mainly women's equal right to freedom of expression—sexual activity and pleasure being considered as one aspect of freedom of expression. "My husband is no more stained by my debauchery than I am by his" (*P.B.*, p. 77), declares Mme de Saint-Ange. This observation perfectly describes the situation of women in the eighteenth century; it points out the difference between what was expected of a man and of a woman. Sade suggests here that women's infidelity is to be regarded, in marriage, in the same way as men's infidelity and that the double standard reflected by the laws of the country against female culprits should not be tolerated. (The punishment for female infidelity then was prison, exile, or sequestration in a convent, while male infidelity was considered a peccadillo.)

When a child is born out of wedlock, Sade suggests that the mother herself should decide whether to keep or reject her child. Speaking of infanticide, Mme de Saint-Ange declares: "There is, on earth, no right more certain than that of mothers upon their children" (*P.B.*, p. 115). If the mother decides to keep her child, Sade, in a revolutionary view, regards her estate as the child's property (*P.B.*, p. 78). In Diderot's *La Religieuse*, Suzanne Simonin was an illegitimate child and, as such, was denied any part of her mother's estate. The positive aspect of Sade's view is to protect the child from any form of prejudice as a result of being a bastard.

However, his criticism of marriage does not mean that Sade wanted the institution abolished. To the contrary, he saw that the secularization of marriage achieved by the Revolutionaries was a positive reform capable of strengthening a useful institution.

Sade's criticism, not only of religious marriage but of the Church in general, was as systematic as that raised by other philosophers, Voltaire and Diderot, for example. He denounced, as they did, the exploitation of religious concepts, principles, cults, ceremonial institutions, etc., for goals that, in the long run, were political in nature or were definitely foreign to the moral and religious interests of the believers (*P.B.*, p. 192). The essential criticism made by Sade against the former monarchic government is that it allowed the interdependence of Church and State powers (*P.B.*, p. 193). In order to avoid this problem in the new Republican state, Sade suggested that the education of the child be first social and civic before being religious (P.B., p. 204): "Civic laws must replace the fear of hell" (P.B., p. 203). "Replace the deific idiocies with which you tire your children's young organs by excellent social principles," he exhorted (P.B., p. 204). Sade did not wish to eliminate all religion or all religious ceremonies, but he wanted to secularize practices that were, in the past, under the sole jurisdiction of the Church. If man had to have a cult, it should be one adapted to the civic condition of the Republican. In this instance, Sade evidently followed in the footsteps of Rousseau. The main idea is that in a Republican state, "religion must be based on ethics, and not the other way around" (P.B., p. 191). In the context of eighteenth-century France, this criticism is more than pertinent. It is directly related to the question of the status of women since religious principles, concepts, and ceremonies were duly exploited as part of the institution of marriage.

The numerous observations made on the civil condition of women earlier in this book amply justify the assertion that *Français, encore un effort si vous voulez être républicains* is not a piece hastily added for political reasons (or, as suggested by some critics, even a piece written by another author). It represents, in fact, the main intentions of Sade, which are to make a plea in favor of the equality of men and women in matters of sexuality and to stress the intolerable situation of women. Sade's stand is explicitly expressed in the following passage, which has too often been overlooked by readers:

> Never can an act of possession be exercised upon a free being; it is equally unjust to exclusively possess a woman as it is to own slaves; all men are born free, all have equal rights: let us never lose sight of these principles; accordingly, no legitimate right can ever be given to one sex, which would allow it to take possession of the other, and never can one sex or one class arbitrarily possess the other. [P.B., p. 231]

It is too easy to forget these denunciations and their political implications. They nevertheless are the outcry of a man who has realized that half of humanity is under the power of the other half and has no way out because the legal and moral powers of the country have no desire to change the status quo.

NOTES

1. *Obliques* 12-13 (1977):277-309.
2. Michel Delon, "Dix ans d'études sadiennes, 1968-1978," *Dix-Huitième Siècle* 11 (1979):393-426.
3. *Yale French Studies* 35 (1965).

4. *Le Marquis de Sade*. Colloque d'Aix-en-Provence sur le marquis de Sade, le 19 et 20 février 1966 (Paris: Armand Colin, 1968).

5. *Tel Quel* 28 (1967).

6. *Europe* 522 (October 1972).

7. *L'Esprit créateur*, 15/4 (Winter 1975).

8. *Obliques* 12-13 (1977).

9. *Dix-Huitième Siècle* 11 (1979):393, 395.

10. The studies published by the scholars assembled in Aix-en-Provence in the summer of 1966 were particularly representative of a new scientific approach to Sade scholarship, which proved most fruitful and inspired many of their colleagues.

11. Jane Gallop, "Impertinent Questions: Iriguay, Sade, Lacan," *Sub-Stance* 26 (1980):57-67.

12. Béatrice Didier has published a number of articles on Sade, among which we find "Inceste et écriture chez Sade," in *Les Lettres nouvelles* 3 (May-June 1972):150-158; "Le Château intérieur de Sade," in *Europe* 522 (October 1972): 54-64; "Sade et Don Juan," in *Obliques* 5 (1974):67-71; "Sade et le dialogue philosophique," in *Cahiers de l'association internationale des études françaises* 24 (May 1972):59-74. She has also written a book entitled *Sade. Une écriture du désir* (Paris: Denoël, Gonthier, 1976). Nancy Miller has published "Novels of Innocence: Fictions of Loss," in *Eighteenth-Century Studies* 2/3 (Spring 1978):325-329, as well as "Juliette and the Posterity of Prosperity," in *L'Esprit créateur* (Winter 1975):413-424. Anne Lacombe has published "Du Théâtre au roman. Sade," in *Studies on Voltaire and the Eighteenth Century* 129 (1975):115-143 as well as "Les Infortunes de la vertu, le conte et la philosophie," in *L'Esprit créateur* 15 (Winter 1975):425-437. Angela Carter has published a book, *The Sadeian Woman* (New York: Pantheon, 1979). Among Beatrice Fink's writings on Sade we find "Food as Subject, Activity and Symbol in Sade," in *The Romanic Review* 65 (1974):96-102; "The Case for a Political System in Sade," in *Studies on Voltaire and the Eighteenth Century* 88 (1972):493-512; "Sade and Cannibalism," in *L'Esprit créateur* 15 (1975):403-412; "Sade's Libertine: A Pluralistic Approach," in *Eighteenth-Century Life* 2 (December 1975):34-37; "Narrative Techniques and Utopian Structures in Sade's *Aline et Valcour*," in *Science Fiction Studies* 7 (March 1980):73-79; "Ambivalence in the Gynogram: Sade's Utopian Woman," in *Women and Literature* 7 (Winter 1979):24-37.

13. Jean Portemer, "Le Statut de la femme en France," in *Recueils de la société Jean Bodin* 12 (1962):447-513.

14. Jean Deprun, "Quand Sade récrit Fréret, Voltaire et d'Holbach," in *Obliques* 12-13 (1977):263-266.

15. Marquis de Sade, *La Philosophie dans le boudoir* (Paris: Union générale d'éditions, Collection 10/18, 1972). All subsequent references will be to this edition, the most recent and readily available, and will be followed, in the text, by the initials *P.B.* and page numbers.

16. Maurice Tourné, "Pénélope et Circé ou les mythes de la femme dans l'oeuvre de Sade," *Europe* 522 (October 1972):71-88.

17. Guillaume Apollinaire, Introduction to *L'Oeuvre du marquis de Sade* (Paris: Bibliothèque des Curieux, 1909), pp. 17, 18, and 20n. The citation and all subsequent ones are my own translation.

18. *Oeuvres complètes du Marquis de Sade*, edited by Gilbert Lely (Paris: Cercle du livre précieux, 1966), vol. 2, p. 50.

19. Denis Diderot, *Éléments de physiologie*, edited by Jean Mayer (Paris: Librairie Marcel Didier, 1964), p. xv.

20. Sade points out the dangers of unchecked demographic progression: "One of the primary vices of this government consists in a much too large population and such surplus can hardly represent riches for the State. These supernumerary beings are like parasitic branches which, because they live at the expense of the trunk, always end up exhausting it" (P.B., p. 62). Malthus had not yet published his *Essay Relative to the Principle of Population*, which appeared in 1798, but we find the same preoccupation expressed by both authors.

21. I have already dealt with this aspect of Sade's production in chapter 3 of my book *Sade romancier* (Neuchâtel: La Baconnière, 1974).

🦋 Vera G. Lee

The Edifying Examples

ACCORDING TO CURRENT DICTIONARIES, to edify means to inspire virtue through an instructive example.[1] Until Rousseau, eighteenth-century French fiction might appear more intent on amusing, exciting, or shocking readers than impressing and teaching them. Yet it contains examples enough of male and female characters throughout the century ostensibly intended to be admired for their goodness and, conceivably, imitated.

Who were the edifying females? In what way were they inspiring? What common denominators did they share? Some answers to these questions can add to our understanding of the fictional and nonfictional female of the French Enlightenment.

Most commonly, to qualify as edifying, female characters fit into two main categories: *virtue rewarded* and *virtue regained* (through repentance, reform, or rehabilitation).[2] Since virtue is a prerequisite in both cases, it would be well to identify the virtuous woman of eighteenth-century French fiction.

To begin with, she would usually exhibit traits that corresponded to the moral views shared by "enlightened" bourgeois *philosophes* and the fashionable society they knew. Virtue, as those intellectuals understood it, had become a vague, elastic, and undemanding quality. For both sexes, it called for indulgence, occasional beneficence, and, above all, an oft-expressed adoration of the ideal of goodness.

Rare is the female character in Voltaire's plays who does not pay tribute to the ideal of virtue. Jocaste in *Oedipe*, Lise in *L'Enfant prodigue*, Artémire, or Marianne are goodness incarnate without necessarily having to perform laudable actions, for they are solidly in favor of the ideal. Rousseau's Julie speaks incessantly of virtue and honor in spite of the clandestine trysts she arranges in her parents' absence. Rosalie of the Chevalier Yon's *Femmes de mérite* has loose morals but a talent for praising and admiring virtue. In the latter part of the century, especially "good" female characters like Rousseau's Julie or Bernardin's Virginie add to their unfailing admiration of virtue concrete demonstrations of beneficence toward deprived or unhappy fellow creatures.

But for females, such vague proofs of goodness do not suffice. Their sex must fulfill first and foremost two stringent prerequisites:

obedience and chastity. Voltaire's compliant Nanine refers to her *devoir* almost as frequently as she does to her *vertu*. An inevitable submission to authority prompts Virginie to utter the words "All you . . . who control my fate,"[3] and almost any admirable daughter or wife in novels and plays will offer proofs of dutiful acquiescence.

More important than obedience, and more directly relevant to the notion of feminine virtue, is the rule of strict abstinence from sexual intercourse except with one's own husband. Even in the permissive Age of Enlightenment, virtue, for females, specifically meant chastity and fidelity. When it came to the stylish upper classes, chastity in young girls seemed far more plausible than fidelity in mature married women, who were expected to take lovers. It stands to reason then that a large number of fictional females are adolescent ingénues whose goodness—more precisely, innocence—rests largely on a technical virginity. But whether young and virginal like Jeannette of Mouhy's *Paysanne parvenue* and Angélique of Challe's *Illustres Françaises* or mature and faithful like Mme Parangon of Restif's *Paysan perverti* and Laclos's Mme de Tourvel, they interest readers less through their chastity or fidelity than through their potential fall. Recognizing the boring nature of continued goodness, an author surrounds his heroine with threatening and inviting pitfalls, tantalizing readers with the implicit question "Will she or won't she?"

Quite naturally, the criteria of obedience and chastity encourage the creation of female characters who mainly project weakness and vulnerability. Although such passive and negative characteristics would not, at first, seem likely qualities for constructing fine moral examples, they can be positive assets when applied to one of the two patterns of edification.

VIRTUE REWARDED

Obedience, chastity, and fidelity will nearly always reap a profit in sentimental comedies. *Nanine, L'Ecossaise, Le Préjugé à la mode, Le Père de famille,* and the myriad *drames* of the late century demonstrate to what extent such moral investments can ultimately pay off. True, in tragedies and novels, the chances of reward for such constraints are far less sure. Nevertheless, in the realm of the novel a resolute virgin has excellent prospects for success. Mouhy's Jeannette, and Angélique of "Angélique et Contamine" in Challe's *Illustres Françaises* are cases in point. To paraphrase Pascal, by betting on virginity, their risks are finite and their potential gains infinite. If they give in to men, they stand to lose everything; if they manage to hold out, they may eventually make a fine match, that is, win the social jackpot. And so they do. Marivaux's Marianne learned the advantages of a hold-out strategy from her dying foster mother; and, clearly, Mme Riccoboni's, or, for that matter, any finished version of Marivaux's novel must have the heroine enter a brilliant marriage with her virginity intact.[4]

Like the staunch virgin, the eternally faithful wife can find happiness and glory at the denouement. Constance in *Le Préjugé à la mode*, the loving spouse in Loaisel de Tréogate's *Dolbreuse*, and other patient, though abused, wives may have the smug satisfaction one day of seeing their errant husbands sink before them on repentant knees.

Since mature wives and mothers of Enlightenment fiction, like the young, nubile female characters, operate out of weakness and vulnerability, their means of achieving their just rewards are limited indeed. According to Nivelle's character Damon, "to defend her rights, a woman has only her fidelity, her weakness, and her tears."[5] So like virgins such as Marianne or Angélique, older women often bend their efforts to manipulating those around them. Marmontel's heroines in *La Femme comme il y en a peu* and *La Bonne Mère* owe their successes entirely to subtle and effective manipulation. In *La Nouvelle Héloïse*, Julie continually (and successfully) maneuvers her lover as though he were a child. Often the rewards of virtue go, not to those with the finest characters, but to those most adept at playing the virtue game.

VIRTUE REGAINED

In defending his love story, Rousseau maintained that a novel that depicts a woman's downfall and subsequent reform is more believable —and, therefore, more morally effective—than one that merely describes her continuing virtue.[6] Although readers may disagree about its effectiveness, Rousseau's own technique was, indeed, to chronicle his heroine's sexual capitulation and, later, her repentance and reform.

Like Julie's redemption, the about-face of many fallen female characters might seem superfluous or contradictory when we consider that sexual surrender could be seen as a virtuous act in itself. Mme de Graffigny, Mme Riccoboni, Baculard d'Arnaud, and other writers of the time constantly impress on their readers that goodness is inextricably tied to sentiment. A virtuous woman can only be one who feels, who sympathizes, who behaves with indulgence and generosity. In novels especially, good, kind hearts can provide justification for scores of right-minded ladies who fall into sin. Says Julie, apropos of her seduction, "love itself would have spared me . . . it was pity that ruined me."[7] Pity breaks the resistance of enamored females in novels of Mouhy or Crébillon. It leads even the most chaste of girls, Virginie, to the edge of the precipice, when she tells Paul: "Do as you will with me. Unvirtuous girl: I could stand your caresses but not your pain."[8] Always the most effective masculine ploy is Valmont's piece of psychological blackmail in his seduction of Mme de Tourvel: "Eh bien! la mort!"

But no matter how powerful the argument that a good woman is a sympathetic, giving one, the traditional moral code still serves as the gauge of proper female behavior, in fiction as in society; thus, the popularity, especially in post-Rousseauist literature, of plots that trace a woman's dramatic fall followed by her repentance and reform. Such reversal of unacceptable conduct appears in a variety of ways. Beaumarchais's *La Mère coupable* concerns a married countess (formerly Rosine of *Le Barbier de Séville*) who, after one single infidelity, spends years anguishing in guilt. Marmontel's *La Mauvaise Mère* describes a mother's rejection of one of her sons and her eleventh-hour change of heart. Such women are joined by an impressive list of repentant prostitutes, including the heroine of the anonymous *Confessions d'une courtisane*, the chevalier Yon's Rosalie, Rousseau's Lauretta Pisana, Diderot's Mme des Arcis and others. For remorseful wayward females of Enlightenment fiction, the prognosis can be excellent. Some ex-prostitutes, such as Lauretta, may not make the fine marriage granted to others, such as Mme des Arcis; but they, like lesser sinners, can don brand new haloes in the last pages of their story. And they often have the last word—albeit from their deathbeds (as, for example, in Elie de Beaumont's *Lettres du marquis de Roselle*).

Virtue regained can appear a facile means of erasing past sin with present probity. In many cases, characters can indulge themselves and not have to mend their ways until the final paragraphs of their story. This eating-one's-cake-and-having-it system may not convert a female public to an exemplary life, but it neatly solves the famous literary *dilemne*[9] by titillating readers and theoretically edifying them in the same work.

If the system of virtue regained does not provide us with profoundly inspirational or edifying examples, virtue rewarded seems hardly more convincing a device. The deserving wives of *Le Préjugé à la mode* or *Dolbreuse*, the sweet and innocent ingénues of *L'Ecossaise* or *Le Père de famille* offer us their histories of long and patient suffering, and their rewards seem less a positive source of joy than a quick end to slow pain. On the other hand, a tale of safeguarded virginity recompensed, customarily also chock full of anguish and danger, impresses us less with the heroine's virtue than with her shrewdness in saving her trump card and winning the game. For a Marianne, strategy and compromise replace the notion of goodness. She prefers the admiration of others to their esteem, and, in order to survive and succeed, she will never carry truth or self-sacrifice to an extreme. "Edifying" and "rewards" in such cases relate merely to the mundane goal of socioeconomic arrival.

All considered, in the search for impressive models of feminine virtue, clearly, it is less the category, less the conventional pattern of edification, that matters than the author's intent and, especially, talent. The two most obvious cases of writers with both the aim and the ability to create memorable edifying female characters are Rousseau and his disciple, Bernardin de Saint-Pierre.

Julie

Julie stands apart from Virginie and from most of the edifying females of her century, in that she has a personality and, indeed, a strong one. The virtuous young ingenues of Voltaire's plays, all frail reeds, are, practically speaking, interchangeable. In novel and theatre, the patient wife and mother, no matter how mature, usually plays a passive, even infantile role, complying with the wishes of her husband, the traditional *paterfamilias* and a sort of surrogate father to her.[10] This is true of characters such as the countess in *La Mère coupable* or Julie's own mother in *La Nouvelle Héloïse*. Yet Julie herself, despite her authoritarian father and the paternal figure who replaces him as her husband, breaks the mold. It is she who, as a young girl, takes all the initiative in her relationship with her tutor-lover. It is she who protests, resists, and revolts against her father, even to the point of planning to use her pregnancy to maneuver the inflexible baron into a shotgun wedding. Later, rather than regret her disobedience, she laments that it did not work. True, Julie does capitulate. She submits to Saint-Preux out of some combination of sensuality, love, sympathy, inexperience, and a lot of free time. She gives in to her father because of pity and guilt. Yet, in each case, she chooses her course of action— indeed, she uses the word *choix* (p. 323) in referring to her sexual surrender—instead of blaming her own blindness, the tyranny of others, or destiny. If Julie agrees to marry the man of her father's choice, she first sets the terms; she will do so only with Saint-Preux's consent. Later, on the subject of her vow of fidelity, she resolutely declares, "I shall keep it until death" (p. 334).

Julie's will and her lucidity represent two sides of the same coin. She rarely deludes herself, but if she does, she eventually sets herself straight. Intent on examining her own motives, she is in constant communication with her super-ego. She may tell herself for years that she no longer loves Saint-Preux. In her final "posthumous" letter to him, however, she explains her self-imposed illusion as a very "practical" and "useful" means of keeping herself out of danger. She had simply manufactured and put on an effective psychological chastity belt. Earlier—and younger—when love was too attractive and compelling for Julie to deal with through her lucidity and will, she "solved" the problem by handing it over to Saint-Preux, that is, by asking him to protect her virginity. Yet, despite Julie's sensuality, her lapses, her self-imposed periods of blindness, or her deliberate renunciation of will, most of her letters throughout the novel impress the reader with her strength and her sober, rational insights. Mature since her hour of birth, Julie is always right—even when she is wrong.

In what way can this strong-minded character serve as an edifying example?

During the course of *La Nouvelle Héloïse*, we find Julie torn between two species of virtue: *virtue as sentiment*, the passion of sacred love, a secular, preromantic religion, and *virtue as honor*, the Christian code of purity, monitored by the ever-watchful eyes of God. Her love for Saint-Preux is, at one and the same time, sacred passion and sheer dishonor. Yet, as she says, "love and innocence were equally necessary to me" (p. 323). Faced with marriage to Wolmar, she finds the Corneillean contradiction unacceptable, and so she sacrifices love. But Julie, a product of the emotional Rousseau and an increasingly sentimental climate, cannot offer readers an unflinchingly Spartan reform. Instead, she must find a way to reconcile the two kinds of virtue, and she finally does. After having had the pleasure of passion and the justification of moral and religious reform, she not only demonstrates her susceptibility to Saint-Preux after she marries, but also, on her deathbed, she openly avows her passion for him. Although still technically Mme de Wolmar, her confession causes her no guilt, since she is leaving this world for another one that will undoubtedly reunite her with her lover (and not her husband). Julie satisfies both definitions of virtue and, in a sense, has the best of both worlds. As she puts it, "my virtue remains spotless and my love without remorse" (p. 729).

According to Rousseau, Julie's example would prove useful (particularly to a mature, female reading public and married couples[11]) because of her moral rehabilitation, her pattern of virtue lost and found once again.[12] But if his heroine came to serve as a model for her time, it was less in the story of her fall and redemption than in her image as a new and admirable species of female. This was the model that served as an inspiration for the late eighteenth- and early nineteenth-century woman, real and fictional: Rousseau's lady of Clarens, admired for her devotion as wife and mother, for her simplicity, sincerity, generosity and sentiment, her love of nature, her modesty and feminine grace.

Virginie

Bernardin de Saint-Pierre's character, like Rousseau's, is "feeling and virtuous" and similarly demonstrates a certain strength in protesting an arranged marriage; but beyond that, she bears no resemblance at all to Saint-Preux's mistress. Virginie's creator, devoting all his efforts to rendering external rather than internal realities, does not endow his heroine with the personality or psychological complexities of a Julie.

If the two-dimensional Virginie is edifying, it is largely because of two things: her beatific morality and her fate in the last pages of her story. As a pre-teen-ager, Virginie obviously deserves high marks for conduct and attitude. It is perhaps unnecessary to recall her sweet, if naïve, befriending of a Negro slave woman, her presents of home-cooked wheat cakes to poor whites, or, in general, her mania for doing good. And it would no doubt be kinder to pass in silence over some of her more unmemorable homilies, such as "one must not do a thing, not even a good deed, without consulting one's parents" (p. 95) or "bread that comes from a wicked person fills your mouth with gravel" (p. 89). Her behavior and moral stance seem so predictably admirable that readers may be surprised to find her feeling less than saintly under the stress of puberty and a hot climate.

More significant than such examples, however, is Virginie's final destiny, that is, her plight at sea and her solution to it, for there is the episode with the deepest moral implications and the greatest dramatic impact on the reader. There Virginie is presented with her most important existential choice: to undress or not to undress. It must certainly have impressed readers throughout the years that Virginie was so chaste she preferred keeping her clothes on to saving her life, and many must have pondered over what conclusions to draw. Did it mean that if society had not dragged Virginie off to corrupt Paris, but let her stay in a state of nature, she would not have killed herself because of an acquired social etiquette that demanded modesty? It is true that as a child, in her island paradise, she was quick to pull her skirt up like an umbrella to shield Paul and herself from the rain. But later, even on that same island, she proved to be a modest adolescent indeed. Whatever Bernardin's intention, it is certain that he did not mean to chastise Virginie for her reluctance to disrobe. Yet Sade could have used the situation to greater advantage.

Julie convinces readers mainly because of her essence; Virginie largely because of her fate. In death, both women, almost saintly figures, edify through their incarnation of *virtue sublime*.[13] Julie's death, however, offers her a complacent happiness and peace, while Virginie's, on the contrary, provides shock and sheer tragedy. Fitting neither the category of virtue rewarded nor virtue regained, in the tradition of Clarissa rather than Pamela, Virginie's goodness for the sake of goodness is sublime because it is tragically doomed.

EDIFICATION IN REVERSE, OR VIRTUE PUNISHED

Nothing seems more "interesting," in the French sense of touching, than oppressed virtue in female characters. To investigate the subject thoroughly would take us outside the bounds of this study and into the realm of victimization. Yet mention should be made of the numerous writers whose ambition was to edify the public with tales of unhappy, though virtuous, women. The aim was ostensibly to elicit sympathy for such characters, thereby encouraging readers to want to help virtue in distress. Diderot's nun Suzanne, Duclos's Mme de Luz, and Laclos's Mme de Tourvel are only a few examples of the system of oppressed virtue. Yet quite naturally, rather than inspire readers with moral attitudes, such tales can logically suggest the conclusion that virtue does not pay. No eighteenth-century writer has demonstrated this moral reversal so clearly, pithily, and wittily as Voltaire in his short story Cosi-Sancta. To summarize it briefly, a young woman, Cosi-Sancta, undergoes misery after misery as long as she remains chaste or faithful. The disgusting old man she is forced to marry suspects her unjustly of a clandestine affair, and her attempts to discourage an assiduous admirer only inflame the young man's passion for her. The husband murders the suitor and is himself condemned to hanging for his crime. In order to save that villain, Cosi-Sancta must give herself to the judge. Then, to save her brother's life, she has to submit to his would-be assassin. And thirdly, to save her dying son's life, she is obliged to sleep with the doctor. Because of her three very helpful sacrifices, Cosi-Sancta is eventually canonized.

Voltaire's moral? As long as Cosi-Sancta persisted in following the rule of chastity, she brought pain and tragedy to those around her. When she consented to share her "sacred treasure" in a trinity of adulteries she could work wonders, inspiring great admiration.

Particularly in the novel, virtue frequently undergoes its "edifying" trial by fire and punishment. Cosi-Sancta and Virginie have much in common with Sade's Justine. They and other heroines may remind us, too, of the medieval Sainte Eulalie, put to the stake for her fidelity to Christianity. "Buona pulcella fut Eulalie. . . ." A good girl and a good virgin, but killed nonetheless.

The idea that feminine virtue does not pay underlies balanced, almost Alexandrine statements made by two heroines at diametrically opposite moral poles: Rousseau's virtuous Julie and Sade's evil Juliette.

Julie says, "Le passé m'avilit, le présent m'afflige, l'avenir m'épou-vante" (The past demeans me, the present pains me, the future frightens me, p. 189); Juliette says, "Le passé m'encourage, le présent m'électrise, je crains peu l'avenir" (The past encourages me, the present electrifies me, I fear not the future).[14]

It would be false to come to the conclusion that the Age of Enlightenment judged traditionally edifying heroines to be laughably wrong. Certainly, during the latter part of the century, figures such as Julie and Virginie, exemplary in life and saintly in death, inspired great admiration in sentimental readers. We can conclude, however, that such sublime examples were exceptional and that, before Rousseau, eighteenth-century fiction—for all its patient, long-suffering, silent, and weak females—offered few women who could qualify as truly inspirational. This is undoubtedly because the Enlightenment's con-cept of virtue was singularly lacking in grandeur and because transmundane ideals had gone quite out of fashion during the myth-exploding age of *philosophes*. Poems about female saints in the Middle Ages could impress the public with examples of sacrifices made to a familiar religious ideal. Stories about Joan of Arc could illuminate through an exalted, transcendental heroism. Corneille's Chimène, with all her human quality, was still admirable in her commitment to *noblesse oblige*.

But the morality of the Enlightenment, an increasingly bourgeois artifact, no longer understood concepts of *gloire*, sacrifice, heroism, or mysticism. A moral philosophy that replaced self-sacrifice with self-fulfillment, *gloire* and heroism with moderation and compromise, could hardly provide fertile ground for female characters to serve as examples of purity or grandeur. For that, French literature would have to await Chateaubriand's Atala or, later, heroines of Péguy, Claudel, and modern drama's revival of ancient Greek myths.

NOTES

1. For example, in French, *Le Petit Robert*, 1979; in English, *The American Heritage Dictionary*, 1973.

2. The term "edifying female" has a more restrictively affirmative thrust than "edifying story." Therefore, a category such as "vice punished" will not be treated in this study.

3. Bernardin de Saint-Pierre, *Paul et Virginie* (Paris: A. Quantin, 1878), p. 151.

4. Here were edifying examples enough for nubile girls of good family, but how many respectable adolescent females were encouraged to read stories about threatened virginity?

5. Nivelle de La Chaussée, *Le Préjugé à la mode*, in Brenner and Goodyear, *Eighteenth-Century French Plays* (New York: Appleton-Century-Crofts, 1927), p. 273.

6. Jean-Jacques Rousseau, *Les Confessions*, edited by Jacques Voisine (Paris: Garnier, 1964), p. 515.

7. Jean-Jacques Rousseau, *La Nouvelle Héloïse*, edited by René Pomeau (Paris: Garnier, 1960), p. 70. Subsequent quotations from this work will be cited in text.

8. Saint-Pierre, p. 148. Subsequent quotations from this work will be cited in text.

9. Cf. Georges May, *Le Dilemme du roman du dix-huitième siècle* (Paris: Presses universitaires de France and Yale University Press, 1963).

10. The passive role corresponds to the Arab concept of *settachia* (child-woman).

11. See "Préface de Julie" in Appendix of *La Nouvelle Héloïse*, p. 743ff.

12. See Rousseau, *Les Confessions*, p. 515.

13. Sublime too (although I lack space to treat them here) are the tender, loving friends of late-century fiction or the sweet, self-sacrificing mothers, whose immaterial but ample reward consists simply in their continuing goodness, the satisfaction it grants them, and the admiration it inspires in those around them.

14. Marquis de Sade, *Oeuvres complètes* (Paris: Cercle du livre précieux, 1966), vol. 9, p. 582.

 # VII

Portrayal of French Women in Other European Literatures

❧ Katharine M. Rogers

The View from England

IN EIGHTEENTH-CENTURY ENGLAND, as in France, there was much discussion of the nature and role of women and increasing protest, direct and indirect, against institutions that remained patriarchal. English women were gradually gaining more intellectual respect from men and more meaningful participation in social life, but they continued to lag behind French women in these areas. The English and French differed most sharply in their attitude toward marriage. In England, marriage based on love, expressed as intimate companionship and demanding absolute fidelity at least from the wife, was an ideal generally professed and increasingly practiced.[1] In France, of course, despite the efforts of certain philosophers and painters to popularize an ideal of domestic affection, marriages continued to be arranged for mercenary reasons, and young men and women so connected were neither expected to be intimate nor forbidden to seek satisfaction through adultery. In accordance with these contrasting views, English girls mixed more freely in society than French ones, so as to meet men they could love; and married English women were more guarded in their behavior with men because, supposedly, they had already found sexual and emotional fulfillment in their marriage.[2]

English observers constantly emphasized the acceptance of adultery in France. Sometimes they simply noted the difference, such as when Philip Stanhope, Lord Chesterfield, assured his son that in Paris a presentable young man could certainly have an affair "with a woman of health, education, and rank," since all the women of fashion had lovers.[3] The bachelor hero of Frances Brooke's novel *Emily Montague*, who is too considerate to endanger a wife's reputation in England, has no qualms about courting married women in France, for there, "marriages . . . being made by the parents, and therefore generally without inclination on either side, gallantry seems to be a tacit condition, though not absolutely expressed in the contract."[4] But other commentators saw the French attitude as evidence of immorality and unmanliness. In a witheringly contemptuous estimate, David Hume charged that the French held adultery "in the highest vogue and esteem . . . every man of education chose for his mistress a married woman, the wife, perhaps, of his friend and companion" and every man, likewise, took "pride in his tameness and facility" in allowing his own wife "full liberty and indulgence."[5]

The more relaxed, less possessive relationships between the sexes in French society not only allowed adulterous affairs but encouraged a general gallantry remarkable to the English. Eliza Haywood contrasted Englishmen's indifference to all women on whom they had no sexual designs with the general attentiveness of French men to women, and Chesterfield confirmed that "a gallant turn prevails in all their companies, to women, with whom they neither are, nor pretend to be, in love."[6] Hence language that was mere gallantry from a Frenchman would be a declaration of love from an Englishman.[7] Hester Thrale remarked that Parisian crowds were less rude and dangerous than London ones, for in Paris "every man thinks himself the protector of every woman."[8]

While most English, particularly women, appreciated the superior politeness of the French, some despised it as typical French effeminacy. Tobias Smollett, contemptuous of both French people and women, reduced the Frenchman's politeness to mindless routine: "He learns like a parrot . . . the whole circle of French compliments . . . and these he throws out indiscriminately to all women without distinction . . . it is no more than his making love to every woman who will give him the hearing." He can be so adept only because, "mingling with the females from his infancy," he "not only becomes acquainted with all their customs and humours, but grows wonderfully alert in performing a thousand little offices, which are overlooked by other men, whose time hath been spent in making more valuable acquisitions."[9]

Perhaps it was this habitual gallantry that convinced Englishmen that women ruled in France, a situation they all deplored. Christopher Wren attributed the fussy over-ornamentation of Versailles to feminine influence: "The women as they make here the language and fashions, and meddle with politics and philosophy, so they sway also in architecture."[10] Frances Burney d'Arblay's small son picked up the commonplace that "the ladies govern . . . entirely" in France, and Arthur Young stated as an obvious fact that women exerted "enormous" influence on political affairs under the ancien régime.[11] Hume agreed that in France "the females enter into all transactions and all management of church and state: and no man can expect success, who takes not care to obtain their good graces." He went so far as to call French society a continuous saturnalia, in which masters not only serve their slaves all year long but also serve slaves who are such not by misfortune but by nature. The French nation

> gravely exalts those, whom nature has subjected to them, and whose inferiority and infirmities are absolutely incurable. The women, though

without virtue, are their masters and sovereigns. . . . in all places and all times, the superiority of the females is readily acknowledged and submitted to by everyone, who has the least pretensions to education and politeness.[12]

While these comments grossly exaggerate the power of French women in society, it is true that they exerted an influence over social life that amazed English observers. They led conversation and taste in a way that was unknown in England, where, at least early in the century, men and women met only for cards, dancing, or flirtation. Even in 1783, a character in Hannah Cowley's play *Which is the Man?* complained that Englishmen reserve "all their passions" for their clubs and "all their wit" for Parliament, while the French marquis learns his politics "in the drawing-room of Mme the Dutchess . . . whilst the sprightly countess dispenses taste and philosophy to a circle of bishops, generals, and abbés."[13] Helen Maria Williams noted with approval that women were admitted to coffeehouses (at least in Revolutionary Paris), "for the English idea of finding ease, comfort, or festivity, in societies where women are excluded, never enters the imagination of a Frenchman."[14] French visitors were shocked by the English custom that required ladies to withdraw after dinner. They attributed this to English contempt or fear of women,[15] but Englishmen typically saw it as proof of the superiority of English males. Samuel Johnson, defending the society of London against that of Paris at the end of an all-male dinner in 1778, pronounced: "They talk in France of the felicity of men and women living together: the truth is, that there the men are not higher than the women, they know no more than the women do, and they are not held down in their conversation by the presence of women."[16] He probably meant that the French attached less importance to Latin and Greek, the great barrier in England between solid masculine learning and feminine superficiality.[17]

Observers more attuned to the graces, however, preferred French conversation to English. Chesterfield found

> the polite conversation of the men and women of fashion at Paris, though not always very deep, . . . much less futile and frivolous than ours here. It turns at least upon some subject, something of taste, some point of history, criticism, and even philosophy, which, though probably not quite so solid as Mr. Locke's, is however better, and more becoming rational beings, than our frivolous dissertations upon the weather or upon whist.

He attributed the inferiority of mixed conversation in England to the fact that "our English women are not near so well informed and cultivated as the French; besides that they are naturally more serious and silent."[18] Frances Brooke confirms his estimate: "A French woman of distinction would be more ashamed of wanting a taste for the *belles-lettres*, than of being ill dressed," and because English ladies fail to adorn their minds, they are "at Paris the objects of unspeakable contempt."[19] Brooke's hero, Colonel Rivers, deplores French ladies' shallowness of feeling, as shown in their preference "of unmeaning admiration to the real devotion of the heart"; but he also believes that respectable English ones "are generally too reserved; their manner is cold and forbidding; they seem to think it a crime to be too attractive."[20]

Elizabeth Montagu, the leading Bluestocking hostess, agreed that French conversation was superior. In Paris, the men of letters "by their vivacity and politeness shew they have been used to converse much with women. The ladies by being well informed and full of those graces we neglect when with each other shew they have been used to converse with men."[21] Maria Edgeworth's social ideal combined "French manners" with "English morals." She would rule out the political and gallant intrigues of French social life; but she approved of the mingling of "feminine and masculine subjects of conversation, instead of separating the sexes . . . into hostile parties, dooming one sex to politics, argument, and eternal sense, the other to scandal, dress, and eternal nonsense."[22] Mary Wollstonecraft, similarly applauding the benefits of French women's greater social freedom, noted that it strengthened their characters as well as improving their conversation. (Only a radical writer, attaching less importance to sexual propriety than most English people and believing that women ought to take an interest in politics, could approve of the *character* of French women.) She found French ladies less insipid than the English because they had freer social contacts with men, were less enslaved to the mind-narrowing occupation of ornamental needlework, and were less restricted by the artificial reserve enjoined by English propriety: "acting more freely, they have more decision of character, and even more generosity." The result is that they are more respected as well as more respectable: the French, admitting "more of mind into their notions of beauty, give the preference to women of thirty . . . they allow women to be in their most perfect state, when vivacity gives place to reason, and to that majestic seriousness of character, which marks maturity."[23]

French men not only enjoyed conversing with women but made a point of sharing knowledge with them. (Formal education for girls was equally inadequate in both countries.) Bernard Le Bouvier de Fontenelle's *Entretiens sur la pluralité des mondes* (1686), the most famous effort to instruct women in a traditionally "masculine" area, was well known in England. A writer in *The Female Spectator* said that women were more respected and better educated in France because they could expect men to share with them the results of their scholarly reading.[24] Oliver

Goldsmith confirmed that a man who would court a lady must be capable of discussing Newton and Locke, coyly adding that he saw "as bright a circle of beauty at the chymical lectures of Rouelle, as at the court of Versailles."[25]

Only with the Bluestocking assemblies of the later eighteenth century did the English have anything comparable to the salons that dominated French fashionable society. But although these assemblies brought women and eminent men together to converse as equals, they never exerted the influence of the salons. They were rigorously limited by the propriety that dictated female behavior in England. Intellectual brilliance was less important than chastity; the assemblies were open only to ladies of unimpeachable respectability. Hannah More's highest praise for Bluestocking conversation was that virtue always controlled what was said, so that, whenever necessary, "virtue sunk what wit inspired." Furthermore, she claimed, competitive display of wit was not encouraged.[26] Frances Burney d'Arblay, sharing her distaste for aggressiveness in women, was relieved to discover that Mme de Laval did not have "the vehement vivacity so usual amongst *les femmes d'esprit*. . . . Her observations were sagacious, and her satire . . . too just to be ill natured."[27] Finally, the assemblies could never serve, like the *salons philosophiques*, as forums for the propagation of new ideas; they had to be conservative and apolitical because even relatively liberal English thinkers considered politics and religion unsuitable topics for women.[28] The Bluestockings did much to raise the intellectual status of English women, but, by French standards, they were restricted; and they never enjoyed the respect and power of the *salonnières*. Hence, France could be called, in contrast to England, "the paradise of lady wits."[29]

Expecting women to confine their interests to private life, matters of taste, and orthodox religion, English observers were surprised to see French women participate in philosophical and political controversy. Laurence Sterne, titillated by the novelty, threw a coy allusion to a *physical précieuse* (a female philosophical materialist) into his *Sentimental Journey*, where he also described the "three epochas in the empire of a French woman" as she goes from coquette to deist to dévote: "When thirty-five years and more have unpeopled her dominions of the slaves of love, she re-peoples it with slaves of infidelity—and then with the slaves of the Church."[30] Despite its facetious tone, revealing his lack of respect for women's ideas, whether freethinking or orthodox, Sterne's remark shows both the acceptability of religious questioning among French women and the prevalent English belief that they ruled French society. Arthur Young was surprised to see two ladies at a political dinner in France in 1787, something that could never happen in England. Unlike most English people, he thoroughly approved: "The conversation of men, not engaged in trifling pursuits, is the best school for the education of a woman."[31]

Most English observers, however, had misgivings about the greater freedom produced in French women by their wider intellectual range and their easier and more flirtatious associations with men. Frances Burney d'Arblay's relationships with Germaine Necker de Staël and Stéphanie-Félicité de Genlis illustrate the mixture of fascination, disapproval, and alarm that French female intellectuals aroused in an intelligent but conventional Englishwoman. D'Arblay admired and was charmed by both women but was compelled by external pressure and her own inhibitions to break off their acquaintance. First, she was reluctantly forced to recognize that they had extramarital affairs. Then, they mixed in politics—even worse, liberal politics. De Genlis, whom she had once admired as "the apparent pattern of female perfection," shocked her by espousing revolutionary ideals to the extent of dining with people of servant rank and permitting a young noblewoman to dance at a ball "with anybody, known or unknown." De Staël put herself forward as an intellectual leader and freely expressed her views on liberal politics and the restrictiveness of English feminine propriety.[32] D'Arblay, on the other hand, was embarrassed and annoyed when the headmistress of a French school tried to present her as a celebrity at a prize-giving ceremony.[33] English women felt they must at least maintain an air of modesty.

Many English writers simply deplored French women's ease with men and desire to shine intellectually as destructive of modesty, chastity, and family affection. Their suspicions were aggravated by such French habits as wearing rouge, riding astride, speaking plainly of natural functions, and receiving male visitors in their bedrooms.[34] Sir James Macdonald complained that French women seemed "not to know what diffidence and modesty mean" because they constantly forced witty flattery from men, and he went on to draw a distinction dear to the English heart: "In France women are more flattered and less esteemed than in other countries."[35]

Jane West, indignantly rejecting "the ostentatious obsequiousness" that the French "practise to a degree of farcical affectation," celebrated "the mild chaste attractions of the British fair . . . simple elegance, domestic habits, and all the graces of discretion, delicacy, and ingenuous attachment."[36] Edgeworth, with almost equal fatuity, explained why a hero who searched through Europe for a woman worthy to be his wife found her in England. Though he admires the wit and elegance of French women and wants an enlarged understanding capable of comprehending his political aspirations, he disapproves of their love of power, political intrigue, and "devouring diseased appetite for admiration . . . which substitutes a precarious, factitious, intoxicated existence in public, for the safe self-approbation, the sober, the permanent happiness of domestic life."[37] Thomas Gisborne agreed with Edgeworth that, though Englishmen wanted intelligent wives, they did not want one intelligent in the Parisian style: erecting "herself into an idol for the votaries of science and taste to worship," giving "audience to a levee of deistical philosophers," or pronouncing "to the listening circle her decision on a manuscript sonnet." And he was shocked by French women's participation in political intrigue, which he attributed to the absolutism of the ancien régime and the disorder of the Revolutionary government.[38] The more liberal Arthur Young, who differed from Gisborne in approving of the early Revolutionary changes, agreed with him about women's participation. He believed that their political influence declined as the French government was becoming more democratic and declared that, as a result, French women "will become more amiable, and the nation better governed."[39]

It was assumed that French women's relative emancipation entailed a loss of domestic virtue. Hume said the French "have resolved to sacrifice some of the domestic to the sociable pleasures; and to prefer ease, freedom, and an open commerce, to a strict fidelity and constancy."[40] Hannah More, indignantly rebutting de Staël's charge that English ladies were insipid, claimed that the reserve and diffidence she deplored were virtues; English ladies were, very properly, educated to fulfill their duties at home rather than to shine in society and compete with men. And, of course, she was horrified by de Staël's view that coquetry is "the flavor which gives to society its poignancy."[41] Anna Barbauld turned with revulsion from the egotistical French mother to the English one, "endowed with talents and graces to draw the attention of polite circles, yet devoting her time and cares to her family and children."[42] Even Wollstonecraft said French women's skill in repartee was necessary "to supply the place of that real interest only to be nourished in the affectionate intercourse of domestic intimacy."[43]

The belief that fashionable French ideals detracted from domestic virtue, which had some basis in actuality, was augmented by vague but powerful suspicions that sexual and intellectual freedom were connected. As Joseph Addison reprehends the French-imported custom of admitting male visitors to a lady's dressing room, he mentions that the lady he visits is talking politics. Going on to warn against the tendency of French manners "to make the sex . . . *more awaken'd,* than is consistent either with virtue or discretion," he gives an example not of sexual looseness but of intellectual assertion: making one's opinions heard in public.[44] Richard Edgeworth made the same association when he cautioned Anna Barbauld:

> As your sex becomes more civilized every day, it is necessary that they should become more circumspect in conversation and in all the paraphernalia of modesty. A married lady in France is allowed one lover,

she is pardon'd for two; three is rather too many—but great delicacy of sentiment, elegant language, decent dress, and a good choice of the objects of her attachments will preserve her from absolute excommunication.[45]

The French Revolution does not appear to have changed the English view of French women, but only confirmed attitudes already held. The political activities of French women during the Revolution reinforced Montagu's previous opinion that they "have too much of the male character, the men of the female."[46] The radical Wollstonecraft, on the other hand, applauded their involvement and hoped it would kindle patriotism, which would inspire them to abjure the coquetry and artifice in which they had been trained. She hoped that the new Revolutionary leadership would

try what effect reason would have to bring them back to nature, and their duty; and allowing them to share the advantages of education and government with man, see whether they will become better, as they grow wiser and become free. They cannot be injured by the experiment; for it is not in the power of man to render them more insignificant than they are at present.[47]

Note that Wollstonecraft, the only feminist among these writers, saw less difference than the others between French and English women; in her view, both groups were powerless and debased by social oppression.

Nevertheless, English observers were responding to some real differences. A domestic ideal of loving marriage and familial intimacy was becoming increasingly predominant in England, while gallantry remained the mode in France, producing both flattering attentiveness to women in general and acceptance of adulterous affairs. French women were less inhibited than English ones, not only sexually, but intellectually. They felt more free to display their wit and knowledge, to take the lead in conversation, and to range into religious and political controversy.

However, subjective elements were at least as important in forming the English attitude. The English conviction that women ruled men in France may be based not so much on actual life as on romances such as those of Madeleine de Scudéry. These works, whose heroes submit to every whim of the lady they love and strive for years to make themselves worthy of her hand, were widely read in England and must have contributed to the impression that French women were treated with exaggerated respect. Jean-Jacques Rousseau's *La Nouvelle Héloïse* reinforced the conviction of its many English readers that the French approved of sexual passion unsanctioned by marriage.

Secondly, the English attitude toward French women was part of their intensely ambivalent attitude toward the French in general:

strong attraction and admiration opposed by contempt required by national pride. Actually, the English stereotype of the French was like their stereotype of women; both groups were supposed to be vain, superficial, frivolous, affected, clever but not solidly learned, and socially agreeable but weak in character. Such a nation would naturally submit to women and emphasize flashy but insubstantial "feminine" values. Hume explicitly concluded that where men associate much with women, as in France, gaiety will be preferred over prudence, politeness over simplicity of manners, taste and delicacy over good sense and judgment.[48]

Finally, English observers projected on French women the exciting but frightening idea of emancipation, which naturally arose as women in England were beginning to develop their minds and aspirations. Even so conservative a woman as Hannah More felt the attraction a little, for—though she detested de Staël's *Corinne* and rejected its values—she could not stop reading it.[49] For many English, however, the beginnings of female emancipation, occurring in both countries but more apparent in France, were simply a source of anxiety. French women were more free to display and claim recognition of their talents; they were also more free to have liaisons and ignore their families. The French example made it easier for English conservatives to associate easy social intercourse with destruction of domestic virtue, intellectual freedom with sexual license, and mental achievement with brazen assertiveness; and, thus, to cast a blighting suspicion of immodesty over any efforts by women to exercise their talents and enlarge their sphere.

NOTES

1. This is not to say that mercenary marriages were no longer made for convenience, that girls were no longer bullied into marriage, that husbands and wives were always congenial and devoted, or that adulteresses were always ostracized; but these were the accepted standards, which were coming to determine social practice. See Lawrence Stone, *The Family, Sex and Marriage in England 1500-1800* (New York: Harper and Row, 1977).

2. The duc de La Rochefoucauld, in 1788, noted that "young girls mix with the company and talk and enjoy themselves with as much freedom as if they were married" and that "husband and wife are always together and share the same society. It is the rarest thing to meet the one without the other." Quoted in Stone, pp. 318, 329.

3. Letters of 1750, Philip Dormer Stanhope, Earl of Chesterfield, *Lord Chesterfield's Letters to His Son*, Everyman's Library (New York: Dutton, 1929), pp. 179, 194.

4. Frances Brooke, *The History of Emily Montague*, 1769 (New York: Garland, 1974), vol. 1, p. 176. Charlotte Smith repeatedly made the point that in France,

unlike England, courtship of married women was acceptable: *Emmeline* (London: Oxford University Press, 1971), p. 53; *Desmond* (London: G. G. J. and J. Robinson, 1792), vol. 1, pp. 226-227; *The Banished Man* (London: T. Cadell and W. Davies, 1794), vol. 2, p. 163.

5. David Hume, "A Dialogue," *The Philosophical Works*, edited by Thomas Hill Green and Thomas Hodge Grose (Darmstadt: Scientia Verlag Aalen, 1964), vol. 4, p. 294. Tobias Smollett confirms this with his usual sour exaggeration: if you make friends with a Frenchman and receive him in your family, he will try to seduce your wife or daughter and call this treachery "simple gallantry, considered in France as an indispensable duty on every man who pretended to good breeding." See *Travels through France and Italy, 1766* (New York: Praeger, 1970), p. 78.

6. Eliza Haywood, *The Female Spectator* (Dublin: George and Alexander Ewing, 1747), vol. 1, pp. 194-195; Chesterfield, p. 184.

7. Smith, *Emmeline*, p. 346.

8. Journal of 1784, *The French Journals of Mrs. Thrale and Dr. Johnson*, edited by Moses Tyson and Henry Guppy (Manchester: Manchester University Press, 1932), p. 95. Arthur Young and Helen Maria Williams agreed that French men were more considerate of women than Englishmen were: see Young, *Travels in France During the Years 1787, 1788, 1789*, edited by M. Betham-Edwards (London: G. Bell, 1913), p. 75; and Williams, *Letters Written in France in the Summer 1790* (London: T. Cadell, 1791), p. 43.

9. Smollett, pp. 75-76. See Laurence Sterne, *A Sentimental Journey and Journal to Eliza, 1768* (New York: NAL, 1964), p. 34.

10. Christopher Wren, letter from Paris, 1665, in *A Calendar of British Taste: From 1600 to 1800*, edited by E. F. Carritt (London: Routledge and Kegan Paul, 1949), p. 69.

11. *The Journals and Letters of Fanny Burney (Mme d'Arblay)*, edited by Joyce Hemlow (Oxford: Clarendon, 1972—), vol. 5, p. 73; Young, p. 294.

12. Hume, vol. 4, pp. 296, 301.

13. Hannah Cowley, *Which is the Man?* (London: C. Dilly, 1783), p. 29.

14. Helen Maria Williams, *Letters from France: Containing Many New Anecdotes Relative to the French Revolution* (London: Robinson, 1792), vol. 2, p. 63.

15. Béat de Muralt and abbé Jean Bernard Le Blanc, quoted in Philippe Séjourné, *Aspects généraux du roman féminin en Angleterre de 1740 à 1800* (Aix-en-Provence: Publications des annales de la faculté des lettres, 1966), pp. 22-24.

16. James Boswell, *The Life of Johnson* (London: Oxford University Press, 1953), p. 918. Chesterfield confirms this: *Letters*, p. 172.

17. Chesterfield supports this interpretation, adding that French people of both sexes were well informed about the history of their own country (p. 191).

18. Chesterfield, pp. 228, 250. He was writing in 1752, when the Bluestocking assemblies were only getting started.

19. Frances Brooke, *The Old Maid* (London: A. Millar, 1764), pp. 18-19.

20. Brooke, *Emily Montague*, vol. 1, pp. 23, 117-118.

21. *Mrs. Montagu, "Queen of the Blues": Her Letters and Friendships from 1762 to 1800*, edited by Reginald Blunt (Boston: Houghton Mifflin, 1923), vol. 1, p. 329. Horace Walpole found French women "the first in the world in everything but beauty; sensible, agreeable, and infinitely informed." See *Selected Letters*, edited by William Hadley, Everyman's Library (New York: Dutton, 1926), p. 453. See also Young, p. 39.

22. Maria Edgeworth, *Patronage, 1814, Tales and Novels* (New York: AMS Press, 1967), vol. 8, p. 165. Elizabeth Carter and Hannah More, both

conservative Bluestockings, protested against men's refusal to discuss substantial subjects with women.

23. Mary Wollstonecraft, *A Vindication of the Rights of Woman*, 1792 (New York: W. W. Norton, 1975), pp. 70, 75-76; idem, *An Historical and Moral View of the Origin and Progress of the French Revolution*, 1794 (New York: Scholars' Facsimiles and Reprints, 1975), p. 311.

24. *The Female Spectator*, vol. 2, pp. 228-229.

25. Oliver Goldsmith, *An Enquiry into the Present State of Polite Learning in Europe*, 1759, in *Collected Works*, edited by Arthur Friedman (Oxford: Clarendon, 1966), vol. 1, p. 300.

26. Hannah More, "Bas Bleu; or Conversation," in *Complete Works* (New York: Harper, 1835), vol. 5, pp. 363, 371.

27. Frances Burney d'Arblay, *Diary and Letters*, edited by Charlotte Barrett (London: Chatto and Windus, 1876), vol. 4, p. 337.

28. See, for example, Edgeworth, *Madame de Fleury, Tales and Novels*, vol. 6, p. 292: "no amiable or sensible woman can wish to interfere" in politics; and Brooke, *Emily Montague*, vol. 1, p. 224: infidelity is "a vice peculiarly contrary to the native softness of woman . . . I should almost doubt the sex of an unbeliever in petticoats."

29. D'Arblay, *Diary and Letters*, vol. 1, p. 197.

30. Sterne, pp. 12-13, 123.

31. Young, pp. 85-86.

32. D'Arblay, *Diary and Letters*, vol. 3, p. 408. De Staël was amazed, in turn, by d'Arblay's dependence on her father's judgment when she was forty years old: "mais est-ce qu'une femme est en tutelle pour la vie dans ce pays?" (but is a woman under guardianship for life in this country?) (vol. 3, p. 498).

33. D'Arblay, *Journals and Letters*, vol. 5, p. 370.

34. See, for example, Smollett, pp. 44, 69; Thrale, p. 100; Sterne, p. 72; Joseph Addison, *Spectator*, no. 45.

35. *Mrs. Montagu, "Queen of the Blues,"* vol. 1, p. 96.

36. Jane West, *Letters to a Young Lady*, 1806 (New York: Garland, 1974), vol. 1, pp. 41-42.

37. Edgeworth, *Patronage, Tales and Novels*, vol. 7, pp. 394-395. See Colonel Rivers' appreciation of Emily, the woman he loves; she combines "the smiling graces of France" with "the blushing delicacy and native softness of England" (Brooke, *Emily Montague*, vol. 1, p. 119).

38. Thomas Gisborne, *An Enquiry into the Duties of the Female Sex*, 1797 (New York: Garland, 1974), pp. 265-266, 323-324.

39. Young, p. 294.

40. Hume, vol. 4, p. 298.

41. More, vol. 3, pp. 268-270. More was scandalized that Mme du Deffand, whom she considered cynical and indelicate, who separated from her husband on grounds of incompatibility and had adulterous affairs, was nevertheless received in the best society of Paris (vol. 3, pp. 276-278).

42. Betsy Rodgers, *Georgian Chronicle: Mrs. Barbauld and Her Family* (London: Methuen, 1958), p. 97.

43. Wollstonecraft, *French Revolution*, p. 510.

44. Addison, *Spectator*, no. 45, 1711.

45. Anna Letitia Le Breton, *Memoir of Mrs. Barbauld* (London: George Bell, 1874), p. 94.

46. Letter of 1792, *Mrs. Montagu, "Queen of the Blues,"* vol. 2, p. 281.

47. Wollstonecraft, *Vindication*, p. 167. Both Wollstonecraft and Helen Maria

Williams deplored the failure of the French Revolutionary leaders to extend the rights of man to women, even to the extent of educating them.

48. Hume, vol. 4, p. 302. Smollett found French men "more ridiculous and insignificant than the women" (*Travels*, pp. 73-74). Surprisingly, it was Wollstonecraft who made this identification most explicit: "The French may be considered as a nation of women; and made feeble, probably, by the same combination of circumstances, as has rendered these insignificant"; both groups are ingenious rather than profound, sentimentally susceptible rather than impassioned (*French Revolution*, p. 247).

49. *The Letters of Hannah More*, edited by R. Brimley Johnson (New York: Lincoln Macveagh, 1926), p. 189.

✑ Charlotte C. Prather

The View from Germany

FRIEDRICH MELCHIOR GRIMM reports an adventure, which he describes as "rather temerous and delicate to be attempted by a young and lovely woman." The heroine of the adventure, which Grimm transforms into a most amusing anecdote, is, in fact, Mme Deshoulières, whose poetry Grimm is pleased to see being published post-humously. He transcribes the episode from a biography of the poet that her editor has provided—a biography that he assures us is otherwise wholly tedious and poorly written:

> Mme Deshoulières, having been told during a visit to friends in the country that one of the wings of their chateau was customarily haunted by night, conceives a great curiosity and determination to witness the said apparition personally. Having insisted upon sleeping in the haunted apartment, she hears her door open in the middle of the night. She addresses the ghost who, however, does not respond. It approaches treading heavily and sighing. A table is upset; the bed curtains part. The young woman, unconcerned, reaches for the visitor to discern whether it has any palpable form. She easily seizes the two ears of the ghost which she finds to be long and velvety, a discovery which causes her some serious thought. Afraid to release the said ears and thus render an escape possible, she persists until dawn in this uncomfortable position. At first light she recognizes her captive as a large dog of quite placid temperament who has developed a preference for sleeping there in comfort rather than out of doors. She is thus able to relieve the fears of her host who wonders at her courage.[1]

This episode from the private life of a woman of some public stature may be seen as emblematic of the eighteenth-century German view of French women and of women in general. The relative weight of personal data, vis-à-vis public information, in this case a presentation or evaluation of the poetry of Mme Deshoulières, is not insignificant, nor is the ambiguous stance of the reporter in his interpretation of the adventure itself. The poetry, in fact, receives neither evaluation nor criticism. The only praise is offered to the editor, who has made, Grimm maintains, a wise choice in his selection rather than burdening the public with the entire corpus of the author's work. The poetry seems not to deserve extensive attention; perhaps it was heartily mediocre. One may judge from evidence throughout the *Correspondance littéraire*, however, that had the author been a man Grimm would not have withheld his witty, stinging, and, at times, ruthlessly devastating criticism of an indifferent production. In the case of a woman, the personal is most frequently simply more interesting to him and also, he assumes, to his readers. The poetry edition is mentioned solely for the sake of a charming biographical note.

How does Grimm perceive the young woman whom he delineates so robustly in this brief passage? She is alone, independent, rational, curious, intelligent, enterprising, and courageous—at least braver than those who have been living in humble submission to an unseen and uninvestigated spirit. Expectations of another kind of femininity surround the narrative, however. Mme Deshoulières' actions, not particularly remarkable to the modern reader, are presented as precisely that. The heroine is viewed, not as an example of the enterprising and educated modern woman, but as an interesting character because of the union within her of two assumedly contradictory characteristics: womanhood and rational, investigative enterprise. Where the individual woman is admired and even, at times, welcomed as a colleague, she is not considered anything other than individual, never the measure of Woman. The literary woman remains for Grimm an oxymoron.

The episode is of particular note because of its inclusion in the *Correspondance littéraire*. Grimm was undoubtedly the most famous and widely read German correspondent living in France in the eighteenth century. Although not of significant literary stature himself, he had contact with an actively productive society of authors, publishers, artists of all sorts, and, of course, the women who conducted the stimulating salons, which were the meeting places of the most well-known *beaux-esprits*. Along with Diderot and Henri Meister, Grimm faithfully produced the *Correspondance* for twenty years (1753-1773). In Germany, a relatively small but influential group, mostly members of the various German courts, subscribed to it. Catherine the Great and Goethe were among its notable readers.[2] Grimm was, therefore, undoubtedly the most prolific and constant source of information in German intellectual circles about French literary and artistic life for two decades. Grimm's comments about women fall into two categories, both of which can be seen in the anecdote about Mme Deshoulières. If he refers to the literary, artistic, and intellectual talent and production of a woman, he considers himself to be addressing her "masculine" attributes and accomplishments. When his discussion revolves upon a woman's or women's personal life and activities, he consciously judges these matters in terms of "feminine" criteria.

To be sure, Grimm occasionally applies quite severe criticism to the works of female authors. About Mme de Bocage, who wrote a work called *Paradis terrestre*, inspired by Milton's *Paradise Lost*, he writes:

> As much as the original possessed interest, nobility and warmth, the copy is cold, servile and boring. The French author, wanting to avoid the faults into which the English author had fallen, has rendered none of the beauties of the English work. She is a house painter who has retouched the canvas of a great master. The work of Mme de Bocage can almost pass for a parody of Milton (1.125).

After this devastating review, Grimm feels obliged, however, to write a few kind words about Mme de Bocage as a private person. He takes care to imply that artistic failure in no way constitutes a substantive criticism when the artist is a woman. In other words, authorship is not to be seen as a woman's profession or as a major expression of herself as an individual. It is, rather, a side issue, a hobbyhorse. The criticism of a woman's art is, thus, also a relatively harmless matter. Of *L'Histoire de Charles VI* by Mlle de Lussan, he says it should have been written in two volumes instead of nine. Later, he writes that her nine volumes do not even merit nine pages. But he is also able to state: "She is one of those women who do the most honor to the fair sex" (2.151, 317).

It is clearly a far more serious matter when Grimm adds to his literary criticism of Mme de Graffigny a personal attack as well; he finds nothing can redeem her *Lettres d'une Péruvienne* and explains, moreover, that she has cast herself upon literature out of financial necessity. Being unable to distinguish herself by anything appropriate to a woman, she has, he maintains, thrown herself with equal failure into the world of letters—an unattractive pretention for a woman (1.132).

There is one justification, however, for a woman's assuming the otherwise male pursuit of literature: success. Grimm expresses no reservations when he mentions Mme de Lambert's celebrity in the literary world. Nevertheless, he still cannot divorce his views about feminine modesty and propriety from an evaluation of literary merit:

> The letters of Mme de Lambert are well formulated, written freely and elegantly. One sees in them that modesty of an intelligent woman who does not wish to be suspected of intellectual ambition, and that reserve in judging the works of others which is the proof of a good heart and a good spirit (1.147-148).

He obviously means to imply a good heart and a good spirit *of a woman*. Certainly, he himself does not hesitate to criticize (at times rather venomously) the works of his contemporaries. Without modesty and reserve, the writings of a woman would appear to Grimm monstrous.

Literary activity is, therefore, a male prerogative and only does credit to a woman when it has been modified by "feminine" characteristics such as delicacy and modesty. Above all else, it must make no claim of intellectual equality, an almost pejorative attribute for a woman.

In general, Grimm's estimate of French women of letters is almost always mixed and expressed with rather biting wit: "Mme Dacier had a mediocre intellect and great erudition . . . Mme de La Suze had little direction and much feeling . . . Mme de Sévigné was devout but not ridiculous . . . Mlle de Scudéry had great intelligence but not much character" (1.182). Often the cause for the praise or blame directly relates to Grimm's perception of the proper literary tone for a lady. Mme Dacier, he says, is admirable, wise, and modest, as is fitting for a woman. He finds fault with Mme de La Suze, on the other hand, for her bad reputation, flippancy, frivolity, and looseness, attributes that might, in fact, add to the stature of a male author. Even in noting the death of Mme du Châtelet, Grimm withholds approbation where he finds that she has behaved in an unfeminine manner. He mentions that in spite of her great celebrity abroad, she has mostly attracted censure at home. Her talent and enterprise seem to impress him, but he finds them, nevertheless, somewhat unnatural: "The real character of Mme du Châtelet was to be extreme in everything" (1.365).

With regard to character and personal life, and completely apart from the unwomanly art of literature, Grimm (like most of his German contemporaries) sees French women in a questionable light. Moral standards are lax; women have a frightening amount of power, influence, and notoriety. Proper family and civic structure is threatened by the position of women in French society. Grimm is distressed by the loose and frivolous life he sees among the French nobility, particularly in the case of women. He concludes rather sarcastically: "Nevertheless, do not believe, on the basis of this account, that all the women in France are models of the one whom I have just portrayed [Mme de Puisieux]; Boileau, the satirist, has previously counted up to three honest women in Paris" (1.167). Almost as disturbing to the German viewer as the libertine social mores that Grimm records are the social influence and political power of French women. He describes with some humor, but not much approbation, the manipulative abilities of Mme de Tencin, who was first adept enough to free herself from the restraints of the cloister and, later, through her privileged position with the duke of Orleans, was in danger of having enormous political impact. The duke, prince regent, was terrified of her will to rule, however, and sent her away after twenty-four hours: "She began by almost wanting to govern the realm . . . and an old courtier has told me that the regent, in speaking of Mme de Tencin, said he did not want a mistress who would talk of politics when alone with him" (1.385).

Jacques Lacant speaks of the German disdain for the ascendancy that women seemed to have in French noble society.[3] A similar situation did not exist in Germany because there was no structure that was the equal of the Parisian salons. Women were not interpreters and arbiters of public life in Germany as they often were in France.

One important reason for the German sense of moral superiority and disapproval of women's freedom and authority in eighteenth-century France was the importance of pietism in both bourgeois life and literary circles. Pietism was a movement with roots in seventeenth-century Protestantism. Although occasionally in conflict with more orthodox theology and church order, pietistic groups existed for the most part within and in harmony with the churches. The movement had a definite mystical element and stressed the personal experience of belief and individual piety. In addition to having an important effect on the daily life of the bourgeois, it attracted a fairly strong literary component. The early pietists were prolific writers. Jakob Spener, considered to be, with August Hermann Franke, the founder of the movement, won a large following with his *Pia Desideria* (1675). Gottfried Arnold's *Unparteiische Kirchen und Ketzerhistorie* (1699-1700) was a radical challenge to orthodox Protestantism. A number of hymn books were published to reflect the new religious orientation, including collections by Zinzendorf and Tersteegen.

The personal, somewhat sentimental, religious experience was very attractive to poets and presented a sharp contrast to the order and rationality of the Enlightenment, which was never so strong in Germany as it was in England and France. A new interest in the state and development of the emotions within a self-analytical religious framework found a literary echo. The personal journal, culminating with Goethe's *Leiden des jungen Werther* (1774), becomes a very popular genre. In fact, Goethe's mother belonged to a pietistic circle, and the philosophy and personalities of that group played a significant role in the author's later work. One of his mother's friends, Susanne von Klettenberg, is the model for the schone Seele, whose confessions form the encapsulated novella in *Wilhelm Meisters Lehrjahre* (1795-1796).

The hegemony of subjectivity, sentiment, and personal religious experience explains the German rejection of what was viewed as artifice, libertinism, and a rather cold calculation replacing true feeling in the French women of the time. Johann Gottfried Herder speaks of what he deems the French coldness in his *Journal meiner Reise im Jahr 1769*. He maintains that the French borrowed much of what they had achieved in the realms of literature, art, and taste in general from the Italians and the Spanish. The French, however, he says, have civilized these acquisitions in diminishing the all too fiery imaginative force of the Latins:

> The all too passionate aspect of love disappeared; it was mellowed; but
> along with the adventurous, also the truly tender was lost: it became
> chilly gallantry. . . . One needs only to consider them in their theater:
> such well studied grimaces! monotonous gallantries!—They have dis-
> carded the heart-breaking: true marital love is not portrayed. . . .[4]

While Herder cannot approve of the emotional violence of the Italians
and the Spanish, as he sees it, he is even less satisfied with the cold
politeness, gallantry, coquettry, and affectation that he views as
dominating French manners and the French theater. He uses the word
zärtlich (tender) several times. This tenderness, along with genuine
marital love, he misses on the French stage. A corresponding absence
of what might be called virtuous family life is directly traced to the
public stature and libertine life of women.

There was a tremendous fear that what was viewed as a French
disregard for morality might infect German society. One sees, therefore, a certain defensiveness in German writings against any infiltra-
tion by things French. In Gottsched's *Die Vernünftigen Tadlerinnen,* a
moral and cultural weekly, written by fictive women editors, one finds
the following satiric parenthesis regarding virgins (*Jungfern*): "if we still
have a few of them among us: for we have gotten nothing but 'ladies'
for quite some time now; and many would consider it an insult if one
were to call them maidens. . . ."[5] Even Grimm, living in Paris, does not
accept the moral tolerance of the society around him. André Cazes
recounts how Grimm, having become the lover of Mme d'Epinay,
proceeds to "reform" her.[6] He makes it clear that their relationship is
to remain monogamous; former lovers are, at his insistence, politely
removed from her house. Moreover, Grimm is also given credit for the
reform and elevation of his mistress' salon:

> In fact, this salon was the work of Grimm. With his constant and firm
> advice, he enabled a woman with a lost reputation to reconquer an
> honorable place in the world. He made her realize at the beginning the
> frivolity of her goals, the inconsistency of her behavior. . . . He
> surrounded her with intelligent company, and developed her taste in
> literature and philosophy with tyrannical vigor.[7]

An excellent analysis of the differing role of women in France and
Germany in the eighteenth century may be found in Paul Kluckhohn's
*Auffassung der Liebe in der Literatur des 18. Jahrhunderts und in der deutschen
Romantik.* Kluckhohn sees the effect of pietistic sentimentality in the
German preference for an emotional definition of love and a domestic
image of women and contrasts this with the more rococo interpretation of women and sexuality in France. Nevertheless, even in
Germany, the sensual, which Kluckhohn sees as the primary theme of
eighteenth-century French literature, receives its due in the literary
world most often through translation of French erotic literature,
which was widely read and imitated.[8]

This disapproval of French manners occurs simultaneously with a strong movement in German literary circles to reject the imitation of French literature, most particularly in the theater. Herder was strongly concerned for the development of a genuinely German literary style and language, and Lessing was bound to win the heated debate with Gottsched over the proper models for a German theater, the English or the French. One point of cultural similarity that serves to strengthen the German leaning away from France and toward the English model is the significance of bourgeois society to literature. Pierre Fauchery notes the contribution of Samuel Richardson to the ennoblement of English middle-class society. Certainly, Clarissa Harlowe gives to her class a stature that also has a profound effect on the German literary world (aside from the latter's already mentioned predilection for the kind of sentimentality that makes Richardson so popular in eighteenth-century Germany). Fauchery sees bourgeois Germany as being even more jealous of its identity and literary hegemony.[9] The class-conscious stance taken by German novelists manifests itself in mistrust and criticism of the aristocracy as a corrupt society, devoted to debauchery. The enfranchised and vocal role of women in the French aristocracy must then appear threatening, if not actually immoral, vis-à-vis the more traditional family and community structures of the German bourgeoisie.

One sees then, especially in the German novel of the eighteenth century, models of the French woman taken from life, but more often from literature. She is portrayed as frivolous, seductive, libertine, irresponsible, and often enormously appealing but definitely dangerous —even fatal. Certainly, the type of Manon Lescaut finds a firmly established place in the German novelist's canon, especially in Goethe's. The theater "girls" from Marianne through Philine, and perhaps most uniquely Mignon, echo aspects of the Manon character. Fauchery points out the similarity, for instance, between the transportation as a criminal of Frau Melina in *Wilhelm Meisters Lehrjahre* and Manon's deportation.[10]

The French woman, specifically the aristocratic French woman, is portrayed by German novelists throughout the eighteenth century as a corrupt and corrupting figure. Fauchery cites a number of examples:

> In Schnabel's *Insel Felsenburg*, it is a French actress who seduces the father of Frau von Barley; in *Rosaliens Briefe*, it is a French marquise who turns the head of the weak Pindorf; a French woman will serve as warden to the innocent Agnes von Lilien who has been sequestered by the enemies of her father and her fiance; again it is a French woman in Tieck's *William Lovell* who, because of the hero's virtue, pushes him into a life of crime.[11]

The French woman as temptress, then, becomes something of a commonplace in eighteenth-century German literature. She may even provide an effective and useful tool for necessary evil, thus enabling the virtuous to remain unsullied. An interesting example is again Schnabel's *Insel Felsenburg*. The Dutch captive, Charlotte van Bredal, has no scruples about allowing a French member of the seraglio to take her place in the sultan's bed. Since the French concubine is willing to serve the "infidels" as well as the Christians, the virtuous heroine of the tale feels free to take advantage of the other's lax standards. (One wonders whether the greater crime was seen in the adultery itself or the fact of its being committed with a heathen.)[12]

In this same novel, one of the villains, Herr Lemelie, is coincidentally the scion of one of the most noble families of France. He eventually confesses the beginnings of a debauched life; at the age of eighteen, he raped his sister. The incest continues and eventually leads to his murdering her.[13] The horror of the tale has a grisly fascination for Lemilie's audience within the novel and undoubtedly for the reader as well, but the author's care is noted in assigning such moral degeneracy to foreigners, whenever possible to the French. As Fauchery concludes, it is possible to extract from the German novel of the eighteenth century a vast quantity of anti-French material: "Almost everything in this literature which is opposed to virtue and to the happiness of women comes from France or makes one think of France."[14]

Of all the French women visible to the German eye in the eighteenth century, perhaps only the writers are truly seen and, in consequence, appreciated. Wieland, who has been generally viewed by critics as one of the most "French" of German authors of the Enlightenment and who was knowledgeable in and appreciative of contemporary French literature, had high praise for a number of French women authors. He writes to his cousin, Sophie von La Roche (also a successful novelist who owed much of her entrance into the literary world to his advice and encouragement): "I very much like Mme de Staël and the prose of Dame Graffigny; but as for Mme Riccoboni, I prefer her to all the others, without even excepting the charming Mlle de La Fayette, who is infinitely better than all the Dames Tencin and Gomez in the universe."[15] Wieland's praise is perhaps not altogether astonishing, given his admiration for the French and his natural sympathy for women.[16]

Johann Christoph Gottsched, whose life work, aside from the *Versuch einer kritischen Dichtkunst* (1730), is the reworking and translation of the masterpieces of the French stage for the German theater, has enthusiastic praise for *Cénie* of Mme de Graffigny.[17] In fact, the play is translated into German in 1753 by Gottsched's wife, Luise Adelgunde Victoria Gottsched. More significant, however, are the laudatory remarks of Lessing in the twentieth essay of the *Hamburgische Drama-turgie* about Mme de Graffigny's play (although he has scant praise for the German translation by Frau Gottsched).[18] Goethe also has great admiration for certain French women of letters, most particularly for Mme de Staël.[19]

Gottsched, who saw the French theater as the only possible model from which to build a respectable and legitimate German theater and who, therefore, felt more at ease with the more active role of women in the intellectual life of the nation than many of his German contemporaries, shows himself to be quite receptive to the achievements of women. He notes with pleasure the announcement of the Paris medical faculty that it has chosen a woman president, the Countess of Boisenon, although, in addition to her erudition and intelligence, he also feels compelled to mention her beauty as reason for her great popularity.[20] Finally, Gottsched sees the *Paradis terrestre* of Mme de Bocage as evidence that the powers of the mind are not limited by sex.[21] Certainly, Gottsched encouraged the literary talent of his own wife, whose plays are, in fact, more genial and entertaining than her brilliant but unoriginal husband's. However, one must note that she remained, nevertheless, always in his shadow. He spoke for her, and she wrote extraordinarily funny, satirical plays mainly to illustrate his literary theories.

It is difficult to assess how much of the German understanding of French women in the eighteenth century—in the literary world and in society as a whole—is based on tertiary information. Certainly, the only French women who were really able to make a direct impact on the German consciousness were the writers. Their works were received by an educated public that spoke French, and were also translated or, in the case of the theater, were reworked for the German stage, which, in its infancy, still relied heavily upon a French repertory. Thus, the products of the French literary world were made available to the German populace as a whole, and not merely to a limited and highly educated group.

The influence of Melchior Grimm in forming an image of France for his fellow citizens should not be underestimated. His *Correspondance* was largely responsible for transmitting a view of the salons where women played a more significant role than their German counterparts in animating the intellectual and artistic life of the nation.[22] The alliance of literary sentimentality, reflected in the popularity of Richardson, with pietism, a religious movement having a strong literary emphasis, helped to apply an aura of corruption to the more worldly and rational French culture. Women, traditionally the guardians of societal virtue, were then especially subject to an indictment of libertinism. The growing importance of the bourgeois community in German economic and cultural life further strengthened the criticism of the pietists. The relatively powerful position of French women in political and cultural affairs was seen as a threat to the harmony of home life, having an undermining effect on the stability of the family and eventually of the economic community as well. Finally, the role of German literature is particularly important in perpetuating an image of French women that may have been derived more from French literature than from life itself. The figure of the dangerous coquette, who is capable of destroying a naïve and virtuous hero, becomes a cliché for the German novel of the Enlightenment and a convenient vehicle through which to portray the conflicts of good and evil, innocence and corruption, youth and experience, which so fascinated the eighteenth century. Although individual French women were applauded for their outstanding accomplishments, they rarely became the model in the German mind for French women in general. They remained a somewhat unpleasant stereotype, useful to the writers of novels and to the builders of public taste and community ethics.

NOTES

1. Friedrich Melchior Grimm, *Correspondance littéraire* (Paris: Garnier, 1877-1882), vol. 1, pp. 90-91. Subsequent references in the text are to this edition and are noted with volume and page number.

2. Jacques Lacant provides an interesting account of the significance of Grimm's *Correspondance* for educated German circles and cites Goethe's appreciation of it: "I also had the privilege of regularly receiving these reports, and I never failed to study them eagerly and to accord them the greatest of credit." *Marivaux en Allemagne* (Paris: Klincksieck, 1975), p. 185.

3. Lacant, p. 116.

4. Johann Gottfried Herder, *Sämtliche Werke* (Berlin: Weidmann, 1878), vol. 4, p. 414.

5. Freytag den 18. Jenner 1726, *Die vernünftigen Tadlerinnen* (Leipzig: Braun, 1727), p. 21.

6. André Cazes, *Grimm et les encyclopédistes* (Paris: Les Presses universitaires de France, 1933), p. 250.

7. Cazes, pp. 268-269.

8. Paul Kluckhohn, *Die Auffassung der Liebe in der Literatur des 18. Jahrhunderts und in der deutschen Romantik* (Halle: Niemeyer, 1922), p. 161.

9. Pierre Fauchery, *La Destinée féminine dans le roman européen du XVIIIe siècle: 1713-1807* (Paris: A. Colin, 1927), pp. 38-39.

10. Ibid., p. 68.

11. Ibid., p. 79. Fauchery speaks of the clichéed figure of the French woman in German literature: "The scene of seduction, by a perverse Parisienne, of a young and ingenuous foreigner, is one of the most wide-spread commonplaces of the eighteenth-century novel; we know that Saint Preux—a French speaker but not French—will be himself the victim of it" (p. 31).

12. Johann Gottfried Schnabel, *Insel Felsenburg*, edited by Ludwig Tieck (Breslau: Max und Komp, 1828), vol. 3, pp. 222-224.

13. Ibid., vol. 2, pp. 33-34.

14. Fauchery, pp. 78-79.

15. Letter of August 1768, in *Neue Briefe Christoph Martin Wielands, vornehmlich an Sophie von La Roche,* edited by Robert Hassencamp (Stuttgart: Cotta, 1894), p. 168.

16. Albert Fuchs traces Wieland's debt to French literature, including to French women authors, in *Les Apports français dans l'oeuvre de Wieland de 1772 à 1789* (Paris: H. Champion, 1934). He also mentions a number of biographical "rescue" essays that Wieland wrote on French women of the Middle Ages and the sixteenth century (pp. 193-274).

17. Johann Christoph Gottsched, *Das Neueste aus der anmuthigen Gelehrsamkeit* (Leipzig: Breitkopf, 1751), pp. 126-133.

18. Gotthold Ephraim Lessing, *Werke* (Baden: Tempel Klassiker, 1965), vol. 2, pp. 595-596.

19. For a good discussion of Goethe's link to the French and of his view of Mme de Staël, see Albert Fuchs, *Goethe und der französische Geist* (Stuttgart: Metzler, 1964), pp. 14-19.

20. *Anmuthige Gelehrsamkeit* (July 1754), p. 558.

21. Ibid. (June 1755), p. 409.

22. An interesting presentation of the women whose salons were of cultural and literary importance in eighteenth-century Berlin is Ingeborg Drewitz, *Berliner Salons: Gesellschaft und Literatur zwischen Aufklärung und Industriezeitalter* (Berlin: Haude und Spener, 1979).

🎇 Carolyn Hope Wilberger

The View from Russia

THE IMAGE of the French woman in Russian literature of the eighteenth century is inextricably linked to the complex and often contradictory relationship between France and Russia during this period. The Russian woman was fundamentally different from her Western European counterpart—socially, politically, economically, and culturally *different*. Just as Russia was trying to join the enlightened community of Western nations, so, too, certain Russian women were striving to emulate the eighteenth-century Western woman. In this quest, the "French woman" would be both model and guide. The fundamental question posed in the literature of this time, a literature produced by men with ambivalent attitudes toward the sweeping changes occurring in Russian family life, was the validity of the French example: were French women paragons of beauty, intelligence, and social grace, or were they models of superficiality, selfishness, and infidelity?

One cannot even begin to understand the Russian woman of this period, let alone her relationship to the French woman, without knowing something of the political, social, and cultural background of Russia. The eighteenth century was a watershed in Russian history. The reigns of Peter the Great (1689-1725) and his successors, especially Catherine the Great (1762-1796), were all dedicated to one goal—making Russia a *Western* nation politically, economically, industrially, militarily, and culturally equal or superior to France, England, and Germany. To this end, Russians systematically broke down the barriers of superstition and isolationism imposed by geography, history (the Mongol invasion), and religion (the xenophobia of the Orthodox Church)—barriers that had left Russia a semi-Oriental, medieval relic in the eighteenth-century world.

Nowhere are the changes imposed by Peter the Great more evident than in the lives of women of the Russian court nobility. The pre-Petrine woman had been reared apart from the contaminating influence of boys; she had been taught prayer, obedience, and a few domestic skills, such as embroidery. Her marriage, often to a complete stranger chosen by her father, culminated in the transfer of the symbolic whip from father to husband. According to the latest manual of household management, the *Domostroi* (1556), her married life consisted of complete obedience to her husband (the symbolic whip was frequently used literally to insure this obedience) and isolation from the outside world in the *terem*, rooms reserved for the women of the household where they spent their lives, even eating apart from the men. The occasional ventures into the outside world were made only to visit relatives or attend church (which the woman entered by a special door and where, again, she sat apart). The origin of the *terem* is variously attributed to the Mongol influence (the Oriental separation of the sexes), the desire to protect women from the dangers and coarseness of Russian life, or the desire to protect Russian men from their women. The latter attitude derives primarily from the traditional religious view of woman as evil temptress:

> Unfortunately, the higher a lady's rank and the more gorgeous her wardrobe, the less likely she was to be seen. The Muscovite idea of women, derived from Byzantium, had nothing of those romantic medieval Western conceptions of gallantry, chivalry and the Court of Love. Instead, a woman was regarded as a silly, helpless child, intellectually void, morally irresponsible and, given the slightest chance, enthusiastically promiscuous. . . . This isolation of women and disdain for their companionship had a grim effect on seventeenth-century Russian men. Family life was stifled, intellectual life was stagnant, the coarsest qualities prevailed. . . .[1]

Peter the Great, while hardly a feminist (his strongest praise for wife Catherine, after all, had been that she "acted like a man"), was influenced by Western ideas about the role of women in society. From 1700 onward, the life of at least a few Russian noblewomen improved. Women certainly never lost their second-class legal status. Peter's "meritocracy" based advancement on service to the state, military service, and the payment of taxes (calculated on the basis of male serfs)—all avenues closed to women. However, the new concern for individual rights and responsibilities did improve women's lot. A 1702 decree established that marriage must be by *consent*, women were allowed to retain rights to their property (admittedly enforcement was difficult), and the whip was replaced by a kiss at the marriage ceremony. Peter declared an end to the *terem* and ordered that women become an integral part of Russian social life. To that end, he decreed in 1718 the holding of *assemblées*, evening parties hosted two or three times per week by his courtiers for the purpose of genteel social intercourse between the sexes:

> Before long, St. Petersburg society flocked to these receptions. In one room there would be dancing, in another people playing cards, in a third a group of men somberly smoking their long clay pipes and drinking

from earthernware mugs, and in a fourth men and women laughing, gossiping and enjoying one another in a way hitherto unknown in Russia.[2]

Men and women, again on imperial order, traded in flowing Oriental robes for the latest Western fashions; women wore as much rouge "as the French"; homes were lavishly redecorated with the best European furnishings; servants were decked out in Western livery; and banquets boasted the best in imported French wines and delicacies.

The Russian noblewoman had a new life, a life *à la française*. The French ambassador to the Russian court, Ségur, would remark in 1785: "One sees already a large number of elegant ladies, young girls remarkable for their graces, speaking equally well seven or eight languages, playing many instruments and familiar with the most celebrated poets and novelists of France, Italy, and England."[3] This was the *problem* as far as many Russian writers were concerned. It seemed that the imitation had not stopped with French fashions, mannerisms, and language. Appallingly, the "new Russian woman" also seemed to be aping the domestic irresponsibility and infidelity of her French sisters.

Before turning to the portrait of "the French woman" in Russian literature, one must first consider the portrait of *"woman"* in Russian literature because the two are interdependent. Pre-Petrine Russian literature was also profoundly different from its Western counterpart. Literature was a complex amalgam of oral and written, religious and secular. The religious tradition predominated until the seventeenth century, and the picture of "woman" in this tradition was an ambivalent one. On one hand, there was Mary, the supreme mother figure, and various female saints. On the other hand, however, there was woman as the source of temptation and the cause of the Fall, described as "insinuating, cunning, stealthy, slanderers, insnarers, heretics, wolverines, serpents, scorpions, vipers . . . the most evil of all evil is an evil woman."[4]

In her fascinating study of women in Old (pre-Petrine) Russian literature, Joan Delaney Grossman traces the image of women in *secular* literature of the period as well, finding again the double image of the Wise Maiden and the *zlaja zena*, the evil temptress. Especially interesting in regard to eighteenth-century portraits of French women are her observations on women in the *bylina* (epic songs of the Kievan period). This masculine genre, not unexpectedly, tended to view women as objects of war and rape. Feminine images included the serpent-witches with magical powers, the all-gracious mother figures, Amazon types (ferocious and valuable companions in arms who had to be tamed before marriage), the unfaithful wives (whores who were a threat to the hero's soul, body, and ego), and the *foreign brides*.

Grossman's observations on the latter are exceptionally thought-provoking and fundamental to the analysis of later portraits of French women:

> Foreign women are shown repeatedly as threats to the hero and through him to the strength of the state. It is no doubt significant that these foreign brides are pagans. Nor are they simply heathens waiting for the light of Christianity. Insidious, immoral, or generally troublesome, they work either openly or covertly for the destruction of the Christian hero. But the case is somehow ambiguous: are these women dangerous because they are foreigners and pagans, or because they are women?[5]

The similarities are striking. French women will be in the same mold: "pagan" (Roman Catholic, not Orthodox) and immoral. The same ambiguity will also have to be considered: were French women "bad" because they were "French" or because they were "women," women par excellence in fact, since for most of eighteenth-century Europe they set the standards of womanhood?

Russian literature of the eighteenth century is a picture of great complexity. Having missed the Western Renaissance, Russian literature had enormous ground to cover. French, German, and English influences swept into Russia together: the baroque, the *précieux*, the neo-classical and the sentimental were being absorbed at one time. Western literary developments of centuries were telescoped into mere decades in Russia. The combination of elements from all these competing traditions formed something uniquely eighteenth-century Russian. At the same time they were striving to absorb foreign literatures and mold a coherent national one, Russian writers were also in search of a literary language. Russian was "not a single language at all, but a congeries of dialects, all somewhat artificial and remote from living speech."[6] In this quest, women and the French language would play important roles. Russian sentimentalist Karamzin would be lamenting as late as 1802 that this linguistic problem was the primary difficulty of Russian authors: "And here again we are in trouble: in better homes they speak primarily French! The charming women to whom one should listen if one wants to adorn a novel or comedy with some pleasant, felicitous expressions, captivate us with non-Russian phrases."[7] Karamzin himself would solve this dilemma by writing as the ladies of good society spoke.

The first literary genre to feature French women was the "Petrine tale." These anonymous popular adventure tales (almost all written after 1725) developed outside the main neo-classical currents of the "new" Russian literature. Most were Russian adaptations of seventeenth-century translations of Western European medieval tales:

From these literary sources came a new notion of women as partners in love relationships that extended beyond the physiological bond between the sexes. This was far from the medieval Western concept of chivalric love, which had no counterpart at any time in Russia; but the idea of an intense mutual devotion between a man and a woman suggested that women were subject to the same feelings and thoughts as men. The recognition of common characteristics and shared experience laid the groundwork for a reappraisal of the relations between the sexes. These new perceptions were refined and idealized, along with images of women, in the expanding world of eighteenth-century Russian literature.[8]

The Petrine tales were primarily concerned with those upwardly mobile groups (merchants, military men, service nobility) that made their fortune by succeeding in Western terms. The hero was typically a young merchant or nobleman who travels West, winning there fame, fortune, and the fair maiden by dint of his own intellect and talent (Petrine equivalents of epic heroism and valor).[9] The foreign women involved seem to be distinguished less by any specifically "French," "Italian," or "German" characteristics than simply by the mere fact of being "Western." They seem important primarily as "proof" that *Russian* men are worthy of the love and loyalty of these supposedly superior Europeans.

The Tale of the Russian Nobleman Alexander is doubtless the most complex of the tales. The precocious son of an important nobleman, Alexander goes to France to see the world and seek honor and glory. He will become the first Russian "knight-errant." There is no attempt at geographical accuracy or local color: "Geographical accuracy was simply not considered an important feature. Often as not the lands the adventure tale hero visits are imaginary and/or legendary. Even when this is not the case geographical accuracy was not considered important."[10] Thus, Alexander reaches France on horseback in only a few days. He soon goes to Lille, a city reputed for its beauty. There is a brief discussion of its walls, fortifications, gates, etc.—information probably derived from a coat of arms or medieval emblamata.

In Lille, Alexander meets and immediately falls in love with the beautiful Eleonora. Their romance of some three years follows courtly conventions with numerous tests of love, the exchange of documents and a ring given to him by his parents. The idyll is rudely interrupted by the evil general's daughter, Gedvig-Doroteja, a typical *zlaja zena*, who seduces Alexander. Eleonora dies of grief at this betrayal; Alexander renounces Gedvig-Doroteja and returns to Paris.

In Paris, he woos and wins the beautiful Tira, daughter of a French "Hofmarschal of the Court," who is the most inaccessible woman in Paris and who especially dislikes foreigners. Their relationship remains chaste. When Alexander decides to return to Russia after fighting a duel with one of her former suitors, Tira dresses in armor and accompanies him. Just a few miles from Paris, the lovers and Alexander's friend, Vladimir, are separated by brigands. Tira's odyssey covers the globe, including a stint as a Spanish shepherdess and a visit to China. Some fifteen years later, the two Russian noblemen are reunited with Tira in Paris and set out again for Russia. Alexander drowns; Tira commits suicide by falling on her sword. Gedvig-Doroteja falls to her death in anger at the graves of Tira and Alexander.

The women protagonists are typical female figures for gallant adventure tales. Eleonora and Tira are both positive feminine images; Tira is the more active of the two, masquerading as a knight-errant herself. Gedvig-Doroteja is exemplary of the threatening woman who betrays her husband to seduce the hero. None seems specifically "French" in any way. Perhaps the most interesting feminine element in the tale is the debate on the question of woman's character: is she evil by nature or is it circumstance (including bad men) that leads her astray? The hero, Alexander, and Vladimir, a misogynist who physically abuses his women, seem to illustrate these two concepts. Alexander, who associates with respectable women, finds true love and devotion; Vladimir, who prefers prostitutes, becomes increasingly bitter and sadistic.

Another tale with a French heroine is *The Tale of Ioann the Russian Merchant and the Beautiful Maiden Eleonora*. Ioann is the precocious son of a prosperous merchant who goes to Paris to study commerce. This tale is more in the tradition of the pseudo-moralistic anecdotal tale than the chivalrous romance. Ioann falls in love with Eleonora, a Parisienne of Spanish background and the ward of Ioann's host. Their love affair is rather casual with few of the conventions of chivalrous tales. Eleonora, who wears expensive clothes, takes the initiative on occasion, serving Ioann sweet vodka in his room. Ioann's host, learning of the relationship, marries Eleonora to another man. Beaten and chased from the house, Ioann returns to Russia where he goes into business with his father, presumably savoring happy memories of Eleonora. As in the *Tale of Alexander*, the heroine seems ruled more by literary conventions than by any consideration of national types.

The relative paucity of French women characters in eighteenth-century Russian literature is no doubt due, at least in part, to the prevailing neo-classical currents. An example in point is Alexander Sumarokov (1717-1777), father of the Russian tragedy. His mentors were Corneille and Voltaire. In his desire to create a national theater, nevertheless, Sumarokov rejected the prevailing predilection for anti-quity and exotic locales in favor of *Russian* subjects in all but two tragedies. Again, the lack of local color is the most obvious feature; still, the tragedies did try to adapt Russian history to neo-classical and eighteenth-century theatrical practices. This obviously ruled out French heroines.

Many other writers, while not using French characters, did make at least passing mention of French women. In Vasilii Maikov's mock epic *Elisei, or Bacchus Enraged* (1769-1770), there is a telling reference to a reformatory for prostitutes: "The place was a miniature Paris. Each girl was an angel in the flesh. That is why the house was always kept bolted."[11] Here Elisei learns that only idiots are constant in love. In Paris, notes Maikov, he could have learned how to dress, how to explain shameless lust, and how to talk nonsense. In his celebrated *Journey from St. Petersburg to Moscow* (1790), Alexander Radishchev notes the effects of French women, if not their actual presence. While Russian country women still display "natural charm . . . without any false front of sophistication," he chastises Frenchified city women with this rebuke: "On your cheeks there is rouge, on your heart rouge, on your conscience rouge, on your sincerity—soot. Rouge or soot, its all the same."[12]

The comic opera often based its plot on problems caused by French influence. Iakov Kniazhnin's *Misfortune from a Coach* (1779) is typical. Admirable peasants Anyuta and Lukian are about to be married when evil landowner Firiulin decides to sell Lukian into the army in order to purchase a new French carriage:

> For the holidays, I absolutely have to have a new coach. Although I have many coaches, this one I have in mind has been imported from Paris. Imagine, Monsieur Clément, the disgrace it would be not only for me but for all of you if your master did not ride in this beautiful coach; and if your mistress did not buy those lovely headdresses that are also imported directly from Paris . . . To unfortunate people like us who have returned from France to this savage country one pleasure has remained, and that is after making a decent turnover on this Russian trash one can get some respectable French thing.[13]

Lukian and Anyuta are saved to become the personal servants of Firiulin when he learns that they know two words of French—"monsieur" and "madame." Kniazhnin must also be given credit for one of the most inventive uses of Francomania ever. In his comedy *The Eccentrics* (1790), one Russian character tries to explain why he must keep his French mistress Zhabot ("to chatter"), even after his marriage, with this memorable line: "I made this contract—it's no great sin—so as not to forget the French language!"[14]

Russian comedy, which developed in the second half of the century along neo-classical lines, frequently had its origin in Francophobia, also. It tended to be didactic and filled with French plot devices, right down to the saucy soubrette and other assorted characters with no real counterparts in Russia. French names like Oronte, Géronte, and Dorante gradually gave way to Russian allegorical ones like Prostakov (simpleton) and Chistoserdov (pure heart). The language was frequently a bizarre mixture of Russian and French. Eighteenth-century Russian comedy reached its pinnacle with Denis Fonvizin's *Brigadier* (1769) and *The Minor* (1782).

Brigadier, the first realistic Russian comedy, is a biting satire on Francomania. Ivanushka is an ignorant fop who has just returned from Paris; he is appalled at the thought of living in Russia and of having a Russian wife. He would prefer the Councillor's wife, Avdotia, who spends three hours per day on her toilette and lives only for her French headdresses. The old charge of French immorality soon surfaces. Ivanushka is disgusted by the thought of a faithful, God-fearing, Russian wife after his liaisons with French women: "Does God really interfere in such matters in Russia? At least in France, gentlemen, He has left such things as loving, changing partners, marrying, and divorcing to the human will." He finds a soul mate in the silly Avdotia, despite the fact she has one almost unpardonable fault: "All my unhappiness consists of the fact you're Russian. It is such a *défaut* that nothing can make up for it . . . My body was born in Russia, that's true, but my soul belongs to the crown of France."[15]

Fonvizin was deeply troubled by the harmful effects of both Francomania and Francophobia. In a question addressed to Catherine the Great in 1783, he summarizes the Russian dilemma: "How might we eliminate two contradictory and equally harmful prejudices: the first, that in our own country everything is bad and everything abroad is good; and the second, that abroad everything is bad and everything in our country is good?"[16]

In this regard, Fonvizin's observations on the French in his *Letters from my Second Journey Abroad* (1777-1778) are especially interesting. Published with the *Journal* from his third trip, these letters were a significant contribution to Russian prose. The Russian traveler is astonished by the filth of French cities. In Montpellier, he remarks: "We have noticed that the feminine sex here is much brighter than the masculine, and besides they are not at all hard to look at. There are no real beauties, but the women do have pleasant, happy faces." They do "screech" a lot, however. In Paris itself, there is no morality, only an "empty brilliance and extravagant insolence in the men, a shameless indecency in the women—apart from these truly I see nothing else." Foreigners flock to Paris only for the theater and the girls. Russian men, however, have not sought out "proud" French women; Russian ladies, such as Mme Shuvalov, find their courtesy calls go unanswered. The feminine landscape is dominated by *les filles*, "indecent wenches covered from head to foot with diamonds." They dress superbly, ride in the best carriages, and live in the most beautiful houses:

> [At the theater] they sit in loges with their lovers, among whom the most prominent personages shame themselves publicly by sitting together with them in the same loges. Their wealth is inestimable . . . the wenches are the ones who are enjoying the treasures of the world. How many entire families have been ruined by them! How many good women made unhappy! How many young people destroyed! Here is a city to rival Sodom and Gomorrah!

He is only slightly less outraged by Mme Rousseau, the *philosophe's* widow, whom he calls the "greediest person the world has ever produced" and whom he blames for what he calls Rousseau's "suicide." Indeed she should be hung![17] In short, French women seem to be greedy, superficial, and immoral in the extreme. If it is any comfort to French national pride, he would later find Italian women even more depraved than the Parisiennes.

Ivan Krylov was also fond of ridiculing Francomania. His comedy *The Fashion Shop* dates from 1807 and shows the persistence of the immorality issue. This fashion shop is owned by a French émigrée Mme Carrée. As with all such establishments in late eighteenth-century Russia, this shop enjoys a deservedly shady reputation as a place for assignations and seductions and as a center for the smuggling of foreign goods into Russia without the payment of excise taxes. Russian women such as Mme Sumburova flock to these shops to squander money on the latest French luxuries. In this play, the dubious French proprietress is denounced to the police by her countryman Trichet, a bailiff who has absconded with his employer's property. Once again the "French connection" is clear—"French" means extravagance, waste, and immorality. Indeed, the Russian characters turn against the fashion shop as "both French and a temptation to feminine extravagance."[18] The Francophobia of the Russian theater (comic opera and comedy) would also be prominent in Russia's newest, most controversial, and most anticlassical genre—the novel.

Misgivings about the French abound in the works of novelist Fëdor Emin: "Emin's fiction is pervaded by a militant gallophobia which clearly announces Fonvizin's pre-romantic and nationalist sentiments . . . ."[19] Emin's last novel, *The Letters of Ernest and Doravra* (1766), is generally recognized as the first attempt at an *original* Russian novel as well as Russia's first epistolary novel. The plot, not surprisingly, recalls *La Nouvelle Héloïse:* an exchange of letters among friends concerning the ill-fated romance of a genteel, wealthy (later married) young noblewoman and a poor but virtuous (also married) young nobleman. Despite the obvious similarities, there are substantial differences in structure and characterization, which made *The Letters* much more than a pale imitation of Rousseau.

One of these original features is the novel's "Russianness," exemplified by both "surging patriotism" and "intensified xenophobia." The French governess, often an unqualified teacher who misleads her young Russian charges, is a favorite target: "When we entrust the education of the child to a French woman and, as the case may be, place him into the hands of someone who came to this country because she was exiled from hers, due to dishonorable behavior, then he will have learned her morals and frivolity." Again the question of French immorality seems to dominate the discussion. Heroine Doravra, reared by an old Russian nurse who instructed her in the ways of traditional Russian morality, laments the deleterious effect French etiquette has had on Russian courtship:

> A large majority of our [Russian] European women try for as long as possible not to divulge to their lovers their true inclination, which is neither too strong nor very effective. Many insist on making their lovers suffer through variously contrived ways of scorn and rejection; in their hearts they rejoice seeing their captive subjected to the cruelest of despairs.[20]

Nikolai Karamzin (1766-1826) was the first Russian writer to gain a reputation in the West. Usually considered the father of Russian sentimentalism, Karamzin wrote in the salon language of Europeanized Russia. At the age of twenty-two, he set out on a trip (May 1789-September 1790) that would take him through Germany, Switzerland, France, and England. His *Letters of a Russian Traveler* (1791-1801) are an important prose contribution to eighteenth-century Russian literature, combining as they do features of a "sentimental journey" à la Sterne with the Enlightenment passion for imparting information.

Karamzin's general attitude toward women in the *Letters* is the shy, restrained one adopted by Sterne. His few brief encounters usually end on an innocent note. This does not prevent him from remarking that there are many dissolute women in Berlin, which has been described by others as a Sodom and Gommorah (there did seem to be quite a few of these).[21] The women of Switzerland are nicely differentiated. The ladies of Basel are ugly, while those of Bern are given to socializing. The women of Lausanne are too "French," and those of Geneva like to tease (pp. 115, 137-138, 143-145). His greatest praise is reserved for the ladies of Zurich, where a woman's role is that of devoted wife and mother. Famous for their fidelity, they dress simply, wear no rouge, and, shades of the *terem*, have little or no social life outside the home (p. 128).

Once in Paris, Karamzin meets women of all social classes. He speaks glowingly of the artisan's wife whose life is spent in rustic toil

(p. 187). On the other hand, there is the actress whose lover, an old marquis, had ruined his family to buy her the best carriage in Paris—not solely an affliction of Russian comic opera characters, it would seem (p. 196). Most of his personal contacts are with salon ladies, although many salons have already closed as their mistresses experience financial ruin or flee the oncoming revolution. Karamzin is impressed by the intelligence of these women; most of them even understand Lavoisier's chemistry. He is not, however, impressed by their literary efforts, finding many expressions "not the words of a lady" and observing that these *femmes écrivains* often put even their lovers to sleep (pp. 191-192, 244).

Karamzin's hostess is Mme Glo . . . , a well-educated woman of about thirty who cultivates writers and serves good food. Her conversation tends to be boring, however, and her critical judgment is dubious since she always disagrees with our Russian traveler (pp. 188, 239). Then there is Mme N . . . , the "young, tender, languid, blonde pretty wife" of a blind, deaf, and crippled old Provencal nobleman. Mme N . . .'s great passion is the theater (p. 189).

It is at the theater that Karamzin has one of his most interesting encounters. He meets a beautiful, young blonde in a black dress, wearing a pale-blue ribbon on her unpowdered fair hair and a corsage of red roses on her lily-white bosom. Karamzin is intrigued by her friendly manner but later wonders about her profession since women of rank do not talk openly with strangers. Still, he cannot bring himself to accept the idea that this haunting beauty could be just another one of *les filles* (pp. 228-232).

On several occasions, French women ask him about Russian women. Mme Konkler in Geneva is informed that the women of Moscow are beautiful, without peer in intelligence, and matchless in the poetry that they write. They also pray a good deal (p. 146). The beautiful blonde at the theater learns that Russian women are beautiful and that "at any rate they are loved." She opines that, unlike French women, they doubtless know more about loving than pleasing (p. 230). Countess D . . ., Mme N . . .'s sister, is considering Russia as a place of exile. She is disturbed, however, by some of the reports she has heard about the harshness of the climate and the coarseness of the people. Karamzin tries to allay her fears about the rigors of a Russian winter by assuring her that Russian women become even more charming when the cold animates their faces. He reassures her that there is indeed a social life in Russia with theater, balls, suppers, cards, and "the charms of your sex." Foreigners are received well. One wonders if Countess D . . . has heard the stories of Russian wife-beating because she asks Karamzin point-blank: "Are women respected in Russia?" His reply is a bit flowery, to say the least: "In our country a woman is seated on the throne. Glory and love, the laurel and the rose, this is the motto of our knights" (pp. 246-248).

In the eighteenth century, French women were renowned as Europe's great beauties while their plainer English sisters paled in their shadow. Perhaps Karamzin's ultimate insult to French woman-hood, therefore, comes during his trip to England. From the moment he steps off the boat from France in Dover, he can think only of women. Karamzin proclaims himself captivated by "the youthful-looking English women, especially after coming from France where there are very few beauties." He wanders the streets for hours "just to feast my eyes on the women of Dover." English pallor bespeaks deep sensibility; these are veritable "lilies" whose languid glances say "I know how to love tenderly" (pp. 261-262). In London, the ladies dress simply and tastefully with no powder or rouge. There are, nevertheless, even more prostitutes than in Paris (pp. 270, 320). It is in English villages where English women truly shine in a land of "little Emiles and little Sophies." These modest, virtuous ladies are trained to be good wives and mothers with a strong sense of domestic responsibility, a sense lacking in society belles who think only of themselves and neglect their husbands and children. Indeed, Karamzin feels this devotion to family happiness is the key to England's Enlightenment (pp. 310-314).

Karamzin was by no means a Francophobe. At this time in his life, he was very much a cosmopolitan Westernizer who defended the reforms of Peter the Great as beneficial to all Russians. It was only after the Revolution and his own study of Russian history that Karamzin would begin to have serious doubts about the Westernization process itself. His concern for Russian women, however, seems unchanging. The French woman, despite her intelligence and charm, seemed to symbolize the disintegration of traditional family values and the abandonment of the sacred female role of faithful wife and devoted mother. (One should perhaps recall that this was also a concern of numerous French social critics as well.) Part of Karamzin's attitude is, of course, sentimental posing—the virtues of the simple, happy peasant life. In Russia, the role of women in the new Westernized society was, nevertheless, a very real problem. Did donning French fashions and adopting French manners mean turning away from Orthodox morality and love of family? For many Russians, the answer would seem to be yes. Karamzin would later (1802) chide Russian women for imitating shameless French women "who danced contredanses on the graves of their parents, husbands, and lovers!"[22] In his prose tale *Natalie the Boyar's Daughter* (1792), he would say: "I, in discussing old and new fashions with them [great-grandmothers], always grant preference to their caps and fur jackets over the present-day bonnets à la . . . and all the Gallic-Albion attire, glittering on the Muscovite beauties of the end of the eighteenth century."[23]

For a Russian writer, the creation of a French character was not a neutral, or even primarily literary, act.[24] So omnipresent was the controversy over the benefits and evils of French influence that the very use of a French character required one to take a position in the nascent Slavophile-Westernizer debate. It was an especially delicate matter when the French character was also a woman because of the passions surrounding the whole question of the "proper" role of the Russian woman. It is possible to see in the Russian criticism a genuine concern for cherished, worthwhile, traditional values. It is also possible, however, to interpret the Slavophile position as a brazen attempt to keep women "in their place"—in the case of Russia, an especially lowly place:

> [Conservative Prince Shcherbatov] lamented in the eighteenth century that the artificial and superficial process of cultural Westernization, in corroding so many of the cherished traditions of the Russian way of life, was unraveling the fabric of traditional sexual relations as well. The fashionable practice of "feminine intrigue," imported from the salons and ballrooms of France, had transformed certain upper class ladies from relatively passive and silent creatures into aggressive and cunning devotees of Les Liaisons dangereuses. What critics such as Shcherbatov deplored was not that woman was a sex object, but rather that she was a conscious participant in the erotic game.[25]

The definitive portrait of the French woman in eighteenth-century Russian literature has yet to emerge. One must await a thorough survey of all Russian plays, novels, tales, etc.—a task clearly beyond the scope of this brief essay. The initial look at a few eighteenth-century master works does give an indication of how complicated the interpretive task will be. The image that emerges to date strikes one as primarily negative—the French woman as a model of frivolity, irresponsibility, and infidelity. Before the final verdict can be returned, however, this portrait will have to be placed beside those of other foreign women. In turn, all these images will have to be studied in the more general context of women, Russian and foreign, in eighteenth-century Russian literature. Woman's special place and problems in Russian religious and literary tradition will have to be carefully evaluated. Perhaps the most important question that will eventually have to be answered is the one posed earlier by Joan Delaney Grossman: are these women dangerous because they are foreigners or because they are women?

NOTES

1. Robert K. Massie, *Peter the Great: His Life and World* (New York: Alfred A. Knopf, 1980), pp. 31-32, 34. See also Dorothy Atkinson, "Society and the Sexes in the Russian Past," in *Women in Russia*, edited by Dorothy Atkinson, Alexander Dallin and Gail Warshofsky Lapidus (Stanford: Stanford University Press, 1977), pp. 3-38. (In this essay, I have tried to cite works of interest to the non-Russian specialist. Excellent Russian bibliographies can be found in many of these works.)

2. Massie, pp. 808-809. Peter would be followed on the throne by four women, who ruled Russia for about seventy years of the century. Catherine the Great especially would try to improve the lot of women with court appointments such as that of Princess Dashkova to the Academy of Sciences, schools for women such as the Smolny Institute, the easement in confiscation laws to help wives and children of dead or exiled nobles, foundling homes for unwed mothers, etc. See Atkinson, p. 29; and J. L. Black, "Educating women in Eighteenth-Century Russia: Myths and Realities," *Canadian Slavonic Papers*, no. 20 (1978):23-43.

3. Black, p. 38.

4. Atkinson, pp. 15-16.

5. Joan Delaney Grossman, "Feminine Images in Old Russian Literature and Art," *California Slavic Studies*, no. 11 (1980):61.

6. William Edward Brown, *A History of Eighteenth-Century Russian Literature* (Ann Arbor: Ardis, 1980), p. 596. See also W. Gareth Jones, "A Trojan Horse within the Walls of Classicism: Russian Classicism and the National Specific," in *Russian Literature in the Age of Catherine the Great*, edited by A.G. Cross (Oxford: Wm. A. Meeuws, 1976), pp. 95-120; and Harold B. Segel, "Classicism and Classical Antiquity in Eighteenth- and Early Nineteenth-Century Russian Literature," in *The Eighteenth Century in Russia*, edited by J. G. Garrard (Oxford: Clarendon Press, 1973), pp. 48-74.

7. Nikolai Karamzin, "Why Are There So Few Talented Authors In Russia," in *The Literature of Eighteenth-Century Russia: A History and Anthology*, edited by Harold B. Segel, 2 vols. (New York: Dutton, 1967), vol. 1, p. 455. See also *Women in Russian Literature*, edited by Carl R. and Ellendea Proffer, no. 9-10 of *Russian Literature Triquarterly* (1974):71-75, 443-446.

8. Atkinson, p. 26.

9. Gary Cox, "Fairy-Tale Plots and Contemporary Heroes in Early Russian Prose Fiction," *Slavic Review* 39, no. 1 (March 1980):85-96.

10. Richard S. White, "The Development of Russian Prose in the Early Eighteenth Century" (Ph.D. diss., University of Michigan, 1971), p. 204, n. 15. The discussion of the Petrine tales follows Mr. White's interpretation.

11. Segel, *Literature*, vol. 2, pp. 145, 161-162.

12. Aleksandr N. Radishchev, *A Journey from St. Petersburg to Moscow*, edited by Roderick Page Thaler, translated by Leo Wiener (Cambridge, Mass.: Harvard University Press, 1958), pp. 131-132, 210-211.

13. Segel, *Literature*, vol. 2, pp. 381, 389.

14. Brown, p. 355.

15. Segel, *Literature*, vol. 2, pp. 325, 342, 344. See also pp. 348-349.

16. Charles A. Moser, *Denis Fonvizin* (Boston: Twayne, 1979), pp. 99-100.

17. Segel, *Literature*, vol. 1, pp. 322, 326-328, 333-334, 343-344.

18. Brown, pp. 373-375. In an earlier Krylov story "Nights" (1792), the

French proprietress of a fashion shop is also a "madame" (p. 563).

19. David E. Budgen, "Fëdor Emin and the Beginnings of the Russian Novel," in Cross, *Russian Literature*, p. 76.

20. Wanda Zielinski-Sorgente, "An Epistolary Novel Reevaluated: *The Letters of Ernest and Doravra* by F. A. Emin" (Ph.D. diss., Northwestern University, 1978), pp. 47, 50-51. This study concentrates on the relationship between *The Letters* and *La Nouvelle Héloïse*. Until recently, Emin has been a neglected figure in Russian literature. His novels, as well as those of his even less celebrated contemporaries, will have to be closely analyzed in future studies of women in Russian literature.

21. N. M. Karamzin, *Letters of a Russian Traveler (1789-1790)*, translated and abridged by Florence Jonas, (New York: Columbia University Press, 1957), p. 69. All further references to this work appear in the text.

22. A. G. Cross, *N. M. Karamzin: A Study of his Literary Career 1783-1803* (Carbondale: Southern Illinois University Press, 1971), p. 212.

23. N. M. Karamzin, *Selected Prose of N. M. Karamzin*, edited by Henry M. Nebel, Jr. (Evanston: Northwestern University Press, 1969), p. 74. See also Nebel, *N. M. Karamzin: A Russian Sentimentalist* (The Hague: Moulton, 1967).

24. It could also be argued that the French were likewise unable to create a truly fictional Russia. Voltaire, Rousseau, and Montesquieu, among others, seemed trapped by history and current political events, limiting most of their comments in *contes* and novels to Peter the Great's exploits and Catherine the Great's reign. See my "Voltaire's Russia: Window on the East," *Studies on Voltaire and the Eighteenth Century*, vol. 164 (Oxford: The Voltaire Foundation, 1976), pp. 185-198.

25. Richard Stites, "Women and the Russian Intelligentsia," in Atkinson, Dallin, and Lapidus, p. 40.

Eva M. Kahiluoto Rudat

The View from Spain: Rococo Finesse and Esprit Versus Plebeian Manners

A una señorita francesa

La bella que prendió con gracioso reir
Mi tierno corazón, alterando su paz,
Enemiga de amor, inconstante, fugaz,
Me inspira una pasión que no quiere sentir.

—Leandro Fernández de Moratín "Epigramas"[1]

THIS EPIGRAM addressed to a French *demoiselle* sets the tone for the prevalent view on the French woman in Spanish eighteenth-century literature. The connotation of frivolity, fugacity, inconstancy, levity, and grace places this brief piece—and the French woman it depicts—within the rococo culture, of which the Spaniards had an example in the Bourbon court since the year 1700.

The view presented by the late eighteenth-century playwright Leandro Fernández de Moratín echoes in style and content the earlier description of a French coquette by José Cadalso in his *Cartas marruecas (Moroccan Letters)*, presumably written before 1780. For Cadalso, *coquetterie* is the favorite pastime of the French women and consists of finding ways to deceive all men who court them. He describes how the coquette has a marvelous time because she has all young men of some merit at her disposal, a fact that truly flatters her self-esteem. Yet, since the French take some matters very lightly—including love—this flirting is not taken seriously, and the young men usually take their incense from one altar to another without giving it much thought.[2]

Similar attributes, such as inconstancy and superficiality—not only in love but also in other matters—appear already in a seventeenth-century assessment of the French character by Carlos García (1617), who claims that "God gave the French nation utmost effort, courage and gentility but accompanied by a remission of variability and inconstancy."[3] This opinion can be substantiated by literary examples, such as Lope de Vega's play *Anzuelo de Feniza (Feniza's Bait)*, in which lack of firmness in women is deemed of French origin. Lope writes, "I know their condition / every woman who professes / this French passion / is not firm at heart."[4]

It is hardly conceivable that the French influence in Spain would have started suddenly, as if by magic, in exactly the year 1700. The Spanish aristocracy was cosmopolitan enough to have absorbed some of the magnificent splendor of Louis XIV and his court. In descriptions of seventeenth-century customs, the French, in fact, receive blame for having introduced luxury and fashions conducive to vice and lack of morals. María de Zayas y Sotomayor, one of Spain's first feminists, in her *Novelas amorosas y ejemplares (Amorous and Exemplary Novels,* 1637), levels a pointed criticism against the French. In a long poem, inserted in one of her novels, she laments the abandonment of the simple customs of yesteryear. The political element is also present as the French are, above all, accused of having introduced the taste for luxury "after they appropriated the Spaniards' courage,"[5] in other words, their position as a world power.

Although early seventeenth-century Spanish commentators tend to stress the contrast between the French superficiality and levity of character and the Spanish severity and more profound way of thinking, a change occurs toward the end of the seventeenth century. According to an eighteenth-century essayist, Juan Pablo Forner, the Spanish severity gives way to a more lively, gallant, and vivacious style. Forner discusses the influence of Phillip IV's luxurious court upon the Spaniards' language and their literary expression. He defines, in fact, the incipient rococo style as he describes how their language became "more rapid, lusty, lively, sonorous, cheerful, gallant, flowery, delicious."[6] These are, no doubt, some of the characteristics that, together with the variability and inconstancy attributed to the French women, identify the opinion both Moratín and Cadalso have of them with the eighteenth-century rococo customs. Helmut Hatzfeld in "Gibt es ein literarisches Rokoko in Spanien?" ("Does a Spanish Literary Rococo Exist?") connects particularly Cadalso's writings with the rococo culture, which he discusses as a lifestyle and fashion.[7] This rococo mode is presented, rather than defined, in Cadalso's account of the *petimetre* (from the French *petit-maître*) or *lindo* (the French *beau*). He talks about a young man of "gallant appearance, gracious conversation, illustrious name, magnificient equipage, courtly behaviour and the right age for love affairs," who, in addition, dares to use rather questionable language in the presence of his distinguished hostess.[8] A similar description could just as well be dedicated to this young man's female counterpart, a *petimetra,* whose copying of French fashions and lifestyle the Spanish writer criticizes.

The eighteenth-century Spaniards' opinion of the French woman is reflected in their reactions to the *afrancesamiento,* or French influence, upon their own customs. Cadalso's *Cartas marruecas*—fictitious oriental letters between two Moroccans following the fashion of Montesquieu's *Lettres persanes,* the *Lettres chinoises* by marquis d'Argens, and many others—is an eloquent example of this type of criticism. Gazel, who travels in Spain, writes to his old Moroccan teacher, Ben Belay, and describes the most varied aspects of life in Madrid. In his answer, Ben Belay denounces the customs as a source of decadence and summarizes, at the same time, some of the most typical elements of the rococo way of life. In his opinion, "a nation used to delicate tables, soft beds, fine food, effeminate manners, amorous conversations, frivolous pastimes and special studies, directed toward refinement of all the elements of luxury does not pay attention when all this is shown as being signs of approaching decadence."[9] Thus, it is the old Moroccan who condemns the frivolity of life in the Spanish court, contrasting in this respect with Nuño, Gazel's Spanish guide and escort, who is evidently a spokesman of the Spanish aristocracy and, possibly, of Cadalso himself.

Nuño seems to accept the decadence of his time as an inevitable evil, a *fait accompli.* He shows the Moroccan a letter written by his sister, another *petimetra afrancesada*—to a certain extent, the Spanish counterpart of the French coquette—who describes her typical daily activities employing language full of "fashionable" half-French expressions. She writes: "Today it did not dawn in my apartment before half past twelve noon [*hasta medio día y medio,* a direct translation of the French *midi et demi*]. I had two cups of tea; I put on a *déshabillé* and a night cap for a *tour* of the garden; and I read about eight stanzas of the second act of *Zaïre* [a play by Voltaire]." Aside from representing a typical picture of the idle life—fashion, fine food, and entertainment are her only preoccupation—this letter also demonstrates the complete change that has occurred in Spanish society. In the preceding century, she would have been confined to her home, literally locked up under the absolute domination of her spouse, whose acts were governed by a strict honor code. Now, on the contrary, it is an accepted fact that a married woman may have a *cortejo*—a young man, obviously her lover, who not only appears as her escort in public but also attends her at breakfast and helps her with her toilet. This explains the presence of a M. Labanda at an early hour in her private quarters. As her letter indicates: "Monsieur Labanda came; I started my toilet; the *abbé* was not there. I gave orders to pay my modiste. I went to the reception room; a few people entered [*entró un poco de mundo,* again a direct imitation of the French expression *un peu de monde*]." The letter reflects the typical function of the Spanish upper-class woman who directs salons, referred to in Spanish as *tertulias*. Her husband is usually not visible, but the *cortejo* is always present, as is often an *abbé de salon* (this time the *abbé* was not there), an elegant clergyman of evidently doubtful morals. Sometimes actors or writers may visit her. In the letter, the *petrimetra* speaks of card games (*piquete* and *quince*) and of her favorite dishes (*crapaudina*, a French dish). She tells how the new *chef*, who is "divine," just arrived from Paris ("*viene de arribar*," a copy of the French *vient d'arriver*). She criticizes the theater presentation as detestable but expects the next play will be *galant*; the actors, however, are deplorable (*pitoyables*, another of her French expressions).[10]

The Spanish salon, however, is criticized in the writings of the time as lacking in refinement and intelligent conversation. The Spaniards themselves are ashamed to be Spaniards due to the triviality and vulgarity as well as lack of manners exhibited in these reunions as compared to the elegant *finesse* and *esprit* of the French women in their salons.

This fact is due, in part, to the Spaniards' "patriotic" reaction against the *afrancesamiento* (Frenchified customs), which brought about a provincialism and plebeianism in dress, entertainment, and art. In other words, a rather superficial change occurred instead of one based on a more profound influence of the Spanish tradition. Thus, the *petimetra afrancesada* becomes the *maja*, and, of course, the *petimetre* turns into a *majo*, when everyone—not only actors and actresses adopting the fashion promoted in plays depicting national customs, but even the aristocrats—adopts the provincial attire. In the theater, the *sainetes*, short one-act plays by Ramón de la Cruz, are the most famous ones for depicting and criticizing these new attitudes of the Spanish society. The same plebeianism also dominates the style of the Spanish *tertulias* in the eighteenth century and is strongly reflected in the art of the period, such as Goya's sketches of *majas* and *majos* in the *Caprichos* series, and, above all, his paintings *Maja desnuda* (The Naked *Maja*; Madrid: Prado, no. 743) and *Maja vestida* (The Clothed *Maja*; Madrid: Prado, no. 744), for which the Duchess of Alba may have served as a model.

In view of this vulgarization of Spanish customs, it is indeed legitimate to ask whether the source of Spanish decadence is really to be sought in France. Foreign travelers in Spain seem to be of a different opinion and are invariably scandalized by the generality of low morals.[11] Carmen Martín Gaïte, in her book on the amorous and marital customs of eighteenth-century Spain, *Usos amorosos del dieciocho en España*, notes that *cortejo* in particular should be seen as a Spanish custom originating as a reaction against the strict sixteenth-century honor code and, thus, as a natural consequence of the Spanish woman's earlier confinement and total alienation from social life, although either French or Italian influence is usually cited as a source of this custom.[12] If, however, foreign influence is to be taken into account, the origins of *cortejo* can be traced to the Italian *cicisbeo*, a custom introduced by the Venetian tradesmen who, during their long absences on business, wanted their wives to be entertained. This expression appears in Spain as *chichisveo* before the term *cortejo* is used.[13] The French *coquetterie*, on the other hand, is distinct in that it involves an element of *finesse* and frivolity as well as a more sophisticated mode of courting: elegant fashions, intelligent conversation or *causerie*, and an aspect of deceit as the coquette enjoys the company of several admirers without ever becoming seriously involved. According to Carmen Martín Gaïte, even the term *coquetería* was, in the eighteenth century, not yet generally accepted as a Spanish word due to the affectation it implied.[14] The image of the French woman as the rococo coquette, on the other hand, appears repeatedly in Spanish literature of the second half of the century.

Cadalso and other contemporaries of his criticize not so much the French customs and the French woman of the rococo period as the Spaniards' vulgarized imitation of this lifestyle, evident in their pseudo-French language and their ostentatious fashions. The fact that this imitation is, above all, superficial and concerned with external appearance and luxury has been noticed by an earlier writer, Diego de Torres Villarroel in his *Visiones y visitas de Torres con Don Francisco de Quevedo por la corte* (1727-1728), also known as *Moral Dreams*. He says the Spaniards always wanted to imitate everything and "without consulting their reason, in love with the superficial, accepted certain extravagances as an improvement."[15]

The social criticism leveled by Torres is presented in the guise of dreams during which he visits Madrid in the company of Don Francisco de Quevedo, whose *Sueños* (*Dreams*, 1627) are evidently his model. When Torres describes the life of his time, his judgment corresponds closely to seventeenth-century morality; and his literary expression echoes the sharp baroque contrasts between good and evil, between moral and corporal beauty on the one hand and ugliness and vice on the other. In the late eighteenth-century authors, however, the outright condemnation of the French moral license is absent; and the tortuous baroque exuberance is replaced by more gracious, softer, and lighter tones, as well as diminutives. An expression like *mi tierno corazón* (my tender heart) would have been unthinkable for a baroque Spaniard.

José Cadalso, educated in France, favors the French intellectual influence and seems not to be disturbed by the fact that in the letter of the young *petrimetra* she includes in the list of her daily pastimes readings of Voltaire's *Zaïre*, which, in a more traditional Spanish view, would have been condemned as a heresy.

A more conservative Spanish opinion is to be found in an early twentieth-century account of Spanish aristocrats residing in the eighteenth-century French court. Father Luis Coloma, a Jesuit, in *Retratos de antaño* (*Portraits of the past*), calls Paris the center of corruption, "the university of the seven deadly sins," dominated by two luminous figures: Voltaire and Mme du Barry. In other words, the intellectual world represented by the heretical deism and women of doubtful morals govern the social life. In a sharp contrast to this entourage, the author presents the figure of Doña María Manuela Pignatelli de Aragón, Gonzaga, Moncayo y Caracciolo, Duchess of Villahermosa. She had been educated in a convent and, at the age of fifteen, married the duke of Villahermosa, who took her to the French court. There, she had to confront problems created by the vicious world for which she was unprepared.[16] She, nevertheless, maintains her integrity despite her husband's neglect and love affairs. In this description, the innocent young Spanish girl with a religious education has to confront the sophistication and malice of the women in the French court.

If, however, we were to judge only by the literary image of the rococo coquette, or by the somewhat biased account of a Jesuit, our view of the Spaniards' opinion of the French eighteenth-century woman would be unfair. It is therefore interesting to see that a person who actually lived in France for some length of time or someone who was familiar with the literary talents of French women offered a very different view. Such persons, in fact, tried their best to destroy the myth of excessive liberality sustained by writers who hardly even had the opportunity to get to know French women. The contrary view is best expressed by Ignacio de Luzán in his *Memorias literarias de Paris* (*Literary Memories of Paris*, 1751), in which he depicts the French woman as modest, well educated, and especially concerned with educating equally both her sons and daughters in modesty and good manners. Luzán writes that people who only pass through Paris occasionally or who only contemplate it from afar necessarily have an erroneous opinion on the liberality of this great court. Only with difficulty will these people believe what he affirms regarding the women's modesty. The positive image, nevertheless, becomes evident when their activities are closely observed "in the churches, in the streets, in the houses, in their conversations, in the dances, at the tables, and in the theaters." The women's modesty, at least in public, is, according to Luzán, "like a general system of the nation, with only rare exceptions."[17]

Another interesting observation deserves to be mentioned: Luzán has noticed how foreigners sometimes use a language that embarrasses the ladies and causes them to appear frightened and surprised at having to listen. This constitutes yet another proof of the fact that the French women's liberality is an opinion people outside France have of her rather than in the country itself (p. 50).

For Luzán, there are other reasons for the liberality of customs in Paris—liberal, in his vocabulary, implies licentiousness—which he prefers not to discuss. If, in fact, such a liberality does exist, the reasons for it are not to be sought in the women's lack of modesty. He reaches these conclusions after discussing women's education, which he considers to be as good as the education men receive (pp. 46-47). Luzán, author of the *Poética* (1737) and himself an educator, states that in Paris one can find women well instructed in geography, history, philosophy, and even mathematics (p. 47). He attributes this to the fact that all girls have the opportunity to learn how to read, write, and calculate in the parochial and convent schools. These rudiments of knowledge grant them the opportunity to continue educating themselves at home through readings that are available to them. Luzán understands that this interest in a wider knowledge is typical not only of the nobility but also of the daughters of artisans and the like. He mentions several books published for this specific purpose, such as *Des études convenables aux demoiselles,* which includes an introduction to French grammar, orthography, rhetoric, poetry, universal history, geography, mythology, and "many other useful instructions written utilizing a clear and easy method" (p. 48). Further examples are *L'Art poétique à l'usage des dames,* rhetoric for women, and Newton's philosophy for women. He singles out the marquise du Châtelet as having defended Newton's philosophy against a great mathematician, M. Mairan. Furthermore, several women writers deserve Luzán's special attention: Mme de Bocage, author of a tragedy the *Amazons* and a poem "The Lost Paradise," written as an epilogue to Milton; and Mme de Graffigny, author of *Peruvian Letters,* another example of exotic letters common in the eighteenth century (p. 49).

The principal issue addressed by Luzán is the necessity of providing equal educational opportunity for boys and girls, a situation already existing in France, where both books and teachers were available for this purpose. In Spain, on the other hand, the traditional convent education failed to teach girls anything beyond domestic skills, not even how to read and write. The old, well-established belief, linked to the notion of original sin, still persisted; it maintained that knowledge for women was not only unnecessary but also dangerous because women did not possess the capacity to distinguish between right and wrong or the will to combat vice.

Luzán's observations reflect not only his awareness of the sharp contrast between the prevailing views on women's education in France and those in Spain but also the knowledge of issues under discussion at the time. Although the debate on the supposed inferiority of the female intelligence was still raging throughout Europe—and France was no exception—the concern for providing for women an adequate lay education beyond the traditional convent school was brought up in France as early as the seventeenth century by François Poulain de La Barre, in *De l'égalité des deux sexes* (Paris, 1673). Poulain's radical view was that "women would be perfectly capable of holding posts in the Church, army, judicature, and so on, normally reserved for men," according to Jean H. Bloch in "Women and the Reform of the Nation."[18] This view, based on the thesis that a woman's intellect could in no way be inferior to a man's since sexual differences were physical, was not yet generally accepted. The more moderate opinion of Fénelon in his *Traité de l'éducation des filles* (1687) was to become the authority for eighteenth-century views on girls' education.[19] The importance of women's preparation for their role in the family and in the society was stressed. Although "Fénelon placed emphasis primarily on extensive religious and moral education" (Bloch, p. 3), he also promoted extensive reading for women. The concept of the virtuous and enlightened woman prevailed in most eighteenth-century writings on the subject of female education (Bloch, p. 4). The Revolution brought about a new concept of the woman as *citoyenne* (citizen), whose education was important for the good of the nation (Bloch, p. 7). Bloch points out, however, that conservative views surprisingly coexisted with the new ideas in the works of many women writers, who tended to echo, for example, the rather traditional stand of Rousseau, who "denied women any public or professional role" (Bloch, p. 5).

In France, where the Church had not been able to prevent the publication of the *Encyclopédie* or of other writings of the *philosophes*, women had access to knowledge, especially toward the end of the eighteenth century. The situation in Spain was antithetical, since all foreign books had been banned for several decades and most of the latest advances in scientific knowledge were omitted from the educational program because they were considered harmful to the Church's doctrine. The education of girls was scarcely regarded as worthy of mention, for a woman's intelligence was still considered as barely surpassing that of a beast. Fray Benito Jerónimo Feijoo, famous for his writings encouraging progress in all fields, had written a *Defensa de las mujeres* (Defense of Women) in 1725, an essay in which he defended the intellectual capacity of women and refuted erroneous opinions with arguments similar to Poulain's in France some five decades earlier.[20] Yet the traditional opinion still prevailed toward the end of the century. When Josefa Amar y Borbón, an exceptionally enlightened woman writes her *Discourse in Defense of Women's Talent and Their Capacity for Government and Other Positions Held by Men* (1786), she still had to contend with defending the female intelligence and utilized Feijoo's eloquent arguments.[21] She did so, however, adding an unusual personal interpretation because she explained original sin not as a propensity toward vice but as a desire for knowledge, since "curiosity is a sign of talent" (p. 407). In her essay, written in support of Spanish women's access to the Sociedad económica de los amigos del país de Madrid—an economic and patriotic society dedicated to promoting scientific and economic progress—she defended women's ability to deal with matters of national economy and politics. She lamented the fact that in her world women were still denied not only the possibility of holding positions commensurate with their knowledge and skills but also their right to instruction. She stated:

> The men, not satisfied after having reserved for themselves positions, honors, compensations for their work, in other words everything that could excite the studiousness and dedication of women, have also deprived the members of our sex of the satisfaction of having an enlightened mind (p. 402).

Thus, the Spanish woman in this enlightened age, far from seeking professional vindication, had to fight for her basic right to learn to read and to educate herself for her own personal pleasure. Josefa Amar's own case was obviously an exception; through her connection with the *Sociedad económica,* she had access to books that otherwise were prohibited and that only members of this and other similar societies were allowed to import. Also, she evidently had a sensible father—a physician—who shared much of his knowledge with his daughter. Josefa Amar's major treatise on the education of women, *Discurso sobre la educación física y moral de las mujeres* (*Discourse on the Physical and Moral Education of Women* (1790), attests to the advanced medical knowledge of its author.[22] Some of her ideas about domestic matters such as infant care, children's clothing and health, breastfeeding, and the like are surprisingly modern. The issues she presents reflect, at the same time, an intimate knowledge of the existing literature on the subject of girls' education. Due to censorship, Spanish writers of the time could not always openly identify their sources, particularly when they quoted the French *philosophes.* The issues Josefa Amar addresses, such as the legal situation of women, the supposed innate characteristics of women, and the prevailing marital customs, link her to the encyclopedists.

The *philosophes,* for example, had introduced the idea of combining the most desirable aspects of bourgeois marriage with the customs of the nobility. Adhering to this ideal, Josefa Amar advocates better understanding and mutual cooperation between the spouses. In this context, she cites John Locke's *Some Thoughts Concerning Education* (pp. xxv-xxvi), a work considered representative of the encyclopedists' position.[23] Another of Josefa Amar's principal sources is Fénelon's *L'Education des filles.* Thus, in spite of her striving toward a situation in which the enlightened woman could contribute to both private and public happiness, Josefa Amar—like many of the French women writers of her time—still maintains a fairly conservative stand. For her, anything beyond the woman's traditional place in the home is still unattainable. This conservatism is also reflected in her recommendations regarding readings suitable for young women. She thinks that novels that deal excessively with love should not be given to young girls. Although the French, according to her, often consider that good morals can be taught by reading novels, her own opinion is that the immorality in such novels would set forth a bad example (p. 192).

On the whole Josefa Amar y Borbón's opinions reinforce Ignacio de Luzán's earlier views on the excellence of the French woman's education and her intelligence. In her writings, she affirms her admiration for the French women who have acquired literary fame. In her essay on women's talent, she mentions the marquise de Sévigné, the comtesse de Lafayette, and Mme Dacier (p. 409), whose translation of Homer she also cites (p. 436). In her treatise on education, she again points out the great number of French women who have excelled in literary endeavors (p. xxiii), particularly Mme de Bocage [sic], who is well known for her poetry and her letters on Italy (p. xxx).

The last chapter of Josefa Amar's *Discourse on the Education of Women* deserves special attention because it is an annotated bibliography of writings dealing with the education of women from Greek antiquity to her own day. Even today, it constitutes an interesting starting point for any research on the subject. Besides extensive erudition, this bibliography shows Josefa's interest in French women writers. The author mentions the marquise de Lambert who, in her *Réflexions nouvelles sur les femmes* and *Lettre sur la véritable éducation* (Paris, 1727), wrote that "women have more taste and understanding for culture and propriety of style than men" (pp. 336-337).[24] Another curious entry is *Emile chrétien ou de l'éducation* by M. de Leveson, which she lists as "contrary to Rousseau's *Emile*" (p. 340). Besides the well-known authorities, such as Locke and Fénelon, already cited, she mentions *Projet pour perfectionner l'éducation* by abbé de Saint-Pierre (p. 338),[25] and a book entitled *De l'éducation phisique [sic] è [sic] morale des femmes* (Brussels, 1779), listed by her as anonymous (p. 341).[26] The identical title might suggest similarity of views with her own *Discourse*. As works of special importance, she also mentions Fénelon's *Aventures de Télémaque* (p. 343) and *Adèle & Théodore, ou Lettres sur l'éducation* by the marquise de Genlis (p. 345).[27] This bibliography deserves more comprehensive comments, which are not within the scope of this study.

The better education and intellectual superiority of the French woman could not completely overshadow the claims of excessive liberality in the minds of the conservative Spaniards. They had to admit, however, that the French rococo coquette had *finesse* and *esprit* not equalled by her Spanish counterpart in spite of certain efforts toward refinement of taste. Lack of education leads to an imitation of trivialities and a vulgarization of manners as the provincial patriotic reaction against everything foreign brings about the plebeian manners and the degradation of nobility. The modesty and good education of the majority of French women, therefore, was appreciated by Spanish eighteenth-century educators and writers who had serious intentions of improving the level of women's education in Spain and needed, for this purpose, a model worthy of their esteem.

NOTES

1. *Obras*. Biblioteca de Autores Españoles 2 (Madrid: Atlas, 1944), p. 606. The epigrams are not dated but Leandro Fernández de Moratín (1760-1828) started his literary production in 1779. All translations from Spanish to English in this study are mine.

To a French Girl
The beauty, who with her gracious laugh
set my tender heart on fire and altered its peace,
enemy of love, fickle, fleeting,
inspired in me a passion, which she herself did not want to feel.

2. José Cadalso, "Carta LXXVI," *Cartas marruecas* (first published posthumously in *Correo de Madrid* from February 4, 1789 to July 25, 1789, and as a volume in Madrid: Sancha, 1793. José Cadalso lived between 1741 and 1782. See Clásicos Castellanos 112 (Madrid: Espasa-Calpe, 1935), pp. 186-187.

3. Carlos García, *La oposición y conjunción de los dos grandes luminares* (Paris, 1617; Madrid : Libros de Antaño, 1877), p. 264. See Miguel Herrero García, "Concepto de los franceses," in *Ideas de los españoles del siglo XVII* (Madrid: Gredos, 1966), p. 408.

4. Lope de Vega, *Anzuelo de Feniza, Obras* XIV (Madrid: Real Academia Española, 1890), 505a. See Herrero García, pp. 408-409.

5. María de Zayas y Sotomayor, *Novelas amorosas y ejemplares* (Paris: Baudry, 1847), p. 297.

6. Juan Pablo Forner, *Exequias de la lengua castellana* (Madrid: Espasa-Calpe, 1956), p. 74.

7. Helmut Hatzfeld, "Gibt es ein literarisches Rokoko in Spanien?" *Iberoromania* 1 (1969):59-72.

8. Cadalso, "Carta LXIX," p. 174. See Hatzfeld, p. 66.

9. Cadalso, "Carta XXXVIII," p. 216. See Hatzfeld, pp. 66-67.

10. Cadalso, "Carta XXXV," pp. 97-99. See Hatzfeld, pp. 65-66.

11. Carmen Martín Gaite, *Usos amorosos del dieciocho en España* (Madrid: Siglo XXI de España Editores, 1972), pp. 1-3.

12. Martín Gaite, p. 15.

13. Martín Gaite, p. 19. See also Werner Krauss, "Gesellschaftlichkeit und Geselligkeit im Spanien der Aufklärung," *Werk und Wort* (Berlin/Weimar: Aufbau-Verlag, 1972), pp. 242-285.

14. Martín Gaite, p. 194.

15. Diego de Torres Villarroel, *Visiones y visitas de Torres con Don Francisco de Quevedo por la corte*, 1727-1728 (Madrid: Espasa-Calpe, 1966), pp. 60-61.

16. P. Luis Coloma, S.J., *Retratos de antaño*, vol. 1 (Madrid: Razón y Fe, 1914).

17. Ignacio de Luzán, *Memorias literarias de Paris: actual estado y método de sus estudios* (Madrid: Gabriel Ramírez, 1751), pp. 51-52. Subsequent references are included in the text.

18. See Jean H. Bloch, "Women and the Reform of the Nation," in *Woman and Society in Eighteenth-Century France: Essays in Honour of John Stephenson Spink*, edited by Eva Jacobs et al. (London: The Athlone Press, 1979), p. 3. Subsequent references to Bloch's work are included in the text.

19. Abbé Salignac de La Mothe Fénelon, *L'Education des filles* (1687), p. 1. See Bloch, pp. 3-4.

20. Fray Benito Jerónimo Feijoo, "Defensa de las mujeres," *Teatro crítico universal*, vol. 1, Discurso XVI, 1st. ed., 1725. See *Obras escogidas*, edited by Vicente de la Fuente (Madrid: Rivadeneyra, 1863).

21. Josefa Amar y Borbón, "Discurso en defensa del talento de las mujeres, y de su aptitud para el gobierno, y otros cargos en que se emplean los hombres," *Memorial Literario*, no. 32 (Madrid, 1786). See also the same text re-edited by Carmen Chaves McClendon in *Dieciocho*, 3 (1980):144-161. Subsequent references to the first version are included in the text.

22. *Discurso sobre la educación física y moral de las mujeres* por Doña Josepha Amar y Borbón, Socia de Mérito de la Real Sociedad Aragonesa y de la Junta de Damas Unida a la Real Sociedad de Madrid (Madrid: Benito Cano, 1790). Subsequent references are included in the text.

23. See Katherine Clinton, "Femme et Philosophe: Enlightenment Origins of Feminism," *Eighteenth Century Studies*, 8 (1975):294.

24. About the importance of the marquise de Lambert and her salon for the intellectual life in Paris at the beginning of the eighteenth century, see Clinton, p. 285.

25. For further comments on abbé de Saint-Pierre's book, see Bloch, p. 4.

26. Bloch, pp. 11-12, refers to this book as a work by Reballier and states, "Reballier put the argument in even stronger terms by insisting, as Poulain had done one hundred years before, on women's natural rights to knowledge."

27. See Bloch, p. 12.

✿ Claire G. Moses

The Legacy of the Eighteenth Century: A Look at the Future

In EIGHTEENTH-CENTURY FRANCE, both the image and reality of women were undergoing profound changes. These changes extended forward into the nineteenth and twentieth centuries and explain the modern concept of French womanhood. Our examination of eighteenth-century views on women will conclude by highlighting the connections that link the experience of eighteenth-century French women to French women's future experiences.

Throughout the eighteenth century, there was great interest in women's issues. The basic liberalism of the writers of that era guaranteed that women's plight would be treated with sympathy. Furthermore, the willingness of the Enlightenment philosophers to question the basic immutability of apparently natural characteristics had revolutionary implications for the status of women.

Voltaire wrote that women's inferiority was contingent upon circumstance, not upon natural necessity.[1] Montesquieu thought-provokingly symbolized human tyranny in the person of a young Persian girl presumed—but falsely—to be happy in her place in the king's harem.[2] In L'Esprit des lois, he advocated equality of treatment of men and women in divorce.[3] In the Encyclopédie, women were judged equal to men in intellectual capacity; it was their limited education that was held responsible for the nonrealization of their potential.[4] According to Samia I. Spencer, calls for improved education for women were a not uncommon part of the general concern for education throughout the century.[5] D'Alembert defended women's rights to an education equal to men's. Diderot, in his treatise on public education, pointed out that improved education for boys would be in vain if effective reforms were not also carried out for the training of girls.[6]

It is not surprising then that fully feminist writings emerged with the Revolution. The years immediately preceding the storming of the

Bastille witnessed a stepped-up pace in the circulation of pamphlets and brochures on a host of social and political issues. The women's issue was not neglected among them. There is evidence that these brochures circulated throughout France, passed along by friends and relatives gathering in provincial salons.[7] The *cahiers de doléances*, prepared in 1789 by the primary electoral assemblies to inform their representatives to the Estates General of their concerns, reveal that the demand for improved female education was widespread.[8] The third estate of Chatellerault sought equality for both sexes.[9] In the primary election (early in 1789) for the third-estate representative from Chevanceaux, women voted, and no one dared prevent them.[10]

The most important of the feminist publicists during the early years of the Revolution were Condorcet, Olympe de Gouges, Etta Palm d'Aelders, and Théroigne de Mericourt. In their writings, the basic concepts of Enlightenment reasoning are made to pertain to women as well as to all men. Their feminism paralleled the Revolution's politics of individual rights. They believed that individuals of both sexes were similar in capacity and character, and they ascribed male-female differences to socialization. Sex, no more so than social position at birth, should not be a cause to deny the basic rights of citizenship. Justice required that all men *and* women be assured the opportunity to develop their full potential.

A phenomenon of nearly equal importance was the development of a collective female consciousness, resulting from women's participation in the Revolution. A few women took part in the disturbances of July 14, 1789, and again of the night of August 4, but they were notable for their singularity. The "October Days" of that same year, however, were a women's affair; and women participated in important numbers in the Champ de Mars demonstration of 1791, as they did again on 4 Prairial (1795). Parisian women participated in politics through the "mixed fraternal societies," which had been created to inform and instruct "passive" citizens—including women—of the actions of the Revolutionary government. In the provinces, clubs of entirely female membership sprang up. Although for the most part, the women in these provincial clubs seemed to have understood their role to be that of auxiliary supporters to the male makers of the Revolution, their activities encouraged the emergence of a sense of the collective power of women.

The opposition likely sensed this nascent collective force. By the fall of 1793, all of the feminist activists found themselves at one or another point along the spectrum of the political opposition, and the Committee on General Security moved to silence them. The prosecution quickly widened from an attack on a frankly feminist group, such as the Société des Républicaines Révolutionnaires, to all women who dared to participate in politics. The violent reaction against women's political activities, frequently believed to have been inspired by Napoleon, was, in fact, already in motion by 1793.

This reaction can, of course, be understood simply as a reemergence of a seemingly eternal patriarchal system, but such an explanation would overlook its historically specific characteristics. Jacobin arguments against women's political activities were not some mere throwback to "unenlightened" times. Rather, Jacobins relied on the quite new reasoning formulated by Rousseau. As Gita May has made clear, Rousseau was unlike earlier patriarchalists.[11] He depicted a middle-class, not upper-class, existence and specifically a kind of middle-class life that had not existed in earlier centuries when workplace and home overlapped. He glorified the separation of private and public spheres and elevated bourgeois women's newly time-consuming maternal preoccupations to an exalted level. Women's role as men's companion was elevated too; they were indispensable to men's happiness, and, in recognition, Rousseau's men loved and respected them. Women's innate aptitude for love and selfish devotion thus assured them dignity, respect, and happiness. In some ways, Rousseau reads more like women's defenders in the earlier, seventeenth-century *querelle des femmes* than their detractors.

But Rousseau's appreciation of women's familial role was central to arguments that actually strengthened older patriarchal values by reformulating them in terms that were relevant to eighteenth-century society. It was women's maternal responsibilities that now required her exclusion from the kind of civil, political, and economic activities that Rousseau championed for all men. Rousseau had changed the patriarchal concept of womanhood from one that was similar in quality but lesser in value to one that was qualitatively different and, if not lesser than, still subordinate to men.

Rousseau is echoed in the 1793 report of the Committee of General Security that was written to respond to the question, "Should women meet in political associations?"

> No, because they would be required to sacrifice to them [the associations] the more important cares to which Nature calls them. Private functions to which women are destined by Nature are necessary to the general order of society; social order results from the difference between men and women.[12]

That the eighteenth century ended in repression is, therefore, neither surprising nor even anachronistic. The uniform legal system that rationalist jurists spent more than a decade drawing up enshrined the Rousseauist concept of the difference of women from men. The Civil Code recognized the rights of all citizens but excluded women from the definition of citizenship. Women were thereby reduced to the status of a legal caste at the same time that the ancien régime's

legal class system was abolished for men. Women's status worsened—
if not in absolute terms, then in relative terms. Indeed, even in
absolute terms, *some* women's status worsened, for when many
different laws had applied differently to French people from different
geographic areas or from different orders there had existed opportunities for women, especially noble women, to escape the full harshness
of patriarchal laws. They could slip through loopholes created by
differing and overlapping legal systems. Those opportunities had now
been erased, and this was the meaning, for women, of the new civil
equality.

Eighteenth-century views on women were contradictory, then,
providing encouragement for the emergence of a feminist movement
but also new weapons to gun it down. On balance, however, the
movement was forward because even seemingly patriarchal views,
like Rousseau's, contained the seeds of new power for women that
bore fruit in the following century.

In nineteenth-century France, the romantic woman—a direct descen-
dant of Rousseau's Julie—was idealized. This rehabilitation of women
in theory was the foundation upon which a feminist movement would
be constructed. Women's self-esteem was elevated by their positive
depiction in popular literature. As a result, some were emboldened to
question the continuing limitations placed on their activities. Not
surprisingly, nineteenth-century feminists were ambivalent about the
image of the good, romantic woman. They recognized that this
literary personnage was no equal to man; she was child-like, dependent
on men's power for her very survival, or self-sacrificing, subordinating
herself to men's interests. Nonetheless, feminists frequently employed
romantic language idealizing women to further their cause. Its
usefulness for feminist purposes was undeniable.

There was a relation, too, between the creation of a legal system
based solely on sex and the reemergence of feminism in the nineteenth
century. The Code served as a rallying point for feminist protest not
only because it discriminated against women but also—and perhaps
more significantly—because it intensified women's sense of sex identification. By proclaiming the political significance of sex, the Code
ironically participated in the shaping of feminist consciousness.

The continuing influence of eighteenth-century thought on women
is evident, too, in the subsequent development of the French feminist
movement. In nineteenth-century France, the utopian socialists were
the first to discuss feminist ideas. During the 1830s and 1840s, their
teachings reached an audience throughout the Western world. Feminism moved beyond isolated concern to become an international
collective force.

The first of the utopian socialists to discuss feminist ideas were the Saint-Simonians, who envisioned a world order ruled over by a "couple-pope," the male to represent "reflection," the female "sentiment." This dichotomization of the human personality is right out of Rousseau. At first reading, then, it appears that Saint-Simonians had accepted a patriarchal prejudice that had been intended to justify women's restriction to a domestic role. But Saint-Simonians really turned Rousseau upside down. Their feminism was integral to a system that actually prized emotion (the female quality) over reason (the male quality). They preached that only sentiment, not reason, could provide a strong and solid bond for a peaceful society. The future direction of the new age could be entrusted only to those who were especially endowed with sentiment: women, but priests and artists as well. In practice of what they preached, both sexes participated in the governance and administration of the group.

By 1848, utopian feminists, whose numbers now included Fourierists as well as Saint-Simonians, were basing their demands for female equality on the glorification of women *as mothers*. In their words, "the mothers of your sons cannot be slaves." This kind of reasoning distinguished nineteenth-century feminism from its Revolutionary predecessor; the equality of women was not merely "just"; now it was "necessary." "It is above all this holy function of motherhood, . . . which requires that women watch over the futures of their children and gives women the right to intervene not only in all acts of civil life, but also in all acts of political life."[13]

Why did feminists choose to coopt a line of reasoning that Jacobin patriarchalists had once used against their predecessors? I relate this shift in nineteenth-century feminist theory to the eighteenth-century cultural revolution that made of childhood a distinct and important phase of life.[14] As each child became a more important individual to the parents and remained at home for a longer number of years, mothers' maternal responsibilities increased. Their power increased, too, because the domestic sphere—along with the child—was elevated in importance and because the separation of workplace and home increasingly removed men from the home and left women more in control there.

The effect of the increasing separation of workplace and home was contradictory; women lost power, too, by being excluded from sharing in the new opportunities for political participation and economic independence that were opening to increasing numbers of men. But feminists protested only their exclusion from the public sphere and *confinement* to the domestic sphere. They did not question women's responsibilities and roles within the home, viewing these rather as a source of empowerment.

During the 1830s, utopian feminists had also taught that women's liberation and sexual liberation were interconnected issues, but by 1848, they had rejected this notion. Here, too, the shift in feminist theory is explained by changes in women's lives dating to the eighteenth century. Utopian visions had been overwhelmed by the reality of a dramatic increase in the ratio of "illegitimate" births to total births that had begun about mid-eighteenth century. Until 1750, illegitimacy had been essentially unknown in ancien régime France; by the mid-nineteenth century, it accounted for between five and ten percent of all births in France, and in certain areas—especially Paris, Lyons, and Bordeaux—illegitimacy accounted for between thirty and fifty percent of all births.[15]

Feminists—many of whom had attempted to live the new morality of "free love"—came to the sad conclusion that sexual liberation without economic liberation or political rights was a chimera. Large numbers of young women were working in large cities far from their parents. Their geographical mobility had left them bereft of traditional familial support systems. Throughout the century, women on their own— even without a child to support—could not earn wages sufficient to support themselves. Exploitative conditions in the work force carried over to sexual relations. Example after example in literature attested to the exploitative nature of sexual relations outside of marriage, which commonly involved a woman from the lower classes and her employer of the upper classes. Almost half of the illegitimate children born in Paris in the 1880s were born to servant mothers, but employers were protected against their servants' claims by the legal system.[16]

The feminist program after 1848 was shaped by this reality. Feminists demanded a legal solution to the problems raised by illegitimacy and supported changes in the Code that would permit divorce and paternity suits, establish inheritance rights for illegitimate children, and eliminate prostitution. At the same time, they insisted that the most obvious solution to illegitimacy was the best solution: sexual abstinence for the unmarried. Their feminism was based on their arguing that this morality apply to men as well as to women.

They demanded, too, the rights and opportunities for an independent existence. At the head of their platform reappeared the centuries-old demand for improved educational opportunities, which after the establishment of a state system of secondary schools for girls, in 1880, became the specific demand that girls' education be made equal to boys'. Next, feminists demanded the right to work. For bourgeois women, this slogan meant opposition to laws that denied them access to the professions. For working-class women, it meant opposition to the so-called protective laws that limited their earning power and the demand that their wages be raised to the level of mens'.

After the Republic was secured in 1879, feminists were hopeful that their demands would be met. They fashioned a kind of politics that was patterned after that of the Opportunist Republicans, whom they challenged. They reasserted the language of individual rights that stressed the "justice" of their cause and focused on issues that could be resolved by legal reforms. At first, their campaign to change the Civil Code highlighted women's exclusion from the rights of citizenship; they demanded that women be allowed to be witnesses to public acts, notaries, and guardians to children in addition to their own and that women be allowed to control their own earnings and share the father's authority over the children and over the community property as well. But, soon, some feminists were urging that the demand for the vote should be put first in their program; in 1909, the Union Française pour le Suffrage des Femmes united formerly fragmented feminists into one block aimed at enfranchising women.

How well did feminists fare? That their struggle was uphill and their victories slow in coming is not surprising given the strength of the patriarchal legacy of the eighteenth century. Nonetheless, the contradictions of that legacy afforded them opportunities as well. Feminists were most successful when those who controlled power shared the liberal values of the Enlightenment or the radicalism of Revolutionists. Unfortunately, this was only intermittently so in nineteenth-century France. Saint-Simonian activities, encouraged by the upheavals of the Revolution of 1830, were curtailed by the government in 1832 and again in 1834. From 1848 to 1850, the feminists could organize clubs and publish newspapers, but, in 1851, the government cracked down on them. An entire generation of feminist leadership was exiled; most never returned to France. Repressive laws on the press and assembly were not lifted until the final years of the Second Empire; and only then did new leaders recommence the propaganda effort. Then came the repression of the Commune uprising, and the working-class participants of the nascent feminist movement were punished, most of them by exile. The rights to organize, lecture publicly, and publish freely were necessary preconditions for further success. The Enlightenment had legitimized these safeguards in theory; in reality, they were not secured for almost another century.

Only in 1879 were the rights of feminists to publish and meet publicly ensured. Their achievements in the decades that followed were significant: 1) 1880: a state system of secondary education for girls; 2) the opening up of the university to women—1866, faculté de médecine; 1870, faculté des lettres, sciences, et droit; 1896, école des beaux-arts; 3) 1884: the reestablishment of divorce; 4) the right to practice certain "public" professions—1881, newspaper publisher; 1885, medicine; 1900, law; 5) 1897: the right to witness public acts (single women only); 6) 1898: the right to vote for judges of the *tribunes de commerce;* 7) 1907: the right to vote for members of the conseils de prud'hommes; 8) 1907: the mother's right to equal authority with father over their children; right of mothers alone, in case of "illegitimate" children, to exercise the "paternal" authority; and right of married women to control their own earnings; 9) 1912: the right to initiate a paternity suit; 10) 1919: the Chamber of Deputies passed a universal suffrage bill; 11) 1924: girls' *lycées* adopted a course of study preparatory for the baccalaureate.

Then the pace of change slowed. The feminist movement proved too weak to withstand the reaction that swept all Western countries, France included, in the period that followed. Most notable was the inaction of the Senate on the suffrage bill. French women had to await the total defeat of the Vichy Right before winning the right to vote. An ordinance of the Provisional Government, dated April 21, 1944, finally recognized their most basic right of citizenship. The eighteenth century agenda had been fulfilled.

Because change is continuous and recognizes no special moment at the turn into a new century, characteristics of the lives of French women in the nineteenth century—and even into the twentieth century—are evident already in the eighteenth century. But the historical record for that time was contradictory. The Revolution, for example, had witnessed the first burst of feminist activity, but this turned out to be short-lived. The codification of civil and criminal laws a decade later froze the inferior position of women into French jurisprudence. It is an irony that history's celebration of the remarkable ideals and slogans advanced by the Revolution overlooks the almost total interdiction of civil and political rights for women.

Yet I have read the record of this historical period and judged their significance for women positively. Such an interpretation requires a look beyond the eighteenth century and into the future. There, we can see how important these years were for the future development of feminism and for the undermining of eighteenth-century arguments against sexual equality. Whereas, prior to 1789, favor for the ideas of the emancipation of women—or at the least, for greater opportunities for women—was restricted to the upper classes and support was usually in the form of approving women's desire for a better education, a feminism more sweeping in its scope and more inclusive in its following had arisen with the Revolutionary upheavals. Eighteenth-century feminists not only added new demands to their program—the rights of full citizen participation in politics and government, the right to work, the right to equality in marriage, and even the right to share the burdens of a nation at war—but they also adopted new methods to obtain their goals. They comprehended that political action was more than a "demand"; it was a means to achieve their demands. They had grasped the potential strength of collective female action. The eighteenth century had bequeathed to the future the *means* to women's liberation.

NOTES

1. François Marie Arouet Voltaire, "Prix de la justice et de l'humanité," *Oeuvres complètes* (Paris: Firmin Didot Frères, 1854-1858), vol. 5, p. 454.
2. See Pauline Kra, "Montesquieu and Women," chapter 17.
3. Charles de Secondat Montesquieu, *L'Esprit des lois* (Paris: Firmin Didot Frères, 1868), pp. 243-245.
4. Denis Diderot and Jean Le Rond d'Alembert, *L'Encyclopédie ou dictionnaire raisonné des sciences, des arts, et des métiers*, 17 volumes (Paris: David Le Breton Durand, 1756), vol. 6, pp. 468-476.
5. See Samia I. Spencer, "Women and Education," chapter 4.
6. Denis Diderot, *De l'éducation publique* (Amsterdam: n.p., 1762).
7. Paule-Marie Duhet, *Les Femmes et la révolution, 1789-1794* (Paris: Julliard, 1971), p. 41.
8. Elizabeth Racz, "The Women's Rights Movement in the French Revolution," *Science and Society* 16 (1952):153.
9. Edwin Randolph Hedman, "Early French Feminism from the Eighteenth Century to 1848" (Ph.D. diss., New York University, 1954), p. 47.
10. Duhet, p. 25.
11. See Gita May, "Rousseau's Antifeminism Reconsidered," chapter 20.
12. Quoted in Duhet, pp. 154-155.
13. Eugénie Niboyet, *La Voix des femmes*, 5 April 1848.
14. See Philippe Ariès, *Centuries of Childhood*, translated by Robert Baldick (New York: Vintage Books, 1962).
15. Edward Shorter, "Illegitimacy, Sexual Revolution, and Social Change in Modern Europe," *The Journal of Interdisciplinary History* 2 (1971):265-267. The best analyses of the causes of the rise in illegitimacy are Joan Scott and Louise Tilly, "Women's Work and the Family in Nineteenth-Century Europe," *Comparative Studies in Society and History* 17 (1975):36-64; and Louise Tilly, Joan Scott, and Miriam Cohen, "Women's Work and European Fertility Patterns," *Journal of Interdisciplinary History* 6 (Winter 1976):447-476. They have compared the values and behavior of nineteenth-century women with those of eighteenth-century women (relying heavily on the work of Olwen Hufton). They are able to show *continuity* of both values and behavior. The rise in the birth rate outside of marriage they ascribe to: 1) a new context in which geographic mobility left the women far from parental protection; 2) economic necessity or opportunity that forced or encouraged the male partner of a sexual union to move on before a marriage was legalized; and especially 3) the increase in absolute numbers of that urban class in which legalized marriage was "traditionally" uncommon.
16. Theresa McBride, *The Domestic Revolution: The Modernization of Household Service in England and France, 1820-1920* (New York: Holmes and Meier, 1976), pp. 102-103.

CONTRIBUTORS

HARRIET B. APPLEWHITE is Professor of Political Science at Southern Connecticut State University. She is co-editor, with Darline Gay Levy and Mary D. Johnson, of *Women in Revolutionary Paris, 1789-1795*. The author of scholarly articles on Revolutionary France and a study of political alignment in the National Assembly, she is currently collaborating with Darline Gay Levy on an analysis of Parisian women's contribution to democratic politics in Revolutionary France.

GERMAINE BRÉE is Kenan Professor of Humanities at Wake Forest University, a "Vilas Professor," and a permanent member of the Institute for Research in Humanities at the University of Wisconsin. She is an authority on modern French literature and philosophy. Her publications include books on André Gide, Albert Camus, Jean-Paul Sartre, Marcel Proust, and women writers in France. She has received honorary degrees from twenty-four colleges and universities and was the 1975 president of the Modern Language Association of America.

SUSAN P. CONNER is Professor of History and Chair of the Department of History at Tift College, a woman's college in Forsyth, Georgia. She has contributed articles to dictionaries on the French Revolution and Napoleonic France and has published articles on the role of women in French history in the *Proceedings of the Consortium on Revolutionary Europe, Laurels*, and the *Proceedings of the Western Society for French History*.

JUDITH CURTIS has taught French language and literature at Scarborough College, University of Toronto, since 1967. She has published a critical edition and articles in the field of eighteenth-century French theatre and is currently a member of a team of researchers preparing an edition of the correspondence of Mme de Graffigny.

CISSIE FAIRCHILDS is Associate Professor of History at Syracuse University and the author of *Poverty and Charity in Aix-en-Provence, 1640-1789* and *Domestic Enemies: Servants and their Masters in Old Regime France*.

ELIZABETH FOX-GENOVESE teaches history at SUNY Binghamton and is the author of *The Origins of Physiocracy: Economic Revolution and Social Order in Eighteenth-Century France* and, with Eugene D. Genovese, of *Fruits of Merchant Capital: Slavery and Bourgeois Property in the Rise and Expansion of Capitalism.* She also translated and edited *The Memoirs of P. S. Du Pont de Nemours Addressed to His Children.* She directs "Restoring Women to History," a project sponsored by the Organization of American Historians.

LINDA GARDINER is the editor of *The Women's Review of Books.* She has published several articles in the field of history of philosophy and the history of ideas. She is currently working on a biography of Emilie du Châtelet.

RUTH GRAHAM, a member of the Institute for Research in History, taught at Queens College, City University of New York, and is now an editor of the *Annals of Scholarship.* Her essays on women in the French Revolution and on the Revolutionary clergy have appeared in many journals and collections. She is presently writing a book on the ecclesiastical deputies to the National Convention.

SUSAN R. KINSEY has taught French at Baruch College, City University of New York, and for the University of Maryland, European Division, in London, England. She has presented papers before the NEMLA and at Marymount College in London. Dr. Kinsey is currently working in program development for continuing education and is Director of the English Language Institute at Long Island University in Brooklyn, New York.

PAULINE KRA is Professor of French at Yeshiva University. Her work on Montesquieu includes studies of structure ("The Invisible Chain of the *Lettres persanes,*" "L'Enchaînement des chapitres de *L'Esprit des lois*") and of oriental and religious themes ("Religion in Montesquieu's *Lettres persanes,*" "The Role of the Harem in Imitations of the *Lettres persanes*"). She has also written on Voltaire and La Bruyère.

ALICE M. LABORDE is Associate Professor of French Literature at the University of California at Irvine. She has published articles and reviews in numerous scholarly journals. Her main contribution to eighteenth-century research consists of four books: *L'Oeuvre de Madame de Genlis, L'Esthétique circéenne, Sade romancier,* and *Diderot et l'amour.* She has also published two volumes of original poetry, *Tendre Tropisme* and *Kaleidoscopes.* She has completed a manuscript on the intellectual relationship between Diderot and Mme de Puisieux and is engaged in an extensive study of Sade's concept of eroticism.

VERA G. LEE is Professor and Chair of the Department of Romance Languages at Boston College. She has received grants from the Mellon Foundation, the American Philosophical Society, and the Carnegie Foundation and holds the title of Chevalier des Palmes Académiques. Her best-known publication in eighteenth-century studies is *The Reign of Women in Eighteenth-Century France*. She is currently researching a book on Beaumarchais.

DARLINE GAY LEVY, Associate Professor of History at New York University, is the author of *The Ideas and Careers of Simon-Nicolas-Henri Linguet: A Study in Eighteenth-Century French Politics* and co-editor (with Harriet B. Applewhite and Mary D. Johnson) of *Women in Revolutionary Paris, 1789-1795*. She is the recipient of an American Council of Learned Societies Fellowship and a Fulbright Senior Research Scholar Award for research on a book (with Harriet Applewhite) to be called "Subjects into Citizens: The Political Participation of Women in Revolutionary Paris."

SARA ELLEN PROCIOUS MALUEG is Professor of French at Oregon State University. She is the author of articles and book reviews on the eighteenth century, as well as co-author of an introductory French text. Her current research interests include Diderot, the *Encyclopédie*, and cross influences between France and America during the eighteenth century.

GITA MAY is Professor of French and Department Chair at Columbia University. She is a Fulbright Fellow, Guggenheim Fellow, NEH Senior Fellow, Chevalier and Officier de l'Ordre des Palmes Académiques. She also served as president of the Northeast American Society for Eighteenth-Century Studies (1981-1982) and Second Vice-President of the American Society for Eighteenth-Century Studies. Her publications include *Diderot et Baudelaire, critiques d'art, Madame Roland and the Age of Revolution, Stendhal and the Age of Napoleon,* and numerous articles and book reviews.

BLANDINE L. McLAUGHLIN received a Doctorat d'Université from the Sorbonne. She has taught at Mary Washington College in Fredericksburg, Virginia, and at Smith College in Northampton, Massachusetts, and is presently Professor of French at the University of Alabama in Birmingham. Among her publications are a monograph, *Diderot et l'amitié,* and articles on Diderot, Laclos, Gabriel Marcel, and others.

BARBARA G. MITTMAN is Associate Professor of French at the University of Illinois, Chicago. She has published articles about various aspects of Diderot's theatre and about the phenomenon of spectators on the stage in seventeenth- and eighteenth-century France. A book on the latter subject will be published in 1985.

CLAIRE G. MOSES teaches women's studies at the University of Maryland, College Park, and is editor and managing editor of *Feminist Studies*. She is the author of *French Feminism in the Nineteenth Century*, published by the State University of New York Press in 1984..

CHARLOTTE PRATHER is Assistant Professor of German at Wellesley College. Her specialization is the eighteenth-century novel, but she also has a strong interest in Medieval and Renaissance literature. She is currently a student at the Weston School of Theology in Cambridge, Massachusetts, and hopes to do ministry in the Roman Catholic Church.

URSULA M. REMPEL is Associate Professor of Music at the University of Manitoba, where she teaches courses in music history and directs early music ensembles. She has published articles on the history of the harp, on women harpists, on Renaissance consort music, and on American music (with W. John Rempel). She is a member of the Board of Readers, *The American Harp Journal*, and is editor of The Manitoba Music Educators' Association *Journal*.

DANIELLE RICE received her Ph.D. in Art History from Yale University, where she specialized in eighteenth-century art and social history. She is currently Curator of Education at the National Gallery of Art in Washington, D.C.

ADRIENNE ROGERS has taught at Russell Sage College in Troy, New York, since 1962. She is presently Professor and Chair of the Department of Modern Languages and Cultures. Her work with Middlebury College was completed in Paris and her teaching experience includes both the secondary and college levels.

KATHARINE ROGERS, Professor of English at Brooklyn College and the City University Graduate School, has published *The Troublesome Helpmate: A History of Misogyny in Literature*, a book on William Wycherley, several anthologies, and numerous articles on eighteenth- and nineteenth-century literature. Her *Feminism in Eighteenth-Century England* appeared in 1982.

EVA M. KAHILUOTO RUDAT is the founder and editor-in-chief of the journal *Dieciocho: Hispanic Enlightenment, Aesthetics, and Literary Theory*. Her publications include *Las ideas esteticas de Esteban de Arteaga* and numerous articles on Hispanic languages and literatures.

ROSEANN RUNTE is President of Université Sainte-Anne. She is President of the Canadian Federation for the Humanities, past President of the Canadian and the Atlantic Societies for Eighteenth-Century Studies, editor of three volumes of *Studies in Eighteenth-Century Culture*, and author of numerous articles.

GLORIA M. RUSSO is the Resident Director in Paris of the Sweet Briar Junior Year in France Program. Her publications include "Sexual Roles and Religious Images in Voltaire's *Pucelle*," *Expanding Communication: Teaching Modern Languages at the College Level*, several other articles on language teaching, and an English libretto for a chamber opera, *Follies and Fancies*, based on Molière's *Les Précieuses ridicules*.

SAMIA I. SPENCER is Associate Professor of French at Auburn University in Alabama and author of *Le Dilemme du roman marivaudien*. Her publications on women in France, French and Quebecois culture, the teaching of languages, and eighteenth-century French literature, have appeared in, among others, *The French-American Review, Contemporary French Civilization, The French Review, The Canadian Modern Language Review*, and *The Proceedings of the Western Society for French History*.

JOAN HINDE STEWART is Professor of French and Assistant Dean for Research in Humanities and Social Sciences at North Carolina State University. She has published books and articles on eighteenth- and twentieth-century French literature, including *The Novels of Mme Riccoboni*, an edition of Riccoboni's *Lettres de mistriss Fanni Butlerd* and *Colette*. She is presently writing a book on novels by eighteenth-century French women.

RUTH P. THOMAS is Associate Professor of French at Temple University and Director of the Temple Sorbonne Summer Program. She has published articles on the fiction of Marivaux, Montesquieu, Diderot, and others as well as on French novels of the seventeenth and nineteenth centuries.

CAROLYN H. WILBERGER is Associate Professor of French at Portland State University, Portland, Oregon, and the author of several studies on eighteenth-century France and Russia, including *Voltaire's Russia: Window on the East*.

INDEX